PREFACE

When we were students at University, the subject of "human rights" was never mentioned; the European Convention on Human Rights was just another Treaty mentioned in the Public International Law class. Students and practitioners now ignore the subject of human rights at their peril. The implementation of the Human Rights Act and the Scotland Act has led to a sea-change in the way in which both lawyers and the public sector bodies work. Public bodies have to be aware that their every action may have implications for the human rights of a citizen and their administrative practices and procedures have to be altered accordingly. There have been many cases, but not the tidal wave some commentators predicted; rather there has been a steady flow. Nonetheless, staying with the watery theme, liquid has a tendency to find a way of escaping from the path set for it, and this has been the case with human rights challenges also. It has been in some unexpected ways that challenges have succeeded, certainly in Scotland. We have tried to examine these "unexpected events" throughout the text.

The text is intended for students and those practitioners who need an overview of the Convention, the jurisprudence of its institutions and the effects, real and possible, on Scots law. Most of the chapters are based on the Convention Articles and we have tried to adopt a style that first defines and discusses the Convention jurisprudence and then the law existing in Scotland and the application and effect of the Convention principles upon that law. Where appropriate we have also included some discussion of the effect upon English law. By adopting this approach we are aware that some topics are discussed twice in different chapters. This means however that each chapter is a separate self-contained entity which we hope the reader will find easier to follow.

The text states the law up to the end of November 2001, but we have been able to make some changes and additions at the proof stage.

We are grateful to our colleagues at Paisley and Napier Universities; their support and encouragement has been very welcome. We are grateful too for the help and understanding (particularly the latter) of Jill Barrington and Luisa Deas at W. Green. The book would not have been completed however without the endless patience of our families and our love and thanks go especially to them.

Val Finch
Chris Ashton
March 2002

CONTENTS

TABLE OF U.K. CASES

TABLE OF EUROPEAN CASES

TABLE OF STATUTES

TABLE OF ACTS OF THE SCOTTISH PARLIAMENT

TABLE OF STATUTORY INSTRUMENTS

TABLE OF EUROPEAN LEGISLATION

DIRECTIVES

CHAPTER 1

INTRODUCTION

This is an exciting time in the development of human rights law. 1.01
Major constitutional changes have taken place throughout the
United Kingdom in the last few years. The process of devolution of
certain legislative powers to Scotland has involved major constitutional and administrative changes. The fact that the incorporation
of the European Convention on Human Rights into the domestic
law of the United Kingdom was taking effect at the same time has
led, inevitably, to a period of increased scrutiny of both substantive
and procedural laws. It is difficult to keep apace with all of the
changes and an exhaustive treatment of the whole field of human
rights law would be a marathon task at this stage. We have decided,
therefore, to concentrate on certain aspects. In particular, this book
is intended to provide an explanation of the legal protection of
human rights in Scotland. It concentrates on those areas where the
substantive or procedural rules are different from the rest of the
United Kingdom. In each chapter we have given a brief explanation
of the relevant Convention rights, looked to a limited extent at the
jurisprudence of the European Convention on Human Rights and
considered the effect of incorporation of the European Convention
on Human Rights on some aspects of current Scots law.

The United Kingdom is an unusual modern democracy as it
comprises more than one jurisdiction but lacks a formal written
constitution. It is usual in a modern Western democracy for the
rights of citizens to be enshrined in a constitutional document and
the United Kingdom does not have such a document. The process
of devolution has, however resulted in increased formalisation of
the relationship between the United Kingdom Government and the
jurisdictions to which some legislative powers have been devolved.
There is still nothing which has the status of an entrenched
constitutional guarantee of fundamental rights. Pressure for a Bill
of Rights has increased year by year and this has led to the major
constitutional change which took effect in 1999 and 2000.[1] The
European Convention of Human Rights and Fundamental Free-

---

[1] Scotland Act 1998, Human Rights Act 1998.

1

doms has now been substantially incorporated into the domestic law of the United Kingdom. Whether this was the most appropriate way to protect human rights in the United Kingdom is still the subject of debate. It has been argued that it would have been preferable to delay the change so that it could be achieved by a Bill of Rights which would be more in tune with the philosophy and culture of the United Kingdom. The "quick fix" of incorporation of the European Convention of Human Rights certainly allowed the development of human rights law to take place several years earlier but the "price" of this strategy may well prove to be several years of uncertainty and a huge increase in litigation until a body of jurisprudence has developed.

RIGHTS AS OPPOSED TO LIBERTIES

1.02   We are not used to a culture of legal rights in the United Kingdom. The law has been concerned with civil liberties rather than individual rights. Civil liberties are residual, not entrenched in a constitution as rights often are in other countries. The citizen enjoys the residue of freedom left behind after the legal restrictions have been imposed. A citizen does nothing wrong if he takes advantage of his liberties but there is no positive duty on any organ of the state to facilitate them. For example, the Civic Government (Scotland) Act 1982 gives local authorities powers to permit public assemblies and to impose conditions in so doing, but it does not impose a duty on local authorities to ensure freedom of association. Thus, a liberty is simply an area of human activity which at present is unregulated by the law. By contrast, if a citizen has a right then there will be some corresponding duty on persons generally or specific organs of the state to ensure that he has opportunity to exercise his right. An example of a right is the right of a person to find out what data relating to him is held by an organisation.[2] There is a corresponding duty imposed on organisations to make the information available.

THE STATUS OF THE EUROPEAN CONVENTION OF HUMAN RIGHTS IN THE UNITED KINGDOM PRIOR TO THE HUMAN RIGHTS ACT 1998

1.03   The European Convention on Human Rights has been incorporated into the domestic law of the United Kingdom by the Scotland Act 1998, which came into force in 1999, and by the Human Rights Act 1998, which came into force in October 2000. Even prior to

---

[2]   Data Protection Act 1998.

incorporation there was evidence of a gradual increase in the willingness of judges to regard the European Convention on Human Rights as a matter which should be taken into account in the course of administrative decision-making. The English courts have lead the way in this approach and the decisions of the Scottish courts in recent years have followed the same trend. The circumstances in which the Convention should be taken into account were however limited to the following categories.

(1) Where Legislation is Ambiguous or the Law is Uncertain

In *R v. Secretary of State for the Home Department, ex parte Brind,*[3] 1.04
it was held that where a statute is clear and unambiguous international principles and standards, such as Convention rights may not be relevant. However, regard ought to be had to the Convention as an aid to interpretation. A presumption should be applied that Parliament must have intended to legislate in accordance with the Convention. This case was an unsuccessful challenge to the decision to ban broadcasts by IRA figureheads which featured their own voices.[4]

A similar presumption was not accepted by the Scottish courts until 1996 when, in the case of *T, Petitioner (sub nom. AMT, petitioners),* Lord President Hope took the opportunity to clarify the extent to which regard should be given to the European Convention on Human Rights in Scots law. T, aged 34 and unmarried, appealed against the refusal of his petition to adopt a child. His petition had been refused because he was a single male living in a homosexual relationship, despite the fact that T was regarded by the adoption panel and the director of social services as offering the best home for the child because he was a registered nurse and had nursed both children and adults with physical and mental disabilities. The appeal was successful on other grounds but Lord President Hope stated that it was also relevant to consider whether a refusal to allow adoption by homosexual applicants would conflict with the European Convention on Human Rights 1950. The Scottish courts should apply the presumption that Parliament intended to legislate in conformity with the Convention. This case brought the judicial interpretation of the relevance of the ECHR to Scots law in line with current judicial reasoning in England and Wales. The previous position in Scotland had been based on the case of *Kaur v. Lord Advocate.*[5] In distinguishing that case, Lord Hope observed:

---

[3] [1991] A.C. 696.
[4] See also *Att.-Gen. v. Guardian Newspapers Ltd. (No. 2)* [1990] 1 A.C. 109.
[5] 1980 S.L.T. 322.

"It is now an integral part of the general principles of European Community Law that fundamental human rights must be protected and that one of the sources to which regard may be made for an expression of rights is international treaties for the protection of rights on which member states have collaborated or of which they are signatories."[6]

(2) Where Legislation has been Passed to Bring the Domestic Law Into Line with the Convention

In the case of *R v. Secretary of State for the Home department, ex parte Norney,*[7] it was held that, where legislation has been passed with the specific purpose of securing conformity with Convention standards in an aspect of domestic law, the court should have regard to the relevant provisions of the Convention. The case involved referral of prisoners serving life sentences to the parole board. In considering the exercise of the discretion to refer prisoners by a government minister it would be perverse to ignore the relevant provisions of the Convention.

(3) Where Administrative Decisions Affect Fundamental Rights

1.05 Where administrators are making decisions affecting fundamental rights and freedoms of individuals it has been held that the European Convention on Human Rights is a relevant consideration which the administrator should take into account before making a decision.[8] This did not mean that public authorities are bound to exercise their discretion consistently with the Convention, only that the procedures followed should show that the Convention rights have been taken into consideration.[9]

THE STATUS OF OTHER INTERNATIONAL TREATIES

1.06 The incorporation of the European Convention on Human Rights represents a major advance in the development of Scots law but it must not be forgotten that the European Convention on Human Rights represents only a very small part of international human rights law. International human rights law consists of a wider range of instruments, ranging from binding Treaties to Recommendations. Some are global in their application, like the United Nations

---

[6] 1997 S.L.T. 724; 1996 S.C.L.R. 897; [1997] Fam. Law 8; [1997] Fam. Law 225.
[7] (1995) 7 Admin. L.R. 681.
[8] *R v. Ministry of Defence, ex p. Smith* [1996] Q.B. 517 (CA).
[9] *R v. Horseferry Road Magistrates' Court, ex p. Bennett* [1994] A.C. 42. *Britton v. Secretary of State for the Environment,* CO/1348/96 and CO/1349/96, October 24, 1996.

Convention Against Torture and Other Cruel, Inhuman or Degrading Treatment or Punishment and the United Nations Convention on the Rights of the Child 1989. Others apply only in a specific region. The American Convention on Human Rights 1969 and the European Convention on Human Rights are in this category. The status of all of the human rights Treaties, apart from the European Convention, has not been changed. The circumstances in which they will be taken into account are those described above.

HUMAN RIGHTS PROTECTION UNDER EUROPEAN COMMUNITY LAW

The founding Treaties of the European Community do not 1.07 specifically include human rights and this caused difficulty in the early years of the Community when cases came before the European Court of Justice concerning human rights principles enshrined in domestic constitutions of the Member States. The European Court of Justice has increasingly adopted the principles of the European Convention on Human Rights in cases before it, thus bringing the Convention rights into Community law "by the back door". There have been discussions for a number of years regarding the possible accession of the Community to the Convention but this has not happened, largely because of the difficulty in reconciling the supreme nature of the decisions of the European Court of Justice in matters of Community law with decisions being taken by the Strasbourg Court which could overturn that supremacy. In an attempt to bring human rights more completely into the Community sphere, the Nice European Council in December 2000 agreed to adopt the European Charter of Fundamental Rights, a composite document of civil and political rights together with social and economic rights. The Charter, however, is not enforceable—largely because social and economic rights were included—and it will be some years before the issue of enforceability will be considered by the Council again. Nonetheless, the Charter sets out the general principles of human rights espoused by the European Court of Justice and is a step towards full recognition of those rights by the Community and, by implication, the Member States themselves.

THE HUMAN RIGHTS ACT AND THE SCOTLAND ACT

Although it is commonly stated that the Convention Rights have 1.08 been incorporated into the domestic law of the United Kingdom the Convention rights have not actually been incorporated into United Kingdom Law. The long title of the Human Rights Act states that it is an Act to give further effect to rights and freedoms guaranteed under the European Convention on Human Rights; to make provisions with respect to holders of certain judicial offices who become judges of the European Court of Human Rights and for connected purposes.

The Act achieves its aim of "giving further effect" to the Convention rights in several ways.

(1) A Requirement That Legislation Should be Interpreted so as to Comply with the Convention

1.09   The Human Rights Act 1998, section 3(1) provides that "[s]o far as it is possible to do so, primary legislation and subordinate legislation must be read and given effect in a way which is compatible with the Convention rights." And subsection (2) provides, *inter alia*, that this section "(a) applies to primary legislation and subordinate legislation whenever enacted". In the case of *J.A. Pye (Oxford) Limited v. Graham*, Mummery L.J. said, in relation to section 3(1):

> "The principle of the interpretation of primary and secondary legislation contained in section 3 of the 1998 Act can be relied on in an appeal which is heard after that Act came into force, even though the appeal is against an order made by the court below before the Act came into force".

And Keene L.J. stated that subsection (1) applies to all cases coming before the courts on or after October 2, 2000 "irrespective of when the activities which form the subject-matter of those cases took place".[10]

(2) A Requirement that Courts and Tribunals take Account of the Jurisprudence of the European Court of Human Rights

1.10   Section 2 states that a court or tribunal determining a question which has arisen in connection with a Convention right must take into account any:

(a) judgment, decision, declaration or advisory opinion of the European Court of Human Rights;
(b) opinion of the Commission given in a report adopted under Article 31 of the Convention;
(c) decision of the Commission in connection with Article 26 or 27(2) of the Convention;
(d) decision of the Committee of Ministers taken under Article 46 of the Convention.

---

[10]   *J.A. Pye (Oxford) Limited v. Graham*, unreported, February 6, 2001.

These judgements, decisions, etc., must be taken into account regardless of when they were made or given, so far as, in the opinion of the court or tribunal, it is relevant to the proceedings in which that question has arisen. There is, however no strict doctrine of judicial precedent with regard to the jurisprudence of the European Convention. There are also principles of interpretation which must be taken into account in deciding whether a judgment or decision should have a strong persuasive value.(See below.)

(3) A Requirement that Public Authorities Act in a Manner Compatible with Convention Rights

Section 6(1) of the Human Rights Act states that it is unlawful for a   1.11 public authority to act in a way which is incompatible with a Convention right. This section does not apply where, as the result of primary legislation, the authority could not have acted differently, or where the authority was acting to give effect to a provision in primary legislation which could not be read as compatible with convention rights. A public authority is defined as

    (a) a court or tribunal,
    (b) any person certain of whose functions are functions of a public nature, but does not include either House of Parliament, or a person exercising functions in connection with proceedings in Parliament.

Parliament in this context does not include the House of Lords sitting in a judicial capacity and so the House of Lords and the Privy Council are included in the definition of public authority when conducting judicial business. Acts include failure to act, but not a failure to lay a proposal for legislation before Parliament or to make any primary legislation or remedial order.

Section 57(2) of the Scotland Act states that a member of the Scottish Executive has no power to make any subordinate legislation, or to do any other act, so far as the legislation or act is incompatible with any of the Convention rights. Section 29(1) states that an Act of the Scottish Parliament is not law so far as any provision of the Act is outside the legislative competence of the Parliament. One of the grounds upon which an Act would be deemed to be outside the legislative competence would be if it is incompatible with any Convention right or with Community Law.[11]

These three methods of giving further effect to Convention rights fall short of incorporating the Convention as part of national law and of creating an entrenched constitutional instrument. The Human Rights Act can be changed in the future by ordinary

---

[11] Scotland Act 1998, s.29(2)(d).

legislative processes. The Human Rights Act is an Act of Parliament like any other and is ultimately subject to the sovereignty of Parliament. It does not give the courts the power to declare that any primary legislation which is incompatible with Convention rights is invalid. Since the courts cannot strike down legislation of the United Kingdom Parliament on grounds of incompatibility with Convention rights, section 10 of the Human Rights Act gives power to ministers to amend offending legislation by remedial order. This special procedure applies only where the minister considers that there are compelling reasons for proceeding under section 10. Where this is not the case amendment will require legislation through the normal procedures. In order to avoid inadvertent insertion of incompatible provisions into legislation, section 19 of the Act requires the minister in charge of a bill to make a statement of compatibility before the second reading or to draw the attention of the House to the desire of the government to proceed with the legislation although a statement of compatibility with Convention rights cannot be made. Parliament may of course choose to enact legislation which is incompatible with the Convention and may refuse to change existing legislation even where there has been a declaration of incompatibility with Convention rights. In such a case the citizen whose rights are infringed would have no remedy in the courts in the United Kingdom but may take a case to the European Court of Human Rights. Acts of the Scottish Parliament, however, may be declared *ultra vires* by the courts.

PRINCIPLES OF THE EUROPEAN CONVENTION ON HUMAN RIGHTS

1.12 The United Kingdom has ratified Articles 1 to 18 and Protocols 1 and 6. Section 1 of the Human Rights Act defines Convention rights as the rights and fundamental freedoms contained in the Articles of the Convention and the two Protocols to the Convention set out in Schedule 1 to the Act. Provision is made for subsequent amendments to the Act whenever the United Kingdom ratifies further protocols.

The United Kingdom is obliged by Article 1 of the Convention to protect the rights therein. The Convention is to be interpreted: "in good faith in accordance with the ordinary meaning to be given to the terms of the treaty in their context and in the light of its object and purpose".[12]

---

[12] Vienna Convention on the Law of Treaties, Art. 31.

The Articles

Article 1—Responsibility of the State

Article 1 simply states that the High Contracting parties (*i.e.* the states) shall secure to everyone within jurisdiction the rights and freedoms defined in the Convention. The state is therefore not only responsible for actions taken by and on behalf of the government but has a duty to provide adequate protection for the citizens from any violations of the convention. This includes an obligation to ensure that the substantive laws and legal procedures are effective in preventing conduct harmful to others. After the stepfather of a nine year old boy had been acquitted of assault, the child applied to the European Court of Human Rights, contending that his treatment constituted a violation of the European Convention on Human Rights 1950 Article 3. It was held that there had been a breach of Article 3 because the child had suffered severe beatings. As to whether the United Kingdom Government should be held responsible for the ill treatment the child received, Article 1 read with Article 3, demanded that contracting states adopt measures to ensure the protection of those within their jurisdiction and prevent them from suffering torture or inhuman or degrading treatment or punishment, with children and the vulnerable deserving particular protection in the form of effective deterrence. The acquittal of the stepfather demonstrated that English law as it stood failed to provide adequate protection for children.[13]

1.13

The Substantive Rights

The rights guaranteed under the Convention are traditional individual rights. The language of the Convention fits in well with the British philosophy of freedom from unjustified interference rather than incontrovertible rights such as those which are found in some written constitutions. The term "Convention rights" as used in the Human Rights Act means the rights and fundamental freedoms set out in—

1.14

 (a) Articles 2 to 12 and 14 of the Convention,
 (b) Articles 1 to 3 of the First Protocol, and
 (c) Articles 1 and 2 of the Sixth Protocol,

as read with Articles 16 to 18 of the Convention.

None of the Convention Articles is absolute. Even the right to life may be infringed in circumstances where it is justified. Articles 8 to 11 may be subject to limitations which are prescribed by law and

---

[13] *A v. U.K.,* 5 B.H.R.C. 137; [1998] 2 F.L.R. 959; [1998] 3 F.C.R. 597; (1999) 27 E.H.R.R. 611; [1998] Fam. Law 733; [1998] H.R.C.D. 870; [1998] Crim. L.R. 892.

which are necessary in a democratic society. Restrictions may be deemed necessary in order to protect national security, to maintain public order, to prevent crime, to protect public health safety or morals, to protect the rights and freedoms of others and to prevent the disclosure of confidential information.

The Articles are as follows:

- Article 2: right to life
- Article 3: prohibition of torture, inhuman or degrading treatment or punishment
- Article 4: prohibition of slavery and forced labour
- Article 5: right to liberty and security of person
- Article 6: right to a fair trial; supplemented by Article 2 of Protocol 7: right of appeal in criminal matters, and Article 3 of Protocol 7: compensation for wrongful conviction
- Article 7: no punishment without law, *i.e.* prohibition of retrospective criminal law; supplemented by Article 4 of Protocol 7: right not to be tried twice
- Article 8: right to respect for private and family life and correspondence
- Article 9: freedom of thought, conscience and religion
- Article 10: freedom of expression
- Article 11: freedom of assembly and association
- Article 12: right to marry and found a family
- Article 13: right to an effective remedy in relation to a violation of Convention rights
- Article 14: prohibition of discrimination in relation to the rights and freedoms set out in the Convention, supplemented by Article 5 of Protocol 7: right to equality between spouses
- Article 16: Restrictions on political activity of aliens
- Article 17: Prohibition of abuse of rights.
- Article 18: Limitation on use of restrictions on rights.

The Protocols to which further effect is given by the Human Rights Act are as follows:

- Protocol 1, Article 1: protection of property
- Protocol 1, Article 2: right to education
- Protocol 1, Article 3: right to free elections
- Protocol 6, Article 1: abolition of the death penalty, but with a possible exception in
- Protocol 6, Article 2: allowing a state to make provision for the death penalty in times of war or where there is an imminent threat of war.

Articles 19 to 51 of the Convention provide for the establishment and operation of the European Court of Human Rights.

Principles of Interpretation of the European Convention

The European Convention was intended to apply international 1.15 standards across diverse jurisdictions. The approach which the Court takes to the interpretation of the Convention is governed by international law rather than the rules of interpretation in the relevant state. In dealing with cases from each jurisdiction, the judges of the European Court of Human Rights have to take into account the national laws and culture of the relevant state. This is done by allowing a "margin of appreciation" when considering issues such as whether or not a restriction on a right is reasonable. When giving effect to Convention rights the courts in the United Kingdom cannot treat cases from Strasbourg as precedents in the same way as cases from within the hierarchy of the national legal systems. The Human Rights Act has expressed this as a principle that the courts must take into account Strasbourg jurisprudence. This does not mean that decisions and judgments from Strasbourg will be regarded as having the same binding authority as, for example, decisions by the House of Lords.

Purpose of the Convention

Any interpretation of the terms of the Convention must give 1.16 consideration to the object and purpose of the Convention. As it is first and foremost an instrument for the protection of individual human beings its provisions should be interpreted so as to make its safeguards practical and effective.[14] This does not mean that there will be no restrictions whatsoever on individual rights or liberties since restrictions will often be justified. The legitimacy of each restriction on individual rights is considered on its own merits.

Uniform Meaning for Convention Terms

The Court of Human Rights interprets terms used in the 1.17 Convention in a manner independent of their meaning under particular national laws. The Court has had to develop its own meanings for words whose meanings vary amongst national legal systems. This is in order to secure consistent application regardless of the national legal systems from which a case originates. The terms used may not have the same meanings as legal or technical terms in any national system. This is known as the principle of "autonomous meaning". The terminology used under national law is taken into account for clarificatioon.

---

[14] *Loizidou v. Turkey* (1995) 20 E.H.R.R. 99, para. 72

Convention as a Dynamic and Evolving Instrument

1.18 The Court of Human Rights has repeatedly stressed that the
Convention is a living instrument which must be interpreted in the
light of present-day conditions.[15] This means that the original
negotiations for the development of the Convention and the
original statements of intent are rarely taken into account. As the
Convention is a living instrument the Court of Human Rights
accepts that the effect of the Convention may change over time. The
Court of Human Rights is aware of developing standards in human
rights protection and its decisions take account of these changes in
standards. In the case of *Brown v. Stott* it was stated that:

> "In interpreting the Convention, as any other treaty, it is
> generally to be assumed that the parties have included the
> terms which they wish to include and on which they were able
> to agree, omitting other terms which they did not wish to
> include or on which they were not able to agree. Thus
> particular regard must be had and reliance placed on the
> express terms of the Convention, which define the rights and
> freedoms which the contracting parties have undertaken to
> secure. This does not mean that nothing can be implied into
> the Convention. The language of the Convention is for the
> most part so general that some implication of terms is
> necessary, and the case-law of the European Court shows that
> the court has been willing to imply terms into the Convention
> when it was judged necessary or plainly right to do so. But the
> process of implication is one to be carried out with caution, if
> the risk is to be averted that the contracting parties may, by
> judicial interpretation, become bound by obligations which
> they did not expressly accept and might not have been willing
> to accept. As an important constitutional instrument the
> Convention is to be seen as a 'living tree capable of growth
> and expansion within its natural limits'[*Edwards v. Attorney
> General of Canada* [1930] A.C. 124] but those limits will often
> call for very careful consideration." [16]

Convention Rights as Minimum Standards

1.19 Articles 52 to 59 of the Convention contain miscellaneous

---

[15] *Loizidou v. Turkey* (1995) 20 E.H.R.R. 99, para. 72.
[16] *Brown (Margaret) v. Stott, (sub nom. Stott (Procurator Fiscal) v. Brown;
Procurator Fiscal, Dunfermline v. Brown; Brown v. Procurator Fiscal, Dunfermline)* [2001] 2 W.L.R. 817; [2001] 2 All E.R. 97; 2001 S.L.T. 59; 2001 S.C.C.R. 62;
[2001] R.T.R. 11; [2001] H.R.L.R. 9; [2001] U.K.H.R.R. 333; (2001) 145 S.J.L.B.
100.

provisions. This includes the very important Article 53, which states that:

> "Nothing in this Convention shall be construed as limiting or derogating from any of the human rights and fundamental freedoms which may be ensured under the laws of any High Contracting Party or under any other agreement to which it is a party."

This Article makes it cleat that the standards for the protection of rights in the Convention are the minimum standards. Where an individual already has a higher level of protection under domestic law, that law will take precedence. Resort to the European Court will only be required where the law of the State concerned has failed to protect an individual's right when judged against the benchmark of the minimum standard in the relevant Article or Articles.

Derogation and Reservation

A few Convention rights are absolute and subject to no possibility of derogation. These are the prohibitions on torture, inhuman and degrading punishment,[17] of slavery,[18] and on retroactive criminal offences.[19] Some other provisions are subject to strictly limited derogation only. A state may, under Article 15, derogate from the right to life in time of war or grave public emergency but only in respect of deaths resulting from lawful acts of war. The only permitted restriction on the abolition of the death penalty is in respect of acts committed in time of war or imminent threat of war.[20] In general, however, the Convention follows a pattern of stating a right in general terms and then permitting restrictions on that right, to take account of other legitimate interests within the state. Following a decision that the United Kingdom had violated Article 5(3), which requires that persons arrested or detained shall be brought promptly before a judge, the United Kingdom entered a derogation from that Article.[21] The court held that a delay of four days and six hours in bringing a person before a judge did not comply with Article 5(3). The four applicants had been arrested by the police in Northern Ireland as persons reasonably suspected of involvement in acts of terrorism. The detention had been authorised by section 12 of the Prevention of Terrorism (Temporary Provisions) Act 1984.

1.20

---

[17]   ECHR, Art. 3.
[18]   *ibid.,* Art. 4(1).
[19]   *ibid.,* Art. 7.
[20]   *ibid.,* Protocol 6, Art. 2.
[21]   *Brogan v. U.K.* (A 145-B (1988)).

Convention cases are analysed in a standard way. The first stage
is for the Court to consider whether there has been an interference
with a right. If it is established that there has been interference with
a right, it is then necessary to consider whether the interference is
justified. In many cases some restriction on rights is justifiable.
Restrictions are deemed to be justified if they meet the following
four criteria:

(1) They must be lawful
(2) They must be intended to pursue a legitimate purpose
(3) They must be "necessary in a democratic society" and
(4) They must not be discriminatory.

Lawful Restrictions

1.21 Interference with Convention rights is *prima facie* unlawful therefore any interference must be specifically authorised. In giving
specific authorisation for an infringement of a right

"the law must indicate the scope of any such discretion
conferred on the competent authorities and the manner of its
exercise with sufficient clarity, having regard to the legitimate
aim of the measure in question, to give the individual
adequate protection against arbitrary interference".[22]

This concept is consistent with the rule that administrative
discretion is never unfettered but must only be exercised within the
confines of the power which has been delegated to the individual
administrator.[23] It is also a restatement of Dicey's first principle of
the rule of law as "the absolute supremacy or predominance of
regular law as opposed to the influence of arbitrary power".[24] The
Court of Session is experienced in judging whether administrative
decisions are within the bounds of the powers which have been
delegated by law and have little difficulty in satisfying itself whether
any restriction on Convention rights is lawful.

Restrictions Intended to Pursue a Legitimate Purpose

1.22 Any interference with individual rights must have a legitimate
objective. It has been very rare indeed for the Court of Human
Rights to find that there has not been legitimate purpose for a
restriction. The Court has been reluctant to find that a national
government may have had an ulterior motive when imposing a
restriction where there is a stated justification which meets the

[22] *Malone v. U.K.* (1985) 7 E.H.R.R. 14, para. 68.
[23] *Padfield v. Minister of Agriculture, Fisheries and Food* [1968] A.C. 997.
[24] A.V. Dicey, *The Law of the Constitution*, (10th ed., Macmillan, 1959), p.202.

criteria. In the case of *Handyside v. United Kingdom*[25] the applicant was unable to prove that his books had been seized for political reasons rather than for the "protection of morals" of a child audience.

Necessity for the Restriction

The restriction must not exceed that which is necessary to meet the stated legitimate purpose. One important issue is the principle of proportionality: According to this principle, in order to be justified, a restriction must be proportionate to the legitimate aim pursued.[26] The extent of the restriction must be sufficient to achieve its aim without restricting individual freedoms any more than is strictly necessary. The law should aim for a fair balance between the rights of individuals, and the needs of the wider community.

    The principle of the "margin of appreciation" is of fundamental importance when restrictions on rights are under consideration. The Court of Human Rights recognises that state authorities are in a better position than the Court to assess what the interest of the society requires in their particular country. In the *Handyside* case the Court recognised the ability of the United Kingdom Government to assess the degree to which morality requires restrictions on obscene expressions. The margin of appreciation is a degree of deference accorded by the Court of Human Rights in recognition of the relative advantage of cultural awareness. This does not mean that states may take advantage to impose restrictions without limit. The restrictions have to be justified in each individual case before the Court. The attitude of the Court takes into account the context in which the restriction operates. A smaller margin of appreciation is allowed where the importance of the right at stake is greater. The Court also takes into account the particular purpose pursued by the state, and the degree to which practice varies among Convention States. In *R v. Director of Public Prosecutions, ex parte Kebilene*, Lord Hope observed as follows:

1.23

> "The doctrine of the margin of appreciation is an integral part of the supervisory jurisdiction which is exercised over state conduct by the international court. By conceding a margin of appreciation to each national system, the Court has recognised that the Convention, as a living system, does not need to be applied uniformly by all states but may vary in its application according to local needs and conditions. This technique is not available to the national courts when they are considering Convention issues within their own country. But

---

[25] *Handyside v. U.K.* (1976) 1E.H.R.R. 737.
[26] *ibid.*

in the hands of the national court also the Convention should be seen as an expression of fundamental principles rather than a set of mere rules. The questions which the courts will have to decide in the application of these principles will involve questions of balance between competing interests and issues of proportionality. In this area difficult choices may have to be made by the Executive or the legislator between the rights of the individual and the needs of society. In some circumstances, it will be appropriate for the courts to recognise that there is an area of judgement within which the judiciary will defer, on democratic grounds, to the considered opinion of the elected body or person whose act or decision is said to be incompatible with the Convention. It will be easier for such an area of judgement to be recognised where the Convention itself requires a balance to be struck, much less so where the right is stated in terms which are unqualified. It will be easier for it to be recognised where the issues involve questions of social or economic policy, much less so where the rights are of high constitutional importance or are of a kind where the courts are especially well placed to assess the needs for protection."[27]

Restrictions Must Not be Discriminatory

1.20 The Convention does not contain a general prohibition against discrimination *per se*. However, Article 14 prohibits discrimination in the enjoyment of the rights and freedoms set forth in the Convention. Under the Convention, discrimination is established where a distinction in treatment has no reasonable and objective justification.[28] The concept of a reasonable and objective justification for a difference in treatment may overlap with the consideration of whether a particular restriction is necessary in a democratic society. In both instances the principle question to be asked is whether a legitimate aim is sufficient to justify the distinction being made. The concept of discrimination relates specifically to circumstances where restrictions that are reasonable when applied uniformly may be unreasonable if applied in a different way to different groups of people.

---

[27] *R v. Director of Public Prosecutions, ex p. Kebilene* [1999] All E.R. 801.
[28] *Belgian Linguistics Case* (1968) Ser. A, No. 6, 1 E.H.R.R. 252, para. 10.

CHAPTER 2

FUNDAMENTAL HUMAN RIGHTS: ARTICLES 2, 3 AND 4

ARTICLE 2—THE RIGHT TO LIFE

"(1) Everyone's right to life shall be protected by law. No one shall be deprived of his life intentionally save in the execution of a sentence of a court following his conviction of a crime for which this penalty is provided by law.

(2) Deprivation of life shall not be regarded as inflicted in contravention of this article when it results from the use of force which is no more than is absolutely necessary:

(a) In defence of any person from unlawful violence;
(b) In order to effect a lawful arrest or to prevent the escape of a person lawfully detained;
(c) In action lawfully taken for the purpose of quelling a riot or insurrection."

Article 2 of the Convention expresses the most basic of all human rights, the right to life. It is a right which is not confined to the European Convention however, it is to be found in all other relevant human rights treaties, such as Article 6 of the United Nations International Covenant on Civil and Political Rights 1966. However, most of these Treaties include the exception of a judicially imposed death penalty. The European Convention includes the exception, but Optional Protocol Number 6 provides for the abolition of the death penalty in peacetime and most of the nation members of the Council of Europe, including the United Kingdom, have ratified this Protocol.[1] Article 2 of Protocol 6 permits the restriction on the abolition of the death penalty in respect of acts committed in time of war or imminent threat of war, and this reflects the original power in Article 15 which allowed 2.01

---

[1] The U.K. ratified this on May 20, 1999.

derogation from the Convention Article 2 in respect of deaths resulting from "lawful acts of war".

The Article is divided into two main aspects: the right to life itself, with the allowable exception of a judicially imposed death penalty after conviction; and three instances when the deprivation of life may be justified. These are

(1) self-defence or the defence of another;
(2) lawful arrest or the prevention of escape from lawful detention; and
(3) during action to quell a riot or insurrection.

In addition to these issues, this chapter will consider other aspects of the right to life which have been brought before the European Court: the investigation and prosecution of agents of the state who take life, including deaths in custody; abortion; euthanasia; and the death penalty. The last three are controversial in most states and the European Court treads carefully in its judgments in these issues.

Article 2 is one of the most fundamental and it must be strictly construed, particularly the exceptions of paragraph 2.[2] However, it is not designed to guarantee all human life, rather it is an instruction to the state and its agents who are required to protect the individual's right to life.[3] There have been many attempts to extend the meaning of Article 2 to encompass areas not perhaps envisaged by the original drafters. The European Court has acknowledged that the Convention is a "living document"[4] to be interpreted in the light of present day conditions. The Court also held that while creative interpretation cannot create a new right,[5] it will consider whether such extensions are appropriate. Two cases against the United Kingdom are of interest here. In the first, the Commission had to consider whether death and brain damage to children caused by vaccination came within the ambit of the Article. The Commission decided that although a small proportion of children had suffered death or injury, the vaccination programme had been conducted responsibly and was not a violation of Article 2.[6] In the second case, a number of children had been murdered by a nurse, Beverley Allitt, while in the care of a hospital. The parents argued that NHS cutbacks had led to inadequate supervision of the nurse and therefore the children's right to life had been violated.

---

[2] *McCann v. U.K.* (1995) 21 E.H.R.R. 97.
[3] P. Ferguson "The Right to Life: some procedural requirements" (2001) N.L.J. Vol. 151, no. 6986, 808.
[4] *Tyrer v. U.K.* (A/26) (1979–80) 2 E.H.R.R. 1, para. 31.
[5] *Johnston v. Ireland* (A/112) (1986) E.H.R.R. 203.
[6] *Association X v. U.K.* (1978) 14 D.R. 31; and see *Boffa v. San Marino* (1998) 92 D.R. 27.

The Commission refused to consider the issue of NHS funding.[7]

There need not be an intention to kill for the violation to occur. 2.02 For instance, in *Stewart v. United Kingdom*[8] a soldier was aiming at the legs of a rioter when he was struck by a brick and his gun misfired. The rubber bullet hit a young boy on the head and killed him. There was no question of a deliberate killing and the Commission found that although Article 2 applied, the soldier's action was lawful under paragraph 2 of the Article. The case highlighted that Article 2 will apply to both intentional killing and the accidental taking of life through the use of force. The words "absolutely necessary" in paragraph 2 indicate that a test of strict proportionality operates.

It is not necessary for the victim to die for the Article to apply; it may be sufficient if the victim's life has been put at material risk.[9] Article 2(1) requires the state to take appropriate steps to safeguard the lives of people living within the jurisdiction and this may amount to a positive obligation to take preventative measures to protect a person or persons who may be at risk because of the criminal acts of another. In *Osman v. United Kingdom*[10] a boy's teacher became obsessed with the boy and committed a number of minor offences pursuing the child. The police knew of the man's obsession but no protective measures were taken and the man murdered the boy's father and another person. A civil suit against the police failed, with the Court of Appeal relying on *Hill v. West Yorkshire Police*[11] saying that the police could not be sued for operational failures. The European Court held that the authorities had known there was a real and immediate threat to life in this case and they should therefore have taken appropriate measures to protect the Osman family.

> "The court notes that the first sentence of art 2(1) enjoins the state not only to refrain from the intentional and unlawful taking of life, but also to take appropriate steps to safeguard the lives of those within its jurisdiction . . . it must be established . . . that the authorities knew or ought to have known at the time of the existence of a real and immediate risk to the life of an identified individual or individuals from the criminal acts of a third party and that they failed to take measures within the scope of their powers which, judged reasonably, might have been expected to avoid that risk".[12]

---

[7] *Taylor Family v. U.K.* (1994) Appl. 23412/94.
[8] (1984) 39 D.R. 162.
[9] *Yasa v. Turkey* (1999) 28 E.H.R.R. 408.
[10] (2000) 29 E.H.R.R. 245.
[11] [1989] A.C. 53.
[12] See also *Danini v. Italy* (1996) 87 D.R. 24.

The Court also noted that the obligation to take preventative measures was not to be interpreted so as to impose an impossible or disproportionate burden on the authorities.[13]

In *Venables and Thompson v. News Group Newspapers Ltd*[14] the two boys convicted of the murder of two-year-old James Bulger when they were 10 years old sought permanent injunctions to prevent the media from disclosing any details of their whereabouts or their adult appearance once they had been released from custody. They based their claim on Articles 2 and 3. The newspapers claimed that the court had no jurisdiction to grant such injunctions in respect of adults and relied on Article 10 of the Convention and section 12(4) of the Human Rights Act 1998. Dame Butler-Sloss granted the permanent injunctions, stating that in exceptional circumstances the court could extend the protection of confidentiality of information where a failure to do so would probably lead to serious physical injury or to the death of the person seeking the injunction. There was a real and serious risk to the rights of the claimants under Articles 2 and 3.

> "In so doing and having regard to articles 2, 3 and 8 it is important to have regard to the fact that the rights under articles 2 and 3 are not capable of derogation, and the consequences to the claimants if those rights were to be breached. It is clear that on the basis that there is a real possibility that the claimants may be the objects of revenge attacks, the potential breaches of articles 2, 3 and 8 have to be evaluated with great care."[15]

2.03 Dame Butler-Sloss made reference to the judgment of Lord Woolf in *R v. Lord Saville of Newdigate, ex parte A.*[16] The case related to the identification of soldiers who had been involved in the events of "Bloody Sunday" in 1972 when 26 people were killed or injured. The tribunal of inquiry set up in 1998 and chaired by Lord Saville had insisted that if the soldiers retained anonymity, the tribunal's openness would be compromised. The Court of Appeal upheld the Divisional Court's decision to quash the tribunal's decision to insist on publication. Lord Woolf said that the tribunal had not considered sufficiently the risk to the soldiers' lives if their anonymity was lost.

> "[W]hen a fundamental right such as the right to life is engaged, the options available to the reasonable decision-

---

[13] See also *Mahmut Kaya v. Turkey*, March 28, 2000, ECtHR (unreported).
[14] [2001] 1 All E.R. 908.
[15] *ibid.*, para. 77.
[16] [1999] 4 All E.R. 860.

maker are curtailed. They are curtailed because it is unreasonable to reach a decision which contravenes or could contravene human rights unless there are sufficiently significant countervailing considerations. In other words, It is not open to the decision-maker to risk interfering with fundamental rights in the absence of compelling justification."

The risk to life must also be specific to the applicant; if it is a general risk, such as was experienced by persons holding high office in Ireland during the "Troubles", then there will be no obligation on the authorities to maintain a bodyguard.[17]

The Use of Force

The second paragraph of Article 2 allows the use of lethal force but only where it is absolutely necessary. The paragraph identifies three situations for the legitimate use of such force: 2.04

    (a) Self-defence or the defence of others;
    (b) To effect a lawful arrest or prevent an escape;
    (c) To quell a riot or insurrection.

   The United Kingdom Government has come under pressure as a result of this paragraph particularly for the activities of the police and armed forces in connection with the civil unrest in Northern Ireland. The European Court held in *McCann v. United Kingdom*[18] that the use of force has to be "strictly proportionate" to the risk. In this case, the action of soldiers in shooting three IRA terrorists in Gibraltar was held to be reasonable because they thought the terrorists were about to detonate a bomb. However, the authorities had had the terrorists under surveillance for some time and could have arrested them earlier; the failure to detain the suspects amounted to unlawful action. The Court stated that the authorities had to consider whether the operation could be "planned and controlled . . . so as to minimise, to the greatest extent possible, recourse to lethal force".[19] The Court noted that soldiers would shoot to kill, as they had been trained to do, whereas police officers were trained to wound and capture where possible. There had been earlier opportunities for the police to have arrested the three terrorists. The authorities had handled the situation poorly and thus there was an excessive use of force.
   In *Kelly v. United Kingdom*[20] a vehicle was being driven

---

[17] *W v. U.K.* (1983) 32 D.R. 190; *M v. U.K. and Ireland* (1986) 47 D.R. 27.
[18] (1995) 21 E.H.R.R. 97.
[19] *ibid.*, para. 194.
[20] (1993) 74 D.R. 139.

aggressively through a checkpoint and was thus putting the soldiers
manning the checkpoint at risk. The use of lethal force in these
circumstances was justified under paragraph 2(a). In similar
circumstances a British soldier shot at a car which drove through
a road block in Northern Ireland and one passenger was killed and
another wounded. The soldier relied on a plea of self-defence but
this was rejected by the Court of Appeal and the House of Lords.
His actions were subject to a reasonableness test and in this
instance, the action was "grossly disproportionate to the mischief to
be averted".[21] His conviction for murder was subsequently
reviewed and after a re-trial he was acquitted on evidential grounds.

2.05   In *McCann* the European Court commented on the investigation
of the deaths by inquest proceedings and it has been held to be
important that there is an effective investigation of any deaths or
injuries caused by the use of force by state authorities. The
minimum requirements for such investigations were set out in
Velikova v. Belgium.[22] The investigation must be thorough, effective
and impartial. In the *Taylor Family v. United Kingdom* case, the
Commission said that although the inquiry into the deaths of the
children murdered by Beverley Allitt was not held in public, it was
sufficient that the families could attend and the report itself was
published. The lack of effective investigation may itself be a breach
of Article 2 as was found in *Salman v. Turkey.*[23] In this case, the
Court said: "When a person is taken into custody in good health
and dies, there is a particularly stringent obligation on the
authorities to provide a satisfactory and convincing explanation
of the death." There was no plausible explanation for the man's
injuries and the government did not account for his death while in
custody, therefore the responsibility for the death lay with them.

On May 5, 2001, the Court ruled on cases where 14 men were
killed by the security forces in Northern Ireland during the period
1982 to 1992.[24] In each case, the Court found that there had been a
violation of Article 2 because there had been no proper investigation by the state of the circumstances in which the deaths occurred.
The incidents had led to charges that there was a "shoot-to-kill"
policy operated by the security forces in Northern Ireland, but the
Court did not rule on this point, saying that it would have entailed
an analysis of the history of the "Troubles". They found that the
investigations had shown a lack of independence of the investigating police officers from the security forces involved in the incidents,

[21] *R v. Clegg* [1995] 1 All E.R. 334 at 338D.
[22] April 27, 2000.
[23] [2001] EHRLR 108; see also *Tanrikulu v. Turkey* (2000) 30 E.H.R.R. 950.
[24] *Jordan v. U.K.*, Appl. 24746/94; *McKerr v. U.K.*, Appl. 28883/95; *Kelly v. U.K.*,
Appl. 30054/96; *Shanaghan v. U.K.*, Appl. 37715/97, all decided May 4, 2001,
ECtHR.

a lack of public scrutiny and information to the victims' families of the reasons for the decision not to prosecute and the non-disclosure of witness statements prevented the applicants from fully participating in the inquests. In addition, the Director of Public Prosecutions failed to give reasons why he had decided not to prosecute; he had no duty to do so but he did have discretion in whether he should supply reasons. In addition, the use of public interest immunity certificates had prevented the investigation of relevant matters at the inquest proceedings.[25] The Court held that there had to be proper transparent procedures for ensuring the accountability of state agents where there has been a use of lethal force. Such procedures were necessary to instill public confidence and dispel any fears of improper motives.

In Scotland, there have been few instances where the police, armed forces or other agencies have had to kill someone while trying to apprehend them or prevent injury to others. Police officers may use force to effect an arrest or to prevent the commission of a crime but the amount of force used must be reasonable in the circumstances.[26] The use of force to arrest is recognised as permissible under Article 2(2) of the Convention but the second reason for force, to prevent the commission of a crime, may not be. The Convention test that the killing is "absolutely necessary" (which suggests the officer has no other alternative) is a stricter test than "reasonable in the circumstances". It is possible in the future that any killing of a person by police officers will be viewed differently by prosecuting authorities and this will lead to more prosecutions. A similar difficulty arises where the plea of justification is made on the grounds of self-defence. Currently a person who kills and pleads self-defence will be entitled to be acquitted if certain conditions are satisfied. The danger to life or limb of the accused or a third party must have been imminent and it must have been necessary to use that force.[27] In addition, the amount of the retaliation must not be excessive and there must have been no opportunity to retreat or escape from the situation.[28] Gane observes that the effect of the Convention rules may cause an anomaly in that the scope of self-defence would be narrower when invoked by a soldier or police officer than by a member of the public.[29] This assumes that Article 2(2) does not have horizontal

---

[25] This has been changed by a Home Office Circular issued in 1999 recommending disclosure 28 days before the inquest is held.

[26] *Marchbank v. Annan*, 1987 S.C.C..R. 718; see also J. Rogers "Justifying the Use of Firearms by Policemen and Soldiers: a response to the Home Office's review of the law on the use of lethal force" (1998) 18(4) L.S. 486.

[27] *Fenning v. H.M. Advocate*, 1985 S.L.T. 540.

[28] *McBrearty v. H.M. Advocate*, 1999 S.L.T. 1333.

[29] C. Gane "The Substantive Criminal Law" in *A Practical Guide to Human Rights Law in Scotland* (Lord Reed (ed.), W. Green & Son, Edinburgh, 2001).

x24 *Human Rights and Scots Law*

effect so as to apply to the actions of private individuals.

2.06   The Convention requires a state to protect a citizen's right to life from infringement by officials. It could be argued that a citizen should also be protected from attack by other citizens.[30] This may lead to the plea of self-defence being more narrowly construed as a result of the Convention's rules being applied in the Scottish courts.[31]

Deaths in Custody

2.07   The state has an obligation to investigate the death of a person who has been held in the custody of the police or prison authorities.[32] That investigation should be sufficiently rigorous and transparent so that an explanation for the death can be given and appropriate action taken.

The issue of transparency was raised in respect of a decision of the Director of Public Prosecutions not to prosecute. The High Court of Justice decided in *R v. D.P.P., ex parte Manning*[33] that where a man on remand had died in prison custody and a coroner's jury had returned a verdict of unlawful killing, naming a certain prison officer, against whom there was *prima facie* evidence, there was an expectation of a plausible explanation for the decision not to prosecute. The Director of Public Prosecutions should in those circumstances supply the reasons for his decision.

Where a death in legal custody has occurred in Scotland, the Procurator Fiscal will be informed and will take charge of the ensuing inquiry to secure evidence and investigate the circumstances of the incident. The fiscal will report his or her findings to the Lord Advocate and a fatal accident inquiry will be held under the Fatal Accidents and Sudden Deaths Inquiry (Scotland) Act 1976[34] unless a trial is to be proceeded with. The holding of a fatal accident inquiry is mandatory in two circumstances: for the death of an employee occurring as a result of an accident at work, and where the person has died while being held in legal custody. The definition of legal custody here does not include the detention of persons who were being held outside a police station. The Act does allow a discretionary fatal accident inquiry to be held in those circumstances. A discretionary fatal accident inquiry may be held where a death is sudden, suspicious or unexplained, or has occurred in

---

[30] Perhaps as a result of the *Osman* ruling, *supra* no. 10.
[31] A. Ashworth "The Human Rights Act and the Substantive Criminal Law: A Non-Minimalist View" [2000] Crim. L.R. 564. For a different view, see R. Buxton "The Human Rights Act and the Substantive Criminal Law" [2000] Crim. L.R. 331.
[32] *supra* no. 23.
[33] [2000] 3 W.L.R. 463.
[34] s.1.

circumstances giving rise to public concern, and where it appears that it is in the public interest to hold such an inquiry. A Fatal Accident Inquiry is held before a sheriff and its purpose is to inquire into the circumstances of the death and any actions or systems that caused or contributed to the death. At the end of the inquiry the sheriff will make a determination in terms of section 6 of the Act. This will set out, so far as it is possible to do so, the details of the occurrence leading to the accident and the cause of death, any reasonable precautions which might have prevented the death and accident, any defects in the working systems and any other relevant facts. The sheriff has no power to make findings of fault or to apportion blame between any persons contributing to the accident. It is also possible for the Lord Advocate to order a fatal accident inquiry at the conclusion of a trial if there are issues still unresolved by the trial.

In England, all incidents of death or serious injury involving police officers are investigated by the Police Complaints Authority set up under the Police and Criminal Evidence Act 1984. However, the investigation is supervised by the Police Complaints Authority but carried out by the police themselves. This practice was criticised by the European Committee for the Prevention of Torture in 1997.[35] The Committee doubted whether the Authority and the investigative procedures would have the confidence of the public. The Stephen Lawrence Inquiry Report reached a similar conclusion[36] and in 2000 the Home Office asked consultants to look at the options for setting up an independent police complaints commission.

There is a requirement to safeguard a prisoner while he or she is in custody and this may extend to taking reasonable steps to prevent him or her from committing suicide. In *Keenan v. United Kingdom*[37] a mentally disturbed prisoner committed suicide while he was being held in segregation on the punishment block. His mother sought a ruling that proper steps had not been taken to safeguard his life and that placing him in the punishment block amounted to inhuman and degrading treatment under Article 3 because of his mental state. The Commission accepted the mother's submission and the case was heard by the Court in April 2001. The medical practitioners in the case disagreed on the diagnosis of paranoid schizophrenia with a high risk of suicide and the Court accordingly was unable to find a violation of Article 2. However,

2.08

---

[35] Report to the U.K. Government on the visit to the U.K. and Isle of Man carried out by the European Committee for the Prevention of Torture and Inhuman and Degrading Treatment or Punishment (CPT), September 8–17, 1997.

[36] *The Stephen Lawrence Inquiry Report* by Sir William MacPherson of Cluny (The Stationery Office, 1999).

[37] Appl. 27229/95, decision April 3, 2001.

the administrative decision to impose a seven day segregation in the punishment block when it was known he was at risk amounted to ill-treatment under Article 3. This particular case may raise a number of issues for the Scottish prison service after the spate of prison suicides in the women's prison, Cornton Vale, and other prison establishments.

Abortion

2.09 This complex and highly controversial procedure has been considered by the Convention bodies on a number of occasions. In *Paton v. United Kingdom*[38] the Commission held that there was no breach of Article 2 if the abortion was carried out at an early stage of the pregnancy to protect the mother's health.

> "The 'life' of the foetus is intimately connected with, and cannot be regarded in isolation of, the pregnant woman. If article 2 were held to cover the foetus and its protection under the article were . . . seen as absolute, an abortion would have to be considered as prohibited even where the continuance of the pregnancy would involve a serious risk to the life of the pregnant woman. This would mean that the 'unborn life' of the foetus would be regarded as being of higher value than the life of the pregnant woman. The 'right to life' of a person already born would thus be considered as subject not only to the express limitations [set out in Article 2(2)] but also to a further, implied limitation."[39]

Reasonable rules to restrict abortion are not incompatible with the Convention and do not violate a woman's rights under Article 8.[40] The judges of the European Court have shied away from pronouncing on the "rights" of the foetus, perhaps because there is no consensus among the States themselves. In *Open Door Counselling and Dublin Well Woman Centre Ltd v. Ireland*[41] a dissenting minority of judges said that Article 2 protected the foetus *in utero* but the majority did not address the issue. The case was in fact dealt with on the basis of the balance between freedom of expression and protection of morals.

The thorny questions in abortion concern the status of the foetus—is the foetus a person, and if it is, can it then become a victim? These questions involve deep ethical issues and it is not the purpose of this book to discuss ethics. However, the issue of

---

[38] (1981) 3 E.H.R.R. 408.
[39] *ibid.*, para. 19.
[40] *Bruggemann and Scheuten v. Germany* (1977) 10 D.R. 100.
[41] (1992) 15 E.H.R.R. 244.

abortion is one which taxes both the European Court and domestic courts. The argument seems to be that a case before the European Court requires the applicant to be a victim. A foetus has the potential for life but it does not experience life "now". Further, it has the potential to become a victim, but if it is aborted then the potential for life ceases as does the potential for becoming a victim.[42]

In Great Britain, abortion is regulated by various statutes, in 2.10 particular section 1 of the Abortion Act 1967 as amended by section 37 of the Human Fertilisation and Embryology Act 1990.[43] The 1967 Act allows termination of pregnancy where the pregnancy has lasted less than 24 weeks and its continuation would involve greater risk to the physical or mental health of the mother or any existing children; or there is grave risk of permanent injury or death to her; or there is a substantial risk that the child would suffer from serious handicap.

The law concerning abortion is a reserved power to the United Kingdom Parliament under the Scotland Act 1998 although this was a highly controversial reservation.

In Scotland, the courts have had to consider whether aborting a foetus was a civil wrong actionable at the instance of the foetus. In *Kelly v. Kelly*[44] the estranged husband of a pregnant woman sought interdict to prevent her having an abortion. The man argued that as he was the biological father he was the unborn child's guardian and should be able to petition the court to prevent damage taking place to the child while still *in utero*. The Court of Session concluded that "Scots law conferred no right on the foetus to continue to reside in its mother's womb".[45] The abortion was not a civil wrong and the father had no right to prevent the abortion taking place.

Euthanasia and Withdrawal of Life-sustaining Medical Treatment

As with abortion, these are issues that raise controversy and 2.11 questions of morality and ethics. There are few European cases on euthanasia. In *Widmar v. Switzerland*[46] the Commission declared that there was no requirement under Article 2 for states to make passive euthanasia a criminal offence. In some cases, the Court has

---

[42] P. Bassen "Present Stakes and Future Prospects: the status of early abortion" (1982) 11 Philosophy and Public Affairs 34.

[43] The 1967 Act does not apply in Northern Ireland where abortion remains unlawful. The law there is still regulated by the Offences against the Person Act 1861 which prohibits the procurement of a miscarriage at any stage of the pregnancy.

[44] 1997 S.L.T. 896.

[45] E. Russell "Abortion Law in Scotland and The Kelly Foetus" 1997 S.L.T. 187 at 188.

[46] Appl. 20527/92 (1993).

ruled that termination or withdrawal of medical treatment may
amount to a breach of Articles 2 or 3. In *D v. United Kingdom*[47] the
Court avoided making a decision on whether Article 2 would be
violated, instead basing its decision on inhuman treatment in
violation of Article 3. D was subject to a deportation order but
challenged the order on the ground that he had an incurable and
terminal disease and the country to which he was to be deported did
not have the necessary medical facilities to ease his suffering.

In September 2000, doctors in England had to make a harrowing
choice; separate conjoined ("Siamese") twins and allow one child to
die, or leave the twin girls joined and see both children die within a
few months. The difficult decision to operate was opposed by the
children's parents. In *Re A (Children)(Conjoined Twins: Medical
Treatment)(No. 1)*[48] the Court of Appeal held that it was lawful for
the separation operation to go ahead even though the death of one
child was the inevitable result of the procedure. The "right" of life
for one child who had a good chance of having a good quality of
life outweighed the right of the other child, who could not survive
since she was dependent on her sister's vital organs. The Court held
that the evil to be inflicted was not disproportionate to the evil
avoided.

In 1996, the Scottish courts considered whether it would be in the
best interests of a woman in a persistent vegetative state to
discontinue the treatment of artificial feeding and hydration.[49] A
court of five judges of the Inner House of the Court of Session held
that the court had jurisdiction on behalf of the sovereign as *parens
patriae* (to protect those who could not protect themselves) to
authorise a medical practitioner to discontinue life sustaining
treatment where the patient was permanently insensate and
unconscious. It was not in the best interests of the patient that
the life sustaining treatment be continued. In addition to this
decision, the Lord Advocate issued a statement to clarify the
criminal law and confirm that no criminal prosecution would follow
a decision to withdraw treatment from a patient in persistent
vegetative state provided the permission of the civil court had been
granted. This case followed the English decision in *Airedale NHS
Trust v. Bland* where a victim of the Hillsborough football stadium
disaster was left in a persistent vegetative state and his parents and
the hospital sought permission to discontinue the treatment he was
receiving.[50] In a more recent case, a hospital trust sought a
declaration to allow it to discontinue the administration of artificial
hydration and nutrition to M, a woman who had been in a

---

[47] (1997) 24 E.H.R.R. 423.
[48] [2001] 2 W.L.R. 480.
[49] *Law Hospital NHS Trust v. Lord Advocate*, 1996 S.C. 301.
[50] [1993] A.C. 789.

persistent vegetative state for more than three years.[51] The Family Division of the High Court of Justice granted the declaration saying that the continuation of treatment was no longer in the best interests of M and its withdrawal did not violate Article 2(1) of the Convention. This latter declaration was based on the European Court's decision in *Osman v. United Kingdom*[52] where the Court said that the positive obligation on a state to protect life was not an absolute obligation to treat a patient if that treatment would be futile. Further, the discontinuance of treatment would not violate Article 3 since that article required the victim to be aware of inhuman or degrading treatment and here M had had no awareness of the treatment for three years and thus would be unaware of its withdrawal. In the *Bland* case the House of Lords had made it clear that their decision applied only to patients in a persistent vegetative state and that any decision to withdraw treatment needed the approval of the High Court.[53]

In *NHS Trust v. D*[54] a child was born with chronic irreversible 2.12 and worsening lung disease. He also had heart failure and dysfunction of the liver and kidneys. His life expectancy was short. The hospital sought a declaration that should he suffer future respiratory or heart failure, the treatment should be palliative only and not include artificial ventilation and resuscitation. The child's parents strongly opposed the application. Three paediatricians reported that it was in the best interest of the child not to be subjected to such invasive procedures. Both parties cited Article 2 in support of their views. The court held that the courts had a strong obligation to take all steps in favour of preserving human life save in the most exceptional circumstances. Withholding life prolonging treatment did not violate Article 2 because it was in the best interests of the child. The court also referred to the European Court's ruling in *D v. United Kingdom*[55] where it was held that Article 3 of the Convention required that a person is not subjected to inhuman or degrading treatment and this includes the right to die with dignity.

The question of whether the state must preserve life, even though the person does not wish this, has been raised in recent years. In *Secretary of State for Home Department v. Robb*[56] a prisoner on hunger strike was recognised as having a right to self-determination

---

[51] *NHS Trust A v. M* [2001] 2 W.L.R. 942.
[52] *supra* no. 10.
[53] Practice Note [1996] 4 All E.R. 766; and see discussion of these cases in G. Laurie and J. Mason "Negative Treatment of Vulnerable Patients: Euthanasia by any other name?" (2000) Jurid. Rev. Pt. 3, 159.
[54] [2000] 2 Fam.L.R. 677.
[55] *supra* no. 47.
[56] [1995] Fam.L.R. 127.

which took precedence over any countervailing interest of the state in preserving life and preventing suicide. In *X v. Germany*[57] the Commission held that force feeding might amount to inhuman or degrading treatment under Article 3, but not where it was carried out to uphold the state's positive obligation to protect life. In a later case, the Court ruled that forcible medical treatment or feeding would not be inhuman or degrading treatment under Article 3 where it was therapeutically necessary.[58]

The issue of consent to medical treatment is increasingly being raised in the courts. Generally the domestic courts have recognised that if an adult is suffering from no mental incapacity, that person has an absolute right to consent to or refuse medical treatment.[59] A number of cases in the early 1990s in England overruled the wishes of pregnant women who were refusing to have a caesarian section to deliver their baby[60] but the Court of Appeal reaffirmed in 1998 that a mentally competent pregnant woman may refuse medical intervention.[61]

2.13   Patients, or their parents in the case of children, may refuse medical treatment because of their religious beliefs. The courts take the view that the interests of the patient or child patient is paramount. Thus where a 15-year-old Jehovah's Witness had refused to give consent to any blood transfusion which might be necessary during a kidney transplant, the High Court in Belfast ruled that the procedure was lawful and in the girl's best interests.[62]

It is possible that there will be challenges to the procedures of the prison authorities where they refuse to issue condoms to homosexual prisoners. It could be argued that there is a positive duty to minimise the risk of these prisoners contracting HIV infection. The Prison Service's Director of Healthcare in England and Wales wrote to Heads of the Prison Healthcare warning that prison doctors may be in breach of their duty of care if they do not prescribe condoms to a prisoner who requests them and then goes on to contract HIV in prison.[63] Even if the breach of the Convention is due to the prisoner's own conduct, the State is not necessarily absolved from responsibility.[64] The European Court has stated that sexual orientation and activity is "an intimate aspect of private life"

---

[57] (1985) 7 E.H.R.R. 152.

[58] *Herczegfalvy v. Austria* (1992) 15 E.H.R.R. 437.

[59] *E.g. Re T (adult)(refusal of medical treatment)* [1992] 4 All E.R. 649.

[60] *E.g. Norfolk and Norwich Healthcare (NHS) Trust v. W* [1996] 2 F.L.R. 613.

[61] *St George's Healthcare NHS Trust v. S (No. 2)* [1998] 3 All E.R. 673.

[62] See also, *supra* no. 48.

[63] J. Levenson "A Hard Act to Follow? Prisons and the HRA" (2000) London, Prison Reform Trust.

[64] *McFeeley v. U.K.* (1981) 3 E.H.R.R. 161.

under Article 8[65] but it is nonetheless debatable whether the rights under Article 8 would include the right of a prisoner to have condoms so that he could indulge in homosexual activity in prison.

The Suicide Act 1961 abolished the crime of suicide in England but retained the crime of aiding and abetting, counselling or procuring the suicide of another, and thus it is an offence to actively assist someone to die—so-called "active euthanasia". This position was reiterated by the House of Lords Select Committee on Medical Ethics in 1994 when it unanimously decided that there should be no change in the substantive law on euthanasia, mercy killing or complicity in suicide.[66] The Committee also recognised that a person of sound mind should be able to refuse invasive medical treatment either now or to take account of future incapacity by completing a "living will".

In Scotland, where someone has assisted another to commit suicide or has committed euthanasia it is likely that they would not be charged with murder but with culpable homicide. The reason is that the *mens rea* will not be present and thus there is no malice or wicked intent on the part of the accused. In Scots law, there must be *mens rea* for a conviction of murder to be made.[67] In late 2001, Mrs Diane Pretty sought judicial review of a decision of the Director of Public Prosecutions that her husband might be subject to a criminal charge if he assisted her to die. Mrs Pretty suffers from the fatal motor neurone disease and needs assistance for all tasks. After her petition was rejected by the House of Lords[67A] Mrs Pretty took her case to the European Court of Human Rights on March 19, 2002 and an early decision is expected.

Euthanasia has been recognised in law in some states of the United States and in the Netherlands, but in 1997, the Australian Supreme Court declared legislation legitimising euthanasia in the Northern Territory was unconstitutional.

Suicide is not a crime in Scotland but a person who tries to commit suicide, particularly in a public place, may be charged with breach of the peace, thus allowing the authorities to seek psychiatric assistance for the person.

In its early days of operation, the Scottish Parliament tackled 2.15 some of the issues surrounding the incapacity of adults who, by reason of mental disorder or inability to communicate, are unable to regulate their own affairs. The Adults with Incapacity (Scotland)

2.14

---

[65] *Laskey v. U.K.* (1997) 24 E.H.R.R. 39; H. Arnott "HIV/AIDS, Prisons and the Human Rights Act" (2001) E.H.R.L.R. 1.

[66] Report of the House of Lords Select Committee on Medical Ethics (1993-94) H.L. Paper 21-I.

[67] M. Christie (ed.) *Gordon's Criminal Law of Scotland* (2000) at 249.

[67A] *R (on the application of Pretty) v. D.P.P.* [2002] H.R.L.R. 10.

Act 2000[68] received the Royal Assent on May 9, 2000 and deals, *inter alia,* with the issue of medical treatment in Part 5. The law of Scotland prior to this Act was uncertain since it was not clear whether the doctor treating an adult patient with an incapacity had the authority to do so. The only way to ensure the doctor had authority was to apply to the courts as in the *Law Hospital* case. Section 47(2) of the Act gives the doctor a general authority to "do what is reasonable in the circumstances . . . to safeguard or promote the physical or mental health of the patient". The Act is clear that the treatment is for safeguarding or promoting the patients' health and that would therefore preclude its use to allow a doctor to withdraw artificial life-supporting treatment. The original bill had defined medical treatment as: "surgical, medical, nursing, optical or dental procedure or treatment; ventilation, nutrition and hydration by artificial means; and any other procedure or treatment designed to safeguard or promote physical or mental health". The second part of the original definition had caused concern and considerable debate within the Scottish Parliament since it was perceived as allowing "passive euthanasia". The Scottish Ministers were at pains to reassure the Parliament that "the common law position relating to patients in persistent vegetative state, established in the judgment of the Law Hospital case, stands and is not superseded by this bill".[69]

Another issue has arisen in recent years with regard to the withdrawal of medical treatment. On occasions, doctors have to decide whether or not to resuscitate a patient who is terminally ill and whose heart stops. The doctor has to consider whether the treatment is futile and they should not prolong the patient's suffering by resuscitation. Some doctors started marking patient's notes with the initials "D.N.R." (do not resuscitate) without the patient or their relatives being aware of this. Where the patient is mentally capable then they should be involved in the non-resuscitation decision. This right comes from Convention rights under Articles 2 and 8. Under Article 8, there is no general right to demand treatment, rather there is a right to be consulted on the treatment or decision being offered. Under Article 2, the state has the obligation to protect the life of patients in its care but the *Osman* decision has limited that obligation to what is reasonable.[70] The European Court has also recognised the concept of futility.[71] The Convention will ensure that decisions involving life and death will have to be properly justified by the medical practitioners and a

---

[68] 2000, asp 4.
[69] Iain Gray, Deputy Minister for Community Care, SPOR, Justice and Home Affairs Committee, February 29, 2000, col. 819.
[70] *Osman v. U.K.* (2000) 29 E.H.R.R. 245 at 306, para. 116.
[71] *LCB v. U.K.* 1999 27 E.H.R.R. 212.

decision not to resuscitate will have to be based on relevant and reasonable considerations. Many D.N.R. decisions operate as a blanket-ban against certain types of people, for instance those who are old, frail and considered likely to die soon. However, if the D.N.R. decision is made on the basis of the age of the patient, this may be a breach of Article 14 as well as Article 2. Article 14 prohibits discrimination on any grounds and then gives a list of examples such as sex and race. The list however is not exhaustive and discrimination on grounds of age may be included in the list.

It is clear from the foregoing that there is no right to demand a certain kind of treatment, particularly where doctors have deduced that the treatment would not benefit the patient. In *R v. Cambridgeshire District Health Authority, ex parte B*[72] a young girl with leukaemia sought an order to compel the health authority to pay for an innovative treatment which she hoped would save her life. The doctors had decided that any further treatment, except palliative care, would be futile. The Court of Appeal held that it had no authority to interfere with the clinical judgment of her doctors. The decisions of the European Court to date would appear to support this view.

An aspect of this discussion not yet answered is where a patient is 2.16 refused specific treatment to prolong his life because its effectiveness would be lessened because of the patients' failure to take medical advice, for instance to give up smoking or drinking. The treatment would benefit the patient but not to the extent expected or desired by the doctors. Such a decision by the doctors might be challengeable as a violation of the patient's human rights.

The Death Penalty

Protocol Number 6, para. 1: "The death penalty shall be abolished. 2.17 No-one shall be condemned to such a penalty or executed."

The European Convention on Human Rights Protocol Number 6 seeks the abolition of the death penalty but the European Court has not stated that the death penalty violates Article 2, the right to life. This was made clear in *Soering v. United Kingdom*[73] where Soering was resisting extradition to the United States to stand trial on a murder charge. If convicted, there was a real danger that he might receive the death penalty and thus be required to spend a number of years on "death row" before all avenues of appeal against the sentence had been exhausted. He submitted that spending years on death row would be inhuman treatment under Article 3. It is notable that Amnesty International was granted special leave by the court to make written submissions on the death penalty itself. The

---

[72] [1995] 1 W.L.R. 898.
[73] (1989) Series A, No. 161.

organisation argued that the death penalty should be held to be an inhuman punishment and a violation of the right to life. However, only one judge supported this view, saying that the extradition would expose Soering to the risk of inhuman treatment and would also "and above all, violate his right to life."[74] The court held that the long wait on death row whilst the appeal procedures were completed amounted to inhuman treatment under Article 3, but was not a violation of Article 2. Kidd points out a paradox here.[75] An extradition to a country where the death penalty sentence would be carried out quickly, without the long drawn-out appeal process of the United States, would not necessarily violate Article 3 in terms of inhuman treatment. In fact, the inhuman treatment in a jurisdiction like the United States would be set in train by the prisoner himself utilising the appeal process which would then subject him to the "death row phenomenon".

Another interesting issue in the *Soering* case was the willingness of the European Court to rule on a *potential* violation of the Convention. In most cases, the Court rules on issues after the damage has been done, but in this case, of course, the damage was likely to be permanent and irreparable. The Commission asked the United Kingdom to suspend its extradition order pending the Court's ruling.[76] The United Kingdom complied with the request, possibly because the death penalty for most capital crimes was abolished in the United Kingdom many years ago. It is interesting to note here that even when the United Kingdom had the death penalty, it was not carried out if there was a delay of more than 90 days between the sentence of death being pronounced and the date of execution. In such circumstances, the Home Secretary had invariably granted a reprieve[77] and thus the United Kingdom avoided the death row phenomenon. The Privy Council has continued to follow this practice in cases from Commonwealth countries. In *Pratt v. Attorney-General for Jamaica*[78] a seven member bench held that the carrying out of the death penalty 14 years after the prisoner had been sentenced to death would amount to inhuman punishment contrary to section 17(1) of the Jamaican Constitution. The court further indicated that a delay of more than five years would be too long.

2.18   The death penalty in the United Kingdom for the remaining civilian offences was abolished by the Crime and Disorder Act 1998,

---

[74] Opinion of Judge de Meyer.
[75] J. Kidd (1994) "Extradition and Expulsion Orders and European Convention on Human Rights: The Soering Decision and Beyond" Bracton Law Journal, Vol. 24, 67 at 71.
[76] This was done under r.36 of the Court's Rules of Procedure.
[77] Report of the Royal Commission on Capital Punishment 1949-1953.
[78] [1993] 3 W.L.R. 995 (P.C.).

while the Human Rights Act 1998 section 21(5) removed the death
penalty as a sentence in the armed forces legislation. The United
Kingdom ratified the Sixth Protocol on May 20, 1999.

Although most of the signatory countries of the Convention have
abolished the use of the death penalty in peacetime, the majority of
the countries of the world continue to use it and indeed some have
extended its use to include offences such as drug trafficking. The
European Court had therefore to take a pragmatic view of the
death penalty and concluded that the death penalty itself was not a
violation of Article 2, but the conditions in which the prisoner
would live, until such a sentence was carried out, would be a
violation of Article 3. In the event, Soering was extradited to the
United States, but not until the prosecuting authorities had
substituted a non-capital murder indictment for the capital
charge.[79]

Conclusion

Most people would consider that the concept of the right to life 2.19
applied mainly to those in prison or in custody, or those who had
been sentenced to death for committing murder. However, the
European Court has not confined its deliberations to such cases and
issues relating to abortion, euthanasia and medical intervention
have now become more common. It could be said that it is the
imprecise nature of the Article which has allowed such deliberations
to take place and thus widen its scope. It is likely that challenges
will occur in the future regarding embryo research, cloning and in-
vitro fertilisation. In the latter, for instance, issues may arise as to
the destruction of unwanted embryos.

The obligation on the state is to protect the right to life and this
has been held to mean not just preventing endangerment to life but
also that the state must take positive action to safeguard life. If the
state is thus required to actively ensure the rights of its citizens, then
it is possible that the environmental issues will give rise to human
rights cases. For instance, the grant of planning permission, or the
grant of a licence, or failure to take enforcement action may give
rise to liability. Environmental disasters such as Chernobyl would
give rise to claims that the public authorities had not safeguarded
the rights of the victims under Articles 2 and 8. In *Guerra v. Italy*[80]
the applicants argued that their lives had been put at risk by the
state's failure to supply information regarding the risks of a nearby
chemicals factory. They alleged that workers from the factory had
died of cancer. The European Court found a violation of Article 8
and so did not pronounce on the claim under Article 2. However,

---

[79] *The Times*, August 2, 1989.
[80] (1998) 26 E.H.R.R. 357.

one judge indicated that he considered the Article had been breached and another commented that the jurisdiction might evolve to develop implied rights. "It may therefore be time for the Court's case law on Article 2 to start evolving, to develop the respective implied rights, articulate serious risk to life, or different aspects of the right to life."

On a smaller, but no less important scale, the issue of smoking in public places may give rise to claims under Articles 2 and 8.[81] These problems remain in the future for now but undoubtedly the European Court would be able to consider them in the context of the "living instrument" that is the Convention.

ARTICLE 3

"No one shall be subjected to torture or to inhuman or degrading treatment or punishment."

2.20   The simple straightforward terms of Article 3 belie its complexity and width of application. The European Court of Human Rights has interpreted this Article to include torture such as electric shocks to the private parts, degrading treatment such as corporal punishment and inhuman treatment such as extradition of an accused to stand trial for murder in a state using the death penalty. The Article is drafted in absolute terms allowing no derogation or infringement in the interests of public safety, welfare or morality. It may not be infringed "even in time of war or other public emergency, threatening the life of the nation".[82] The central idea of Article 3, as for many of the rights in the Convention, was to ensure that there could be no repeat of the atrocities perpetrated by the Nazis throughout Europe during 1933 to 1945.

Article 3 has ancient roots. It is seen for instance in Article 10 of the English Bill of Rights 1688 which declares: "excessive bail is not to be required nor excessive fines imposed nor cruel and unusual punishments inflicted". A similar provision was included in 1791 by the eighth Amendment in the United States Constitution. The Universal Declaration of Human Rights forbids torture or "cruel, inhuman or degrading treatment or punishment". The word "cruel" was omitted from the European Convention on Human Rights. The draft Convention put forward by the Consultative Assembly specified prohibited punishments including "excess of light, darkness, noise or silence as to cause mental suffering". The final draft omitted these specific prohibitions leaving it to the Court

[81]   R. Purchas and J. Clayton "A Field Day for Crackpots? The Human Rights Act 1998, Development Projects and Control" [2001] J.P.L. (Feb.) 134.
[82]   Art. 15.

to decide the limits of the Article.

The European Convention for the Prevention of Torture and Inhuman or Degrading Treatment or Punishment set up in 1987 the European Committee for the Prevention of Torture (CPT). The Committee comprises a body of independent experts nominated by the states parties but who act without national ties. Their remit is "to examine the treatment of persons deprived of their liberty with a view to strengthening, if necessary, the protection of such persons from torture and from inhuman or degrading treatment or punishment". The Committee is entitled to visit any place where a person may be detained as a result of the decision of a public authority. The places can include police stations, prisons and immigration detention centres and the public authority can include judges, immigration officials and prisons. A report of their visit is sent to the state concerned and this report remains confidential unless the state agrees to its publication. Most states now allow publication.[83] The Committee has no formal powers of enforcement but it may publish its reports if the state fails to act on its recommendations.

There are three types of mistreatment identified in the article:

(1) Torture;
(2) Inhuman treatment or punishment; and
(3) Degrading treatment or punishment.

It will be seen from the discussion that follows that the terms are not synonymous and that the European Court has not yet fully settled the limits of each.

(1) Torture

In the *Greek Interstate* case[84] the Commission first distinguished the 2.21
different degrees of prohibited conduct, in particular stating that a "certain roughness of treatment" such as slaps to the face or head would not necessarily contravene the Article. The Commission further declared that torture did not necessarily require a physical element; mental suffering could amount to torture.

The United Kingdom were accused by the Irish State of violations of Article 3 in *Ireland v. United Kingdom*[85] which concerned 14 people who were interrogated by the United Kingdom security forces in 1971. The security forces used a number of

---

[83]   See J. Murdoch "The European Convention or the Prevention of Torture and Inhuman and Degrading Treatment or Punishment: Activities in 1996 and 1997" (1998) 23 E.L. Rev. H.R. Supp. 199.

[84]   (1969) 11 Yearbook 501.

[85]   (1979-80) E.H.R.R. 25.

different methods of interrogation including sleep deprivation, deprivation of food and drink, hooding and subjection to noise. None of the internees were physically injured but some suffered psychiatric symptoms. The United Kingdom Government suspended the use of these methods in March 1972 and argued that the case should not be brought because the United Kingdom did not dispute the facts and had taken steps to resolve the issue. The European Court decided to consider the non-contested allegations so that they could define the rules more clearly.

The Court defined torture as "deliberate inhuman treatment causing very serious and cruel suffering". This definition followed the terms of a Resolution of the General Assembly of the United Nations which had been adopted in 1975: "Torture constitutes an aggravated and deliberate form of cruel, inhuman or degrading treatment or punishment".[86] The subsequent UN Convention against Torture and other Cruel Inhuman or Degrading Treatment or Punishment[87] referred to torture as requiring "the intentional infliction" of the treatment or punishment. The purpose of the torture might be to obtain information or a confession although no particular purpose need be the motivation for the maltreatment to amount to torture.

2.22　　The Court decided that the United Kingdom's actions in the *Ireland v. United Kingdom* case did not reach the level of suffering of particular intensity and cruelty implied by the word "torture". The level of severity will depend on all the circumstances of the case and the Court will take into account such factors as the duration of the maltreatment, its physical or mental effect on the applicant, and where appropriate the sex, age and health of the applicant.

The Court's definition of "very serious and cruel suffering" is not fixed and has been developing since the 1970s to include actions which previously did not reach the threshold. However, this development is a reflection of the increase in the standards of behaviour expected by the international community as a whole. The European Court has found that there is a special stigma attached to torture which would only apply to deliberate inhuman treatment causing very serious and cruel suffering.[88] This could be reached by an accumulation of acts of physical and mental violence, such as occurred in *Aydin v. Turkey*.[89] The victim was a 17-year-old Kurdish girl who was suspected of being a Kurdish separatist or sympathiser. She was detained at a police station where she was blindfolded, beaten, stripped, placed inside a tyre and sprayed with a high-pressure hose and finally raped.

---

[86]　General Assembly of the UN: Resolution 3452(XXX).
[87]　Adopted December 1984, effective from June 26, 1987.
[88]　*Mahmut Kaya v. Turkey*, March 28, 2000, ECtHR.
[89]　(1997) 25 E.H.R.R. 251.

In *Selmouni v. France*,[90] a man suspected of being a drugs trafficker was arrested and questioned over a period of 40 hours by the French police. On release, he was examined by a doctor who reported "lesions of traumatic origin on the skin". Police officers were subsequently convicted of assault. The European Court held that the conduct of the police amounted to torture. There was now a greater emphasis on human rights in the international community and higher standards of conduct were being demanded so that democratic societies were less likely to tolerate breaches of fundamental rights. Actions which had previously been classified as "inhuman and degrading treatment" as opposed to "torture" may now be classified differently because the Convention is a "living instrument" and standards may therefore change over time.

In *Selmouni* the actions of the police were designed to obtain information or a confession from the victim. Such actions would indicate that the threshold of torture had been reached. In *Dikmi v. Turkey*[91] the applicant had been subjected to electric shocks applied to his feet, ears and genitals. The acts of violence had amounted to torture when taken with the length of time they had been applied and the fact that their purpose was to obtain information or a confession. 2.23

The use of torture is never justified by the end results. In *Tomasi v. France*[92] reports from four independent doctors cited injuries to the applicant for which there was no satisfactory explanation. The European Court said that although T was an alleged terrorist and murderer, the State could not use the fight against terrorism to reduce the protection to his physical well-being. The Court has interpreted the Article to mean that a suspect must leave custody in as good health as s/he arrived. In *Aksoy v. Turkey*[93] a terrorist suspect was systematically beaten, electrocuted and suspended by the arms with his hands tied behind his back. The European Court held that this was of "such a serious and cruel nature that it can only be described as torture".[94]

It is now accepted that there is a duty not to extradite or deport a person to a state where he would have a justified fear of being subjected to torture. This is now enshrined in Article 3(1) of the UN Torture Convention 1985. Torture is recognised as something more serious than inhuman or degrading treatment. There is an intensity of cruelty and suffering which is different from other forms of mistreatment and the European Court has said that a special stigma

---

[90] (2000) 29 E.H.R.R. 403.
[91] (2000) Appl. 20869/92, July 11, 2000.
[92] (1992) 15 E.H.R.R. 1.
[93] (1997) 23 E.H.R.R. 553.
[94] *ibid.*, para. 64.

attaches to it.[95] If torture is abhorred to this extent in states which are signatories to the Convention, it is obvious that it could not be tolerated if the state were to allow a person to be extradited to a non-signatory state where torture was used.

2.24   The *Soering* case[96] took this issue one stage further by stating that it was not possible to extradite someone to a non-signatory state where he would be subject to treatment regarded as inhuman or degrading by the Convention. It is, however, a decision the repercussions of which could be to undermine international extradition law. The law of extradition is to prevent criminals from escaping justice by fleeing to another country. The United Kingdom could not have allowed Soering's extradition to the United States and thus the European Convention on Human Rights states would have, in effect, become "safe havens" for fugitives from jurisdictions with the death row phenomenon. In the event, the United States authorities changed the indictment to a non-capital charge and the United Kingdom (and the other European states) was spared the embarrassment of being unable to allow the extradition of a criminal.

In the United Kingdom, persons with United Kingdom citizenship who commit acts of torture may be prosecuted in the United Kingdom wherever the offence was committed. Non-United Kingdom citizens who enter the United Kingdom may also be prosecuted. The United Kingdom ratified the UN Convention against Torture on December 8, 1988 by enacting the Criminal Justice Act 1988. Section 134 of the Act gives universal jurisdiction for torture and this was used in the extradition action by Spain against General Pinochet Ugarte of Chile. Pinochet could not be extradited to face charges of murder but the House of Lords held that he could face extradition where he had authorised or organised torture or similar activities after December 8, 1988. Pinochet was returned home to Chile when it was found that he was medically unfit to face extradition proceedings.[97]

(2) Inhuman treatment or punishment

2.25   The European Court has differentiated the various aspects of Article 3, treating torture as a more serious violation than inhuman treatment and in turn treating inhuman treatment as more serious than degrading treatment. In the *Soering* case,[98] the possible punishment did not amount to torture but it was within the

---

[95]   *Ireland v. U.K.* (1978) 2 E.H.R.R. 25 at 80.
[96]   *Supra* no. 73.
[97]   *R v. Bow Street Stipendiary Magistrate, ex p. Pinochet Ugarte (No. 3)* [2000] 1 A.C. 147.
[98]   *supra* no. 73.

meaning of inhuman treatment. The expectation is that the European Court would not prevent extradition where the treatment amounted to a "lesser" violation, degrading treatment, since this would threaten the international concept of extradition as a means of enforcing the law.

The European Court has however extended the *Soering* decision to deportation orders where the applicants claimed they would be at risk of torture. In *Vilvarajah v. United Kingdom*[99] the claimants were Tamil Sri Lankan nationals who opposed their deportation to Sri Lanka. They were unable to show that there was a real risk of mistreatment under Article 3. Whilst awaiting the European Court's decision, the applicants were deported back to Sri Lanka where they did not suffer the treatment they had feared. This illustrates that the United Kingdom was under no obligation to postpone deportation while awaiting the Court's decision, although it may use its discretion to do so. The treatment or punishment will be inhuman if it "causes intense physical or mental suffering".[1] Examples of this include prolonged ill-treatment and sensory deprivation,[2] and deportation of a person suffering from a terminal illness to a country which did not have the medical facilities required to treat his condition.[3] In *Tomasi v. France*[4] the applicant was subjected to ill-treatment for 40 hours and the European Court held that where the applicant was held in custody the threshold for holding that the treatment was inhuman was lowered.

> "Although the injuries observed might appear to be relatively slight, they nevertheless constitute outward signs of the use of physical force on an individual deprived of his liberty and therefore in a state of inferiority. The treatment had therefore been both inhuman and degrading."[5]

In *Selcuk & Asker v. Turkey*[6] two middle-aged applicants had to stand and watch as the security forces destroyed their homes and property by burning. As a result, they had to leave the village they had lived in all their lives and seek work and shelter elsewhere. The Court held that the ill-treatment was of sufficient severity as to be categorised as inhuman treatment.

In *Z and A v. United Kingdom*[7] four children had sought damages   2.26

---

[99] (1992) Series A, No. 215.
[1] *Ireland v. U.K.* (1978) 2 E.H.R.R. 25 at para. 167.
[2] *ibid.*
[3] *D v. U.K.* (1997) 24 E.H.R.R. 423.
[4] *supra* no. 92.
[5] *ibid.*, para. 113.
[6] (1998) 26 E.H.R.R. 477.
[7] Appl. 29392/95, May 10, 2001, ECtHR, *The Times*, May 31, 2001.

42

Human Rights and Scots Law

from a local authority for failing to protect them from severe
neglect and emotional abuse. The children's situation had been
known to the local authority from 1987 but nothing was done by
the social services department until 1992 when the mother
threatened to batter them. Eventually the children were taken into
care. The action for damages against the local authority for breach
of statutory duty and negligence was struck out by the House of
Lords, where it was held that there needed to be clear statutory
language to give rise to the potential for damages for breach of
statutory duty.[8] At Strasbourg, the European Court held that the
neglect suffered by the children reached the threshold necessary for
a finding of inhuman or degrading treatment. The local authority
had failed to protect the children from serious long-term harm and
neglect for five years and thus there had been a breach of Article 3.
In addition, there was a breach of Article 13 in that they had been
denied an effective remedy for the damage they had suffered.

The applicants in *R v. North West Lancashire Health Authority,
ex parte A, D and G*[9] argued that a refusal by the health authority to
fund treatment for trans-sexualism amounted to inhuman and
degrading treatment under Article 3 and interference with their
right to respect for private life under Article 8. The Court of Appeal
found that Article 3 did not cover these kinds of circumstances. The
challenge was to "a health authority's allocation of finite funds
between competing demands".[10] The issue of finite funds was
discussed previously in *R v. Cambridge Health Authority, ex parte
B*[11] where Justice Laws had allowed the judicial review application
at first instance. He held that the health authority could not
lawfully exercise its discretion in a way that would undermine the
child's right to life. The Court of Appeal overruled that decision,
criticising the implication that a public body would be liable to
subject its accounts to judicial scrutiny. However, the courts may
now have difficulty in reaching such a decision as that of the Court
of Appeal in *ex parte* (No. 1) *B*[11]. It is likely that if there is grave
and immediate risk to life, the health authority will have to do more
than plead poverty. They may have to establish how their resources
are deployed to show that fundamental human rights are not
breached.

(3) Degrading treatment or punishment

2.27 The concept of degrading treatment or punishment is not a static
one; as in the other two types of prohibited action, the European

---

[8] *X v. Bedfordshire County Council* [1995] 2 A.C. 633.
[9] (1999) 2 C.C.L.R. 419.
[10] *ibid.*, Auld L.J.
[11] [1995] 2 All E.R. 129.

Court has pushed back the boundaries on what may be regarded as degrading. However, a certain level of severity has to be reached before the treatment or punishment becomes degrading. If the Article 3 threshold is not reached, the ill-treatment may still breach the Convention under Article 8, which also covers the physical integrity of the person.

The treatment or punishment will be degrading if the victim has feelings of fear, anguish or inferiority which are capable of breaking down physical or mental resistance.[12] The victim's vulnerability is also important, so that a prisoner who is subjected to violence will be able to claim a violation of Article 3, unless the violence was caused by and was proportionate to his own conduct.[13] The handcuffing of a prisoner will not necessarily be a breach of Article 3 where "it does not entail the use of force or public exposure exceeding what is reasonably considered necessary in the circumstances".[14] Where a person is sedated, handcuffed and strapped to a security bed, the Article will not be breached if it can be shown to be "therapeutically necessary".[15]

In *Tyrer v. United Kingdom*[16] a 15-year-old boy on the Isle of Man pleaded guilty to assault and was sentenced to be birched the same day. However, he had to wait some hours until the police doctor arrived and then he was held down by two police officers and birched. When the birch broke at the first stroke, his father had to be restrained from intervening. The European Court did not find the action to be torture or inhuman treatment or punishment but did find it to be degrading punishment.

> "It constituted institutionalised violence, carried out by total strangers; it constituted an assault on precisely what it is one of the main purposes of Article 3 to protect, namely a person's dignity and physical integrity."

The punishment could be regarded as degrading even though it did not outrage public opinion and did not leave any lasting injury. To be considered as degradation the punishment had to have more than the usual element of humiliation that a judicial punishment would normally invoke.

The issue of corporal punishment of children has given us some interesting cases. A number of factors are taken into account: the circumstances, the nature and context of the punishment and the manner and method of its execution. In *Campbell and Cosans v.*   2.28

---

[12] *Ireland v. U.K.* (1978) 2 E.H.R.R. 25.
[13] *Rubitsch v. Austria* (1995) 21 E.H.R.R. 573.
[14] *Raninen v. Finland* (1998) 25 E.H.R.R. 563.
[15] *Herczegfalvy v. Austria* (1993) 15 E.H.R.R. 437.
[16] (1978) 2 E.H.R.R. 1.

United Kingdom (No. 2),[17] Mrs Campbell wanted the local education authority to guarantee that her son would not be punished by the use of the tawse. Mrs Cosans' son had refused to take the tawse and she had then refused to allow her son to return to school because there was no guarantee of a recurrence. The tawse was a leather strap commonly used by teachers in Scotland to punish children. The European Court held that neither boy could be said to have been humiliated or debased. Indeed, it was submitted that the threat of the tawse in Cowdenbeath in 1982 was not degrading because it was a common punishment to which many pupils were subjected. There was an absence of real or imminent threat to the boys and the Court held that the mere possibility of corporal punishment being inflicted on them did not amount to a breach of Article 3.

In *Warwick v. United Kingdom*[18] a 16-year-old girl was given one stroke of the cane across her hand. The punishment was administered by the male headteacher in the presence of another male teacher and another girl. The Commission held that the punishment was not of a trivial nature and caused humiliation serious enough to amount to degrading punishment. Of importance here was the age of the girl; under English law she was considered to be a woman of marriageable age. Where a 15-year-old boy was caned across his clothed buttocks and needed medical treatment, the Commission found violations of Articles 3 and 13.[19] In *Costello-Roberts v. United Kingdom*[20] a seven-year-old boy attending a private school was told that he would receive three slaps from a rubber-soled gym shoe on the clothed bottom. This punishment was carried out three days later. The European Court held that the punishment was not degrading since the punishment had not reached the level of severity to justify that term and it did not have a lasting effect on the boy. The use of corporal punishment was abolished in all United Kingdom schools, both public and private, in 1998.

An issue which remains to be resolved in the United Kingdom's domestic law is that of the use of corporal punishment by parents or guardians of children. In *A v. United Kingdom*[21] a nine-year-old boy was regularly beaten by his stepfather, using a garden cane. The man was prosecuted for assault causing actual bodily harm, but was acquitted after the jury accepted his defence that he had used reasonable force to chastise a difficult child. The boy applied to the European Court claiming that the state had failed to protect him from ill-treatment by his stepfather, this amounting to a breach of

---

[17] (1982) 4 E.H.R.R. 293.
[18] (1986) 60 D.R. 5.
[19] *Y v. U.K.* (1994) Series A, No. 247A.
[20] (1995) 19 E.H.R.R. 112.
[21] (1998) 27 E.H.R.R. 611.

Article 3. The Court held that the ill-treatment reached the Article 3 threshold and the law relating to reasonable chastisement did not provide adequate protection against treatment or punishment which was contrary to Article 3. By failing to provide adequate legal protection against the conduct prohibited by Article 3, the Court further stated that the State became responsible for it under Article 1 which states, "[t]he High Contracting Powers shall secure to everyone within their jurisdiction the rights and freedoms defined in Section 1 of this Convention." Since Article 1 is not brought into United Kingdom law by the Human Rights Act 1998 the right recognised in *A v. United Kingdom* is not one recognised under the Human Rights Act, which limits such rights to rights against the state and rights against public bodies for which the state is responsible.[22]

The Commission had emphasised in its findings that Article 3 was 2.29 not to be "interpreted as imposing an obligation on States to protect, through their criminal law, against any form of physical rebuke, however mild, by a parent of a child". The Court did not seek to prevent the physical punishment of children either.

The United Kingdom Government acknowledged the problem highlighted by *A v. United Kingdom* and undertook to amend the law on parental chastisement. The current law relating to parental chastisement in Scotland is contained within the Children and Young Persons (Scotland) Act 1937, section 12(7) which specifically recognises "the right of any parent, teacher or other person having the lawful control or charge of a child or young person to administer punishment to him". It is for the court to decide whether or not the punishment is reasonable. The common law gave a teacher the right to reasonably chastise a pupil but this was restricted by section 48A(1) of the Education (Scotland) Act 1980. The exercise of the rights under the 1937 Act has to be in accordance with the Children (Scotland) Act 1995 section 1, which declares that parental responsibility must be exercised in the interests of the child. At common law, the force used must be moderate and the person must not have acted with evil intent.[23] In *B v. Harris*[24] it was found that hitting a nine-year-old with a belt was reasonable, while in *Peebles v. MacPhail*[25] hitting a child so that he fell over was unreasonable. Where the court decides that the punishment has been excessive, the person may be guilty of an offence under section 12 of the 1937 Act as well as guilty of common law assault. The 1995 Act may also be invoked since the offence will constitute grounds for compulsory measures of

---

[22]   See R. Buxton "The Human Rights Act and Private Law" (2000) 116 L.Q.R. 48.
[23]   *Gray v. Hawthorn* 1964 J.C. 69.
[24]   1990 S.L.T. 208.
[25]   1990 S.L.T. 245.

supervision under section 52 of the 1995 Act.

At the time of writing, no legislation has been enacted on parental chastisement but the relevant departments in Scotland and in England and Wales[26] have issued consultation papers on the matter. The Scottish Paper, *The Physical Punishment of Children in Scotland*, was issued in February 2000 and it appears to start from the premise that the defence of reasonable chastisement should remain. Indeed the main aim of the paper seems to be a consideration of what would constitute "reasonable".[27] The paper suggests that the courts should have regard to certain factors when deciding what reasonable chastisement would be. These would include the nature and context of the punishment, how long it lasted and whether it was a frequent occurrence, any physical or mental effects and the sex, age and state of health of the child.[28] The paper asked whether there should be additional factors such as the reason for the punishment, the person involved and the vulnerability of the child.

2.30   The Scottish Law Commission's Report on Family Law[29] had recommended that corporal punishment should only be administered by those who have parental responsibility and rights and there should be no defence where implements such as a stick or belt were used. The recommendation was rejected during the passage of the Children (Scotland) Act 1995. The 2000 Consultation Paper asks, strangely given the Scots case law and the jurisprudence of the European Court of Human Rights, whether the new law should state that certain forms of punishment "could never be capable of being considered reasonable". These include blows to the head, shaking a child or using an implement.[30] The paper also suggests that a list of unacceptable types of punishment might mislead people, since they might then conclude that a type of punishment not listed would be acceptable.

Compensation

2.31   If a person has been ill-treated in breach of Article 3, the European Court has held that in addition to a thorough and effective investigation, the payment of compensation may be appropriate.[31]

---

[26]   Protecting Children, Supporting Parents (2000) Department of Health, http://www.doh.gov.uk/scg/pcspca.htm.
[27]   A. Stafford "Children are Unbeatable" (2000) SCOLAG no. 269, 5.
[28]   These were identified by the European Court in *A v. U.K.* (1998) 27 E.H.R.R. 611 at para. 22.
[29]   Scot. Law. Com. No. 135, 1992.
[30]   *ibid.*, para. 5.9.
[31]   *Assenov v. Bulgaria* (1998) 28 E.H.R.R. 652.

Life Sentences

The issue of life sentences imposed for murder or serious crimes has 2.32
been raised under Article 3. The cases have involved a number from
the United Kingdom relating to indeterminate sentences imposed
on children and young people. In *T v. United Kingdom, V v. United
Kingdom,* [32] the boy murderers of two-year-old James Bulger
sought a decision that their Article 3 rights had been breached by an
unjustifiable and persistent failure to fix a tariff, the length of time
they could expect to remain in custody before their case would be
reviewed by the Parole Board. An earlier case had found that a life
sentence imposed on children aged between 10 and 18 might breach
Article 3 if no account was taken of changes in their characters as
they matured.[33] The same would not however apply if a life
sentence was imposed on a young person aged 18 to 21.[34] Such
sentences may breach other Articles and there is further discussion
of these issues in chapters 3 and 4.

In *Kotalla v. Netherlands*[35] the Commission found that there was
no requirement under Article 3 to review a life sentence, although
this would be desirable. Again there is no breach of Article 3 where
a policy change results in a life sentence prisoner being required to
serve a minimum period on the basis of deterrence and retribution,
even though the prisoner had to serve a longer period than he
originally expected. In *Hogben v. United Kingdom*[36] the prisoner
was in an open prison after serving 13 years. His tariff was set at 20
years and he was therefore transferred back to a closed prison. His
"disappointed hopes" did not amount to inhuman treatment.

In England and Wales, the Powers of Criminal Courts (Sentencing) Act 2000 allows the imposition of an automatic life sentence
on someone who has committed a serious offence for a second time.
The courts have some discretion where there are "exceptional
circumstances" which justify not imposing the life sentence. This
legislative provision, originally in the Crime (Sentences) Act 1997, is
not as draconian as it appears, although it can be argued that it may
be arbitrary. Under the 2000 Act, the offender will be detained only
for a period specified under section 28 of the 1997 Act, which
calculates that he is eligible for release at the same time as he would
have been if sentenced to a determinate sentence. He may not be
lawfully detained longer unless the Parole Board considers his
confinement is necessary to protect the public. The 2000 Act may
fall foul of Article 3 because the imposition of a life sentence may be

---

[32] (1999) 30 E.H.R.R. 121.
[33] *Singh and Hussain v. U.K.* (1996) 22 E.H.R.R. 1.
[34] *Ryan v. UK* (1998) Appl. 32875/96.
[35] (1978) 14 D.R. 238.
[36] (1986) 46 D.R. 231.

considered to be arbitrary and capricious since such a sentence is the most severe that can be imposed on an offender and should therefore be reserved for very serious crimes. It is likely that the English Court of Criminal Appeal will have to adopt a wide definition of the phrase "exceptional circumstances" in order to ensure compliance with the Convention. Recently, however, the Court of Appeal declared that the mandatory life sentence for murder under the Murder (Abolition of Death Penalty) Act 1965 did not contravene Articles 3 and 5 of the Convention.[37]

2.33   In late 2000, the Court of Appeal considered four cases where the defendants had been given life sentences after being convicted of a second serious offence. The Court said that the imposition of a life sentence would contravene the Convention if it were wholly inappropriate to impose such a sentence to protect the public. The Court could take into account factors such as the risk to the public, any difference in kind between the two offences, and the time that had elapsed between them.[38]

The Status of Prisoners

2.34   The conditions under which prisoners are detained must not be inhuman or degrading and a number of cases have been brought complaining about prison conditions. The threshold is whether the conditions of imprisonment fall below the conditions normally found in Europe. The Council of Europe Minimum Rules for the Treatment of Prisoners sets out the standards to be used in assessing conditions but breach of these rules will not necessarily indicate a breach of Article 3.[39] However, they can be used to support a contention that the conditions fall below Convention standards. A European Committee for the Prevention of Torture Report criticised the standards in which prisoners with psychiatric problems were being held. The Commission found that there was a breach of Article 3 and the failure to provide an adequate treatment regime breached Article 5(1).[40] In *McFeeley v. United Kingdom*[41] the applicants were convicted of offences under anti-terrorist legislation and they complained that their Article 3 rights had been breached because of disciplinary proceedings against them. They had been protesting about the removal of "special category" status which meant that they would be treated as ordinary prisoners. They refused to wear prison uniform or to work, or to use the toilet and

---

[37] *R (on the application of Lichniak) v. Secretary of State for Home Department* [2001]All E.R. 22.

[38] *R v. Offen* (No. 2); *R v. McGuillard; R v. McKeown; R v. Okwnegbunam*, Court of Appeal, November 9, 2000.

[39] *X v. Germany* (1985) 7 E.H.R.R. 152.

[40] *Aerts v. Belgium* (1998) 29 E.H.R.R. 50.

[41] (1981) 3 E.H.R.R. 161.

washing facilities provided. As a result they were confined to their cells for up to 23 hours each day although this was not in the punishment block. The Commission held that the treatment suffered did not attain a level of severity sufficient to indicate a violation of Article 3. In addition, the harsh conditions of detention developed from the applicants' own decision not to comply with prison regulations and these could not be the responsibility of the United Kingdom Government. The government's responsibility was to ensure that their reaction to the prisoners was kept under constant review to safeguard the health and well-being of the prisoners so far as was possible in the circumstances.[42]

Solitary confinement will not necessarily breach Article 3; it may be justified on the grounds of security, order, discipline or the prevention of crime.[43] In *Wardlaw v. United Kingdom*[44] a prisoner challenged his detention in the segregation unit at Inverness Prison claiming that the conditions were in violation of Article 3. The Commission struck out the claim for want of interest on the part of the applicant.

The conditions in police cells and prisons were raised in *Price v. United Kingdom*.[45] The applicant was severely disabled by kidney problems and had to use a wheelchair. She was committed to prison for seven days for contempt of court. She was detained overnight in a police cell which had no suitable facilities for a disabled person and she had to sleep in her wheelchair. On her transfer to prison, she was detained in the health centre which had disabled facilities but she had to have the assistance of male officers to use the toilet because the duty nurse was unable to lift her. As a result of these conditions, she had to be catheterised and her kidney condition worsened. The government said that while the health professionals and the prison governor were aware of her potential and actual difficulties, they were unable to transfer her because she was not suffering from a particular medical complaint. The European Court held that although there was no positive intention to humiliate and debase her, the detention of a severely disabled person in such conditions constituted degrading treatment. The applicant was awarded £4,250 for non-pecuniary damage because she had suffered moral damage which could not be compensated solely by the finding of a violation. The decision in this case imposes an obligation on police and prison authorities to ensure that a prisoner is not subjected to intolerable treatment. The decision also raises the question as to whether the sentence itself for contempt of court would be violation of the Convention since the European Court

---

[42] See also *B v. Germany* (1998) 55 D.R. 271.
[43] *X v. Denmark* (1982) 27 D.R. 50.
[44] (1989) 60 D.R. 71.
[45] European Court, July 10, 2001.

noted that the sentence was particularly harsh in the circumstances of the case.

2.35   The imprisonment of an elderly infirm person will not necessarily be a violation of the Convention, provided that appropriate medical care is available. In *Sawoniuk v. United Kingdom*[46] a 79-year-old man was convicted under the War Crimes Act 1991 but the European Court declared his application inadmissible because his imprisonment was not disproportionate or arbitrary where there was no evidence of ill-treatment or exceptional hardship.

Medical treatment must be provided to persons in custody.[47] In *Lockwood v. United Kingdom*[48] the prisoner was diagnosed by the prison doctor as having a tumour but there was a delay of four months before this was confirmed by a second medical opinion. During this time treatment was begun and further tests carried out. The applicant contended that the delay in confirming the diagnosis was inhuman and degrading treatment. The Commission, however, said that the delay had not been sufficient to constitute a violation of Article 3.

The Prison Service in both Scotland and England maintain that their current practices are "Convention compliant" although some changes were made before the Human Rights Act came into effect on October 2, 2000. The use of "strip cells" was discontinued; these were used for prisoners who were deemed to be at risk from suicide or self harm. The practice was identified as one which would fall foul of Article 3 as being degrading treatment. The lack of sanitary facilities within cells has been raised in Scotland as a violation of Article 3. In a petition for judicial review, a remand prisoner at H.M.P. Barlinnie challenged the conditions under which he was detained.[49] In particular he averred that the process of "slopping out" whereby he had to use a bucket to relieve himself and then empty the bucket two or three times a day, amounted to inhuman and degrading treatment. He said that these conditions exacerbated a long-standing medical condition for which he needed further medical treatment. The conditions in the remand wing had been known to be unsatisfactory for a number of years and the European Committee for the Prevention of Torture (CPT) had been told in 1994 by the prison service that internal sanitation should be provided in all prison cells by 1999. Lord MacFadyen found in Napier's favour, making an order for the Scottish Ministers to secure his transfer to a prison which complied with Article 3 of the Convention within a period of 72 hours. The decision has been appealed by the government but in August 2001, further cases were

---

[46] Appl. 63719/00.
[47] *Hurtado v. Switzerland* (1994) 280 Series A 16.
[48] (1992) 15 E.H.R.R. CD 48.
[49] *Napier v. The Scottish Ministers* (2001).

raised in the Court of Session by prisoners at Barlinnie seeking compensation for the poor conditions in the prison.

Other issues identified as possible actions include enforced 2.36 withdrawal from drink or drugs, compulsory medical treatment and long disciplinary procedures.

Search Procedures

Both the police and prison authorities have to carry out procedures 2.37 which may be sufficiently degrading to reach the European Convention threshold. For instance, a non-consensual intimate search might be a breach of the Article, particularly if it included the vagina or rectum. Any search carried out in inappropriate circumstances may be a violation, for instance a search carried out by a man on a woman. Most cases before the European Court have involved violations of Article 8 rather than Article 3. However, it is possible that a prisoner subjected to a strip search may no longer have to rely on an argument that the prison officer's action was unlawful or irrational. He may be able to argue in the United Kingdom courts that there had been a violation of the right not to be subjected to "inhuman or degrading treatment or punishment". The *Wednesbury* doctrine used by the British courts where actions have to be deemed irrational may have to be reconsidered in favour of the doctrine of proportionality. Such searches may therefore be overturned if they are not "aimed at meeting a pressing social need and are not proportionate to the aim of meeting that need".[50]

Deportation

It has already been observed that it is considered inhuman 2.38 treatment to extradite a person to return to a jurisdiction where it was likely that he would have to spend many years on death row—*Soering v. United Kingdom.*[51] It is also inhuman to deport a terminally ill person to a country which does not have adequate medical facilities to deal with his condition—*D v. United Kingdom.*[52]

In *Vilvarajah v. United Kingdom*[53] five Tamils who were illegal immigrants were expelled to Sri Lanka despite claims that they would be subject to ill-treatment. Three of the applicants were beaten and tortured after their return. The European Court however found that there was no violation of Article 3. The

---

[50] F. Klug, R. Singh and M. Hunt "Rights brought home: a briefing on the Human Rights Bill with amendments" (1997) Human Rights Incorporation Project, King's College, London.
[51] (1989) 11 E.H.R.R. 439.
[52] (1997) 24 E.H.R.R. 423.
[53] (1991) 14 E.H.R.R. 248.

existence of a risk to the men had to be assessed according to the facts known, or facts ought to have been known, at the time of their expulsion. Improvements in the political and military situation had led to the voluntary repatriation of Tamils to their homes and there were no special aspects which might have alerted the United Kingdom authorities to the possibility that some of the applicants would be badly treated. In *Hilal v. United Kingdom*[54] the Court found a violation of Article 3 where the United Kingdom proposed the expulsion of a Tanzanian citizen back to his homeland. The applicant was a member of the opposition party and had provided substantiated evidence of torture in police detention.

In *Chahal v. United Kingdom*[55] the applicant was ordered to be deported on the grounds of national security. He was a Sikh activist who was suspected of involvement in various terrorist crimes. He maintained that he would be in danger if he were returned to India. The European Court accepted that at least some of the Punjab police did not respect the human rights of Sikh militants and this risk of inhuman or degrading treatment or torture meant that deportation would be contrary to Article 3. The lack of judicial involvement in the decision to deport him on national security grounds mean that there was also a breach of Article 6. The United Kingdom Government had argued that the State's interest in expelling the applicant should be taken into account but the Court held that Article 3 rights were not subject to the limitations of Article 15. "The activities of the individual in question, however undesirable or dangerous, cannot be a material consideration."

2.39   An Iranian woman granted refugee status by the United Nations was nonetheless due to be deported from Turkey back to Iran, where she feared that she would be subjected to punishment because of her adulterous behaviour.[56] In Iran, adultery was still punishable by stoning to death, or flogging or whipping. The European Court held that a mandatory five day time limit to seek asylum, which she had not met, was contrary to her fundamental human rights under Article 3 and her claims had not been investigated before the deportation order was made. The Court found there had been a breach of Articles 3 and 13.

In *TI v. United Kingdom*[57] a Sri Lankan Tamil was refused asylum in Germany. He travelled to the United Kingdom and claimed asylum. The Home Secretary rejected the claim and certified the case under the Asylum and Immigration Act 1996, section 2, ordering his removal back to Germany. That country

---

[54] Appl. 45276/99, March 6, 2001, European Court.
[55] (1997) 23 E.H.R.R. 413.
[56] *Jabari v. Turkey*, July 11, 2000.
[57] [2001] I.N.L.R. 211.

acknowledged its responsibility for his claim under the Dublin Convention of 1990. The applicant claimed that as Germany would return him to Sri Lanka, the United Kingdom was in breach of the European Convention on Human Rights. The European Court held that although T could make a fresh application in Germany, his previous application would be taken into account and Germany did not recognise non-state agents of persecution. The United Kingdom could not rely on the provisions of the Dublin Convention because of the prohibition against torture and ill-treatment was too important to allow such a derogation of responsibility. However the German Government had granted asylum to Tamils in the past and their standards were not so unreasonably high that T's application would not receive proper consideration. The United Kingdom was not therefore in breach of Article 3.

The Immigration and Asylum Act 1999, sections 10 and 63 effectively remove the right of appeal against deportation from most deportees. The grounds for deportation are found in the Immigration Act 1971, section 3 and include: those who overstay their visit or breach a condition of entry; those whose deportation is deemed to be conducive to the public good, usually after a conviction for a criminal offence; spouses and children of a deportee; and those recommended by a court for deportation. The Immigration Rules[58] require the Home Secretary to balance the public interest against the compassionate circumstances of each case.

Nationals of the European Economic Area may only be deported 2.40 on one of the grounds listed in the Directive 68/360/EEC which are public policy, public health and public security. An European Union national may only be deported if the person causes a genuine and sufficiently serious threat to public policy affecting one of the fundamental interests of society.[59]

The 1999 Act provides at section 63 that appeals against deportation will only be possible in cases where the deportation is deemed to be conducive to the public good or in family cases. An express right of appeal is also granted under section 65 where the person contends that their human rights have been breached by a public authority contrary to section 6(1) of the Human Rights Act 1998.

The British courts have indicated that the Home Secretary should balance the public interest against the human rights of the deportee[60] and the greater the interference with human rights the more the court would require by way of justification. If the Home

---

[58]   H.C. 395.

[59]   *R v. Bouchereau* [1977] E.C.R. 1999.

[60]   *R v. Secretary of State for Home Department, ex p. Gangadeen* [1998] Imm. A.R. 106.

Secretary fails to undertake this balancing exercise, the decision
may be struck down as *ultra vires.*

2.41   The Geneva Convention on the Status of Refugees 1951 has not
been incorporated directly into United Kingdom law, but the
Asylum and Immigration Appeals Act 1993, section 1 annexed the
Convention into domestic law. Thus anyone who can substantiate a
claim for asylum under Article 1 of the Geneva Convention will not
be removed from the United Kingdom. The Article applies to
people who have experienced persecution on account of their race,
religion, nationality, political opinion or membership of a social
group. The Geneva Convention, Article 33 allows removal of a
person whose presence constitutes a danger to national security or
who have committed a serious non-political crime. The Home
Secretary is required to conduct a balancing test into the
circumstances of the case.[61] The Special Immigration Appeals
Commission Act 1997 was passed after the *Chahal v. United
Kingdom* decision to establish a new appeals process for national
security cases, thus allowing Article 3 Convention issues to be
addressed.

The grounds for removal under Article 33 of the Geneva
Convention are narrower than the rights of Article 3 of the
European Convention. A person, who might experience persecution
on grounds of the sex or sexuality if they were deported, may still be
able to argue that their expulsion would contravene Article 3
ECHR even though the reason does not fall within the terms of the
Geneva Convention. The scope of the Human Rights Act and the
absolute nature of Article 3 rights may combine to encourage the
United Kingdom courts to look at wider issues.

ARTICLE 4: PROHIBITION OF SLAVERY AND FORCED LABOUR

"(1) No one shall be held in slavery or servitude.
 (2) No one shall be required to perform forced or compulsory labour.
 (3) For the purposes of this article the term 'forced or
compulsory labour' shall not include:

(a) any work required to be done in the ordinary course
of detention imposed according to the provisions of
Article 5 of this Convention or during conditional
release from such detention;
(b) any service of a military character or, in case of
conscientious objectors in countries where they are

---

[61] *Rigastraie v. Secretary of State for the Home Department,* Court of Appeal, May
2, 1995.

recognised, service exacted instead of compulsory
military service;
(c) any service exacted in case of an emergency or
calamity threatening the life or well-being of the
community;
(d) any work or service which forms part of normal civic
obligations."

Article 4(1) is an absolute right which cannot be restricted even in   2.42
time of war or other public emergency.[62] Articles 4(2) and 4(3) are
special rights in that they can be restricted where the public interest
so requires. Article 4(2) prohibits forced labour but Article 4(3)
gives a list of exceptions to that prohibition.

There have been few complaints under this Article and none of
them has been upheld. The complaints considered by the Convention institutions have fallen into two main categories: prisoners and
professional people who have been compelled to provide their
services free to the community.

Slavery was defined in the Slavery Convention 1926, Article 1(1)
as "the status or condition of a person over whom any or all of the
powers attaching to the right of ownership are exercised". In *Barar
v. Sweden*[63] a Mauritanian citizen applied for asylum stating that he
had left Mauritania to escape slavery. It was accepted that he was a
slave although he was only obliged to visit his father's master once a
year and carry out some minor tasks. Slavery was illegal in
Mauritania but it was claimed that vestiges of it remained. He
claimed that he would be at real risk of torture or death if he
returned. The European Court declared the application inadmissible because it was not substantiated that he would risk being killed
or tortured on his return to Mauritania or that he would risk
treatment contrary to Article 4.

Servitude on the other hand does not include the idea of   2.43
"ownership". In *Van Droogenbroeck v. Belgium*[64] the European
Court defined servitude as "the obligation to provide another with
certain services (and) the obligation on the part of the 'serf' to live
on another's property and the impossibility of changing his
condition". Servitude does not include military service even where
the enlistment period is a long one without prospect of early
discharge.[65] A soldier enlists by choice and has a duty to abide by
his terms of engagement.

---

[62] By virtue of Article 15(2), the Contracting States may not derogate from Article
4(1).
[63] [1999] E.H.R.L.R. 330.
[64] (1982) 4 E.H.R.R. 443.
[65] *W, X, Y and Z v. U.K. (The Boy Soldiers Case)* (1968) 11 Yearbook 562
(European Commission).

Article 4(2) prohibits forced or compulsory labour but the definition of this does not include work done in the ordinary course of detention imposed by Article 5 or during conditional release from such detention.[66] Convicted and remand prisoners may be required to do such work. For instance in *X v. Switzerland*[67] the Commission allowed that a juvenile could be required to work during his placement under observation in a closed institution. Prison work need not be remunerated[68] but it should have a rehabilitative element if it is not to breach the Article.[69] In *Ackerl v. Austria*[70] a number of judges complained that at certain times they were obliged to take over the functions of other judges without receiving additional remuneration. The European Commission dismissed their arguments that this was in breach of Article 4(2) as forced or compulsory labour. The work was carried out in pursuance of freely negotiated terms of employment and could not therefore fall within Article 4(2).

The Convention does not positively define the term "forced or compulsory labour" but gives a number of exceptions which are not included in the definition. The European Court referred to international conventions to find a definition in *Van der Mussele v. Belgium*.[71] The International Labour Organisation Convention Number 29 defines forced or compulsory labour as "all work or servitude which is exacted from any person under the menace of any penalty and for which the said person has not offered himself voluntarily".

2.44   Forced labour requires some form of physical or mental constraint[72] while compulsory labour will include work "exacted under the menace of any penalty" and is performed against the will of the person. The European Court has taken the view that Article 4 will evolve over time and has to be interpreted "in the light of the notions currently prevailing in democratic states".[73] Thus providing legal aid work on limited fees is not compulsory labour[74] and the requirement for a trainee barrister to provide free legal services as part of that training is not compulsory labour.[75]

Prior to *Van der Mussele v. Belgium* the Commission had required that two cumulative conditions had to be satisfied; these

---

[66] Art. 4(3)(a).
[67] (1980) 18 D.R. 238.
[68] *21 Detained Prisoners v. Germany* (1968) 11 Yearbook 528, European Commission.
[69] *De Wilde, Ooms and Versyp v. Belgium* (No. 1) (1979–80) 1 E.H.R.R. 373.
[70] Appl. 20781/92, 78-A D.R. 116.
[71] (1983) 6 E.H.R.R. 163.
[72] *Van der Mussele v. Belgium* (1984) 6 E.H.R.R. 163.
[73] *ibid.*, para. 32.
[74] *X and Y v. Germany* (1978) 10 D.R. 224, European Commission.
[75] *supra* no. 72.

were based on the International Labour Organisation's Conventions. First, the work or service had to be performed by the worker against his will and second, the obligation to carry it out was unjust or oppressive or its performance constituted "an avoidable hardship." After the *Van der Mussele* case, the test was altered but still comprised of two stages:

(1) Was the labour performed by the individual against his will, taking into account whether he entered the service voluntarily but also whether the specific work was outside the normal scope of the service, and

(2) Was the obligation unjust, oppressive or an unavoidable hardship taking into account whether the work was outside the ambit of the individual's normal activities, whether it was required in the public interest and whether it imposed a disproportionate burden on the individual.

In the first case on Article 4, the Commission had to consider whether a newly qualified dentist should be required by his government to work for two years in the public service.[76] The government's intention was to improve dental care in remote areas. The applicant claimed that this was forced labour. The Commission dismissed the application saying that "the service was for a short period, provided favourable remuneration and did not involve any diversion from his chosen professional work." The Commission further concluded that the service was covered by Article 4(3)(c) as being service exacted in case of "an emergency or calamity threatening the life or well-being of the community".

The Article is not infringed where a person refuses a job offer and   2.45
then has his unemployment benefit withdrawn.[77] Similarly, there is no breach where the payment of unemployment benefit is dependent on the applicant seeking suitable work.[78]

The compatibility of community service orders for offenders has come under scrutiny in the context of Article 4(3)(a). The Criminal Procedure (Scotland) Act 1995, section 238(2) requires that a community service order is imposed only if the offender consents to it. Arguably the offender's choice is limited since the alternative is imprisonment or detention, but it is sufficient to show that the convicted person has not been forced or compelled.

In England the Crime (Sentences) Act 1997, section 38 removed the requirement of need for consent to community service and probation orders except where a probation order includes a

---

[76] *Iverson v. Norway.*
[77] *X v. The Netherlands* (1976) 7 D.R. 161, European Commission.
[78] *Talmon v. The Netherlands* (1997) E.H.R.L.R. 448, EComHR.

requirement for psychiatric treatment or treatment for alcohol or drug dependency.

2.46   The European Court has adopted a flexible approach to such provisions, stressing that the notion of compulsory labour is a changing one to be interpreted in the light of changing circumstances. A community service order is therefore unlikely to be considered a violation particularly where it is a realistic alternative to custody and there is a rehabilitative aim.

Article 4(3)(b) refers to conscientious objectors but does not give them the right to exemption from military service.[79] The Commission had declared in an earlier case that by including the words "in countries where they are recognised" in Article 4(3)(b) "a choice is left to the High Contracting parties to the Convention whether or not to recognise conscientious objectors and, if so required, to provide some substitute service for them".[80]

The right to conscientious objection to military service falls within the protection of Article 9 where refusal to perform military conscription is based on one's well-formed beliefs. However Article 4 allows states to require military serve regardless of conscientious objections. If the state does recognise such objection, alternative service may be required, even if the conscientious objection still applies to this form of civilian service.

2.47   Finally, paragraph (d) of Article 4(3) refers to "normal civil obligations" and this has been held to include such activities as an obligation to undertake compulsory fire service. In *Schmidt v. Germany*[81] all male adults in the district of Baden-Wurttemberg were required to serve in the fire brigade or pay a fire service levy. The European Court held that the levy was a compensatory charge which was closely linked to the obligation to serve and was within the scope of the Article. The Court did find a violation of Article 14 because women were excluded from the obligation without justification.

---

[79]   *Johansen v. Norway* (1985) 44 D.R. 155 EComHR.
[80]   *X v. Austria*, Appl. 5591/72, 43 Coll 161 EComHR.
[81]   (1994) 18 E.H.R.R. 513.

CHAPTER 3

LIBERTY AND SECURITY OF THE PERSON

ARTICLE 5—RIGHT TO LIBERTY AND SECURITY

"(1) Everyone has the right to liberty and security of person. No one shall be deprived of his liberty save in the following cases and in accordance with a procedure prescribed by law:

    (a) the lawful detention of a person after conviction by a competent court;

    (b) the lawful arrest or detention of a person for non-compliance with the lawful order of a court or in order to secure the fulfillment of any obligation prescribed by law;

    (c) the lawful arrest or detention of a person effected for the purpose of bringing him before the competent legal authority on reasonable suspicion of having committed an offence or when it is reasonably considered necessary to prevent his committing an offence or fleeing after having done so;

    (d) the detention of a minor by lawful order for the purpose of educational supervision or his lawful detention for the purpose of bringing him before the competent legal authority;

    (e) the lawful detention of persons for the prevention of the spreading of infectious diseases, of persons of unsound mind, alcoholics or drug addicts or vagrants;

    (f) the lawful arrest or detention of a person to prevent his effecting an unauthorised entry into the country or of a person against whom action is being taken with a view to deportation or extradition.

(2) Everyone who is arrested shall be informed promptly, in a language he understands, of the reasons for his arrest and of any charge against him.

(3) Everyone arrested or detained in accordance with the

provisions of paragraph 1(c) of this Article shall be brought promptly before a judge or other officer authorised by law to exercise judicial power and shall be entitled to trial within a reasonable time or to release pending trial. Release may be conditioned by guarantees to appear for trial.

(4) Everyone who is deprived of his liberty by arrest or detention shall be entitled to take proceedings by which the lawfulness of his detention shall be decided speedily by a court and his release ordered if the detention is not lawful.

(5) Everyone who has been the victim of arrest or detention in contravention of the provisions of this Article shall have an enforceable right to compensation."

3.01 This Article has given rise to a great number of cases, partly because the complexity of the Article has led to problems of interpretation. The Article had to be drafted in such a way as to be applicable across a wide range of criminal jurisdictions.

The right to liberty and security of person under Article 5 is a special right which can be restricted in time of war or other public emergency. It is "free-standing" and can be invoked outside the trial process of Article 6. The facts of the case must indicate that there was a deprivation of liberty, not just a restriction on the applicant's freedom of movement.[1]

Article 5(1) deals with the legitimacy of depriving a person of their liberty while the rest of the Article sets out minimum rights for a person in detention. The first sentence of Article 5(1) provides for the right to liberty and security of person, but the second sentence then gives the six circumstances in which this right can be restricted. The list that follows has been held to be exhaustive[2] and any restriction not included will constitute a breach.[3] The word "lawful" is used in this Article and under the European Convention this word has a specific meaning. A restriction on a Convention right will only be lawful if: the domestic legislation or special rules have provided a legal basis for it; the rule is "accessible" to those affected by it; and it is "foreseeable" so that those affected by it are able to understand it and so regulate their behaviour accordingly.[4]

3.02 Article 5(2) requires the person arrested to be informed of the reasons for arrest while Article 5(3) requires the arrested person to be brought before the court promptly and then to be tried within a reasonable time. Where arrest or detention has taken place, Article

---

[1] *S.F. v. Switzerland* (1994) 76-A D.R. 13.
[2] *Monnel and Morris v. U.K.* (1987) 10 E.H.R.R. 205.
[3] *Ciulla v. Italy* (1991) 13 E.H.R.R. 346.
[4] K. Starmer, *Human Rights Digest* (Blackstone Press, London, 2001), p.4.

5(4) requires that the arrested or detained person will have the right to seek judicial consideration of the lawfulness of the detention. Finally, where a person has been unlawfully arrested or detained, there will a right under Article 5(5) to compensation.

At this point it is useful to note that children and young people enjoy the same fair trial rights under Articles 5 and 6 as adults do. However, the European Court has also stated that children have special status and the standards to be applied have to be adjusted to take account of this.[5] The adaptations for children were stated in *T v. United Kingdom, V v. United Kingdom*[6] and are discussed fully in Chapter 4.

The Anti-Terrorism, Crime and Security Act 2001 introduced measures to ensure the safety of British citizens after the terrorist atrocities of September 11, 2001 in the United States of America. Sections 21 to 32 of the Act allow the detention of those certified by the Home Secretary to be threats to national security and who are suspected of being international terrorists but their removal from the United Kingdom is not presently possible. The detention will be subject to regular review. The current law follows the provisions of Article 5(1)(f) by allowing detention where action is being taken to remove the person from the United Kingdom. The new Act will contravene Article 5 and so the United Kingdom Government announced a derogation from the Article on December 18, 2001. The derogation was made under Article 15 which allows measures to be taken "in time of war or other public emergency threatening the life of the nation . . . to the extent strictly required by the exigencies of the situation". The government considers that the terrorist threat has created a public emergency within the meaning of Article 15.

Article 5(1)

This first part of the Article is concerned with deprivation of liberty and the circumstances under which that deprivation can be considered lawful.   3.03

In *R v. Chief Constable of Kent Constabulary, ex parte Kent Police Federation Joint Branch Board*[7] the Chief Constable had proposed that the conduct of reviews of police detention under section 40 of the Police and Criminal Evidence Act 1984 should be by video link. The case was heard before the Human Rights Act 1998 came into effect and it is one of the first domestic decisions in which reliance was placed on Article 5. Lord Bingham recognised the importance of the rule of law that a person's liberty should only be taken away

---

[5] *Nortier v. Netherlands* (1993) 17 E.H.R.R. 273.
[6] (1999) 30 E.H.R.R. 121.
[7] [2000] Crim. L.R. 857.

in accordance with the law. The 1984 Act gave certain safeguards to the suspect, including a requirement that a written record of the grounds of detention should be made by the review officer "in the presence of the person whose detention is under review".[8] That condition could not be fulfilled if the reviewer was in one place and the detained person in another. The Act provided for "face-to-face" contact and it was for Parliament to decide whether this important safeguard for the person was to be changed.

The right to liberty is not concerned with a mere restriction on freedom of movement; that is governed by the Fourth Protocol, Article 2, and is discussed in Chapter 9. The distinction between deprivation of liberty and restrictions of liberty has been found to be a fine one, based on degree or intensity rather than substance.[9] Thus confining military personnel to barracks was not a deprivation of liberty, but locking them up would be.[10] It is also notable from the decisions of the European Court, particularly *Ashingdane v. United Kingdom*,[11] that Article 5 is concerned with actual liberty rather than with the particular place of lawful detention, although detention in an inappropriate place may breach the Article.

3.04   A person who surrenders voluntarily to custody will not lose the protection of the Convention rights by doing so. The European Court stated that

> "the right to liberty is too important in a 'democratic society' within the meaning of the Convention for a person to lose the benefit of the protection of the Convention for the single reason that he gives himself up to be taken into detention. The detention might violate Article 5 even though the person concerned might have agreed to it."[12]

The length of detention is important but a breach can occur in even a very short period of detention. For instance, a detention to allow a blood test to be taken was found to be a violation.[13] In most circumstances the detention will be in prison or a police station, but it can be in other situations. In May 2001, hundreds of people were "corralled" by the police in the Oxford Circus area of London for several hours. Many of the people had been involved in the "May Day protests" and they were trying to continue their protests elsewhere in the city. Some of the people were not involved in the protests; they were tourists or people going about their normal

---

[8]   Police and Criminal Evidence Act 1984, s.37(5).
[9]   *Guzzardi v. Italy* (1980) 3 E.H.R.R. 333.
[10] *Engel v. The Netherlands* (1979-80) 1 E.H.R.R. 647.
[11] (1985) 7 E.H.R.R. 528.
[12] *De Wilde, Ooms and Versyp v. Belgium* (1971) 1 E.H.R.R. 373, para. 65.
[13] *X v. Austria* (1979) 18 D.R. 154.

business. All of them were detained because the police feared breaches of the peace would occur. Some acts of vandalism, criminal damage and unruly behaviour did take place and there were some arrests. However, the majority of the crowd were well behaved and non-violent. It remains to be seen whether any of these people caught up in the detention will seek redress since the reasons given by the police, *i.e.* a fear of a breach of the peace, may be unjustified. Normally the police must suspect a particular individual or individuals of being about to commit a breach of the peace; they could hardly suspect this in respect of hundreds of people.

In Scotland, a person may not be detained indefinitely. It must cease as soon as there are no longer grounds for reasonable suspicion that the person committed the offence. The period of detention is deemed to end if the suspect is arrested for the offence or detained under any other statutory provision. In any case the detention must be terminated after six hours. A person may be detained under more than one enactment provided that the cumulative period of detention remains less than six hours. Detention is not to be used as a means of delaying arrest and charge. Once there is sufficient evidence to justify an arrest the suspect must be arrested and charged. In *Grant v. H.M. Advocate*[14] the accused was detained for longer than six hours. However, during the six-hour period he made an incriminating statement and this was led in evidence. He objected to the use of the statement on the grounds that the detention had lasted longer than six hours and was therefore unlawful. The High Court of Justiciary held that the fact that the detention has exceeded the limit did not invalidate things which were lawfully done during the six hour period.

In general, a person has not been deprived of their liberty if they are free to leave the area of confinement. For instance, in *SM and MT v. Austria*[15] the applicants were free to leave an airport transit area to go to another country. However, this will not apply to persons seeking asylum if their only option is to leave for a country where their safety cannot be guaranteed. In this circumstance they do not have a genuine freedom to leave.[16] If the person is free to leave detention but does not know this, or feels constrained from leaving, then this may amount to a violation of Article 5.[17]   3.05

The detention must also be necessary and there should be no alternative to the detention. In *Litwa v. Poland*[18] the applicant was taken into detention to sober up. This was held to be unjustified

---

[14] 1990 J.C. 77; 1990 S.L.T. 402; 1989 S.C.C.R. 618.
[15] (1993) 74 D.R. 179.
[16] *Amuur v. France* (1996) 22 E.H.R.R. 533.
[17] But see *Guenat v. Switzerland*, Appl. 24722, April 10, 1995, EComHR.
[18] Appl. 26629/95, April 4, 2000, ECtHR.

because the alternative of taking him home had not been considered.

The Legality of Detention

3.06 The detention "must essentially comply with national law and the substantive and procedural rules thereof".[19] It follows therefore, that if the detention is unlawful under Scots law, it will also be in breach of Article 5.

The detention must fall within one or more of the requirements in Article 5(1)(a) to (f). The list is exhaustive and each ground for detention is construed narrowly.[20] Each requirement provides that the detention must be lawful and it must be carried out in accordance with a procedure prescribed by law. This means that there must be a basis for the detention in domestic law, it must conform to the general requirements of the Convention and it must not be arbitrary.[21] The general requirements of the Convention dictate that the domestic law must be accessible and precise.

> "[W]here deprivation of liberty is concerned it is particularly important that the general principle of legal certainty be satisfied. It is therefore essential that the conditions for deprivation of liberty under domestic law be clearly defined and that the law itself be foreseeable in its application, so that it meets the standard of 'lawfulness' set out by the Convention, a standard which requires that all law be sufficiently precise to allow the person—if need be, with the appropriate advice—to foresee . . . the consequences which a given action may entail."[22]

The common law rules of the United Kingdom jurisdictions have been held to be adequate in principle to satisfy this requirement of Article 5(1).[23]

Arbitrary deprivation of liberty is prohibited so that the clandestine transportation of a person from one jurisdiction to another to circumvent a court order would be a breach of Article 5.[24] If the detention is lawful under domestic law it may nonetheless be arbitrary because it has been used in bad faith or was not proportionate. However, it appears that the lawfulness of the state action may be "fudged" where circumstances dictate. In *Sanchez-*

[19] *Herczegfalvy v. Austria* (1993) 15 E.H.R.R. 437 at para. 63.
[20] *Winterwerp v. The Netherlands* (1979) 2 E.H.R.R. 387.
[21] *supra* no. 4 at 204.
[22] *Baranowski v. Poland,* March 28, 2000, ECtHR, para. 52.
[23] See *CR v. U.K., SW v. U.K.* (1995) 21 E.H.R.R. 363.
[24] *Bozano v. France* (1986) 9 E.H.R.R. 297.

Ramiriz v. France,[25] "Carlos the Jackal" was captured in the Sudan and flown to a French military air base where an arrest warrant was served on him. He claimed his deprivation of liberty was unlawful and challenged the involvement of French officials at his capture in Sudan. The Commission declared the application inadmissible because the actions of the Sudanese officials fell outwith the scope of the Convention while the French arrest warrant was lawful. Collaboration between French and Sudanese authorities did not raise an Article 5 violation, particularly where this was in the fight against terrorism.

The state can however incur responsibility if they co-operate with   3.07
private individuals to deprive a person of their liberty. In *Riera Blume v. Spain*[26] members of a religious sect were arrested by the Catalan police and taken to a hotel where they were handed over to their families. They were kept in the hotel for eight days undergoing "deprogramming" until they were questioned by a senior police officer and allowed to leave. They brought criminal complaints against the police for unlawful imprisonment. The police officers were acquitted on the grounds that their actions had been legitimate and well intentioned. The European Court found there was no legal basis for the deprivation of liberty and the national authorities had acquiesced in that deprivation. There was therefore a violation of Article 5(1).

The procedure laid down by the domestic law must be followed, or a breach of Article 5(1) will occur. The normal rules of fairness will apply so that where a person was not given an opportunity to be heard before being confined in a psychiatric hospital, this was held to be unlawful.[27] If there is bad faith on the part of the authority or the detention was not proportionate, then there may be a violation of the Article on the ground that it is arbitrary.[28]

Pre-trial Detention

The United Kingdom has been brought before the Convention   3.08
institutions on a number of occasions because of the Northern Ireland situation and the United Kingdom's attempts to control the movements of suspected terrorists. The Article, however, does not include reference to prevention of offences against public order or state security and thus the United Kingdom has invoked the right to derogation under Article 15. In *McVeigh, O'Neill and Evans v. United Kingdom*[29] the applicants were arrested in Liverpool when

---

[25] Appl. 28780/95, June 24, 1996, EComHR.
[26] (2000) 30 E.H.R.R. 632.
[27] *Van der Leer v. The Netherlands* (1990) 12 E.H.R.R. 567.
[28] *R v. Governor of Brockhill Prison, ex p. Evans (No. 2)* [2000] 4 All E.R. 15.
[29] (1983) 5 E.H.R.R. 71, Council of Europe Report 1982.

they arrived from Ireland. They were detained for about 45 hours
under the Prevention of Terrorism (Supplemental Temporary
Provisions) Order 1976, but were later released without charge.
The Commission decided that the detention was not improper or
arbitrary and had been used to secure the fulfillment of an
obligation prescribed by law, namely to submit to examination
under the 1976 Order.

The second case involved the application of the Northern Ireland
(Emergency Provisions) Act 1978 where two men and a woman
were detained for periods ranging between 30 and 44 hours.[30] They
claimed that they had not been arrested on reasonable suspicion of
having committed an offence (as in Article 5(1)(c)) but had been
arrested to gather information. The Court discussed the notion of
"reasonable suspicion" and noted that the authorities should be
required to supply sufficient facts or information to satisfy the court
that grounds for reasonable suspicion existed that the person
arrested had committed the alleged offence. The Court also stated
that where terrorist activities were involved, it was not always
appropriate to disclose such sources. However, there must always
be sufficient information to indicate on what basis the genuine
suspicion was held. In this case, the United Kingdom Government
failed to meet the minimum standards set out in Article 5(1)(c) and
there had therefore been a violation of Article 5(1).

Detention after conviction—Article 5(1)(a)

3.09   The lawful detention of a person convicted by a competent court is
upheld in Article 5(1)(a). The person may also be lawfully detained
while awaiting the hearing of an appeal. In *Douiyeb v. Netherlands*[31]
the European Court held that a subsequent finding by a domestic
court that the conviction was based on error in fact or law will not
affect the lawfulness of the detention. The Article does not require a
lawful conviction but a lawful detention. However, the court must
have had jurisdiction over the matter and this has raised questions
regarding magistrates' courts in England and Wales. In *Perks v.
United Kingdom*[32] the Court accepted the House of Lords ruling
where the Lords had distinguished between errors within the
jurisdiction of the magistrates' court and those where that
jurisdiction had been exceeded.

The conviction must be the cause of the detention to satisfy
Article 5(1)(a). In *Weeks v. United Kingdom*[33] the applicant had
been sentenced in 1966 to an indeterminate life sentence; he was

[30] *Fox, Campbell and Hartley v. U.K.* (1992) 14 E.H.R.R. 108.
[31] August 4, 1999, ECtHR.
[32] (1999) 30 E.H.R.R. 33.
[33] (1988) 10 E.H.R.R. 293.

aged 17 at the time. Three years later he suffered a mental breakdown and was treated in a psychiatric hospital. In 1976, he was released on licence but then committed a number of minor offences, leading to the revocation of his licence by the Home Secretary in 1977 under the provisions of section 62(2) of the Criminal Justice Act 1967. The Parole Board considered his case and recommended his release in 1982. He claimed that the minor offences were not sufficient to justify his re-detention and he was not able to challenge the recall in court. The life sentence had been imposed on W because he was considered to be "dangerous" and had mental problems although these did not warrant committal by the court to a mental hospital. The life sentence was the only sentence whereby his condition and progress could be monitored so that he could be released when he was no longer a danger to society. The government submitted that W's release on licence in 1976 did not break the chain of sentence; he was on licence, living outside prison as a result of a privilege and his right to liberty had not been restored to him. The European Court rejected this view saying that whether W had regained his liberty for the purposes of Article 5 was a question of fact. He was lawfully at large and thus in an actual state of liberty, so that his recall by the Home Secretary was a removal from the state of liberty to the state of custody. However, the Court was prepared to allow domestic authorities some discretion on whether there was a sufficient causal link between the two instances of imprisonment. The connection between the original conviction in 1966 and the recall in 1977 was sufficiently established to indicate that there was no violation of Article 5(1)(a).

Weeks had also claimed that he was unable to challenge the recall in court and this breached Article 5(4). The Court held that the Parole Board did not meet the requirements of Article 5(4) with regard to its independence, impartiality and its powers and procedures. The remedy of judicial review did not provide the review required by the Article and thus there had been a violation of Article 5(4).

In *Gordon v. United Kingdom*[34] the applicant had been confined 3.10 to a mental hospital by the Mental Health (Scotland) Act 1960, sections 55 and 60. He later had a period in an ordinary mental hospital with leave privileges but was then returned to a secure hospital. He challenged this on the ground that he had not had an opportunity for periodic review of the need for his continuing detention and this was contrary to Article 5(4) as found in *X v. United Kingdom*.[35] The Commission applied the European Court's decision but Scots law had already been amended by the Mental

---

[34] (1985) 47 D.R. 36.
[35] (1982) 4 E.H.R.R. 188.

Health (Amendment)(Scotland) Act 1983, section 21 and no further action was required.

The question of recall to complete a determinate sentence was raised in *Varey v. The Scottish Ministers*.[36] In 1984, V was sentenced to a *cumulo* total of 29 years for assault and robbery. The Parole Board recommended his release on licence in 1998 and he then established a new life and new business for himself. In 1999, he appeared in court on drugs offences and was refused bail. He appealed against the bail decision and the day before the bail appeal was to be heard, the licence was revoked by the Scottish Ministers and he was returned to prison. The Parole Board confirmed the revocation on the grounds of risk to the public. V sought judicial review of the decision of the Scottish Ministers arguing that it was in breach of Article 5 and there was no causal connection between the circumstances leading to that decision and his original sentence. The petition for judicial review was held to be incompetent because the decision complained of was not made by the Scottish Ministers but by the Parole Board. At the time of the court's decision, the Human Rights Act 1998 had not come into effect but the court made observations on the European Convention on Human Rights argument. The Convention cases, which supported the proposition that the recall had to be based on the rationale of the original sentences, such as *Weeks v. United Kingdom*,[37] were concerned with discretionary life sentences, not mandatory life sentences or determinate sentences. The guarantee of Article 5(4) (judicial determination of the lawfulness of the detention) was fulfilled by the original trial and sentence procedure. There was no additional right conferred on V to challenge the lawfulness of the continuing detention or re-detention after revocation of his licence. The Court also found that the Parole Board fulfilled the functions of a court under the Prisons (Scotland) Act 1989 section 28(5).

The question of what constitutes a court was discussed in *De Wilde, Ooms and Versyp v. Belgium*[38] where it was held that the word implies independence of execution and of the parties to the case, together with guarantees of judicial procedure. Here the police court in which the detention of vagrants was ordered did not satisfy the Convention definition of court.

3.11   Additional days in custody imposed on a prisoner because he failed a mandatory drugs test was neither a deprivation of liberty nor unlawful detention contrary to Article 5. The Divisional Court of the High Court of Justice held in *Greenfield v. Secretary of State for the Home Department*[39] that the additional days were imposed

---

[36]   2000 G.W.D. 30–1205.
[37]   *supra* no. 33.
[38]   (1979-80) 1 E.H.R.R. 373.
[39]   *The Times*, March 6, 2001.

as a disciplinary measure not as a criminal charge, which would have required a fair and public hearing by an independent tribunal.

Court orders and obligations prescribed by law—Article 5(1)(b)

Article 5(1)(b) contains two parts. The first concerns lawful arrest 3.12
or detention where the person has not complied with an order of the court. An example of this would be a finding of contempt of court. A person may not be imprisoned because s/he has failed to comply with a contractual obligation. This is specifically excluded by the Fourth Protocol to the Convention. The United Kingdom has not ratified this protocol but it accepted that imprisonment for debt is not permitted in the United Kingdom. The Convention will not be violated if a person is imprisoned because of a failure to pay a fine lawfully imposed by a court.[40]

The second part of Article 5(1)(b) allows detention to ensure that a person fulfills an obligation prescribed by law.[41] However, the person must have had an opportunity to fulfill the obligation but failed to do so. It appears from the case *Perks v. United Kingdom*[42] that the sanction of imprisonment for non-payment of the community charge (the poll tax) was justifiable to ensure the legitimate aim of payment was met.[43]

In the *Lawless case*[44] the European Court held that there had to be a specific and concrete obligation. Once that obligation was identified, the person could be detained to fulfill the obligation. In *McVeigh, O'Neill and Evans v. United Kingdom*[45] a requirement to submit to an examination on arrival in the United Kingdom was found not to be a violation because the obligation was sufficiently specific and concrete. However, the Commission stated that its finding was based on the premise that the obligation in question arose in limited circumstances and for a limited purpose, namely to combat terrorism. Article 5(1)(b) is therefore more restrictively interpreted than it perhaps appears.

In the United Kingdom the new Terrorism Act 2000 section 89 3.13
requires a person to submit to questioning and this would appear to be specific and concrete enough to satisfy the Convention.

Arrest or detention on suspicion of having committed a crime—Article 5(1)(c)

Under this Article it is permissible to arrest or detain a person in 3.14

---

[40] *Airey v. Ireland* (1977) 8 D.R. 42.
[41] *supra* no. 10; *Steel v. U.K.* (1998) 28 E.H.R.R. 603.
[42] *supra* no. 32.
[43] See also *Benham v. U.K.* (1996) 22 E.H.R.R. 293.
[44] (1961) 1 E.H.R.R. 15.
[45] *supra* no. 29.

order to bring them before a competent court because one of three factors is present. The first is that there is reasonable suspicion that the person has committed an offence. The second is that it is necessary to prevent the commission of an offence, and the third factor is that it is necessary to prevent the person fleeing after committing an offence. The offence must be one known to the domestic law.[46]

If you take a literal interpretation of the Article, the person who is kept in custody on suspicion would always have to be brought before a competent court. If the police decided to release the person before s/he had been to court, then the police would be in breach of this Article.[47] The European Court considered this problem in *Brogan v. United Kingdom*.[48] The four applicants were arrested under section 12 of the Prevention of Terrorism (Temporary Provisions) Act 1984 which gave a seven-day detention power to the police. The applicants argued, *inter alia*, that since they had been released without charge, the purpose of their arrest was not to bring them before a court but to gather information and harass them. The European Court rejected this contention, saying there was

> "no reason to believe that the police investigation in this case was not in good faith or that the detention of the applicants was not intended to further that investigation by way of confirming or dispelling the concrete suspicions which . . . grounded their arrest."[49]

The Court later gave a definition of the phrase "reasonable suspicion". It would occur where the facts or the information would satisfy an independent adviser that the person might have committed an offence.[50] What would be regarded as "reasonable" would depend upon all the circumstances of the case.

> "In this respect, terrorist crime falls into a special category. Because of the attendant risk of loss of life and human suffering, the police are obliged to act with utmost urgency in following up all information, including information from secret sources."[51]

3.15 Full proof is not necessary[52] and the information giving rise to the

[46] *Loukanov v. Bulgaria* (1997) 24 E.H.R.R. 121.
[47] A. Brown, *Law Basics: Human Rights* (W. Green & Son, Edinburgh, 2000), p.33.
[48] (1989) 11 E.H.R.R. 117.
[49] *ibid.*, at 131 para. 53.
[50] *supra* no. 30; and see *Margaret Murray v. U.K.* (1995) 19 E.H.R.R. 193.
[51] *ibid.*, para. 32.
[52] *X v. Austria* (1989) 11 E.H.R.R. 112.

suspicion might remain confidential where a security situation existed, such as in Northern Ireland.[53]

Although there must be honesty and good faith in the suspicion, honest belief will not be enough to satisfy the Convention requirement. There must be an objective basis which justifies the detention or arrest.[54] The Scottish courts have considered the meaning of "reasonable suspicion" on a number of occasions. For instance, in *Dryburgh v. Galt*[55] Lord Wheatley noted that it did not matter whether the information given to the police officer turns out to be ill-founded. "The circumstances known to the police officer at the time he formed his suspicion constitute the criterion, not the facts as subsequently ascertained."[56]

In Scotland, there is no statutory definition of detention but it has been described as a form of limited or temporary arrest.[57] Detention can range from stopping a person in the street for a few minutes to taking a suspect to a police station to be held in custody. The power to detain a suspect and to require the co-operation of witnesses at the scene of a crime is given in sections 13 and 14 of the Criminal Procedure (Scotland) Act 1995.

Section 13(1)(b) relates to witnesses and provides that where a 3.16 police constable has reasonable grounds for suspecting that an offence has been committed and he believes that a person has information about the offence, the constable may require that person to give his name and address. The constable may not use force to require the person to remain at the scene but if the witness refuses to give his name and address he may then be arrested.

Section 13(1)(a) provides that where a police constable has reasonable grounds for suspecting that the person has committed or is committing an offence he may require that person to give his name and address and an explanation of "the circumstances which have given rise to the constable's suspicion". It is worth noting here that no form of caution is yet required. The constable must explain his suspicions and require the suspect to remain while his particulars are checked. This must be carried out "quickly" according to subsection 3 and the constable may use reasonable force to ensure that the person remains while the information is being checked.[58]

The section does not use the word "detain" but merely "requires the person . . . to remain" with the constable while the particulars

---

[53] *Margaret Murray v. U.K.* (1995) 19 E.H.R.R. 193, paras 58–9.
[54] *supra* no. 30.
[55] 1981 S.C.C.R. 26.
[56] *ibid.*, at 29.
[57] C. Ashton and V. Finch, *Constitutional Law in Scotland* (W. Green & Son, Edinburgh, 2000), p.431.
[58] Criminal Procedure (Scotland) Act 1995, s.13(4).

are being verified.[59] The status of the person is therefore in doubt at this point. Presumably if he attempted to leave he would be prevented from doing so by the constable using reasonable force under section 13(4). However, he is not legally detained according to section 295 of the Act; this gives the definition of legal custody as occurring where a person "is required or authorised by or under this Act or any other enactment to be taken to any place, or to be detained or kept in custody". In section 13(2) the suspect has to remain; he is not taken anywhere or held to be taken elsewhere.

3.17   The power to detain a suspect is given in section 14 and from the moment a person is detained, he is in legal custody.[60] A constable who has reasonable grounds to suspect that a person has committed, or is about to commit, an offence punishable by imprisonment may detain that person.[61] The detention has two purposes: first to allow investigation of the offence, and second to investigate whether criminal proceedings should be instigated against that person. The question of what constitutes "reasonable ground" to detain a person was considered in *Wilson and Nolan v. Robertson*.[62] The accused were convicted of theft and appealed against the conviction on the basis that their conviction had depended largely on their own alleged admissions when they were detained. They submitted that they had been illegally detained as there were no reasonable grounds for suspecting that they had committed the offences. The police had thought that a fire exit in the premises had been tampered with and there was evidence that the accused could have done so. There was therefore reasonable suspicion and the detention was lawful, thus allowing the admissions to be admitted as evidence.[63]

The police officer must tell the suspect the grounds for detention, *i.e.* the nature of his suspicions and general details of the offence. This has to be done at the time of the detention and a statutory caution must also be given at this time. The statutory caution requires the suspect only to give his name and address; he need not answer any further questions.[64] The police officer must then take the detained suspect as quickly as is reasonably practicable to a police station or other premises to carry out the investigations into the offence. Reasonable force may be used both to detain the person[65] and to search his person.[66] The requirement to take the

[59] Criminal Procedure (Scotland) Act 1995, s.13(2).
[60] *ibid.*, s.295.
[61] *ibid.*, s.14(1).
[62] 1986 S.C.C.R. 700.
[63] See also *Keegan v. Gilchrist*, 1999 J.C. 185.
[64] See discussion in Chap. 5.
[65] Criminal Procedure (Scotland) Act 1995, s.14(8).
[66] *ibid.*, s.14(7).

accused as quickly as is reasonably practicable to a police station does not mean the nearest station. For instance, in *Menzies v. H.M. Advocate*[67] the suspect was detained near Airdrie but taken to Dunfermline.

The officer effecting the detention must have a reasonable suspicion that the person had committed an offence. In *Woodward v. Chief Constable of Fife*[68] a woman sought damages against the police for wrongful detention. She had been detained under the Criminal Justice (Scotland) Act 1980, section 2(1) on suspicion of having committed theft. The officer who detained her had not been involved in the investigation but had been informed by colleagues that she was under suspicion. After detention of four hours, she was handed over to other officers who continued the detention. She was then arrested and charged with theft and held in custody for a further four hours. She alleged that the original detention was unlawful because the detaining officer has no reasonable grounds for suspecting that she had committed a crime, her knowledge being derived from colleagues. The Court held that the initial detention was unlawful and the subsequent detention was equally unlawful. There was however no malice on the part of the officers and therefore no damages were payable.

On arrival at the police station, the statutory caution must be 3.18 given again as well as the common law caution before formal questioning begins. In *Tonge v. H.M. Advocate*[69] the High Court of Justiciary advised that the common law caution should be given before any interviews conducted within the six hour detention period under section 14.

From the moment of detention, the clock runs. The suspect must be released from detention at the end of six hours unless he is arrested, or detained in pursuance of some other enactment, or there are no longer grounds for suspecting that he has committed an offence.[70] A record of the detention must be kept by the constable, such record giving the information required by section 14(6). The information required is:

(a) The time, date and place at which the detention commenced;
(b) The suspected offence or offences;
(c) The reason for the suspicions:
(d) The time at which the suspect has been read the cautionary statement and informed of his rights;
(e) Name and address of the suspect;

---

[67] 1995 S.C.C.R. 550.
[68] 1998 S.L.T. 1342.
[69] 1982 S.C.C.R. 313.
[70] Criminal Procedure (Scotland) Act 1995, s.14(2).

(f) Any reply made by the suspect;

(g) The police station to which he is being taken;

(h) The time of arrival at the police station;

(i) The time and place of any subsequent move during detention.

Evidence collected during the six hour period of detention is admissible provided the proper cautions have been given. If the detainee is released without charge, the police may still charge him later in connection with that offence but will not be able to detain him again under section 14(3). Arrest and charge would be the only way of dealing with him.

Where a person is detained under a specific enactment, the period of detention allowable may vary from the 1995 Act. Thus the Prevention and Suppression of Terrorism (Supplementary Temporary Provisions) Order 1984[71] allowed an initial period of detention of 12 hours. This could be extended if the examining officer had reasonable grounds for suspecting that the person detained was or had been involved in terrorist acts.

The Home Secretary then had power to extend the period for up to five days while consideration was given to the making of an exclusion order.[72]

3.19 A person who has been detained (or arrested) has a number of rights. There is a common law right not to be mistreated in custody, a right now protected by the Convention. Under section 14(9) of the 1995 Act, the person detained does not have to answer any questions but must give his name and address. A person who is aged 16 or over and who has been detained has the right to have intimation of his detention sent to a solicitor and one other person reasonably named by him.[73] There should be no delay in this intimation being made except where delay is necessary in the "interests of the investigation or the prevention of crime or the apprehension of offenders" but this delay should be no longer than is necessary. The solicitor and the other named person should be informed of where he is being detained. The entitlement to have a solicitor or other person informed of the detention must be intimated to the detained person as soon as he arrives at the police station or other place. The details of the intimation must be recorded giving the time when the request was made and the time it was complied with.

Where the police decide not to intimate the detention immediately to a solicitor or the named person, there is no requirement on them to record their reasons for the delay. This would however be

---

[71] S.I. 1984 No. 418.

[72] See *Breen v. Chief Constable of Dumfries and Galloway,* 1996 S.L.T. 822.

[73] Criminal Procedure (Scotland) Act 1995, s.15(1)(b).

in the spirit of the Act, and arguably the spirit of Articles 5 and 6 of the Convention. At this stage the suspect does not have the right to have access to a solicitor, merely to have his detention intimated to the solicitor. There is no right, for instance, to have the interview stopped so that he can consult with his solicitor.

The police may search the suspect,[74] take fingerprints, palm prints and other prints and impressions as are deemed appropriate.[75] The types of prints and samples which may be taken under section 18 were extended by this Act and defined more fully by the Crime and Punishment (Scotland) Act 1997. The 1995 Act also allows the police to take samples such as hair, fingernail, blood and body fluids and swabs of saliva[76] but the taking of these must be authorised by a police officer of the rank of at least inspector. The police may not take samples of a more intimate or invasive nature, such as an internal physical examination, and such procedures require the authority of a sheriff's warrant obtained by the procurator fiscal.[77] Thus the physical measurement of a suspect[78] would probably be permitted under section 18 but the obtaining of a dental impression would probably require a sheriff's warrant.[79] In *G v. Lees*[80] a warrant was sought to enable a blood sample to be taken from a man charged with the rape and assault of his wife. However, the man had a phobia of needles and it was held that it was acceptable to modify the warrant to allow a sample to be obtained by means of pinpricks.

Section 18(8)(b) allows for the taking possession of evidence 3.20 where there is imminent danger of it being lost or destroyed. In *Bell v. Hogg*[81] the police stopped a van in the early hours of the morning. The police were investigating the theft of copper and the four occupants of the van were told of the reason for stopping them and were cautioned. The officer noticed marks on the men's hands and suspected that these were made by copper. They were taken to the police station where they were asked to give hand-rubbings on paper. They had not been arrested or charged and they were told they need not give the samples. The samples matched the stolen copper and they were prosecuted. Objection was made to the hand rubbings but the court held that the officer was justified in taking the samples because of the urgency in preserving the evidence. When deciding whether or not evidence is admissible the court

---

[74] Criminal Procedure (Scotland) Act 1995, s.14(7).
[75] *ibid.*, s.18.
[76] *Curley v. Fraser*, 1997 S.C.C.R. 705.
[77] *Morris v. MacNeill*, 1991 S.L.T. 607.
[78] *Smith v. Cardle*, 1993 S.C.C.R. 609.
[79] *Hay v. H.M. Advocate*, 1968 S.L.T. 334.
[80] 1992 S.C.C.R. 252.
[81] 1967 J.C. 49; 1967 S.L.T. 290.

takes into account the public interest in the effective investigation of crime and the protection of the accused from arbitrariness, dishonesty or oppression.

Search before arrest may be authorised by a specific statute. For instance, the Civic Government (Scotland) Act 1982, section 60 gives power to a police constable to search a person suspected on reasonable grounds of being in possession of stolen property. The property and any other evidence of the theft may be seized by the police. A uniformed police officer may stop and search vehicles where there is reasonable suspicion of involvement in such a crime.

A person may be detained and searched where a police constable has reasonable grounds to suspect that the person is in possession of an offensive weapon.[82] The person must be informed of the reason for the search and detention. There are similar powers under the Misuse of Drugs Act 1971, section 23(2) to detain and search a person if there are reasonable grounds to suspect the person is in possession of drugs. The suspicion need not be based on the actions of the person but can be based on the evidence of another person who is present or from an anonymous informant.[83] The person detained may be taken to a police station for the search to be carried out. Such searches made under statutory powers must be carried out strictly in accordance with the relevant statutory procedure.[84]

3.21   Generally speaking, the powers of detention are poorly defined in Scotland, particularly when compared to the powers in the English statute, the Police and Criminal Evidence Act 1984. Thus there are no Scottish Codes dealing with the meaning of reasonable suspicion, or treatment while in custody, or sanctions where a code is breached.[85]

The Codes published under the 1984 Act regulate the circumstances in which a police officer may stop and search a person "on suspicion" and it is submitted that in some circumstances these powers may breach the Convention. For instance, Code A paragraph 1.7A states that a police officer may stop and search a person whom he has reasonable grounds to suspect is in innocent possession of a stolen or prohibited item. There is an absence of a power to arrest in these circumstances and it is likely that such a stop and search would be unlawful under Article 5(1)(c).

Further problems arise with the requirement that the purpose of the detention is to bring the person before a competent legal authority. Powers exercised under the Terrorism Act 2000 section 43 and under the 1984 Act are meant to determine whether there is

[82] Criminal Law (Consolidation) (Scotland) Act 1995.
[83] *Weir v. Jessop*, (No. 1) 1991 S.C.C.R. 242.
[84] *Normand v. McCutcheon*, 1994 S.L.T. 327.
[85] *Grant v. H. M. Advocate*, 1989 S.C.C.R. 618.

sufficient evidence to justify an arrest. That would appear to be contrary to the Article.

Where a person is arrested on the grounds of reasonable 3.22 suspicion but the police have no belief in the guilt of the person, the arrest will be unlawful and contrary to section 6 of the Human Rights Act 1998. If the person is co-operative, there may be no justification for arresting him and the purposes of Article 5(1)(c) could be served by interviewing the person at home.

Under this Article the test requires reasonable suspicion regarding the commission of an *offence*. This draws into question whether the provisions of section 41 of the Terrorism Act 2000 are incompatible with the Convention because section 41 refers to suspicion that a person is a terrorist and allows for arrest without reasonable suspicion that an offence has been committed. The compatibility will depend on the interpretation of section 41 and Article 5(1)(c) and the interpretation of the *Brogan* case.[86] The European Court had decided that the definition of acts of terrorism in the Prevention of Terrorism (Temporary Provisions) Act 1984 was "in keeping with the idea of an offence" and the applicants had been asked about specific offences after their arrest. However, the definition of acts of terrorism in the 1984 Act referred to the use of violence for political ends. The definition in section 1 of the 2000 Act is wider, covering the use or threat "for the purpose of advancing a political, religious or ideological cause" of action designed to influence the government or intimidate the public. The action has to involve serious violence against a person or serious damage to property, or seriously disrupt an electronic system, endanger life or create serious risk to health and safety. The destruction of genetically modified crops or hacking into a computer do not equate in scope with the use of violence as in the 1984 Act and thus an arrest based on section 41 of the 2000 Act may be a breach of the Convention. If the person is arrested as part of an investigation but not questioned about specific offences such as those given in section 1, a breach of the Convention seems inevitable.

The detention of minors—Article 5(1)(d)

There are two aspects to Article 5(1)(d). The first is the ability to 3.23 detain a minor for educational purposes and the second is to bring the minor before a competent legal authority. The second part is equivalent to the provisions for adults in Article 5(1)(c).

The detention of a young person for educational supervision will require the state to prove that some educational facilities are available to the minor in the place of detention. Thus detaining a

---

[86] *Brogan v. U.K.* (1989) 11 E.H.R.R. 117.

16-year-old in a remand prison, which had no educational facilities, for a total of 119 days over a period of one year, was not justified.[87]

In *Re K (a child)*[88] the Court of Appeal in England had to consider whether an order placing a child in secure accommodation (under the Children Act 1989, section 25) was a deprivation of liberty under Article 5. The court held that the order had to be justified by one of the exceptions in Article 5(1). The appropriate exception was Article 5(1)(d). Since education was compulsory for any child under 16, it followed that section 25 did not have to refer to education and the secure unit was obliged to provide him with education. The concept of "educational supervision" went beyond academic lessons in the classroom. The court also based its decision on a case which had been declared inadmissible by the European Court but in which that Court had found in similar circumstances to *Re K* that a secure accommodation order was permissible under Article 5(1)(d).[89] In the *Re K* case, the Court of Appeal said that its duty under the Human Rights Act 1998 was to try to find compatibility between the United Kingdom statute and the Convention.

3.24   In Scotland, where the person detained is a child under 16 years[90] the police have a duty to contact the child's parent or guardian and allow them access to the child.[91] If the parents or guardian are unavailable a social worker or some other responsible person should be informed. Access to the child by the parent or guardian may be restricted under section 15(5) where it is essential for the furtherance of the investigation or the well being of the child. Any such restriction or refusal of access should be recorded by the police officers involved or any admission or statement made by the child may be inadmissible.[92] The Act assumes that generally a child will not be detained in custody but will be released to appear at court in due course. Section 43 details the procedures following the arrest of a child. The child does not have the right to have a solicitor or other named person informed of their detention; the police have a discretion as to whether they inform a solicitor.

Mental illness and vagrancy—Article 5(1)(e)

3.25   Article 5(1)(e) covers five groups of people: those who must be confined to prevent the spread of infectious disease, mentally ill people, alcoholics, drug addicts and vagrants. The objectives of this

---

[87]   *Bouamar v. Belgium* (1989) 11 E.H.R.R. 1.
[88]   [2001] 2 All E.R. 719.
[89]   *Koniarska v. U.K.*, Appl. 33670/96, October 12, 2000, unreported.
[90]   But over eight years, the age at which criminal responsibility arises according to Criminal Procedure (Scotland) Act 1995, s.41.
[91]   *ibid.*, s.15(4).
[92]   *H.M. Advocate v. G.B. and D.J.M.*, 1991 S.C.C.R. 533.

Article include the protection of the public and the individual himself and the wording of the Article should therefore be interpreted accordingly.

In Scotland, the spread of infectious disease is controlled by the Public Health (Scotland) Act 1897, as amended by various National Health Service (Scotland) Acts. The 1897 Act allows the detention in hospital of a person with an infectious disease; under section 54 a designated medical officer must sign a certificate which is presented to the sheriff by the local authority for an order of detention to made. The person can only be detained so long as they remain infectious.

A person who is detained because of mental illness must be kept in a suitable hospital or clinic[93] and receive suitable treatment. The psychiatric wing of a prison would not be suitable for someone of unsound mind.[94] If the person is detained under an emergency admission, this would only be acceptable while the person's condition was being assessed. In *Winterwerp v. Netherlands*[95] a period of six weeks appeared to be the limit. The Court also found that the term "person of unsound mind" would not apply to someone whose views or behaviour deviated from the norms upheld by society. A person who voluntarily surrenders to detention in a psychiatric hospital will still have the protection of the Article. If a person has mental health problems but has been convicted of a criminal offence, the detention will be governed by Article 5(1)(a) unless the conviction results in an order for treatment.

In *Ashingdane v. United Kingdom*[96] the Court gave three 3.26 minimum conditions which had to be satisfied before a person could be lawfully detained under Article 5(1)(e). First, a competent authority had to establish that a true mental disorder existed, this being based on objective medical expertise. Second, the disorder had to be such as to warrant compulsory confinement. The Court had previously approved the practice of the Netherlands Government in only detaining those who were a danger to themselves or to others.[97] Finally, the disorder had to be persistent to warrant continued detention.

These standards will require that the grounds for the person's detention are reviewed at regular intervals and if there is a change in the person's circumstances then s/he must be released.

Release from detention should only be refused if there is medical evidence establishing that continued compulsory hospitalisation is necessary or appropriate. In Scotland, under the Mental Health

[93] *Ashingdane v. U.K.,* (1985) 7 E.H.R.R. 528
[94] *Aerts v. Belgium* (1998) 29 E.H.R.R. 50.
[95] *Winterwerp v. The Netherlands* (1979) 2 E.H.R.R. 387.
[96] *supra* no. 93.
[97] *supra* no. 95.

(Scotland) Act 1984 compulsory detention is only permitted where a person is suffering from a treatable mental illness and is receiving treatment. It has been held that patients must be released if they are not receiving treatment. Detention to protect the rest of society from a dangerous person is not lawful under that Act. In the case of *Reid v Secretary of State for Scotland*[98] a patient who had been convicted of culpable homicide, and who had a psychopathic personality, applied for discharge from hospital under section 64(1)(a) of the Mental Health (Scotland) Act 1984 on the ground that it was no longer appropriate for him to be detained for treatment as he suffered from a persistent mental disorder which was not treatable. The case eventually came before the House of Lords on appeal. The House of Lords held that a sheriff was bound to grant an application for discharge if treatment was not likely to "alleviate or prevent a deterioration of his condition". In this case, there was agreement among experts that medical treatment was not likely to lead to a cure but the treatability test was wide enough to include things other than medication and psychiatric treatment. The fact that the structured and controlled environment of the hospital resulted in an improvement in Reid's anger management could be considered as amounting to treatment. His continued detention was therefore lawful. This approach was not followed in the sheriff court case of *Ruddle v. Secretary of State for Scotland.*[99] The sheriff ordered the release of a potentially dangerous patient because his condition was not being alleviated by treatment in a secure institution.[1]

The lawfulness of the detention of an autistic man by a hospital trust was discussed in *R v. Bournewood Community and Mental Health NHS Trust, ex parte L*[2] where the applicant was autistic and incapable of giving consent. L had attended a day care centre where one day he became so agitated that his carers were called. They, however, could not be contacted and so a doctor was called and L was admitted to the mental health behavioural unit of the hospital. The trust told L's carers that he had been admitted on an informal basis. When L applied through his legal representative for judicial review and *habeas corpus* the trust said that he was not being detained, but if he was then the detention was lawful under the common law of necessity, which was applicable since treatment was in his best interests. The Court of Appeal said that it was clear that L was not permitted to leave the hospital and therefore was being

---

[98] *Reid v. Secretary of State for Scotland* [1999] 2 W.L.R. 28; [1999] 1 All E.R. 481; 1999 S.C. (H.L.) 17.
[99] *Ruddle v. Secretary of State for Scotland*, 1999 G.W.D. 29–1395.
[1] See also *Johnson v. U.K.* (1999) 27 E.H.R.R. 296; (1998) 40 B.M.L.R. 1; [1998] H.R.C.D. 41.
[2] [1998] 1 All E.R. 634.

detained. There was no informal basis to the detention because that would require L's consent and he was incapable of giving it. The detention was held to be unlawful.

If the person is found to have an untreatable personality disorder 3.27 but no identifiable mental disorder, will this justify the person's detention on grounds of risk to the public? The European Court has stressed the importance of judicial review of the circumstances of a person's detention on grounds of mental disorder. It could be argued that the United Kingdom's mental health laws are contrary to the Convention because in both Scotland and England, the statutes encourage the detention of people who have a mental disorder and are considered dangerous but who still have the capacity to understand what is happening to them. The question is whether the detention, which is driven by considerations of public policy, is lawful, since no health interest for the patient is being served.[3]

The Scottish courts had an opportunity to consider such an issue in *A v. The Scottish Ministers*.[4] The case concerned three restricted patients held at the State Hospital Carstairs. They sought a review of the first Act of the Scottish Parliament to be passed, the Mental Health (Public Safety and Appeals)(Scotland) Act 1999, saying that it was outwith the legislative competence of the Scottish Parliament by virtue of section 29(2) of the Scotland Act 1998. They put forward three arguments. First, the 1999 Act was incompatible with their rights under Article 5(1) of the European Convention on Human Rights. Secondly, their detention was a form of preventative detention which was not justified in terms of Article 5(1)(e). Thirdly, the test for the original detention was less stringent than the one which now obtained to their discharge, namely a "serious harm" test. This test, made under the Criminal Procedure (Scotland) Act 1995, section 59, made it more difficult for them to be discharged than admitted. Two of the men had lodged their appeals before the 1999 Act was passed and the Act had retrospective effect. This, they argued, constituted an interference with the judicial process inconsistent with their right to equality of arms.

The Court of Session held that the principles of Article 5(1)(e) had been met. The Article did not require the detention to be for the purposes of treatment and it could be justifiable for a legitimate purpose such as the protection of the public. The Lord President, Lord Rodger, said:

"The right to liberty which Article 5 enshrines is undoubtedly a high constitutional right. But it is not an absolute right and

---

[3]   R. Horton "Health and the UK Human Rights Act 1998" (2000) The Lancet, Vol. 356, 1186.
[4]   2001 S.C. 1.

the exceptions which the Convention recognises arise in areas where social policy comes into play."[5]

3.28 The court held that Article 5(1)(e) did not require detention to be for the purposes of treatment. It was justifiable for a legitimate social purpose such as protection of the public.

The 1999 Act was passed in September 1999 using the emergency procedure in the Scottish Parliament. It was rushed onto the statute book as a result of *Ruddle v. Secretary of State for Scotland*.[6] The Mental Health (Scotland) Act 1984 did not allow the sheriff to consider the wider issue of the protection of the public as regards people with personality disorders, such as Ruddle. The 1984 Act did not give a right of appeal against the sheriff's decision and judicial review was not possible. The 1999 Act sought to remedy these problems by adding a public safety ground for refusing to discharge a restricted patient, and broadened the meaning of "mental disorder". An appeal route from the sheriff's decision was also added. In *A v. The Scottish Ministers*[7] the Court of Session held that the retrospective application to pending proceedings of the Act did not violate the patient's Convention right to equality of arms in terms of Article 5(4). "The need to avoid danger to the safety of members of the public was an important public interest which justified a measure of retrospection as a proportionate means of achieving the protection of the public."[8]

In England, the Court of Appeal made a declaration of incompatibility of the Mental Health legislation with Article 5. The case turned on the fundamental issue of how the tribunal functioned. The burden of proof is placed on the restricted patients in seeking release whereas Convention jurisprudence on Article 5 suggests that the state must justify detention. The court was unable to interpret the law in line with Article 5 and made a declaration of incompatibility.[9]

3.29 The term "vagrant" was not defined in the Convention but the European Court has appeared to accept a Belgian definition of a vagrant as being "a person with no fixed abode, no means of subsistence and no trade or profession".[10] The term did not extend to members of the mafia who had no identifiable sources of income.[11]

[5]   *A v. The Scottish Ministers*, 2001 S.C. 1, para. 51.
[6]   *supra* no. 99.
[7]   *supra* no. 4.
[8]   *ibid.*, Lord Rodger. See also: *A v. The Scottish Ministers*, 2001 S.L.T. 1331 (Privy Council).
[9]   *H v. Mental Health Review Tribunal North and East London Region* (2001) *The Times*, April 4, 2001.
[10] *De Wilde, Ooms and Versyp v. Belgium* (1979–80) 1 E.H.R.R. 373.
[11] *Guzzardi v. Italy* (1980) 3 E.H.R.R. 333.

Alcoholics may also be detained under this Article and the scope of the Article will also extend to those temporarily under the influence. However the Court has held that detention is only acceptable where other measures, such as taking the person home, have been considered. In *Litwa v. Poland*[12] the applicant who had been drunk and behaving offensively was taken by the police to a sobering-up centre where he was held for six and a half hours. This was held to be a breach of the Article.

Where a person has been arrested in Scotland and the police have reasonable grounds for suspecting that the person is drunk, the police officer may take him to "any place designated by the Secretary of State . . . as a place suitable for the care of drunken persons".[13] The person cannot be compelled to stay in such a place. This provision was intended to allow for the treatment of a drunken person in a detoxification centre rather than through the criminal justice system. However, the government has only set up a few pilot schemes.

Immigration and Extradition—Article 5(1)(f)

The European Court has recognised the right of states to control 3.30 entry, residence and the expulsion of aliens[14] and Article 5(1)(f) authorises lawful arrest and detention in three circumstances: to prevent unlawful entry to the country; to deport a person; or to hold a person while extradition proceedings are under way.

The lawfulness of the expulsion or extradition process is important in this context. In *Bozano v. France*[15] the applicant had been convicted of a number of serious offences, including murder, in his absence and the State of Italy had requested his extradition from France. The French Court refused the extradition request because there was no requirement in Italian law for the applicant to be retried in his presence, and this was contrary to French public policy. The applicant was then released. However, one month later, he was taken by plain clothes police officers to a police station, served with a deportation order, and then driven to the Swiss border, some 12 hours' drive away. The closest border to the police station was Spain. The Italian authorities sought and obtained his extradition from Switzerland. The European Court held that the deprivation of liberty was not lawful and not compatible with the right to security of person.

Where deportation or extradition is impossible, the detention

---

[12] Appl. 26629/95, April 4, 2000, ECtHR.
[13] Criminal Procedure (Scotland) Act 1995, s.16(1).
[14] *Chahal v. U.K.* (1997) 23 E.H.R.R. 413.
[15] (1986) 9 E.H.R.R. 297.

cannot be lawful under Article 5(1)(f).[16] The deportation or
extradition proceedings must be in progress for this part of the
Article to apply. The Article requires that "action is being taken
with a view to deportation" and "it is therefore immaterial for the
purposes of Article 5(1)(f) whether the underlying decision to expel
can be justified under national or Convention law".[17]

If there is delay, the detention may be unlawful and the person so
detained will have the right, under Article 5(4) to have the legality of
the detention reviewed by a court.[18] Various decisions of the
European Court have indicated that there should be no undue delay
in the deportation proceedings.[19] However, in *Chahal*[20] the
European Court held that a detention of six years was not excessive
because it was necessary to ensure that such decisions were not taken
hastily without due regard to all of the relevant issues and evidence.

Minimum Rights for Persons Detained

3.31 The rest of Article 5 is concerned with stating the minimum rights
for persons who are detained. They fall under three headings:
reasons for detention (Article 5(2)); trial within a reasonable time or
release pending trial (Article 5(3)); and judicial determination of the
lawfulness of the detention (Article 5(4)). Article 5(5) then provides
for compensation to be paid in the event of unlawful detention.

Article 5(2)

3.32 In Article 5(2) the person detained is entitled to be told promptly, in
a language he can understand, the reason for his arrest and the
charge against him. The person should be told these reasons as soon
as possible, but the promptness will depend on the circumstances of
the case. The reasons need not be given in their entirety at the
moment of the arrest, particularly where terrorist offences are
suspected. In *Fox, Campbell and Hartley v. United Kingdom*[21] the
European Court held that the person should be told the "essential
legal and factual grounds for his arrest" to allow him to apply to a
court to challenge the lawfulness of the detention. Making a highly
legalistic statement of the charge to the person may not be sufficient
to discharge the requirements of Article 5(2). If the process of
questioning makes the charge clear, then the requirements of the
Article will be met. In *Dikmi v. Turkey*[22] the Court held that words

---

[16] *Ali v. Switzerland,* Appl. 24881/94 EComHR.
[17] *supra* no. 14 at para. 112.
[18] *Zamir v. U.K.* (1985) 40 D.R. 42.
[19] *Quinn v. France* (1996) 21 E.H.R.R. 529.
[20] *supra* no. 14.
[21] (1992) 14 E.H.R.R. 108.
[22] (2000) Appl. 20869/92, July 11, 2000.

which gave a fairly precise indication of the nature of the charge were sufficient to satisfy Article 5(2). A police officer had said to the applicant: "You belong to Devrimci Sol (a terrorist group) and if you don't give us the information we need the only way for you to get out of here will be as a corpse." The mention of the terrorist organisation should have alerted the applicant that he was suspected of prohibited activities. In *Margaret Murray v. United Kingdom*[23] the Court held that there was no violation of Article 5(2); the reason for the detention would have quickly become apparent and the lack of more probing questions was caused by the applicant's refusal to answer questions.

The English common law power of arrest for breach of the peace came under scrutiny in *Steel v. United Kingdom*.[24] The European Court found the common law sufficiently clear to find that the actions of some of the suspects amounted to a breach of the peace. Two applicants had attempted to disrupt a grouse shoot and this would have caused others to become violent. The arrests and initial detention were consistent with Article 5. However, they refused to be bound over to keep the peace and were detained for non-compliance with a court order. That order was sufficiently precise and specific as to enable the applicants to foresee the consequences of their actions and so there was no violation of Article 5(1). Three other applicants were arrested while handing out leaflets protesting at the sale of weapons. The Court held that their action was peaceful and there was nothing to justify the police fear of violence or breach of the peace. The arrest and detention for seven hours was in breach in the Convention.

Under the Police and Criminal Evidence Act 1984, section 28, there is a requirement for the officer to state the person is under arrest and to give reasons for the arrest either at the time or as soon as practicable thereafter. In *D.P.P. v. Hawkins*[25] the Court of Appeal found that an arrest becomes unlawful when it is practicable to inform the defendant of the reason for arrest but reasons are not given. The unlawfulness will commence at the point of failure to give reasons and will not have retrospective effect so as to include acts done by the officer earlier.

Article 5(3)

The provisions of Article 5(3) lie at the heart of criminal process protection. The Article requires two main issues to be addressed: prompt appearance before a judicial authority and trial within a reasonable time or release pending trial. 3.33

---

[23] (1995) 19 E.H.R.R. 193.
[24] (1998) 28 E.H.R.R. 603.
[25] [1988] 1 W.L.R. 1166.

If an accused person is to be kept in custody, Article 5(3) of the Convention requires that there are relevant and sufficient grounds for doing so. The grounds for the detention have to be tested in court and upheld by a judge or other authorised person. The domestic court must consider "all the facts arguing for and against the existence of a genuine requirement of public interest".[26] The general requirement of public interest must justify "a departure from the rule of respect for the accused's liberty".[27]

As a result of losing a number of cases before the European Court in relation to the procedures used in courts martial, the government amended the Army Act 1955 by enacting the Armed Forces Act 1996 which came into force on April 1, 1997. Regulations were made under the 1996 Act to specify the procedure to be used when a soldier was detained under open or closed arrest.[28] The regulations gave a right of review against the decision to detain and a right of appeal against sentence as well as conviction. However the case of *Hood v. United Kingdom*[29] illustrated that there were still problems with the court martial procedure. Hood had been arrested on a charge of being absent without leave and he was brought before his commanding officer and later the unit adjutant. He was then held under close arrest until his court martial 127 days later. The European Court held that although the commanding officer put Hood into custody, he was not a judicial authority in terms of Article 5(3), because "he could play a central role in the subsequent prosecution of the case against the applicant".[30] In this case, both Articles 5(3) and 5(5) were breached. The government then enacted the Armed Forces Discipline Act 2000 and this requires that the detention of a serviceman or woman before or during trial must be authorised by a person who satisfies the requirements of Article 5. The 2000 Act operates by inserting amendments in the three service statutes: the Army Act 1955, the Air Force Act 1955, and the Naval Discipline Act 1957.

3.34   Article 5(3) is clear that the appearance before a judge should be prompt and any delay, even where made under prevention of terrorism legislation, may be a violation. In *Brogan v. United Kingdom*[31] the applicants were held for four days and six hours without charge. This was held to be too long and the United Kingdom subsequently indicated a derogation from Article 5(3) for situations where public emergency occurs. The derogation was

---

[26] *Letellier v. France* (1992) 14 E.H.R.R. 83.
[27] *CC v. U.K.* (1999) Crim. L.R.228.
[28] Investigation and Summary Dealing (Army) Regulations 1997, regs 20–24.
[29] (2000) 29 E.H.R.R. 365.
[30] *ibid.*, para. 57.
[31] (1989) 11 E.H.R.R. 117.

made on December 23, 1988 under the prevailing legislation.[32] The derogation was confirmed by the Human Rights Act 1998, section 14(1)(a) and Schedule 3, Part I, for a period of five years from October 2, 2000 and might be renewed for a further period under section 16. The European Court accepted the derogation was justified in *Brannigan and McBride v. United Kingdom*.[33] The United Kingdom domestic legislation therefore governs the length of time terrorist suspects may be held without charge. However, the peace settlement in Northern Ireland has changed the emergency situation and therefore, arguably, the grounds under which the derogation was made. The Terrorism Act 2000 addresses some of this by providing for judicial authorisation of detention rather than decreasing the length of time a terrorist suspect can be held. The maximum period of detention is still seven days for a person arrested under section 41 but this must be under a warrant issued by a judicial authority.[34] The warrant can be issued where there are reasonable grounds for believing the detention is necessary to question the person or to preserve evidence. The person so detained or their solicitor has the right to make written or oral representations. As a result of the implementation of the Terrorism Act the government withdrew its derogation on February 19, 2001.

The wording of Article 5(3) refers to the right "to trial within a reasonable time or to release pending trial". Despite this wording, the right to trial and the right to release pending trial are not alternatives. The accused person is entitled to a trial which is held within a reasonable time and, while awaiting that trial, s/he is entitled to be released on bail unless the prosecution persuades the court that there are relevant and sufficient grounds for refusing bail.

The court should consider bail at the earliest opportunity.[35] The English statute, the Police and Criminal Evidence Act 1984, limits detention times in sections 41 to 46 and these would appear to be Convention compliant. Section 46 of the Crime and Disorder Act 1998 requires the Custody Sergeant to bail a detained person to the next court sitting and this is seen as an encouragement to an early hearing.

The European Court has recognised that there are certain 3.35 circumstances where bail can validly be refused. First, bail can be refused if there are reasonable grounds for believing that the accused will abscond. Although the gravity of the offence is a factor in considering this, other factors such as the character of the

---

[32] Prevention of Terrorism (Temporary Provisions) Act 1984.
[33] (1994) 17 E.H.R.R. 539.
[34] Schedule 8, para. 29—judicial authority is sheriff in Scotland, senior district judge in England and Wales and county court judge in Northern Ireland.
[35] *Aquilina v. Malta* (1999) 29 E.H.R.R. 185

accused, his assets and community ties, will also be relevant.[36] Second, there may be a fear that the accused will interfere with the course of justice, such as interference with witnesses. There must be specific allegations indicating that interference is likely.[37] There is an obligation here on the authorities to ensure that the risk of interference is kept under review and if that risk disappears, then the accused is entitled to be released from custody.[38] Third, there may be grounds for believing that the accused will commit further offences. This refusal will usually be based on the fact that the accused has previous convictions. However, the European Court has held that the previous convictions and the current charge must be similar;[39] if they are not, there are no grounds for assuming that the accused will commit further offences.[40] In *Caballero v. United Kingdom*[41] the applicant had been convicted in 1987 of manslaughter. In 1996, he was arrested on suspicion of rape and the magistrates automatically refused him bail because of his previous conviction. In proceedings before the European Court, the United Kingdom Government conceded that there had been a violation of Articles 5(3) and 5(5). The Law Commission commented on section 25 that it would be "liable to be misunderstood and applied in a way which would violate the Convention, namely as dispensing with the need to take all relevant circumstances into account".[42] The Criminal Justice and Public Order Act 1994 was subsequently amended by section 56 of the Crime and Disorder Act 1998.

The fourth circumstance recognised by the European case law is to preserve public order. In *Letellier v. France* the accused was suspected of having committed a high profile premeditated murder. His detention was justified on the grounds that public reaction to his release might have given rise to public disorder. The court indicated however that the detention would only be justified where the crime was sufficiently grave and it was based on "facts capable of showing that the accused's release would actually disturb public order". For instance, in *Tomasi v. France*[43] the authorities were concerned that the applicant had been involved in terrorist offences. The final circumstance is to protect the accused. This may be closely related with the previous circumstance or it may be that the accused requires appropriate medical or mental health care to prevent him from committing further offences.

---

[36] *supra* no. 25 at para. 35.
[37] *Clooth v. Belgium* (1991) 14 E.H.R.R. 717.
[38] A. Brown, *supra* no. 47 at 37.
[39] *Toth v. Austria* (1992) 14 E.H.R.R. 551.
[40] *supra* no. 26.
[41] (2000) Appl. 32819/96, February 8, 2000.
[42] Law Commission Consultation Paper No. 157 "Bail and the Human Rights Act 1998" at para. 9.30.
[43] (1992) 15 E.H.R.R. 1.

The last sentence of Article 5(3) states that "[r]elease may be conditional by guarantees to appear for trial". The European Court has held that bail with conditions may be used in preference to pre-trial detention.[44] Conditions which have been held to be permissible include the surrender of a passport, the imposition of a residence requirement and the provision of a surety although the amount required must be based on the accused's means.

The Scots law on bail was scrutinised in *Burn and McQuilken v.* 3.36 *Procurator Fiscal, Glasgow*.[45] Earlier caselaw[46] had indicated that the judge did not need to go behind a statement by the procurator fiscal that Crown enquiries were proceeding and it was therefore necessary in the public interest that the accused was remanded in custody while these were proceeding. The High Court of Justiciary recognised that the court had a duty to consider whether there were good reasons, based on legal criteria, for a remand in custody. The court should not just rely on what it is told by the prosecutor. This will mean that the prosecution will have to justify their opposition to bail by giving an explanation of the reasons for their opposition. The court overturned the earlier case and applied the European Court decision of *TW v. Malta*.[47] The High Court further noted that where bail was refused and the enquiries were completed before the next scheduled hearing, the prosecution should bring the matter back to the court so that a review of the custody could be held.

Bail proceedings must be fair and there must be "equality of arms", *i.e.* the defence must know what documents and evidence the prosecution holds and these must be disclosed before the bail hearing.[48] The European Court held that the minimum requirement was that "each party must be afforded a reasonable opportunity to present his case—including his evidence—under conditions that do not place him at a substantial disadvantage vis-à-vis his opponent".[49]

The court hearing the bail application should give reasons for refusing bail.[50] While the Convention does not require an appeal system where bail is refused, if one is provided then the same principle of equality of arms is required.[51]

In Scotland, the Scottish Executive has reformed Scots law to 3.37 ensure compliance with the Convention. The Bail, Judicial Appointments etc. (Scotland) Act 2000 was passed to amend

---

[44] *Wemhoff v. Germany* (1979–80) 1 E.H.R.R. 55.
[45] 2000 S.L.T. 538.
[46] *Boyle v. H.M. Advocate*, 1995 S.L.T. 162.
[47] (2000) 29 E.H.R.R. 185.
[48] *Lamy v. Belgium* (1989) 11 E.H.R.R. 529.
[49] *Dombo Beheer B.V. v. The Netherlands* (1993) 18 E.H.R.R. 213 at para. 33.
[50] *Tomasi v. France* (1992) 15 E.H.R.R. 1.
[51] *Toth v. Austria* (1992) 14 E.H.R.R. 551.

sections of the Criminal Proceedings (Scotland) Act 1995. The 2000 Act removed statutory exclusions to the granting of bail in cases of murder or treason, culpable homicide, attempted murder, rape or attempted rape. Previously the 1995 Act did not allow bail for an accused who had a previous conviction for murder or treason, or for those with a prior conviction for the other crimes mentioned where the current charge was one of those crimes. The new requirement is that the sheriff or judge considers the question of bail within 24 hours of the first appearance of the accused, whether or not an application for bail has been made.[52] The Act also gives the accused the right to appeal against a decision to refuse bail.[53] The Convention caselaw recognises a number of reasons for refusal.[54] However, in Scots law, factors such as the seriousness of the crime, the strength of the case against the accused and the accused's previous criminal record, were previously taken into account and these would appear to be insufficient in themselves to justify the refusal of bail under Article 5(3).

There are no criteria specified in the 2000 Act which will limit the right to bail; this was deliberate. The Scottish Executive maintained that setting out limits on the statutory right would be challenged as incompatible with the Convention case law. Thus it is left to the sheriff or judge to weigh the circumstances in each case on its merits.

Finally, the Immigration and Asylum Act 1999 introduced new procedures regarding the detention of those seeking asylum. The powers of the Immigration Service to detain a person are set out in the Immigration Act 1971, Schedules 2 and 3; a general power is given to detain a person while a decision on their case is pending. The 1999 Act section 44 requires that a person detained under the 1971 Act must be referred to the court no later than the eighth day after the commencement of the detention. A bail hearing must be heard no later than the tenth day after the commencement of the detention. Further referrals to the court are required at given intervals.

3.38   Section 46 introduces a presumption in favour of bail for those detained, thus ensuring the Act's compliance with the European Convention and the International Covenant on Civil and Political Rights, Article 9. The Secretary of State may direct where the bail hearing will be held[55] and this may be in prison or a detention centre. Such a hearing would deny detainees a hearing in public and may therefore violate the right to a fair hearing under Article 6. The

---

[52]   1995 Act, s.22A as inserted by the 2000 Act.
[53]   1995 Act, s.32 as amended by the 2000 Act.
[54]   see para. 3.35 above.
[55]   Immigration and Asylum Act 1999, s.45.

hearing may be held via a live television link between a detention centre and the court.[56]

Article 5(4)

This part of the Article allows the person in custody to challenge the lawfulness of the detention in court as speedily as possible. At first sight, it may appear similar to Article 5(3), but this paragraph challenges the lawfulness of the detention itself, not whether or not the detention is appropriate. 3.39

The challenge to the detention must be allowed as speedily as possible. Thus in *Oldham v. United Kingdom*[57] the applicant had been convicted of manslaughter in 1970 and sentenced to life imprisonment. He was released on licence for the third time in 1993, but was recalled in 1996. In November 1996, the Parole Board confirmed the recall and stated that the next review would be in 1998. The European Court held that this two year delay was unreasonable and the detention was unlawful because there had not been a speedy determination for the purposes of Article 5(4). Such determination had to be made in the light of individual circumstances.[58]

The issue of equality of arms arises here as in Article 5(3) and the European Court had indicated that this would apply to any appeal process as well. In *Aerts v. Belgium*[59] the Court held that legal aid should be available where the parties are required to be represented on appeal. Legal aid should not be refused because the legal aid authorities perceive that the prospects for a successful appeal are low. That decision is for the court to make.

In Scotland, the Crown has adopted procedures so that the defence is not put at a disadvantage at committal proceedings and that the principle of equality of arms is satisfied. The Crown will provide a custody statement to the accused. This is a written statement of the evidence on which the Crown case is based. The accused may then challenge the sufficiency of the evidence at the committal hearing but not the reliability of the evidence since this is a matter for the trial itself. 3.40

The review by the domestic court is important to assure those arrested or detained that the detention is lawful. The scope of the review will depend on the circumstances. A full review by a court would be required in two particular instances, first, where the initial decision to detain was not taken by a court or tribunal and second

[56] D. Stevens "The Immigration and Asylum Act 1999: a missed opportunity?" [2001] M.L.R. Vol. 64(3) 413.
[57] Appl. 36273/97, *The Times*, October 24, 2000.
[58] see also *Hirst v. U.K.*, Appl. 40787/98 ECtHR.
[59] *supra* no. 94.

where the grounds for detention are likely to change over time. The latter type would apply in respect of people who are detained on mental health grounds and prisoners who have served the "preventative" part of their sentence.

In *Thynne, Wilson and Gunnell v. United Kingdom*[60] each of the three applicants had been sentenced to life imprisonment for various grave sexual offences and assaults. Each applicant had also been diagnosed as suffering from a mental or personality disorder. This case came after the decision of the European Court in *Weeks v. United Kingdom*, where the Court had declared that the taking of a discretionary decision by the Home Secretary as to the release of a life prisoner was contrary to Article 5(4). The Court had held that the issue of release should be subject to an adequate level of judicial control. Since the United Kingdom Government had not changed its system, the issue was brought again before the European Court by these three applicants. The United Kingdom Government had argued that it was impossible to untangle the punitive and security aspects of the life sentence. The Court dismissed this argument saying that the English courts had already recognised the "protective purpose of this form of life sentence". The Court went on,

> "it seems clear that the principles underlying such sentences, unlike mandatory life sentence, have developed in the sense that they are composed of a punitive element and subsequently of a security element designed to confer on the Secretary of State the responsibility for determining when the public interest permits the prisoner's release. This view is confirmed by the judicial description of the 'tariff' as denoting the period of detention considered necessary to meet the requirements of retribution and deterrence."[61]

3.41 The Court was satisfied that in each case, the punitive element of the discretionary life sentence had expired. Their mental conditions were likely to change over time and thus the lawfulness of their continued detention had to be subject to review by a court at reasonable intervals.

The European Court made it clear in *Wynne v. United Kingdom*[62] that a mandatory life sentence was not to be treated in the same way as a discretionary life sentence. In *Wynne*, the applicant had been convicted of murder and received a mandatory life sentence. He was released on life licence but committed a further killing, pleading guilty to manslaughter on the grounds of diminished responsibility.

---

[60] (1990) 13 E.H.R.R. 666.
[61] *ibid.*, para. 73.
[62] (1994) 19 E.H.R.R. 333.

He received a discretionary life sentence for this conviction and his life licence for the original offence was revoked. He claimed that since he had served the punitive element of the mandatory life sentence, there was a breach of Article 5(4) because the lawfulness of his detention could not be reviewed by a court. The European Court, however, ruled that for mandatory life sentences "the guarantee of Article 5.4 was satisfied by the original trial and appeal proceedings and confers no additional right to challenge the lawfulness of continuing detention or re-detention following revocation of the life licence".[63] A mandatory life sentence imposed on a person aged 18 to 21 has been held to attract a similar approach.[64]

The issue of a sentence "during Her Majesty's pleasure" imposed on a juvenile has been raised on a number of occasions in the European Court. A 16-year-old youth was convicted of the murder of his two-year-old brother and received a mandatory sentence for detention "at Her Majesty's pleasure".[65] He claimed, relying on Article 5(4), that he was entitled to have his detention reviewed by a court as reasonable intervals. The Court had to consider whether the juvenile detention equated to an adult mandatory life sentence or a discretionary life sentence. An indeterminate sentence such as detention at Her Majesty's pleasure could only be justified by considerations based on the need to protect the public. The young person's personality and attitude would change as he or she matured and these would have to be taken into account when assessing the risk they posed to society. If this did not happen then these young people "would be treated as having forfeited their liberty for the rest of their lives".[66] The United Kingdom Government responded to the decision by providing oral hearings once every two years by section 28 of the Crime (Sentences) Act 1997. The *Hussein* case and the later case of the boys who killed James Bulger[67] set out the principle that they were entitled to have their cases reviewed at reasonable intervals and these reviews should be conducted at an oral hearing with legal representation available and the possibility of the hearing of the evidence of witnesses. The principle of "equality of arms" was also shown in *Kampanis v. Greece*[68] where a violation of Article 5(4) occurred when the applicant was not allowed to respond to submissions made by the prosecution.

In Scotland, the High Court has held that a discretionary life sentence has both a security and a punitive component, and the   3.42

---

[63] (1994) 19 E.H.R.R. 333, para. 36.
[64] *John Ryan v. U.K.* (1998) Appl. 32875/96 EComHR.
[65] *Hussain v. U.K.* (1996) 22 E.H.R.R. 1.
[66] *ibid.,* at para. 53.
[67] (1999) 30 E.H.R.R. 121; see also *Curley v. U.K.* (2001) 31 E.H.R.R. 14.
[68] (1996) 21 E.H.R.R. 43.

latter covers both retribution and deterrence.[69] The punitive
component should not take into account the need to protect the
public; it is the task of the Parole Board to decide when a prisoner
may be released and whether it is safe to do so.[70]

The Scottish Parliament enacted the Convention Rights (Compliance)(Scotland) Act 2001 which aims to bring the sentencing and
release arrangements for mandatory life prisoners into line with
those of discretionary life prisoners and murderers aged under 18
years. The Act repeals various sections of the Prisoners and
Criminal Proceedings (Scotland) Act 1993. Section 1 removes the
role of the Scottish Ministers in deciding the length of time a
mandatory life prisoner will spend in prison. Courts must set a
"punishment" period for both the mandatory and discretionary life
prisoners and the Parole Board must review the continuing need for
imprisonment at the end of the punishment period and thereafter at
regular intervals. The "punishment" period is appealable. Although
the government believed that the existing legislation was compatible, the Act was introduced to ward off any challenge by an
existing mandatory life prisoner. The Act removes the political
element of sentencing and places the responsibility for assessing the
risk of release upon the Parole Board sitting as a tribunal.

The Act also makes provision for children who are sentenced to
detention without limit of time. A punishment period must be set
and the Scottish Ministers are obliged to release such prisoners on
licence if so directed by the Parole Board.

3.43   Where a person is mentally ill and has been detained as a result of
this, there may still be a right under Article 5(4) to have the
lawfulness of the detention tested at reasonable intervals. The
European Court stated in *Winterwerp v. The Netherlands* that such
a person should still have access to a court and to "some form of
representation" failing which " he will not have been afforded the
fundamental guarantees of procedure applied in matters of
deprivation of liberty".[71] It may be that special procedural
safeguards will be necessary to ensure that those who are not fully
capable of acting for themselves have their interests protected. In
this case the applicant had not engaged with the proceedings
leading to his detention, he had not been legally represented and he
was not notified of the outcome of the hearings, and not given an
opportunity to argue his case before the courts. These facts
indicated a violation of Article 5(4).

The review must be held at regular intervals because detention is
only lawful so long as the mental illness persists and with sufficient
intensity to warrant the person's detention.

---

[69] *Murray, Hartley and Simpson v. H.M. Advocate*, 1999 S.C.C.R. 946.
[70] *John O'Neill v. H.M. Advocate*, 1999 S.L.T. 958.
[71] (1979) 2 E.H.R.R. 387, para. 60.

"A person of unsound mind who is compulsorily confined to a psychiatric institution for an indefinite or lengthy period is in principle entitled, at any rate where there is no automatic periodic review of a judicial character, to take proceedings 'at reasonable intervals' before a court to put in issue the 'lawfulness'—within the meaning of the Convention—of his detention."[72]

The initial review should take place speedily and should not exceed a few weeks. Thus in *Winterwerp v. The Netherlands*[73] six weeks was too long. The length of time acceptable will however depend on the conduct of the applicant and his or her legal representative.[74]

In England, where a patient has applied for discharge from a restriction order made under the Mental Health Act 1983, there is a reversed burden of proof. The authorities are required to show reliably that he is of "unsound mind".[75] In *R (on the application of C) v. Mental Health Tribunal*[76] the Court of Appeal confirmed that a person is entitled to a speedy decision on the lawfulness of the detention even if suspected of being mentally ill. The practice adopted by the Mental Health Tribunal of listing applications after eight weeks for administrative convenience was therefore unlawful.[77]

3.44

The status of the court or body which hears the case has been questioned in various cases. In *Weeks v. United Kingdom*[78] the Parole Board was under scrutiny. The European Court held that whilst the members were independent and impartial, the Board's powers were advisory in that it could only make recommendations to the Home Secretary which he could reject if he so chose. The Board's procedure did not require them to disclose any adverse material it held about the prisoner. The scope of judicial review of Board's recommendations and the Home Secretary's decisions was not wide enough to ensure that the detention "was consistent with and therefore justified by the objectives of the indeterminate sentence imposed on him".[79] In *X v. United Kingdom*[80] the European Court held that mental health review tribunals created under the Mental Health Act 1959 were not judicial bodies within

---

[72] *Megyeri v. Germany* (1992) 15 E.H.R.R. 584, at para. 22.
[73] (1979) 2 E.H.R.R. 387.
[74] *Boucheras v. France* (1991) 69 D.R. 236.
[75] R (*on the application of H*) v. *Mental Health Review Tribunal N. and E. London Region* [2001] Civ. 415 (CA).
[76] [2001] EWCA, June 30, 2001.
[77] See *E v. Norway* (1994) 17 E.H.R.R. 30.
[78] (1987) 10 E.H.R.R. 293.
[79] (1982) 4 E.H.R.R. 188, para. 69; see also *Thynne, Wilson and Gunnell v. U.K.* at note 60.
[80] *ibid.*

the meaning of Article 5(4) because they had advisory functions only. This was amended in England by the Mental Health Act 1983 and in Scotland by the Mental Health (Scotland) Act 1983 so that the review tribunals have power to release a detained patient from custody. The right of appeal is now found in section 63 of the Mental Health (Scotland) Act 1984 which allows a patient to appeal at regular intervals against their detention. In *A v. Scottish Ministers*[81] the Court of Session held that the amendments to the 1984 Act made by the Mental Health (Public Safety and Appeals) (Scotland) Act 1999 gave patients additional rights of review to challenge the legality of a decision by the Scottish Ministers not to discharge them. The patients had also challenged the validity of the 1999 Act on the grounds that it had retrospective effect to pending proceedings and thus violated the right of equality of arms under Article 5(4). However, the court held that interference with the right under Article 5(4) could be justified on compelling grounds of general public interest subject to the principle of proportionality. Here the measure of retrospection was a proportionate means of achieving the protection of the public and so there was no violation of Article 5(4).

The issue of detention under the United Kingdom's immigration laws was tested in *Chahal v. United Kingdom*[82] where the applicant was unable to seek judicial review of the detention because the government said that issues of national security were involved. The European Court held that this was a violation of Article 5(4), pointing out that other countries had procedures whereby they could address national security concerns but still provide "a substantial measure of procedural justice" to applicants.[83] The length of time (five years) for the deportation proceedings had also been excessive.

3.45   The provision of an effective remedy to challenge the legality of the detention is part of Article 5(4). In *Harkin v. United Kingdom*[84] the applicant was a citizen of Northern Ireland who arrived from the province at a Scottish port and was detained under the anti-terrorism laws. He claimed that he did not have an effective remedy to challenge the legality of his detention. The Commission confirmed the decision of *McVeigh, O'Neill and Evans v. United Kingdom*[85] that the remedy of *habeas corpus* was sufficient to meet the Article 5 requirement. Needless to say this particular decision caused some confusion since the remedy of *habeas corpus* is not one known to Scots law.

---

[81]   *supra* no. 4.
[82]   *supra* no. 14.
[83]   *ibid.*, at para. 133.
[84]   (1986) 48 D.R. 237.
[85]   (1981) 5 E.H.R.R. 71.

It follows from the various rulings of the European Court that once a remedy has been granted, it must be carried out quickly.[86]

Article 5(5)

The final part of Article 5 deals with the provision of compensation. 3.46 It is distinct from the power of the European Court to award just satisfaction under Article 41. Article 5(5) gives a right to compensation so that an award of an *ex gratia* payment would not be sufficient for the purposes of the Article. The European Court has held that a rule that compensation is only payable where there is proof of damage would not violate the Article.[87] However, the term "damage" includes pecuniary and non-pecuniary damage and the latter will include "moral" damage such as distress, pain and suffering.[88]

The detention must be in breach of Article 5 for compensation to become payable. In *Perks v. United Kingdom*[89] the detention of people who had refused to pay their poll tax levies was held not to be unlawful and therefore compensation was not payable. In *Hood v. United Kingdom*[90] there was no domestic right to compensation in respect of the unlawful detention of a soldier facing court martial, and so as well as a breach of Article 5(3) there was a breach of Article 5(5).

The Human Rights Act 1998, section 9(3) allows the award of damages in respect of a judicial act done in good faith only in cases of "arrest or detention in contravention of" Article 5. Such an award is made against the Crown. Where the judicial act is not made in good faith section 8 of the Act applies and damages should be awarded as appropriate. The level of damages to be awarded in a case of false imprisonment was addressed by the English Court of Appeal in *Thompson v. Commissioner of Police for the Metropolis*.[91] The court laid down guidelines for the award of damages starting with a basic award of £500 for the first hour, followed by decreasing amounts for subsequent hours. Aggravated damages could be added if there were special circumstances such as oppressive or humiliating conduct by the arresting officer. Exemplary damages of £5,000 or more could also be available if the total amount of the basic award plus aggravated damages did not provide sufficient punishment. The exemplary damages should not exceed the amount of the basic damages multiplied by three and the overall total amount should not normally exceed £50,000. These amounts should

---

[86] *Roux v. U.K.* (1986) 48 D.R. 263.
[87] *Wassink v. The Netherlands* (1990) A/185-A.
[88] *Huber v. Austria* (1976) 6 D.R. 65.
[89] (1999) 30 E.H.R.R. 33.
[90] *supra* no. 29; see also *Jordan v. U.K.* (2000) *The Times*, March 17, 2000.
[91] [1997] 2 All E.R. 762.

satisfy the requirements of Article 5(5) because the European Court is likely to allow a wide margin of appreciation for states to decide the levels of compensation available.[92]

---

[92] H. Fenwick, *Civil Rights: New Labour, Freedom and the Human Rights Act* (2000).

CHAPTER 4

RIGHT TO A FAIR AND PUBLIC HEARING

EUROPEAN CONVENTION ON HUMAN RIGHTS ARTICLE 6(1)

The European Convention provides in Article 6(1) as follows:

> "(1) In the determination of his civil rights and obligations and of any criminal charge against him, everyone is entitled to a fair and public hearing within a reasonable time by an independent and impartial tribunal established by law. Judgement shall be pronounced publicly but the press and public may be excluded from all or part of the trial in the interests of morals, public order or national security in a democratic society, where the interests of juveniles or the protection of the private life of the parties so require, or to the extent strictly necessary in the opinion of the court in special circumstances where publicity would prejudice the interests of justice."

Article 6 concerns the right to a fair trial. There have been more 4.01 applications to the European Court of Human Rights concerning Article 6 than any other Article in the Convention. Article 6(1), which is discussed in this chapter, concerns a general right in relation to both civil rights and obligations and criminal charges. Articles 6(2) and 6(3) are concerned with the rights of persons charged with criminal offences. Article 6(1) is complex and contains several different elements. The sphere of its application is "civil rights and obligations" and "criminal offences." These terms are not necessarily given the same meanings by the European Court of Human Rights as they are by the Scottish Courts. The right to a hearing within a reasonable time is a right, which applies to civil as well as criminal proceedings and does not depend on a person being in custody. The right to a hearing before an independent and impartial tribunal is a right which has been raised as a devolution issue in several cases following the implementation of the Scotland Act. The right to a fair hearing involves concepts such as the right to be heard, the right to know reasons as well as a general right to fair treatment. The right to a hearing in public is a qualified right and the Article therefore provides for exceptions when the press and public may be lawfully excluded from trials.

DEFINITION OF CIVIL RIGHTS AND OBLIGATIONS

4.02 The rights under Article 6 arise in the determining of civil rights and obligations. The meaning of "civil rights and obligations" does not depend on the legal classification assigned to the right or obligation by the legislators. The question is whether the content and effect of the right or obligation allows the meaning "civil right" or "civil obligation" to be assigned to it.[1] Judicial processes will fall easily within the definition of "determining civil rights and obligations" but it will not always be easy to determine which aspects of administrative decision-making fall within this category. Whether it will be a more effective discriminating factor than the existing categorisation of administrative decision-making into judicial, quasi-judicial and administrative decisions remains to be seen. It is sometimes difficult to decide whether a case concerns what the European Court of Human Rights would regard as a civil right.

The right to claim compensation in relation to property is a civil right. This includes claims arising from shareholding. In *Lithgow v. United Kingdom*, the Court held that the shareholders in shipbuilding companies nationalised by the Aircraft and Shipbuilding Industries Act 1977 were entitled to rely on Article 6(1). The right to compensation derived from owning shares was undoubtedly a civil right. However, the court held that Article 6(1) did not guarantee shareholders an absolute right to a court for the determination o f the right to compensation: The arbitration tribunal set up by the 1977 Act met the requirements of Article 6(1).[2]

Planning determinations affect property rights and so fall within the ambit of Article 6(1). In *Lafarge Redland Aggregates Ltd v. Scottish Ministers*, Redland Aggregates, raised a petition for judicial review against the Scottish Ministers, challenging procedural matters in relation to Redland's application for planning permission for the development of a "superquarry" on the Isle of Harris. Redland argued that the Scottish Ministers were in breach of Article 6. The Scottish Ministers argued, *inter alia*, that there was no dispute or "contestation" and so Article 6 did not apply. It was held that Article 6 was applicable as Redland's property rights,

---

[1] *Ringeisen v. Austria* (1971) 1 E.H.R.R. 455.
[2] *Lithgow v. U.K.* (1986) 8 E.H.R.R. 329.

were clearly a civil right within the meaning of Article 6(1), and if an appeal against refusal of planning permission was protected by Article 6 it would be astonishing if proceedings resulting from the calling in of an application were afforded less protection. There was a dispute involving Redland's civil rights, evidenced by an inquiry, which heard evidence for and against the application. A breach of Article 6(1) had occurred in respect of the procedures followed.[3]

Some matters in relation to education, such as admission to a school, may involve a civil right but matters of academic judgment will not. In the case of *Hanuman v. United Kingdom*, Hanuman sought a declaration of admissibility in respect of his application to the Court arising from his appeal to a University academic appeals committee's decision and the rejection, without reasons, of his complaint to the University Visitor. It was held that the matters complained of did not involve either a civil right or a criminal charge in terms of the European Convention on Human Rights 1950 Article 6. The application was refused.[4]

4.03

Decisions involving the entry or deportation of immigrants are generally not regarded as civil rights. *Maaouia v. France*, a Tunisian citizen living in France, was made the subject of a deportation order in 1990 on completing a French prison sentence for armed offences against the person. He did not comply with the order and an exclusion order was made against him. In 1994 the deportation order was quashed, but the exclusion order was not rescinded until 1998 and Maaouia complained that the length of time taken to rescind the order was unreasonable under Article 6(1). It was held that Article 6 did not apply. An exclusion order was a legitimate immigration measure that was not related to criminal proceedings. The procedure involved did not constitute a civil right capable of protection under Article 6.[5]

Matters concerning the employment contracts of public employees are not generally considered to concern civil rights. In *Neigel v. France*, a shorthand typist employed by a local authority complained to the Court on the grounds of excessive delay in resolving an employment issue. She was granted one year's leave of absence for personal reasons in 1983. She was entitled to reinstatement as of right, conditional on a suitable vacancy existing at the time she sought reinstatement. However, no such vacancy existed in 1984 when she applied for reinstatement and she was informed that she had been given unpaid leave of absence pending a suitable vacancy. A subsequent re-application in 1985 was met with the same response. Neigel brought legal proceedings against the

---

[3] *Lafarge Redland Aggregates Ltd v. Scottish Ministers*, 2001 S.C. 298; 2000 S.L.T. 1361; [2001] Env. L.R. 27; [2000] 4 P.L.R. 151; [2000] N.P.C. 109.
[4] *Hanuman v. U.K.* [2000] E.L.R. 685.
[5] *Maaouia v. France* (2009) 9 B.H.R.C. 205.

local authority for reinstatement, but the claim failed and her final appeal was dismissed in 1991. She then complained that she had not had a hearing within a reasonable period of time, contrary to Article 6. It was held that reinstatement was a right recognised under domestic law. However, the matter complained of was concerned with Neigel's recruitment and career and did not entail a civil right, as required by Article 6.[6] Disciplinary proceedings by professional organisations, which determine a person's right to engage in his profession, qualify as the determination of civil rights.

DEFINITION OF CRIMINAL CHARGE

4.04 If a national court classifies an act as a criminal offence the European Court of Human Rights will not challenge this determination. There may be uncertainty however, in relation to activities which are not classed as crimes. The Court regards the fact that an act is not classed as a crime or offence under national law as a relevant factor but not a definitive test. In the case of *Engel v. Netherlands*, the Court decided that even the fact that a person may be imprisoned as a punishment is not enough to categorise a matter as a criminal offence. Engel had committed offences against military discipline and had been punished by two days' arrest.[7] In *McFeeley v. United Kingdom*, the Commission decided that a disciplinary hearing within a prison was not a determination of a criminal charge even though the consequences could include extended loss of liberty.[8]

It was held in the case of *R (on the application of Fleurose) v. Securities and Futures Authority*[9] that the Securities and Futures Authority 's disciplinary proceedings did not involve the determination of a criminal charge for the purposes of the Human Rights Act. Fleurose, who had been found guilty of improper conduct as a trader in securities by the Securities and Futures Authority 's disciplinary tribunal, applied for judicial review of the dismissal of his appeal against the decision to suspend him from acting as a registered person. It was contended that, as the Securities and Futures Authority 's disciplinary proceedings involved a "criminal charge" he was entitled to the protection afforded by Articles 6(2) and 6(3) and that he should have had the right not to incriminate himself and the right to legal representation. The application was refused. The condition of criminal proceedings had not been fulfilled in so far as it was not being alleged that Fleurose had

---

[6] *Neigel v. France* (2000) 30 E.H.R.R. 310.
[7] *Engel v. Netherlands* (1979–80) 1 E.H.R.R. 647.
[8] *McFeeley v. U.K.* (1981) 3 E.H.R.R. 161.
[9] [2001] EWHC Admin. 292.

breached his personal obligations to the state in his capacity as a citizen. Fleurose had chosen to become a trader and so had voluntarily elected to become subject to the proceedings of the Authority. In any event, as the function of a regulatory authority was to protect the public, it would be a grave impediment to an investigation if traders could refuse to co-operate on the ground of self-incrimination.[10]

INDEPENDENT AND IMPARTIAL TRIBUNAL

Independence

In the determination of his civil rights and obligations and of any   4.05
criminal charge against him, everyone is entitled to a fair and public hearing by an independent and impartial tribunal established by law. The requirement for independence is an aspect of fairness, which was not so clearly established in Scotland prior to the implementation of the Scotland Act. The Scots law on fairness concentrated rather on the twin pillars of natural justice, *i.e.* absence of bias in the mind of the judge and a right to be heard. There was emphasis therefore on impartiality and procedural fairness but the issue of independence was not given much importance. In order for a court or tribunal to be independent and impartial in terms of Article 6(1) there are several conditions which must be met:

(1) Security of tenure of the members
(2) Absence of bias amongst the members of the tribunal
(3) Absence of procedural unfairness

(1) Security of Tenure of the Members

In deciding whether a tribunal can be said to be independent, regard must be had to the following matters:

(a) The manner of appointment of its members,
(b) Their term of office,
(c) The existence of guarantees against outside pressures,
(d) Whether the body presents an appearance of impartiality.[11]

---

[10] *R (on the application of Fleurose) v. Securities and Futures Authority* [2001] EWHC Admin 292. See also *Engel v. Netherlands (No.1)* (A/22) (1979-80) 1 E.H.R.R. 647.
[11] *Findlay v. U.K.* (1997) 24 E.H.R.R. 221. See also *Starrs v. Ruxton*, 2000 J.C. 208; 2000 S.L.T. 42; 1999 S.C.C.R. 1052; [2000] H.R.L.R. 191; [2000] U.K.H.R.R. 78; 8 B.H.R.C. 1.

They must not be subject to removal or reappointment at the whim of the government

4.06 **Judicial appointments.** Following the implementation of the Scotland Act 1998, one of the fist indications of the momentous nature of the change in status of the European Convention on Human Rights in Scots Law was a challenge to the impartiality of the sheriff court when presided over by a temporary sheriff. The Lord Advocate is a member of the Scottish Executive and so his acts must be compatible with Convention rights.[12] There is an exemption from this requirement where he is carrying out functions as the head of public prosecution in Scotland. His actions may not be challenged on the basis of non-compliance with convention rights where he could not have acted differently as the result of one or more provisions of primary legislation. The Lord Advocate played a key role in the appointment of temporary sheriffs and this was not part of his exempt activities as head of the system of prosecutions. On November 11, 1999 the High Court of Justiciary upheld a challenge under Article 6 of the European Convention of Human Rights which brought to an end the system of temporary sheriff appointments in Scotland. A prosecution before Temporary Sheriff David Crowe in Linlithgow Sheriff Court was challenged on the basis that a temporary sheriff could not be regarded as impartial when his future employment prospects were subject to influence by the Lord Advocate. The Lord Advocate had a key role in the appointment, dismissal and non-reappointment of temporary sheriffs. He is also head of the public prosecution system in Scotland. Temporary sheriffs may be reluctant to reach decisions that may cause the Lord Advocate to look upon them with disfavour. Consequently temporary sheriffs could not be regarded as sufficiently independent of the Executive to meet the requirements of Article 6 that an accused have a fair hearing before an "independent and impartial tribunal". It was held that the independence of a member of a court was to be established by reference to the manner of appointment, the term of office, the guarantees against outside pressure and the appearance of independence. Temporary sheriffs were appointed by the Secretary of State for Scotland,[13] however, the Lord Advocate played an important role in that he decided what appointments were required and advised the Scottish Courts Administration on selection. Appointments were generally for one year only. Appointment as a temporary sheriff was widely regarded as a step towards

---

[12] Scotland Act 1998, s.44(1)(c).
[13] Sheriff Courts (Scotland) Act 1971, s.11.

appointment as a permanent sheriff. Possible hopes of such advancement, as well as the short-term nature of the office, compromised the independence of the temporary sheriff. The absence of security of tenure was the most important factor in casting doubt on the independence of temporary sheriffs. While there was no suggestion that the Scottish Executive had ever acted contrary to the principles of judicial independence, it was necessary that legal guarantees of the independence of the judiciary be in place.[14]

The situation was held to be different in the case of temporary judges. An action of damages went to proof before a temporary judge. During *avizandum* the decision in *Starrs v. Ruxton* was issued. On the basis of that decision one of the parties in the damages action sought to raise as a devolution issue that a temporary judge was not an independent and impartial tribunal. It was held that the appointment and use of temporary judges to hear cases, where the Crown itself was not involved in the claim, did not breach a party's Convention rights. Temporary judges have security of tenure and enjoy the same status and immunities as a permanent judge. The absence of a guarantee of reappointment did not affect a temporary judge's independence. The Lord President decided whether or not to use a temporary judge and had laid down restrictions on the use of temporary judges in potentially sensitive cases, such as judicial review. Though the temporary judge remained in practice, given the institutional safeguards of the judicial oath and declinature, in particular where a conflict of interest arose, this factor did not breach Article 6.[15]

These two cases brought the issue of judicial appointments into the limelight and caused the Scottish Ministers to recognise the need for a review of the process of judicial appointments. Public unease over the procedures for judicial appointments was increased by one or two instances of Lord Advocates appointing themselves to the Bench. Following a process of consultation, the Justice Minister announced judicial appointment reforms, which include the advertising of all appointments of the Court of Session judges, sheriff principals and sheriffs and an independent Judicial Appointments Board. The Judicial Appointments Board will scrutinise candidates and recommend the best person for nomination to the First Minister. The Board will contain a balance of legal and lay people and be chaired by a senior non-legal figure. The scheme should be in operation by the end of 2001. The reforms will lessen the role of the Lord Advocate in the judicial appointment procedure.

---

[14]   *Starrs v. Ruxton (sub nom. Ruxton v. Starrs)* 2000 J.C. 208; 2000 S.L.T. 42; 1999 S.C.C.R. 1052; [2000] H.R.L.R. 191; [2000] U.K.H.R.R. 78; 8 B.H.R.C. 1.
[15]   *Clancy v. Caird (No.1)*, 2000 S.L.T. 546; 2000 S C.L.R. 526.

4.07   The use of temporary sheriffs has now been abolished.[16] The flexibility and support that the temporary sheriffs provided will remain but in the form of part-time appointments which will be in line with the European Convention on Human Rights. In order to ensure maximum independence, part-time sheriffs will be appointed for a period of five years. Any part-time sheriff coming to the end of a five-year appointment will be automatically re-appointed with limited exceptions and the Lord President will appoint the tribunal authorised to remove part-time sheriffs.

The status of the district court in relation to the requirements of Article 6(1) came under consideration in the case of *Clark v. Kelly*.[17] Proceedings had commenced against Kelly on charges of theft and breach of the peace, to which Kelly pled not guilty. Kelly raised a devolution issue alleging that Kirkcaldy District Court was not an independent and impartial tribunal under the European Convention on Human Rights 1951 Article 6(1). The district court is presided over by a Justice of the Peace who has no legal qualifications and who determines both questions of fact and law. He or she is advised by a clerk of the district court, who acts as legal assessor in the district court, on matters of law, practice and procedure. The clerk of the district court is appointed in terms of section 7 of the District Court (Scotland) Act 1975. He is not a member of the court and does not share the responsibility of the court for its decision. He is an official who is appointed and employed, on a full-time or part-time basis, by the local authority. The clerk does not offer judgment and takes no part in deliberations on conviction or sentence. On sentencing he is only concerned to advise on the powers of the court. All fines imposed in a district court in respect of common law offences and fines under the Civic Government (Scotland) Act 1982 accrue to the local authority concerned.[18] Justices of the Peace are appointed and may be removed by the Scottish Ministers.[19]

The justices referred the matter to the High Court under the Scotland Act 1998, section 98, Schedule 6. They asked the following five questions:

(1) Is the district court, as constituted an independent and impartial tribunal in terms of Article 6(1) of the European Convention on Human Rights?

(2) Is the clerk of the district court acting in a judicial capacity or performing a judicial role in the exercise of his function of providing advice to the Justice of the Peace?

---

[16] Bail, Judicial Appointments etc. (Scotland) Act 2000.
[17] *Clark v. Kelly*, 2001 J.C. 16; 2000 S.L.T. 1038; 2000 S.C.C.R. 821.
[18] District Courts (Scotland) Act 1975, s.23(2).
[19] District Court (Scotland) Act 1975, s.9(2).

(3) Is the clerk of the district court in law part of the tribunal for the purposes of Article 6(1)?

(4) Is the act of a Procurator Fiscal in calling a case for trial before the district court as at present constituted an act which is compatible with the Convention right of the accused in terms of Article 6(1)?

(5) Since communications between clerks and justices are private and outwith the presence of the accused and his legal advisers, does the accused have a fair hearing in public?

It was held that the clerk of the district court does not act in a judicial capacity but only in an advisory capacity. He is not, therefore part of the tribunal for the purpose of Article 6(1). There was nothing objectionable in the practice of private communication between clerks and justices provided that care was taken to confine such communication to the provision of legal advice. Any matter on which the defence or prosecution might wish to make material comment should be raised in open court. The legal adviser to the district court was employed by the district council and was totally independent in every way of the procurator fiscal's department.

The independence of a reporter to a planning enquiry came under consideration in the case of *County Properties Ltd v. Scottish Ministers*. The case arose when the Scottish Ministers called in an application by County Properties Ltd for listed building consent to demolish an historic house and appointed a reporter to hold a public inquiry. The house, an A-listed building, was built as a town house and later extended to form offices for the architect Alexander Thomson. Edinburgh City Council granted planning permission and listed building consent for demolition of the house and replacement with a new office building but ministers intervened and called-in the application. County Properties sought judicial review arguing that the Scottish Ministers did not qualify as an independent and impartial tribunal when they made the decision to call-in the application and that the reporter was not independent or impartial. The planning application had been opposed by Historic Scotland, which was part of the Scottish Administration. The reporter was appointed and paid by the Scottish Ministers. The Scottish Ministers admitted that neither they nor the reporter were independent or impartial, but averred that the requirements of Article 6(1) were satisfied because County Properties had a right to appeal the outcome of the inquiry to the Court of Session, both on matters of fact and of law. The court held that, although there would be instances when the existence of a right of appeal or review would satisfy the requirements of Article 6(1) in relation to administrative decisions, the right of appeal under the Planning (Listed Buildings and Conservation Areas) (Scotland) Act 1999,

4.08

section 58 may not satisfy the requirements. It was not clear whether such an appeal could cover questions of fact as well as legal issues.[20]

The issue of whether a right to fair hearing was contravened where a policy maker also acting as adjudicator in planning appeals was considered by the House of Lords in *R (on the application of Holding & Barnes Plc) v. Secretary of State for the Environment, Transport and the Regions.* The Secretary of State appealed against a declaration that his powers to determine planning applications were incompatible with Article 6(1), given his involvement in the formulation of planning policy. It was held, allowing the appeal, that the courts were able to exercise sufficient control over the decision making portion of the Secretary of State's role by means of judicial review. It was possible for the courts to set aside a particular decision for a multiplicity of reasons. The courts could control the lawfulness of the decision but had no function to review the policy-making portion of the Secretary of State's role. It was not necessary that, in order to comply with Article 6; a hearing had to be capable of review on its merits.[21]

4.09 **Parole Board for Scotland.** One specific result of the need to secure compliance with Article 6(1) is the proposed reconstitution of the Parole Board for Scotland. The Convention Rights Compliance Act, Part 2, includes a proposal to reform the Board so that it meets the criteria for independence. Parole was introduced to Scotland by the Criminal Justice Act 1967, which also established the Parole Board for Scotland. The Parole Board is currently regulated by section 20 of the Prisoners and Criminal Proceedings (Scotland) Act 1993. The Parole Board includes a Lord Commissioner of Justiciary and at least three other members. There are currently 14 members including a sheriff and a retired sheriff. Members are appointed by the Secretary of State. They receive remuneration and allowances determined by the Secretary of State. It has been recognised that, to

---

[20] *County Properties Ltd v. Scottish Ministers,* 2000 S.L.T. 965; [2000] H.R.L.R. 677; [2000] 4 P.L.R. 83; [2001] J.P.L. 170.

[21] *R (on the application of Holding & Barnes Plc) v. Secretary of State for the Environment, Transport and the Regions, (sub nom. R v. Secretary of State for the Environment, Transport and the Regions, ex p. Holdings & Barnes Plc. Joined cases: R (on the application of Premier Leisure UK Ltd) v. Secretary of State for the Environment, Transport and the Regions; R (on the application of Alconbury Developments Ltd) v. Secretary of State for the Environment, Transport and the Regions; Secretary of State for the Environment, Transport and the Regions v. Legal and General Assurance Society Ltd)* [2001] UKHL 23; [2001] 2 W.L.R. 1389; [2001] 2 All E.R. 929; [2001] U.K.H.R.R. 728; [2001] 20 E.G.C.S. 228; (2001) 98(24) L.S.G. 45; (2001) 151 N.L.J. 727; (2001) 145 S.J.L.B. 140; [2001] N.P.C. 90.

fulfil the requirements of Article 6(1) members of the Parole Board must have some degree of security of tenure.

The Convention Rights Compliance Act provides that members should be appointed by the Scottish Ministers for a fixed term of between six and seven years. The regulations for appointment would be established by Ministers but laid before the Scottish Parliament. Re-appointment would be possible but only for one further period of six or seven years and only after a gap of at least three years. Originally the proposal had been for a gap of at least six years between appointments but it was amended as the Deputy Justice Minister stated that a gap of three years is sufficient to remove any legitimate doubt about the independence and impartiality of members.[22] Removal from office will only be possible for specified breaches, such as inability, neglect of duty or misbehaviour.[23] Decisions to remove members from office will be made by a specially established tribunal. Membership of this tribunal will be for a fixed period. Members will be appointed by the Lord President of the Court of Session. The three members of the tribunal must be,

> "(a) either a Senator of the College of Justice or a sheriff principal, (who shall preside);
> (b) a person who is, and has been for at least 10 years, legally qualified;
> (c) one other person who shall not be legally qualified."[24]

In order to ensure that members cannot be informally dismissed by Ministers simply ceasing to allocate work to them, work will be allocated to members, up to a guaranteed level, by the chair of the Parole Board.

Another reform, which has been brought about to ensure compliance with the Convention, is the proposed reform of the procedures for appointing the procurator fiscal of the Lyon Court. The Lyon Court is the Scottish court that deals with the law of arms and heraldry. It is presided over by the Lord Lyon King of Arms. The Lord Lyon appoints a Procurator Fiscal, whose function is to raise complaints and petitions in the Lyon Court when an infringement of heraldic law has occurred.[25] The fact that the Lord Lyon appoints the Procurator Fiscal as well as presiding over the court could be seen to be a breach of Article 6. Part 5 of the Convention Rights (Compliance) (Scotland) Act proposes a new procedure for appointment.[26] The person appointed must be an

---

[22] Meeting of Justice Committee, April 25, 2001.
[23] Convention Rights Compliance (Scotland) Act, s.3(A).
[24] *ibid.*, s.5.
[25] Lyon King of Arms Act 1867, s.9.

advocate or solicitor. He or she will be appointed by the Scottish Ministers "on such terms and conditions as they determine." The current Procurator Fiscal will cease to hold office when Part 5 of the new legislation comes into force.

(2) Impartiality

4.10 Impartiality has two aspects:

(1) subjective freedom from bias or personal prejudice
(2) impartiality from an objective viewpoint.

Should the court or tribunal fail either test, then it is not to be regarded as impartial in terms of Article 6(1).[27] In *Piersack v. Belgium* the European Court of Human Rights stated:

> "Whilst impartiality normally denotes absence of prejudice or bias, its existence or other wise can, notably under Article 6(1) of the Convention, be tested in various ways. A distinction can be drawn in this context between a subjective approach, that is endeavouring to ascertain the personal conviction of a given judge in a given case, and an objective approach, that is determining whether he offered guarantees sufficient to exclude any legitimate doubt in this respect . . . However, it is not possible to confine oneself to a purely subjective test. In this area even appearances may be of a certain importance . . . any judge in respect of whom there is a legitimate reason to fear a lack of impartiality must withdraw."[28]

Prior to the implementation of the Scotland Act and the Human Rights Act the existing Scots law already had a well-established and clear set of principles to ensure procedural fairness in the operation of courts and tribunals. The issue of impartiality was already well-established in the Scots law principles of natural justice.

4.11 **Natural justice**. The principles of natural justice derive from the ordinary rules of civil and criminal procedure, which serve to ensure that every party to proceedings in a court has the opportunity of knowing the case which he has to meet and of presenting his case before an impartial judge. The superior courts in their supervisory role over tribunals and administrative agencies require natural justice to be observed by many bodies which are not courts but

---

[26] Convention Rights (Compliance) (Scotland) Act, s.11(3) inserts a new s.9A into the Lyon King of Arms Act 1867.
[27] *De Cubber v. Belgium* (1985) 7 E.H.R.R. 236.
[28] *Piersack v. Belgium* (1983) 5 E.H.R.R. 169. See also *Hauschildt v. Denmark* (1990) 12 E.H.R.R. 266.

which exercise powers which involve consideration of facts and making decisions that directly affect the rights and interests of individuals. Breach of a rule of natural justice in which a body is required to act judicially will lead to its decisions being declared *ultra vires*.

Judicial functions. It is a well-established principle that the rules of natural justice must be observed when a judicial function is being exercised. The extent to which the concept of a judicial function equates to the term "determination of civil rights and obligations" under Article 6(1) remains to be seen. The Donoughmore Committee on Ministers' Powers in 1932 tried to analyse and differentiate between different types of functions carried out by way of government. They categorised decisions into three types: administrative, judicial and quasi-judicial. An administrative decision puts no legal obligation upon the person charged with the duty of reaching the decision to consider and weigh submissions and arguments or to collate any evidence or to solve any issue. The grounds on which he acts and the means he takes to inform himself of the surrounding circumstances before acting are left entirely to his discretion. A judicial decision is one reached on a dispute following presentation of the case by each party, including the taking of evidence, submission of legal argument and the application of law to the facts. It is clear that the rules of natural justice will apply to judicial decision-making according to this definition. The Committee also identified a type of decision-making which has judicial characteristics and which they called quasi-judicial. A quasi-judicial decision is one that resolves a dispute following a presentation of the case by each party, the adducing of evidence and the possible submission of legal argument. The consequence of the decision is administrative action based on ministerial discretion. The committee recognised the similarity between administrative and quasi-judicial decisions saying, "[i]ndeed generally speaking a quasi-judicial decision is only an administrative decision, some stage or some element of which possessed judicial characteristics". Natural justice is an inherent part of this sort of decision-making. This was held to be so in the case of *McDonald v. Lanarkshire Fire Brigade Joint Committee*. Thomas McDonald and other firemen brought an action against Lanarkshire Fire Brigade Joint Committee for a reduction of a decision of their disciplinary tribunal. McDonald had been charged with an offence under the Schedule to the Fire Service (Discipline) (Scotland) Regulations 1953. The regulations stated that a brigade member who has been charged will be informed in writing as soon as possible of the charge and receive other reports or written allegations on which the charge may be founded. McDonald received written notification of the charge and reports only days

4.12

before his hearing. At the hearing McDonald complained that the regulations had not been complied with. He requested an adjournment due to the shortage of notice given. The Fire Brigade Joint Committee considered that the regulations had not been breached and the request for adjournment was rejected. McDonald brought a petition for judicial review. It was held that the decision of the Joint Committee should be reduced since it was a quasi-judicial body that should have adhered to the principles of natural justice.[29] The principles of natural justice are not confined solely to judicial decision-making. There is a general duty to act fairly in a wide range of administrative activities, although specific aspects such as a right to a hearing and a right to representation may not apply in every case.

In the case of *McDonald v. Burns*, it was held that the principles of natural justice should be observed where church authorities are making decisions which affect individual rights and interests. Several nuns were dismissed from their convent in Edinburgh but refused to leave. An action was brought in the Court of Session for a decree for their removal. The sisters claimed that no charges had been made against them and that they had been given no right of reply, contrary to the rules for dismissing sisters. The Lord Ordinary allowed the decree for their removal and the sisters appealed. The Inner House held that, although religious authorities have privative jurisdiction within their own sphere, the courts can entertain an action where the religious body has acted beyond its constitution in a manner calculated to affect the civil rights and patrimonial interests of any of its members. The fact that the principles of natural justice had not been adhered to meant that the decision was *ultra vires* and void.[30]

4.13 **Justice must be seen to be done**. The two main principles of natural justice are: *audi alteram partem* (hear the other side), known as the right to a hearing, and *nemo judex in causa sua (potest)*, (no one can be a judge in his own cause), known as the rule against bias. Underlying these there is a third principle that justice must not only be done but must manifestly be seen to be done. This is an objective test for bias which does not require any proof of actual bias in the mind of the decision-maker. The case of *Barrs v. British Wool Marketing Board* related to circumstances where there had probably been no unfairness but an opportunity had been created in which unfairness could have taken place. The British Wool Marketing Scheme 1950 provided that wool delivered to the Marketing Board should be valued by appraisers. A producer who

---

[29] *McDonald v. Lanarkshire Fire Brigade Joint Committee*,1959 S.C.141.
[30] *McDonald v. Burns*, 1940 S.C. 376.

was aggrieved by the valuation by the appraisers had a right of appeal to a tribunal consisting of five members. One producer, Barrs, whose wool was valued at 3d per pound below the maximum price, appealed to the tribunal. The tribunal examined the wool in the presence of a representative of the producer and the two appraisers who had originally valued it. The tribunal then retired for consideration. The representative of the producer was excluded at this stage but the two appraisers retired with the tribunal members although they took no part in the discussions. The tribunal dismissed the appeal and reduced the value of the wool by another penny per pound. Barrs sought reduction of the tribunal's decision on the ground that it had reached its decision in circumstances that were contrary to natural justice. It was held that the tribunal was a body that was required to act judicially. By creating a situation in which one side may have had an opportunity to put forward arguments without giving an equal opportunity to the other, they had transgressed the principles of natural justice and the decree of reduction was granted. Lord Clyde said, "[t]he test is not, has an unjust result been reached? but, was there opportunity afforded for injustice to be done? If so the decision cannot stand".[31]

This same principle applies where there has been a possibility that a person making a judicial decision has been biased. Such were the circumstances in the case of *Bradford v. McLeod*. During a prolonged national strike by coal miners a conversation took place at a social function in Ayr in which the strike was discussed. A sheriff and a solicitor were both present. At one point the sheriff made remarks to the effect that he "would not grant legal aid to miners". Subsequently a miner represented by that solicitor appeared before that same sheriff accused of breach of the peace on a picket line. The solicitor moved that the sheriff should declare himself disqualified from hearing the case because of the views that he had expressed. The sheriff declined to disqualify himself. The miner was convicted of the offence, as were 13 others in similar circumstances. They all sought to have their convictions and sentences suspended. It was held that there had been a miscarriage of justice. Although the sheriff himself might have been satisfied that he was not biased and would not act in a manner contrary to his judicial oath, circumstances existed which could create in the mind of a reasonable man a suspicion of the impartiality of the sheriff. It was not enough that justice was done, it must also be seen to be done. Lord Ross quoted from the judgment of Justice Eve in *Law v. Chartered Institute of Patent Agents.*[32]

---

[31] *Barrs v. British Wool Marketing Board,* 1957 S.C. 72.
[32] *Law v. Chartered Institute of Patent Agents* [1919] 2 Ch. 276 (at p.289).

"If there are circumstances so affecting a person acting in a judicial capacity as to be calculated to create in the mind of a reasonable man, a suspicion of that person's impartiality, those circumstances are themselves sufficient to disqualify although in fact no bias exists."

Lord Ross said, "[t]hat dictum, also represents the law of Scotland upon this matter." He also said:

"This case may serve as a reminder that the law of Scotland is jealous of its reputation for doing justice and for ensuring that justice is seen to be done; it may also serve to remind judges that if justice is not merely to be done but is to be visibly done, they like Caesar's wife, must be above suspicion."[33]

Although there are few Scottish cases in which natural justice is mentioned prior to *Barrs v. British Wool Marketing Board*, that case made it clear that English developments in the caselaw of natural justice applied equally within Scotland. The House of Lords decision in the English case of *Ridge v. Baldwin (No.1)*[34] marked a revival of interest in the principles of natural justice. This was followed in the judgment on the Scottish case of *Malloch v. Aberdeen Corporation (No.1)*.[35] The principles English law diverged from those of Scots Law when, in the case of *R v. Gough*, the test that justice must be seen to be done was replaced with a test of real danger of bias.[36] This case was not followed in Scotland and is probably out of line with the test of independence and impartiality in Article 6(1). The principles of natural justice apply to a broader sphere of decision-making than decisions made by public bodies. The right of an individual to be heard applies in principle to a wide range of domestic tribunals including some which are not actually public authorities, an example being the ruling bodies of sports.[37]

4.14 **The rule against bias—*nemo judex in causa sua*.** The principles of natural justice confer a right to be judged by a person who is impartial. Erskine said, "[i]t is a rule founded in nature itself that no man can be a judge in his own cause".[38] The risk of bias may arise because of, (a) the identity of the decision-maker or, (b) because of his relationship with, or (c) knowledge of the parties. A risk of bias

[33] *Bradford v. McLeod*, 1986 S.L.T. 244.
[34] *Ridge v. Baldwin* [1964] A.C. 40.
[35] *Malloch v. Aberdeen Corporation* (No. 1), 1971 S.C. (H.L.) 85.
[36] *R v. Gough* [1993] A.C. 646.
[37] *St Johnstone Football Club v. Scottish Football Association Ltd*, 1965 S.L.T. 171.
[38] Erskine *Institutes* 1, 2–25.

may also arise where, (d) the interests of the decision-maker may be affected by the decision with which he is entrusted or, (e) because of the procedures that have been followed.

(a) Bias arising from the opinions of the decision-maker. Evidence of 4.15 bias in the mind of one member of a tribunal may be sufficient to call into doubt the impartiality of the whole tribunal. The case of *Hoekstra v. H.M.Advocate*, arose from an appeal against conviction on drug offences by four men. The men appealed to the High Court of Justiciary, to a bench of three judges chaired by Lord McLuskey. A devolution issue was raised on the ground that the court was not impartial as Lord McLuskey had expressed very strong disapproval of the European Convention on Human Rights in a series of newspaper articles. Leave to appeal to the Privy Council was refused and the men appealed against this decision. Lord McLuskey said, in relation to the question as to whether he should decline any further involvement with the case:

> "If I were to take part as a member of the bench that had decided to consider for itself whether or not it should decline jurisdiction I would . . . find myself in the position of having to reach a conclusion as to what view a fair-minded and informed member of the public might make of my capacity to act impartially . . . I am not persuaded that I could sufficiently detach myself from the matters that might have to be considered."

In relation to the objective test of impartiality, Lord Rodger observed:

> "Under the objective test, it must be determined whether, quite apart from the judge's personal conduct, there are ascertainable facts which may raise doubts as to his impartiality . . . What is at stake is the confidence which the courts in a democratic society must inspire in the public and above all, as far as criminal proceedings are concerned, in the accused. Accordingly, any judge in respect of whom there is a legitimate reason to fear a lack of impartiality must withdraw."

The appeal was therefore referred to a differently constituted bench.[39]

This case is notable because it is the first time that a decision in a

---

[39] *Hoekstra v. H.M.Advocate (No.3)* 132354, *(Joined Cases: Van Rijs (Jan) v. H.M.Advocate; Van Rijs (Ronny) v. H.M.Advocate; Van Rijs (Hendrik) v. H.M.Advocate)*, 2000 J.C. 391; 2000 S.L.T. 605; 2000 S.C.C.R. 367; [2000] H.R.L.R. 410; [2000] U.K.H.R.R. 578; 2000.

court of appeal has been set aside on the grounds of bias. It is also the first time that such a decision was made when there was neither bias exhibited in the course of the judgment nor in opinions expressed in the context of or with relevance to the case in question. It should not be taken as a precedent for a view that objective bias would be lacking whenever a judge makes a critical comment on a legal matter. The circumstances of this case were special. Lord McLuskey had criticised the incorporation of the European Convention on Human Rights into United Kingdom law in scathing terms in a national newspaper.

4.16   In criminal cases the impartiality of the proceedings may be called in to questions if there is evidence of bias amongst the jury as in the case of *Sander v. United Kingdom*. Sander, an Asian, was convicted of conspiracy to defraud. The trial had been adjourned following a complaint by a juror of racist comments from two other jury members. The following day the judge received two letters, one of which contained an apology from a jury member as to his conduct and an assurance of that he was not racially biased. The other was a collective letter from the jury refuting all allegations of racial bias. The judge subsequently redirected the jury but chose not to discharge them. Sander appealed unsuccessfully to the Court of Appeal contending that the judge should have discharged the jury, as there had been a real danger of bias. Sander applied to the European Court of Human Rights complaining that he had not been tried before an impartial tribunal contrary to the European Convention on Human Rights 1950 Article 6(1). It was held that the trial judge had not been in a position, having established that racist comments had been made by at least one jury member, to inquire into the nature of the comments. Accordingly, the court had failed to establish from a subjective position that the jury had not been impartial. There was some doubt as to the credibility of the collective letter considering that the jury member who had first raised fears as to racial bias had signed it. The letter could not be viewed as reliable as it was natural that upon accusation a person would deny racist views. Whether or not members of the jury were actually biased, the decision of the judge to redirect the jury rather than to dismiss it did not remove the suspicion of racial bias. The judge had both been informed of a serious allegation and received an indirect admission that racist remarks had been made. The judge had not, given the importance of removing doubts concerning impartiality, taken all steps necessary to ensure that there was no risk of bias. It had not been adequate merely to accept the collective letter as ground that the jury had purged themselves of any prejudices they might have had.[40]

---

[40]   *Sander v. U.K.*, 8 B.H.R.C. 279; [2000] Crim. L.R. 767.

(b) Bias arising from the status or identity of the decision-maker.
A judge may not hear a case if he is related to one of the parties. 4.17
The Declinature Acts 1594 and 1681[41] specified the prohibited
degrees of relationship within which a judge should decline to hear
a case. A judge may not sit in cases involving his father, son,
brother, uncle, nephew or son-in-law. (This also included mother,
daughter, etc.) Breach of these rules lead to the nullity of all
proceedings whether or not any objections were raised to the judges
at the time the case was heard. In the case of *Moncrieff v. Lord
Moncrieff*, the Lord President declined to sit on the bench, as he was
the brother-in-law of the appellant in the case. Where the
relationship is between a decision-maker and a party to an action
who is appearing in the capacity of a public official there may not be
a need for disqualification.[42] In *McGilvray v. Oban Assessor*, it was
held that a distinction could be made as the interest rose through
discharge of a public duty. The case was an appeal to the Lands
Valuation Court against a decision by the Valuation Committee.
One of the members of the committee was the brother-in-law of the
assessor. It could not be supposed that he would be biased in favour
of his brother-in-law when a decision to change the valuation
decision would have no detrimental impact on him.[43]

In the case of *Stott v. Minogue*, an allegation of bias was made on
the basis that judges and police officers might be Freemasons.
Thomas Minogue was charged with theft. He claimed that two
thirds of Scottish sheriffs and judges are Masons and this could
breach his right to a fair trial under the European Convention of
Human Rights. At the intermediate diet, he lodged a plea that, as
some police witnesses might be freemasons, unless the court could
guarantee impartiality in relation to freemasonry, his right to an
impartial and independent hearing under the European Convention
on Human Rights 1950 Article 6(1) would be violated. Minogue
contended that he was entitled to ask the trial judge whether he was
connected to the freemasons and that the judge would be obliged to
answer. It was held that there was no entitlement for accused
persons to request positive declarations regarding membership of
organisations, nor any duty for judges to reply to such requests.
The judicial oath should be given the greatest weight and, if deemed
insufficient in itself, then taken together with the ethical duty upon
judges to disclose any conflict of interest in hearing a case, these two
safeguards should provide sufficient proof of impartiality to satisfy
the terms of Article 6(1).[44] In the case of *Lafarge Redland
Aggregates Ltd v. Scottish Ministers*, Redland Aggregates chal-

---

[41] Repealed by Court of Session Act 1988, Sched. 2.
[42] *Moncrieff v. Lord Moncrieff* (1904) 12 S.L.T. 267.
[43] *McGilvray v. Oban Assessor*, 1916 S.C. 665.
[44] *Stott v. Minogue*, 2001 S.L.T. (Sh.Ct) 25.

lenged the Scottish Ministers decision to refer the question of whether a potential quarry site the site should be a candidate special area of conservation (sac) to Scottish Natural Heritage. Redland argued that Scottish Natural Heritage could not give an impartial judgment. It was held that a breach of Article 6(1) had occurred in respect of the partiality issue.[45]

4.18 *(c) Bias arising from previous involvement with the case or the parties.* Bias may arise from a person's previous connection with one of the parties or because of a pre-judgment of the case. In *Free Church of Scotland v. McRae*, it was held that a judge should be disqualified if he had previously acted as counsel for one of the parties.[46] In the case of *McPherson v. Hamilton* a sheriff fined the accused for contempt of court (non-attendance for a court appearance). In doing so he expressed the view that he did not believe the explanation for non-attendance. The actual case was called before the same sheriff later that day. It was decided that the sheriff should have declined to sit, as he had expressed a view as to the credibility of the accused, and this was an issue in the case.[47] A judge should also decline to hear a case if he holds an extra-judicial public office, which may give rise to a conflict of interests. In the case of *Jex-Blake v. Edinburgh University Senatus*, Lord President Inglis declined to hear a case involving Edinburgh University because he was Chancellor of the university. Lord Justice-Clerk Moncrieff also declined to preside but his declinature was repelled because he was only a member of the university court and that was not such a direct connection.[48]

Prior involvement with the matter to be decided may also give rise to a risk of bias. In the case of *London and Clydeside Estates Ltd v. Secretary of State for Scotland*,[49] the Secretary of State for Scotland was deciding an appeal against a refusal of planning permission after a public local inquiry. Some time prior to these events the Secretary of State, as the local Member of Parliament, had written letters supporting an objection to development of the site on behalf of one of his constituents. At the opening of the inquiry counsel for the developers raised the issue of bias and invited the reporter to adjourn the inquiry. He did so, but the Secretary of State instructed him to re-open the inquiry. The developers then presented a petition under the judicial review procedure for reduction of the direction that the Secretary of State

---

[45] *Lafarge Redland Aggregates Ltd v. Scottish Ministers*, 2001 S.C. 298; 2000 S.L.T. 1361; [2001] Env. L.R. 27; [2000] 4 P.L.R. 151; [2000] N.P.C. 109.
[46] *Free Church of Scotland v. McRae* (1905) 13 S.L.T. 77.
[47] *McPherson v. Hamilton*, 1991 S.L.T. 611.
[48] *Jex-Blake v. Edinburgh University Senatus* (1873) 11 M. 784.
[49] *London and Clydeside Estates v. Secretary of State for Scotland*, 1987 S.L.T. 459.

should himself decide the appeal and reduction of the appointment of the reporter. The petitioners claimed that the previous involvement of the Secretary of State raised a suspicion in a reasonable man that he could not decide the appeal impartially. It was held that a minister was not disqualified from exercising a quasi-judicial function merely because of previous support for a particular policy in relation to a particular development. It was possible, however, that such disqualification would occur where a minister expressed such support so intransigently that a reasonable man might suspect that he would be unable to weigh up proven facts in a fair way. The nature of the minister's previous support was, however, not of that character and the evidence at the present inquiry was likely to differ from that of the previous inquiry. There was therefore no basis for suspicion that the Secretary of State would not consider the petitioner's application fairly; and the application was dismissed.[50] This case seems to reflect a move away from the idea that a person should not preside wherever there is a small risk that it might appear that there was pre-judgment of the issues. It introduced a standard whereby a person only needs to refrain from making a decision if there is actual evidence that he has formed a pre-judgment. In *Brown v. Executive Committee of Edinburgh Labour Party*, interim interdict and suspension were granted where members of a disciplinary committee who were due to deal with a complaint against nine local labour party councillors had, in the course of a council meeting, voted to pass a motion critical of the conduct of the nine councillors. It was held that a risk of bias in the minds of some members of a body would invalidate a decision by the whole body.[51] The likelihood of a pre-judgment having been made was also very strong in the case of *Lockhart v. Irving*. Lockhart and other police officers presented a petition for suspension and interdict against Irving, the Chief Constable, to prevent him investigating complaints in which he was personally concerned. Lockhart and others had made a report to the Coatbridge Town Clerk about the Chief Constable using the police patrol car for his personal use. They were then suspended from duty for offences against discipline. If they appealed an investigation would have been held by the Chief Constable. Interdict was granted.[52] The case of *Harper of Oban Engineering Ltd v. Henderson* was a prosecution of a company for actions in contravention of certain statutes. The case was heard by a justice who had previously worked for the company and who had been dismissed. Although the company had submitted a plea of guilty to the offences and

---

[50] See also *Black v. Scott Lithgow Ltd*, 1990 S.L.T. 612 and *Anderson v. Hillary*, 1991 S.L.T. 521.
[51] *Brown v. Executive Committee of Edinburgh Labour Party* 1995 S.L.T. 985.
[52] *Lockhart v. Irving*, 1936 S.L.T. 567.

taking into account that in a small community it would be a
common occurrence for a justice to have a connection with at least
one of the parties. It was held that it would be contrary to natural
justice for this particular case to be heard by the justice, as there
was a risk of bias arising from a personal grievance.[53] The rule
against bias has been held to apply to arbitration. An arbiter must
carry out his duties impartially and fairly. It was held in the case of
Edinburgh Magistrates v. Lownie,[54] that an arbiter may be
disqualified if he accepts employment or has business dealings with
one of the parties after his employment as arbiter.

4.19   *(d) Bias arising from interest.* A judge should decline to hear a case
if he has an interest in the outcome of the case. This applies to any
case in which he has a pecuniary interest, which might be likely to
influence him, or which others might think would influence him. In
the English case of *Dimes v. Grand Junction Canal Proprietors*, a
judgment of Lord Chancellor Cottenham was set aside, as he was a
shareholder in the Canal Company. Lord Campbell said:

> "No one could suppose that Lord Cottenham could be . . .
> influenced by the interest that he had in this concern but . . . it
> is of the last importance that the decision that no man is to be
> a judge on his own case should be held sacred."[55]

In the Scottish case of *Sellar v. Highland Railway Company*, Lord
Buckmaster said:

> "The importance of preserving the administration of justice
> from anything which can even by remote imagination infer a
> bias or interest in the judge upon whom falls the solemn duty
> of interpreting the law is so grave that any small incon-
> venience experienced in its preservation may be cheerfully
> endured."[56]

A direct and personal interest or holding in a company seeking a
remedy or a license will always disqualify. In the case of *Ower v.
Crichton*, where licensing magistrates had taken part in a decision
affecting premises in which they had a financial interest the court
held that the decision was a nullity on the ground that there had
been a breach of natural justice.[57] However, a less direct interest

---

[53] *Harper of Oban Ltd v. Henderson*, 1989 S.L.T. 21.
[54] *Edinburgh Magistrates v. Lownie* (1903) 10 S.L.T. 752.
[55] *Dimes v. Grand Junction Canal Company* (1852) 3 H.L. 759. A similar case in
     Scotland was *Caledonian Railway Company v. Ramsay* (1897) 4 S.L.T. 267.
[56] *Sellar v. Highland Railway Company*, 1919 S.C. (H.L.) 19.
[57] *Ower v. Crichton* (1902) 10 S.L.T. 271. See also *Blaik v. Anderson* (1900) 7 S.L.T.
     299, *McDonald v. Finlay*, 1957 S.L.T. 81.

does not always lead to disqualification. In the case of *Houston v. Ker*, it was held that a magistrate who was the owner of a public house in a burgh was not disqualified from deciding applications regarding other licensed premises in the burgh despite the interest which he might have in minimising competition.[58] In *Gray v. Fowlie*, a case concerning a parish's provision for paupers, it was held that a judge should not decline to hear a case merely because he owned property in the parish and may have to pay more through possible rate increases depending on the outcome of the case.[59] In the case of *Hercules Insurance Company v. Hunter*, six judges were disqualified from hearing a case because they held policies with the insurance company bringing the action. As this would mean that the case could not be heard, it was necessary to disregard the disqualifications.[60] Similar problems arose in other cases and eventually the problem was resolved by the Court of Session Act 1868, section 103 which stated that merely holding fire insurance or life insurance policy with a company, or holding stock in an unincorporated company merely as a trustee, was not to be ground for declinature by a judge. Direct personal interest such as holding shares in a personal capacity continued to be a ground for declining to hear a case.

The general rules relating to bias were explained in the judgment of Lord Justice-Clerk Moncrieff in the case of *Wildridge v. Anderson*. Wildridge was convicted of a charge of malicious mischief and fined seven shillings and sixpence. It was alleged that he had damaged a cushion of the billiard room of the Moffat Library in Port Glasgow. Later, Wildridge discovered that Niven, the magistrate who had convicted him, was one of the trustees of the library and therefore one of the proprietors of the damaged property. He sought suspension of his conviction and sentence before the High Court claiming that Niven was disqualified because of interest from presiding at his trial. It was held that:

> "The general and salutary principle is that no man can be a judge in his own cause, and that rule within certain limits is vigorously applied. The reason of it is obvious, to ensure not merely that the administration of justice shall be free from bias but that it shall be beyond suspicion. It is subject however, to qualifications and exceptions."

The result of the authorities, which were cited in the judgment, was summarised as follows:

---

[58] *Houston v. Ker* (1890) 28 SLR. 575.
[59] *Gray v. Fowlie* (1847) 9 D. 811.
[60] *Hercules Insurance Company v. Hunter* (1837) 15 S. 800.

> "(1) As a general rule a pecuniary interest, if direct and individual, will disqualify, however small it may be.
> (2) An interest although not pecuniary may also disqualify, but the interest in that case must be substantial.
> (3) Where the interest which is said to disqualify is not pecuniary, and is neither substantial nor calculated to cause bias in the mind of the judge, it will be disregarded, especially if to disqualify the judge would be productive of grave public inconvenience."

4.20 Lord Moncrieff decided, on applying these guidelines to the case, that the presiding magistrate had no pecuniary interest, and no appreciable personal interest in the outcome of the case. If he were disqualified, then so were all the other magistrates in Port Glasgow as they were all *ex officio* trustees of the Moffat Library. Having to bring in the sheriff from Greenock every time there was a case involving the Library would be inconvenient. Therefore it was held that any breach of natural justice could be disregarded.[61]

This doctrine of grave public inconvenience will apply in circumstances where all of the judges who would otherwise be available to hear a case would be disqualified.[62] It has also been recognised that in smaller jurisdictions, it is more likely that the judge will know some of the parties.[63] If disqualification were to result from every instance of a person making a judicial decision also holding a public office there would be interference with the operation of many of the functions of public offices, particularly at a local level. Disqualification will, however, always result where a person is personally or individually interested in the particular matter or question before him.[64]

An interest that is not pecuniary will not lead to disqualification unless it appears to create a risk of real bias. In *McGeehan v. Knox*, McGeehan, who had held a licensing certificate for a number of years, was refused a licence one year by the Licensing Court in Airdrie. Knox, the chairman of the Licensing Court was Chief Templar of the Independent Order of Good Templars and had published a pamphlet on temperance. Three other members of the Licensing Court were also active members of temperance organisations. McGeehan sought reduction of the court's decision to refuse his licence on the ground that these members were disqualified through bias from sitting on the court. The Inner House held that

---

[61] *Wildridge v. Anderson* (1897) 25 R. (J) 27.
[62] See also *Downie v. Fisherrow Harbour Commissioners* (1903) 11 S.L.T. 250, *Martin v. Nicholson*, 1920 1 S.L.T. 67.
[63] *Harper of Oban (Engineering) v. Henderson*, 1989 S.L.T. 21.
[64] Court of Session Act 1988, s.4.

there had been no breach of natural justice.[65] It is not impossible for someone to administer faithfully a law of which he disapproves.

(e) Bias arising from improper procedure. The conduct of 4.21 proceedings should be such as to ensure that there has been an impartial consideration of the matter to be decided. In the case of *Macdougall v. Millar*, it was held that a magistrate was not allowed to canvass other magistrates urging them to oppose the grant of a licence.[66] In the case of *Goodall v. Shaw*, an apparently unfair procedure was held to be acceptable. In an area where there were too many licences in operation the licensing court adopted a policy of granting all of the unopposed licences before considering the licenses which had been opposed by temperance organisations. It was held that this was competent because the court exercised its discretion in each case and not all of the licences that had been opposed were withdrawn.[67] It does seem though that this is an example of pre-judging the applications in a way that gives an unfair advantage to objectors.

The need to balance the requirement for natural justice for the individual against practical convenience was a factor in the case of *Laughland v. Galloway*, Laughland was convicted of theft in a JP court and sought to suspend the conviction on the ground that the clerk of that court and the procurator fiscal were also partners in the same firm of solicitors. The Court of Session held that their public official duties should be distinguished from their connection in the legal firm, holding that the test laid down in *Wildridge v. Anderson* should be applied in this case. There was therefore no breach of natural justice.[68] In that case all of the proceedings were held in public, but in the case of *Low v. Kincardineshire District Licensing Court*, where the solicitor of one party and the clerk to the court, his father, were partners in the same firm and the proceedings took place partly in private it was held that there had been a breach of natural justice.[69]

Participation in an appeal or subsequent litigation by a person who was involved in the making of the original decision probably also creates a real likelihood of bias. In the case of *McDonnell, Petr*,[70] an applicant for housing benefit from Cumbernauld Development Corporation appealed in terms of the Housing Benefits Regulations 1985 to the Cumbernauld Development

---

[65] *McGeehan v. Knox* (1913) S.C. 688.
[66] *Macdougall v. Millar* (1900) 8 S.L.T. 284.
[67] *Goodall v. Shaw*, 1913 S.C. 630.
[68] *Laughland v. Galloway* (1968) S.L.T. 272.
[69] *Low v. Kincardineshire District Licensing Court*, 1974 S.L.T. (Sh.Ct) 54.
[70] *McDonnell, Petr*, 1987 S.L.T. 486. See also *Barrs v. British Wool Marketing Board*, 1957 S.C. 72; *R v. Sussex Justices* (1924) 1 K.B. 256.

Corporation review board. At the hearing the applicant's representatives left the room after the parties' submissions and the
representatives of the corporation remained while the members
deliberated. The applicant presented a petition for judicial review
for the reduction of the decision of the review board on the ground
that the presence of the corporation's representatives constituted a
breach of natural justice. He did not claim that these representatives
had taken any part in the deliberations. It was held that natural
justice required that a tribunal exercising a quasi-judicial function
must offer a fair and equal opportunity to the parties before it. The
presence of one party alone during the deliberations of the tribunal
was sufficient to invalidate the decision regardless of whether the
party was present accidentally and took no part in the proceedings
and the decision was reduced.

4.22   Scots law does not rely on a particular test to establish whether or
not bias exists. It is a matter for consideration in the context of each
case. The criteria for disqualification have been prioritised as
follows, the factor most likely to lead to bias is a personal
relationship, followed by shareholding, personal pecuniary interest,
and prior involvement with the parties. Non-pecuniary interest is
the least likely to lead to disqualification. This must be considered
in the context of the nature of the function of the decision-maker
and the remoteness of the interest.[71]

Bias caused by pre-trial publicity. Where juries are involved in a
trial there is also a risk of bias arising from pre-trial publicity. This
is prevented to some extent by the rules relating to contempt of
court, which prevent the publication of information prejudicial to a
trial.[72] The risk of bias from pre-trial publicity came under
consideration by the Privy Council in the case of *Montgomery v.
H.M.Advocate.* Montgomery and another, who had been charged
with murder, appealed against the decision of the High Court of
Justiciary dismissing their appeal in relation to a minute raising a
devolution issue. It was submitted that prejudicial publicity prior to
the trial meant that the acts of the Lord Advocate in indicting them
had been contrary to the Scotland Act 1998, section 57(2) given that
their right to a fair trial under the European Convention on Human
Rights 1950 Article 6 had been impinged. Montgomery was later
acquitted of the murder charge. It was held that the question of
impartiality had to be considered objectively. Consideration had to
be given not just to the consequences of the publicity on the
members of the jury, but also to the role of the judge in securing a
fair trial so far as it was open to him to do so. There were no
grounds in this case to alter the findings of the High Court of

---

[71] S. McMurtie, "The Principle of Nemo Judex in Causa Sua" Juridical Review
      1996 [5] pp. 304–320.
[72] Contempt of Court Act 1981.

Justiciary that the publicity had not prevented the jury from being impartial.[73]

ACCESS TO JUSTICE

Article 6 contains no express right of access to a court but in *Golder* 4.23 *v. United Kingdom*[74] the European Court held that it would be inconceivable that Article 6 should describe in detail the procedural guarantees afforded to parties in the course of litigation and should not first protect that which makes it possible to benefit from such guarantees, namely access to a court. In *Ashingdane v. United Kingdom*,[75] the court ruled that

> "the right of access to the courts is not absolute but may be subject to limitations; these are permitted by implication since the right of access, "by its very nature calls for regulation by the State, regulation which may vary in time and place according to the needs and resources of the community and of individuals". In laying down such regulation, the Contracting States enjoy a margin of appreciation. Whilst the final decision as to observance of the Convention's requirements rests with the Court, it is no part of the Court's function to substitute for the assessment of the national authorities any other assessment of what might be the best policy in this field."[76]

Access to justice may not therefore require that every dispute is settled by a court. Resolution of disputes may be by other means, such as hearings before administrative tribunals or even consideration by an individual minister. The fairness of the procedure is more important than the status of the body making the decision.

A complete failure to provide any forum for adjudication may amount to a breach of Article 6. In *W v. United Kingdom*,[77] it was held that there had been a breach of Article 6 as the procedures for parents to appeal against the decisions of local authorities were

---

[73] *Montgomery (David Shields) v. H.M.Advocate* [2001] 2 W.L.R. 779; 2001 S.C. (P.C.) 1; 2001 S.L.T. 37; 2000 S.C.C.R. 1044; [2001] U.K.H.R.R. 124; 9 B.H.R.C. 641.

[74] *Golder v. U.K.* (1979–80) 1 E.H.R.R. 524.

[75] *Ashingdane v. U.K.* (1985) 7 E.H.R.R. 528.

[76] See also *Fayed v. U.K.* (1994) 18 E.H.R.R. 393; *National & Provincial Building Society v. United Kingdom (Joined Cases: Leeds Permanent Building Society v. United Kingdom; Yorkshire Building Society v. United Kingdom)* [1997] S.T.C. 1466; (1998) 25 E.H.R.R. 127; 69 T.C. 540; [1997] B.T.C. 624; [1998] H.R.C.D. 34.

[77] *W v. U.K.* (1988) 10 E.H.R.R. 29.

inadequate. The Court considered that this was a domain where despite the difficult discretionary decisions to be made by the authorities, there was a great need for protection against arbitrary interference with parental rights. The decision-making process must ensure that the views and interests of parents were made known and taken into account by the local authorities. This was not a situation in which it was sufficient for an aggrieved parent to institute judicial review proceedings since the reviewing court would not be able to examine the merits of the local authority's decision on parental access. What was required by Article 6(1) in relation to the rights in question was that parents must be able to have the decision taken by a local authority with regard to access reviewed by a tribunal with jurisdiction to examine the merits of the matter. The powers of the courts in the United Kingdom did not extend to this and a breach of Article 6(1) had occurred.

One of the five principles recommended by the Committee of Ministers of the Council of Europe is that a person concerned with an administrative act which is likely to affect directly and adversely his rights, liberties or interests should have a right to be heard. He should be informed of this right and be given the opportunity to put forward facts and arguments and (where appropriate) evidence. All this should be taken into account by the administrative authority before deciding.[78] There are two aspects to the principle that everyone is entitled to a right to a hearing. First, every party to judicial proceedings has the right to reasonable notice of the case against him and secondly, every party is entitled to the opportunity to make submissions to the hearing and to bring evidence to it.

4.24   In the case of *Inland Revenue Commissioners v. Hood Barrs*, Lord Reid said, "[n]o tribunal, however informal, can be entitled to reach a decision against any person without giving to him some proper opportunity to put forward his case". Barrs, who owned a sawmill on the island of Mull, claimed that his business had suffered heavy losses and that he was, as a consequence, entitled to large refunds of income tax. The inspectors disputed his figures. When the Commissioners of Income Tax for Mull met to consider the amount of Barr's losses, without any further procedure and without holding any hearing, they issued loss certificates for an amount greater than the losses that Barr had claimed. The House of Lords held that the Commissioners were performing a judicial function and therefore the principles of natural justice should have been followed. Their procedures had not allowed the tax inspectors a proper right to be heard and the decision to issue the loss certificates was reduced.[79]

---

[78] Committee of Ministers of the Council of Europe, Resolution (77) 31, *On the Protection of the Individual in Relation to the Acts of Administrative Authorities.*
[79] *Inland Revenue Commissioners v. Hood Barrs*, 1961 S.C. (H.L.) 22.

A person should not be denied a hearing on the basis that the hearing would be futile unless it can be clearly demonstrated that such is the case. In the case of *Malloch v. Aberdeen Corporation*, Malloch and other teacher appealed against a decision of the Court of Session in which it had been held that, although guidelines issued by the Secretary of State had been *ultra vires*, the decision by the local council to dismiss the teachers was not *ultra vires*. An education sub-committee had dismissed Malloch, and other teachers, upon the passing of a resolution on the ground that he was not a registered teacher as required by regulations made under statute. He claimed that his dismissal had been a breach of natural justice, as he had not been granted a hearing. It was held that the appellant had a general right to be heard before being dismissed. It had been argued that a hearing would be futile but the House of Lords decided that any such hearing would not necessarily be futile because the relevant legislation was sufficiently ambiguous for the appellant to make out a case.[80]

EQUALITY OF ARMS

The right to a hearing need not confer rights such as the right to call 4.25 witnesses, the right to legal representation and the right to cross-examine witnesses. Such rights may be conferred by an individual statute or regulation but if there is no such provision there is no right to insist on a particular type of procedure being followed. The essential right is to a hearing that is fair and which affords an equal opportunity to both sides to put their case. This is known as equality of arms. In the case of *Board of Education v. Rice*, it was held that a government department, in determining an appeal from the decision of a local authority must act in good faith and listen fairly to both sides. This is a duty that lay on everyone who decided anything. The department was not, however required to treat such a question as a trial and was not required to follow the procedure of a court of law.[81]

Right to Notice

In the case of *Moss Empires Ltd v. Glasgow Assessor*, it was held 4.26 that it is a breach of natural justice to fail to give proper notice of procedures, especially if this means that a right of appeal may be lost. In *St Johnstone Football Club v. Scottish Football Association Ltd*,[82] a decision was held to be *ultra vires* because of a failure to

---

[80] *Malloch v. Aberdeen Corporation* (No. 1) [1971] 1 W.L.R. 1578 (H.L.).
[81] *Board of Education v. Rice* [1911] A.C. 179.
[82] *St Johnstone Football Club v. Scottish Football Association Ltd*, 1965 S.L.T. 171.

notify a football club of proceedings being taken against it. The
football club had arranged a benefit match for one of its players.
The Association wrote to the club criticising its arrangements for
the match and informing it that the Executive and General
Purposes Committee had decided to censure and fine St Johnstone.
In a later letter it was stated that the decision of the Executive and
General Purposes Committee had been confirmed by the Association's council and that the club, if it was dissatisfied with this
decision, should have challenged the decision at the meeting of the
Council. When the Association pressed for payment of the fine, the
club brought an action for declarator that the fine and censure were
illegal and *ultra vires*. It was held that the Council, acting as a
judicial authority should have observed the principles of natural
justice. As it had acted contrary to natural justice declarator that
the decision as *ultra vires* was granted. The notice must be given in
sufficient time to allow a person to prepare his answers to the case
against him.[83]

Right to Submit Argument

4.27 If proceedings are to be conducted fairly it is important that a
person who will be affected by a decision should be provided with
an opportunity to make representations either before the decision is
made or before it is implemented to his detriment. This right to
submit argument need not always involve a right to be heard in
person. It is important, however, that both parties are treated
impartially and are given an opportunity to state their case in some
form. In the case of *R v. Army Board of the Defence Council, ex
parte Anderson*, a soldier sought judicial review of a decision by the
Army Board rejecting his complaint of racial discrimination. It was
held that the Board should have made a specific finding as to
discrimination in accordance with the Race Relations Act 1976.
Also, given the importance of its function, the Board should ensure
that there is a high standard of fairness in its procedures. It should
have considered whether to hold an oral hearing. Material should
have been made available to the complainant and he should have
been given an opportunity to respond.[84] In the case *R (on the
application of Ponting) v. Governor of Whitemoor Prison* the court
considered whether a dyslexic person should be entitled to resources
to assist him in submitting his case. Ponting, a dyslexic life prisoner,
challenged a decision of the prison governor to restrict his access to
computing facilities. He contended that he needed more time to
enable him to conduct litigation in which he was engaged. He
claimed that his right of access to the courts and his right to a fair

---

[83] *Moss Empires Ltd v. Glasgow Assessor*, 1917 S.C. (H.L.) 1.
[84] *R v. Army Board of the Defence Council, ex p. Anderson* [1992] 1 Q.B. 169.

trial was impeded because, although he was competent to conduct oral argument, his grammar and spelling would disadvantage him without full access to word processing facilities. It was held that the imposition of restrictions on the use of the computing facilities was not sufficient to prevent Ponting from communicating the nature of his case nor did it represent such a significant disadvantage as to affect the "equality of arms". The restrictions were not unreasonable, as they were required to prevent unauthorised use by Ponting or by other prisoners.[85]

Right to Know of Evidence Submitted by Others

The principles of openness and fairness require that each party   4.28
should know the case that he has to answer and the basis on which a decision is made. A right of access to information is one of the five principles recommended by the Committee of Ministers of the Council of Europe. The resolution states that a person concerned, in order effectively to exercise his right to be heard, should on request be given access, by appropriate means, to the relevant factors on which the administrative act is intended to be based before the act is taken.[86] If a decision of a judicial nature is being made in a forum where the parties tender arguments on which a decision is made no other considerations should be taken into account unless the parties know about them and have an opportunity to comment. In *Freeland v. Glasgow District Licensing Board*, Freeland challenged the legality of the board's decision to refuse to grant him a licence. One of the reasons for the board's decision was that "[t]he Board drew on its own knowledge of the area in which the premises are situated and had regard to information supplied by the police about the general pattern of disorder in the vicinity of the premises." It was held that the rules of natural justice are contravened if a Board takes a decision on the basis of its own previous knowledge without disclosure of that fact or those facts to the party for his comments.[87]

Where there is no statutory procedure laid down the person making a decision will usually have discretion as to how the proceedings are conducted as long as the proceedings are fair to all parties. In the case of *Stewart v. Secretary of State for Scotland*, a former sheriff sought judicial review of an order made by the

---

[85] *R (on the application of Ponting) v. Governor of Whitemoor Prison* [2001] EWHC Admin. 241.
[86] Committee of Ministers of the Council of Europe, Resolution (77) 31, *On the Protection of the Individual in Relation to the Acts of Administrative Authorities.*
[87] *Freeland v. Glasgow District Licensing Board*, 1979 S.C. 226. See also *Tomkins v. Glasgow District Licensing Board*, 1994 S.L.T. 34; *William Hill Scotland (Ltd) v. Kyle and Carrick District Licensing Board*, 1991 S.L.T. 559; *General Medical Council v. Spackman* [1943] 2 All E.R. 337.

Secretary of State removing him from office. Section 12(1) of the Sheriff Courts (Scotland) Act 1971 provides that an investigation into a sheriff's fitness for office may be undertaken by the Lord President and the Lord Justice Clerk who may then report to the Secretary of State for Scotland. The Secretary of State may make an order removing a sheriff from office if the report is to the effect that the sheriff is unfit for office. An investigation had been undertaken at the request of the Secretary of State, which took the form of a general investigation into the sheriff's conduct since 1980. Particular examples of the sheriff's conduct were identified and investigated in detail. Statements were taken from a number of persons with experience of his conduct. At the completion of their preliminary inquiries the senior judges provided the sheriff with a list of the cases relevant to his conduct, which they were to investigate together with short details of each case, and appended documentation where appropriate. He was invited to answer a number of questions and make observations. Following the sheriff's written response the senior judges interviewed a number of persons before interviewing the sheriff. Thereafter the senior judges submitted their report to the Secretary of State. The sheriff sought reduction of the order and the report on grounds which included an allegation that there had been a failure to comply with the requirements of natural justice. He argued that he should have been told who had spoken both for and against him, been informed what evidence had been rejected and for what reasons, been given copies of all the witnesses' statements, have had the opportunity to examine the relevant court processes, and been informed of the senior judges' preliminary conclusions. It was held that as no rules were laid down by statute as to the procedure to be followed, the senior judges were the masters of their own procedure subject only to the requirement to act fairly. They were not required as a matter of fairness to do more than they had done to give him notice of the case that he had to meet. The petition was dismissed. It was observed that the question whether the requirements of natural justice had been met by the procedure adopted in any given case had to depend to a great extent on the case's own facts and circumstances.[88]

Right to be Heard in Person

4.29   Whether or not there is a right to be heard in person will depend on the context in which the decision is being made. This was discussed in the case of *Local Government Board v. Arlidge*.[89] Section 17 of the Housing, Town Planning, etc. Act 1909 authorised local authorities to make an order if a dwelling was unfit for human habitation.

---

[88]   *Stewart v. Secretary of State for Scotland*, 1995 S.L&T. 895.
[89]   *Local Government Board v. Arlidge* [1915] A.C. 120ᵗ(H.L.).

There was a right to appeal against such an order to the Local Government Board. In 1911 Hampstead Borough Council issued a closing order on Arlidge's house. He appealed to the Local Government Board, which appointed an inspector to hold a public local inquiry. The inspector visited the house and reported to the Local Government Board who confirmed the closing order. Arlidge appealed on the basis that;

(1) The notice of refusal of appeal did not show which officers of the Local Government Board had considered the appeal.
(2) Arlidge was entitled to be heard in person by the Local Government Board and he had not been invited to the inquiry.
(3) Arlidge had not seen the inspector's report.

It was held that;

(1) There was no procedural requirement to inform Arlidge who had heard the appeal.
(2) The rules of natural justice do not necessarily require that a party should be invited to be heard in person. Arlidge's written submission of evidence had been considered.
(3) Arlidge was not entitled to insist on seeing the inspector's report.

Viscount Haldane said,

"when the duty of deciding an appeal is imposed, those whose duty it is must act judicially. They must deal with the question referred to them without bias, and they must give to each of the parties the opportunity of adequately presenting the case made. But it does not follow that the procedure of every tribunal must be the same."

Procedures laid down by Parliament must, of course, be followed but due regard must also be given to administrative efficiency. Lord Shaw of Dunfermline said,

"when a central administrative board deals with an appeal from a local authority it must do its best to act justly, and to reach just ends by just means. If a statute prescribes the means it must employ them. If it is left without express guidance it must still act honestly and by honest means. In regard to these certain ways and methods of judicial procedure may very likely be imitated; and lawyer-like methods may find especial favour from lawyers. But that the judiciary should presume to impose its own methods on administrative or executive officers is a usurpation. And the assumption that the methods of natural justice are ex necessitate those of courts of justice is wholly unfounded."

The matter had been determined in a judicial spirit in compliance with the principles of substantial justice and so the decision was held to be valid.

More recently, in *Malloch v. Aberdeen Corporation* (No. 1), the education committee dismissed Malloch and 37 other teachers because they were unregistered in terms of the Schools (Scotland) Code 1956, as amended. Malloch sought reduction of the resolution of the education committee and the notices of dismissal on the ground that, contrary to natural justice, the committee refused to receive written representations or to afford Malloch the right to be heard in person before the resolution was passed. The House of Lords held by a majority of three to two that there had been a breach of natural justice.[90] This case differed from Arlidge in that Malloch had been denied an opportunity to submit his arguments in any form either in writing or in person at a hearing. In the case of *Young v. Criminal Injuries Compensation Board*, Young challenged a decision by the Criminal Injuries Compensation Board (CICB). He had asked for an oral hearing but the CICB refused to grant such a hearing. Young argued that the refusal contravened the scheme and the provision of the scheme entitling the board to refuse an oral hearing was itself contrary to natural justice. It was held that as there was no dispute about the material facts on which the decision to refuse compensation was based, the applicant was not entitled to an oral hearing. There was a distinction between a right to a hearing and a right to be heard. In a scheme, which was administrative and non-adversarial, the refusal of a hearing was not contrary to natural justice where the applicant had the opportunity of presenting the board with all relevant information in writing.[91]

Right to be Represented

4.30 The Committee of Ministers of the Council of Europe stated that it should be possible for a person concerned to be assisted or represented in the administrative process. It is not clear whether they were recommending that legal representation should be allowed or whether less formal advice and representation was what they had in mind.[92] In the case of *Enderby Town Football Club v. Football Association Ltd*, it was held that natural justice did not

---

[90] *Malloch v. Aberdeen Corporation (No. 1)*, 1971 S.C.(H.L.) 85.
[91] *Young v. Criminal Injuries Compensation Board*, 1997 S.L.T 297.
[92] Committee of Ministers of the Council of Europe, Resolution (77) 31, *On the Protection of the Individual in Relation to the Acts of Administrative Authorities*.

necessarily require that a person should be entitled to legal representation. However, although there is not always a right to legal representation the broader principles of natural justice, that proceedings should be carried out fairly and that justice should be seen to be done may require that representation be permitted.[93] In the case of *R v. Leicester City Justices, ex parte Barrow*, Barrow challenged the refusal to allow him to have a friend to sit with him and give advice and assistance when he was prosecuted for non-payment of poll tax. It was held that the administration of justice had to be open and fair and had to be seen to be fair. Fairness required that a party conducting proceedings in person should be afforded all reasonable facilities to enable him to represent himself, including a friend to give advice, unless this would be contrary to the interests of justice. The conviction was quashed.[94] In the case of *Pett v. Greyhound Racing Association (No. 2)*, a greyhound trainer who was the subject of an inquiry into the illegal use of drugs applied for a declaration that the association was acting *ultra vires* in refusing to allow legal representation at a hearing. His application was refused on the basis that natural justice related to the elementary principles of fairness, whereas legal representation was a sophisticated procedural matter. The right to legal representation will therefore only exist if such a right has been conferred by statute or if the matter in question is so serious that to deny legal representation would be unfair.[95]

JUDICIAL PRECEDENT AS A BARRIER TO ACCESS TO JUSTICE

The rigid application of a precedent without considering the impact in subsequent cases may amount to an infringement of the right of access to justice. The principle that an action in negligence could not be taken against the police when they had failed to prevent a crime was considered in the case of *Osman v. United Kingdom*. Osman, a teenage boy, was seriously injured and his father was killed after being shot by Osman's former teacher, who had become obsessed by Osman. Prior to the shooting, a number of disturbing incidents had occurred, including damage to Osman's home. The teacher had been interviewed by the school authorities and the police. The teacher, who had also shot and injured a deputy headmaster and killed his son, was convicted of manslaughter. Osman and his mother brought an action for negligence against the police in respect of their conduct of the investigation into the teacher's activities. The Court of Appeal ordered the action to be

4.31

[93] *Enderby Town Football Club v. Football Association Ltd* [1970] 3 W.L.R. 1021.
[94] *R v. Leicester City Justices, ex p. Barrow* [1991] 2 Q.B. 260.
[95] *Pett v. Greyhound Racing Association (No. 2)* [1970] 1 Q.B. 46.

struck out as disclosing no reasonable cause of action on the ground that for reasons of public policy, no action in negligence could lie against the police in respect of the investigation and suppression of crime.[96] Osman and his mother applied to the European Court of Human Rights, contending that the state had failed to protect the lives of Osman and his father and to protect the family from harassment contrary to Article 2 and Article 8, and that Osman and his mother had been denied access to a court in respect of that failure, contrary to Article 6(1). It was held that there had been no violation of Article 2. The state was not in breach of its positive obligation to take preventative measures to protect an individual whose life was at risk from another. There was no reason for the police to know or suspect that there was a real and immediate threat to Osman and his fathers' lives. None of the incidents prior to the shootings were life threatening and there was no proof that the teacher was responsible for those acts. There was no evidence that the teacher was mentally ill or prone to violence. For the same reasons the state was not in breach of its positive obligations under Article 8, but there had been a violation of Article 6(1). The rule in *Hill v. Chief Constable of West Yorkshire*[97] appeared to operate as an absolute defence to an action in negligence against the police. This prevented a court considering the competing public interests in each case before it and constituted a disproportionate interference with a person's right to have a determination on the merits of an action against the police in a deserving case in breach of ArticLE 6(1).[98]

STATUTORY EXCLUSION OF JUDICIAL CONTROL

4.32 Statutory provisions that prevent or restrict legal challenge by affected individuals are known as ouster clauses. The courts have always given the narrowest possible interpretation to ouster clauses although they have been obliged to give effect to them where they are clear and unambiguous. The impact of Article 6(1) in this area is likely to be significant, for example, provisions of the Consumer Credit Act 1974 have been declared to be incompatible with Article 6(1) on the grounds that they deny a right of access to justice. In the case of *Wilson v. First County Trust Ltd* the court considered whether the restrictions on enforcement under the Consumer Credit

---

[96] Following the House of Lords' ruling in *Hill v. Chief Constable of West Yorkshire* [1988] 2 All E.R. 238; [1989] A.C. 53.
[97] *Hill v. Chief Constable of West Yorkshire* [1988] 2 All E.R. 238; [1989] A.C. 53.
[98] *Osman v. U.K.* (2000) 29 E.H.R.R. 245; (1999) 1 L.G.L.R. 431; 5 B.H.R.C. 293; (1999) 11 Admin. L.R. 200; [1999] 1 F.L.R. 193; [1999] Crim. L.R. 82; [1998] H.R.C.D. 966; [1999] Fam. Law 86; (1999) 163 J.P.N. 297.

Act 1974, section 127(3) infringed F's human rights as being a disproportionate restriction on a lender's right to have the enforceability of its loan determined by the court. The Act provides that a lender cannot enforce repayment of a loan where the loan agreement was defective in form. The court granted a declaration of incompatibility on the basis that an order made after the Human Rights Act came into force which deprived a person or body of the right to a fair trial would conflict with Article 6(1). The guarantee of a fair trial under Article 6(1) of the Convention was of no substance if the 1974 Act prevented enforcement where that was just and where there was no prejudice to the debtor. The Consumer Credit Act deprived First County Trust Ltd of its ability to enjoy the benefit of the contractual rights arising from the agreement or of the rights arising from the delivery of the security. That did not strike a fair balance between the rights of an individual and the public interest.[99] In *Hatton v. United Kingdom*,[1] Mrs Hatton sued the United Kingdom Government as she had suffered loss of sleep caused by night flights in and out of Heathrow airport. She was unable to bring a claim for damages for nuisance before the courts in the United Kingdom because section 76 of the Civil Aviation Act 1982 provided statutory immunity from such actions. She and other applicants were awarded damages of £4,000 each. The European Court of Human Rights ruled that the United Kingdom was in breach of its obligation to provide a sufficient remedy to the applicants. Judicial review of the decision to allow night flights would not provide a sufficient remedy since it did not allow the courts to weigh up the merits of the decision. In judicial review proceedings a court could not consider whether the restriction on the applicants right to home and family life under Article 8 could be justified on the grounds of economic well-being of the country.[2]

VEXATIOUS LITIGANTS

When a person persistently instigates litigation that is without merit 4.33
there is a procedure under the Vexatious Actions (Scotland) Act 1898[3] by which a person can be declared a vexatious litigant. The aim of this provision is to prevent a person wasting the courts' time. A procedure that prevents a person bringing a case to court could amount to a denial of the right to a hearing. However, invoking the procedure does not mean that the person is barred thereafter from

---

[99] *Wilson v. First County Trust Ltd (No.2)* [2001] EWCA Civ. 633.
[1] October 2, 2001, unreported.
[2] *Hatton v. U.K.*, October 2, 2001, unreported. See also, *Z and A v. U.K.*, May 11, 2001.
[3] Vexatious Actions (Scotland) Act 1898, s.1.

instituting legal proceedings. Instead it requires that he needs to obtain leave from a Lord Ordinary before instigating litigation. He may be required to find caution, *i.e.* to pay funds into court in advance of the action. In the case of *H.M.Advocate v. Bell*,[4] the Inner House considered a petition by the Lord Advocate to have James Bell declared a vexatious litigant after he had raised a large number of actions, several of which related to issues already settled by litigation. One of the grounds raised in defence to the petition was that the provisions of the 1893 Act were incompatible with Article 6(1) of the Convention. The court should therefore make a declaration of incompatibility, since the right of access to a court of justice was impeded. The same argument was made about the requirement of caution as the need to raise funds in advance of an action could also be regarded as an impediment to the right of access to justice. The Inner House held that an order under the 1893 Act does not prevent the respondent from raising actions altogether. As it only requires that he should obtain leave from a Lord Ordinary before doing so he is not denied his right of access to justice under Article 6. It was also held that the requirement of caution was not inconsistent with Article 6.[5]

Costs as Bar to Access

4.34   The requirement that costs are lodged in advance of a trial may, however, amount to a denial of the right of access to justice if the sum involved is excessive. This was the case in *Pordea v. Times Newspapers Ltd.* Pordeau had brought a defamation action in England against Times Newspapers. The action was dismissed when Pordeau failed to provide security for costs. Times Newspapers obtained an order for costs and sought to enforce it in France. The Cour de Cassation refused to enforce the order on the ground that the costs order was contrary to public policy because the costs were set at a disproportionately high level and prevented Pordeau obtaining access to justice, contrary to Article 6(1) of the Convention.[6] A similar decision was reached by the European Court of Human Rights in *Ait-Mouhoub v. France*. Ait-Mouhoub had been convicted and imprisoned for offences of armed robbery. He appealed and also lodged civil and criminal actions against two *gendarmes* alleging perjury, extortion and forgery. He was refused legal aid and an order was made against him requiring him to give security for costs. He complained of a breach of Article 6, on the grounds that he had been refused access to a court. The French

---

[4]   *H.M.Advocate v. Bell*, March 23, 2001, Inner House, Extra Division, unreported.
[5]   *H v. U.K.*, 1985 45 D.R. 281.
[6]   *Pordea v. Times Newspapers Ltd* [2000] I.L.Pr. 763.

Government contended that Article 6 did not apply because there were no civil rights at stake. It was held that the proceedings were concerned with a civil right. The amounts of the security for costs orders were manifestly excessive in view of Mouhoub's lack of means and were designed to prevent him from lodging a complaint against the policemen. There had accordingly been a breach of Article 6.[7]

Legal Aid

Legal Aid is s system whereby financial assistance is provided to enable persons to secure legal advice and representation. Legal aid is widely available in relation to criminal prosecutions but its availability in relation to civil matters is more restricted. The European Court of Human Rights has interpreted Article 6 to the effect that cases which affect an individual's civil rights should attract legal assistance in certain circumstances. These circumstances include the complexity of the case; the need for expert witnesses to establish facts and the degree of emotional involvement of the applicant in the case.[8] Part 3 of the Convention Rights (Compliance) (Scotland) Act extends Advice and Assistance and Civil Legal Aid to cases where Article 6 is likely to require it. 4.35

Currently there are three forms of legal aid available in relation to civil cases.

(1) Advice and Assistance

Advice and Assistance, under the Legal Aid (Scotland) Act, Part II[9] allows an individual with limited financial means to obtain advice from a solicitor, or, in certain circumstances, an advocate, on matters of civil or criminal law. It does not usually include financial assistance for representation at a court or tribunal 4.36

(2) Advice by Way of Representation

Advice by Way of Representation, under the Advice and Assistance (Assistance by way of Representation) (Scotland) Regulations,[10] is available in relation to petitions for the appointment of an executor to a deceased person, Parole Board hearings, proceedings under the Proceeds of Crime (Scotland) Act 1995, certain proceedings under the Mental Health (Scotland) Act 1984, petitions by a debtor for his own sequestration, proceedings arising 4.37

---

[7] *Ait-Mouhoub v. France* (2000) 30 E.H.R.R. 382; [1998] H.R.C.D. 976.
[8] *Airey v. Ireland (No.1)* (1979-80) 2 E.H.R.R. 305.
[9] Legal Aid (Scotland) Act 1986, Pt II.
[10] Advice and Assistance (Assistance by way of Representation) (Scotland) Regulations 1997 (S.I. 1997 No. 3070, s.197.

from a failure to pay a fine or other sum or obey an order of the court and proceedings in Employment tribunals.

(3) Civil Legal Aid

4.38 Civil Legal Aid under the Legal Aid (Scotland) Act[11] is available in relation to proceedings in the House of Lords, the Court of Session, the sheriff court, the Employment Appeal Tribunal, the Lands Valuation Appeal Court, the Scottish Land Court, the Lands Tribunal for Scotland and the Restrictive Practices Court. It is not available for proceedings in any other tribunals in Scotland. It is available for appeals from tribunal decisions to the Court of Session.

The Convention Rights (Compliance) (Scotland) Act extends the availability of civil legal aid and advice by way of representation to any proceedings before any court or tribunal where a person's civil rights and obligations are to be determined. The Act provides that the Scottish Ministers will set "factors" for eligibility for legal aid, which the Scottish Legal Aid Board will consider. These factors will be considered in conjunction with the current tests of the potential success of the action, reasonableness and financial legibility. The new factors are likely to relate to those identified in the case of *Boner v. United Kingdom* and *Maxwell v. United Kingdom*, wherein it was held that the interests of justice required legal aid to be granted bearing in mind factors including, the nature of the proceedings and the limited capacity of an unrepresented appellant to put forward a legal argument. The most important factor is the importance of the issue at stake.[12]

PUBLIC HEARINGS

4.39 The right to a hearing in public is the only part of Article 6(1) which is a qualified right. Article 6(1) states that the press and public may be excluded from all or part of the trial. The Article lists the legitimate aims for which such exclusions may take place. They are as follows,

(1) in the interests of morals, public order or national security in a democratic society;

(2) where the interests of juveniles or the protection of the private life of the parties so require; or

(3) to the extent strictly necessary in the opinion of the court in special circumstances where publicity would prejudice the interests of justice.

---

[11] Legal Aid (Scotland) Act 1986, Pt III.
[12] *Boner v. U.K.* and *Maxwell v. U.K.* (1995) 19 E.H.R.R. 246.

These exceptions provide a basis on which the competing interest of the individual and the public interest can be balanced. In relation to qualified Convention rights the Court analyses the case against four tests in order to establish whether or not the right has been contravened;

(1) Has there been any interference with a substantive right?
(2) Is the act amounting to interference carried out in accordance with the law?
(3) Does the interference purport to have a legitimate aim?
(4) Is the interference necessary in a democratic society?

The legitimate aims in relation to interference with the right to a hearing in public are only those specified in Article 6(1). The concept of action which is necessary in a democratic society involves a test of proportionality. The action taken must not exceed that which is strictly necessary to achieve the legitimate aim. It may be the case, therefore, that exclusion of the public from part of a trial may be justified, whereas exclusion from the whole course of the proceedings would not be regarded as necessary. In the case *R v. Bow County Court, ex parte Pelling*, Pelling sought to have the Civil Procedure Rules 1998, Part 39 rule 39.2(3)(c), which provided for hearings to be held in private in certain circumstances, declared *ultra vires*. He contended that it was a principle of the highest importance that courts should sit in public which, by virtue of the principle of legality, could not be undermined by legislation except in express terms, and that the Civil Procedure Rules breached his human rights, in particular, his right to a fair trial under the Human Rights Act 1998, Schedule 1 Part I Article 6. It was held that the rules were permissive and did not breach the principle of legality as they did not comprise a blanket ban upon publicity but simply permitted judges to sit in private in very limited circumstances. The rules were subject to a general principle that hearings were ordinarily to be held in public. Article 6 was not absolute and the Convention acknowledged the existence of a certain scope for discretion in the approach of national courts to the issue of Article 6.[13]

---

[13] *R v. Bow County Court, ex p. Pelling* (No.2) [2001] U.K.H.R.R. 165. See also *Hakansson v. Sweden* (1991) 13 E.H.R.R. 1.

TRIAL WITHIN A REASONABLE TIME

4.40 Delays in the resolution of legal disputes have given rise to a large number of cases before the European Court of Human Rights. Article 6(1) is not concerned with the need for a prompt trial where a person has been deprived of their personal liberty while awaiting a criminal trial. This is dealt with in Article 5. Article 6 is more concerned with a general principle of prompt administration of justice. In civil proceedings the reasonable time referred to in Article 6(1) normally refers to the elapsed time from the moment the action was instituted before the tribunal until the remedy is provided.[14] In criminal cases the relevant time begins when the person is officially notified that they have committed a criminal offence by a competent authority.[15] In *H.M.Advocate v. P*, two boys, aged 13 years, were indicted for the rape of a 14-year-old girl with learning difficulties. The rape allegedly took place on March 11, 1999 and the accused were charged on March 16, 1999. The case was allocated for trial on February 19, 2001. The boys lodged a minute of notice of devolution issue in which they raised pleas in bar of trial on the grounds of unreasonable delay, relying on their rights under Article 6(1). It was held that the cumulative history of the case gave the impression that it was not dealt with as urgently as was required and there had been no priority afforded to the case given the involvement of children. The overall period of time lapsed was much longer than normal in a case like this, even where the complainer had learning difficulties. The delay was particularly unusual given the involvement of children and there had been no satisfactory explanation given for the delay.[16]

The criteria for determining whether a delay is reasonable were considered in the case of *Pailot v. France*. Pailot, a haemophiliac infected with the HIV virus by blood transfusion, brought proceedings against the government in France in May 1990, seeking compensation for the medical complaints he suffered from because of the HIV infection. The Administrative Court rejected the claim in March 1993 and Pailot's appeal was dismissed in February 1994. Pailot pursued a further appeal before the Conseil d'Etat in April 1994. In December 1994, Pailot lodged an application with the European Court of Human Rights, contending that the delay amounted to a breach of the Article 6(1). In June 1995 the Commission noted that Pailot and France had reached a friendly settlement under Article 28(1)(b). Pailot had accepted FF200,000 for non-pecuniary damage. Pailot's appeal was subsequently

---

[14]   *Poiss v. Austria*, 1987 10 E.H.R.R. 231.
[15]   *Dyer v. Watson*, 2001 S.L.T. 751; 2001 S.C.C.R. 430.
[16]   *H.M.Advocate v. P (sub nom. H.M.Advocate v. DP; DP v. SM)*, 2001 S.L.T. 924; 2001 S.C.C.R. 210.

allowed by the Conseil d'Etat in April 1997, which ordered compensation in the sum of £862,250, plus interest. It was held that, in assessing whether the length of proceedings exceeded a reasonable time, consideration had to be given to;

(1) the state of the proceedings at the start of the period under consideration,
(2) the nature and complexity of the dispute,
(3) the conduct of the parties and
(4) the seriousness of the case.

It was held that Article 6 had been breached, notwithstanding the friendly settlement, as the case had been pending before the Conseil d'Etat for more than three years with no explanation for the delay being given.[17]

Article 6(1) imposes a duty on contracting states to organise their legal systems so that the courts will be able to comply with the requirements of Article 6(1). This includes an obligation to provide sufficient courts to deal with cases within a reasonable time. A temporary backlog in cases, caused by an unusual increase in business will not however amount to a breach of Article 6(1) provided that the state can show that prompt action has been taken to reduce the backlog.[18]

In *Robins v. United Kingdom* the court held that the requirement for a trial within a reasonable time means that all ancillary matters, such as the resolution of disputes over costs must be resolved within a reasonable period after the substantive dispute has been decided. In that case, Exeter County Court had given judgment against the applicants in a civil action for damages in relation to sewage pollution in 1991. Disputes over the liability of the applicants to pay costs were not resolved until 1995. It was held that the costs proceedings were a continuation of the original substantive legal proceedings which related to the determination of civil rights and obligations. The court found that the state had been in violation of its obligations during two periods of 10 months and 16 months when no action had been taken to resolve the outstanding matters.[19]

Long delays between events and the legal actions resulting from them will not always amount to a breach of Article 6(1). A breach of Article 6(1) arises only where the state has failed to act to bring a case to trial within a reasonable time. In the case of *Reilly (Elizabeth Liddle) v. H.M.Advocate* the High Court of Justiciary considered the question of delay in relation to rights under Article

4.41

---

[17] *Pailot v. France* (2000) 30 E.H.R.R. 328; [1998] H.R.C.D. 451.
[18] *Buchholz v. Germany* (1981) 3 E.H.R.R. 597.
[19] *Robins v. U.K.* (1997) 26 E.H.R.R. 527.

6(1). Ms Reilly was charged with embezzling a large sum of money from her employers in 1991. The crime was reported to the police in 1992 but, because of the large number of potential witnesses, proper investigation took some time and produced a large amount of evidence. Reilly was questioned in December 1996. An accountant's report was commissioned in June 1998 and the final report was submitted in March 1999. Reilly appeared on petition warrant on June 28, 1999. She had raised a devolution issue claiming that a substantial delay in bringing her case to trial breached her right under Article 6(1) to have her case heard within a reasonable time, but that claim was rejected by the sheriff. Reilly appealed. The High Court of Justiciary held that Article 6(1) applied to the period from the time of Reilly's interview in 1996. The case was not a simple matter and required a substantial investigation. Consequently, there was no breach of Article 6(1). Given the volume of material acquired during the inquiry, the delay between December 1996 and March 1997 was quite ordinary, and there was no suggestion that between then and February 1998 anyone involved had been dilatory in their handling of the case.[20] Periods of inactivity during the process of investigation and prosecution will not always mean that a delay contravenes Article 6(1). A delay of 17 months in the investigation of a case was held not unreasonable in the case of *Gibson (David Blair) v. H.M.Advocate.* Gibson was charged with stealing a trailer in December 1996 (charge 1) and between August and September 1998 (charge 2). The Crown spent 17 months investigating charge 1 and in May 2000 Gibson was indicted for trial. He lodged a devolution minute on the ground of unreasonable delay with regard to charge 1. The sheriff accepted the Crown's explanation as to the delay. There had been difficulties in investigating the ownership of the trailer. Gibson appealed to the High Court wherein it was held that the lapse of 17 months was unusual by general standards but a Crown investigation could be expected to take some time, and a period of inactivity, *prima facie*, would not bring about a finding of unreasonable delay. Delay implied a departure from the norm. The Crown was found not to have acted unreasonably.[21]

Where a case is complex and the interests of justice require that extended investigations are necessary a longer period of delay will be deemed to be reasonable than in more straightforward cases. Delay may also be justified where the investigations are protracted because of technical considerations. In *Crummock (Scotland) Ltd v. H.M.Advocate,* contractors, while resurfacing a road, allowed diesel

---

[20] *Reilly (Elizabeth Liddle) v. H.M.Advocate,* 2000 S.L.T. 1330; 2000 S.C.C.R. 879. See also *Mitchell (Alexander Todd) v. H.M.Advocate,* 2001 S.C.C.R. 110.
[21] *Gibson (David Blair) v. H.M.Advocate,* 2001 J.C. 125; 2001 S.L.T. 591; 2001 S.C.C.R. 51; 2001.

oil to escape from a bowser and pollute the water supply to parts of Edinburgh. The environment agency initially investigated and informed Crummock that the case would not be referred to the fiscal. A year later an indictment was served on Crummock. He argued that the delay contravened his right under the European Convention on Human Rights 1950 Article 6(1) in that the indictment was not served within a reasonable time and no explanation was given for the delay. It was held that, as it was a scientifically complex case, the delay was not so unreasonable as to contravene Article 6(1).[22]

The case *H.M.Advocate v. Little (William Maxwell)* involved **4.42** considerable periods of delay in relation to sexual offences, which had allegedly been committed between 1978 and 1989. In this case the Crown could not provide a satisfactory explanation for the delay and there was held to be a breach of Article 6(1). It was not necessary for Little to show that he had actually suffered prejudice by reason of the breach of his Article 6(1) rights, but such prejudice would be relevant to any compensation claim.[23] The delay could not be considered to be reasonable when there was no justification for long periods of inactivity. In *H.M.Advocate v. Workman* where there had been delays totalling three years, including a period when charges were progressed against two other parties for the same offence. It was held that the length of delay called for an explanation and no satisfactory explanation had been given but a breach of Article 6 had to be assessed on the whole facts and circumstances and not just the length of any delay. The circumstances included the consequences of the delay for the individual. The delay for Workman was not so serious as to amount to a breach of Article 6(1).[24]

---

[22] *Crummock (Scotland) Ltd v. H.M.Advocate*, 2000 J.C. 408; 2000 S.L.T. 677; 2000 S.C.C.R. 453.
[23] *H.M.Advocate v. Little (William Maxwell)*, 1999 S.L.T. 1145; 1999 S.C.C.R. 625.
[24] *H.M.Advocate v. Workman*, 2000 J.C. 383.

CHAPTER 5

RIGHTS IN CRIMINAL LAW: PART I
ARTICLES 6(2) AND 7

ARTICLE 6(2)

"Everyone charged with a criminal offence shall be presumed innocent until proved guilty according to law."

5.01 The basic premise of this paragraph of Article 6 is that the courts and public authorities should start from the standpoint that the accused is innocent and it is for the prosecution to prove their guilt to the standard required by law. "The presumption of innocence is a fundamental tenet of our criminal procedure. It follows that the burden of proof rests on the Crown to displace this presumption."[1] In Scotland, of course, that standard is guilt "beyond reasonable doubt". This means that at least two independent pieces of evidence must be provided in respect of "every material issue in the case against the accused".[2]

The premise was seen in *Barberra, Messegue and Jabardo v. Spain*[3] where the European Court declared the meaning of Article 6(2) as:

"Paragraph 2 embodies the principle of the presumption of innocence. It requires, *inter alia,* that when carrying out their duties the members of the court should not start with the preconceived idea that the accused has committed the offence charged and any doubt should benefit the accused. It also follows that it is for the prosecution to inform the accused of the case that will be made against him so that he may prepare and present his defence accordingly and to adduce evidence sufficient to convict him."[4]

---

[1] Lord Justice Clerk Thomson in *Mackenzie v. H.M.Advocate,* 1959 J.C. 32 at 36–7; for general discussion of presumption of innocence, see S. Summers "Presumption of Innocence" (2001) Juridical Review 37.
[2] T. Jones and M. Christie, *Criminal Law* (2nd ed., 1996).
[3] (1989) 11 E.H.R.R. 360.
[4] *ibid.,* para. 77.

The Court has held that it is possible to infringe the presumption of innocence in a number of ways. For instance, in *Allenet de Ribemont v. France*[5] the Court found that unqualified public statements by the police or the prosecution referring to an individual as the perpetrator of an offence could amount to a violation of the Article.

The Article also addresses a number of other issues, including the use of presumptions of fact or law and the right to silence, and these will be discussed below. The presumption of innocence extends to the awarding of costs or compensation in the event of an acquittal. For instance, in *Sekanina v. Austria*[6] a man was acquitted of his wife's murder but he was denied reimbursement of his costs and compensation because there was still considerable suspicion that he was guilty.

> "The voicing of suspicions regarding an accused's innocence is conceivable as long as the conclusion of the criminal proceedings has not resulted in a decision on the merits of the accusation. However it is no longer admissible to rely on such suspicions once an acquittal has become final."

In *Minelli v. Switzerland*[7] the applicant had been the subject of a criminal defamation action, which was discontinued after it ran out of the limitation period. The Swiss Trial Court charged M with most of the trial costs, basing its decision on the reason that had the case gone ahead the applicant "would in all probability have been convicted". On appeal, the federal court approved the "substance of the decision on the essential points". The European Court held there had been a violation of Article 6(2). 5.02

> "The presumption of innocence will be violated if, without the accused's having previously been proved guilty according to law and, notably, without his having had the opportunity of exercising his rights of defence, a judicial decision concerning him reflects an opinion that he is guilty . . . It suffices that there is some reasoning suggesting that the court regards the accused as guilty."[8]

In compensation proceedings following an acquittal of the accused person, there must be no statements made voicing suspicions about whether that person was in fact guilty. "Once an acquittal has become final . . . the voicing of any suspicions of guilt, including

---

[5]   (1995) 20 E.H.R.R. 557.
[6]   (1993) 17 E.H.R.R. 221.
[7]   (1983) 5 E.H.R.R. 554.
[8]   (1983) 5 E.H.R.R. 554, para. 37.

those expressed in the reasons for the acquittal, is incompatible with the presumption of innocence."[9]

The European Court has, however, concluded that Article 6(2) is not violated where there is a refusal of payment of costs after a criminal action had been discontinued.[10] The Article was not breached where the costs were not awarded to an applicant because her actions in not disclosing her defence prolonged the proceedings.[11]

The general right of a "fair trial" is given in the first paragraph of Article 6 and the second paragraph has been interpreted as being part of that general right. Accordingly, where a breach of Article 6(1) is found, the European Court may not enquire further to ascertain whether or not there has been a breach of Article 6(2). The Court appears to take a holistic view, with the principle being that if the right to a fair trial has been breached, for instance for want of an impartial hearing, then this may have been evidenced by assumptions made by the judge which showed that he thought the accused was not innocent from the outset.

5.03   The principle of presumption of innocence has had a chequered history in Scots law and it was not until 1928 that it became a fundamental procedural rule.[12] In *Slater v. H.M.Advocate*[13] evidence was led that the motive for the murder of an old lady was the theft of her jewellery and that the accused made a living from gambling and dealing in jewels. In his direction to the jury, the judge referred to the man's poor character saying that the presumption of innocence applied less to him than to an "upright" citizen. The conviction was quashed. Lord Justice Clerk Clyde stated that "[t]he presumption of innocence applied to every person charged with a criminal offence in precisely the same way, and it can be overcome only by evidence relevant to prove the crime with the commission of which he is charged."

In Scotland, there is a misconception that the verdict of "not proven" is somewhat less than a verdict of "not guilty". Juries have been known to return the verdict in the belief that somehow it will show their doubt as to the accused's innocence. The effect of the verdict is of course the same as a "not guilty" verdict but there is a stigma attached to the verdict which might prove difficult to justify in terms of Article 6(2).

---

[9]   *Rushiti v. Austria,* March 21, 2000 ECtHR, para. 31.
[10] *Lutz v. Germany* (1988) 10 E.H.R.R. 182.
[11] *Byrne v. U.K.* [1998] E.H.R.L.R. 628.
[12] S. Summers, *supra* no.1, p.48.
[13] 1928 J.C. 94.

Presumptions

The European Court has recognised that presumptions regarding   5.04
fact and law operate in every legal system and the Convention does
not prohibit their use. However, they must be confined to
reasonable limits and must maintain the rights of the defence.[14]
Where the prosecution proves an offence was committed by the
accused, the burden of avoiding criminal liability may pass to the
accused but this burden must again be within reasonable limits. The
issue of a "reverse onus" clause will only arise where the legal or
persuasive burden of proof is placed on the accused. It will not
apply where it is an evidential burden—that is the accused has to
prove some defence—for instance, self-defence, by means of
evidence. In *R v. Lambert, Ali and Jordan*[15] the Court of Appeal
held that the burden on the defence of proving diminished
responsibility did not offend Article 6(2) because the burden only
arose once the prosecution had proved unlawful and intentional
killing. The defendants had not been required to prove an essential
element of the offence, but had been given an opportunity to
establish a special defence. In Scotland, the burden of proof will
pass to the accused where he pleads either diminished responsibility
or the special defence of insanity. The standard of proof of insanity
is not "beyond reasonable doubt"; instead, the accused has only to
establish his insanity at the time of the offence on the balance of
probabilities, the standard used in civil actions.[16]

In *Lambert, Ali and Jordan* the Court of Criminal Appeal in
England applied the European Court's decision in *Salabiaku v.
France*.[17] Article 392(1) of the French Customs Code stated that
once the prosecution had proved possession of drugs in certain
circumstances, the accused would be presumed guilty of smuggling
drugs unless they could prove it was impossible for them to have
known about the drugs. The European Court held that the
presumption was not beyond what was reasonable, having regard
to the objectives of the offence (dealing with a serious social
problem) and the accused was not left without a means of defence.
The Convention had to be interpreted purposively to strike a
balance between the rights of the individual and the rights of
society.

The use of such "reverse onus" clauses was considered by the
House of Lords in *R v. Director of Public Prosecutions, ex parte
Kebilene*.[18] Section 16A(1) of the Prevention of Terrorism

---

[14] *Salabiaku v. France* (1991) 13 E.H.R.R. 379. See also *Tefner v. Austria*, March 20, 2001, ECtHR.
[15] [2001] 2 W.L.R. 211.
[16] *H.M.Advocate v. Mitchell*, 1951 S.L.T. 200.
[17] *supra* no.14.
[18] [1999] 4 All E.R. 801.

(Temporary Provisions) Act 1989 created an offence of possession of articles for purposes connected with terrorism. Section 16A(2) provided a defence to subsection (1) by allowing the defendant to prove that the possession was not for such a purpose. The defendant submitted that this burden of proof was contrary to Article 6(2) and the Director of Public Prosecutions should not have consented to the prosecution. The House of Lords by majority found against Kebilene, on the basis that decisions of the Director of Public Prosecutions were not subject to review except where dishonesty, *mala fides* or other exceptional circumstances were present. The judges, however, felt that the European Convention on Human Rights caselaw did not completely ban "reverse onus" clauses and that each case had to be assessed on its merits. It was also thought that section 16A(2) could be treated as placing an evidential, rather than persuasive, burden on the accused and in this regard the section would not infringe the Convention. Lord Hope applied a balancing approach between the interests of the accused and those of society as a whole:

> "It is not immediately obvious that it would be imposing an unreasonable burden on an accused who was in possession of articles from which an inference of involvement in terrorism could be drawn to provide an explanation for his possession of them which would displace that inference."[19]

On the issue of statutory presumptions he said:

> "Statutory presumptions which place an 'evidential' burden on the accused, requiring the accused to do no more than raise a reasonable doubt on the matter with which they deal, do not breach the presumption of innocence. They are not incompatible with Article 6(2) of the Convention. They take their place alongside the common law evidential presumptions which have been built up in the light of experience."

5.05 The Privy Council had to consider the use of presumptions within the Proceeds of Crime (Scotland) Act 1995, section 3(2) in *H.M.Advocate v. McIntosh.*[20] The High Court of Justiciary had found that a prosecutor would be acting contrary to the presumption of innocence under Article 6(2) if in applying for a confiscation order he invited the court to rely on those presumptions. Section 3(2) allowed the court to assume that property held or transferred to a person convicted of drug trafficking had been a

---

[19] s.16A of the 1989 Act is now re-enacted in s.57 of the Terrorism Act 2000.
[20] 2001 S.L.T. 304.

payment or reward for such trafficking. The Crown appealed against the ruling to the Privy Council and they allowed the appeal saying that the making of a confiscation order did not of itself amount to a person being charged with a criminal offence and it therefore followed that Article 6(2) did not apply. The assumptions of the 1995 Act only arose where there was a significant discrepancy between the property and expenditure of the defender and his known income. These assumptions were proportionate and in the public interest.[21]

The Drug Trafficking Act 1994 contained a statutory presumption that property held by the convicted person during the preceding six years represented the proceeds of drug trafficking. In *Phillips v. United Kingdom*[22] the European Court noted that the purpose of the 1994 Act was to enable the national court to assess the amount of the confiscation order. There was no further criminal charge and so Article 6(2) did not apply to confiscation proceedings. The presumption here could be rebutted if the accused could show on the balance of probability that he acquired the property by other means. In addition the trial judge had the discretion not to apply the presumption if it gave rise to a serious risk of injustice.

There are a considerable number of statutes containing "reverse onus" sections and the government continues to create new ones. In the Terrorism Act 2000, a number of sections have a reversed burden of proof where the suspect has to prove that information he has obtained is not to be used for purposes outlawed by the statute. For instance, it is an offence under section 58 for anyone to collect, possess or make a record of information of the kind likely to be useful to a person committing or preparing an act of terrorism. Thus, a journalist collecting information about a controversial group would have to prove that the information was not being collected for criminal purposes; failure to do so could result in imprisonment.

An accused's previous convictions may not normally be 5.06 introduced in evidence, thus ensuring that they do not unduly influence either the jury or the judge. Evidence of previous convictions will normally only become relevant after conviction during the sentencing stage. A recent attempt to invoke the Convention was made in *Andrew v. H.M.Advocate*[23] where a witness unexpectedly referred to the accused's previous convictions. The High Court refused his appeal since such a "breach" did not

---

[21] In his judgment, Lord Bingham referred to the provisions of the United Nations Convention Against Illicit Traffic in Narcotic Drugs and Psychotropic Substances 1988.

[22] Appl. 41087/98.

[23] 2000 S.L.T. 402.

justify quashing the conviction either under the Convention or in existing Scots law.

There is generally a presumption of sanity, but, where the accused pleads the special defence of insanity or makes a plea of diminished responsibility, the onus of proving his mental state will pass to him.[24]

The Right to Silence and the Right not to Incriminate Oneself

5.07   The basic premise of Article 6(2) is that a person is innocent and the prosecution must prove their guilt to the required standard. From this the European Court has derived a right to silence; an accused person need not say anything at the trial because it is not for him to prove his innocence. The prosecution has to prove his guilt. In *Funke v. France*[25] the Court said that a fair trial includes "the right of anyone charged with a criminal offence . . . to remain silent and not to contribute to incriminating himself."

The right to silence, or not to incriminate oneself, is not specifically mentioned in Article 6, but it is "a generally recognised international standard" whereby the accused is protected against improper compulsion by the authorities.[26] It is seen in Article 14(3)(g) of the International Covenant on Civil and Political Rights, "[e]veryone facing a criminal charge is entitled not to be compelled to testify against himself or to confess his guilt". The right not to incriminate oneself will be violated if an accused is coerced against his will to make statements and these are then used against him. The Court has made it clear that it is not the compulsory questioning which contravenes the Convention, rather it is the use of those statements to incriminate the person in criminal proceedings.[27]

In *Saunders v. United Kingdom* the prosecution made extensive use at his trial of answers he had been required to give under the Companies Act 1985, sections 432 and 442. The applicant thus lost his privilege against self-incrimination and he argued that this was unfair and an abuse of process. He was convicted of fraud. The European Court found that there was a threat of a penalty for remaining silent and the introduction of the interviews into the trial proceedings thus amounted to a violation of Article 6(2). The Court stated, "[t]he right not to incriminate oneself, in particular, presupposes that the prosecution in a criminal case seek to prove their case against the accused without resort to evidence obtained through methods of coercion or oppression in defiance of the will of the accused".[28] The Court also appeared to reject the consideration

---

[24]   *Lambie v. H.M.Advocate*, 1973 S.L.T. 219.
[25]   (1993) 16 E.H.R.R. 297.
[26]   *Saunders v. U.K.* (1997) 23 E.H.R.R. 313 at para. 68.
[27]   *ibid.*, and see also *Abas v. Netherlands*, Appl. 27943/95, EComHR.

of the public interest in the application of freedom from self-incrimination, "[t]he public interest cannot be invoked to justify the use of answers compulsorily obtained in a non-judicial investigation to incriminate the accused during the trial proceedings".[29]

The United Kingdom Government responded to the decision by enacting section 59 and Schedule 3 of the Youth Justice and Criminal Evidence Act 1999. This provides that in relation to statutory powers requiring compulsory answers to questions, including those under the Companies Act 1985, the answers may not be used in a subsequent trial, except a prosecution for perjury.

5.08

In *Murray (John) v. United Kingdom*[30] the European Court held that the right to silence is not absolute. Murray had been arrested under the Prevention of Terrorism (Temporary Provisions) Act 1989 and taken to a police station where a senior officer decided to delay access to a solicitor for 48 hours. During this period, Murray repeatedly stated that he had nothing to say and once he was granted access to a solicitor he said that he had been advised not to answer questions. Under Northern Ireland regulations, a criminal court may exercise its discretion to draw adverse inferences from an accused's failure to mention a fact during police questioning. The court drew such an inference once the prosecution had established a *prima facie* case against Murray and he was convicted. The European Court found that based on the facts there had been no breach of Article 6(2) since Murray had been able to remain silent. There was also strong evidence against him and the drawing of inferences was not therefore unfair.

In *Condron v. United Kingdom (No. 2)*[31] the applicants were convicted of supplying heroin and possession of heroin with intent to supply. After their arrest their solicitor maintained that they were not fit to be interviewed because of heroin withdrawal symptoms but the police doctor disagreed with this. The applicants were cautioned but refused to reply to questions put by police officers and did not offer an explanation of their activities. At their trial they said that they did not answer questions on the advice of their solicitor and they then gave an explanation of their activities. The trial judge indicated to the jury that they might draw an adverse inference from the applicant's silence during the police interview. The judge referred to the applicants' explanation but did not indicate to the jury that they might be satisfied with the plausibility of the explanation and thus would not need to draw an adverse inference. The European Court found that particular caution was required before an accused's silence could be invoked against him.

---

[28] *Saunders v. U.K.* (1997) 23 E.H.R.R. 313 at para. 68.
[29] *ibid.*, para. 74
[30] (1996) 22 E.H.R.R. 29.
[31] (2001) 31 E.H.R.R. 1.

It would be incompatible with the Convention to base a conviction solely or mainly on an accused's silence or refusal to answer questions or give evidence on his own behalf. However, the Court also recognised that where the circumstances clearly required the accused to give an explanation and where he did not do so, then his silence might be taken into account when the persuasiveness of the prosecution's evidence was being assessed. As a result of the decision in *Condron* the English courts have amended the form of words used to direct the jury on the inference to be drawn.

5.09   The right not to incriminate oneself came under scrutiny in Scotland in *Brown v. Procurator Fiscal, Dunfermline*[32] where the accused was suspected of driving while intoxicated. She had been detained on suspicion of theft but was asked how she had arrived at the superstore. She said that she had travelled by car and pointed the car out. She was advised that it was an offence under the Road Traffic Act 1988 section 172 to refuse to tell the police who was driving the car at the time of the alleged offence. A breath test then proved positive and she was charged with driving the car while intoxicated. She was subsequently convicted of this charge. On appeal the conviction was quashed as being contrary to Article 6. The use of the statement made under the coercion of section 172 was a breach of Article 6 and the section had to be interpreted to prevent the use of statements so obtained as evidence in criminal proceedings.

The decision was appealed by the Crown to the Privy Council and judgment was given on December 5, 2000.[33] The case was one of the first tests of the Human Rights Act before the Privy Council and its implications for road traffic law throughout the United Kingdom were considerable. The Privy Council analysed the nature of the rights protected by Article 6 and whether or not they were absolute in nature. The right to a fair trial was considered to be absolute and central to the Convention itself. Other rights under the Article, including implied rights such as the right to silence, would not be absolute but would be "open, in principle, to modification or restriction so long as this is not incompatible with the absolute right to a fair trial".[34] Thus, the freedom from self-incrimination might be subject to qualification in the public interest. The judges then considered whether section 172 was a proportionate response to the legitimate public interest in road traffic regulation and particularly to the serious social problem of death and injury on the roads. The judges stressed that section 172 was narrow in scope since it aimed only to obtain information on the identity of the driver and did not

---

[32] 2000 S.L.T. 379.
[33] *Procurator Fiscal Dunfermline and H.M. Advocate General for Scotland v. Margaret Anderson Brown*, 2001 S.L.T. 59.
[34] *ibid.*, Lord Hope at p.51 of transcript.

authorise further questioning by the police. The Privy Council thus found that there was no breach of Article 6 by the requirement under section 172 to give the name of the driver of the vehicle.

The decision in *Brown* was based on its facts and particularly the regulatory nature of the offence. Section 172 is part of a regulatory scheme and the legislation limits the type of questioning the police may use. The Privy Council distinguished the situation in *Brown* from that in *Saunders v. United Kingdom* saying that in the latter case there had been prolonged questioning of the applicant. The European Court had identified the rationale of the freedom from self-incrimination as the "prevention of improper compulsion".[35] The European Court held in *Heaney and McGuinness v. Ireland*[36] that where the offence is non-regulatory and serious, interference with the right not to incriminate oneself would be subject to greater scrutiny. There was a degree of compulsion under the emergency anti-terrorism legislation which destroyed the very essence of the right not to incriminate oneself and this was a breach of Article 6. The Irish Government's argument that the provision was a proportionate response to its security and public order concerns was rejected.

The right to remain silent will be violated if the accused is not allowed access to a solicitor before interview.[37] If the solicitor then advises the accused to remain silent, the domestic court should give this fact appropriate weight.[38] The directions given to the jury by the judge must conform to the Convention principles; if they do not, it is unlikely that the defect can be remedied at the appeal stage. The European Court made this clear in *Condron v. United Kingdom (No. 2)*[39]:

> "The Court of Appeal had no means of ascertaining whether or not the applicants' silence played a significant role in the jury's decision to convict. The Court of Appeal had regard to the weight of evidence against the applicants. However it was in no position to assess properly whether the jury considered this to be conclusive of the guilt."[40]

There is no right to costs for a defendant under the Convention and a refusal to reimburse costs to the defendant does not offend the presumption of innocence.[41] In *Byrne v. United Kingdom*[42] the

5.10

---

[35] *supra* no.25, *per* Lord Steyn at p.39 of transcript.
[36] Appl. 34720/97, judgment December 21, 2000.
[37] *supra* no.30.
[38] *supra* no.31.
[39] (2001) 31 E.H.R.R. 1.
[40] *ibid.*, para. 63.
[41] *Lutz v. Germany* (1988) 10 E.H.R.R. 182.

defendant did not disclose her defence and thus prolonged the proceedings against her. The domestic court refused to award her costs and the European Commission held that this did not infringe her right to presumption of innocence.

In normal circumstances, a person who is under suspicion of having committed an offence will be cautioned by the police officers investigating the matter. The principle behind the use of the caution is that of "the right to silence". It warns the suspect that he does not have to say anything and the investigating officers are under a duty to ensure that the suspect understands the meaning of the words. In Scotland, there is no duty on a person to answer police questions but giving false information to the police may amount to an attempt to pervert the course of justice.[43] The law in Scotland on self-incrimination is equally clear as Lord Gillies pointed out in *Livingstone v. Murray*,[44] "[i]t is a sacred and inviolable principle that no man is bound to incriminate himself". The right is now set out in statute. The Criminal Procedure (Scotland) Act 1995, section 14(9) states that a person detained by the police "shall be under no obligation to answer any question other than to give his name and address, and a constable shall so inform him both on so detaining him and on arrival at the police station or other premises". Thus, a suspect in Scotland is under no obligation to answer questions but must supply his name and address. The statutory form of caution should be administered both at the time of detention and at the place of detention. The High Court of Justiciary has also recommended that the caution be administered before questioning.[45]

The detained person has to be told that he is being detained because he is suspected of having committed an offence punishable by imprisonment, the general nature of the offence and the reasons for suspecting him. He must also be told he is being detained pending further investigation, that he is being taken to a police station and that he will then be informed of his further rights. This is the extent of the statutory caution. However, the caution will normally end with the words: "You are not obliged to answer any further questions but anything you do say will be recorded and may be given in evidence". This part of the caution has its roots in the common law and is given to ensure fairness to the suspect. In *Scott v. Howie*[46] the statutory caution was not read to the accused on arrival at the police station. However, before he was questioned, both the statutory and a full common law caution were given. The

---

[42] [1998] E.H.R.L.R. 628, EComHR.
[43] *Dean v. Stewart*, 1980 S.L.T. (Notes) 85.
[44] (1830) 9 Shaw 161.
[45] *Tonge v. H.M.Advocate*, 1982 S.C.C.R. 313.
[46] 1993 S.C.C.R. 81.

accused then made a statement which was used in evidence at his trial. He appealed his conviction averring that the statement was inadmissible but the High Court of Justiciary held that although there had been a procedural defect, there had been no unfairness to him. The full common law caution had ensured that the person was treated fairly.

In *Custerson v. Westwater*[47] the police asked Custerson if he had a knife in his possession. He had not yet been cautioned but the court held that the evidence that he had a knife was admissible. In *Young v. Friel*[48] a suspect volunteered information about another offence of which the police were then unaware. His conviction for this offence was upheld and the court held that it was not necessary to administer a second caution in these circumstances.[49] 5.11

Of course it is the case that other public servants have the authority to question people. Generally such public servants must use the same fair procedures as the police. In *Walkingshaw v. McIntyre*[50] a post office enquiry officer visited the accused because his name was on a list which showed that there was no record of him having a television licence. The enquiry officer asked him if he had a licence; she gave no words of caution before asking the question. The court held that it was unfair to invite the suspect to incriminate himself without the benefit of caution and his incriminating reply was therefore inadmissible.

In English law, the form of caution is set out in the Codes of Practice made under the Police and Criminal Evidence Act. Code C, paragraph 10.4 gives the wording to be used:

> "You do not have to say anything. But it may harm your defence if you do not mention when questioned something which you later rely on in court. Anything you do say may be given in evidence."

The right to silence was the subject of political controversy in 1993 when the Conservative Home Secretary, Michael Howard, announced to his Party Conference that he intended to remove "the so-called right to silence", his intention apparently was to compel suspects to answer questions and incriminate themselves. The Criminal Justice and Public Order Act 1994, section 34 modified the right by providing that a court may draw "such inferences as appear proper" if the accused failed to mention something during questioning which he then relied on in his defence. The effect of the 1994 Act is that a person may remain

---

[47] 1987 S.C.C.R. 389.
[48] 1992 S.C.C.R. 567.
[49] See also *Pennycuick v. Lees*, 1992 S.L.T. 763.
[50] 1985 S.C.C.R. 389.

silent but will run the risk that his defence will not be believed. In *R v. Bowden*[51] Lord Bingham, C.J. said that the laws had to be given proper effect, but since they "restrict rights recognised at common law as appropriate to protect defendants against the risk of injustice, they should not be construed more widely than the statutory language requires". In *Averill v. United Kingdom*[52] the European Court did not find a violation of Article 6(2) where the domestic court had drawn adverse inferences from the accused's silence. However, "the extent to which adverse inferences can be drawn from an accused's failure to respond to police questioning must be necessarily limited". In *Condron v. United Kingdom*[53] the Court held that silence could not be the sole or main basis for any conviction but was relevant in assessing the persuasiveness of the evidence presented by the prosecution.

5.12   Two other sections in the 1994 Act allow adverse inferences to be drawn from a person's failure to explain. Section 36 refers to a failure by the accused to explain marks on his clothing or items in his possession when he is arrested close to the scene of a crime, while section 37 refers to a failure by the accused to explain his presence at or near the scene. In *Averill v. United Kingdom*[54] the applicant failed to give a satisfactory account of his presence near the scene and also an account of the presence of fibres on his clothing and in his hair. The European Court accepted that these were factors justifying an adverse inference.[55]

ARTICLE 7—NO PUNISHMENT WITHOUT LAW

"(1) No one shall be held guilty of any criminal offence on account of any act or omission which did not constitute a criminal offence under national or international law at the time when it was committed. Nor shall a heavier penalty be imposed than the one that was applicable at the time the criminal offence was committed.

(2) This Article shall not prejudice the trial and punishment of any person for any act or omission which, at the time when it was committed, was criminal according to the general principles of law recognised by civilised nations."

---

[51] [1999] 2 Cr.App.R 176 at 181, Court of Appeal.
[52] (2001) 31 E.H.R.R. 36.
[53] (2001) 31 E.H.R.R. 1.
[54] *supra* no.52.
[55] A. Jennings, A. Ashworth and B. Emmerson "Silence and Safety: The Impact of Human Rights Law" [2000] Crim. Law Rev. 879.

Article 7 confers absolute rights which cannot be restricted even in   5.13
times of war or other public emergency[56] and it relates exclusively
to criminal proceedings.

The Article is divided into two paragraphs, the first dealing with
the broad principles of criminal law. The second paragraph allows
the prosecution of people for crimes of an international nature such
as war crimes, so that such people cannot escape punishment
because the crime was not specified in the domestic legislation at the
time it was committed but it was nevertheless an affront to general
international legal principles. Thus the War Crimes Act 1991was
protected from challenge under Article 7(1) by the qualification of
Article 7(2). The Act allowed the prosecution of individuals for
their alleged criminal actions during the Second World War. The
offences had to have been committed in Germany or in German
occupied territory.

Article 7(1) requires that a person has to be convicted of a crime
which existed at the time it was allegedly committed and that the
penalty imposed should not be more severe than the penalty which
applied at the time of the offence. It has to be noted that the
prohibition on the creation of retroactive offences applies to those
created by legislation and by the development of the common law.
However, the gradual clarification of the rules of criminal liability
through judicial interpretation of cases may be allowed provided
that the development is consistent with the offence and is
reasonably foreseeable. In *SW v. United Kingdom* and *CR v. United
Kingdom*[57] the applicants had been charged with the rape or
attempted rape of their wives. At the time the offences were
committed a husband was immune at common law from prosecution for the rape of his wife. That immunity had been eroded
through various judicial decisions until it no longer existed. The
applicants claimed a violation of Article 7 in that the crime of which
they were convicted did not exist at the time they committed the act
for which they were prosecuted. The European Court held that
there was no violation of Article 7 because in this case the law had
evolved in a consistent and foreseeable way. The Court also
observed:

> "The abandonment of the unacceptable idea of a husband
> being immune against prosecution for the rape of his wife was
> in conformity not only with a civilised concept of marriage
> but also, and above all, with the fundamental objectives of the

---

[56]   Similarly Arts 2, 3 and 4(1).
[57]   (1996) 21 E.H.R.R. 363.

Convention, the very essence of which is respect for human dignity and human freedom."[58]

The issue of judge-made-law is one which applies to both the Scots and English jurisdictions. A common law offence may be clarified or developed by the judges and the European Court has indicated that this is possible so long as the rule-making function remains within reasonable limits. In *Gay News Ltd and Lemon v. United Kingdom*[59] a private prosecution was brought against the editor and publisher of a magazine. The charge was blasphemous libel by publishing an obscene poem and illustration. The trial judge directed the jury that to satisfy the requirements of the common law offence, it was necessary only to establish that the publication had vilified Christ in His life and crucifixion. There was no need to establish an intention beyond an intention to publish. The applicants were convicted and appealed to the House of Lords where the judges by majority held that intention to blaspheme was not a necessary element of the offence, although the law was unclear. The applicants complained to the European Court saying that their conviction was based on legal principles which did not exist, or were not sufficiently clearly defined at the time the offence was committed. The Commission rejected the claim as manifestly ill-founded because all of the domestic courts involved had confirmed the existence of the offence and had interpreted the law in a reasonable way. The question of *mens rea* had been raised but had been answered in the same way by each court. The law was accessible to the applicants and its interpretation was reasonably foreseeable. Accordingly there was no violation of Article 7(1).

5.14   In *Times Newspapers Ltd and Neil v. United Kingdom*[60] the *Sunday Times* newspaper published extracts of a book, *Spycatcher*, written by Peter Wright, a former MI5 officer. The publication on July 12, 1987 was timed to coincide with publication in the United States of America. However, the Attorney General commenced proceedings against the applicants for contempt of court on the ground that the publication frustrated the purpose of original injunctions granted in July 1986 to prevent publication on grounds of national security. The book was published in the United States the day after the Attorney General commenced proceedings, but the United Kingdom Government did not take legal action to restrain publication in the United States. The original injunctions had been granted against two other newspapers. A number of papers published summaries of the allegations given in the book and they were cited for contempt of court on the grounds that they had

---

[58] (1996) 21 E.H.R.R. 363, para. 44. See also *X Ltd and Y v. U.K.* (1982) 28 D.R. 77.
[59] (1983) 5 E.H.R.R. 123.
[60] (1992) 14 E.H.R.R. 229.

known the injunctions existed. In June 1987, those contempt proceedings were heard in court and it was held that no contempt had been committed by the newspapers not covered by the injunctions. The Attorney General appealed that decision and it was while this appeal was pending that the *Sunday Times* decided to publish, after receiving legal advice that no contempt proceedings would be possible. The decision in the June 1987 proceedings was overturned on appeal and in 1989 the *Sunday Times* and others were tried for contempt and found guilty. A fine of £50,000 was imposed. The Court of Appeal upheld the conviction but quashed the fine. The applicants sought redress in the European Court, alleging that at the time of the publication they were not guilty of any offence and to find them guilty was contrary to Article 7. The European Commission found that the constituent elements of the common law offence of contempt were sufficiently clear at July 12, 1987. The fact that established legal principles were applied to novel circumstances did not render the offence retroactive.

In Scotland, the High Court of Justiciary retains a declaratory power which allows it to declare the ambit of a known crime, or to criminalise an action which was formerly not known to be criminal. The power is probably contrary to Article 7(1) although it has not yet been tested against the Convention. The origins of the declaratory power are shrouded in history but two of the Scots institutional writers, Hume and Alison, acknowledge its existence and assume that it is necessary to create new crimes. Both writers were of course writing in a time when the criminal law was almost entirely common law and the intervention of Parliament to make criminal legislation was comparatively rare. They said that new crimes should be created by Parliament and by the courts, but do not explain the court's power to make such laws. The judiciary has tried to explain why such power is given to them. "I hold it to be law, that the right of enquiring into all injuries to individuals by criminal acts, as well as defining in such cases the nature and extent of the punishment, is constitutionally entrusted to this Court."[61] Hume preferred the courts to make new criminal laws because Parliament was too slow to do so. However, in modern times it could not be said that Parliament, whether of the United Kingdom or the Scottish variety, is too slow to react to new circumstances where public safety issues are involved.

The declaratory power continues to exist but it is exercised in very limited circumstances. Alison in *Principles*[62] stated that the power might be exercised in respect of an act or omission which was both in itself wrong and hurtful to the persons or property of

[61] Lord Meadowbank in *Rachel Wright* (1809) Burnett, app. no. vii.
[62] *Principles of the Criminal Law of Scotland* (1832-33) i, 624.

others. The High Court has accepted these principles but has not in recent years exercised the power to any great extent. The judges have instead used the breadth of the common law to bring certain activities into the sphere of the criminal law. In *Strathern v. Seaforth*[63] the crime of clandestinely taking and using another's property was created. The ground for creating the offence was the adverse social consequences of failing to punish such conduct. In *McLaughlin v. Boyd*[64] the crime of shameless indecency was recognised by reference to Hume's *Commentaries* where the definition of crime as a doleful or wilful violence against society in the matter of "violence, dishonesty, falsehood, indecency, irreligion" was set out.[65] The power was asserted by the Crown and accepted by the High Court in *Khaliq v. H.M.Advocate*.[66] Later, Lord Justice Clerk Ross recognised the existence of the declaratory power in *Grant v. Allan*[67] but declined to exercise it. The accused was employed by a commercial firm and obtained computerised information regarding the firm's clients, which he then offered for sale to a competitor. He was charged with theft of the information but the relevance of the charge was challenged. The High Court declined to exercise the power on the ground that it was for Parliament to decide the punishment of immoral acts.

5.15   There is little doubt that the declaratory power offends the principles set out in Article 7 of the Convention. In any legal system, it is implicit that an action which is not prohibited will be permitted. The courts should not therefore have the power to withdraw the implied permission for acts which have already been done.[68] "The declaratory power so starkly conflicts with the legal principles which lie at the heart of criminal jurisdiction in the western tradition that its continuing existence can only be considered anomalous in a modern legal system."[69]

Article 7(1) refers both to offences and to penalties imposed as a result of criminal conviction. The issue of what constitutes a penalty has been raised a number of times before Convention institutions. In *Kokkinakis v. Greece*[70] the European Court pointed out that Article 7(1) embodied a more general principle that

"only the law can define a crime and prescribe a penalty . . . it follows from this that an offence must be clearly defined in

---

[63] 1926 J.C. 100. See also *Kerr v. Hill*, 1936 J.C. 71, wasting the time of the police.
[64] 1934 J.C. 19.
[65] *Commentaries on the Law of Scotland Respecting Crimes* (1797) at page 22.
[66] 1983 S.C.C.R. 483.
[67] 1987 S.C.C.R. 402.
[68] R. McCall Smith and D. Sheldon, *Scots Criminal Law* (2nd ed., 1997).
[69] *ibid.*, at 11.
[70] (1993) 17 E.H.R.R. 397.

law. This condition is satisfied where the individual can know from the wording of the relevant provision and, if need be, with the assistance of the court's interpretation of it, what acts and omissions will make him liable."[71]

The Scots law therefore needs to be as precise and definite as possible if it is not to run foul of the Convention. Gane suggests that two offences are particularly vague and therefore may not be Convention compliant.[72] Breach of the peace—"the fiscal's friend"—requires either proof of an actual disturbance or proof of "something done in breach of public order or decorum which could reasonably be expected to lead to the lieges being alarmed or upset".[73] The offence has been very broadly interpreted and covers a wide range of circumstances, such as "peeping" through a hole in a partition wall to watch women using a solarium[74] to sitting on a felled tree while protesting that it had been felled.[75]

The second offence identified by Gane is shameless indecency. Again there is a broad range of circumstances where this offence had been charged. It ranges from an indecent assault by a man on other men[76] to showing an obscene video recording to two teenage girls in private.[77]

However, it also seems that the European Court has recognised that the criminal law may be imprecise because of the nature of the offence. In *Gillow v. United Kingdom*[78] the Court stated:

5.16

"The Court recognises that the offence of blasphemy cannot by its very nature lend itself to precise legal definition. National authorities must therefore be afforded a degree of flexibility in assessing whether the facts of particular case fall within the accepted definition of the offence."[79]

If the circumstances surrounding the offence are within the boundaries previously established by the case law, then arguably the offences of breach of the peace and shameless indecency will not

[71] (1993) 17 E.H.R.R. 397, para. 52.
[72] C. Gane "The Substantive Criminal Law" in Lord Reed (ed.) *A Practical Guide to Human Rights Law in Scotland* (W. Green & Son, 2001), p.78.
[73] *Rafaelli v. Heatly*, 1949 J.C. 101; *Young v. Heatly*, 1959 J.C. 66; *Donaldson v. Vannet*, 1998 S.C.C.R. 421.
[74] *MacDougall v. Dochree*, 1992 S.C.C.R. 531.
[75] *Colhoun v. Friel*, 1996 S.C.C.R. 497; for detailed study of breach of the peace see P. Ferguson "Breach of the Peace and the European Convention of Human Rights" (2001) Edin. L.Rev. Vol. 5, 145.
[76] *McLaughlan v. Boyd*, 1934 J.C. 19.
[77] *Carmichael v. Ashrif*, 1985 S.C.C.R. 461.
[78] (1989) 11 E.H.R.R. 335.
[79] *ibid.*, para. 41.

fall outside the bounds of the Convention. The problem may occur
if the Scots courts seek to extend these boundaries to circumstances
not previously envisaged.

The European Court has decided that the word "penalty" has a
wider meaning than fine or imprisonment; for instance, a penalty
can include confiscation of assets. The courts must be able to assess
for themselves whether a particular measure amounts to a penalty
in fact.

In *Welch v. United Kingdom*[80] the applicant was arrested and
charged in November 1986 with drug trafficking offences. In
January 1987, the Drug Trafficking Offences Act 1986 came into
force. This Act allowed the courts to impose confiscation orders. In
February and May 1987, W was charged with five more offences
and he was eventually tried and convicted in August 1988. A term
of imprisonment was imposed together with a confiscation order.
He maintained that the imposition of the confiscation order was a
retroactive criminal penalty prohibited by Article 7. The government argued that the confiscation order was not a penalty because
its purpose was to deprive the person of his ill-gotten profits and to
prevent their use in future drugs trade. The European Court held
that the starting point for assessing whether or not the confiscation
order was a penalty was to ask whether the measure was imposed
after conviction for a criminal offence. Here the accused had to be
convicted of a drugs trafficking offence before a confiscation order
was imposed. The 1986 Act was designed to prevent the use of
funds for future drug trafficking but it had nonetheless an
additional aim of punishing the offender. The Court considered
that the reality of the situation indicated that the applicant faced a
more far-reaching detriment as a result of the order than any
detriment he faced at the time of the commission of the acts for
which he was convicted. The Court held that there was a breach of
Article 7 in the retrospective application of the 1986 Act; however
the Court stressed that the decision did not question the powers of
confiscation given to courts as a method of fighting the scourge of
drug trafficking.

5.17   The European Court indicated in *Welch* that the factors to be
considered in deciding whether a measure is a penalty would
include: the nature and purpose of the measure; its characterisation
under national law; whether it was imposed following a criminal
conviction; the procedure for making and implementing the
measure; and the severity of the measure.

In *Taylor v. United Kingdom*[81] the Commission declared
inadmissible an argument that a confiscation order, made after

---

[80]   (1995) 20 E.H.R.R. 247.
[81]   [1998] E.H.R.L.R. 90.

the 1986 Act and relating to earlier offences, was a breach of Article 7. The applicant knew when committing the later offences that a confiscation order could be applied. The Court of Appeal (Criminal Division) in England held in *R v. Malik*[82] that there was no breach of Article 7 where a term of imprisonment was imposed for non-compliance with a confiscation order. The default term was simply a means of enforcing the order and did not constitute the imposition of a more severe penalty.

A requirement to register under the Sex Offenders Act 1997 was held not to be a penalty within the meaning of Article 7.[83] The Crime (Sentences) Act 1997, section 2 allows the imposition of a statutory life sentence where an offender has already been convicted of an earlier similar serious offence. The Commission was satisfied that the provisions were preventative in nature only. In *R v. Offen*[84] the Court of Appeal held that Article 7 was not engaged because the statutory sentence was for the second offence not the first. The penalty imposed for the first offence remained the same, so there was no retrospectivity.

An attempt by a convicted prisoner to have the conditions in which he was held declared to be a penalty was rebuffed by the Northern Ireland courts. In *Re Fulton's Application for Judicial Review*[85] the prisoner had been placed in the Punishment and Segregation Unit of the Maze Prison for his own safety. He sought transfer to another prison but this was refused because the prison policy was to house prisoners convicted of terrorist offences in the Maze Prison following the Good Friday Agreement. The prisoner contended that the conditions in which he was held were in breach of Articles 3, 7 and 8. On the issue of Article 7, it was held that the court did not decide on the conditions in which he would be held after conviction and such conditions were not a "penalty" in terms of Article 7. His contentions under Articles 3 and 8 were also dismissed.

5.18

The second sentence of Article 7(1) refers to a prohibition on "a heavier penalty" being imposed than the one applicable at the time the offence was committed. It is assumed in both Scots and English law that a statute increasing a penalty for an offence will not take effect retrospectively unless there is clear statutory language indicating that it does. However, it should be remembered that while this may be the case in domestic law, such provisions may still be incompatible with the Convention, as in *Welch v. United Kingdom*.[86] Since 1995 and the *Welch* decision, the United

---

[82] *The Times*, May 30, 2000.
[83] *Ibbotson v. United Kingdom* [1999] E.H.R.L.R. 218, EComHR.
[84] November 9, 2000.
[85] [2000] N.I. 447.
[86] (1995) 20 E.H.R.R. 247.

Kingdom Government has tried to ensure the avoidance of any provision which might be construed as a retrospective increase in punishment. Thus in the Proceeds of Crime Act 1995, the power to make confiscation orders for non-drug trafficking offences will apply only if every offence of which the accused is convicted in the same proceedings was committed on or after the commencement date of the Act.

CONCLUSION

5.19 The prohibition on retrospectivity may cause problems within the United Kingdom jurisdictions. For instance, an offence may have been committed several years before the person is charged and brought to trial. DNA testing has become highly advanced and increasingly accurate and many cases are now being solved as a result of the scrutiny and testing of physical evidence gathered at the time of the offence. The prosecution may therefore have to be conducted under the legislative provisions which were in force at the time of the offence but which are now repealed. Sentencing legislation in Scotland and particularly in England is continually being enacted. Almost as soon as one statute is brought into force a new bill is introduced to Parliament. Prosecution authorities face an unenviable task ensuring that an accused is prosecuted under the legislation pertaining at the time of the offence and the sentencing authority will also have to ensure that the sentence imposed is no greater than that which would have been applicable at the time of the offence.

CHAPTER 6

RIGHTS IN CRIMINAL LAW: PART II

ARTICLE 6(3)

"Everyone charged with a criminal offence has the following minimum rights:

(a) to be informed promptly, in a language which he understands and in detail, of the nature and cause of the accusation against him;
(b) to have adequate time and facilities for the preparation of his defence;
(c) to defend himself in person or through legal assistance of his own choosing or, if he has not sufficient means to pay for legal assistance, to be given it free when the interests of justice so require;
(d) to examine and have examined witnesses against him and to obtain the attendance and examination of witnesses on his behalf under the same conditions as witnesses against him;
(e) to have the free assistance of an interpreter if he cannot understand or speak the language used in court."

"States must ensure that everyone charged with a criminal offence benefits from the safeguards provided by Article 6(3)."[1]

The minimum rights espoused by this part of Article 6 are not 6.01 unknown to the domestic law of Scotland and England and have been recognised as being established in Scots law long before the implementation of the Human Rights Act and the Scotland Act.[2]

---

[1] *Vacher v. France* (1996) 24 E.H.R.R. 482 at para. 28.
[2] See *Anderson v. H.M.Advocate* 1996 S.C.C.R. 114.

The rights are also found in other international conventions, such as the International Convention on Civil and Political Rights, Article 14(1)(a) and are guaranteed by organisations such as the United Nations Human Rights Committee.

This part of Article 6 is closely connected with the first and second paragraphs and it gives the basic rights which must be available if the trial is to be considered fair. It applies only to criminal actions and applies to persons who have been charged and are subject to criminal proceedings. It will apply to people who have been convicted but not yet sentenced.[3]

To some extent, the European Court has taken a broad view of what constitutes a "criminal offence". In *Benham v. United Kingdom*[4] the Court said that three criteria had to be taken into account when deciding whether a person is "charged with a criminal offence" for Article 6 purposes. These are:

- the classification of the proceedings in national law;
- the nature of the proceedings; and
- the nature and degree of severity of the penalty.

The case was concerned with the imprisonment of the applicant for non-payment of the community charge. He complained, *inter alia,* that legal aid had not been available to him during the committal hearings before the magistrates' court. The European Court held that there had been a breach of Article 6(3)(c) when taken with Article 6(1). The nature of the proceedings and the punitive penalty of up to three months' imprisonment suggested it was a criminal offence. The law on the community charge was complex and the applicant had no entitlement to be legally represented. This suggested that he should have had the benefit of free legal representation particularly since his liberty was at stake.

6.02   The rights of Article 6(3) will apply to children as well as adults. In *Re M (a child)*[5] an application for a secure accommodation order under the Children Act 1989 section 25 was held not to be a criminal charge within the meaning of Article 6(3). The section 25 jurisdiction is protective and at common law the child is entitled to the five specific minimum rights described in Article 6(3) however the application is classified.

The minimum rights protected by Article 6(3) are not, however, absolute but a breach of them may be an indication that Article 6(1) has been violated. The right to a fair trial in Article 6(1) is considered to be absolute and therefore any breach of another part

---

[3]   *X. v. U.K.* (1972) 15 Yearbook 394.
[4]   (1996) 22 E.H.R.R. 293.
[5]   [2001] EWCA Civ. 458.

of Article 6 may be sufficient to show that the proceedings were not fair. In *Procurator Fiscal of Dunfermline and H.M.Advocate General for Scotland v. Brown*[6] Lord Steyn said "[o]nce it has been determined that the guarantee of a fair trial has been breached, it is never possible to justify such a breach by reference to the public interest or on any other ground."

Article 6(3)(a)—the right to be informed of the charge

The wording of this paragraph is similar to that of Article 5(2), which applies to persons who have been arrested. This paragraph applies after a charge has been made and it requires the accused to be given detailed information of the nature and cause of the accusation which has been made against him. The purpose of the paragraph is to enable the accused to begin preparing his defence.[7] If the offence is specific in nature, it may be sufficient to provide a brief description of the offence, the date, place and the alleged victim.[8] Otherwise, the Convention requires detailed information to be provided. In *Pelissier v. France*[9] the European Court held that the paragraph requires the defendant to be informed not only of the cause of the accusation, *i.e.* the acts he is alleged to have committed, but also the legal characterisation given to those acts. 6.03

> "The provision of full, detailed information concerning the charges against the defence and consequently the legal characterisation that the court might adopt in the matter, is an essential prerequisite for ensuring that the proceedings are fair."[10]

The amount of detail required will depend on the circumstances of the case. Thus where the charge gives a period in which the offence is alleged to have occurred rather than a specific date, this will satisfy the requirements of the Article. The High Court of Justiciary remarked in *McLean v. H.M.Advocate*[11] that "there will be many cases in which the Crown cannot know the precise date on which a crime was committed". So long as a time frame is indicated and this is specific enough to allow the accused to prepare a defence, then the Convention requirement will be satisfied.

In *Mattoccia v. Italy*[12] the applicant was convicted of rape. The charge had stated that the rape had occurred "in Rome in

---

[6] 2001 S.L.T. 59.
[7] *G.S.M. v. Austria* (1983) 34 D.R. 119.
[8] *Brozicek v. Italy* (1989) 12 E.H.R.R. 371.
[9] March 25, 1999, ECtHR.
[10] *ibid.,* para. 52.
[11] November 3, 1999.
[12] [2001] E.H.R.L.R. 89.

November 1985" but no further specification of the date and place
was given. The applicant contended that the charge was too vague
and he was unable to defend himself. The European Court stated
that the provision of full detailed information was "an essential
prerequisite to ensure that the proceedings were fair. The extent of
detailed information would vary depending on the particular
circumstances of each case."[13] The Court also found a violation
of Article 6(3)(b) in that the inadequacy of the information of the
charge had not given the applicant sufficient time to prepare his
defence. The government authorities had been in possession of
further information on the date and place of the alleged incident but
this was not given to the applicant.

The accused person cannot use a clerical error to escape
prosecution where it was obvious to all parties that an error had
been made. In *Gea Catalan v. Spain*[14] the applicant had been
charged with obtaining property by deception. In pre-trial
submissions, the prosecutor referred to a statutory aggravation of
the offence but a typing error gave the wrong Article of the
Criminal Code. The European Court held that the applicant could
not claim that he had not been informed of all the components of
the charge against him when the prosecution case was obvious from
the pre-trial submissions.

Article 6(3)(b)—the right to have time to prepare the defence

6.04   The Article assumes that information will be made available to the
accused and it is obvious that it is necessary for a fair trial that the
accused has the right to see any and all material before the trial,
where this may help him to establish his innocence. The issue is one
of "equality of arms".[15] The prosecution has greater facilities for
investigation than the defence and so the accused person should be
able to see all relevant information which has been or could be
collected by the prosecuting authorities. The Commission maintained in *Jespers* that the authorities must be under an obligation to
gather evidence in favour of the accused as well as against him. In
Edwards v. United Kingdom[16] the applicant argued that the police
had failed to disclose two pieces of evidence at his trial. The first
was the evidence of a witness who had maintained that she would
be able to recognise her assailant but had then failed to recognise
him from a photograph. The second was the existence of a set of
fingerprints found at the scene of the crime. The European Court
held that it was "a requirement of fairness under Article 6(1),

---

[13]   [2001] E.H.R.L.R 86, p.90.
[14]   (1995) 20 E.H.R.R. 266.
[15]   See *Jespers v. Belgium* (1981) 27 D.R. 61.
[16]   (1992) 15 E.H.R.R. 417.

indeed one which is recognised under English law, that the prosecution authorities disclose to the defence all material evidence for or against the accused".[17] The Court concluded that there had been a violation of both domestic law and Article 6 at the trial stage. However, this defect was remedied before the appeal stage and thus Article 6 was not violated overall.

It can be argued that the right under Article 6(3)(b) will have effect "throughout the proceedings" and will mean that the accused person has the right to disclosure of evidence during interrogation, pre-trial interviews, the trial itself and any appeal hearings. When a person is questioned by the police, it would obviously be helpful to the person to know what evidence the police has against him so that he can counter the accusations. However, from the police point of view, it is better if the suspect does not know everything and if in fact he can be led to believe that the police know more than they do. The police are therefore able to exert great influence, perhaps even coercion, on the suspect and thus encourage him to confess. In the seminal decision of *Miranda v. Arizona*[18] the United States Supreme Court acknowledged that custodial interrogation was "created for no other purpose than to subjugate the individual to the will of the examiner". The European Convention seeks to equalise the balance of resources between the police and the suspect. The jurisprudence of the European Court indicates that the safeguards of Article 6 apply to pre-trial investigations including custodial interrogation. The Article applies to people subject to a criminal charge and the word "charge" has been interpreted by the European Court as "the official notification given to an individual by the competent authority of an allegation that he has committed a criminal offence".[19] In both Scots and English law the notification could be constituted by arrest or charge by the police or the receipt of a summons to attend a district or magistrates' court.[20]

The European Court has interpreted the wording of Article 6(3)(b) in respect of "adequate facilities" as meaning that the accused must have access to the results of investigations undertaken throughout the proceedings.[21] In *Jespers v. Belgium*[22] the European Commission stated that investigating and prosecuting authorities were obliged to disclose to the accused any information which might assist him in exonerating himself or obtaining a reduction in

---

[17] (1992) 15 E.H.R.R. 417, para. 36.
[18] 384 US 436 (1966).
[19] *Corigliano v. Italy*, A 57 (1982) at para. 34.
[20] For discussion see R. Toney "Disclosure of Evidence and legal assistance at custodial interrogation: what does the European Convention on Human Rights require?" (2001) *International Journal of Evidence and Proof*, Vol. 5(1) 39.
[21] *Can v. Austria*, A 96 (1985) Comm. Report para. 53.
[22] (1981) 27 D.R. 61.

sentence. The Commission has further stated that a strict approach should be taken where the prosecuting authorities wilfully suppressed evidence.

6.05   In *Jasper v. United Kingdom*[23] the prosecution withheld certain documents on the grounds of public interest immunity and sought an *ex parte* application to the court to uphold the public interest immunity certificate. The defence was informed of the application but not of the contents of the materials to be withheld. The trial court allowed the defence to indicate the nature of their defence so that the trial judge could assess whether any of the documents included evidence material to the defence. The documents were withheld. The European Court held that there was no violation of the Article 6 right to disclosure in this case because there had been substantial procedural safeguards to assure overall fairness to the accused. From this decision it is clear that the Convention requires that there are identifiable procedural safeguards for the suspect at the interrogation. However, it is also clear that the Convention is concerned with the effect of the procedural safeguards on the overall fairness of the proceedings.[24]

The right to see information held by the prosecution is limited by a need to ensure the rights of others. Thus, in *Hardiman v. United Kingdom*[25] the Commission held that the applicant did not have the right to see the prison psychiatric reports of a co-accused even though it may have had potential relevance to the credibility of the co-accused's testimony. Such reports were not referred to normally unless a medical issue arose. In addition the co-accused had not been cautioned and did not have legal representation while meeting with the psychiatrist. Non-disclosure was not unfair or arbitrary.

In Scotland, the courts considered that the Crown has a duty to disclose any information to the defence that tended to exculpate the accused. In addition the Crown is required to disclose information or evidence which the defence considers to be material to their case. The defence however has to explain why the evidence is significant to the defence.[26] If the prosecution declines to release the information or evidence, the defence may petition the court for the recovery of the documents. It is, however, a fairly rare occurrence for such a petition to be made. In *Maan, Petitioner*[27] the petitioner sought recovery of parts of the criminal records of some prosecution witnesses. He intended to plead self-defence to a charge of assault. The High Court of Justiciary held that the Crown had a duty to disclose information which might exculpate the

[23]   Appl. 27052/95, February 16, 2000.
[24]   *Murray v. U.K.* (1996) 22 E.H.R.R. 29.
[25]   [1996] E.H.R.L.R. 425.
[26]   *McLeod v. H.M.Advocate (No. 2),* 1998 S.L.T. 233.
[27]   2001 G.W.D. 6–194.

accused and this included information bearing directly or indirectly on the guilt or innocence of the accused.[28] This would include information tending to undermine the credibility of Crown witnesses.[29] If the information was relevant to a legitimate attack on the character or credibility of the witness and thus relevant to the defence, the accused was entitled to have it disclosed prior to the trial to allow for proper preparation. In addition it was unsatisfactory for the defence to have to rely on the Crown to intervene or to rely on the judgment of the prosecutor.

In England, the prosecution is required under the Criminal 6.06 Procedure and Investigations Act 1996, section 3 to disclose automatically any material not previously disclosed which, in the prosecution's opinion, might undermine the prosecution case against the accused. When the defence case statement is received by the prosecution, the prosecution must then disclose any prosecution material which may reasonably be expected to assist the accused's defence as disclosed in the defence case statement. However, the 1996 Act also provides that comments and inference may be drawn where the accused gives evidence which differs from the contents of the defence statement.

The 1996 Act refers to the prosecution and to the situation where the accused either pleads not guilty or is indicted and committed for trial. The Act does not therefore cover the disclosure of evidence during the police questioning phase of an investigation (discussed above). This would appear to leave a suspect unprotected. In *R v. Argent*[30] the Chief Justice noted that the police disclosure was more limited than in normal circumstances but dismissed the defence argument that this had interfered with the defence lawyer's ability to advise her client fully. This case, His Lordship noted, was not a very complex one but the situation might be different if it had been complex. In *R v. Imran and Hussein*[31] the Court of Appeal stated that the police were under a duty not to actively mislead a suspect but rejected a defence submission that the police are required to fully disclose their evidence under the Criminal Justice and Public Order Act 1994, sections 34 to 37.

In *Rowe and Davis v. United Kingdom*[32] the European Court recognised that the entitlement to have relevant evidence disclosed is not an absolute right. The case involved evidence which was withheld on the authority of public interest immunity certificates. The judgment, the first in which such public interest immunity certificates were considered, mentioned three "compelling interests"

---

[28] See also *H.M.Advocate v. Ward*, 1993 S.C.C.R. 595.
[29] *Jespers v. Belgium* (1981) 27 D.R. 61.
[30] [1997] 2 Cr. App. R. 27.
[31] [1997] Crim. L. R. 754.
[32] (2000) 30 E.H.R.R. 1.

which might lead to the withholding of evidence: national security, protection of witnesses and preserving secrecy in police investigations. Any restrictions on the rights of the defence should be "strictly necessary" and "sufficiently counter-balanced by procedures followed by judicial authorities". In this respect the procedure in *Rowe and Davis* was unsatisfactory. "The prosecutor's failure to lay the evidence in question before the trial judge and permit him to rule on the question of disclosure deprived the applicants of a fair trial."

6.07   The "preparation of his defence" will include the preparation of an appeal against conviction. The convicted person must be given details of any time limits regarding the lodging of the appeal[33] and, in order to prepare his appeal properly, he has to know the basis upon which he was convicted. In other words, he has to know the judge's reasons. This raises a difficulty in respect of appeals under Scots law, particularly where the person is convicted of a summary offence in either the sheriff or district courts. Normally the sheriff or justice of the peace will not give detailed reasons for the decision at the time of handing down the verdict. If the accused subsequently appeals against the conviction, the judge will prepare a stated case in which the findings of fact and the reasoning for the verdict will be given in detail. However, the accused must indicate his grounds for appeal before the stated case is prepared. The European Commission found that the failure of a court of first instance to provide reasons for its decision until after the appeal was lodged amounted to a violation of Articles 6(1) and 6(3)(b). However, the European Court subsequently found no violation on the lack of access to a written copy of the fully reasoned first instance judgment.[34] In an earlier case, the trial court's reasons were made available on appeal but the appeal exposed the applicant to a risk of an increased sentence.[35] This was found by the European Court to be incompatible with Article 6. In United Kingdom criminal appeals, it is open to the appeal court to increase or reduce the sentence given by the trial court.

The giving of reasons is gradually becoming more commonplace in United Kingdom courts but it is still not necessarily regarded as a duty. In *R v. Higher Education Funding Council, ex parte Institute of Dental Surgery*,[36] Justice Sedley tried to define when there was a common law duty to give reasons. Although the case involves public law issues, his comments are still wide enough to encompass this discussion. He said:

---

[33] *Vacher v. France* (1996) 24 E.H.R.R. 482.
[34] *Zoon v. The Netherlands*, Appl. 29202/95 [2001] E.H.R.L.R. 17.
[35] *Hadjianastassiou v. Greece* [1993] 16 E.H.R.R. 219.
[36] [1994] 1 W.L.R. 242.

"There is no general duty to give reasons for a decision, but there are classes of case where there is a duty. One such class is were the subject matter is an interest so highly regarded by the law (e.g. personal liberty) that fairness requires that reasons . . . be given as of right."

Article 6(3)(c)—Right to defend oneself or have legal assistance

The right to defend oneself suggests that one must be allowed to be 6.08 present in court in order to put that defence. However, the European Court has taken the view that trial in absence is not incompatible with Article 6(3)(c) if the person is able to seek a fresh determination of the charges against him.[37] If there is a trial or other proceedings at which the accused is not present, the court must ensure that the accused's legal counsel is given the opportunity to defend the accused in his absence.[38]

The right to conduct one's own defence is inherent in Article 6(3)(c). Although the old adage of "he who defends himself has a fool for a client" is probably correct, nonetheless it is still open to an accused to examine and cross-examine witnesses. In summary trials where the offence is a minor one, it is possible that the accused will not qualify for legal aid and will therefore be forced to represent himself. However, the Convention is clear that free legal assistance should be available "where the interests of justice so require" and certainly Scots law has long made provision for legal aid to be available where an accused is in danger of losing his liberty. For instance, a system of free legal aid for the poor was instituted in Scotland in 1424 and a system of assistance was available through the Faculty of Advocates until 1950 when the modern legal aid scheme was implemented.[39]

The "interests of justice" will involve consideration of the complexity of the case, the ability of the accused to present his case unaided and the severity of any possible penalty.[40]

In recent times, the issue of "self-representation" has arisen in 6.09 both Scotland and England where men accused of rape and other serious sexual offences have dismissed their lawyers and cross-examined the alleged victims personally.[41] The English legal response to the "abuse" of the right to represent oneself was to take away the right. The Youth Justice and Criminal Evidence Act

---

[37] *Poitrimol v. France* (1994) 18 E.H.R.R. 130; *Dombo Beheer B.V. v. The Netherlands* (1993) 18 E.H.R.R. 213.
[38] *Lala v. The Netherlands* (1994) 18 E.H.R.R. 586.
[39] See D. Walker, *The Scottish Legal System* (8th ed., W. Green & Son, Edinburgh, 2001).
[40] *Benham v. U.K.* (1996) 22 E.H.R.R. 293.
[41] *E.g.* a woman was subjected to six days of cross-examination by her attacker, Ralston Edwards.

1999 has removed the right of a person charged with a sexual offence to cross-examine in person the alleged victim in connection with that or any other offence with which he is charged in the same criminal proceedings. Section 34 of the Act allows the court to prevent the accused from cross-examining the complainant and section 35 prevents such cross-examination of child complainants and child witnesses. It is possible to prevent the cross-examination by the accused of other witnesses where "it is in the interests of justice".[42] If the accused is banned from questioning a witness, section 38 provides for a legal representative to be appointed by the court. The judge may issue a warning to the jury not to be prejudiced by this procedure being carried out.

The European Court ruled in *Croissant v. Germany*[43] that the accused's right under Article 6(3)(c) was not an absolute one, and it can be restricted if there is sufficient justification for doing so. However, the restriction must be to the minimum extent necessary. In *X v. Austria*[44] the Commission commented that Article 6(3)(c) "does not confer on the person charged . . . the right to decide in what way provision should be made for his defence". The decision remained with the "competent authorities" and the court's task was "to ascertain whether the method they [the competent authorities] have chosen is consistent with the requirements of a fair trial". The right is to have an adequate defence available and not to have the right to personally cross-examine witnesses. In *Imbrioscia v. Switzerland*[45] the Court observed that the Article did not specify how the right is to be exercised and it is up to the State to choose how the right is to be secured. This might be through legal assistance or by allowing the accused to defend himself in person. Whatever method is chosen by the state it must comply with the requirements of a fair trial.

The European Court in *Croissant* held that the right could be restricted if it was in the interests of justice to do so. Both the European Court and the Commission recognised that trials for rape or serious sexual offences were different because of the effect of giving evidence on the victim. If the victim is cross-examined by the accused, the ordeal is compounded. The Commission in *Baegen v. The Netherlands*[46] commented that in ensuring the accused's right to a fair trial, account has to be taken of the victim's right to respect for her private life. "The Commission accepts that in criminal proceedings regarding sexual abuse certain measures may be taken for the purpose of protecting the victim, provided that such

---

[42]   1999 Act, ss. 36–37.
[43]   (1992) 16 E.H.R.R. 135.
[44]   (1968) 11 Yearbook 322.
[45]   (1993) 17 E.H.R.R. 441.
[46]   1994, unreported.

measures can be reconciled with an adequate and effective exercise of the rights of the defence." In *Baegen* the victim of a rape had been allowed to remain anonymous both to the accused and his lawyer. The investigating judge had examined her and asked her questions submitted previously by the defence lawyer. The Commission held that there had been no breach of Article 6(1) or 6(3)(a) because the applicant had been "sufficiently informed".

Following two Scottish trials in 1999 and 2000 where the accused personally cross-examined their victims[47] the Scottish Executive made it clear that there would be no immediate change in the law because of the possible difficulties with Convention rights. However, in November 2000, the Scottish Executive published a consultation paper "*Redressing the Balance*" which contained proposals to prevent the cross-examination of witnesses by the accuse himself, and the Sexual Offences (Procedure and Evidence) (Scotland) Act 2002 was passed on March 6, 2002.   6.10

Currently, where an accused is indicted with rape or any other serious sexual offence, the accused may examine in person any witness, including the alleged victim. The court has the right to intervene where the questioning is either abusive or is designed to obtain inadmissible evidence. However, the line between acceptable questioning and that which is unacceptable may be a fine one and the accused will usually receive the benefit of any doubt. The Bill proposes to ensure that such a confrontation between the accused and his accuser cannot occur, to minimise the distress and humiliation to the victim but also to ensure the rights of the accused in presenting a robust defence to the charge. Upon arresting a man for an offence of the type stated in the Bill, the police will give the accused an oral warning that he will require to be legally represented at any trial and if he fails to appoint a solicitor, the court will do so. This warning will be given in writing when the accused is indicted or cited to appear in court. Further warnings will be given at the first appearance in court. A mandatory hearing will be introduced to ensure that the accused is legally represented. The court will appoint a solicitor if the accused has failed or refused to do so. Provision will be made under the legal aid provisions to identify solicitors who are willing to act for such an unrepresented accused and legal aid will automatically be available. The appointed solicitor is required to seek his client's instructions but if these are not forthcoming then the solicitor has to proceed to represent the accused to the best of his ability given the material available. The accused has no power to dismiss a court-appointed solicitor or counsel.

---

[47] *McFadyen v. Austin*, February 1999, unreported; and *H.M.Advocate v. Anderson*, June 2000, unreported.

The Bill lists the types of offences to be covered by the ban. The list duplicates an existing list found in the Criminal Procedure (Scotland) Act 1995, section 274(2) which prevents evidence being led of the complainer's sexual habits and experience. The list is not intended to be exhaustive and the Bill gives power to the Scottish Ministers to vary the list as necessary to reflect developments in the law.

6.11   The proposals in the Bill differ from the practice adopted in England and Wales under the Youth Justice and Criminal Evidence Act 1999, where the accused is able to self-represent except in the cross-examination of the victim and certain other witnesses. For this cross-examination the court may appoint a legal representative. The Scots legislation will require the accused to be legally represented throughout the trial, not just for the cross-examination of the victim. The Scottish Executive, in the Policy Memorandum published with the Bill, gave the reason for the different procedure. In England and Wales, there is more pre-trial disclosure of statements and evidence than in Scotland where much of the evidence is disclosed orally in court. A court-appointed lawyer drafted in for the cross-examination would not have heard all the evidence and the accused would therefore be disadvantaged. The Memorandum also pointed out that the complainer would be "marked out" by the different procedure being used for her evidence and this might disadvantage the accused by drawing extra attention to her evidence. This might prejudice the accused to the extent of undermining the presumption of innocence under Article 6(2) of the Convention.

The wording of Article 6(3)(c) stipulates that there should be legal assistance of the accused's "own choosing" and the Scottish Bill does not appear to meet that requirement. However, the Bill gives the accused the opportunity at various times to appoint his own solicitor and it is only when he fails or refuses to do so that a solicitor is appointed. In *Croissant v. Germany* the European Court had commented on the use of court appointed counsel, pointing out that "the national courts must certainly have regard to the defendant's wishes . . . However they can override these wishes when there are relevant and sufficient grounds for holding that this is necessary in the interests of justice".[48]

It has been argued that the right to defend oneself in person or through legal assistance of one's own choosing means that there is a right to have a solicitor present at any interview conducted by the police. In Scotland, at common law and by statute, a person who is detained or arrested by the police does not have the right to have

---

[48]   *supra* no.43, para. 29.

their solicitor present at any interview. The Criminal Procedure (Scotland) Act 1995, section 17 gives an arrested person the right to immediate access to a solicitor and the right to have a "private interview" before examination or appearance in court. This, however, comes too late to have an impact on the questioning made by the police and the right relates to legal advice on the future court process. In practice, the lack of legal advice during police interview may cause difficulty for the prosecution, since there is greater likelihood of evidence being declared inadmissible.[49] A person detained has the right under section 15 of the 1995 Act to have a solicitor informed that he has been detained but it is then up to the solicitor to decide whether or not he will attend at the police station to interview his client. The solicitor does have the right to attend any identification parade and there are exceptional rights available where the solicitor's client has been charged with murder, attempted murder or culpable homicide.

In *H.M.Advocate v. Robb*[50] the High Court of Justiciary 6.12 discussed the decision reached by the European Court of Human Rights in *Murray v. United Kingdom*[51] and concluded that the case turned on the particular legal regime of Northern Ireland and could not therefore be extrapolated to Scotland. In *Paton v. Ritchie*[52] the High Court held that Article 6(3)(c) did not create a universal right to have access to a solicitor before or during questioning by the police. However, in *Condron v. United Kingdom*[53] the European Court observed that the presence of a solicitor at the interview was a "particularly important safeguard"[54] for dispelling any compulsion to speak which the caution may have encouraged. The denial of access to a solicitor within the first 24 hours of detention generally was considered in *Averill v. United Kingdom*[55] to be a violation of Article 6(3)(c). "The concept of fairness enshrined in Article 6 requires that the accused has the benefit of the assistance of a lawyer already at the initial stages of police interrogation."[56]

The security legislation in place in Northern Ireland was further challenged in *Magee v. United Kingdom*[57] where the applicant was arrested in connection with terrorist activities. He requested his solicitor but this was refused under the Northern Ireland (Emergency Provisions) Act 1987. Over the course of two days, he was interviewed eight times. In the sixth interview he broke his

---

[49] *Forbes v. H.M.Advocate*, 1990 S.C.C.R. 69.
[50] 1999 S.C.C.R. 971.
[51] (1996) 22 E.H.R.R. 29.
[52] 2000 S.L.T. 239.
[53] (2001) 31 E.H.R.R. 1.
[54] *ibid.*, para. 60.
[55] (2001) 31 E.H.R.R. 36.
[56] *ibid.*, para. 57. See also *Magee v. U.K.* (2001) 31 E.H.R.R. 35.
[57] (2001) 31 E.H.R.R. 822.

silence and gave detailed answers including a full confession of his part in the conspiracy to bomb military personnel. After this interview he was allowed access to his solicitor. He complained about ill-treatment during the various interviews although there was no medical evidence to support these. He complained to the European Court alleging breach of Articles 6(1) and 6(3)(c). The European Court found violations of both parts of Article 6, saying that access to a solicitor should have been available during the initial stages of the interrogation to "provide a counterweight to the intimidating atmosphere".

The applicant may choose a lawyer or have one appointed for him under a legal aid scheme. That lawyer must be able to act for the applicant and provide effective representation. The European Court has indicated that the state is not responsible for the quality of the representation unless it is apparent that it is poor or it is brought to the attention of the state in some way. However, if a lawyer appointed under legal aid fails to represent the accused effectively, the state is required under Article 6(3)(c) to intervene.[58] The domestic court should ensure that the defence lawyer has sufficient time and facilities to prepare for the case, including adjourning the case if necessary.[59] If the accused and his lawyer cannot agree on the line of the defence, the accused should be allowed time to seek another lawyer. He should not be required to proceed unrepresented.[60]

6.13   Another aspect of this sub-paragraph is that communications between the accused and his lawyer should be confidential. Thus in *S v. Switzerland*[61] the European Court held that if the lawyer and client could not communicate without surveillance, this would remove much of the usefulness of the lawyer's assistance. The Convention is intended to guarantee rights that are practical and effective. It may, however, be legitimate to intercept lawyer/client communications where crime or disorder is feared.

Finally, in two recently decided cases before the European Court, the State of Belgium was found to be in breach of Articles 6(1) and 6(3)(c) because the Court of Cassation had refused to allow the applicants' lawyers to represent them because they had failed to surrender to custody.[62]

The availability of legal aid in appeals was considered in *Granger v. United Kingdom*.[63] That decision of the European Court found that the refusal of legal aid and representation during an appeal

[58] *Kamasinski v. Austria* (1989) 13 E.H.R.R. 36; *Artico v. Italy* (1981) 3 E.H.R.R. 1.
[59] *Goddi v. Italy* (1984) 6 E.H.R.R. 457.
[60] *Venters v. H.M.Advocate*, 1999 S.L.T. 1345.
[61] (1992) 14 E.H.R.R. 670.
[62] *Goedhart v. Belgium; Stroek v. Belgium* [2001] E.H.R.L.R. 373.
[63] (1990) 12 E.H.R.R. 469.

hearing was contrary to the Convention. The position in Scotland at the time was that anyone convicted had an automatic right of appeal to the High Court of Justiciary; there was no need for leave of the court or requirement to show probable cause. However, there was such a requirement if the person was to obtain legal aid. If the grounds of appeal failed to meet the criterion that there was a reasonable prospect of success, the person would not receive legal aid and would have to represent himself before the court. The Crown however would be represented by an Advocate Depute. The European Court found that such practices violated Article 6(3)(c).[64]

As a result of these cases, the Criminal Procedure (Scotland) Act 6.14 1995 contained provisions to end the automatic right of appeal. The appellant must now seek leave to appeal and if this is granted legal aid and representation will automatically become available.[65]

Where a person charged with an offence requires legal aid to prepare and present his defence, this is available in all Scottish criminal courts.[66] However in Edinburgh Sheriff Court and Edinburgh District Court, the accused may not be able to choose his own solicitor.

The Public Defence Solicitor's Office was set up as a pilot scheme in 1998 to try to reduce the costs of legal aid. In order to ensure that accused people used the scheme, originally those accused who had their birthdays in January or February were directed to the public defence solicitor. If they did not wish the public defence solicitor they had to give good reason and obtain a waiver of direction. Since July 2000, this direction has been removed and an accused person may choose to have a public defence solicitor or a solicitor from a private firm. The European Court has recognised that an accused does not have an unqualified right to choose their own lawyer where legal aid is provided.[67]

Article 6(3)(c) refers to "legal assistance" and this raises the question as to whether the legal assistance has to be given by someone who is legally qualified. The European Court has not stipulated this requirement but it is apparent that the assistance must be "effective assistance". In England, it is the practice of many law firms to send a clerk or trainee to assist clients in the custodial interrogation phase of the investigation. Although this can be detrimental to the client's interest it is no more detrimental than a qualified lawyer acquiescing in the hostile style of questioning sometimes adopted by the police, or recommending a guilty plea to

---

[64] See also: *Boner v. U.K.* (1995) 19 E.H.R.R. 246; *Maxwell v. U.K.* (1995) 19 E.H.R.R. 97.
[65] 1995 Act, s.42.
[66] Legal Aid (Scotland) Act 1986 as amended by the Legal Aid Act 1988.
[67] *Croissant v. Germany, supra* no.43.

ensure a "through-flow"' of legal aid funding.[68] The courts have the ability to quash a conviction on the grounds of the flagrant incompetence of the defence counsel but the conduct of the counsel would have to be very obviously incompetent.

6.15   The granting of free legal aid is subject to "the interests of justice". In *McDermitt v. United Kingdom*[69] a stipendiary magistrate had refused an application for legal aid where the applicant was accused of breach of the peace and assaulting a police officer. The magistrate considered that, as a matter of policy, the "interests of justice" did not apply to such charges. The government accepted that the application for legal aid had not been dealt with appropriately and a friendly settlement was reached.

The availability of legal aid was also discussed by the European Court in *Benham v. United Kingdom*[70] and more recently in *Perks v. United Kingdom.*[71] In *Benham* the Court had found that there was a breach of Article 6(3)(c) because legal aid had not been available to the applicant at the committal hearing in the magistrates' court and he had been imprisoned for non-payment of the community charge. In *Perks,* the applicant had failed to pay a community charge bill and was not legally represented at the magistrates' court hearing. Legal aid was not available to him despite the government having assured the Court that it was available in such cases.

The Scottish courts have come close to finding the government's legal aid rules contrary to Article 6(3)(c). Regulations made in 1999 set up a system of fixed fee payments for criminal legal aid work in summary complaints.[72] In *Buchanan v. McLean*[73] Lord Prosser referred to concerns from the defence that the fixed fee payment was insufficient to pay for a robust defence. He said:

> "The concerns of an individual accused, if founded upon facts which objectively justify such concerns, might in our opinion provide a sufficient basis for saying that there was a breach of Article 6(3)(c). But again this would depend on the particular facts of particular cases."

In the event, the court found that the accused's defence had not been prejudiced by the restriction on the fee paid, but the prospect of such a finding in the future was raised by Lord Prosser's statement.

6.16   The Scottish Parliament passed the Convention Rights (Com-

---

[68] R. Toney, *supra* no.20.
[69] (1985) 52 D.R. 244.
[70] (1996) 22 E.H.R.R. 293.
[71] (2000) E.H.R.L.R. 190.
[72] Criminal Legal Aid (Fixed Payments) (Scotland) Regulations 1999 (S.I. 1999 No.491).
[73] 2000 S.L.T. 928.

pliance) (Scotland) Act 2001, Part 3 of which has made amendments to the provision of legal aid. The Act adds new subsections to section 33 of the Legal Aid (Scotland) Act 1986. The new provisions allow a solicitor to ask the Scottish Legal Aid Board for a waiver from fixed fees where prescribed conditions exist that such fixed fees would prevent the client from receiving a fair trial. The kind of cases where such a waiver would be necessary would include cases where there were a large number of prosecution witnesses to be interviewed, or where the services of an interpreter were required, or where one of the participants (complainer, accused or eye-witness) had a profound learning difficulty or is mentally ill. The preparation of a defence in these circumstances would be time-consuming and therefore expensive.

The rules applying to the system of children's hearing also had to be changed after the Court of Session found that there was a requirement for legal representation for the child where deprivation of liberty was at stake. In *S v. Miller (No. 1)*[74] the key consideration was whether the person involved in the litigation could effectively conduct their own case and the lack of free legal representation could significantly impair the child's ability to affect the outcome of the proceedings.

Article 6(3)(d)—Examination of witnesses   6.17

The principle of this sub-paragraph is again that of equality of arms, *i.e.* the accused must have the same opportunity to prepare and present his case as the prosecution. The right to cross-examine witnesses may be subject to conditions and restrictions so long as they apply equally to both sides. Witness anonymity may not accord with this sub-paragraph but the European Court has left some discretion to the national court in its interpretation.

The European Court has taken the view that, while the provision is specifically stated in the Convention, there will be no breach if the overall procedure was conducted fairly.[75] Moreover, in *Doorson v. The Netherlands*[76] the Court noted that although the interests of witnesses and victims were not specifically covered by Article 6, such people were protected by other provisions of the Convention, including Article 8. Article 8 implies that the state should organise its criminal proceedings to ensure that the interests of victims and witnesses are not unjustifiably imperilled. It may be more likely that the defence will be able to cross-examine a witness in person where the witness is an undercover officer.[77]

---

[74] 2001 S.L.T. 531.
[75] *Asch v. Austria* (1993) 15 E.H.R.R. 597.
[76] (1996) 22 E.H.R.R. 330.
[77] *Van Mechelen v. The Netherlands* [1998] E.H.R.L.R. 517.

The accused is entitled to examine witnesses against him; this implies that hearsay evidence is excluded. In *Unterpertinger v. Austria*[78] the two victims of assault made statements to the police but declined to give evidence. The applicant was convicted mainly on the basis of those statements. The European Court held that the applicant had not had a fair trial under Article 6(1) and 6(3)(d). The Austrian Court had treated the statements as proof of the accusations whereas the European Court referred to them as "information". The European Court however indicated that the reading out of the statements was not, *per se*, inconsistent with the Convention.

6.18   In Scotland, the law relating to hearsay is found in section 259 of the Criminal Procedure (Scotland) Act 1995. The Act gives exceptions to the rule that hearsay evidence is inadmissible. Thus evidence of a statement made by a person may be admissible if the judge is satisfied that the person is not able for a reason given in section 259(2) to give evidence in person, and the evidence would have been admissible if given in person, and there is evidence that the statement was made. The reasons in section 259(2) are:

- the person who made the statement is dead or mentally or physically unfit to give evidence personally, or
- the person is outside the United Kingdom and it is not reasonably practicable for them to attend, or
- the person cannot be found despite reasonable steps being taken to find him, or
- the person is entitled to refuse to give evidence on the ground that the evidence might incriminate him, or
- the person has been called as a witness but has refused to take the oath or to give evidence.

Where the judge is satisfied that the party tendering the evidence, or someone connected to him, have colluded to bring about the unavailability of the witness, section 259(3) states that the evidence will not be admissible.

If hearsay evidence is to be led, and it is clear that the witness will not attend in person, then all parties must be given notice before the trial.[79] Notice is not required if the witness attends but then refuses to give evidence on the ground of self-incrimination or if he fails to testify. If there is a challenge to the evidence, this will normally occur before the trial commences[80] and the judge will decide the issue on the balance of probabilities. If there is no objection to the admission of evidence of a statement, under section 259(1) the

[78] (1991) 13 E.H.R.R. 175.
[79] 1995 Act, s.259(5).
[80] 1995 Act, s.259(8).

evidence is admissible without the judge having to be satisfied as to the issues in that sub-section. In *H.M.Advocate v. Nulty*[81] the alleged victim of a rape had given evidence on a tape-recording of the event. At the trial in 1999, she had revealed in cross-examination that she had had previous sexual experience, a fact previously unknown to both the Crown and the defence. That trial was deserted for unconnected reasons. By the time of the second trial, the woman had become mentally unfit to give evidence and the prosecution applied for the tape recording to be entered in evidence. The accused objected, arguing that the court had discretion to refuse the application on the ground of fairness. When the judge rejected this, the accused raised a devolution issue, stating that the admissibility of the tape breached his right to a fair trial under Article 6(1) and 6(3) of the Convention. He argued that the woman's credibility was crucially important and the jury would not be able to judge her demeanour. The only direct evidence of the crime was that of the woman and corroboration was only possible by applying the *Moorov* doctrine.[82] In addition he had been unable to cross-examine the woman at the first trial regarding the information on the tape. The High Court of Justiciary said that the question of fairness had to be approached in an overall manner and there was no unfairness to the accused in admitting the tape. There were sufficient safeguards in place, namely the requirement of corroboration of evidence, the right of the defence to question the witness's credibility and the ability of the judge to deal with any difficulties by giving appropriate directions to the jury.

In *Asch v. Austria*[83] the European Court found no breach of 6.19 Article 6(3)(d) where a conviction was partly based on a statement made by the complainer to the police. The complainer, the accused's cohabitee, subsequently refused to give evidence at the trial. However, there was additional evidence corroborating the woman's statement and the evidence of the accused himself gave rise to doubts as to his truthfulness.

Where the witness is dead or ill, corroboration will be an important consideration on the overall fairness of the proceedings. In *Ferrantelli and Santengelo v. Italy*[84] a witness committed suicide in prison and his hearsay evidence was admitted. The European Court held that this was acceptable particularly since there was a series of other items of evidence which corroborated the statement he had previously given.

The United Kingdom Government enacted legislation in 1998 to tackle the problem of bad neighbours. The Crime and Disorder Act

---

[81]   2000 S.L.T. 528.
[82]   *Moorov v. H.M.Advocate*, 1930 J.C. 69.
[83]   (1993) 15 E.H.R.R. 597.
[84]   (1996) 23 E.H.R.R. 288.

1998, section 1 provides for the imposition of an anti-social behaviour order (ASBO). The order is made using the civil rules of procedure[85] but breach of an order carries criminal penalties including imprisonment. The procedure for applying for an ASBO allows hearsay evidence, although the court may call the maker of the original statement to be cross-examined. Where the evidence of an "anonymous witness" is allowed in the proceedings, it is possible that a breach of Article 6(3)(d) will be found since the person against whom the ASBO is sought will not have had the opportunity to examine witnesses against him.

6.20   The European Court has stated that the evidence of anonymous witnesses should be treated with caution. In *Kostovski v. The Netherlands*[86] the Court held that reliance on anonymous witnesses at the investigation stage of criminal proceedings was not precluded by the Convention. However, using anonymous statements as sufficient evidence to found a conviction is a different matter. Such evidence may be relied on so long as there are "counterbalancing factors" to protect the accused by enabling him "to challenge the evidence of anonymous witnesses and attempt to cast doubt on the reliability of the statements".[87] Where the anonymous witness is an undercover officer, the evidence must be treated with caution. The proceedings will be unfair if the undercover officer, or an informant, incited the commission of the offence.[88]

Article 6(3)(e)—Assistance of an interpreter

6.21 Just as a person accused of a crime must be able to understand the nature and cause of the accusation to enable him to construct his defence, so he needs to be able to understand what is happening in court and instruct his defence lawyer. Both situations are covered in Article 6(3) but in separate paragraphs. The right to have the charge explained in a language the accused understands is given in Article 6(3)(a) while the right to have the free assistance of an interpreter is given in Article 6(3)(e). Both provisions must be complied with if the trial is to be considered fair.

The European Court clarified its thoughts on the right to have an interpreter in *Kamasinski v. Austria*.[89] The right to an interpreter means that the accused should have someone to help him understand the oral part of the trial and to assist him in understanding the contents of documentary evidence. It does not extend to the accused having a written translation of the

---

[85] See *R v. Manchester Crown Court, ex p. McCann* [2001] 1 W.L.R. 1085, where it was recognised that an application for an ASBO is a civil proceeding.
[86] (1989) 12 E.H.R.R. 434.
[87] *Doorson v. The Netherlands* (1996) 22 E.H.R.R. 330, para. 75.
[88] *Teixeira de Castro v. Portugal* (1999) 28 E.H.R.R. 101.
[89] (1991) 13 E.H.R.R. 36.

documentary evidence. However, the Court was clear that under Article 6(3)(a) the indictment had to be given to the accused in a language he understood and this might require a written translation to be made available to him. The exact amount of translated material required for the trial to be conducted fairly would depend on various factors, such as the complexity of the indictment and the amount of questioning by the police and investigating judges. In *Kamasinski* the questioning was lengthy and therefore the accused must have been aware of the case against him. In addition, he did not ask for a translation of the indictment, had challenged the indictment on insufficiency of evidence and had told the trial court that he understood the charges.

The right in this sub-paragraph does not allow an applicant to seek to conduct proceedings in the language of his own choice. Thus an applicant who understood French did not have the right to conduct his defence in the Breton language.[90]

In *Luedicke, Belkacem and Koc v. Federal Republic of Germany*[91] 6.22 the applicants were foreign nationals with limited knowledge of German. They were convicted and ordered to pay costs including the cost of interpreters. They complained that this was a breach of Article 6(3)(e). The European Court looked at the translations of the Convention in both English and French where the words "free" and "gratuitement'" were used respectively. The ordinary meaning of these words was not contradicted by the object and purpose of the Article or its context and accordingly there had been a violation of the Article.

---

[90] *K v. France* (1984) 35 D.R. 203.
[91] (1979-80) 2 E.H.R.R. 149.

CHAPTER 7

THE RIGHT TO PRIVATE AND FAMILY LIFE AND THE RIGHT TO MARRY AND FOUND A FAMILY

ARTICLE 8—RIGHT TO RESPECT FOR PRIVATE AND FAMILY LIFE ONE'S HOME AND CORRESPONDENCE

"(1) Everyone has the right to respect for his private and family life, his home and his correspondence.

(2) There shall be no interference by a public authority with the exercise of this right except which as is in accordance with the law and is necessary in a democratic society in the interests of national security, public safety or the economic well-being of the country, for the prevention of disorder or crime, for the protection of health or morals, or for the protection of the rights and freedoms of others."

7.01 This Article protects the rights of the individual in two distinct ways. He or she is entitled to respect for his or her private life and relationships. He or she is also entitled to privacy and non-intervention by the state. The right to respect for private and family life, home and correspondence is a qualified right. This means that it subject to several exceptions. Interference with the exercise of the right of privacy will be lawful on the following conditions:

(1) it is in accordance with the law, and ;

(2) it is necessary in a democratic society in the interests of—

(a) national security, or

(b) public safety, or

(c) the economic well-being of the country, or

(d) for the prevention of disorder or crime, or

(e) for the protection of health or morals, or

(f) for the protection of the rights and freedoms of others.

These exceptions provide a basis on which the competing interest of the individual and the society in which he lives can be balanced. There are therefore four tests which are used to establish whether or not Article 8 has been contravened:

(1) Has there been any interference with a substantive right?
(2) Is the act amounting to interference carried out in accordance with the law?
(3) Does the interference purport to have a legitimate aim?
(4) Is the interference necessary in a democratic society?

The European Court of Human Rights has been unwilling to lay down a definitive interpretation of the concept of private life, preferring to leave it open to interpretation to meet the needs of individual circumstances. In *Niemietz v. Germany*, it was stated, with regard to the concept of family life, that

> "it would be too restrictive to limit the notion to an 'inner circle' in which the individual may live his own personal life as he chooses and to exclude therefrom entirely the outside world not encompassed within that circle. Respect for family life must also comprise to a certain degree the right to establish and develop relationships with other human beings."

It was also made clear in that judgment that private life could include business or professional activities engaged in by an individual.[1] The right to respect for private life under the Convention has a much wider meaning than the traditional meaning of privacy in Scotland, where it tends to focus on the right to be protected from intrusion by the press. It also includes the right to live in a manner suited to ones own personal beliefs and inclinations.

There will be interference with private and family life whenever state action has a direct impact on an individual, for example when property is searched. A law which may result in future infringements may also be contrary to Article 8, as in the case of a law banning homosexual activities. Article 8, however, has come to be regarded as requiring more from the states than that they should simply refrain from interfering with the private lives of citizens without justification. The notion of respect for privacy may be interpreted as including a positive obligation on the state to ensure that the privacy of the individual is protected. A state may be in contravention of Article 8 if it does not provide adequate legal

---

[1] *Niemietz v. Germany* (1993) 16 E.H.R.R. 97.

safeguards to protect the privacy of individuals through measures such as Data Protection legislation.

RESPECT FOR PRIVATE LIFE

7.02 Scots law does not recognise a right of privacy, *per se*, although the privacy of the home is protected by regulation of the police powers of entry and search. The Calcutt Report noted that a common law right to privacy could possibly develop in Scotland where there is a more general concept of *culpa* (legal wrong) in comparison with the more narrowly drawn English torts.[2] There may be situations where the publication of private information may be restrained, for example, under Press Codes of Practice,[3] publication of information may be prevented where it has been obtained in breach of confidence.[4] Breach of confidence was considered in the English case of *Douglas v. Hello! Ltd.* The actor Michael Douglas had entered into a contract with *OK* magazine for the exclusive right to publish photographs of his wedding to Catherine Zeta-Jones. *Hello!* magazine had obtained photographs which they intended to publish. *Hello!* successfully appealed against an interim injunction restraining them, until trial or further order, from publishing the photographs. *OK* argued that publication of the photographs by *Hello!* would amount to a breach of confidence. It was held that this could have been the case if *Hello!* had obtained the photographs by subterfuge. *Hello!* claimed that they had bought the photographs from a wedding guest the day after the wedding. It was held that by virtue of the Human Rights Act 1998, section 12(3) it was likely that Douglas would be able to establish that *Hello!* should not be allowed to publish the photographs because *Hello!* had breached the Code of Practice of the Press Complaints Commission 1997, Clause 3. If a breach of the Code had occurred, *Hello!*'s right to freedom of expression was restricted by Schedule 1 Part I Article 10(2) of the Act. This would have been the case if the photographs had been obtained illicitly. The rights of Michael Douglas and Catherine Zeta-Jones would have been infringed and they would possibly have had a case for an injunction. However, they had already sold their privacy for commercial gain and the current case was really no more than a dispute between two competing

---

[2] The Calcutt Report, *Privacy and Related Matters*, Cm. 1102 (1992).
[3] For example, Press Complaints Commission Code of Practice, 1997, ITC Code, BBC "Producers' Guidelines".
[4] *Quilty v. Windsor*, 1999 S.L.T. 346.

commercial interests.[5] In his judgment Lord Justice Sedley concluded that a right of privacy between individuals should now be recognised as well as between public authorities and individuals. He said:

> "What a concept of privacy does, however, is accord recognition to the fact that the law has to protect not only those people whose trust has been abused but those who simply find themselves subjected to an unwarranted intrusion into their personal lives. The law no longer needs to construct an artificial relationship of confidentiality between intruder and victim: it can recognise privacy itself as a legal principle drawn from the fundamental value of personal autonomy."

The Press Complaints Commission's Code of Practice provides that everyone is entitled to respect for his or her private life, home, health and correspondence. It does not ban intrusions however, but states that a publication will be expected to justify intrusions into any individual's private life without consent. It declares that it is unacceptable to use long lens photography to take pictures of people in private places without their consent. The Code provides that publication is justified where it is in the public interest. Public interest is defined as including the detection of crime, the protection of public health and safety and preventing the public from being misled by a statement or action by an individual or organisation. The Press Complaints Commission qualifies as a public authority in terms of the Human Rights Act and is therefore obliged to have regard to Convention jurisprudence in adjudicating complaints. In the course of parliamentary debates on the Human Rights Act the Lord Chancellor made it clear that the Press Complaints Commission has primary responsibility for ensuring that the media respect individual privacy rather than relying on the courts.[6] In other words legislation to protect privacy will not be introduced unless the Commission fails to persuade newspaper editors to respect the Human Rights Act. The Press Complaints Commission has not been very successful in restraining the press in the past. It can also be criticised on the basis that there is very little it can do if a newspaper does not co-operate. Publicising its findings does not seem to be a strong deterrent. An individual whose rights have been infringed may be able to claim that the Code of Practice does not provide an adequate remedy in terms of Article 13.

The rights conferred by the Convention are individual rights which can be relied on by an individual in a relationship with a

---

[5] *Douglas v. Hello! Ltd* [2001] 2 W.L.R. 992; [2001] 2 All E.R. 289; [2001] E.M.L.R. 9; [2001] U.K.H.R.R. 223; 9 B.H.R.C. 543.

[6] 585 H.L. Deb. 786 (November 24,1997).

public authority but not by a commercial organisation. In *R v. Broadcasting Standards Commission, ex parte BBC*, the BBC applied for judicial review of the decision of the Broadcasting Standards Commission which had upheld a complaint brought by an electrical retailer, against the BBC for breach of its right to privacy in the making of a consumer affairs television programme. The programme involved the secret filming of several transactions at a number of shops to investigate their alleged selling of second-hand goods as new. The BBC questioned whether a right to privacy existed in relation to a company. The BBC also questioned whether any such right was infringed by secret filming in a place open to the public where the event itself was not of an essentially private nature. It was held that the European Convention on Human Rights 1950, Article 8 was designed to protect individuals rather than corporate bodies. The filming did not in itself constitute an infringement of privacy, as the event was not an intrinsically private matter. The application was successful, as no infringement of the privacy of an individual had occurred.[7]

7.03   The concept of private life encompasses the physical and moral integrity of the person, including his or her sexual life.[8] In the case of *X and Y v. Netherlands*, Article 8 was found to have been violated by the failure of Dutch criminal law to provide effective protection for a mentally handicapped 16-year-old who had been subjected to a serious sexual assault.

In the case of *Dudgeon v. United Kingdom*,[9] it was held that legislation in Northern Ireland which criminalised homosexual activities between consenting adult males was in breach of Article 8. Laws were eventually passed to legalise homosexual activities between consenting adult males. In Scotland, the relevant legislation is the Criminal Law (Consolidation) (Scotland) Act 1995 which provides that a homosexual act in private shall not be an offence provided that the parties have consented and have attained the age of 18 years.[10] (In order to provide for equality with heterosexual relationships the age of consent was reduced to 16 by the Sexual Offences (Amendment) Act 2000.)[11] The Act defines "in private" as a situation in which no more than two persons are taking part or are present.

In July 2000, the European Court of Human Rights considered the equivalent legal measures in England and Wales. A homosexual man complained to the European Court of Human Rights that his

---

[7]   *R v. Broadcasting Standards Commission, ex p. BBC* [1999] E.M.L.R. 858; [2000] H.R.L.R. 15; [2000] U.K.H.R.R. 158; [1999] C.O.D. 472.
[8]   *X & Y v. Netherlands* (1986) 8 E.H.R.R. 235.
[9]   *Dudgeon v. U.K.* (1982) 4 E.H.R.R. 149.
[10] Criminal Law (Consolidation) (Scotland) Act 1995, s.13.
[11] Sexual Offences (Amendment) Act 2000, s.1(3).

conviction for gross indecency, relating to sexual acts with four other men which was depicted in a videotape seized from his home, infringed Article 8. Although the acts took place in private, he was convicted under the Sexual Offences Act 1956, section 13 which made it an offence for a man to "commit an act of gross indecency with another man", whether in private or in public. Although the Sexual Offences Act 1967 had decriminalised private homosexual acts between consenting adults, section 1(2)(a) of the 1967 Act retained the prohibition on such acts where more than two men were present or taking part. He asserted that his conviction amounted to a violation of his right to a private life and was contrary to Article 8. As there were no corresponding statutory provisions regulating private acts between consenting homosexual women nor an equivalent provision for heterosexuals the law was discriminatory. It was held that there had been a violation of Article 8. The existence of legislation prohibiting consensual sexual activity between adult males imposed unnecessary restrictions on private life in a democratic society. Whilst state interference might be justified in certain circumstances including the protection of morals or health, the activities had involved only a limited number of friends and it was unlikely that anyone else would have become aware of them. Although the acts were recorded on videotape, it was unlikely that the video would have become available to the public. The acts were, therefore, purely private. As there were no public health issues to be considered, no interference with the right to engage in such activities was justified. The court awarded damages of almost £21,000 and costs and expenses.[12] A consequence of this decision is that the equivalent provision under Scots law could be challenged on the grounds of its incompatibility with Article 8. Part 4 of the Convention Rights (Compliance) (Scotland) Act therefore repealed section 13(2)(a) of the 1995 Act. This will mean that it will no longer be an offence for more than two adult males to take part in homosexual acts in private. The provisions of section 13(2)(b), which state that activities will not be deemed to be in private where they take place in a public lavatory or other place to which the public have, or are permitted to have, access will remain in force.

Investigations into the private lives of service personnel came under scrutiny in the case of *Smith v. United Kingdom*. The Ministry of Defence had operated a policy of excluding homosexuals from service in the armed forces. Several service men and women sought compensation after they had been dismissed from the armed forces on the grounds of their sexual orientation. Eventually, after applications for judicial review of the Ministry of Defence policy

---

[12] *ADT v. U.K.* [2000] 2 F.L.R. 697; 9 B.H.R.C. 112; [2000] Crim. L.R. 1009.

were unsuccessful, as was a subsequent appeal to the House of
Lords, the group of service personnel brought a case to the
European Court of Human Rights. All four applicants contended
that the investigations into their private lives undertaken by the
Ministry of Defence constituted an infringement of their right to
respect for their private lives under the European Convention on
Human Rights 1950 Article 8. The investigations had included
detailed interviews with them and with their partners on matters
relating to their sexual orientation and practices. The European
Court of Human Rights held that the investigations, interviews and
discharges amounted to an "exceptional intrusion" into the
applicants' private lives, constituting a violation of Article 8. The
court accepted that some operational difficulties might arise where
there were homosexual military personnel but that an adverse
attitude to homosexuals could not of itself justify intrusions into the
private lives of personnel. As a consequence of this decision the ban
on homosexuals in the armed forces has been lifted.[13] In the course
of the judgment it was stated there must be particularly serious
reasons for such intrusions into a person's private life in order for it
to be regarded as necessary in a democratic society. The discharges
from the forces were also not considered to be necessary in a
democratic society and so also contravened Article 8. Not every
sexual activity carried on behind closed doors falls within the scope
of Article 8. Investigations for a legitimate purpose such as the
protection of children are regarded as necessary in a democratic
society.

7.04   Applications have been made to the European Court of Human
Rights by transsexuals who have been refused permission to change
their birth certificates to reflect their change of gender. In *Rees v.
United Kingdom*, Mr Rees, a transsexual, claimed that the United
Kingdom were in breach of Article 8. Mr Rees was born with the
physical and biological characteristics of a female baby. As a child
he exhibited masculine behaviour and was ambiguous in appearance. Mr Rees underwent treatment for sexual conversion and lived
as a male. He claimed that the United Kingdom authorities' refusal
to change his entry in the register of births or to issue a birth
certificate so as to reflect his change of sexual identity was contrary
to Article 8. It was held that Article 8 had not been violated as the
mere refusal to alter the register of births or to issue birth
certificates whose contents differ from those of the birth register
could not be regarded as arbitrary interference by public authorities
in a person's right to respect for his private and family life. This was
an area in which contracting states had a wide margin of

---

[13] *Smith v. U.K.* [1999] I.R.L.R. 734; (2000) 29 E.H.R.R. 493; (1999) 11 Admin.
L.R. 879.

appreciation.[14] Another case came before the European Court four years later. In *Cossey v. United Kingdom*, a person who was registered at birth as a male but later underwent treatment and gender reassignment surgery and thereafter lived a full life as a woman, applied to the European Court for a declaration that the United Kingdom had violated Article 8. The fact that she could not be issued with a fresh birth certificate showing her to be a female was a violation of her right to privacy. It was held that when determining the existence of positive obligations on a contracting state which were inherent in the notion of respect for private life, a balance must be struck between the general interest of the community and the interests of the individual. The United Kingdom was not under a positive obligation to modify its birth-registration system.[15]

In *B v. France*, B, a male to female transsexual sought a declaration from the French court that although registered as male, she was in reality of feminine constitution and female sex, that she should henceforth bear feminine forenames and an order rectifying her birth certificate. The court dismissed her application on the grounds that her change of gender had been brought about intentionally by psychological tendencies and medical intervention and that she was biologically of the male sex. She appealed to the European Court of Human Rights alleging a violation of her right to respect for her private life. She claimed that by failing to rectify her sexual status in the civil register and on her official identity documents, the French authorities forced her to disclose intimate personal information to third parties which caused her embarrassment and difficulties in her professional, economic and everyday life and that refusal to allow her to change her forenames was a relevant factor on the question of violation. A majority held that there had been a violation of Article 8 as a result of the frequent necessity to disclose personal information to third parties. B had suffered sufficient distress and inconvenience amounting to a violation of Article 8. A fair balance between the public interest and the interests of the individual had not been struck.[16] The case of *Sheffield and Horsham v. United Kingdom* was brought by two male-to-female transsexuals who complained that failure under United Kingdom to grant recognition of their acquired gender constituted an interference with their rights to respect for their private lives under Article 8. They also claimed a breach of Article 14 in conjunction with Article 8, contending that transsexual people alone were compelled to describe themselves in public by a gender which did not accord with their personal appearance. The court

---

[14] *Rees v. U.K.* (1987) 17 Fam. Law 157.
[15] *Cossey v. U.K.* [1991] 2 F.L.R. 492.
[16] *B v. France* [1992] 2 F.L.R. 249.

found in favour of the United Kingdom Government by a margin of 11 to nine on Article 8. They also held that there was no case to answer on Article 14. It was recognised that although both applicants had experienced incidents which had caused embarrassment and distress, there were occasions when justification of proof of gender might be necessary, and these did not occur so frequently as to infringe disproportionately on the right to respect for private life.[17] In that case the dissenting judges said:

> "It is no longer possible, from the standpoint of Article 8 of the Convention and in a Europe where considerable evolution in the direction of legal recognition is constantly taking place, to justify a system such as that pertaining in the respondent State, which treats gender dysphoria as a medical condition, subsidises gender re-assignment surgery but then withholds recognition of the consequences of that surgery thereby exposing post-operative transsexuals to the likelihood of recurring distress and humiliation."

This dissenting judgment may be a precursor of a narrowing of the margin of appreciation granted to states in this area in the future.

7.05   The disclosure of medical records by state health authorities will amount to a breach of the right to respect for a person's private life but it may be justifiable if the conditions in Article 8(2) are met. In *Z v. Finland*, the applicant had been married to a man who had been charged with serious sexual offences. He was subsequently also charged with attempted manslaughter on the ground that he had known that he was HIV positive at the time when he committed the offences. In order to find out when he knew that he was HIV positive, the court ordered Z's doctor to provide evidence about her health. He disclosed that she was HIV positive. The proceedings were held in private and records of the case were to be kept secret for 10 years. The man appealed and a copy of the appeal court judgment, which identified the applicant and disclosed her HIV status, was given to the press and published in several newspapers. The Court found that there had been a breach of Article 8.[18] The Court stated that the protection of personal, data, not least medical data, is of fundamental importance to a person's enjoyment of his or her right to respect for private and family life. A majority of judges held that the access to the data by the court for the purpose of a criminal prosecution was justified in terms of Article 8(2). However, the Court found unanimously that the limited 10-year

---

[17]   *Sheffield and Horsham v. U.K.* [1998] 2 F.L.R. 928; [1998] 3 F.C.R. 141; (1999) 27 E.H.R.R. 163; 5 B.H.R.C. 83; [1998] H.R.C.D. 758; [1998] Fam. Law 731.
[18]   *Z v. Finland* (1997) 25 E.H.R.R.371.

time-limit and the public judgment could not be justified under Article 8(2).

DATA PROTECTION

Laws regulating the ways in which people can find out what 7.06
information is being held about them by public authorities and
commercial organisation are an important element of the protection
of rights under Article 8. In the United Kingdom the process of
collecting, storing, processing and distributing information is
regulated by the Data Protection Act 1998.[19] The Act protects
the right to privacy by giving rights to individuals to find out what
information is being held about them by organisations. The Act
places obligations on those who record and use personal data (data
users). They must be open about that use (through the Data
Protection Register) and follow sound and proper practices (the
Data Protection Principles). The Data Protection Act 1998 replaces
the scheme embodied in the Data Protection Act 1984. A
substantial proportion of the present law is preserved in the 1998
Act. Two important changes are that trans-border data flows are
now regulated and data protection law is extended to manual data
in "relevant filing systems" by virtue of section 1(1) of the 1998 Act.
The impact of these changes will be lessened by long lead-in
periods. In the case of manual data, all manual data held in a
"relevant filing system" was exempt from the main operative
provisions of the new Act during the "first transitional period"—*i.e.*
from commencement until October 23, 2001. Manual data held on a
"relevant filing system" prior to October 24, 1998 will be exempt
from control during the "second transitional period"—*i.e.* from
commencement until October 24, 2007.

Data Protection Principles

The first principle is that personal data shall be processed fairly and 7.07
lawfully. The data subject should be informed of the purpose or
purposes for which the data are intended to be processed. Data
controllers should consider the extent to which the use of personal
data by them is or is not reasonably foreseeable by data subjects. To
the extent to which their use of personal data is not reasonably
foreseeable, data controllers should ensure that they provide such
further information as may be necessary. Data must be obtained
fairly, *i.e.* without deceiving or misleading any data subject.
Personal data are not to be treated as processed fairly unless the
following information is provided to the data subject:

---

[19] To implement European Union Data Protection Directive (95/46/EC).

- The identity of the data controller,
- If it has nominated a representative for the purposes of the Act, the identity of that representative,
- The purpose or purposes for which the data are intended to be processed, and
- Any further information which is necessary, taking into account the specific circumstances in which the data are or are to be processed, to enable processing in respect of the data subject to be fair.

Personal data may contain a "general identifier" such as a number or code used for identification purposes. The Secretary of State will prescribe conditions which must be complied with to ensure the fair and lawful processing of personal data containing a general identifier.

Data controllers should consider what processing of personal data they shall be carrying out once the data are obtained and consider whether or not data subjects are likely to understand the following:

(a) the purposes for which their personal data are going to be processed,
(b) the likely consequences of such processing, and
(c) more particularly, whether particular disclosures can reasonably be envisaged.

It would be expected that the more unforeseen the consequences of processing the more likely it is that the data controller will be expected to provide further information. Data subjects themselves must be fully aware of the ways in which their personal data may be processed in order for that processing to be considered as fair.

The fair processing information should also be provided to data subjects in cases where the data have been obtained from someone other than the data subject, unless one of the exceptions applies. The exceptions are:

(a) where providing the fair processing information would involve a disproportionate effort;
(b) where it is necessary for the data controller to record the information to be contained in the data or to disclose the data to comply with any legal obligation to which the data controller is subject, other than an obligation imposed by contract;
(c) in addition, the Secretary of State may prescribe further conditions, by way of "appropriate safeguards", which must also be met for the exception to be available.

The second principle is that personal data shall be obtained only for   7.08
one or more specified and lawful purposes, and shall not be further
processed in any manner incompatible with that purpose or those
purposes. Compliance with the second principle cannot be
established simply by registering the purpose(s) for which personal
data are processed, as was possible under the 1984 Act. There are
two means by which a data controller may specify the purpose or
purposes for which the personal data are obtained, either in a notice
given by the data controller to the data subject in accordance with
the fair processing code or in a notification given to the
Commissioner under the notification provisions of the Act. In
deciding whether any disclosure of personal data is compatible with
the purpose or purposes for which the data were obtained,
consideration will be given to the purpose or purposes for which
the personal data are intended to be processed by any person to
whom they are disclosed.

The third principle is that personal data shall be adequate,
relevant and not excessive in relation to the purpose or purposes for
which they are processed. The efficacy of this principle is limited by
the fact that many commercial organisation declare a broad range
of purposes for which data will be processed and members of the
public nevertheless choose to supply data to them. The fourth
principle is that personal data shall be accurate and, where
necessary, kept up-to-date. Data are inaccurate if they are incorrect
or misleading as to any matter of fact. Now data controllers may
have to take reasonable steps to ensure the accuracy of the data
themselves. Whether or not a data controller would be expected to
take such steps will be a matter of fact in each individual case. The
fifth principle is that personal data processed for any purpose or
purposes shall not be kept for longer than is necessary for that
purpose or those purposes.

The sixth principle is that personal data shall be processed in
accordance with the rights of data subjects under this Act. A person
will contravene this principle if they fail to supply information
pursuant to a subject access request under section 7 of the Act, or
fail to comply with notices given under the following provisions of
the Act:

- section 10 (right to prevent processing likely to cause
  damage or distress);
- section 11 (right to prevent processing for the purposes of
  direct marketing); or
- section 12 (rights in relation to automatic decision taking).

The seventh principle is that appropriate technical and organisa-   7.09
tional measures shall be taken against unauthorised or unlawful
processing of personal data and against accidental loss or

destruction of, or damage to, personal data. Matters which should be taken into account in deciding whether security measures are "appropriate" include:

(1) the state of technological development at any time;
(2) the cost of implementing any measures;
(3) the measures must ensure a level of security appropriate to the harm that might result from a breach of security;
(4) the nature of the data to be protected;
(5) the reliability of staff having access to the personal data.

When the processing of personal data is carried out by a data processor on behalf of the data controller the data controller must:

(a) choose a data processor providing sufficient guarantees in respect of the security measures they take;
(b) take reasonable steps to ensure compliance with those measures; and
(c) ensure that the processing by the data processor is carried out under a contract which is made or evidenced in writing, under which the data processor is to act only on instructions from the data controller. The contract must require the data processor to comply with obligations equivalent to those imposed on the data controller by the seventh principle.

The eighth principle is that personal data shall not be transferred to a country or territory outside the European Economic Area, unless that country or territory ensures an adequate level of protection for the rights and freedoms of data subjects in relation to the processing of personal data. The European Economic Area ("The EEA") consists of the 15 European Union member states together with Iceland, Liechtenstein and Norway. In determining what amounts to an adequate level of protection consideration will be given in particular to the following:

(1) the nature of the personal data;
(2) the country or territory of origin of the information contained in the data;
(3) the country or territory of final destination of that information;
(4) the purposes for which and period during which the data are intended to be processed;
(5) the law in forces in the country or territory in question;
(6) the international obligations of that country or territory;
(7) any relevant codes of conduct or other rules which are enforceable in that country or territory; and

(8) any security measures taken in respect of the data in that country or territory.

Where the European Commission makes a finding that a country or territory outside the European Economic Area does, or does not, ensure an adequate level of protection any question which may arise as to whether an adequate level of protection exists shall be determined in accordance with that finding. At present there are no such findings in force. The eighth principle does not apply to a transfer where:

(1) the data subject has given their consent to the transfer;
(2) the transfer is necessary—

    (a) for the performance of a contract between the data subject and the data controller; or
    (b) for the taking of steps at the request of the data subject with a view to their entering into a contract with the data controller.

(3) the transfer is necessary—

    (a) for the conclusion of a contract between the data controller and a person other than the data subject which is entered into at the request of the data subject, or is in the interests of the data subject; or
    (b) for the performance of such a contract.

(4) the transfer is necessary for reasons of substantial public interest. The Secretary of State may specify the circumstances in which a transfer is to be taken to be necessary for reasons of substantial public interest (no such orders are in place as yet).
(5) the transfer—

    (a) is necessary for the purpose of, or in connection with, any legal proceedings (including prospective legal proceedings);
    (b) is necessary for the purpose of obtaining legal advice; or
    (c) is otherwise necessary for the purposes of establishing, exercising or defending legal rights.

(6) the transfer is necessary in order to protect the vital interests of the data subject;
(7) the transfer is part of the personal data on a public register and any conditions, subject to which the register is open to inspection, are complied with by any person to whom the data are or may be disclosed after the transfer;
(8) the transfer is made on terms which are of a kind approved

by the Commissioner as ensuring adequate safeguards for the rights and freedoms of data subjects.

The transfer has been authorised by the Commissioner as being made in such a manner as to ensure adequate safeguards for the rights and freedoms of data.

Right of Access to Personal Data

7.10 Individuals have the right to see the information which is held about them by any organisation. This includes information held by public authorities as well as private sector organisations. The right to see information held by local authorities on manual files was previously provided by the Access to Personal Files Act 1987, which has now been repealed.[20] If the information is inaccurate there is a right to apply to a court for the rectification, blocking, erasure or destruction of inaccurate data.[21] Courts may also order that third parties who have already received the inaccurate data be notified.[22] There are exceptions to the obligation on the data controller to disclose data.[23] These include national security, crime and taxation, journalism and literature. The total exemption in respect of national security arises where a Minister has issued a certificate. Under the 1984 Data Protection Act there was no appeal against such a certificate but, under the 1998 Act, there is a right of appeal to the data protection tribunal.[24] The Secretary of State or the Scottish Ministers may also by order exempt data from disclosure, for example in relation to the mental health of the data subject. There is an exemption from subject access rights for;

(1) education and employment references
(2) data concerning honours
(3) management forecasts and plans
(4) intentions formed in relation to negotiations
(5) examination scripts

Data Commissioner

7.11 The data commissioner maintains a register of data controllers. Registration is required before data can be processed. It is an

---

[20] Access to Personal Files Act 1987. Detailed provisions are in the Access to Personal Files (Social Work) (Scotland) Regulations 1989 (S.I. 1989 No.251), Access to Personal Files (Housing) (Scotland) Regulations 1992 (S.I. 1992 No.1852).

[21] Data protection Act 1998, s.14(1).

[22] *ibid.*, s.14(3).

[23] *ibid.*, Pt IV.

[24] *ibid.*, s.28.

offence to process data unless the data controller is registered.[25]
There is a duty on data controllers to notify data holdings[26] unless
processing is unlikely to prejudice the rights and freedoms of data
subjects.[27] Notification of data holdings is also excused where the
data controller has an approved "in-house" supervision scheme.[28]
Processing pending registration is banned where it is likely to cause,
"[s]ubstantial damage or substantial distress to data subjects"; or,
"[o]therwise significantly prejudice the rights and freedoms of data
subjects".[29] The data protection commissioner may use an
enforcement notice to ensure that a data controller registers. A
data protection tribunal provides a forum for appeal by data
controllers. Appeal can be made against decisions such as a refusal
to register a data controller or decisions to take enforcement action.
Under Part 1 of the Freedom of Information Act 2000 the data
protection commissioner shall be known instead as the information
commissioner and the data protection tribunal shall be known as
the information tribunal.[30]

Relationship between Data Protection Legislation and Freedom of Information Legislation

The Data Protection Act is intended to ensure privacy of personal   7.12
data. It obliges data controllers to ensure that data subjects' privacy
is protected as far as is reasonably possible. Freedom of
Information legislation is designed to secure openness and
accessibility to information held by public authorities. There is
obvious scope for conflict and overlap between the two regimes.
Rights of access to personal data about oneself will continue to be
under the Data Protection Act.[31] Rights of access to information
about third parties will be under the Freedom of Information Act,
but there will be no right to any data which contravenes the data
protection principles. Under the Freedom of Information Act 2000,
the data protection commissioner becomes the United Kingdom
information commissioner. In Scotland, however the Scottish
information commissioner, who will administer the Scottish freedom of information regime, will not be a Scottish data protection

---

[25] Data Protection Act 1998, ss. 17, 21.
[26] *ibid.*, s.17(1).
[27] *ibid.*, s.17(3).
[28] *ibid.*, s.23(1).
[29] *ibid.*, s.22.
[30] Freedom of Information Act 2000, s.18.
[31] "Freedom of Information: Consultation on Draft legislation," Cm 4355, May 1999, para. 32.

commissioner and will need to liase with the United Kingdom data protection commissioner.

RESPECT FOR THE PERSON — POLICE POWERS TO SEARCH PERSONS

7.13 Unless a person has been arrested there is no power to search them under common law. Evidence obtained from a search to which a person has voluntarily consented to be searched will, however be admissible in a trial.[32] Apart from any statutory power, the police have no power to search a person prior to his arrest. There is no common law power to search a person in order to discover evidence for grounds of arrest. In situations of extreme urgency searches carried out before arrest may be excused and the evidence obtained may be used at trial. In *Bell v. Hogg*[33] it was held that searching or taking samples of substances from a person may be justified where the evidence was in danger of being destroyed. While investigating a suspected theft of copper in the early hours of the morning, the police stopped a van, told the four occupants the reason and cautioned them. The officer noticed marks, which he suspected, were made by copper on their hands, and took them to the police station. Before they were arrested or charged of any offence he asked them to give hand-rubbings on paper. They were not told that they need not do so. The substance from their hands matched the stolen wire and the four were prosecuted. Objection was taken to the evidence of the rubbings. It was held that in view of the urgency of preserving evidence, the officer was justified in taking the hand rubbings. There had been no unfairness to the accused; and so the evidence was admissible.[34] When deciding whether or not evidence is admissible account is taken both of the public interest in the effective investigation of crime and the protection of the accused from arbitrariness, dishonesty or oppression. The court has a discretion in each case whether to allow the evidence and avoid an accused person being acquitted on a technicality or whether to disallow it and avoid condoning departures from procedures by the police.

Search before arrest may be authorised by a specific statutory provision such as the Civic Government (Scotland) Act 1982 which provides that a police constable has power to search a person suspected on reasonable grounds of being in possession of stolen property.[35] A constable may seize any suspected stolen property

---

[32] *Devlin v. Normand*, 1992 S.C.C.R. 875, *Davidson v. Brown*, 1990 S.C.C.R. 304, 1991 S.L.T. 335.
[33] *Bell v. Hogg*, 1967 J.C. 49; 1967 S.L.T. 290.
[34] See also *Miln v. Cullen*, 1967 J.C. 21.

and any other evidence of the commission of theft. This power also enables police to stop and search vehicles and vessels in similar circumstances, although only uniformed officers are allowed to stop vehicles.[36] Before carrying out any power of search plain-clothes officers must produce identification. The Criminal Law (Consolidation) (Scotland) Act 1995 provides the police with power to search a person reasonably suspected of being in possession of an offensive weapon. The person may be detained for that purpose and must be informed of the reason for the search and detention. Under the Misuse of Drugs Act 1971,[37] a person may be detained and searched if a constable has reasonable grounds to suspect that he is in possession of drugs. The police need not have seen a person acting in a suspicious manner in order to have reasonable grounds to suspect that he is in possession of drugs. Their suspicions may be based on evidence from other persons present or even from anonymous informants. In the case of *Weir v. Jessop*[38] it was held that there were reasonable grounds for suspicion based on information from an anonymous informant. The police had been told that a person was misusing drugs and had gone to the specified location. Weir was the only person there. When he was questioned he denied misusing drugs but did admit that, in the past, he had been involved with drugs. It was held that the police were justified in detaining him for the purposes of a search.

A person detained under this provision may be taken to a police station for the purpose of being searched. Statutory powers of search must be exercised strictly in accordance with the procedures laid down by the relevant statute.[39] Once they have been arrested the police have a power at common law to search a person. The power of search after arrest includes a power to photograph a person and to make a physical examination. This may include including taking fingerprints, palm prints or other such prints and impressions of an external part of the body as the constable considers it appropriate to take, having regard to the circumstances of the suspected offence in respect of which the person has been arrested or detained.[40] On the authority of an officer of the rank of inspector or above, a constable may take samples of hair, fingernail or toenail clippings or scrapings, a sample of blood or other body fluids, a sample of saliva or body tissue obtained from an external

---

[35] Civic Government (Scotland) Act 1982, s.60.
[36] See *Chassar v. Macdonald*, 1996 S.L.T. 1331; 1996 S.C.C.R. 730.
[37] Misuse of Drugs Act 1971, s.23(2).
[38] *Weir v. Jessop*, 1991 S.C.C.R. 242.
[39] *Normand v. McCutcheon*, 1994 S.L.T. 327.
[40] Criminal Procedure (Scotland) Act 1995, s.18(2).

part of the body by means of swabbing or rubbing.[41] Reasonable
force may be used, if required to obtain samples. Swabs may be
taken from the mouth for the purpose of DNA fingerprinting where
the circumstances of the offence justify this.[42]

7.14　　　Where a sample is sought before arrest or detention, or if samples
are required which are not provided for in the statutory provisions,
a warrant from a sheriff is required as authority. Such a warrant
will only be granted where the circumstances are special and where
the delicate balance that must be maintained between the public
interest on the one hand and the interest of the accused on the other
will not be disturbed. In the case of *Morris v. MacNeill*,[43] an
accused person sought suspension of a warrant granted by a sheriff.
A procurator fiscal had obtained from the sheriff a warrant to take
a blood sample from a person suspected of having committed theft
by housebreaking. There was blood found at the scene of the same
blood group as blood found on the accused's clothing. The sheriff
had regard to the facts that the crime was serious and that the blood
analysis would greatly assist in clearing up the crime. The minimal
invasion of the accused's body by a highly qualified doctor in
obtaining a blood sample was outweighed by the public interest in
solving crime. The sheriff accordingly granted the warrant and the
accused thereafter sought suspension of it. It was held that the
circumstances of the case were sufficiently special to justify taking a
blood sample. Since the sheriff had considered balance of the public
interest against the accused's interest he was entitled to grant the
warrant.[44] In a case where a warrant had been granted to take
blood from man charged with rape and assault of his wife it was
held that the warrant could be modified in the interests of the
accused. The accused had a phobia of needles. The warrant was
amended to the taking of a sample of blood by means of finger
pricks.[45]

Activities such as collecting and keeping secret files about
individuals amount to an interference with such person's lives. In
Leander v. Sweden, the applicant was prevented from continuing his
job at a naval museum because he had been refused personnel
control. The military authorities refused to sanction his position
after they had been shown a secret file on him maintained by the
National Police Board. It was held that both the storing and the
release of such information amounted to an interference with

[41] Criminal Procedure (Scotland) Act 1995, s.18(6).
[42] *ibid.*, s.58; *Curley v. Fraser*, 1997 S.C.C.R. 705.
[43] *Morris v. MacNeill*, 1991 S.L.T. 607.
[44] See also *Brodie v. Normand*, 1995 S.L.T. 739; 1994 S.C.C.R. 924; *Walker (Stuart David) v. Lees*, 1995 J.C. 125; 1995 S.L.T. 757; 1995 S.C.C.R. 445; *Hughes v. Normand (No.1)* 1993 S.L.T. 113.
[45] *G v. Lees*, 1992 S.C.C.R. 252.

Leander's private life as guaranteed by Article 8(1). The Court then went on to declare unanimously that the interference was no more than was necessary for the protection of national security. This fact, coupled with the fact that there were adequate procedural safeguards satisfied the requirements of Article 8(2).[46]

In the United Kingdom surveillance in the interests of national security may be carried out with lawful authority by two organisations. MI5 is the internal security service and MI6 deals with overseas security. The operations of MI5 and MI6 are co-ordinated by an intelligence co-ordinator, based in the Cabinet Office. MI5 was established in 1909 under royal prerogative powers as part of the defence of the realm. It was not regulated by statute until the Security Services Act 1989 was brought into force. The service is headed by the director general who is responsible to the Secretary of State for the Home Office. The security service is not incorporated into the Home Office and so apart from the line of responsibility it stands alone. The director general reports directly to the Prime Minister on matters of importance. The service is mainly concerned with gathering information in order to suppress terrorist activities. It holds about 440,000 files but many of these are historical as the service keeps files of all investigations over the last 90 years. About 13,000 files are active dossiers on British citizens.[47] The remit of MI5 has been extended to include investigations of serious crime, particularly the import and distribution of illegal drugs.[48] This role is intended to support, rather than replace the work of the conventional law enforcement agencies. The service is not, however, accountable to local police authorities and the actions of its members may not be the subject of complaints under the police complaints procedures.

Surveillance practices in the United Kingdom were considered by 7.15 the Commission in *Hewitt v. United Kingdom*. The applicants had both worked for the National Council for Civil Liberties (now known as Liberty). They complained that the Security Service had kept files on them as "communist sympathisers". A majority of the Commission gave the opinion that the Security Service had interfered with the applicant's private lives and was in breach of Article 8(1). The interference could not be brought within the exceptions in Article 8(2), because, at the relevant time the Security Service did not have lawful authority for its actions.[49] The Security Services Act 1989 provided the necessary lawful authority.

The Security Services Act 1989 defines the functions of the security service and gives statutory authority for the issuing of

---

[46] *Leander v. Sweden* (1987) 9 E.H.R.R. 433.
[47] Hansard, HC Vol. 317 col.251.
[48] Security Services Act 1996.
[49] *Hewitt v. U.K.* (1992) 14 E.H.R.R. 657.

warrants. The function of MI5 is defined as being:

> "The protection of national security and, in particular, its protection against threats from espionage, terrorism and sabotage, from the activities of agents of foreign powers and from actions intended to overthrow or undermine Parliamentary democracy by political, industrial or violent means.
> It shall also be the function of the Service to safeguard the economic well being of the United Kingdom against threats posed by the actions or intentions of persons outside the British Islands."[50]

The duties of the director general of the service are defined in section 2. He is responsible for the efficiency of the service.[51] He is also obliged to ensure that the service only collects information which is necessary for the proper discharge of its functions.[52] He must also ensure that the service does not take any action to further the interests of any political party.[53] The Intelligence Services Act 1994 established a Parliamentary Intelligence and Security Committee to scrutinise the work of the security services. This provides for the Parliamentary scrutiny of the work of the security services for the first time but there is still provision for information to be withheld from Parliament. Information may be withheld if the Secretary of State has determined that it should not be disclosed.[54]

The security service has power to interfere with property.[55] Interference with property includes forcing entry and bugging premises. Interference with property is lawful if it is authorised by the Secretary of State. The Secretary of State may issue a warrant to obtain information which he considers to be likely to assist the service to carry out any of its functions. He may only do so if the information cannot be obtained by other means. Warrants are only effective for a period of six months. Warrants may be issued by an authorised senior civil servant where the matter is one of urgency.

The Commissioner

7.16   The Prime Minister is under a duty to appoint a Security Services Commissioner.[56] He must be a person who holds or has held high judicial office. His function is to keep under review the exercise of the powers to interfere with property. All members of the Security

---

[50]   Security Services Act 1989, s.1.
[51]   *ibid.*, s.2(2).
[52]   *ibid.*, s.2(2)(a).
[53]   *ibid.*, s.2(2)(b).
[54]   Intelligence services Act 1994, Sched.3, para. 3(1)(b)(ii).
[55]   Intelligence Services Act 1989, ss. 5, 6.
[56]   Security Services Act 1989, s.4.

Service and all departmental officials of the Home Office are under a duty to disclose information to him when requested. The Commissioner makes an annual report to the Prime Minister. This report is laid before parliament but information may be excluded from the report if it appears to the Prime Minister, after he has consulted the Commissioner, that disclosure of the material would be "prejudicial to the continued discharge of the functions of the Service".[57] The Commissioner may instigate the investigation of complaints made by individuals.

The Tribunal

The purpose of the tribunal is to investigate complaints about the service.[58] Any person may complain to the tribunal if he is aggrieved by anything which he believes the Service has done in relation to him or to any property of his.[59] The tribunal is under a duty to investigate all complaints except those which are frivolous and vexatious. The scope of the investigations which the tribunal may make is very limited. It may investigate whether the service had reasonable grounds to investigate the complainant. If the service has disclosed information about the complainant to a third party, such as his employer, the tribunal may ascertain whether the information was true. Complaints about the issue of warrants are referred to the Commissioner who considers whether the Secretary of State was acting properly in issuing the warrant. There is no appeal from a decision of the tribunal and its decisions are not liable to be questioned in any court.

7.17

The Secret Intelligence Service MI6

MI6 is the security service which deals with matters overseas. It gathers information for the defence of the realm and carries out espionage and covert operations outside the United Kingdom. The nature of its work requires a strict regime of secrecy. The existence of the Secret Intelligence Service was acknowledged officially for the first time in 1992. The Secret Intelligence Service is under the control of the Foreign and Commonwealth Office. The function of the Secret Intelligence Service is to obtain and provide information relating to the actions of persons outside the British Islands, and to perform other tasks relating to the actions or intentions of such persons. The actions which it carries out must be in the interests of national security, with particular reference to defence and foreign policies, or in the interests of the nation's economic well being and

7.18

---

[57] Security Services Act 1989, s.4(6) and(7).
[58] *ibid.*, s.5.
[59] *ibid.*, Sched. 1, para. 1.

assisting in the prevention or detection of serious crime.[60] Actions
are carried out under the authority of warrants from the Secretary
of State in the same way as actions by the Security Service.
Complaints may be investigated by the Commissioner and tribunal.
Where actions have been carried out under the authority of a
warrant from the Secretary of State outside the British Islands, the
authorised agent will be immune from any civil or criminal liability
in the United Kingdom.[61]

Regulation of Investigatory Powers

7.19 Two new statues now regulate surveillance whether the surveillance
is for the purpose of protecting national security or preventing
crime or disorder. The main purpose of both Acts is to ensure that
the exercise of these powers is compatible with the provisions of the
Human Rights Act 1998. The Regulation of Investigatory Powers
(Scotland) Act 2000 mirrors the provisions of Part II of the
Regulation of Investigatory Powers Act 2000 which deals with the
regulatory framework of a range of investigatory powers including
the interception, acquisition and disclosure of communications
data, the use of covert and intrusive surveillance and of human
intelligence gathering. However, the Acts have been challenged on
the ground that they deprive people who suspect that they have
been under surveillance from recourse to a remedy in the ordinary
courts. The remedy is provided instead by a tribunal.

The Regulation of Investigatory Powers Act

7.20 The Regulation of Investigatory Powers Act 2000, which received
Royal Assent on July 28, 2000, updates the law on the interception
of communications to take account of changing technology such as
the Internet; puts other intrusive investigation techniques on a
statutory footing for the first time; gives new powers to counter the
criminal use of encryption; and ensures independent judicial
scrutiny of the powers contained in the Act. Parts I, III, IV and
V of this Act apply throughout the United Kingdom. A separate
but complementary Act to regulate the use of surveillance powers
and covert human resources has been developed in Scotland.[62] The
Regulation of Investigatory Powers Act introduces provisions to
regulate:

---

[60] Intelligence Services Act 1994, s.2.
[61] Security Services Act 1989, s.7.
[62] The U.K. Government's can still legislate on devolved matters in the U.K.
Parliament when agreement has been reached under the concordat (memorandum of understanding, para. 13), and in Devolution Guidance Note 1
(common working arrangements, para 5.2).

(1) the interception, acquisition and disclosure of communications data (Part I);
(2) the use of surveillance powers and covert human resources (Part II);
(3) the disclosure and use of encryption keys (Part III); and,
(4) to create new commissioners and a Tribunal to oversee the use of the investigatory powers established under the new legislation (Part IV).

The Intelligence Services, H.M. forces, the Ministry of Defence, Customs and Excise and the British Transport Police can grant or renew authorisations which extend to Scotland. The use of detection equipment for detecting the use of unlicensed television receivers in houses, in contravention of the Wireless Telegraphy Act 1949, section 1, does not come within the scope of the Act.[63] The scope of the Act has been extended to authorise further interceptions of telecommunications including monitoring or recording communications. Monitoring may be carried out to establish the existence of facts, to ascertain compliance with regulatory or self-regulatory practices or procedures or to ascertain or demonstrate standards which are or ought to be achieved, to prevent or detect crime, to investigate or detect unauthorised use of telecommunication systems, and in the interests of national security.[64]

The Regulation of Investigatory Powers (Scotland) Act

The Scottish Act is concerned principally with the use of surveillance powers and covert human intelligence sources by the police and the Scottish crime squad operating in Scotland. Currently the Police Act 1997 regulates the use by the police of intrusive surveillance measures for the prevention and detection of serious crime. The Police Act requires, in all but urgent cases, prior approval of a surveillance commissioner, also established by this Act, of all surveillance operations involving intrusion into a person's home, offices or hotel bedrooms or in certain other cases. A code of practice on intrusive surveillance was introduced on February 22, 1999. These provisions will be superseded by the Regulation of Investigatory Powers (Scotland) Act. 7.21

A general principle under the Act is that surveillance will only be authorised if it is necessary and proportionate. The Act covers three types of activity.

---

[63] Regulation of Investigatory Powers (British Broadcasting Corporation) Order 2001 (S.I. 2001 No. 1057).
[64] Telecommunications (Lawful Business Practice) (Interception of Communications) Regulations 2000 (S.I. 2000 No. 2699).

7.22 **(1) Directed surveillance.** This is defined as covert surveillance
undertaken in relation to a specific investigation in order to obtain
information about, or identify a particular person or to determine
who is involved in a matter under investigation. This type of
surveillance can only be authorised on one of the following
grounds:

> (a) to prevent or detect crime or to prevent disorder;
> (b) in the interests of public safety;
> (c) in order to protect public health.[65]

Authorisations can be granted only by a designated person
holding an office, rank or position with one of the relevant public
authorities prescribed by order of the Scottish Ministers and can
only be made in relation to an application made by a member of the
same force or service.[66] Relevant public authorities include: a police
force; the Operational and Intelligence Group of the Scottish Drug
Enforcement Agency[67]; the Scottish Administration; a council; the
Common Services Agency for the Health Service; a health board; a
special health board, a National Health Service Trust and the
Scottish Environment Protection Agency.

In the Bill there was a fourth ground authorising surveillance for
any other purpose specified by an order of the Scottish Ministers.
This "catch all" clause was removed from the legislation as it was
deemed by the Scottish Parliament to be unsuitable for modern day
democracy. The changes mean that the law on surveillance in
Scotland is now different from that of England and Wales.

7.23 **(2) Intrusive surveillance.** This means covert surveillance carried out
in relation to residential premises or a private vehicle. Intrusive
surveillance will only be authorised for preventing or detecting
crime or preventing disorder. It may be authorised by a chief
constable or, in urgent cases, by a designated person holding the
rank of assistant chief constable in relation to an application by a
member of his or her own force or service. Where the application
relates to residential premises these must be in the area of the
authorising person's force or service. Except in cases where the need
for urgency can be shown, an authorisation for intrusive
surveillance must be approved by a surveillance commissioner
before it can take effect.[68]

---

[65] Regulation of Investigatory Powers (Scotland) Act 2000, s.7.
[66] *ibid.*, s.8.
[67] Regulation of Investigatory Powers (Prescription of Offices, Ranks and Positions)
      (Scotland) Amendment Order 2001 (S.S.I. 2001 No. 87), to the Scottish Crime
      Squad has been replaced in this context by the Operational and Intelligence
      Group of the Scottish Drug Enforcement Agency.
[68] Regulation of Investigatory Powers (Scotland) Act 2000, s.14.

(3) Covert human intelligence sources. A person is a covert human   7.24
intelligence if they establish or maintain relationships in order to
use, covertly, the relationship to obtain information or to provide
access to any information to another person; or to disclose covertly,
information obtained by the use of such a relationship, or as a
consequence of the existence of such a relationship.[69] Such persons
are usually known as source informants, agents or undercover
officers. Covert human intelligence sources may be authorised in the
same way as direct surveillance.

Tribunal

The Tribunal has jurisdiction in relation to matters covered by both   7.25
Acts. Individuals who believe they have been wrongly treated
through the use of interception or surveillance techniques will have
recourse to this Tribunal which also replaces existing remedies for
complaints, provided under the Police Act 1997, the Intelligence
Act 1994 and the Security Services Act 1989. The Act states that the
jurisdiction of the Tribunal shall be the only appropriate tribunal
for the purposes of section 7 of the Human Rights Act 1988
(proceedings for actions incompatible with Convention rights).[70]
There is a time limit of one year for bringing complaints.

The Regulation of Investigatory Powers Act requires the
Secretary of State to have regard to the need to ensure that matters
brought before the Tribunal are "properly heard and considered"
when making procedural rules but this is qualified by the need to
secure that information is not disclosed to an extent or in a manner
that is contrary to the public interest or prejudicial to national
security, the prevention or detection of serious crime, the economic
well-being of the United Kingdom or continued discharge of the
functions of the intelligence services.[71]

Workplace Surveillance

During the period of development of the Regulation of Investiga-   7.26
tory Powers Act the Government pointed out that the existing
legislation did not cover the interception of communications within
private networks. This was seen by the United Kingdom Government as an important gap in the law as it means that there was no
lawful way of intercepting communications over private networks.
There was also no right of legal redress for individuals whose
communications had been unlawfully intercepted on such networks.

---

[69] Regulation of Investigatory Powers (Scotland) Act 2000, s.1(7).
[70] Regulation of Investigatory Powers Act 2000, s.65(2)(a).
[71] *ibid.*, s.69(6).

The issue of workplace surveillance has been a subject of some controversy. There is obvious conflict between the Regulation of Investigative Powers Act, which gives legal sanction to a person with a right to control a private telecommunication network to intercept their own network for lawful business purposes, and the Data Protection Act and the Human Rights Act which are intended to protect privacy. A draft code on workplace privacy, was issued in 2000 with the final version to be launched Easter 2001. Implementation has been delayed due to strong opposition from industry, which claims that the code is too complicated. Employers also object to the barring of blanket monitoring of employee's electronic communications and the opening of staff email. The code conflicts with the Regulation of Investigative Powers Act. The Data Protection Commissioner has insisted email is private and has refused to modify the code, which bars employers from opening personal messages received at work. She also states employees should have the power to delete emails to prevent their being retrieved from hard disks. However, the Department of Trade and Industry has expressed a view that the Regulation of Investigative Powers Act takes precedence, with the only outlet for employees being a civil action against an employer who has not told its staff that email "may or will be intercepted".

RESPECT FOR FAMILY LIFE

Definition of "family"

7.27	The concept of family life is not restricted to situations where there is a traditional family in which the parents are married to each other. It is the right to live as a family or to have personal relationships which the Convention aims to protect. In a case before the European Court of Human Rights, the father and mother of a young child, who were not married at the time of his birth, complained that their rights under the European Convention on Human Rights 1950, Article 6(1) and Article 8 had been violated when they had been denied access to social reports, during care proceedings in respect of the child, who had been taken into care. Children's hearings took a number of decisions concerning custody and access arrangements and eventually freed the child for adoption. The parents had married by this time. European Court of Human Rights held that the failure to give the mother access to the social reports was a breach of Article 6(1). Article 8 had been violated in respect of the right to respect for family life as there was evidence that the parents led a joint family life and acted together in their efforts to gain custody of the child.[72] In *Keegan v. Ireland*,[72A] a case in which an unmarried father complained that his rights under Article 8 had been infringed as he had no right to be heard by the Statutory Adoption Board, the Court considered the nature of family life. After commenting that the conception of the child was a deliberate decision and that the parents had intended at that time to get married the Court said that their relationship had all the hallmarks of family life for the purposes of Article 8. The fact that the relationship later broke down does not alter the nature of the relationship any more than it would for a couple who were lawfully married. In *Kroon v. Netherlands*, the applicants challenged the Dutch system for registration of births as interfering with rights to a family life under Article 8. Mrs Kroon had been married but when that marriage ended she had a stable relationship with Mr Zerrouk, although she did not live with him, and they had a child. Mr Zerrouk wanted to register the child as his son but this was not possible under the rules for registration of births. The Court held that, although, as a rule, living together may be a requirement for a family relationship, exceptionally other factors may serve to demonstrate family ties. Respect for family life requires that biological and social reality prevail over legal presumption. The Netherlands had failed to secure to the applicants the respect for their family life to which they were entitled.[73] In the case of *R v. Secretary of State for Health, ex parte L (M)*, a convicted prisoner serving a life sentence applied for judicial review of a rule which restricted visits by children unless a limited category of relationship existed. The categories of permitted relationship included those where the patient was the parent or relative of the child. The term relative included uncles and aunts but visits by nephews were not permitted until a risk assessment had been carried out. The prisoner argued that this rule interfered with the right to family life under Article 8. It was held that restrictions on child visits to patients at high security were wholly justified and compatible with Article 8. No category of child was entirely excluded from visiting, as it was always possible to have recourse to the courts for a contact order. It was not obvious that the relationship between uncles and aunts and nieces and nephews necessarily fell within the meaning of family life under Article 8. Family life was a flexible concept and depended on the facts of each case. The purpose of the Circular was protect children and, in that regard, it was well balanced.[74]

---

[72] *McMichael v. U.K.* [1995] 2 F.C.R. 718; (1995) 20 E.H.R.R. 205; [1995] Fam. Law 478.
[72A] [1994] 3 F.C.R. 165.
[73] *Kroon v. Netherlands* (1994) 19 E.H.R.R. 263.
[74] *R v. Secretary of State for Health, ex p. L (M)* [2001] 1 F.L.R. 406; [2001] 1 F.C.R. 326; (2001) 58 B.M.L.R. 101; [2001] Fam. Law 101.

The closure of a home for severely disabled people was held to contravene Article 8 in the case of *R v. North and East Devon Health Authority, ex parte Coughlan*. Coughlan, a tetraplegic, was moved from a hospital which was closing to Mardon House, a purpose built property owned by the health authority, which provided facilities for the severely disabled. Coughlan, who had been told that Mardon House would be a permanent home for her, successfully applied for judicial review of a decision of to close Mardon House. The authority appealed. It was held by the Court of Appeal that the decision to close Mardon House was in breach of Article.8 and also of a legitimate expectation brought about by the health authority's own promise. The closure decision was unfair and could not be justified by an overriding public interest.[75]

Adoption of Family Life

7.28 The right to family life may also arise as an issue in cases involving adoption, custody and parental access. In the case of *B v. P*, a child aged two, appealed against the making of a sole adoption order in favour of her natural father. The child's mother had kept the pregnancy secret from the father, with whom she had had only a short relationship and had given her up for adoption at birth. Later the father was informed of the birth and the proposed adoption and the child was successfully placed with him. He was granted parental responsibility with the consent of the mother who wished to have no involvement in the child's life. The guardian *ad litem* argued that adoption was not to the child's benefit as it unnecessarily deprived her of a legal relationship with one of her natural parents and her extended family, and there was insufficient reason to justify the mother's exclusion. It was held that an adoption order would also arguably be in contravention of B's right to family life under Article 8. There was little risk of the mother seeking to interfere in B's life considering her stance in the proceedings but it was not in the child's interests to put an end to any possibility of her mother playing a role in her upbringing in the future.[76]

The rights of the fathers of children who are the subjects of adoption orders have been considered in a number of English cases since the implementation of the Human Rights Act. The prospective adoptive parents of child appealed against the decision to join the child's father, to the adoption proceedings in *Re S (A Child) (Adoption Proceedings: Joinder of Father)*. It was contended

---

[75] *R v. North and East Devon Health Authority, ex p. Coughlan* [2000] 2 W.L.R. 622; [2000] 3 All E.R. 850; (2000) 2 L.G.L.R. 1; [1999] B.L.G.R. 703; (1999) 2 C.C.L. Rep. 285; [1999] Lloyd's Rep. Med. 306; (2000) 51 B.M.L.R. 1; [1999] C.O.D. 340; (1999) 96(31) L.S.G. 39; (1999) 143 S.J.L.B. 213.

[76] *B v. P (Adoption by Unmarried Father)* [2001] 1 F.L.R. 589; [2001] Fam. Law 174.

that it was a misuse of the court's discretion to include the father, as there was no relationship between him and the child. It was held that the judge had properly balanced the interests of the child against those of the father and had acted wisely in the exercise of his discretion, as it pre-empted any future attempt by the father to exploit his rights under the Human Rights Act 1998. Although under the Adoption Act 1976 it was not a requirement that the natural father be joined as a respondent in the proceedings, the father clearly had strong views on the subject of the child's adoption. It was arguable that his right to family life under Article 8 would be infringed if he were not joined as a respondent. The judge was entitled to take account of the recent incorporation of the Convention into domestic law, since any future challenge to the child's adoption would be disastrous for her stability and should be avoided. The appeal was dismissed.[77] This case was prior to the implementation of the Human Rights Act but the decision took into account the imminent changes in the law. In *Re B (A Child) (Adoption Order)*, a father appealed against the making of an adoption order in favour of the foster parents of his son, with whom he had maintained a close relationship. The order had been made despite the father's refusal to consent to it. It was contended that inadequate consideration had been given to the father's right to family life under the Article 8. It was held that there was no apparent proportionality between the order made and the interference with the father's right to family life under Article 8.[78] Two local authorities applied for guidance regarding the notification of the respective fathers of two children in the case *Re H (A Child) (Adoption: Disclosure)*. Both children were subject to adoption proceedings initiated by their unmarried mothers, who had refused to disclose the identities of the fathers. Both mothers had placed the children for adoption at birth. It was held that, if there were close family ties then Article 8 was applicable. The court found that one of the children was part of a family unit with the father and therefore the absence of notice of the adoption would breach his rights under Article 8. It was not necessary for a father to be given notice or be joined in the proceedings where there were no family ties.[79]

The procedures followed in relation to adoption may amount to a breach of Article 8 if the rights of all of the family members are not respected. In *White v. White*, a husband appealed to the Inner House against the sheriff principal's decision to allow an appeal by

---

[77] *Re S (A Child) (Adoption Proceedings: Joinder of Father)* [2001] 1 F.L.R. 302; [2001] 1 F.C.R. 158; [2001] Fam. Law.
[78] *Re B (A Child) (Adoption Order)* [2001] EWCA Civ. 347.
[79] *Re H (A Child) (Adoption: Disclosure)* [2001] 1 F.L.R. 646; [2001] 1 F.C.R. 726; [2001] Fam. Law 175.

his ex-wife against an award of contact in his favour in respect of their youngest child. The approach had been taken, following the principle established in *Sanderson v. McManus*,[80] that the parent applying for access should prove that it was in the best interests of the child. The husband argued that Article 8 supported the view that interference with access between him and the child had to correspond with a pressing social need and be proportionate to the aim pursued. It was held that courts should have regard to the general principle that it was conducive to the welfare of children if their absent parents maintained personal relations and direct contact with them on a regular basis. This principle required to be applied with discrimination; there could be circumstances where the discharge by a parent of his parental responsibilities would not operate in the child's interest. The structure of the law complied with the requirements of Article 8 since it respected family life and contained provisions enshrined in legislation for balancing competing interests of the various members of the family. In making regard for the child's welfare paramount, Scots law was in conformity with the approach laid down by the European Court.[81]

Interference with Parental Rights

7.29 In *T. and P. v. United Kingdom*, the European Court of Human Rights held that there were violations of the European Convention on Human Rights 1950, Articles 8 and 13 where a parent was not treated fairly in the course of the proceedings. The applicants were a mother and daughter who alleged that the daughter had been unjustifiably taken into care and separated from her mother. They had no access to court or an effective remedy in respect of the interference with their rights. A video recording of an interview with the child had not been made available to the mother. The Court held that this should have been determined quickly to allow the mother an effective opportunity to answer the allegations that her daughter could not be returned safely to her care.[82] In *W v. United Kingdom*, the applicant challenged the process by which his child had been placed with long-term foster parents and he and his wife had been denied access to the child. The couple had a history of serious marital and financial difficulties. When the child was born his parents placed him in voluntary care as his mother was suffering from post-natal depression and alcoholism. Without informing the parents, the local authority passed resolutions assuming parental rights over the child. One year later, again without consulting the

---

[80] *Sanderson v. McManus*, 1997 S.C. (HL) 55.
[81] *White v. White*, 2001 S.L.T. 485; 2001 Fam. L.R. 21. See also *Elsholz v. Germany* [2000] 2 F.L.R. 486.
[82] *T. and P. v. U.K.*, unreported, May 10, 2001, ECHR.

parents, the local authority approved a proposal to place the child with foster parents and restrict the access rights of his parents. A month after that, the Director of Social Services decided, for the benefit of the child, that his parents should not be allowed to visit him. The couple instigated legal proceedings but the High Court held that it would not be in the child's interests to return him. Subsequently the local ombudsman held that there had been maladministration in relation to the procedures followed. The Court held that the mutual enjoyment by parent and child of each other's company constitutes a fundamental element of family life. The natural family relationship does not terminate when a child is taken into public care. The authority's procedures amounted to interference with the applicant's right to respect for his family life. The Court found that the interference was in accordance with the law and that they had the legitimate aim of protecting the health or the rights of others—the child. The Court then considered whether the interference was necessary in a democratic society and found that by failing to involve the parents in the decision-making process the local authority had exceeded what was necessary in a democratic society. There was therefore a breach of Article 8.[83] The procedures for taking children into care in England and Wales were subsequently amended.

The procedures in Scotland came under scrutiny in *McMichael v. United Kingdom*. The applicants both had a history of mental illness. In 1987 the wife had given birth to a son. She denied that he was McMichael's child although they had been living together at the time. A children's hearing granted a warrant for the child to be kept in a place of safety because the mother was suffering a recurrence of her illness. The parents attended a children's hearing where a report was considered which had been drawn up by the local social work department. The parents were not given copies of the report but they were informed of the substance of the documents. The children's hearing decided that the child was in need of compulsory care. The Court found that the fact that the applicants did not have access to the documents amounted to a breach of their right to respect for family life.[84]

The European Court has consistently held that Article 8 includes a positive obligation upon states to enable contact between a divorced or separated parent and his or her children. This was outlined in *Glaser v. United Kingdom*. There is a right for a parent to have measures taken with a view to his or her being reunited with the child and an obligation for the national authorities to take such measures. This applies not only to cases dealing with the

---

[83]   *W v. U.K.* (1987) 10 E.H.R.R. 29.
[84]   *Ibid.*

compulsory taking of children into public care, but also to cases where contact and residence disputes concerning children arise between parents and/or other members of the children's family. The obligation to facilitate access is not absolute. The rights and freedoms of all concerned must be taken into account, and more particularly the best interest of the child and his or her rights under Article 8. In the *Glaser* case the Court concluded that the English and Scottish authorities had achieved a fair balance between the competing interests of the applicant, his ex-wife and their children.[85]

Immigration and Deportation

7.30 When citizens of different countries marry, it goes without saying that they wish to live together as a family. One of the barriers to this is the fact that the right to live in a country depends on the laws of the country concerned. Immigration into Scotland is a matter of United Kingdom law. Cases frequently come before the Court of Session challenging decisions relating to immigration and deportation. Infringement of Article 8 is frequently raised as a ground of challenge where one spouse is being denied leave to enter or where a parent is facing deportation.

Ahmed (Nisar), Petitioner was a case in which a Pakistani citizen sought judicial review of a decision to refuse to grant him leave to enter the United Kingdom. He had married an United Kingdom citizen subsequent to action being taken against him in relation to immigration. It was argued successfully on behalf of the Secretary of State that Article 8 of the European Convention on Human Rights does not confer an unrestricted right to enter or remain in a country. This had been stated frequently by the European Commission. The European Court of Human Rights has also stated that the duty imposed by Article 8 cannot be considered as amounting to a general obligation on the part of a state to respect the choice made by married couples of the country of their matrimonial residence and to accept the non-national spouse for settlement in that country.[86] There are provisions within the immigration rules for a person to enter as the spouse of a British citizen or person settled here, if the criteria set out within the rules are met. In the *Ahmed* case the rules had not been met as the marriage had taken place after action had been instigated against Ahmed. There was no breach of Article 8.[87]

The threat of deportation may involve a difficult choice for the family of the person being deported. The family could remain in the

---

[85] *Glaser v. U.K.* [2000] 3 F.C.R. 193.
[86] *Abdulaziz, Cabales and Balkandali* (1985) 7 E.H.R.R. 471.
[87] *Ahmed (Nisar), Petitioner*, 2000 S.C.L.R. 761.

United Kingdom or leave with the person being deported. The attitude of the courts is that a decision to deport a parent is not necessarily an infringement of the right to respect for family life as the family is also free to leave. Modern lifestyles, where couples have separated and then remarried create circumstances where the choice may not be quite so straightforward. In *Ahmed v. Secretary of State for the Home Department*, Ahmed, a Pakistani citizen, sought judicial review of a decision of the Secretary of State, refusing leave to remain in the United Kingdom. In January 1997 Ahmed married an United Kingdom citizen with custody of a child from a former marriage, X. X had contact with her natural father who also lived in the United Kingdom. Ahmed and his wife had another child in October 1997. Ahmed argued that the decision to deport him was *Wednesbury* unreasonable in light of the European Convention on Human Rights 1950, Article 8. Interference in Article 8 rights had to be proportionate to the legitimate aim of the interference and the exceptional circumstances presented by the child of his wife's first marriage had not been taken into account. If Ahmed were removed while his wife remained so that the child could maintain contact with her father, Ahmed would be separated from them but if the whole family moved to Pakistan that contact would be broken. Whatever option was taken involved an interference in Article 8 rights. It was held that there was not such disproportion between the continuation of enforcement action in the public interest and the consequent interference with family relationships. An important factor in the case was that the family relationship only came into existence after enforcement action against Ahmed had been instigated.[88] In *Akhtar, Petitioner*, Akhtar sought judicial review of a decision to refuse him leave to remain in the United Kingdom. He had entered the United Kingdom as a visitor in 1995 and had sought political asylum, which was refused. Enforcement action for his removal started in September 1996. He married an United Kingdom citizen and had a child in 1998. Akhtar argued that the decision breached Article 8. His wife had two children by a previous marriage to whom her ex-husband was permitted contact under a residence order. She would have to seek permission of the courts to take them abroad and if refused would be unable to go with Akhtar. It was held the application of Article 8 in such cases as this involved balancing considerations and an exercise of discretion. In a judicial review the question was whether the decision taker's view that Article 8 had not been infringed was one at which he might reasonably have arrived. The decision of the European Court of Human Rights in similar cases was that it had been the parent's choice to remarry someone whose immigration

[88] *Ahmed v. Secretary of State for the Home Department*, 2000 G.W.D. 12–433.

status was in doubt that had brought about the adverse affect, and not the state. It was a matter for the immigration officer to consider whether the circumstances were sufficiently exceptional to merit departure from the published policy and as these circumstances were implicit in the decision to marry in the knowledge that enforcement action had been taken, his decision was not irrational and unreasonable.[89]

A contrasting case, where the applicant's family ties with the country were long established was *Mehemi v. France*.[90] Mehemi was an Algerian national, was born in France in 1962 and lived there until his deportation in 1995 following his conviction for drug trafficking. In addition to his parents and siblings, some of whom were French nationals, he also left behind his wife, an Italian national resident in France since 1978, and their three children, who were all French nationals. M complained that his permanent exclusion had interfered with his right to family life, contrary to the European Convention on Human Rights 1950, Article 8(2). The complaint was allowed as Mehemi had shown that his established French private life had been interfered with by the order. The use of deportation in such cases had to strike a balance between crime prevention and the preservation of public order and the individual's rights under Article 8. On the facts, Mehemi had no connection with Algeria apart from his nationality, which was outweighed by his French birth, education and upbringing. His links with France were strong in terms of his parents, siblings and his wife and children. Although his conviction weighed against him, his right to family life under Article 8 had been breached by the deportation.

RESPECT FOR ONES HOME

7.31 The definition of home implies that it is the place which is ones principle residence, but in the context of Article 8 the meaning may be wider. This was considered in the case of *Gillow v. United Kingdom*. Mr and Mrs Gillow had moved to Guernsey in 1956 so that Mr Gillow could work there. They bought a plot of land and built a house. They lived in it until 1960 when Mr Gillow took a job overseas. They did not sell the house but rented it. People could only live on Guernsey if they had a resident's licence. In 1979 the Gillows returned to Guernsey but were refused a resident's licence. They lived in the house without a licence but they were prosecuted and had to sell the house and leave. It was held that the house in Guernsey was the Gillow's home. They had not established any other home in the United Kingdom and they had maintained links with the Guernsey house. The fact that they were prevented from living in their home was an interference with their right to respect for their home. It was legitimate for the authorities to try to control the population of Guernsey so as to promote the economic well-being of the island. The action taken was however disproportionate to that aim in the Gillow's case.[91]

In *Buckley v. United Kingdom,* the United Kingdom Government asserted that the term "home" only applied to a residence which had been legally established according to national law. The applicant was a gypsy who had bought a piece of land and then lived on it with her family in three caravans for a number of years. She applied for planning permission to build a house but permission was refused. When she refused to move her caravans enforcement proceedings were taken against her. The Court, following the *Gillow* case, decided that the caravans were her home. It was held however, that the interference with her home was justified in this case, as it was necessary for the economic well-being of the country and for the protection of the health and rights of other persons.[92]

States can be held liable under Article 8 for causing, or failing to prevent, environmental pollution which interferes with a person's right to respect for their home. In *Lopez Ostra v. Spain,* the applicant claimed that her rights under Article 8 had been infringed by pollution. A tannery reprocessing plant had been built, with a state subsidy, 12 metres from her flat. This caused adverse effects on the health of the family and they had to move. The Court held that severe environmental pollution could interfere with the right to respect for a person's home even where the pollution was not highly toxic. The state argued that the interference was justified in the interests of the economic well-being of the area but the Court held that the state had not achieved a fair balance between the interests of the community and the rights of the applicant. It was held that there was a breach of Article 8 and damages were awarded.[93] In *Guerra v. Italy,* the state was held to be in breach of Article 8 for failing to warn local residents of the risk of danger from a nearby chemical plant and to advise on the procedures which should be followed in an emergency.[94] The regulation of environmental pollution is one of the areas where the state has a positive obligation to protect the rights under Article 8, as well as a negative obligation to refrain from interference.

Noise and disruption from neighbours is another area where it 7.32 could be argued that the state should be aware of this positive

---

[91] *Gillow v. U.K.* (1986) 11 E.H.R.R. 335.
[92] *Buckley v. U.K.* (1996) 23 E.H.R.R.101.
[93] *Lopez Ostra v. Spain* (1995) 20 E.H.R.R. 277.
[94] *Guerra v. Italy* (1998) 26 E.H.R.R. 357.

obligation. In recent years the law in Scotland has responded to this issue and local authorities now have two specific powers which enable them to protect the right of the citizen to peaceful enjoyment of his home. Potentially a failure by a local authority to exercise these powers could lead to a challenge under the Human Rights Act by a person whose private home life is disrupted by the conduct of neighbours.

Under the Crime and Disorder Act 1998,[95] a local authority may make an application for an anti-social behaviour order if it appears to the authority that a person of or over the age of 16: has acted in an anti-social manner or pursued a course of anti-social conduct likely to cause alarm or distress to one or more persons outside his household in the authority's area. The purpose of an anti-social behaviour order is to protect persons in the authority's area from further anti-social acts or conduct by him. The provision has been introduced to protect residents from "neighbours from hell" whose behaviour infringes on the rights of those around them to enjoy a peaceful existence. An application is made to a sheriff who can make an order prohibiting the person from doing anything described in the order. An order can last for a specific period, or indefinitely, but that either the local authority or the party named in the order can apply for its variation or revocation.[96]

Local authorities also have specific powers arising from their role as landlords. The Crime and Disorder Act 1998,[97] entitles a local authority to take account of a broad range of anti-social behaviour by a tenant, his companions or visitors at the house, or in its vicinity, as grounds for terminating a secure tenancy. Under Schedule 3 to the Housing (Scotland) Act 1987[98] the landlord of a secured tenant can apply to the sheriff or an eviction order to remove the tenant from the premises. The 1998 Act widens the categories of people whose conduct at the tenanted house, or its vicinity, can give rise to an eviction. A tenant may be evicted not only because of his own conduct or that of other people living in his house but also because of the actions of visitors. An eviction order may be granted if visitors to the premises have directed actions against the tenant's neighbours, or if they have committed criminal offences.

7.33   The right to respect for one's home and family life is a qualified right and so interference with the right may be lawful. Interference with the right of respect for ones home may be authorised by law for the purpose of law enforcement. The police, for example, have powers to search and enter premises. This power can only be

---

[95] Crime and Disorder Act 1998, s.19.
[96] Crime and Disorder Act 1998, s.21(7).
[97] Crime and Disorder Act 1998, s.23.
[98] Housing (Scotland) Act 1987, Sched. 3.

exercised in specific circumstances and is strictly regulated with respect to procedures.

Power of Entry to Premises

In order to enter private premises the police must have either the 7.34 authority of the courts in the form of a warrant or be fully justified in their actions. At common law a constable is justified in entering premises only in certain limited circumstances. He can enter premises if he is in close pursuit of a person who has committed or attempted to commit a serious crime. Serious crimes include murder, rape, robbery, and theft by housebreaking. In *Cairns v. Keene,*[99] the police followed a car because they suspected the driver of being under the influence of alcohol. After stopping his car the man ran into his house pursued by the police officers. He took a bottle from the fridge and drank from it. He claimed that there had been vodka in the bottle and that any breath test, which he took, would not be reliable. At his trial he argued that neither the breath test not the subsequent blood test were admissible as evidence. The police were trespassers in his house and the breath test was not lawfully administered. He was convicted by the sheriff, appealed against the decision and the appeal was dismissed. The sheriff had not regarded the police as being justified in entering private premises because they were not in pursuit of a person suspected of being the perpetrator of a serious crime. He did, however, consider that the evidence was admissible despite this because vital evidence should not be excluded because of a technical flaw. The factors to be taken into account in deciding whether or not evidence is admissible are:

(a) the urgency of the need to secure evidence;
(b)   the gravity of the crime;
(c) the authority and good faith of those who obtained the evidence;
(d) the general principle of fairness to the accused.[1]

A police officer may enter private premises to quell a disturbance which is actually proceeding,[2] if he hears cries of distress or if he is invited to enter by the occupant. In an emergency the police officer may force entry but only after first knocking loudly, stating that it is the police, indicating the nature of the business and demanding admission. Only then after the occupant fails to admit him, may he force entry. In *Campbell v. Vannet,*[3] police officers saw a woman

---

[99] *Cairns v. Keene,* 1983 S.C.C.R. 277.
[1] *per* Lord Cooper in *Lawrie v. Muir,* 1950 J.C. 19.
[2] *Moffat v. McFadyen,* 1999 G.W.D. 22–1038.
[3] *Campbell (Sharon) v. Vannet,* 1997 S.C.C.R. 787.

kneeling by the letterbox of Campbell's front door receiving a package which they believed to contain heroin. One of the police officers shouted, "police, open the door" and saw Campbell run into the bathroom and lock the door. The police then forced open the front door and also the bathroom door where they found Campbell kneeling by the toilet with a brush in her hand. She was convicted of drug offences and appealed on the basis that the police had acted unlawfully. It was held that, as the police officers had just seen a serious crime being committed, they were entitled to enter the premises to detain the person suspected of that crime.

Several statutes authorise a police officer to enter premises without warrant. In each case the police may only take the specific actions which are authorised by the statute. Under the Licensing (Scotland) Act 1976 the police may enter licensed premises to investigate breaches of the licensing conditions. If premises are on fire the Fire Services Act 1947 gives authority to police officers to enter the premises, using force if necessary. Under the Betting, Gaming and Lotteries Act 1963 police may enter premises to investigate breaches of licensing conditions. The Crime and Disorder Act 1998, section 24 amends the Civil Government (Scotland) Act 1982 to empower the police to enter premises without warrant where reasonable grounds exist for believing that an offence involving the use of noise-making equipment has occurred. This section authorises police to enter to premises and to seize musical instruments, televisions and stereo equipment where there is reasonable ground for belief that their use is causing annoyance to others. This power can be exercised without the need for a warrant. The provision operates without prejudice to any other common law or statutory power of entry, search and seizure. Problems of noise caused by loud music might previously have been dealt with as a breach of the peace but difficulties could arise over retention of the property seized, pending any trial, particularly if the accused was not also the owner of the articles seized.[4] Where articles are seized a report must be submitted to the Procurator Fiscal. Once that is done the items can be retained until the prosecutor certifies that they are not needed as evidence, or until the conclusion of proceedings.

7.35   Where the police enter a person's home without appropriate lawful authority it will amount to interference with a person's right to respect for their home. In the absence of circumstances to justify this interference such interference will be in breach of Article 8. In *McLeod v. United Kingdom*,[5] the Court considered a situation in which unauthorised entry into a home had taken place. Following

---

[4]   Crime and Disorder Act 1998, s.24(3) and Sched. 1, enacted as Civic Government (Scotland) Act 1982, Sched. 2A.
[5]   (1999) 27 E.H.R.R. 493.

divorce proceedings the applicant had been ordered to give her husband certain items of furniture from the former matrimonial home, in which she lived with her mother. Thinking that she had agreed to allow him to collect the items her husband arrived at the home accompanied by relatives and a solicitor's clerk. He also arranged for two police officers to be present because he was afraid that there might be a breach of the peace. Mrs McLeod was not at home but her mother let Mr Mcleod and his relatives into the house and they removed the furniture. The policemen then went into the house and checked the items taken against the list in the court order. Mrs McLeod returned to the house and objected to the removal of the property. One of the policemen intervened in the argument and insisted that she allow her husband to leave. The Court recognised that police had power to enter property if a breach of the peace was occurring or to prevent a breach of the peace occurring. The policemen had not taken any steps to check whether or not Mr McLeod was entitled to enter his ex-wife's house on the day in question. As soon as it became apparent that Mrs McLeod was not at home the policemen should not have entered the property, as there was then no risk of a crime or disorder occurring. The Court held that the policemen's actions had been disproportionate to the legitimate aim and there has been a violation of Article 8.[6]

Search of Premises

The police have no general power to search premises without a   7.36
warrant. They may only search premises without a warrant if they have the full and free consent of the occupier of the premises. There must be corroborative evidence that consent has been given and the search must be conducted in the presence of the occupier. If, at any time, the consent is withdrawn the search must be terminated. Where a person has been arrested on a serious charge and a delay in carrying out a search may defeat the ends of justice a search without a warrant may be justified. Searches of premises may be carried out under specific statutory powers[7] or under the authority of a warrant. A general warrant to search premises or to remove articles is incompetent.[8] A warrant must be specific and its terms must be strictly adhered to.[9] If a search is carried out without a warrant any items seized may not be admissible in evidence. In *Graham v. Orr*,[10]

[6]   *McLeod v. U.K.* (1999) 27 E.H.R.R. 493.
[7]   e.g. Civic Government (Scotland) Act 1982, s.60. See *Druce v. H.M.Advocate,* 1992 S.L.T. 1110.
[8]   *Webster v. Behune* (1857) 2 Irv. 596; *Bell v. Black and Morrison* (1865) 5 Irv. 57.
[9]   *Leckie v. Miln*, 1982 S.L.T 177; *Drummond v. Lord Advocate,* 1992 S.C.C.R. 290; *Thomson v. Barbour,* 1994 S.C.C.R. 485; *Bell v. McGlennan,* 1992 S.L.T. 237.
[10] *Graham v. Orr*, 1995 S.C.C.R. 30.

an accused person's car had been driven to a police station following his arrest on a drink-driving charge. It was held that a police constable, who opened the car door and looked inside the car, had carried out a search without having had the power to do so. Evidence of what he had found within the car was inadmissible. However, the public interest in obtaining the evidence may outweigh minor procedural irregularities in the absence of unfairness An example of this is the case of *H.M.Advocate v. Megrahi (No.3)*. An accused, charged with murder of the persons killed in the Lockerbie air disaster in 1988, objected to the Crown's attempts to introduce as evidence the contents of a diary belonging to him. He claimed that the manner in which it was recovered rendered it inadmissible. Two Scottish police officers, an FBI special agent and a Maltese police officer had interviewed a business associate of Megrahi in an office in Malta under an agreement with the Maltese authorities which meant that Maltese criminal law and procedures applied. In the course of the interview the diary was found, apparently during a search. There was no objection to the search or the removal of the diary. No warrant had been produced. There was evidence that under Maltese law a search was lawful if carried out in the presence of an inspector of police or under a warrant signed by him, although a warrant was normally required to take possession of property. It was held that the search was not unlawful as the owner of the premises had consented. The Crown had not proved that it was lawful under Maltese law to take the diary, but the Crown would be permitted to lead the evidence given the public interest in the prosecution of a murder and as what occurred had been excusable. No device or trick had been employed and there was no evasion of the law; and the diary had been left there for about seven months.[11]

An application for a warrant must specify the places to be searched, including outhouses and vehicles and the articles to be seized. The officers who are authorised to carry out the search must not actively search for any items other than those specified. In the case of *Leckie v. Miln*,[12] officers who were searching a suspect's house removed a number of articles which were outside the terms of the warrant. The officers had not seen the warrant nor had they been told what they were searching for. It was held that they had been unlawfully obtained and therefore could not be used in evidence. The conviction for theft was quashed. It often happens, however that police, when conducting a search unexpectedly discover articles of an incriminating nature. In *Tierney v. Allan*,[13] the police found a typewriter, which matched the description of one

---

[11] *H.M.Advocate v. Megrahi (No.3)*, 2000 S.L.T. 1401.
[12] *Leckie v. Miln*, 1982 S.L.T 177.
[13] *Tierney v. Allan*, 1989, S.C.C.R. 334.

which had been stolen, while they were searching for stolen gas cylinders. It was held that the police were justified in seizing the typewriter. In *H.M.Advocate v. Hepper*,[14] the seizure of a briefcase was held to be justified. The initials on the briefcase did not match those of the occupier of the premises and so it was deemed to be plainly incriminating or of very suspicious character. In *Drummond v. H.M.Advocate*,[15] it was held that the evidence of a police constable was not admissible when, operating under a warrant to search for the goods stolen from a furniture warehouse, he had admitted to searching also for and finding clothing stolen from another place. The evidence of another constable operating under the same warrant was admissible. He stated that he opened a wardrobe looking for small items such as pictures and table lamps stolen from the furniture warehouse and he happened to find woollen goods, which he suspected had been stolen from another place. A police officer was not prevented from taking possession of other articles of a plainly incriminatory character, which he happened to come across in the course of a search. In the case of *Rollo v. H.M.Advocate*,[16] it was held that a warrant to search for documents included data files held on computer. Rollo was convicted of being concerned in the supply of drugs. Information crucial to his conviction was seized by police acting on a warrant. The information was stored on a Memomaster electronic notepad and Rollo argued that such a device was not a "document" in terms of the section in terms of which the warrant was issued and that its contents were inadmissible in evidence and accordingly his conviction should be quashed. It was held that the essential essence of the term "document" was the information recorded on it and the seizure was within the terms of the warrant.

Only those authorised by the warrant may carry out a search and seize items as evidence. In *Hepburn v. Brown*,[17] a warrant was obtained by Strathclyde police authorising a search of Hepburn's house. Information supplied by City of London police was used to obtain the warrant and a constable from London was involved in the search. During the search the English policeman found drugs. Hepburn objected to that evidence on the basis that the warrant authorised only the constables of the Strathclyde police force to carry out the search. Hepburn was convicted and appealed. It was held that the search was irregular because the English police officer had conducted part of the search himself. However, as the police officers had been acting in good faith and there had been no deceit

---

[14] *H.M.Advocate v. Hepper*, 1958 J.C.39.
[15] *Drummond v. H.M.Advocate*, 1993 S.L.T. 476.
[16] *Rollo v. H.M.Advocate*, 1997 J.C. 23; 1997 S.L.T. 958; 1996 S.C.C.R. 874.
[17] *Hepburn v. Brown (sub nom. Hepburn v. Vannet)*, 1998 J.C. 63; 1997 S.C.C.R. 698.

on their part, the irregularity could be excused and the evidence could be ruled to be admissible.

7.37   The procedures by which warrants are applied for and granted are an important factor in ensuring that unjustified interference with the right of respect for one home is prevented. The procedures came under scrutiny as a devolution issue in the case of *Birse v. H.M.Advocate*. Birse sought the suspension of a search warrant issued under the Misuse of Drugs Act 1971, section 3(3) on the ground that the granting and enforcing of it had violated his rights under Article 8. As the granting of warrants was an act of the Lord Advocate, this raised a devolution issue. Birse argued that there was not a proper ground for suspecting that someone was in possession of controlled drugs. He also claimed that the procedure for granting the warrant had not provided sufficient safeguard against the possible abuse of the police powers of search. It was held that provided that a justice had acted correctly within the provisions of section 23(3), the granting of a warrant could not breach Article 8. There were reasonable grounds for suspecting that someone was in possession of a controlled drug. The whole point of the procedure under section 23(3) is to interpose an independent judicial figure who actually considers the circumstances and decides whether to grant the warrant. Before granting the warrant, the sheriff or justice must be satisfied that there is a reasonable ground for suspecting that controlled drugs are in the possession of a person on the premises. This does not mean that the sheriff or justice has to carry out further enquiries of his own.[18] It was accepted that a search of a person's home was an interference with the complainer's right to respect for his home. However, provided that the search was conducted under a warrant, and the warrant was granted in accordance with section 23(2), then the search conducted under the warrant was in accordance with the law. It was also accepted that the purpose of the search was for the prevention of crime and that a warrant to search could be necessary in a democratic society for the purpose of preventing drugs offences.[19]

RESPECT FOR ONE'S CORRESPONDENCE

7.38   The interception of communications is permitted in a wide range of circumstances. There must, however be clear, specific unambiguous legal authority for any invasion of privacy. In *Klass v. Germany*, the Court held that the West German law permitting the interception of postal and telephone communications in national security cases was

---

[18]   *Baird v. H.M.Advocate*, 1988 S.C.C.R. 55; *Bell v. H.M.Advocate*, 1989 S.C.C.R. 292, 1988 S.L.T.820.

[19]   *Birse v. H.M.Advocate*, 2000 S.L.T. 869; 2000 S.C.C.R. 505 2000 J.C. 503.

consistent with Article 8. Although it was an interference by a public authority with the right to respect for a person's private and family life and his correspondence it was justified as being necessary in the interests of national security or for the prevention of disorder or crime and that the controls and safeguards built into the German system were sufficient to prevent abuse. The Court accepted that interception of communications was permissible to prevent espionage or terrorism.[20] In *Malone v. United Kingdom*,[21] it was held that Article 8 had been violated by intercepting telephone conversations without specific legal authorisation. The law regarding interception of communications was unclear at the time. It was then clarified by the Interception of Communications Act 1985. The interception, acquisition and disclosure of communications data is now regulated by the Regulation of Investigatory Powers Acts. Whether the law should protect the interception of communications within private premises was considered in the case of *Halford v. United Kingdom*.[22] Telephone conversations of Alison Halford, Assistant Chief Constable in Merseyside, were intercepted by senior officers. She applied to the European Court of Human Rights, alleging a breach of her right to privacy, as guaranteed under Article 8. It was ruled that the Convention had been violated and she was awarded compensation of £10,000. The government argued unsuccessfully that interception of communications within government property was not a violation of the Convention. The Court stated that it is clear that telephone calls made from business premises as well as from the home may be covered by the notions of "private life" and "correspondence" within the meaning of Article 8. There was no evidence of any warning being given to Ms Halford, as a user of the internal telecommunications system, that calls made on the system would be liable to interception. She would have a reasonable expectation of privacy for her calls. The Court stated,

> "any interference by a public authority with an individual's right to respect for private life and correspondence must be 'in accordance with the law' . . . this expression does not only necessitate compliance with domestic law, but also relates to the quality of that law, requiring it to be compatible with the rule of law. In the context of secret measures of surveillance or interception of communications by public authorities, because of the lack of public scrutiny and the risk of misuse of power, the domestic law must provide some protection to the

---

[20] *Klass v. Germany* (1979–80) 2 E.H.R.R. 214.
[21] *Malone v. United Kingdom* (1985) 7 EHRR 14.
[22] *Halford v. U.K.* [1997] I.R.L.R 471, (1997) 24 E.H.R.R. 253; 3 B.H.R.C. 31; [1998] Crim. L.R. 753; (1997) 94(27) L.S.G. 24.

individual against arbitrary interference with Article 8 rights. Thus, the domestic law must be sufficiently clear in its terms to give citizens an adequate indication as to the circumstances and conditions on which public authorities are empowered to resort to any such secret measures."

When communications are intercepted the resulting infringement of Convention rights may affect other individuals as well as the person against whom the action was taken. The rights of such a third party were considered in the case of *Lambert v. France*. An acquaintance of Lambert had been the subject of an order authorising the tapping of his telephone line. The order was extended by a judge issuing standard form written instructions. As a result of the tapping and interception of conversations, Lambert was charged with handling stolen property. Lambert sought an order that the extensions were invalid, contending that the written instructions had been given without reference to offences capable of justifying the continued tapping. The application was refused and that decision was upheld on appeal, where it was also held that Lambert had no standing to challenge the order allowing the extension. Lambert complained that the decision was in breach of the European Convention on Human Rights 1950, Article 8. It was held that the tapping of the telephone line constituted an interference with Lambert's right to a private life and respect for his correspondence. Such interference would contravene Article 8 unless it was in accordance with national law and was in a form that was necessary in a democratic society. The interference in this case had a valid legal basis, but it exceeded what was necessary as such a requirement presupposed a guarantee against abuse. This was lacking as the finding that Lambert had no standing meant he could not bring a challenge as his own line had not been tapped. This meant that he had been deprived of a remedy.[23] The importance of fairness was emphasised in the case of *Amann v. Switzerland*. Amann complained that his right to private life under Article 8 had been breached by the tapping of a telephone conversation between himself and a person who had called him from the former Soviet embassy to order an appliance sold by his company. A record of the conversation had been retained on a card index system, noting that Amman was an embassy contact. It was held that the surveillance interfered with Amman's rights under Article 8. The national law relating to such surveillance activities was not sufficiently clear as to allow those who might be affected to be aware of the risk that it could occur. The surveillance did not therefore accord with the law in its fullest

---

[23] *Lambert v. France* (2000) 30 E.H.R.R. 346; [1998] H.R.C.D. 806.

sense. The keeping of the card had also interfered with Amman's right to privacy.[24]

In the case of correspondence of prisoners it may be difficult to balance the rights of the individual to privacy for his correspondence and the legitimate aim of preventing crime. Whilst it may be justified to intercept the correspondence between convicted criminals and their associates. Interference with correspondence for the purposes of access to justice, such as correspondence with a court, may not be justified. In *Campbell v. United Kingdom*, the applicant was in prison in Scotland, serving a life sentence for murder. He was involved in several sets of proceedings in the civil courts and two applications to the European Commission. His letters were opened and read by prison authorities. The correspondence included letters from his solicitor and from the European Commission. Interception of general correspondence was lawful in terms of the prison rules, however, correspondence with a legal adviser about legal proceedings to which the prisoner was already a party could not be read unless the Governor had reason to suspect that it contained other material. In such a case it should be examined in the presence of the prisoner but only so far as is necessary to ensure that there is no other material in the letter. The Court held that the opening of letters to Campbell had been in accordance with the law. There was also a legitimate aim of preventing crime or disorder. However, correspondence between a lawyer and his client is privileged under Article 8. That such letters be intercepted and read is not in keeping with the principles of confidentiality and professional privilege attaching to relations between a lawyer and his client. The reading of a prisoner's mail to and from a lawyer should only be permitted when the authorities have reasonable grounds to suspect that the privilege is being abused and that the contents of a letter may endanger prison security or the safety of others. In the absence of such evidence, opening letters between a solicitor and his client is not necessary in a democratic society. There was no justification for letters from the Commission being opened. There had, therefore been breaches of Article 8.[25]

Even where the correspondence is not between a prisoner and his solicitor, not every interference with correspondence will be in conformity with the rights under Article 8. Whilst it may be justified to scrutinise letters, to delay and even withhold them may exceed what is necessary in order to achieve a legitimate aim. In *McCallum v. United Kingdom*,[26] the United Kingdom Government made a referral to the European Court of Human Rights following the Commission's findings of violations of the 1950 Convention in

7.39

---

[24] *Amann v. Switzerland* (2000) 30 E.H.R.R. 843.
[25] *Campbell v. U.K.* (1993) 15 E.H.R.R. 137.
[26] (1991) 13 E.H.R.R. 597.

respect of restrictions imposed on McCallum's letters during his prison sentence. The prison authorities had stopped five letters written by McCallum, delayed two others, withheld copies of two letters written on his behalf and imposed a 28-day restriction on his correspondence under a disciplinary award. The Commission decided that, with the exception of the two delayed letters, the interference with McCallum's correspondence constituted a violation of the European Convention on Human Rights 1950, Article 8 of the Convention. The European Court of Human Rights affirmed that the United Kingdom Government was in breach of the right to respect for correspondence embodied in Article 8 of the Convention. McCallum's claim for £3,000 compensation under Article 50 (now Article 41) for distress and isolation suffered was dismissed, but £3,000 costs were granted.[27] In *Herczegfalvy v. Austria,* Herczegfalvy complained of various violations of the European Convention on Human Rights, including Article 8. He had been convicted of various criminal offences and was detained from 1978 until November 1984. The latter part of his detention was in a psychiatric hospital. There were numerous hearings and appeals in Austria. While he was detained all of his letters were sent to the curator who would then decide which, if any to pass on to him. It was held that Article 8 had been violated as Herczegfalvy 's right with respect to his correspondence had been wrongly interfered with. He was awarded 100,000 Austrian schilling compensation and costs.[28]

ARTICLE 12 — RIGHT TO MARRY AND FOUND A FAMILY

7.40   Men and women of marriageable age have the right to marry and to found a family, according to the national laws governing the exercise of this right.

This Article recognises that states may have different laws relating to capacity to marry and the formalities which may be required. The right to marry and to found a family does not confer a right to end a marriage by divorce. In *Johnston v. Ireland* an applicant claimed that his right to marry and found a family was violated by Irish law which prevented him divorcing his first wife and marrying the woman with whom he lived.[29] Prisoners are entitled to marry but the right to marry does not extend to the right to conjugal visits whilst in prison.[30]

The right of to marry has not been extended transsexuals in the

---

[27]   *McCallum v. U.K.* (1991) 13 E.H.R.R. 597.
[28]   (1993) 15 E.H.R.R. 437.
[29]   *Johnston v. Ireland* (1987) 9 E.H.R.R. 203.
[30]   *X v. U.K.*, No.6564/74, 2 D.R. 105(1975).

United Kingdom or in terms of the European Convention, although rights have now been given to transsexual couples elsewhere in the world. In *Rees v. United Kingdom,* Mr Rees, a transsexual, claimed that the English law, which made it impossible for him to enter into a valid contract of marriage with a woman, was contrary to Article 12 of the Convention. Mr Rees was born as a female baby. He underwent treatment for sexual conversion and lived as a male. He referred to the fact that English law only permitted marriage between persons of the opposite sex and that biological criteria were used to determine a person's sex. It was held that Article 12 had not been violated as the right to marry, which was enshrined therein, referred to the traditional marriage between persons of opposite biological sex.[31] A similar case was brought before the Court four years later. The case *Cossey v. United Kingdom*, was an application by a person who was registered at birth as a male but later underwent treatment and gender reassignment surgery and thereafter lived a full life as a woman. She purported to marry a man but the relationship ended shortly thereafter. She applied to the European Court for a declaration that the United Kingdom had violated Article 12 as she was unable to contract a valid marriage with a man, which amounted to a violation of the right to marry. It was held that the United Kingdom was not under a positive obligation to modify its birth-registration system. There had been no significant scientific developments which would justify a departure from the ruling in the *Rees* case. There was no evidence of any general abandonment of the traditional concept of marriage, which in English law involved two persons of the opposite biological sex, and attachment to that concept provided sufficient reason for the continued adoption of biological criteria for determining sex for the purposes of marriage. Therefore it was not open to the Court to take a new approach to the interpretation of Article 12 [32]

The case of *Sheffield and Horsham v. United Kingdom* was 7.41 brought by two male-to female transsexuals who complained that Article 12 was contravened as they were prevented from contracting a valid contract of marriage with a man. The Court found in favour of the United Kingdom Government by a margin of 18 to two on Article 12. As in earlier cases, it noted that Article 12 referred to traditional marriage between persons of opposite biological sex and was concerned to protect marriage as the basis of the family. The prohibition on marriage between two people of the same biological sex in the United Kingdom therefore did not constitute a violation of Article 12. However, the Court also said that;

---

[31]   *Rees v. U.K.* (1987) 17 Fam. Law 157.
[32]   *Cossey v. U.K.* [1991] 2 F.L.R. 492.

"despite its statements in the *Rees* and *Cossey* cases on the importance of keeping the need for appropriate legal measure in this area under review, having regard in particular to scientific and legal developments, it would appear that the responding state has not taken any steps to do so . . . Even if it finds no breach of Article 8 in this case, the Court reiterates that this area needs to be kept under review by contracting states."[33]

There are now medical advances, which need to be taken into account, and it may be that future cases before the European Court will be decided differently. In the English case of *W v. W (Nullity: Gender)*, a husband sought a decree of nullity of marriage on the ground that the marriage was void because his wife was not a woman but a physical inter-sex. It was held, refusing the application, that where the gonadal, chromosomal and genital tests gave differing results, the biological test was inadequate so that additional developmental, psychological, and hormonal factors together with the secondary sexual characteristics could be considered. Mrs W had been registered as a boy at birth on the basis of chromosomal and gonadal evidence and a diagnosis of partial androgen insensitivity together with evidence of her ambiguous genitalia showed that Mrs W was not a transsexual but a physical inter-sex. From the time Mrs W could choose her sexuality she had lived as a woman and had undergone gender reassignment surgery, which had allowed the marriage to be consummated, and that was sufficient to demonstrate that W was a woman for the purposes of the marriage.[34]

---

[33] *Sheffield and Horsham v. U.K.* [1998] 2 F.L.R. 928; [1998] 3 F.C.R. 141; (1999) 27 E.H.R.R. 163; 5 B.H.R.C. 83; [1998] H.R.C.D. 758; [1998] Fam. Law 731.

[34] *W v. W (Nullity: Gender)* [2001] 2 W.L.R. 674; [2001] 1 F.L.R. 324; [2001] Fam. Law 104.

CHAPTER 8

FREEDOM OF THOUGHT AND EXPRESSION

ARTICLE 9—OF FREEDOM OF THOUGHT, CONSCIENCE AND RELIGION

"(1) Everyone has the right to freedom of thought, conscience
and religion: this right includes freedom to change his
religion or belief and freedom, either alone or in
community with others and in public or private, to
manifest his religion and belief, in worship, teaching,
practice and observance.

(2) Freedom to manifest one's religion or beliefs shall be
subject only to such limitations as are prescribed by law
and are necessary in a democratic society in the interests
of public safety, for the protection of public order, health
or morals, or for the protection of the rights and freedoms
of others."

There can be no doubt about the importance of this right, 8.01
particularly when it is set in a historical and political context.
Freedom of religious observance has been a matter of fundamental
importance throughout Europe for several centuries. In the United
Kingdom it has to be considered in the context of a multi-cultural
society in which the Christian religion holds a dominant position
and in which there is still a close link between the established church
and the state.

Article 9 has three distinct elements

(1) Freedom of Belief

The Convention establishes an absolute right to freedom of 8.02
thought, conscience and religion. The right is not limited to
religious beliefs but can be applied equally to moral and political
ideologies. It is unlikely that this right will come under any threat in
the United Kingdom.

(2) Right to Act in Accordance with the Belief

8.03 Article 9 establishes a freedom, either alone or in community with others and in public or private, to manifest his religion and belief, in worship, teaching, practice and observance. This right to carry out activities associated with religion and other beliefs distinguishes Article 9 from Article 10, which gives a right to express views and opinions. Article 9 can be seen as a limitation on the freedom of expression in that, in order to allow people to observe their religious beliefs without interference, it may be necessary to limit the freedom of expression of others (for example by blasphemy laws). The right to manifest ones religion or belief is a qualified right. It may be subject to such limitations as are prescribed by law and are necessary in a democratic society:

(1) in the interests of public safety;
(2) for the protection of public order;
(3) for the protection of health or morals; or
(4) for the protection of the rights and freedoms of others.

Thus, for example, it would not be contrary to Article 9 for a local authority to refuse permission to a religious group to hold a procession on the grounds that there is a strong risk of sectarian violence. In *X v. United Kingdom*, the Commission considered an application from a prisoner who had been refused permission to have a religious book in his cell. The book in question contained a section on martial arts. The prison authorities considered that this could be dangerous to the general prison population. It was held that the prisoner's right under Article 9(1) had been interfered with but that the interference was for the legitimate purposes of protecting public safety and public order. The action was not disproportionate to the purpose and so was justified in terms of Article 9(2).[1]

Questions have arisen with regard to the activities which can be classified as manifestations of a belief. The Article itself specifies worship, teaching, practice and observance as manifestations of belief. In *C v. United Kingdom* it was held that withholding a portion of income tax so as not to support the research and production of weapons did not qualify as a manifestation of belief. Consequently action to enforce payment of the tax was not an interference with rights contrary to Article 9.[2] In *Valsamis v. Greece*, Valsamis' parents who were Jehovah's Witnesses, objected to Valsamis taking part in parades to celebrate National Day commemorating the outbreak of war between Greece and Italy.

---

[1]   *X v. U.K.* (1976) 5 D.R. 100.
[2]   *C v. U.K.* (1983) 37 D.R. 142; also *X v. U.K.* (1984) 6 E.H.R.R. 558.

Valsamis' request to be excused attendance was refused but she did not take part in the school parade. She was suspended for one day. Her parents applied to the Commission in alleging, *inter alia*, breaches of the right to freedom of religion, contrary to the European Convention on Human Rights Article 9. It was held that, since the obligation to take part in the school parade did not offend her parents' religious convictions, there was no breach of Article 9.[3]

(3) Collective Right

Article 9 states that a person has freedom, either alone or in community with others and in public or private, to manifest his religion and belief. This gives collective rights in addition to individual rights. This means that the Convention right can be relied on by organisations representing people collectively, for example schools or charitable societies. 8.04

Article 9 merits a specific provision in the Human Rights Act. Section 13 states that if a court's determination of any question arising under this Act might affect the exercise by a religious organisation (itself or its members collectively) of the Convention right to freedom of thought, conscience and religion, it must have particular regard to the importance of that right. Section 13 was inserted to meet concerns expressed by religious groups that one consequence of the Human Rights Act might be that the state would begin to interfere in matters of religious doctrine, for example by requiring churches to perform marriage ceremonies for homosexual couples. The direction that courts should have regard to the importance of the right is not intended to give any special status to Article 9 over and above any of the other rights. It is still open to a court to decide, for example that the right of free expression under Article 10 takes precedence over rights under Article 9 in the circumstances under consideration at the time.

Article 9 does not give protection against discrimination on religious grounds. That is given by Article 14, but only in connection with other Convention rights. The Council of Europe has agreed a new Protocol 12 to the European Convention on Human Rights which will replace Article 14 with a separate non-discrimination provision. This Protocol opened for signature in November 2000, but the United Kingdom Government has not yet ratified it. The new Charter of Fundamental Rights from the Intergovernmental Conference at Nice is also a potential source of reform. The case of *R v. Chief Metropolitan Stipendiary Magistrate, ex parte Choudhury*, was an application for judicial review of the refusal to grant a summons against the author Salman Rushdie for the offences of blasphemous libel and seditious libel. Rushdie had

---

[3]   *Valsamis v. Greece* (1997) 24 E.H.R.R. 294; [1998] E.L.R. 430.

written a novel called *The Satanic Verses*, which Choudhury found offensive to Islam. The summons was rejected on the ground that the English common law offence of blasphemy was not applicable to Islam. Choudhury argued that blasphemy should be extended to cover Islam and that its failure to do so contravened the right to religious freedom guaranteed under the Convention. It was held that having examined the authorities carefully and in detail, the common law offence of blasphemy applied only to the Christian religion. There was no justification to extend its applicability. That was for Parliament. That blasphemy did not apply to Islam did not mean that the United Kingdom was in breach of its responsibilities under the Convention.[4] This case may well have been decided differently if there was a free-standing Article on religious discrimination.

A Right Not to Hold Religious Beliefs

8.05 It was made clear in *Kokkinakis v. Greece*, that the protection afforded by Article 9 is not only protection for established, organised, traditional religions but also for the right to hold unconventional beliefs which are not shared by others. The Court said in that case:

> "As enshrined in Article 9, freedom of thought, conscience and religion is one of the foundations of a 'democratic society' within the meaning of the Convention. It is, in its religious dimension, one of the most vital elements that go to make up the identity of believers and their conception of life, but it is also a precious asset for atheists, sceptics and the uncon-cerned."[5]

In *Kokkinakis v. Greece* laws prohibiting attempts to persuade others to join a religious group were held to contravene Article 9. Jehovah's witnesses who had been fined for entering peoples' homes and attempting to recruit new members applied successfully to the European Court of Human Rights. The Court held that freedom of religion includes the right to try and convince one's neighbour, provided that the means by which this is achieved are not improper.[6] The Court has also said: "[t]he right to freedom of religion as guaranteed under the Convention excludes any discre-tion on the part of the State to determine whether religious beliefs

---

[4] *R v. Chief Metropolitan Stipendiary Magistrate, ex p. Choudhury* [1991] 1 Q.B. 429; [1990] 3 W.L.R. 986; 91 Cr. App. R. 393.
[5] *Kokkinakis v. Greece* (1994) 17 E.H.R.R. 397, para. 31.
[6] *ibid.*

or the means used to express such beliefs are legitimate".[7] In the census of the United Kingdom population carried out in April 2001, people were asked, for the first time, whether they belonged to a religious organisation and, if so, which one. It was not compulsory to answer the question, but there was some disquiet in some sectors of the population about being asked.

ARTICLE 10 FREEDOM OF EXPRESSION

"(1) Everyone has the right to freedom of expression. This 8.06 right shall include freedom to hold opinions and to receive and impart information and ideas without interference by public authority and regardless of frontiers. This Article shall not prevent States from requiring the licensing of broadcasting, television or cinema enterprises.

(2) The exercise of these freedoms, since it carries with it duties and responsibilities, may be subject to such formalities, conditions, restrictions, or penalties as are prescribed by law and are necessary in a democratic society, in the interests of national security, territorial integrity or public safety, for the prevention of disorder or crime, for the protection of health or morals, for the protection of the reputation or rights of others, for preventing the disclosure of information received in confidence, or for maintaining the authority and impartiality of the judiciary."

Article 10 gives only a qualified right to freedom of expression. The wording of Article 10 suggests a relatively wide set of circumstances in which freedom of expression may be restricted. The purposes of protection of territorial integrity, the reputation of others, preventing the disclosure of information received in confidence and maintaining the authority and impartiality of the judiciary are exclusive to this Article. It has long been accepted by jurists that individual rights may be overridden in circumstances where the infringement of the right is justified. Dworkin argued that there are circumstances in which infringement with rights is justified.[8] One such occasion is where interference is required because of competing rights. This would provide the justification for restricting freedom of expression where harm would occur to others, for example where the other person would suffer harm

---

[7] *Manoussakis v. Greece* [1997] E.H.R.R. 387, para 47.
[8] Dworkin, *Taking Rights Seriously* (1977).

because of defamatory statements or where a trial may be prejudiced by pre-trial publicity. Another occasion in which infringement of a right may be justified is where the exercise of the right may pose a real danger to society. The concept of "danger to society" is not given the same interpretation by all. Some would argue that it includes moral danger and therefore publications which may offend the sensibilities of others on moral or religious grounds are justified. Others would argue that restrictions on free expression on the ground of moral danger are not justified. The margin of appreciation afforded to state law in the context of freedom of expression is therefore wider than with other qualified rights. The general approach of the European Court of Human Rights in relation to Article 10 is shown in the case of *Handyside v. United Kingdom*.[9] Handyside was a publisher who obtained the United Kingdom rights to publish a book called *The Little Red Schoolbook*. It was written and published originally in Denmark and had been published in several other European countries. The book included a section on sex education. After review copies were sent out Handyside was charged with having an obscene publication in his possession. He was fined and the books were forfeited. (A prosecution in Scotland was unsuccessful). The European Court of Human Rights held that there had been no violation of Article 10. It was held that there had been interference with his right to freedom of expression but the interference was for the legitimate aim of protecting morals. In relation to whether the action taken against Handyside was within the boundaries of what is necessary on a democratic society the Court held that the English courts had not exceeded what was reasonably necessary in the context of the views on ethics and education in the United Kingdom. The fact that the book was published elsewhere without challenge was not an argument which the Court could accept. The Court had to consider the national margin of appreciation and the optional nature of the restrictions referred to in Article 10(2). The fact that other States decided to allow the publication of the book does not mean that the decision to prevent publication in the United Kingdom was a violation of Article 10.

Freedom of Expression

8.07　Everyone is entitled to have their own opinions and beliefs and one measure of the extent to which individual liberty is valued in society is the extent to which citizens are able to express their opinions without fear of retribution. Freedom of expression is an essential element of democracy. The ability of citizens to exercise informed choice between political parties depends on members of each party

---

[9]　(1976) 1 E.H.R.R. 737.

being free to publicise their views. Without a reasonable degree of freedom of expression citizens are denied their role in the democratic process. Accountability of a government in power is diminished if criticism of the actions of the government can be suppressed.

Freedom of expression is also important in wider spheres of life than those which affect the processes of democratic government directly. Freedom of speech allows informed discussion on religion ideologies and ethics. Scientific developments can be impeded by rules which suppress the sharing of ideas. Nevertheless, freedom of expression is never completely without restriction. The right of one individual to express his views has to be balanced against the rights of others. The rights which may need to be protected include national security, the right to a fair trial and the right not to be offended or shocked by obscene materials. Freedom of expression exists in the United Kingdom to the extent that anyone is free to express his views except where there is a law which prevents expression of a particular view or disclosure of certain types of information. The current restrictions on freedom of speech in the United Kingdom are broadly compatible with the permitted restrictions under Article 10. Although Article 10(2) lays down a broad range of legitimate aims for restrictions on the freedom of speech the only restrictions which are justified are those which are absolutely necessary. If there is no risk of harm to national interests, free speech should not be repressed. Restrictions were held to be justified in the case *BBC, Petitioners*. After their first petition to the *nobile officium* for consent to broadcast by television the proceedings in the Lockerbie trial had been refused the BBC presented a second petition to the *nobile officium*. The BBC argued that, as the court had already given consent to broadcasting the trial by way of television to four remote sites, refusing to allow broadcasts to the general public breached its rights under the European Convention on Human Rights 1950 Article 10. It was held that there was no devolution issue as the decision to refuse consent was not an "exercise of a function" by the Lord Advocate, but if a devolution issue had arisen, the restrictions would have been justified under Article 10(2).[10]

The Human Rights Act has made special provision for freedom of expression. Section 12 applies if a court is considering whether to grant any relief which, if granted, might affect the exercise of the Convention right to freedom of expression. The court must have particular regard to the importance of the Convention right to freedom of expression and, where the proceedings relate to material which the respondent claims, or which appears to the court, to be

---

[10]   *BBC, Petitioners (No.2)*, 2000 S.L.T. 860; 2000 S.C.C.R. 533.

journalistic, literary or artistic material (or to conduct connected with such material), to

>   (a) the extent to which—
>
>   >   (i) the material has, or is about to, become available to the public; or
>   >   (ii) it is, or would be, in the public interest for the material to be published;
>
>   (b) any relevant privacy code. [11]

In this section court includes a tribunal; and relief includes any remedy or order (other than in criminal proceedings).

8.08   The section is inspired by the purpose of ensuring freedom of the press. It was introduced as a result of concern expressed during the passage of the Act that the incorporation of the European Court of Human Rights would lead to a right of privacy, modelled on Article 8, which would restrict press freedom. It will not be sufficient to show that the material is for example, journalistic and that it is about a public figure, the court will need to look at the specific material and decide whether it should be published.

The Act now embodies in statutory form the rules of court practice that an interdict will not be awarded unless appropriate steps have been taken to notify the respondent, unless there are compelling reasons why such notification is inappropriate. The effect of section 12(3) was considered in the English case of *Douglas v. Hello! Ltd*. The actor Michael Douglas had entered into a contract with *OK* magazine for the exclusive right to publish photographs of his wedding to Catherine Zeta-Jones. *Hello* magazine had obtained photographs which they intended to publish. *Hello!* appealed against the continuation of an interim injunction restraining them, until trial or further order, from publishing the photographs. *Hello!* contended that the judge had failed to give any or sufficient reasons for his decision to grant the injunction and that, if the injunction was upheld, they would suffer damage because the opportunity to publish the photographs in a specific edition of the magazine would be lost. *OK* argued that publication of the photographs by *Hello!* would amount to a breach of confidence.

It was held, that by virtue of the Human Rights Act 1998 section 12(3), publication of the photographs could not be restrained unless it was established that the claimants were likely to succeed at trial. It was likely that Douglas would be able to establish that *Hello!* should not be allowed to publish the photographs because *Hello!*

---

[11] Human Rights Act 1998, s.12(4).

had breached the Code of Practice of the Press Complaints Commission 1997 Clause 3. Since a breach of the Code had occurred, *Hello!*'s right to freedom of expression was restricted by Schedule 1 Part I, Article 10(2) of the Act. However, if the injunction continued and Douglas failed at trial, *Hello!* would suffer damages which it would be extremely difficult to quantify in financial terms and the balancing exercise should be exercised in favour of *Hello!*. The appeal was allowed and the injunction discharged.[12]

There will always be potential conflict between the rights to privacy under Article 8 and the rights to freedom of expression under Article 10. The Human Rights Act has not made freedom of expression an absolute right but it has created an obligation on the courts to give a high priority to freedom of expression. This does not mean that Article 10 will always override Article 8. In order to ensure that the right to privacy is not ignored the Act does directs that courts have regard to any privacy codes. This will include the codes of practice produced by self-regulatory bodies such as the Press Complaints Commission and the Broadcasting Standards Council.

RESTRICTIONS ON FREEDOM OF EXPRESSION

Defamation

The restrictions which the law of defamation imposes on freedom of expression are for the purpose of protecting the reputation of others which is a legitimate purpose in terms of Article 10(2). Provided that the restriction does not exceed that which is necessary in a democratic society, restrictions for this purpose will not contravene the Convention. The purpose of the law of defamation is to protect individuals against false statements, which may cause harm to their reputations and to provide a mechanism for compensation where such harm has occurred. Defamation is the communication of a false statement which is defamatory. The law of defamation has been criticised as providing inadequate protection for the individual from unwarranted intrusion by the press into private lives. The process of gaining compensation for defamatory remarks is expensive and slow. People are often reluctant to undertake the expense of litigation. 8.09

The law of defamation could, however, be a serious threat to free and open debate in the course of debates in Parliament and to judicial proceedings. For this reason the protection of absolute privilege is given to:

---

[12] *Douglas v. Hello! Ltd* [2001] 2 W.L.R. 992; [2001] 2 All E.R. 289; [2001] E.M.L.R. 9; [2001] U.K.H.R.R. 223; 9 B.H.R.C. 543.

(a) Words spoken in proceedings in the Westminster Parliament,[13]
(b) Statements in the course of judicial proceedings
(c) Statements made by the Parliamentary Commissioner for Administration. [14]
(d) Statements made in the course of proceedings in the Scottish Parliament.[15]
(e) Publications made under the authority of the Westminster or Scottish Parliament, *e.g.* official reports of debates, committee papers and radio or television broadcasts of proceedings.

Absolute privilege means that whatever the accuracy of the statement or the intent with which it was made, no action for defamation can be based on it.

Qualified privilege is given to reports of Parliamentary or judicial proceedings. Qualified privilege applies where a statement is a fair and accurate report of the proceedings and it is made without malice.[16] In recent years the media has been inclined to take greater risks in reporting the falls from grace of public figures. The need to balance the right of a political celebrity to privacy against the right of free expression has been under consideration on several occasions. There has been a tendency in the press to assert that the public interest in knowing the truth about politicians justifies invasions of privacy. The House of Lords considered this issue in *Reynolds v. Times Newspapers.* Reynolds, a former Taoiseach (Prime Minister) of Ireland, had sued for damages for libel in respect of a story in the *Sunday Times.* The article was sub-headed; "Why a fib too far proved fatal for the political career of Ireland's peacemaker and Mr. Fixit". A small sum of damages had been awarded and Reynold's appealed on the ground of inadequacies in the judges summing up. *The Times* cross-appealed on the ground that the judge had refused to allow it to use qualified privilege as a defence. It was held, dismissing the appeal by majority, that although the law was concerned to ensure the dissemination of information properly in the public interest, the creation of a new category covered by qualified privilege would afford insufficient protection to individual reputations. It would also be wrong to single out political matters from other matters of public importance. If there were to be a separate category of qualified privilege covering political reporting, a newspaper would be able to publish factually incorrect defamatory statements with impunity, and the

---

[13]   Bill of Rights 1689.
[14]   Parliamentary Commissioner Act 1967, s.10(5).
[15]   Scotland Act 1998, s.41.
[16]   Defamation Act 1996, s.15.

reader would be unable to discern truth from fiction. The existing common law approach to the issue of privilege was to investigate all the circumstances of the case in order to determine its public interest value. The flexible approach to individual cases enabled free speech to be hindered only to the extent absolutely necessary in any given case.

Matters to be given careful consideration dependant on the individual facts of each case include: 8.10

(1) the level of seriousness of the allegation;
(2) the type of information;
(3) the source;
(4) verification attempts;
(5) status of the information;
(6) urgency;
(7) whether any attempt to obtain comment from the claimant had been made;
(8) whether both sides of the story were included in the publication;
(9) the tone of the published material, and
(10) the background to, and timing of, the publication.

Protection of free speech underpins all those considerations, which were not exhaustive. A refusal to identify sources should not result in any adverse inference being drawn.

Obscenity

The laws which interfere with freedom of expression on the grounds of obscenity can be regarded as lawful in terms of Article 10(2) as being for the legitimate aim of protecting morals. This is one of the areas where the importance of regarding the European Convention on Human Rights as a living instrument can be appreciated. Restricting freedom of expression because of obscenity or indecency raises difficult constitutional questions. Can such restrictions be justified by the need to protect society as a whole or certain sectors of society from being shocked or offended? Arguments in favour of restrictions tend to emphasise the need to protect members of society from corrupting influences. Definitions of obscenity depend on contemporary standards of decency taste and morality. It is difficult to apply an objective standard of acceptability for publications. Some publications which were regarded as obscene as little as 40 years ago are considered acceptable today.[17] Obscene publications are those which; "possess the liability to corrupt and 8.11

---

[17] For example the novel, *Lady Chatterley's Lover,* D.H. Lawrence.

deprave those to whom they are sold and exposed".[18]

The majority of cases involving obscene publications are heard before the courts in England and Wales because the majority of publishers are within the jurisdiction of the English courts. The control of obscene material is becoming increasingly difficult now that electronic communications and access to the internet make it possible for individuals to import material directly from outside the United Kingdom.

It is an offence under the Civic Government Scotland Act[19] to display any obscene material in any public place, or in any other place where it can be seen by the public. Material is defined as any book, magazine, bill, paper, print, film, tape, disc or other kind of recording (whether of sound or visual images or both), photograph, drawing, painting, representation, model or figure. In a recent prosecution under this section a man was charged with operating computer bulletin board systems which contained visual images and text files of an obscene nature. The accused argued that "text files" did not fall within the definition of "material" provided by the 1982 Act. He was convicted and appealed unsuccessfully. It was held that text files could be considered to be a recording of a visual image and so were included in the definition of obscene material.[20]

8.12   Performances of plays or television and radio broadcasting are not restricted by this section although they are subject to controls through the licensing system. Performances of films and video recordings are subject to a classification system. It is also an offence under the Civic Government (Scotland) Act to publish, sell or distribute any obscene material or to keep any obscene material with a view to its eventual sale or distribution. In the case of *Rees v. Lees*[21] the accused argued that he had not committed an offence if it could not be proved that he had sold any materials. A large quantity of sex articles had been seized from his shop during two police raids but he argued that there was no evidence that any actual sale had taken place and so he had not "sold" obscene material. He also argued that since the magazines were sealed in clear wrappers, they were not liable to corrupt or deprave. It was held that the word "sells" in section 51(2) included "offers for sale", and the sheriff had been entitled to infer that the articles were available for sale from evidence of sale on other occasions. Obscene magazines and videos visibly displayed with no warnings or age restrictions were liable to corrupt and deprave unsuspecting members of the public who found themselves exposed to the explicit and obscene covers visible through the wrappers. There is a

---

[18] *Ingram v. Macari (No. 2)*, 1983 S.L.T. 61.
[19] Civic Government (Scotland) Act 1982, s.51.
[20] *Ross (Crawford David) v. H.M.Advocate*, 1998 S.L.T. 1313; 1998 S.C.C.R. 359.
[21] *Rees v. Lees*, 1997 S.L.T. 872; 1996 S.C.C.R. 601.

defence of inadvertence. A person will escape conviction if he can prove that he used all due diligence to avoid committing an offence.[22]

Contempt of Court

The purpose of the law relating to contempt of court is to protect 8.13 the judiciary and judicial proceedings from actions or words which would impede or adversely affect the administration of justice.[23] Article 10(2) provides that one of the grounds on which interference with freedom of expression may be justified is maintaining the authority and impartiality of the judiciary. The prevention of crime is another legitimate aim. Laws which protect judicial processes from publicity which would make them ineffective contribute to both of these legitimate aims. The law of contempt is used to prevent publicity which may prejudice a trial both prior to and during the trial. Contempt of court is not strictly a crime but it is treated as a crime as penalties may be imposed on a party in contempt. The law of contempt of court restricts freedom of expression, particularly on the part of newspaper journalists and radio and television broadcasters by preventing the reporting of anything which could be prejudicial to court proceedings. This type of contempt of court is regulated by statute.[24] The Contempt of Court Act applies to publications. A publication is defined as including any speech, writing, broadcast or other communication in whatever form, which is addressed to the public at large or to a section of the public.[25] An example of the effect of the law of contempt on newspaper reporting was the case of *H.M.Advocate v. NewsPaper Group Newspapers.*[26] Following the shooting of a Yugoslavian in Kirkcaldy two newspapers published articles of a fairly sensational nature relating to the incident. These articles were published the day after the shooting and prior to the subsequent arrest of a suspect, and the Lord Advocate presented petitions against both newspaper companies on the ground that the articles were in breach of the Contempt of Court Act 1981 section 2. Both newspapers were held to be in contempt of court. The article in one newspaper was fairly specific in its allegations, implying the suspect was guilty but not naming him. A heavier fine was imposed on that newspaper. The system of criminal justice in Scotland depended upon the proposition that jurors should arrive in the jury box without knowledge or impressions of facts, or alleged facts, relating

---

[22] Civic Government (Scotland) Act 1982, s.51(4).
[23] *Report of the Phillimore Committee on Contempt of Court*, Cmnd. 5794 (1974), p.2.
[24] Contempt of Court Act 1981.
[25] Contempt of Court Act 1981, s.2(1).
[26] *H.M.Advocate v. News Paper Group Newspapers*, 1989 S.C.C.R. 156.

to the crime charged. The articles in question had undermined this. The newspaper companies were not able to plead in defence that they had no intention to interfere with the course of justice. Nor could it be a defence that they had procedures in place to vet articles to ensure that they did not create a risk of causing bias in court proceedings. The 1981 Act lays down a rule of strict liability and any publication which creates a substantial risk that the course of justice—in particular legal proceedings—will be seriously impeded or prejudiced will be a contempt of court regardless of the intent of the persons responsible for publication. The strict liability rule applies only when proceedings are active. Criminal proceedings are active from the time of arrest without warrant, or the time of granting of a warrant of citation, or the time when an indictment or other document specifying the charge is served on the accused. Civil proceedings become active in an ordinary action in the Court of Session or the sheriff court when the record is closed, or when a motion or application is made. In other proceedings the date when they become active is when the date of a hearing is fixed or a hearing is allowed.[27] A case remains active until it is disposed of or abandoned, discontinued or withdrawn. A publication which is a considerable time before a trial is due to take place could still amount to contempt of court. The case of *H.M.Advocate v. Scotsman Publications Ltd* concerned a publication several months before a trial was expected to take place. Mohammed Sarwar, Member of Parliament for a Glasgow constituency was charged with electoral fraud and attempting to pervert the course of justice. An article was published in the *Scotsman* newspaper under the headline, "Sarwar charge witnesses ask for protection". The article alleged that two witnesses had sought police protection as a result of fears about intimidation. The Lord Advocate applied to the court to make findings of contempt in respect of the publisher, the editor and two journalists. It was held that there had been contempt of court. An ordinary reader was likely to conclude that it was intimidation by Sarwar which was to be feared. The likelihood of this was increased by the fact that Sarwar was well known. The suggestion that he would intimidate witnesses lead people to suppose that he must be guilty. There would be a material risk of serious prejudice if any juror had read the article. [28]

The way in which the competing rights of the press, the courts and an accused person are regarded by the European Court of Human Rights can be seen in the case of *News Verlags GmbH & Co KG v. Austria*. A company which owned and published a magazine complained to the European Court of Human Rights that national

---

[27] Contempt of Court Act 1981, Sched. 1.
[28] *HM Advocate v. Scotsman Publications Ltd*, 1999 S.L.T 466; 1999 S.C.C.R. 163.

court decisions prohibited it from publishing a picture of a person who was suspected of involvement in a letter bomb campaign. News Verlags GmbH argued that the prohibition amounted to a violation of its rights to freedom of expression under Article 10. It was held that the prohibition on publication of the pictures in the context of reports on criminal proceedings, was an interference with rights to freedom of expression, which was a breach of Article 10 unless it satisfied the requirements of Article 10(2). The judgments of the domestic courts showed that the injunction against News Verlags GmbH was intended to protect the individual against insult and defamation and against violations of the presumption of innocence. The interference was for the purpose of protecting the reputation or rights of others and also the authority and impartiality of the judiciary and, therefore, satisfied Article 10(2). Although the press must not overstep certain bounds, in particular in respect of the reputation and rights of others or of the proper administration of justice, its duty was nevertheless to impart, in a manner consistent with its obligations and responsibilities, information and ideas on all matters of public interest. Interference with publicity of trials had to be considered in the context of Article 6(1), which provided that hearings be public. Not only did the media have the task of imparting such information and ideas: it had a right to receive them. The right of a suspect under Article 6(2) to be presumed innocent was a factor which had to be taken into account but the absolute prohibition on publication of the suspect's pictures went further than was needed to protect him. In this case it was held that the injunctions granted by the national court were disproportionate to the legitimate aims pursued.[29]

In Scotland actions for contempt of court are usually brought by the Lord Advocate. They may also be brought by a party to a trial who considers that the course of justice will be impeded. An action for contempt of court may be brought by an accused person in a criminal trial. This happened in the case of *Robb v. Caledonian Newspapers Ltd*. Robb had been arrested and charged in August 1993 with lewd, indecent and libidinous practices. He petitioned the court to make a finding of contempt against a newspaper company and its editor in respect of an allegedly prejudicial article published that month. It was held that the application was competent but should be dismissed on the ground of delay. It was argued that an accused person could not petition in this way without the consent of the Lord Advocate. It was held that there was no requirement for Scotland in the Contempt of Court Act 1981 similar to section 7, which required the consent of the Attorney General for proceedings

---

[29] *News Verlags GmbH & Co KG v. Austria* (2001) 9 B.H.R.C. 625. See also *Bladet Tromso v. Norway* (2000) 29 E.H.R.R. 125; *Worm v. Austria* (1998) 25 E.H.R.R. 454.

in England. The common law had never imposed such a requirement. Contempt of court is not a crime and so bringing an action for contempt is not the same as trying to bring a private prosecution for a crime.[30]

8.14   There are defences against an action for contempt of court. It is a defence to prove that, at the time of publication, or distribution of the publication, he or she does not know and has no reason to suspect that relevant proceedings are active.[31] Fair and accurate reports of legal proceedings, held in public, and published contemporaneously and in good faith do not attract the strict liability rule.[32] In *H.M.Advocate v. Danskin*, the sheriff made an order under the Contempt of Court Act 1980 section 4(2) restricting reporting of proceedings until return of the jury's verdict, to counteract concerns that details of a previous trial might be reproduced in reports of the present trial, leading to substantial risk of prejudice to Danskin's right to a fair trial. The press and media sought reduction of that order contending that, provided the reports of the present case were fair and accurate, there was no risk of substantial prejudice to Danskin. The court decided that the order should be restricted to reporting of proceedings taking place outwith the presence of the jury. It was necessary to balance Danskin's Convention rights under Article 6 and the rights of the press under Article 10. There was no substantial risk of prejudice to Danskin's right to a fair hearing if reporting was fair and accurate. Any reporting which was not fair and accurate would be dealt with under section 2(2) of the Act.[33]

A publication which is a discussion in good faith of public affairs or matters of general public interest will not be held to be in contempt if the risk of impeding or prejudicing legal proceedings is merely incidental to the discussion.[34] In the case of *H.M.Advocate v. Scottish Media Newspapers Ltd*, a television actor, had been charged with deforcing a sheriff officer, presenting an axe to him and preventing him executing a warrant. On the same date as his first court appearance, an article appeared in a newspaper published by Scottish Media Newspapers. The article stated that the actor had been arrested over claims that he had threatened sheriff officers with an axe when the officers had called to carry out a poinding. The article also stated that the actor had a history of drink problems and that neighbours had complained about disturbances at his home. The Lord Advocate presented a petition to the High Court asking that the court punish Scottish Media Newspapers as well as

---

[30]   *Robb v. Caledonian Newspapers Ltd*, 1995 S.L.T. 631; 1994 S.C.C.R. 65.
[31]   Contempt of Court Act 1981, s.3(1), (2).
[32]   Contempt of Court Act 1981, s.4.
[33]   *H.M.Advocate v. Danskin*, 2000 S.C.C.R. 101.
[34]   Contempt of Court Act 1981, s.5.

the editor of the newspaper and the journalist who wrote the article. The petition was dismissed. It was held that the court could only find Scottish Media Newspapers in contempt if the article had created a substantial risk of prejudice to the course of justice. The trial was unlikely to take place until more than nine months after the article's publication and the court must assume that a jury would follow the judge's direction only to consider the evidence heard in court. In those circumstances it could not be said that the article was in contempt of court.[35] In the case of the *Sunday Times v. United Kingdom*, the *Sunday Times* complained of a violation of the right to freedom of expression under Article 10, when they were prevented by an injunction from publishing an article which was critical of the Distillers drugs company during negotiations for compensation for victims of the drug thalidomide. The Court held that there was interference with rights under Article 10(1) but that interference was in accordance with the law. It was held by a majority that the legitimate aim of maintaining the authority and impartiality of the judiciary included protecting the rights of litigants who are involved in the machinery of justice. This aim is not one for which the same margin of appreciation is afforded to states as the protection of morals. The protection of the authority of the judiciary is an area of law where there is a great deal of common ground between the approaches of different states. The Court held that the interference with the right to freedom of expression was not necessary in a democratic society. There was no social need sufficiently pressing to outweigh the public interest in freedom of expression. The article contained information on a matter of undisputed public concern. Article 10 confers not only a right on the press to inform the public but also a right on the public to be informed.[36]

Section 10 of the Contempt of Court Act regulates the disclosure of sources. The court may not require disclosure, and a person will not be guilty of contempt as a result of failure to disclose a source of information, unless the court is satisfied that "disclosure is necessary in the interests of justice or national security or for the prevention of disorder or crime".[37] When a penalty is imposed on a person in circumstances where he refuses to disclose sources and disclosure is not necessary for the stated purposes there may be a violation of Article 10 or the Convention. This was held to be the case in *Goodwin v. United Kingdom*. Goodwin had been employed by a journal called *The Engineer*. A person contacted him and provided information about the financial problems of a company

[35] *H.M.Advocate v. Scottish Media Newspapers Ltd*, 2000 S.L.T. 331; 1999 S.C.C.R. 599.
[36] *Sunday Times v. United Kingdom (No. 1)* (1979) 2 E.H.R.R. 245.
[37] Contempt of Court Act 1981, s.10.

called Tetra Ltd. He contacted Tetra for confirmation of this information whereupon Tetra obtained an injunction preventing publication. The High Court ordered Goodwin to identify the source of his information so that Tetra could take action against him or her. Goodwin refused and was found guilty of contempt of court and fined £5,000. The European Court of Human Rights held that protection of journalistic sources is one of the basic conditions for press freedom. Without such protection sources may be deterred from assisting the press in informing the public on matters of public interest. This would undermine the vital public watchdog role of the press. The interference was lawful and was for a legitimate purpose but the purpose was not sufficiently important to justify the interference with the right to protect sources. There was therefore an infringement of Article 10.[38] This approach in the *Goodwin* case has now been followed in the post-Human Rights Act case of *Ashworth Security Hospital v. MGN Ltd.* It was held that, in interpreting section 10 of the Act the court should equate the specific purposes for which disclosure of the source was permitted under section 10 with "legitimate aims" under Article 10 of the Convention. The courts in the United Kingdom should apply the same test of necessity as that applied by the European court. In that case MGN, a newspaper group, appealed against an order that it disclose the identity of a person who had supplied information relating to a well-known offender from the database of a special security hospital. It was held that interference with the right to protect the source of information was justified in this case because the disclosure of confidential medical records to the press was misconduct which was contrary to the public interest.[39]

Restrictions on publication of prohibited material in reports of judicial proceedings

8.15 The Judicial Proceedings (Regulation of Reports) Act 1926 makes provision for restrictions to be placed on the reporting of certain matters arising in judicial proceedings. It is an offence to print or publish indecent material in a report of judicial proceedings.[40] In relation to divorce proceedings it is an offence to publish any particulars of actions of divorce other than certain limited particulars specified in the Act. The only people who can be prosecuted under this Act are proprietors, editors, master printers and publishers. In the case of *Gilchrist v. Scott* it was held that the offence is only committed at the point when a newspaper has been

---

[38] *Goodwin v. United Kingdom* (1996) 22 E.H.R.R. 123.
[39] *Ashworth Security Hospital v. MGN Ltd* [2001] 1 W.L.R. 515; [2001] 1 All E.R. 991; [2001] E.M.L.R. 11; (2001) 98(6) L.S.G. 46.
[40] Judicial Proceedings (Regulation of Reports) Act 1926, s.1.

printed and is distributed for circulation. Jurisdiction is therefore limited to the court which has jurisdiction over the publisher, which may not necessarily be the court in which the proceedings took place.[41] These restrictions are for the purpose of protecting the reputations of the parties to the proceedings and also protecting the morals of the community. These are legitimate aims according to Article 10(2) and the interference will not contravene the right of freedom of expression in Article 10(1) provided that it is not disproportionate.

Restrictions on freedom of expression during court proceedings

The behaviour of people present at court hearings may also be restricted by the law of contempt of court. Anything which amounts to disrespectful words or conduct may be held by a judge to be contempt of court. An example of this type of contempt arose in the case of *Young v. Lees*.[42] Young was present at the trial of his partner. When she was remanded in custody Young shouted "you guffy" at the sheriff. The sheriff found him in contempt of court. He was sentenced to 60 days' imprisonment. The laws which confer such powers on members of the judiciary are for the purpose of maintaining the authority of the judiciary. 8.16

Restrictions on freedom of expression imposed by court action

It is within the power of the courts to grant interdicts to prevent the publication of material. This can be done, for example, to prevent the publication of obscene material, material which would amount to a contempt of court, or material which would prejudice national security. It is not possible, however, to obtain an interdict against the world at large. Interdict will only be granted against those who have received a *caveat* and therefore have an opportunity to defend themselves against the action. This is in contrast to the position in England where an injunction can be awarded with universal effect. In the English case of *Venables v. News Group Newspapers*, Venables and Thompson who, at the age of 11, had been convicted of the murder of a child, applied for injunctions protecting them from being identified upon their release from detention. The injunctions were granted as there was a real possibility that Venables and Thompson would be in danger of revenge attacks if their identities were disclosed. It was held that, in exceptional cases, the court had jurisdiction to widen the scope of the protection of confidentiality of information, even to the extent of placing restrictions on the press. The exceptional circumstances could arise, for example, where if no restrictions were imposed there was a 8.17

---

[41] *Gilchrist v. Scott*, 2000 S.C.C.R. 28.
[42] *Young v. Lees*, 1998 S.C.C.R. 558.

probability that the person seeking confidentiality would suffer serious physical injury or even death. The injunction was granted openly against the world.[43]

Restrictions on freedom of political expression

8.18   Broadcasting during elections is controlled by sections 92 and 93 of the Representation of the People Act 1983. The purpose of the restrictions is to preserve equality between the candidates from different parties. In particular the aim is to protect the rights of individuals or groups with limited financial resources. Expenditure on national party election broadcasts is met out of the central funds of each party. Party election broadcasts may only be made by the British Broadcasting Corporation and under the authority of the Independent Broadcasting Authority. Political advertising is not permitted on television or radio. Following the case of *Grieve v. Douglas-Home*[44] the law was amended to allow broadcasting authorities to incur expenditure in disseminating material relating to elections provided that the material does not take the form of advertisements.[45] No broadcast may be made without the consent of any candidate who appears in the programme.[46] If a candidate participates in a broadcast for the purpose of promoting his own election, every other candidate in the constituency must consent to the broadcast. Participation in a broadcast is taken to mean active participation. In *Marshall v. BBC*,[47] an objection was raised because a candidate who had refused to take part in a broadcast was filmed while canvassing in the streets. It was held that the broadcast did not breach any regulation. No offence had been committed because to "take part" in a broadcast about a constituency means to take an active part in the programme.

Independent broadcasting authorities are under a duty to maintain accuracy and impartiality.[48] Although direct television advertising by political parties is prohibited, each party is allowed a number of party political broadcasts.[49] The amount of time allocated to each party is determined according to the proportion of the overall vote which the party secured at the previous election. This allocation applies during election campaigns and during other

---

[43]   *Venables v. News Group Newspapers Ltd* [2001] 2 W.L.R. 1038; [2001] 1 All E.R. 908; [2001] E.M.L.R. 10; [2001] H.R.L.R. 19; 9 B.H.R.C. 587; [2001] 1 F.L.R. 791; [2001] Fam. Law 258; (2001) 98(12) L.S.G. 41(2001) 151 N.L.J. 57; (2001) 145 S.J.L.B. 43.

[44]   *Grieve v. Douglas-Home*, 1965 S.L.T. 186; 1965 S.C. 315.

[45]   Representation of the People Act 1983, s.75(1)(c)(i).

[46]   *Marshall v. BBC* [1979] 3 All E.R. 80.

[47]   [1979] 3 All E.R. 80.

[48]   Broadcasting Act 1990, s.6.

[49]   Registration of Political Parties Act 1998, ss. 13–15 disallow any political broadcast from a party which is not registered.

political campaigns such as political broadcasting prior to referenda. In 1979 a successful challenge was brought against the allocation of party political broadcast time prior to the Scottish devolution referendum. Allocation of time had been made to four political parties, three of which were campaigning in favour or the referendum proposals. The opponents of the referendum proposals argued successfully that they were being treated unfairly.[50] During the 1987 general election campaign the Scottish National Party challenged their allocation of party political broadcast time. The SNP claimed that they were being treated less favourably in Scotland when compared to other parties who campaigned throughout the United Kingdom.[51]

The European Court of Human Rights has taken a vigorous approach in protecting media comment on political ideas and politicians. A violation of Article 10 was held to have occurred in the case *Lingens v. Austria (No. 2).*[52] Lingens had published articles which contained strong criticism of Bruno Kreisky, the Austrian Chancellor. He had been found guilty of criminal defamation because he was unable to prove that his statements were true. The Court found that the interference with his right to freedom of expression was lawful and for a legitimate aim, (the protection of the rights of others). The Court held that the limits of acceptable criticism are wider as regards a politician than a private individual. The requirements for protection of the reputation of politicians have to be weighed in relation to the interest of open discussion of political issues. His comments were of matters of opinion rather than fact and freedom of opinion is a fundamental part of the right secured by Article 10. The criminal prosecution was disproportionate to the aim pursued and was therefore a violation of Article 10.[53]

Incitement to Racial Hatred

A person may not speak or act in a public place in a manner which 8.19 is likely to engender racial hatred.[54] An offence is committed by a person who, in a public place or at a public meeting, with the intention of stirring up hatred against a racial group in the United Kingdom, uses words or gestures which are threatening, abusive or insulting. It is also an offence to use threatening, abusive or insulting words or gestures in the knowledge that hatred against a

---

[50] *Wilson v. IBA,* 1979 S.L.T. 279.
[51] *Wilson v. IBA (No. 2),* 1988 S.L.T 276. See also *Scottish National Party v. Scottish Television,* Court of Session (1997) Outer House Cases, April 15, 1997.
[52] (1986) 8 E.H.R.R. 407.
[53] *Lingens v. Austria (No. 2)* (1986) 8 E.H.R.R. 407. See also *Oberschlick v. Austria (No. 2)* (1998) 25 E.H.R.R. 357 and *Incal v. Turkey* (1998) 29 E.H.R.R. 449.
[54] Public Order Act 1986, s.17.

racial group is likely to be stirred up. A racial group is defined as a group of persons defined by reference to colour, race, nationality or ethnic or national origins. Nationality in this context includes citizenship, so a racial group could consist of the members of a state with a multi-racial community. The provisions of the Public Order Act apply to written material, videos, films and sound tapes as well as to the original words or gestures. This restriction serves several purposes in the context of Article 10(2). It can protect public safety, prevent disorder, and protect the rights of others.

Discriminatory Advertisements

8.20　Under the Sex Discrimination Act, discriminatory advertisements are unlawful.[55] The use of job descriptions which might be taken to indicate an intention to discriminate, and the use of job descriptions with a sexual connotation such as "sales girl" or "barman" contravenes the Act. The Equal Opportunities Commission may bring proceedings against the publisher of such advertisements within six months of publication. A non-discrimination notice may be issued and an interdict may be sought from the sheriff court to restrain a person from repeating the unlawful act at any time within five years of a non-discrimination notice. This restriction on the right to freedom of expression is for the purpose of protecting the rights of others not to suffer discrimination.

ACCESS TO INFORMATION

8.21　Article 10 is worded so as to include the right to receive information as well as the right to impart information and to express ones ideas and beliefs to others. Where a person wishes to have access to private information about themselves, the issue is really a privacy one and is therefore dealt with in Chapter 7. However, the right of access to information is also important where a person wishes to receive information with the intention of putting the information into the public domain. The workings of democracy require that a citizen will be able to understand as fully as possible the working of government so that he or she may render it accountable. The interests of the individual in receiving information about the workings of government have to be balanced against the interests of the government in withholding the information, often on the grounds of national security. The United Kingdom Government has been criticised as being more obsessed with keeping government

---

[55] Sex Discrimination Act 1975, s.38.

information secret than any other western democracy.[56] The United Kingdom has used various methods to keep information out of the public domain including:

(1) Public interest immunity, a doctrine whereby official information may be withheld from court proceedings;
(2) Criminal sanctions under the Official Secrets Act 1989;
(3) Codes of Practice which restrict Civil Service personnel;
(4) Statutory measures providing for secrecy in specific areas;
(5) Civil actions for breach of confidence.

A move to an approach which allows a reasonably free flow of information so that citizens can be informed as to the processes of government has been seen as a necessary reform for many years. There is now a Freedom of Information Act for the United Kingdom[57] and consultations are in progress on a Freedom of Information Bill in Scotland.

Official Secrecy

Government information was protected until 1989 by the Official   8.22 Secrets Act 1911. Section 1 of that Act dealt largely with espionage and is generally regarded as containing measures which are proportionate to the legitimate aim in Article 10(2) of protecting national security. Section 2, however, imposed a complete prohibition on the unauthorised dissemination of official information, however trivial. It was so wide in its terms that that it protected leaks of any kind of official information, whether or not it was connected with national security. Technically it was unlawful, for example for a civil servant to tell someone what he had for lunch. Section 2 made it an offence to receive official information without authority as well as to impart it. Section 2 became the subject of public criticism after the conviction of Sarah Tisdall, a civil servant who leaked information to a newspaper. The leaked information revealed that contrary to official statements, American cruise missiles had already arrived in the United Kingdom. She was sentenced to six months imprisonment.[58] This was seen by many as an unduly harsh penalty. Even more criticism was aroused by the prosecution of Clive Ponting, a senior civil servant who provided information to Tam Dalyell M.P., which related to the sinking of the Argentinian ship the Belgrano.[59] Ponting's intention was to prevent the suppression of information which he felt was in the

---

[56] Robertson, *Freedom, the Individual and the Law* (1989), pp. 129–131.
[57] Freedom of Information Act 2000.
[58] *R v. Tisdall* (1984) 6 Cr. App. R. (S.) 155.
[59] *R v. Ponting* [1985] Crim. L.R. 318.

public interest. The jury acquitted Ponting. It was felt that the Official Secrets Act 1911, particularly section 2, had now lost its credibility and was perceived by the public as an instrument supporting a culture of secrecy. The House of Commons Treasury and Civil Service Committee[60] reported that section 2 was unenforceable after the fiasco of the Ponting trial.[61]

This finally lead to a reform which was heralded as a big step towards achieving openness in government but which in reality was not a radical change. Section 2 of the Official Secrets Act 1911 was repealed and a new Official Secrets Act was introduced in 1989. Section 1 of the 1911 Act is still available to punish spies.

The Official Secrets Act 1989 did indeed remove criminal sanctions for the disclosure of some types of official information but it made no provisions for access to government information. It does not allow for defences such as public interest, or prior disclosure or lack of *mens rea*, and therefore introduces a stricter liability in relation to the categories of information to which it applies. The Act applies to Crown Servants and government contractors. To a limited extent it also applies to journalists. Crown servants are ministers of the Crown, civil servants, diplomats, police constables and members of the armed forces. The following categories of information are protected by the Act:

(a) information relating to security and intelligence[62];
(b) information relating to defence[63];
(c) information relating to international relations and any confidential information obtained from a state other than the United Kingdom or an international organisation[64];
(d) information the disclosure of which results in, or is likely to result in, the commission of an offence, to facilitate escape from lawful custody, or to impede the prevention or detection of offences or the apprehensions or prosecution of suspected offenders[65];
(e) any information obtained by reason of action taken under a warrant issued either under the Interception of Communications Act 1985, section 2 or the Intelligence Services Act 1994,sections 5 and 7, or relating to such a warrant.

Not every disclosure of information will automatically amount to a criminal offence. In some cases it is necessary to prove that the

---

[60] 7th Report 1985-86, HC 92-1.
[61] *R v. Ponting* [1985] Criminal L.R. 318.
[62] Official Secrets Act 1989, s.1.
[63] *ibid.*, s.2.
[64] *ibid.*, s.3.
[65] Official Secrets Act 1989, s.4(1).

disclosure was damaging. A disclosure relating to defence, for example, will be regarded as damaging if it reduces the capabilities of the armed forces, endangers life or equipment or endangers the interests of the United Kingdom, or of British citizens abroad, or is likely to have any of these effects.[66] In the case *Lord Advocate v. Scotsman Publications Ltd,* which concerned the publication of a book by a former member of the intelligence and security services, the Lord Advocate claimed that the book contained information which was covered by the 1989 Act. It followed therefore that the author, Cavendish, was prohibited from disclosing it. The Crown had already conceded that the information was harmless. The court held that Cavendish was in breach of the Act but that when he circulated the memoirs to third parties, they did not commit an offence by disclosing harmless information. A third party would only be guilty of the offence if the information was damaging in the sense defined by the Act.[67]

Some disclosures will be classed as criminal offences whether or not they are potentially damaging. Any disclosure by a member or former member of the security or intelligence services of information relating to security or intelligence is an offence, whether or not the disclosure is damaging.[68] The disclosure of information connected with warrants under the Interception of Communications Act and the Intelligence Services Act will also be an offence even if the disclosure is not damaging. A member of the security or intelligence services, or a GCHQ officer, is prohibited for his whole life from disclosing information obtained by virtue of his position.[69] Criticism has been levelled at this provision since it would have prevented information being disclosed about several high profile cases, including the spying activities of Anthony Blunt. There can be no doubt that these restrictions are for legitimate purposes as defined by Article 10(2). Whether a prohibition of a disclosure which is not damaging is necessary in a democratic society is less certain.

Section 5 of the Act applies to persons other than crown servants. Where a third party such as a newspaper has received information which was disclosed in contravention of the Official Secrets Act it is not an offence merely to receive the information provided that it is not published. It is an offence, however, to fail to comply with an official direction for the return or disposal of written information.[70] Any subsequent disclosure by the third party will be an offence if it is made either knowing, or having reasonable cause to believe, that

8.23

---

[66] Official Secrets Act 1989, s.1(1).
[67] [1989] 2 All E.R. 852 (HL).
[68] Official Secrets Act 1989, s.4.
[69] s.1(1) and (2).
[70] Official Secrets Act 1989, s.8(4).

the information is protected under the Official Secrets Act. The maximum penalty for disclosing protected information is a period of imprisonment of up to two years, or a fine, or both.

There are defences to a prosecution under the Official Secrets Act. Where disclosure would only amount to an offence if it is damaging it will be a defence to prove that at the time of the alleged offence the accused did not know and had no reasonable cause to believe that disclosure would be damaging.[71] It will also be a defence to show that, a the time of the alleged offence, the accused did not know and had no reasonable cause to suspect that the information disclosed related to one of the protected categories. It will also be a defence for a person to prove that, at the time of the disclosure he believed that he had lawful authority to disclose the information and had no reason to believe otherwise. The Act contains no explicit public interest defence so a person who has made a disclosure in order to reveal wrongdoing by public officials would have no defence. Alternative methods have been provided for a civil servant to pursue a grievance within their own department under civil service codes. Civil servants who wish to "blow the whistle" on illegal practices now share the same protection as other employees, under the Public Interest Disclosure Act 1998.

Breach of Confidence

8.24 Breach of confidence is a civil remedy which provides protection against the disclosure of information where the information has been entrusted to another, in circumstances giving rise to an obligation not to disclose the information. It is a remedy which is commonly used by commercial organisations where employees have leaked commercially sensitive information. The remedy may also be used by public authorities. In *Attorney General v. Jonathan Cape Ltd*[72] the duty of confidentiality was effectively extended to "public" secrets and the Lord Chief Justice stated that the courts had jurisdiction to restrain publication of official information if it could be shown that the public interest demanded it. The civil law has proved to be more attractive than criminal prosecutions for a number of reasons. One reason is that the standard of proof is lower. In civil cases the standard of proof is the balance of probabilities instead of the criminal standard which is that proof must be beyond reasonable doubt. Another factor which makes civil law remedies more attractive, in this context, is that there is no jury to sympathise with a public interest defence. A further advantage is that civil actions can be brought to prevent publication

---

[71] Official Secrets Act 1989, s.1(1).
[72] [1976] Q.B. 75.

whereas criminal prosecution can only be brought after the offence has been committed and the harm done.

This does not mean that civil courts will always find in favour of restraining publication. There is a balance to be drawn between the interests of the government in protecting the information and the public interest in disclosure. The leading case in this area is *Attorney-General v. Guardian Newspapers*[73] in which it was held that publication is excusable where there is a serious and legitimate public interest in the information. Injunctions had been issued to prevent publications of extracts from the *Spycatcher* novel which included allegations of illegal activity engaged in by MI5. The House of Lords decided that the public interest in knowing about the allegations in *Spycatcher* outweighed the interest in maintaining confidentiality. It was also decided that an injunction to restrain future publications of matters connected with the security service would undermine the operation of determining the balance of public interest in deciding whether each publication was to be prevented. The fact that the novel had, by this time, been widely published outside the United Kingdom was also a material factor in this case. In *Lord Advocate v. Scotsman Publications Ltd*, the House of Lords upheld the refusal of interdicts against the publication of extracts from "Inside Intelligence" by Antony Cavendish. There had been prior publication of some of the materials and the risk of damage to national security was very remote.[74]

The *Observer* and the *Guardian* applied to the European Commission of Human Rights complaining about the injunctions. The Court accepted that the injunctions had aims that were legitimate under Article 10(2) as they were deemed to be necessary in order to protect national security. However, the court was less convinced that the injunctions were actually necessary for the whole period of time during which they had been applied. The injunctions were necessary initially but they ceased to be justified when the purpose was no longer to protect confidential information but rather to protect the reputation of the security service. Once the information was published outside the United Kingdom the injunctions were no longer necessary either to protect national security or to maintain the authority of the judiciary.[75]

---

[73] *Att.-Gen. v. Guardian Newspapers (No. 2)* [1990] 1 A.C. 109; [1988] 3 W.L.R. 776; [1988] 3 All E.R. 545; [1989] 2 F.S.R. 181; (1988) 85(42) L.S.G. 45; (1988) 138 N.L.J. 296; (1988) 132 S.J. 1496.

[74] *Lord Advocate v. Scotsman Publications Ltd* [1990] 1 A.C. 812; [1989] 3 W.L.R. 358; [1989] 2 All E.R. 852; 1989 S.C. (H.L.) 122; 1989 S.L.T. 705; [1989] 1 F.S.R. 580; (1989) 86(38) L.S.G. 32; (1989) 139 N.L.J. 971.

[75] *Observer and Guardian v. U.K.* (1991) 14 E.H.R.R. 153.

262 Human Rights and Scots Law

Freedom of Information

8.25   A number of statutory measures govern public access to specialised
       information, such as the Data Protection Act 1998, the Access to
       Medical Reports Act 1988 and the Access to Health Records Act
       1990. However, there is currently no general freedom of informa-
       tion legislation giving a general statutory right of access to
       information held by public authorities in Scotland, or across the
       United Kingdom as a whole. When the Labour party came into
       government in 1997 one of its manifesto commitments was to
       encourage an open, democratic political culture. A White Paper,
       Your Right to Know, was published in December 1997.[76] This
       promised a new relationship between the government and people,
       recognising the public as legitimate stakeholders in the running of
       the company. It is however, a lot easier to support freedom of
       information when in opposition than it is when in government and
       the Draft Bill did not fulfil the promise of the White Paper and the
       Freedom of Information Act 2000 follows the general approach
       adopted in the Draft Bill. Access to information is a reserved matter
       under the Scotland Act 1998 but there is an exclusion of the
       reservation in relation to information held by certain bodies. This
       meant that the Scottish Executive was at liberty to develop a
       freedom of information regime separate from the United Kingdom
       scheme. The Scottish Executive's programme for 2000/2001
       includes a commitment to introduce a Freedom of Information
       Bill in Scotland, preceded by a Draft Bill for consultation. The
       Draft Bill was published in March 2001.
           An individual who wishes to gain access to information will need
       to know whether the public authority which holds the information
       is governed by the United Kingdom Freedom of Information Act
       or the proposed Scottish legislation as the two freedom of
       information regimes are to operate separately. It has been proposed
       that public authorities should each be subject to only a single
       freedom of information regime. Information held by devolved
       bodies in Scotland, or bodies with a combination of reserved or
       devolved information, will be subject to the Scottish regime. This
       includes the Scottish Parliament, any part of the Scottish
       Administration, the Parliamentary Corporation and any Scottish
       public authority, with mixed functions or no reserved functions,
       except as regards information supplied by a Minister of the Crown
       or government department and held in confidence.[77] Information
       held by United Kingdom public bodies classed as "reserved bodies"
       operating in Scotland, such as the Department of Social Security
       and the Ministry of Defence will be subject to the United Kingdom

---

[76]   White Paper, *Your Right to Know* (1997) Cm. 3818.
[77]   Scotland Act 1998, Sched. 5, s.B13.

regime. Cross-border public authorities such as the Forestry Commission will also be subject to the United Kingdom regime. Although sections 4(1) and 5 of the Freedom of Information Act 2000 give the United Kingdom Government power to extend the list of public authorities to which that Act applies, section 80 provides that no order under those sections may be made with relation to the public authorities specified in the Scotland Act. Until both regimes are implemented, rights of access to information will operate under the Public Records Acts and the relevant Codes of Practice; the United Kingdom Code of Practice On Access to Government Information and the Code of Practice on Access to Scottish Executive Information.

The Public Records Acts 1958 and 1967

The main purposes of legislation in this area is to ensure the selection of public records which should be preserved, to safeguard these for posterity and to make them available for public inspection.[78] Most departmental records are destroyed at the first review held after 5 years because they are regarded as unimportant; only about one per cent of records are kept to the next review at 25 years and it is at this time that their historical context will be considered. Some records may be disclosed earlier than the norm because they are part of a government inquiry, for instance, material on the Falklands War became available very quickly because of the Franks Inquiry.[79]

The Public Records Act 1958[80] provided that the records of courts, government departments and some non-governmental public bodies are to be transferred to the Public Records Office before they become 30 years old and they then become available for public inspection when they are 50 years old. The Public Records Act 1967 reduced the closed period to 30 years.[81] There are different time periods for certain types of document. Those which are highly sensitive may be kept in departments for 30 years or more, if the Lord Chancellor approves[82]. The documents must be reviewed at 30 years and periodically thereafter. Examples of such documents are Cabinet Office records, Ministry of Defence records and the records of the United Kingdom Atomic Energy Authority. Other sensitive documents may be transferred to the Public Records Office

8.26

---

[78] Roper, "Access to Public Records" in *Open Government* (Chapman and Hunt ed., Routledge, London, 1987).
[79] *Franks Inquiry on the Falklands war*, Cmnd. 8787 (1983).
[80] This Act, and the 1967 Act, do not apply to Scotland although the provisions of the Acts are adopted procedure for public records in Scotland. Scottish legislation is Public Records (Scotland) Act 1937.
[81] 1958 Act, s.5(1) as amended by 1967 Act.
[82] 1958 Act, s.3(4).

but withheld beyond the 30 years with the approval of the Lord Chancellor. Three types of document were covered by this provision: exceptionally sensitive papers, information received in confidence, and documents about individuals where disclosure would cause distress or endanger them. The period of closure varied although 50 years was the most common length of time. Documents about individuals could be closed for 75 years and documents on the affairs of the Royal family may be closed for 100 years.

Two reviews of the criteria for withholding documents have been undertaken in recent years. In 1981, the Wilson Committee[83] recommended preventing disclosure beyond the 30 years if documents: were exceptionally sensitive and disclosure was likely to harm the public interest; contained information supplied in confidence; or contained information about individuals, disclosure of which would distress them or endanger lives. In 1992, another review of the criteria was ordered by the Lord Chancellor, Lord Mackay of Clashfern. The three criteria for withholding information recommended by the Wilson Committee were retained.

8.27	More recently, documents have been released earlier than expected as a result of the White Paper on Open Government.[84] The White Paper lays down one basic principle regarding the publication of information. This general principle is that information should be released after 30 years unless, (a) it is possible to establish that actual damage will be caused by the release, and (b) the damage would fall within the listed criteria in Annex C of the White Paper "Guidelines on Extended Disclosure". The White Paper also brings the closure time down to 40 years for most documents but retains longer times for information such as that given in confidence, or concerning tax data (75 years) or population census records (100 years). The release of Joint Intelligence Committee records is now possible and many wartime records have been reviewed in order to allow their release.[85]

Code of Practice on Access to Government Information

8.28	The Code of Practice on Access to Government Information is a non-statutory scheme which requires Government Departments and other public authorities under the jurisdiction of the Parliamentary Commissioner for Administration to make certain information available to the public and to release information in response to specific requests. The code was introduced in 1994 and revised in 1997.[86] The Code cannot override existing statutory

---

[83] Modern Public Records (1981). *Report of Wilson Committee*, Cmnd. 8204 (1981).
[84] Cm. 2290, (1993).
[85] *ibid.*, Annex D.
[86] *Code of Practice on Access to Government Information* (2nd ed., 1997).

restrictions on disclosure; some 250 of these were listed in the White Paper.[87]

The Code is intended to ensure that:

- information is handled in way which will promote informed policy-making and debate and efficient delivery of service;
- "timely and accessible" information will be provided to explain the government's policies, actions and decisions; and
- access will be restricted only where there are good reasons for doing so.

No legal remedies are provided for citizens if the code is breached. The government felt that using a Code of Practice instead of legislation would allow for greater flexibility. Legislation, they maintained, would be too cumbersome; of course it would also be subject to judicial scrutiny, which the government wanted to avoid.

Departments were allowed to devise their own criteria and decide which requests should be classified as requests made under the Code. Departments were encouraged not to introduce new form or new bureaucracy. This led to differences in the classification of requests among the departments and thus to difficulties in determining the true number of Code requests made by citizens.

A number of matters are excluded from the Code. There are three main categories of exemption: 8.29

- Those requiring a "harm test" to justify exemption such as documents relating to defence and national security, international relations and proceedings of Cabinet and Cabinet Committees.
- Those which do not require the "harm test", for instance information regarding immigration and nationality. The Government indicated that these records should be exempt because of the nature of the information contained in them for instance, sensitive information provided by third parties. The exemptions apply only to individual cases, not to information on government policy on immigration and nationality.[88]
- Other grounds for refusing access include personal privacy, information given in confidence, unreasonable requests and premature disclosure.

---

[87] White Paper, *Open Government*, Cm. 2290 (1993), Annex B, Pts I and II.
[88] *ibid.*, para. 5.16.

The amended Code gives an undertaking that departments will publish or make available explanatory material on the department's dealings with the public except where publication will prejudice any matter which should be kept confidential. The material will include rules, procedures, internal guidance and administrative manuals. In cases where the harm test is used, the Code states that:

> "In such cases it should be considered whether any harm or prejudice arising from the disclosure is outweighed by the public interest in making information available. The exemptions will not be interpreted in a way which causes injustice to individuals."[89]

The Code is concerned with access to information not documents. The Guidance on Interpretation of the Code justifies withholding the documents by saying that there is an increasing number of different ways in which information is held, for instance paper, computer records, and so it is more appropriate that information is released rather than documents.[90] The PCA has recommended that documents be revealed since this may be the easiest way to deal with a request.

Where a request for information is refused, the Code states that an appeal should first be made through the department's internal resolution procedure; should the complainant still be dissatisfied, a further complaint can be made to the PCA using the MP filter.[91] In normal complaints to the PCA, the complainant has to show that he has suffered injury or injustice because of maladministration by the department. In complaints under the Code, it is enough that he has not been given the information he should have received.[92] The PCA has wide investigatory powers although it is not clear whether he will have the power to override a departmental decision and recommend the release of a document considered confidential. If the decision to refuse access shows maladministration, then conceivably the PCA has the power to override the decision and disclose the information. However, the minister does have the power to certify that the PCA should not make the information public.[93] It is unlikely that the courts will become involved very often in disputes, given that the PCA has been designated as the avenue of redress, although it will still be possible to argue on the basis of abuse of discretion or legitimate expectation and so on. The

---

[89] White Paper, *Open Government*, Cm. 2290 (1993), Preamble to Exemptions.
[90] *Guidance on Interpretation* (1994) paras 50–52.
[91] Parliamentary Commissioner Act 1967, s.5(1).
[92] Second Report of PCA (1994–95) H.C. 91, Access to Official Information: The First Eight Months, para. 3.
[93] Parliamentary Commissioner Act 1967, s.11(3).

PCA has in fact observed that it is the Code not he who will say what information is and is not to be made available:

> "I regard it as very much my task to see that access to official information which is in principle supported by the Code is not narrowed in practice. More than that, if . . . I conclude that the line has been drawn too restrictively in places I shall make my views known."[94]

As previously mentioned, the PCA has no enforcement powers. The   8.30
White Paper stated why enforcement powers were considered unnecessary[95]:

> "The Ombudsman approach has shown to be effective in the UK; although the Parliamentary Ombudsman has no power to enforce his decisions, there is a very high level of compliance with his recommendations."

It should also be noted that the lack of enforcement powers of the PCA is in direct contrast with the powers of the Data Protection Commissioner who receives complaints regarding access to information and who has power to enforce her decisions.

The amended Code does not allow citizens access to public records held under the 1958 and 1967 Acts. The merits of decisions of the Lord Chancellor, Secretary of State for Scotland and the Secretary of State for Northern Ireland are not reviewable by the PCA if the decision is taken without maladministration.[96] The Code does not apply to information held by the courts or contained in court documents.

The operation of the Code falls within the traditional conventions of British Government: a minister is responsible to Parliament for the decisions of officials made under the Code. Further it has been suggested that Parliamentary oversight was retained because of the political nature of the judgments which may have to be made and Parliament is more appropriate than the courts for resolving such matters. The Code does not require departments to acquire information they do not have, or provide information which has already been published, or provide information the government does not consider reliable, or provide information for which an existing service is available at a cost. The target response rate from a department for a simple request is 20 working days. Departments

---

[94]   Annual Report of PCA for 1993, H.C. 290 (1993–94), para. 3.
[95]   White Paper, *Open Government* Cm 2290 (1993), para. 4.21.
[96]   Parliamentary Commissioner Act 1967, s.12(3).

may charge for providing the information.[97] In the United Kingdom, a number of departments offer a few hours' free time, then charge per hour thereafter. It has been suggested that the charging rate could differ between requests for personal files and general information, where the majority of requests come from businesses and the media.[98]

8.31   The PCA in evidence to his Select Committee said that there was an insufficient level of awareness of the Code by citizens.[99] In 1996, he reported that "I continue to find a degree of confusion amongst those responsible for operating the Code, particularly in relation to the application of the exemptions in Part II".[1] A later witness pointed out that the small number of complaints might be explained by the lack of publicity of the Code by the government.[2] One of the inferences which was drawn from the Scott Report was that a Freedom of Information Act is necessary in a modern democracy. The report commented on the lack of openness in government and the fact that the system appeared to accept unquestioningly the need to keep politically sensitive subjects out of the public gaze.[3]

Code of Practice on Access to Scottish Executive Information

8.32   The Scottish Code is based on the United Kingdom code. The United Kingdom Code applies in Scotland in respect of official information held by United Kingdom Government organisations operating in Scotland and cross-border public bodies.

The Scottish Parliament gave a commitment to open government in the *Partnership for Scotland* agreement.[4] The Code of Practice on Access to Scottish Executive Information was issued in July 1999. It governs the regulation of access to information held by Scottish Executive departments and a range of other Scottish public bodies. The code lists these organisations, which include the organisations within the Scottish Executive and other Scottish public authorities such as the Scottish Qualifications Authority, the Parole Board for Scotland, the Accounts Commission for Scotland, the Scottish

---

[97]   The charges appear to range from no charge to £50 *per* A4 page (National Rivers Authority). The PCA has said that he will investigate charges only if someone makes a complaint to him. See Code of Practice on Access to Government Information 1995 Report, pp. 33–34.

[98]   The Constitution Unit (1996) *Introducing Freedom of Information*, London, Constitution Unit.

[99]   H.C. 290, i–iii (1994–95) op.cit., p.1.

[1]   House of Commons (1996) Sixth Report of PCA Access to Official Information, H.C. 593 (1995-96) Introduction.

[2]   H.C. 290 i-iii (1994-95), p.39, Evidence of Maurice Frankel.

[3]   *Enquiry into Exports of Defence Equipment and Dual-Use Goods to Iraq and Related Prosecutions*, H.C. 1151 (1995-96).

[4]   Scottish Executive, *Partnership for Scotland: An Agreement for the First Scottish Parliament*, May 14, 1999.

Higher Education Funding Council and the Scottish Legal Aid Board.

The purposes of the Code are:

(1) to facilitate policy-making and the democratic process by providing access to the facts and analyses form the basis for the consideration of proposed policy and

(2) to protect the interests of individuals and companies by ensuring that reasons are given for administrative decisions, except where there is statutory authority or established convention to the contrary.[5]

The Code states that these two purposes have to be balanced against the following needs:

(1) to maintain high standards of care in ensuring the privacy of personal and commercially confidential information; and

(2) to preserve confidentiality where disclosure would not be in the public interest or would breach personal privacy or the confidences of a third party, in accordance with statutory requirements and Part II of the Code.

The Code imposes certain obligations on the relevant government 8.33 departments and public authorities:

(1) to publish the facts which Scottish Ministers consider relevant and important in framing major policy proposals and decisions;

(2) to publish, or otherwise make available, explanatory material on the Scottish Executive's and other public bodies' dealings with the public except where publication could prejudice any matter which should properly be kept confidential under Part II of the Code;

(3) to give reasons for administrative decisions to those affected;

(4) to publish:

(a) full information about how public services are run, how much they cost, who is in charge, and what complaints and redress procedures are available; and

(b) full and, where possible, comparable information about what services are being provided, what targets are set, what standards of service are expected and the results achieved.

---

[5] Code of Practice on Access to Scottish Executive Information (July 1999) Pt 1.

(5) to release, in response to specific requests, information relating to their policies, actions and decisions and other matters related to their areas of responsibility.

A person who wishes to gain access to information should submit a request in writing to the organisation concerned, referring to the Code. There is a target response time of 20 working days, after which a response must be given. Such a response may:

(1) provide the information requested,
(2) refuse to provide the information requested, or
(3) indicate that further time is needed to provide the information.

Certain categories of information are exempt from the duty to provide access. Some types of information are only exempt where the harm likely to arise from disclosure would outweigh the public interest in making the information available. The Code states that the exemptions will not be interpreted in a way which causes injustice to individuals. The operation of the Code is overseen by the Scottish Parliamentary Commissioner for Administration.

8.34   If access to information is refused the applicant should make a second request to the public authority asking them to review their initial decision. If the applicant is still dissatisfied he may complain, through his Member of the Scottish Parliament or to the Scottish Parliamentary Commissioner for Administration on one of the following grounds:

(1) a failure to provide the requested information in full or in part;
(2) a failure by the organisation to respond;
(3) a delay in dealing with the request;
(4) excessive charges being imposed for providing access to the information.

United Kingdom Freedom of Information Act

8.35 This Act received the Royal Assent on November 30, 2000. Although some elements came into force when the Act was passed there is a long transition period of up to five years for the majority of the provisions. Rights of Access to Information will continue to operate according the Code of Practice on Access to Government Information which will be superseded when the Act is fully in force. The Act provides for a right of access to recorded information held by public authorities. It creates exemptions from the duty to disclose information and it establishes arrangements for enforcement and appeal. The Act amends the Data Protection Act 1998 and the Public Records Act 1958.

The Act creates a statutory right of access which, when compared with the United Kingdom code of practice, provides for a more extensive scheme for making information publicly available. It covers a much wider range of public authorities including: local government, National Health Service organisations, schools and colleges, the police and other public bodies and offices. The provisions in the Act will be regulated by a Commissioner to whom the public will have direct access, rather than access only through the intervention of their Member of Parliament as under the Code. The Act gives the right to apply for access to documents or copies of documents as well as to the information itself.

The Act is in eight parts.

Part I. Access to information held by public authorities—Part I 8.36 governs the principles and operation of the general right of access to information held by public authorities and specifies the conditions which need to be fulfilled before the authority is obliged to comply with a request. An applicant has a right to be told whether the information requested is held by that authority and, if it is held, to have it communicated to him. A request must be made in writing, must state the name of the applicant and an address for correspondence, and must describe the information requested. A request transmitted by electronic means will be treated as being a request in writing.[6] A public authority to which a request for information has been made may charge fees in accordance with regulations made by the Secretary of State. The applicant must be sent a notice in writing specifying the amount of the charge. This is called a "fees notice". Having issued a fees notice, the public authority is not obliged to comply with a request for information unless the fee is paid within a period of three months. Time limits are imposed for complying with access request. The normal time limit is 20 working days from the date of the request, or where a fee has been charged, 20 working days from receipt of the fee.[7]

The information must be provided by the means requested by the applicant wherever this is reasonably practicable. This may be, for example by provision of a copy of a document, by providing a reasonable opportunity to inspect a record, or providing a digest or summary of the information.[8] A public authority is not obliged to comply with a request for information if the cost of supplying the information would exceed the appropriate limit. The appropriate

---

[6] Freedom of Information Act 2000, s.8.
[7] *ibid.*, s.10.
[8] *ibid.*, s.11.

limit means such amount as may be prescribed and so different
limits may apply in different cases.[9] A public authority is not
obliged to comply with a request for information if the request is
vexatious, or where an applicant has repeatedly requested access to
the same information.[10] Where the information has been transferred to the Public Record Office, the request for access to
information must be passed on to the appropriate records
authority.[11] The Act imposes a duty on public authorities to
provide advice and assistance to persons who have made requests
for information.[12] Where a public authority decides to refuse a
request for access to information, for example if it is considered that
the information is exempt information, the applicant must be given
a notice which states the basis for the refusal of the request.

Part 1 of the Act also renames the Data Protection Commissioner, who shall be known instead as the Information Commissioner. The Data Protection Tribunal shall be known as the
Information Tribunal.[13] The Act *places* public authorities under a
duty to publish information in line with a publication scheme which
they must adopt. The scheme must specify:

(1) the classes of information which the public authority
    publishes or intends to publish;
(2) the manner in which information of each class is to be
    published;
(3) whether the material is intended to be available to the
    public free of charge or on payment of a fee.

Approval of the scheme by the Information Commissioner is
required. Such approval will not be necessary where a public
authority chooses to adopt a model publication scheme proposed
by the Information Commissioner.[14]

8.37 **Part II. Exempt information**—Part II sets out the areas of
information, which are exempt from the freedom of information
provisions, either whole classes of information or specific information whose release would be prejudicial to the interest protected.
The classes of exempt information include:

(1) information readily accessible by other means[15];

---

9   Freedom of Information Act 2000, s.12.
10 *ibid.*, s.14.
11 *ibid.*, s.15.
12 *ibid.*, s.16.
13 *ibid.*, s.18.
14 *ibid.*, ss.19-20.
15 *ibid.*, s.21.

(2) information intended for future publication[16];

(3) information supplied by, or relating to, bodies dealing with security matters[17];

(4) information where the exemption is required for the purpose of safeguarding national security[18];

(5) information relating to honours[19];

(6) environmental information which is already available to the public in accordance with regulations, or which is exempt under regulations[20];

(7) information which is personal data, in which case the Data Protection Act applies[21];

(8) information provided to the public authority in confidence[22];

(9) information subject to confidentiality of communications or legal professional privilege[23];

(10) information which the public authority is prohibited by law from disclosing.[24]

The information which is exempt if the specific information request would be prejudicial to the interests protected includes:

(1) information which would be likely to prejudice defence[25];

(2) information which would be likely to prejudice international relations[26];

(3) information which would be likely to prejudice relations between any administration in the United Kingdom and any other such administration. An example would be the relationship between the Scottish administration and the Government of the United Kingdom[27];

(4) information which would be likely to prejudice the economic interests of the United Kingdom or any part of the United Kingdom;

(5) information relating to investigations and proceedings conducted by public authorities[28];

---

[16] Freedom of Information Act 2000, s.22.
[17] *ibid.*, s.23.
[18] *ibid.*, s.24.
[19] *ibid.*, s.37.
[20] *ibid.*, s.39.
[21] *ibid.*, s.40.
[22] *ibid.*, s.41.
[23] *ibid.*, s.42.
[24] *ibid.*, s.44.
[25] *ibid.*, s.25.
[26] *ibid.*, s.27.
[27] *ibid.*, s.28.
[28] *ibid.*, s.30.

(6) information which would be likely to prejudice law enforcement[29];

(7) information for which an exemption is required for the purpose of avoiding an infringement of the privileges of either House of Parliament[30];

(8) information on the formulation of government policy[31];

(9) information which would be likely to prejudice the effective conduct of public affairs[32];

(10) information which would endanger the health and safety of any individual[33];

(11) information or which would be likely to prejudice commercial interests.[34]

8.38 **Part III. General functions of Secretary of State, Lord Chancellor and Information Commissioner**—Part III sets out the functions and duties of the Secretary of State, the Lord Chancellor and the Information Commissioner in relation to operation of the freedom of information regime. The Secretary of State is required to issue a code of practice providing guidance to public authorities on various administrative matters, including the practices to follow when dealing with request for information.[35] It also requires the Lord Chancellor to issue a code of practice providing guidance to public authorities on the keeping, management and destruction of their records.[36] Part III places a duty on the Commissioner to promote good practice and to encourage public authorities to comply with the Act and to produce publication schemes and codes of practice. He is also obliged, where he considers it expedient to provide information about the Act for the public. The Commissioner must lay an annual report before Parliament.[37]

8.39 **Part IV. Enforcement**—Part IV provides for enforcement of the freedom of information regime and the powers of the Information Commissioner in respect of this function. An applicant who is not satisfied with the response by a public authority to a request for information may apply to the Information Commissioner for a decision on whether the authority has acted in accordance with the provisions of the Act. Where the Commissioner finds that a public authority has failed to communicate information when required to

[29] Freedom of Information Act 2000, s.31.
[30] *ibid.*, s.34.
[31] *ibid.*, s.35.
[32] *ibid.*, s.36.
[33] *ibid.*, s.38.
[34] *ibid.*, s.43.
[35] *ibid.*, s.45.
[36] *ibid.*, s.46.
[37] *ibid.*, ss.47–49.

do so he can issue a decision notice to the complainant and the public authority specifying the action required to comply with the obligation to provide information.[38] Where he needs further information to decide whether a public authority has complied with the Act she may issue an information notice requiring it to provide information.[39] He can also issue enforcement notices containing a statement of measures required for a public authority to comply with Part I of the Act.[40] Where a decision notice or an enforcement notice has been served on a public authority it can be countered by a certificate from the accountable person in relation to that authority to the effect that there was no failure to comply with the Act. The accountable person must notify the complainant and must give reasons for his decision unless he has decided that the information is exempt information.[41] The accountable person is the First Minister or deputy First Minister in Northern Ireland, the Assembly First Secretary in Wales and, in relation to any other public authority, a Minister of the Crown who is a member of the Cabinet, the Attorney General, the Advocate General for Scotland or the Attorney General for Northern Ireland. There is a degree of political accountability as the certificate has to be laid before both Houses of Parliament.

Where no certificate has been issued and a public authority has not complied with a notice from the Commissioner, the Commissioner may certify in writing to the court that the public authority has failed to comply with the notice. The court may inquire into the matter and may deal with the authority as if it had committed contempt of court. The courts which can exercise this function are the High Court in England and Wales and the Court of Session in Scotland.[42] The Act does not confer any right of action in civil proceedings and so no action for breach of statutory duty under the Court of Session Act can be brought by an individual who has been denied access to information.[43] Petitions for judicial review of a decision may be used to challenge decisions with regard to access to information.

Part V. Appeals—Part V gives details of the circumstances and 8.40 operation of appeals procedures through a new Information Tribunal, and sets out the circumstances in which an appeal on a point of law can be made to the courts. Where a decision notice has been served, either the complainant or the public authority may

---

[38] Freedom of Information Act 2000, s.50.
[39] *ibid.*, s.51.
[40] *ibid.*, s.52.
[41] *ibid.*, s.53.
[42] *ibid.*, s.54.
[43] Court of Session Act 1988, s.45(b).

appeal to the Information Tribunal against the notice. A public authority may appeal against an enforcement notice. The Tribunal may review the facts and may allow the appeal or substitute another notice or dismiss the appeal. There is an appeal from a decision of the Tribunal on a point of law to the Court of Session. (High Court in England and Wales).[44]

8.41 **Part VI. Historical records and records in the public record office**—Part VI provides a statutory regime for access to public records previously covered by a discretionary scheme under the Public Records Act 1958, and provides for enhanced access to information contained in records which are more than 30-years-old by disapplying some of the exemptions otherwise applicable under the Freedom of Information Act. A record becomes a historical record at the end of a period of 30 years from the date it was created. In general, historical records cannot be exempt information after 30 years, but, in the case of honours the period is 60 years, and in the case of information prejudicial to law enforcement the period is 100 years.

8.42 **Parts VII and VIII**—Part VII extends the provisions on access and data accuracy in the Data Protection Act to all personal records held by public authorities. Part VIII contains a number of miscellaneous provisions, including provisions to prevent the extension of the legislation to the Scottish Parliament and certain devolved bodies, as well as provisions in relation to defamation, copyright and access to environmental information. It also creates a new offence of altering, blocking, erasing, destroying or concealing records held by a public authority with the intention of preventing its disclosure to an applicant who has made a request for the information and is entitled to receive it. The offence applies to the public authority and anyone who is employed by, is an officer of, or is subject to the direction of the public authority. A person found guilty may be fined. (The current level of fine is £5000.) The offence can be committed by civil servants but not by government departments.[45]

Freedom of Information (Scotland) Bill

8.43   The draft Freedom of Information (Scotland) applies to a wider range of public authorities than the current code of practice. It applies to the Scottish Parliament and the Parliamentary Corporation as well as to the Scottish Ministers. It applies to non-ministerial office-holders in the Scottish administration, local authorities, the

---

[44] Freedom of Information Act 2000, ss.57–59.
[45] *ibid.*, s.77.

National Health Service, colleges and universities receiving public funding, joint police boards and chief constables, tribunals and a long list of other bodies carrying out public functions. The Bill is intended to make provision for the disclosure of information held by Scottish public authorities or by persons providing services for them or organisations exercising functions of a public nature.

According to section 1, a person who requests information from a Scottish public authority is entitled to be given it by the authority. Information is defined as information in any form.[46] This will include documents held in manually-recorded form as well as electronic data. The Bill contains similar provisions to the Freedom of Information Act with regard to a duty on public authorities to adopt and maintain publication schemes. These will be subject to review by the Scottish Information Commissioner. The statutory right of access will be retrospective, giving rights of access to recorded information of any age. Applications must be made in writing, giving a contact name and address and identifying the information required. A decision must be made within 20 working days and may be:

(1) the information requested;
(2) an offer to supply information on payment of a fee;
(3) a refusal of a request giving details of the decision not to provide the information.

A request may be refused if:

(1) the request was vexatious;
(2) there had been repeated recent requests from the same applicant;
(3) further information needed to enable the authority to locate the information had not been received;
(4) the applicant had not paid the fee which had been requested;
(5) the authority estimates that the cost of providing the information would exceed the amount prescribed in regulations.

An authority need not provide information if it is already available from another source. There are a number of exemptions, which are classified in the same way as the Freedom of Information Act into three types:

(1) content exemptions;

---

[46] Freedom of Information (Scotland) Bill, s.69.

(2) class exemptions;

(3) absolute exemptions.

8.44   Content exemptions are subject to a test of substantial prejudice. If an organisation believes that the release of information would cause substantial prejudice to interest protected by an exemption, they must then go on to prove that it is not in the public interest to publish. This is a more stringent test than the "likely to prejudice" test in the United Kingdom Freedom of Information Act. The Scottish test requires proof of a probability of substantial prejudice rather than just a possibility of prejudice. This factor, combined with the fact that factual policy information prepared for Scottish Ministers will be included will make it much more difficult for information to be withheld from the public in Scotland.[47] There is, as yet, no definition of public interest but it has been stated that guidance will be provided on criteria for assessing public interest. Consideration will be made on a case by case basis.[48]

Class exemptions apply to a whole category of information without any test of harm being required in order to withhold information. There is a presumption that such information would not normally be released, but the draft Bill proposes that the majority of class exemptions will be subject to a public interest test.

Absolute exemptions apply where disclosure could not be justified by public interest; one example would be where disclosure would contravene current legislation.

The Bill proposes similar investigation and enforcement powers for the Scottish Information Commissioner to those of the Information Commissioner under the United Kingdom legislation. The draft Bill also includes proposals for Ministerial certificates which would override decision notices and enforcement notices issued by the Scottish Information Commissioner. Such certificates could only be issued in relation to certain categories of information, such as formulation of policy, international relations, investigations, confidentiality, and honours. The intention is that they should only be used to protect information of exceptional sensitivity. A copy of the certificate must be laid before the Scottish Parliament within 40 days of the issue of the decision or enforcement notice. The Scottish Information Commissioner's decision on any appeal will be final, although it could be challenged through judicial review procedures in the Court of Session.

---

[47] Scottish Human Rights Centre, "Opening Scotland", *Rights*, January 2000.

[48] SPOR, Justice and Home Affairs Committee, February 16, 2000.

RIGHT TO FREE ELECTIONS

Article 3 of the First Protocol provides:

> "The High Contracting Parties undertake to hold free elections at reasonable intervals by secret ballot, under conditions which will ensure the free expression of the opinion of the people in the choice of the legislature."

This Article differs from other substantive Articles in the Convention in that it does not use a term such as "everyone has a right". Instead it states that the High Contracting Parties have an obligation. It has sometimes been implied from this that the Article does not give rise to individual rights and freedoms but solely to obligations between states. However, the preamble to Protocol 1 states that its purpose is to ensure the collective enforcement of certain rights and freedoms other that those already included in the Convention. Moreover, the European Court of Human Rights has held that Protocol 1, Article 3 implies two distinct rights; to vote for the legislature and to stand as a candidate for election to the legislature.[49] 8.45

The European Court of Human Rights generally accords states a wide margin of appreciation in relation to the detailed provisions of their domestic electoral law. This is because the law in each country has to be considered in the context of national political history and current constitutional practices. To many people the right to vote in elections is regarded as the most important, or possibly the only way, in which they can participate in the government of their country. The opportunities for the citizen living in Scotland to use this power have been increased by entry into the European Community and by the establishment of a Scottish Parliament. We now have four levels of government in which democratically elected members represent the people of Scotland:

(1) The United Kingdom Parliament at Westminster.
(2) The European Parliament.
(3) The Scottish Parliament.
(4) Local Councils.

The right of citizens to participate in democratic elections is the primary indicator that a government is truly accountable to the members of the society it represents. Unlike in certain other countries,[50] there is no legal duty to vote in the United Kingdom,

---

[49] *Mathieu-Mohin and Clerfayt v. Belgium* (1987) 10 E.H.R.R. 1.
[50] For example, Australia, Belgium, Greece and Italy.

although there is a duty to register as a voter in a constituency. The European Court of Human Rights has stated that one of the purposes of the European Convention is to ensure that effective political democracy can be maintained.[51] In a modern democratic state every adult member of society should have an equal right to participate in the electoral process. It is therefore of fundamental importance that the electoral system is conducted in a way which will ensure fairness and integrity, in particular;

(a) there should be a full franchise with only limited restrictions; *i.e.* every adult should have the right to vote;

(b) the voting system should be designed so as to result in both a government which is representative of the electorate and a government which will be able to govern effectively;

(c) the value of each vote cast should be equal to every other vote;

(d) the conduct of the elections should be regulated to ensure legality and fairness.

RIGHT TO VOTE

8.46 Every person over the age of 18, who is resident in a parliamentary constituency on the previous qualifying date and who is not subject to a legal incapacity, has the right to vote.[52] The franchise is not restricted to British citizens but includes citizens of the republic of Ireland and citizens of E.U. and Commonwealth countries, provided that residence requirements are satisfied.[53] Commonwealth citizens include British overseas citizens, British Dependent Territories citizens and citizens of various Commonwealth countries.[54] The qualifying date is currently October 10.[55] A temporary absence on the qualifying date does not necessarily prevent a person being recorded as resident at his main address.[56]

Persons who qualify as resident but who are unable to attend within the constituency on polling day may apply for a postal vote.[57] In the case of *MacCorquodale v. Bovack*,[58] it was confirmed

---

[51] *Matthews v. U.K.* (1999) 28 E.H.R.R. 361; 5 B.H.R.C. 686.
[52] Representation of the People Act 1983, s.1.
[53] *ibid.*, s.1(1)(b)(ii).
[54] British Nationality Act 1981, ss.37 and 50.
[55] See also *Daly v. Watson*, 1960 S.L.T. 271; 1960 SC 216; *Dumfries Electoral Registration Officer v. Brydon*, 1964 S.L.T. 266; 1964 SC 242; *Keay v. MacLeod*, 1953 S.L.T. 144; 1953 S.C. 252.
[56] *William Marr v. Derek K Robertson*, 1964 S.C. 448.
[57] Representation of the People Act 2000.
[58] *MacCorquodale v. Bovack*, 1984 S.L.T. 328.

that students who are normally resident in university accommodation but who have to vacate their accommodation during vacations
are entitled to register as absent voters in the university
constituency. In the case of *Dumble v. Electoral Registration Officer
for Borders*,[59] it was held that Parliament envisaged the possibility
of a person having a qualifying address in more than one
constituency. Where a person had two careers, each of which was
a major interest in his life and each of which required an address in
a separate constituency, it was allowable that the name of that
person should appear in the register of electors for each
constituency.[60] Students therefore may be registered in the
constituency where their university or college is located and in the
constituency where their permanent home is located. Naturally they
are only entitled to vote in one of the constituencies in which they
are registered.[61] Absent voting was previously permitted for people
who were unable to attend at a polling station but is now available
to anyone who chooses to apply.[62]

Each year the electoral registration officer in each constituency
draws up a Register of Electors. The maintenance of the register is
the responsibility of the local council. After canvassing all house-
holds in the constituency a draft register is published. At this stage
amendments may be made. There is a right of appeal against
decisions in relation to the register to a sheriff, and then to an
Electoral Registration Appeal Court, which comprises three Court
of Session judges.[63] Regulations may be made requiring registration
officers to produce two versions of the electoral register, a complete
one and an edited version omitting the names of those who have
asked to have their names excluded from it. The complete version is
to be used for electoral purposes and the edited version may be
made more widely available.[64]

A gap in the provision for the registration of electors for elections   8.47
to the European Parliament became apparent in 1994 when a
resident of Gibraltar, Ms Matthews, applied to the Electoral
Registration Officer for Gibraltar to be registered in the forthcoming elections to the European Parliament. She was told that the
1976 European Communities Act excluded Gibraltar from the
franchise. Ms Matthews applied to the European Court of Human
Rights, claiming that there had been a breach of her right to

---

[59] *Dumble v. Electoral Registration Officer for Borders*, 1980 S.L.T. (Sh.Ct) 60.
[60] See also *Scott v. Phillips*, 1974 S.L.T. 32; *Fox v. Stirk* (1970) 3 All E.R. 7; *Ferris v. Wallace*, 1936 S.C. 561; 1936 S.L.T 292.
[61] See also *Strathclyde Electoral Registration Officer v. Boylan*, 1980 S.C. 266 (prisoner on remand).
[62] Representation of the People Act 2000.
[63] *ibid.*, ss.10 and 57.
[64] *ibid.,*, Sched. 2, para. 10.

participate in elections to choose the legislature contrary to Protocol 1, Article 3. The Government maintained that Article 3 of protocol 1 was not applicable in relation to elections to the European Parliament in Gibraltar. The Court addressed five questions.

(1) Whether the United Kingdom could be held accountable under the Convention for the failure to hold elections to the European Parliament in Gibraltar.

It was held that, notwithstanding their membership of the European Union, contracting states were still responsible for guaranteeing Convention rights. Article 1 of the Convention requires the High Contracting Parties to secure to everyone within their jurisdiction the rights and freedoms defined in the Convention. The Convention was extended to the territory of Gibraltar in 1953. Legislation emanating from the European Union affected the people of Gibraltar in the same way as domestic legislation and therefore the United Kingdom was responsible for guaranteeing the rights in Article 3 of Protocol 1 in respect of both domestic and European elections.

(2) Whether Article 3 of Protocol 1 applied to the European Parliament.

The Government claimed that the legislature in Gibraltar was the House of Assembly, and it was to that body that Protocol 1 Article 3 applied in the context of Gibraltar. The European Parliament itself and its basic electoral procedures were provided for under its own legal system, rather than the legal systems of its member states. The Court held that no reason had been made out which could justify excluding the European Parliament from the ambit of the elections referred to in Article 3 of Protocol 1. The fact that it is a supranational rather than a purely domestic representative organ is not relevant. Neither is it relevant that the European Parliament did not exist when the Convention was agreed. The Convention is a living instrument which must be interpreted in the light of present conditions.

(3) Whether the European Parliament had the hallmarks of a "legislature" in Gibraltar at the material time.

The Court held that the European Parliament must be considered as part of the legislative process in the European Union framework. The fact that it did not share all the characteristics of a state legislature does not prevent it being part of the legislative process. It is no longer purely an advisory and supervisory body.

(4) Whether Article 56 of the Convention (formerly Article 63), applied.
Article 56 provides that states can extend Convention rights to territories for whose international relations they are responsible but that provisions of the Convention shall be applied in such territories with due regard to local requirements. It was held that the position of Gibraltar did not give rise to local requirements which could restrict the application of the Convention under Article 56.
(5) Whether the failure to hold elections in Gibraltar in 1994 violated Article 3 of Protocol 1.
The Government claimed that the margin of appreciation should mean that the Court should not interfere with the details of the electoral processes. Gibraltar was too small in terms of its population to justify a separate constituency and it had no historical ties with any other constituency. Ms Matthews said that she had been completely deprived of the right to vote. The protection of her fundamental rights should not depend on whether or not there were attractive alternatives to the current electoral system. It was held that there had been a violation of Article 3 of Protocol 1 as the very essence of Ms Matthews' right to vote to choose the legislature had been denied.[65]

Legal Incapacity

There are certain categories of people who are not entitled to vote 8.48
because they suffer from a legal incapacity. They include minors (those under the age of 18), mental patients who are compulsorily detained, aliens, peers other than Irish peers and convicted persons in detention.[66] Anyone who is found guilty of certain election offences is not entitled to vote for five years.[67] This is an area where the European Court of Human Rights accords a wide margin of appreciation to states to make rules. A violation of Protocol 1, Article 3 was held to have occurred where a person who was suspected, but acquitted, of being a member of a Mafia organisation was struck off the electoral register. The Court accepted that suspending voting rights of Mafia members was a legitimate aim but that it was disproportionate to continue to suspend voting rights once a person was acquitted of the criminal charges.[68]

[65] *Matthews v. U.K.* (1999) 28 E.H.R.R. 361; 5 B.H.R.C. 686.
[66] Representation of the People Act 1983, s.3, as amended by Representation of the People Act 1985, Sched. 4.
[67] Representation of the People Act 1983, s.60.
[68] *Labita v. Italy*, April 6, 2000.

Elections to the Westminster Parliament

8.49 The maximum term of years for any Parliament is five years and so general elections have to be held every five years.[69] The Prime Minister controls the timing of general elections. There is no constitutional regulation specifying an exact term for a Parliament or a fixed time of year for a general election. Although the dissolution of Parliament and the power to order the issue of writs for the election of a new Parliament is a prerogative power of the Crown, it is a power exercised in practice at the behest of the Prime Minister. This gives the Prime Minister the power to decide to hold a general election at a time which will be politically advantageous to his party. As long as the election is held within the five year period he can decide to hold an election at any time of the year and may even choose to hold it a year or more in advance of the end of the maximum term. In 1974 the Parliament lasted less than one year. In theory the Crown could refuse to dissolve Parliament if it were considered that a second general election within a short time would be contrary to the public interest.

Elections to the European Parliament

8.50 The system of elections based on individual constituencies returning a single member on the basis of territorial representation and "first past the post" has been replaced by a system of proportional representation similar to that used for the Scottish Parliament, with effect from the June 1999 European Parliamentary election. Scotland is a single region of the United Kingdom returning eight members from party lists. Individual candidates may also be listed.[70] In *Prince v. Secretary of State for Scotland*,[71] voters in the elections to the European Assembly sought declarator of their right to a system of proportional representation against the Secretary of State and interdict against the returning officer from conducting the election. The basis of the claim was that the existing system was *ultra vires* and contrary to section 2 of the European Communities Act. The interim interdict was refused because it had not been established that the election system was *ultra vires.*

Elections to the Scottish Parliament

8.51 The first election was held on May 6, 1999. Elections to the Scottish Parliament normally take place every four years. If circumstances

---

[69] Septennial Act 1715, as amended by Parliament Act 1911, s.7.
[70] 1985 S.L.T. 74.
[71] European Parliamentary Elections Act 1978, s.3, as substituted by the European Parliamentary Elections Act 1999.1985 S.L.T. 74.

arise which cause an extraordinary general election to be held before the four-year term has expired it does not affect the normal quadrennial cycle. Therefore if an extraordinary general election is held after three years, the new Scottish Parliament will only last for one year. If, however, an extraordinary general election is held within six months before an ordinary general election would be due the extraordinary general election replaces the ordinary general election.

Right To Stand As A Candidate For Election

There is no statutory definition of the qualifications for membership   8.52 of the House of Commons. However, the House of Commons Disqualification Act 1975 disqualifies certain persons from membership of the House of Commons.[72] These are:

- (a) holders of judicial office;
- (b) civil servants;
- (c) members of the armed forces;
- (d) members of police forces;
- (e) members of non-commonwealth legislatures;
- (f) members of the Boards of Nationalised Industries, Commissions, Tribunals and other bodies whose members are appointed by the Crown.[73]

In addition to these specific disqualifications there are several other restrictions on eligibility:

(a) Persons under the age of 21. The Family Law Reform Act 1969 reduced the age of majority from 21 years to 18 years for many purposes, including the right to vote in elections, but the qualifying age for membership of the House of Commons remains at 21 years.

(b) Persons suffering from mental illness. If an elected member of Parliament is authorised to be detained on grounds of mental illness, the Speaker of the House is notified and, if the illness is confirmed, the Member's seat is declared vacant.[74]

(c) Members of the clergy. A person may not stand for election to the House of Commons if he or she has been ordained to the office of priest or deacon or who is a Minister of the Church of Scotland.[75] A clergyman or clergywoman may relinquish his or her office and thus become eligible to stand for election.[76]

---

[72] House of Commons Disqualification Act 1975, s.1 and Sched. 1.
[73] *ibid.*, Sched. 1, Pt II.
[74] Mental Health Act 1983, s.141.
[75] House of Commons Disqualification Act 1975, s.10(2).
[76] Clerical Disabilities Act 1870.

(d) Bankrupts. A person who is declared bankrupt may not be elected to the House of Commons. If an existing Member is declared bankrupt he is barred from sitting or voting in Parliament until the bankruptcy is discharged by the court or the adjudication annulled.[77]

(e) Persons convicted of certain crimes. Those sentenced to more than one year in prison are disqualified during their sentence or while unlawfully at liberty.[78] Persons convicted of treason are disqualified from election to Parliament. If a Member of the House of Commons is convicted of treason he or she may not sit or vote until a pardon has been received or the sentence of the court has expired.[79]

(f) Persons found guilty of corrupt practices during elections. If a person is found guilty of corrupt practices during an election they may be disqualified from taking up their seat in the House. If the corrupt practice was only discovered after the election, the Member may be disqualified from sitting in Parliament. In December 1997 charges of election fraud were made against Mohammed Sawar, the Member of Parliament who had been elected to represent the Govan Constituency. He was suspended for the House but was reinstated on his acquittal in 1999. A disqualification for corrupt practices lasts for a period of five years for any constituency and for an additional five years in relation to the constituency in which the offence took place.

The rules relating to disqualification for election to the Scottish Parliament are broadly similar to the rules for the Westminster Parliament.[80] Most of the disqualifying categories apply to the Scottish Parliament as well as to the Westminster Parliament.[81] The following groups are disqualified:

(a) those holding judicial office;
(b) civil servants;
(c) members of the armed forces;
(d) members of police forces;
(e) members of a legislature outwith the commonwealth.

The major differences in eligibility are that:

(i) citizens of the European Union resident in Scotland can be members of the Scottish Parliament,[82]

---

[77] Insolvency Act 1986, s.427.
[78] Representation of the People Act 1981, s. 1.
[79] Forfeiture Act 1870, ss. 2 and 7.
[80] Scotland Act 1998, s.15.
[81] House of Commons Disqualification Act 1975, s.1 and Sched. 1.
[82] Scotland Act 1998, s.16(2).

(ii) clergymen and women are not disqualified.[83]

Those disqualified because they hold judicial office include judges in 8.53
the Court of Session and sheriffs. The Lords of Appeal in Ordinary
are expressly excluded from membership of the Scottish Parliament.[84] The Scotland Act makes provision for further disqualifications for the holders of certain public appointments to be made by
Order in Council. This list may differ from the equivalent list of
disqualifications for the Westminster Parliament.[85] Certain posts
will be incompatible with membership of the Scottish Parliament
but not with membership of the Westminster parliament and vice
versa. It is also possible to have disqualifications which relate only
to office holders in a particular region or constituency. The Scottish
Parliament may resolve to disregard a disqualification in an
individual case.[86] This can only be done if the following conditions
are met:

(1) The ground for disqualification no longer exits.
(2) Parliament considers that it is proper for the disqualification to be disregarded.
(3) The disqualification has not been determined by the courts.
(4) The disqualification is not the subject of current legal
proceedings.

The practical consequence of this provision is that a member of
Parliament who holds a disqualifying office may continue as a
member provided that he resigns the other office. The general
disqualifications which apply both to the House of Commons and
to the Scottish Parliament cannot be disregarded by the Scottish
Parliament. The following persons are disqualified:

- Persons under 21 years of age
- Persons suffering from severe mental illness
- Bankrupts
- Persons convicted of certain crimes, and
- Persons convicted of election offences

The disqualification of civil servants from a state's national
elections was considered by the European Court of Human Rights
in *Gitonas v. Greece*. Certain grades of civil servants were
disqualified from election to the Greek Parliament for a period of
three years after they left public service. The Commission found

---

[83] Scotland Act 1998, s.16(1).
[84] *ibid.*, s.15(1)(c).
[85] House of Commons Disqualification Act 1975, Sched. 1.
[86] Scotland Act 1998, s.16 (3)–(5).

that this was a violation of Protocol 1, Article 3, but the Court held that there had been no violation. The Court stated that; "[s]tates enjoy considerable latitude to establish in their constitutional order rules governing the status of parliamentarians, including criteria for disqualification". In this case the disqualifications did not violate Convention rights as they were neither disproportionate nor arbitrary. They served a legitimate purpose in preventing high ranking public servants from abusing the powers and prestige of their previous public offices.[87] In the case of mental illness the Presiding officer has to arrange for the member to undergo a medical examination. Disqualification will take effect if a member has been detained on the ground of mental illness and six months have elapsed without him or her recovering sufficiently to be released.[88] Members who are declared bankrupt are suspended when the court order is made. Their seat is declared vacant after six months unless the order has been recalled.[89]

If a disqualified person is returned as a member his or her election is void and the seat is then vacant. If a member becomes disqualified during office he or she ceases to be a member and the seat becomes vacant. In the case of bankruptcy and insanity, where there is a six month delay before the disqualification takes effect the member is suspended from office in the interim period and cannot participate in any Parliamentary proceedings. The Parliament may withdraw his or her rights and privileges.[90]

8.54   In relation to local government, under the Local Government Officers (Political Restrictions) Regulations 1990, the right of local government officers holding "politically restricted posts" to participate in political activities is restricted. In the case of *Ahmed v. United Kingdom*, Ahmed challenged these rules in the European Court of Human Rights. As a result of the Regulations, Ahmed, a local authority solicitor and holder of a politically restricted post, was unable to stand as a Labour candidate in municipal elections. He applied unsuccessfully for judicial review of the Regulations and, when the appeal was dismissed, Ahmed applied to the European Court of Human Rights, His arguments included a contention that the Regulations were a violation of his right to participate fully in the electoral process, contrary to Article 3 of Protocol 1. It was held that the Regulations pursued the legitimate aim of protecting the rights of both council members and the electorate to effective local political democracy, which required political neutrality on the part of officers. Furthermore, the

---

[87]   *Gitonas v. Greece* (1997) 26 E.H.R.R. 691.
[88]   Mental Health Act 1983, s.141, as amended by Scotland Act 1998, Sched. 8 para. 19.
[89]   Insolvency Act 1986, s.427.
[90]   Scotland Act 1998, s.17(4).

Regulations were "necessary in a democratic society", since they were intended to reduce the risk of abuse of power by local government officers. When balanced against this important aim, the Regulations did not represent a disproportionate interference with Ahmed's rights. Taking into account the margin of appreciation enjoyed by the state, there had been no violation of Article 3 of Protocol 1. The rights under Article 3 were not absolute and the state was entitled to prevent senior local government officers such as Ahmed from contesting seats at elections. The object of the Regulations was the legitimate aim of preserving officers' political neutrality and, in any event, the Regulations only applied so long as Ahmed held a politically restricted post. If he left his post his rights to participate in political activities would be restored.[91] Unfortunately, the Court did not rule on whether or not local government elections fall within the ambit of Protocol 1, Article 3. Presumably this will not be decided until a situation arises in which an infringement of a Convention right has occurred.

Proceedings for Disqualification

(a) Disqualification Claims During Election Proceedings

A claim that a candidate is disqualified is dealt with by an election 8.55 petition under the Representation of the People Act.[92] A petition must be lodged within 21 days after the election. Petitions are considered by an Election Court which consists of two nominated judges of the Court of Session. Depending on the grounds of challenge the respondent to the petition will be either the returning officer or the member whose eligibility is being contested.[93] In order to discourage frivolous applications there is a requirement that the applicant must provide caution of up to £5,000 for the expenses of the proceedings.

(b) Disqualification Claims at Times other than an Election Period

A person who wishes to claim that a member is disqualified may apply to the Court of Session for a declarator to that effect.[94] The defender in such an action will be the member in person. The Court of Session may not make such a declarator if the Parliament has already resolved that the disqualification should be disregarded.[95] Parliament may not resolve to disregard a disqualification which

---

[91] *Ahmed v. U.K.* [1999] I.R.L.R. 188; (2000) 29 E.H.R.R. 1; 5 B.H.R.C. 111; (1999) 1 L.G.L.R. 94; [1998] H.R.C.D. 823.
[92] Representation of the People Act 1975, s.12(5).
[93] Stair Memorial Encyclopaedia, Vol. 15, paras 1436–1492.
[94] Scotland Act 1998, s.18.
[95] Scotland Act 1998, s.18(3)(b).

has been declared by the Court of Session.[96] There is no appeal to the House of Lords from a Court of Session declarator that a member is disqualified. The decision is final. In the same way as for proceedings before an Election Court the applicant must provide security of up to £5,000 for the expenses of the action.

REGULATION OF THE CONDUCT OF ELECTIONS

8.56 The returning officer for each constituency is responsible for ensuring the proper conduct of elections. He is normally an official of the local council.[97] The purpose of the regulation of the conduct of elections is to ensure that there is fairness and a reasonable degree of parity between the candidates regardless of their financial resources. The regulations control the amount of expenditure and the manner in which it can lawfully be spent, proscribing certain unlawful practices and providing procedures for challenge in the event of irregularities during a campaign. Where there has been a failure to follow prescribed procedures the court may grant relief for failure to follow procedures in certain circumstances. The case of *Curran v. Lord Advocate* concerned a failure on the part of an election agent to have the return and declaration signed in the presence of a justice of the peace as required by sections 81 and 82 of the Representation of the People Act 1983. An election agent, who had acted for Mohammed Sarwar in the 1997 general election petitioned for relief from the failure to comply with the terms of the Act. Evidence was accepted that the failure resulted from inadvertence on her part caused mainly by allegations against the candidate and the stressful and unpleasant media attention. It was held that relief could be granted where the failure to follow prescribed procedures was attributable to;

    (a) inadvertence,
    (b) absence of bad faith, and
    (c) that it was just and equitable in the circumstances that relief be granted.[98]

Each candidate must be nominated by 10 registered electors from the constituency in which he intends to stand. The sum of £500 must be deposited. The purpose of this requirement is to deter

---

[96] Scotland Act 1998, s.16(5).
[97] Representation of the People Act 1983 s.25.
[98] *Curran v. Lord Advocate*, 1999 S.L.T. 332. See also: *Clark v. Sutherland* (1897) 24 R. 821; (1897) 4 S.L.T. 363; *Munro v. Mackintosh*, 1920 S.C. 218; 1920 1 S.L.T. 93; *Pole and Scanlon, Petitioners*, 1921 S.C. 98; 1921 1 S.L.T. 38; *Smith v. Mackenzie*, 1919 S.C. 546; 1919 2 S.L.T. 29.

frivolous candidates. The deposit is refunded after the election provided that the candidate has secured five per cent of the votes cast.[99] Once a candidate has been nominated he or she must then nominate an election agent. The candidate may however nominate himself. A declaration that he or she is not disqualified from membership of the House of Commons is also required at this stage.

In the case of elections to the Scottish Parliament, the Secretary of State for Scotland has the power to make detailed rules governing the conduct of elections.[1] These cover such matters as registration of electors, the appointment of returning officers, limitations on election expenditure by individual candidates and by parties and challenges to election results. The Secretary of State can apply with or without modification, the rules found in existing legislation regulating local, Parliamentary or European elections although some matters, such as the management of the counting of the regional list votes need specific consideration.

Corrupt Practices

Corrupt practices include bribery, treating and undue influence. 8.57
Undue influence may be caused by threats or attempts to intimidate electors. Although a completely secret ballot is preferable in order to give the voter confidence in the election process some concessions are made in order to ensure that investigations may be carried out if there is a suspicion that corrupt practices have taken place. It is possible to trace the identity of each voter from the serial number on the ballot paper. This number is recorded opposite the voter's name on the electoral register by the polling clerk at the time of voting.[2] Allegations of election fraud were made in 1997 against the candidate elected in the Glasgow Govan constituency. The allegations, which were not upheld, included a charge that personation of voters had taken place. There were also allegations of financial irregularities. Breaches of the restrictions on expenditure are the most common subject of allegations of corrupt practices.

Expenditure

Expenditure by or on behalf of candidates for election is strictly 8.58
limited. The purpose of this restriction is to promote fairness by preventing the wealthy candidate gaining an unfair advantage by spending large amounts of money on the campaign in the constituency. A maximum limit is placed on expenditure on behalf

---

[99] Representation of the People Act 1985, s.13.
[1] Scotland Act 1998, s.12
[2] Representation of the People Act 1983, s.66.

of each candidate.[3] The Secretary of State is permitted to set and to raise the permitted amounts of expenditure, in line with inflation, by way of statutory instrument. Every candidate must appoint an election agent and all expenditure to promote the election of a candidate must be authorised by the candidate or his agent. A breach of this requirement is classed as a corrupt practice under electoral law.[4] Accounts must be kept of all expenditure on public meetings, advertisements and circulars, or other means by which the candidate or his opinions are made known to the electors. A return of these accounts must be submitted to the Returning Officer within 21 days of the election result.

Where expenditure limits have been exceeded the result of the election may be challenged by petition to an Election Petition Court comprising two judges of the Court of Session. In 1965 such a challenge was made to the election of Sir Alexander Douglas-Home who was at that time the Prime Minister and leader of the Conservative Party.[5] The defeated Communist Party candidate petitioned to have the election declared void on the ground that national party political broadcasts made by Douglas-Home were not authorised in writing by the candidate's election agent nor were they included in the statutory return of expenses. It was held that the broadcasts were not made with a view to promoting the election of the individual candidate in his constituency but rather to inform the public about the party's national policies and therefore there had been no infringement of the statute by the respondent and the petition was refused.

An alternative way to challenge excessive expenditure is to seek an interdict to prevent or to halt expenditure which contravenes the statutory restrictions. An interdict was granted to prevent unauthorised expenditure in relation to local government elections in Lothian Region in 1983.[6] Members of one political party petitioned the Court of Session to interdict the local authority, which was run by another political party, from distributing a publication known as the Lothian Clarion. They alleged that an article in the publication was calculated to promote the election of the majority party's candidates and to disparage candidates of the petitioners' party. An interim interdict was granted on the ground that the article complained of was calculated to promote the election of the majority party's candidates.[7]

---

[3]   Representation of the People Act 1983, ss. 76 and 76A, as amended by the Representation of the People Act 1985.
[4]   Representation of the People Act 1983, s.75.
[5]   *Grieve v. Douglas-Home*, 1965 S.L.T. 186; 1965 S.C. 315.
[6]   *Meek v. Lothian Regional Council* (No. 2), 1983 S.L.T. 494.
[7]   See also *R v. Tronoh Mines Ltd* [1952] 1 All E.R. 697 and *Director of Public Prosecutions v. Luft* [1977] A.C. 962.

More recently two local election candidates sought interdict 8.59
preventing a trade union from carrying on an advertising campaign
against the national government and its policies with a view to
discouraging electors from voting for the political party for which
the petitioners were standing. The interdict was refused on the
ground that the statutory provisions were not contravened by an
advertisement in the form of a generalised attack on one or more of
the policies of a political party at the time of a general election or of
local government elections throughout Scotland.[8]

The matter of restriction of election expenses has been considered
by the European Court of Human Rights. Mrs Bowman, who had
been prosecuted under section 75 for incurring expenditure with a
view to promoting or procuring the election of a candidate in the
1992 general election whilst she was not authorised so to do, applied
to the European Court of Human Rights. She claimed that there had
been a breach of Article 10 of the European Convention on Human
Rights which protects freedom of expression. She had in fact been
acquitted because of a delay in bringing the prosecution. Mrs
Bowman was executive director of the Society for the Protection of
the Unborn Child. She distributed 25,000 leaflets in Halifax shortly
before the 1992 general election outlining the views on abortion of
the three main candidates. She alleged that section 75 of the
Representation of the People Act 1983 amounted to a restriction on
her freedom to express her views. The European Court of Human
Rights recognised that the intention behind section 75 was not to
restrict freedom of expression but rather to regulate expenditure so
as to promote equality between candidates. This aim was considered
to be legitimate as it protected the rights of others. However, the
means of achieving this legitimate aim need to be balanced against
the fundamental democratic principle of freedom of expression and
in particular, freedom of political debate during the period of an
election campaign. The court ruled (by a majority of 14 to 6) that
Mrs Bowman had no other effective means of communicating
information to the electorate on an issue which could affect the
public perception of the candidates. Section 75, which limited the
expenses which Mrs Bowman could legitimately incur to a
maximum of £5, effectively operated as a total ban on her freedom
of expression during the election period. This was made more unfair
by the lack of any financial controls on the expenditure by political
parties at a national level. There were also no restrictions upon the
freedom of the press to support or oppose the election of a particular
candidate. The restriction was held to be disproportionate to the
purpose intended and was therefore a violation of Article 10.[9]

---

[8] *Walker v. Unison*, 1995 S.L.T. 1226.
[9] *Bowman v. U.K.* (1998) 26 E.H.R.R. 1.

Registration of Political Parties

8.60 Problems have arisen when candidates have been nominated for election as representatives of groups with titles which are designed to cause confusion on the part of the voters because of the similarity with the name of an established political party.

The case of *R v. Acting Returning Officer For the Devon and East Plymouth Constituency, ex parte Sanders*[10] was a challenge by Sanders, who was the Liberal Democrat candidate for the Devon and East Plymouth constituency to the acceptance of the nomination of another candidate. This other candidate was nominated as the "Literal Democrat" candidate. Sanders applied for leave to move for judicial review of the returning officer's decision to accept the nomination papers as valid. The action failed for technical reasons, but it was held that it was arguable that the returning officer should not have accepted the nomination. This problem has now been resolved by the requirement for political parties to register their names and their pictorial symbols, which appear on ballot papers.[11] This decreases the risk that voters will be confused by parties with similar names. The register of political parties is used for the following elections, namely, Parliament, the European Parliament, the Scottish Parliament, the National Assembly for Wales, the Northern Ireland Assembly and Local Authorities.

Irregularities in election procedures

8.61 Where there has been an irregularity in the conduct of the election procedures the election of a candidate may be declared void and the election has to be repeated.

An example of procedural irregularity arose in the case of *Miller v. Dobson.*[12] At a local government election two ballot papers were rejected at the count because polling officials at the polling stations had inadvertently omitted to stamp them with the official mark when issuing them to voters. After several recounts the candidate declared duly elected had a majority of one. The candidate who had narrowly lost petitioned the court for a declaration that the other candidate was not duly elected, by virtue of the Representation of the People Act 1983 section 48(1), as the breach of the officials' duty had affected the result. The petitioner also sought a declaration under section 145(1) that she had been duly elected, or alternatively that the election was invalid and that a further election should be

---

[10] *R v. Acting Returning Officer For the Devon and East Plymouth Constituency, ex p. Sanders* [1994] C.O.D. 497; *Times*, May 30, 1994.
[11] Registration of Political Parties Act 1998.
[12] *Miller v. Dobson*, 1995 S.L.T. (Sh.Ct) 114.

held. It was held that the election had to be declared invalid as the omission by the polling officials had affected the result. The court could not determine that another person had been duly elected and so a further election would have to be held.[13]

ARTICLE 17 PROHIBITION OF ABUSE OF RIGHTS

Nothing in this Convention may be interpreted as implying for any state, group or person any right to engage or perform any act aimed at the destruction of any of the rights and freedoms set forth herein or at their limitation to a greater extent than is provided for in the Convention.   8.62

According to the Commission the purpose of this Article is to prevent exploitation of the Convention rights by totalitarian groups. Rights under Article 10, for example, cannot be used to protect those who possess literature promoting racial hatred. This principle was considered by the European Court in *Jersild v. Denmark*. In that case it was held by the majority that the conviction of a Danish journalist for broadcasting racist material was a contravention of Article 10. A decisive factor in the decision was that the journalist did not have a racist purpose when compiling his report. Taken as a whole his programmes could not objectively be viewed as having a racist purpose and therefore his conviction was not necessary in a democratic society. The minority of judges considered that this decision did not accord sufficient protection to those who had to suffer racist hatred. The common ground between all members of the Court was that the international promotion of racist opinions would not be granted the protection of Article 10. [14]

In the later case of *Lehideux v. France* the Court elaborated on the types of expression that will be denied protection under Article 10. That case concerned a finding of the Paris Court of Appeal that the publication of an advertisement defending the actions of Marshall Petain, in collaborating with the Nazis during the war, was an offence. The Court found that there had been breach of Article 10. The advertisement did not promote or support the Nazi cause. The types of expression which will be denied protection under Article 10 include:

(1) Intentionally racist statements;
(2) Expressions supporting Nazi ideology;
(3) Revisionist views seeking to deny historical facts concern-

---

[13]   See also *Fitzpatrick v. Hodge*, 1995 S.L.T. (Sh.Ct) 118); *Morgan v. Simpson* [1975] 1 Q.B. 151.
[14]   *Jersild v. Denmark* (1995) 19 E.H.R.R. 1.

ing major human rights abuses, such as the Holocaust;[15]
(4) Defamatory statements.[16]

---

[15] *Lehideux v. France* (2000) 30 E.H.R.R. 665; 5 B.H.R.C. 540; [1998] H.R.C.D. 89.
[16] *Tolstoy Miloslavsky v. U.K.* [1996] E.M.L.R. 152; (1995) 20 E.H.R.R. 442.

CHAPTER 9

FREEDOM OF ASSOCIATION AND ASSEMBLY

ARTICLE 11 — FREEDOM OF ASSEMBLY AND ASSOCIATION

"1. Everyone has the right to freedom of peaceful assembly and to freedom of association with others, including the right to form and join trade unions for the protection of interests.

2. No restrictions shall be placed on the exercise of these rights other than such as are prescribed by law and are necessary in a democratic society, in the interests of national security, or public safety, for the prevention of disorder or crime, for the protection of health or morals, for the protection of the rights and freedoms of others."

This Article shall not prevent the imposition of lawful restrictions 9.01 on the exercise of these rights by members of the armed forces, of the police, or of the administration of the state.[1]

The right to freedom of assembly and freedom of association is socially and culturally linked to the right to freedom of expression. The European Court of Human Rights has recognised the affinity between Article 11 and Article 10, referring to Article 11 as a specific application of the general principles of freedom of expression in Article 10.[2] Article 11 protects two distinct types of activity. A person is entitled to meet with others as a group in public places. He or she is also entitled to join or to become affiliated to organisations. Article 11 specifies that this includes trade unions but other types of organisations are not excluded. The right to freedom of peaceful assembly and to freedom of association with others is a qualified right. This means that it is subject to several exceptions, these are similar to the exceptions in relation to

---

[1] See *Artze fur das Leben v. Austria* (1991) 13 E.H.R.R. 204.
[2] *Ezelin v. France* (1991) 14 E.H.R.R. 362.

the other qualified rights under the Convention. Interference with the exercise of the right to freedom of assembly and to freedom of association with others will be lawful on the following conditions:

(1) it is in accordance with the law, and;
(2) it is necessary in a democratic society in the interests of;

   (a) national security, or
   (b) public safety, or
   (c) for the prevention of disorder or crime, or
   (d) for the protection of health or morals, or
   (e) for the protection of the rights and freedoms of others.

The economic wellbeing of the country is not a legitimate aim in relation to Article 11, unlike Article 8. These exceptions provide a basis on which the competing interest of the individual and the society in which he lives can be balanced. The four tests for qualified Convention rights are used to establish whether or not Article 11 has been contravened;

(1) Has there been any interference with a substantive right?
(2) Is the act amounting to interference carried out in accordance with the law?
(3) Does the interference purport to have a legitimate aim?
(4) Is the interference necessary in a democratic society?

This Article only protects assemblies which are peaceful. There is no violation of the Article if the state regulates assemblies which are not peaceful or which are unlikely to be peaceful. Article 11 contains a positive obligation on states to protect the exercise of the rights contained therein. In *Plattform Artze fur das Leben v. Austria*, it was held that the state had a duty to protect participants in a peaceful demonstration from interference by a violent group with opposing views. The Court held that:

> "Genuine effective freedom of peaceful assembly cannot . . . be reduced to a mere duty on the part of the State not to interfere: a purely negative conception would not be compatible with the object and purpose of Article 11 . . . Article 11 sometimes requires positive measures to be taken, even in the sphere of relations between individuals, if need be."[3]

The general approach of the European Court of Human Rights to rights under Article 11 is illustrated by the case of *United Communist Party of Turkey v. Turkey*. The United Communist

---

[3] *Plattform Artze fur das Leben v. Austria* (1988) 13 E.H.R.R. 204.

Party of Turkey, TBKP, was formed on June 4, 1990. On that day, its constitution and programme were submitted to the Court of Cassation for assessment of their compatibility with the Constitution and Law 2820 on the Regulation of Political Parties. In July 1991 the Constitutional Court made an order dissolving the TBKP, which entailed the liquidation of the party and the transfer of its assets to the Treasury. The order was based on the inclusion in its name of the prohibited word "communist" and the alleged encouragement of Kurdish separatism. The officials of the party were banned from holding similar offices in any other political party. The TBKP and its leaders applied to the Commission, complaining that the dissolution of the party infringed their right to freedom of association as guaranteed by the European Convention on Human Rights 1950, Article 11. The Commission upheld the application and the Court held that in view of the importance of democracy within the Convention system, there could be no doubt that political parties came within the scope of Article 11. An association was not excluded from the protection afforded by the Convention simply because its activities were regarded by the national authorities as undermining the constitutional structures of the state. Article 11 was applicable to the present case. The dissolution of the TBKP constituted an interference with that party's right to freedom of association. The interference was prescribed by law and, inasmuch as the dissolution was based on a distinction drawn in the TBKP's programme between Turks and Kurds, it could be said to have been ordered with the aim of protecting national security and thus pursued one of the legitimate aims set out in Article 11(2). The only type of necessity which might justify an interference with the rights under Article 11 was one which may claim to spring from democracy, and democracy was the only political model compatible with the Convention. The exceptions set out in Article 11(2) had to be construed strictly in relation to political parties. In the instant case, a political party's choice of name could not in principle justify dissolution in the absence of other relevant and sufficient circumstances, and there was no evidence that the TBKP represented a real threat to Turkish society or the Turkish state. A scrutiny of the TBKP's programme showed that it intended to resolve the Kurdish issue through dialogue. As such, it was penalised solely for exercising freedom of expression. In the circumstances, the drastic measure of the dissolution of the TBKP was disproportionate to the aim pursued and consequently unnecessary in a democratic society. Accordingly, the measure infringed Article 11.[4] The judgment clearly demon-

---

[4] *United Communist Party of Turkey v. Turkey* (1998) 26 E.H.R.R. 121; 4 B.H.R.C. 1; [1998] H.R.C.D. 247.

strates that the Court follows the same analytical framework in applying Article 11 as it does in relation to Articles 8, 9 and 10. First, the Court decides whether or not interference with a right has taken place. Secondly, the Court considers whether the interference was in accordance with law. Thirdly, the Court considers whether the interference was in pursuit of a legitimate aim, and finally, the Court considers whether the interference was necessary in a democratic society. The first three elements are essentially matters of fact but the fourth element involves more judgment in order to ascertain whether the interference is proportionate to the legitimate aim.

9.02   Freedom of assembly has always been regarded as an essential element in a society that claims to implement principles of civil and political freedom. The need for individuals to gather together in groups may be less important now that there are other means of communication such as television, telephones and the Internet but two types of mass public meetings continue to be held:

(a) Public meetings are still important in industrial disputes where mass rallies and picketing of organisations are seen as a useful method of attracting publicity for a cause. During the miners' strike in the mid 1980s large numbers of pickets gathered at the steelworks at Ravenscraig and at Hunterston power station. The police diverted vehicles carrying pickets while they were some distance from either destination.

(b) Processions are still a popular way to attract the attention of the mass news media to a political or environmental cause. Certain traditional processions such as marches by members of Orange Orders still take place in parts of Scotland.

Scots Law does not recognise a right of public protest. Freedom of assembly only exists to the extent that people can assemble together in circumstances which are not subject to regulations or restrictions.[5] People may gather together in groups and may talk but the police could disperse them if they were obstructing the passage of others or if it was deemed likely that a breach of the peace may occur.[6] The European Court of Human Rights considered the right to peaceful assembly in the case of *Ezelin v. France*. Ezelin was a lawyer who had taken part in a public demonstration. The demonstration started as a peaceful protest but became rowdy and some buildings were daubed with graffiti. The Public

---

[5] *Aldred v. Miller*, 1925 J.C. 21.
[6] *Duncan v. Jones* [1936] 1 K.B. 218, *Aldred v. Miller* 1925 J.C. 21.

Prosecutor could not identify those responsible for the insulting behaviour or graffiti but he asked the Bar Council to take disciplinary action against Ezelin who had remained at the scene, although he had not participated in the rowdy behaviour. He was sentenced to a formal reprimand which was upheld on appeal. The Court found that there was an interference with his right of peaceful assembly. The interference was in accordance with law and was for the legitimate aim of preventing disorder. However, the proportionality principle demands that a balance be struck between the requirements of the purposes listed in Article 11(2) and those of free expression by word, gesture or even silence by persons assembled on the streets or in other public places. The pursuit of a just balance must not result in lawyers being discouraged, for fear of disciplinary sanctions, from making their beliefs clear on such occasions. The sanction was excessive and was therefore not necessary in a democratic society.[7] This was the first case in which the Court found a breach of the right of peaceful assembly. The judgment does not distinguish between assemblies which take the form of protest marches and those which are static assemblies or rallies. The fact that the assembly as a whole ceased to be peaceful does not remove the protection from an individual whose actions did not overstep the boundaries of peaceful protest.

PROTECTION OF ASSEMBLIES IN SCOTLAND

Where meetings are held on private property the regulation of the meeting is a matter for the owner of the property. Many meetings are held on premises belonging to local authorities and local authorities have statutory duties to make premises available for political meetings in the period prior to an election.[8] The law also takes steps to protect meetings from disruption by others. It is an offence for a person to attend a public meeting and to act in a disorderly manner for the purpose of impeding the business of the meeting.[9] There is a specific sanction in relation to political meetings in the period leading up to elections. The representation of the People Act 1983 provides that a person who, at a political meeting held in any constituency between the date of issue of a writ for the return of a Member of Parliament and the date of the election, acts or incites others to act in a disorderly manner for the purpose of disrupting the meeting shall be guilty of an illegal practice.[10] 9.03

---

[7] *Ezelin v. France* (1991) 14 E.H.R.R. 362.
[8] Representation of the People Act 1983, ss. 95, 96.
[9] Public Meeting Act 1908.
[10] Representation of the People Act 1983, s.97.

Restrictions on the Freedom of Assembly

Regulation of Processions

9.04 Public processions are regulated by the Civic Government (Scotland) Act 1982 and the Public Order Act 1986 (as amended by the Criminal Justice and Public Order Act 1994). Local Councils have the power to permit a procession to take place or to prohibit the holding of a procession.[11] Seven days notice must be given prior to a procession taking place. Notice must be given to both the council and the chief constable.[12] There are exceptions to this requirement. Advance notification is not required for processions which are customarily or commonly held. The authority may decide to remove this exemption in the case of a particular procession or particular types of procession. A local authority may grant exemption from the requirement to give notice to certain types of procession or the processions of specific organisations. The local authority is also empowered to waive the full period of notice, but not the requirement for notification, in respect of processions which are spontaneous or organised urgently in response to a particular event where there is insufficient time to give the full seven days' notice.

When permission is given to hold a procession the council may impose conditions as to its date, time duration and route. It may also prohibit the procession from entering into any public place specified in the order. A council may, for example, prohibit a march by an Orange Order from entering a predominantly catholic street. Notice of the conditions must be given in writing at least two days before the procession is due to be held. Appeal against a prohibition of a procession or any conditions imposed may be made to a sheriff. Such an appeal must be lodged within 14 days of receipt of the order.[13] The grounds on which an appeal can be made are limited. The only ground is that the council has exceeded its powers. The sheriff may therefore only uphold an appeal if he considers that, in deciding to restrict or ban the procession, the council erred in law or based its decision on a material error of fact, or exercised its discretion unreasonably. The sheriff may not consider the merits of the decision, only whether the council was acting within its authority under the Civic Government (Scotland) Act.

It is an offence to hold a procession without permission or to contravene the conditions which have been laid down.[14] Any person who takes part in an unauthorised procession and who refuses to desist when required to do so by a policeman in uniform is also

---

[11] Civic Government (Scotland) Act 1982, s.63.
[12] *ibid.*, s.62.
[13] *ibid.*, s.64.
[14] *ibid.*, s.65.

guilty of an offence. The powers of a council relate mainly to regulating the holding of processions in advance of them taking place. Regulation of processions at the time when they are taking place falls within the powers of the police.

Requiring that permission be obtained before an assembly takes place or imposing conditions on an assembly will not necessarily amount to a contravention of Article 11 provided that the restrictions are imposed for a legitimate purpose. In the case of *Rassemblement Jurassien and Unite Jurassienne v. Switzerland*[15] the applicants were political organisations seeking independence for the Jura region. They organised a demonstration in the town of Moutier. An anti-separatist group organised a meeting in a restaurant in the town on the same day. The council then banned all political meetings in the town for two days. Having failed to have the ban lifted by the Swiss courts the applicants applied to the Commission claiming that there had been a breach of Article 11. The Commission stated that the right of peaceful assembly was a fundamental right. The right applies to both private meetings and meetings in public places. The fact that meetings in public places are subject to an authorisation procedure does not normally encroach on the essence of the right. Such authorisation procedures are in compliance with the Convention as long as they are for the purpose of ensuring the peaceful nature of a meeting. The ban in Moutier was for a very short duration and was not disproportionate. A longer ban on public processions was imposed in London in 1978. An application to the Commission was made on the grounds that this contravened Article 11 in the case of *Christians against Racism and Fascism v. United Kingdom*. The association of Christians against Racism and Fascism was an ecumenical Christian association which had been set up to oppose fascism and racist conduct. This was a time when the National Front was very active. There had been riots and disturbances resulting from several public processions by the National Front and counter demonstrations by other organisations. The National Front was planning more demonstrations. The Metropolitan Police Commissioner decided to ban all public processions in London for two months. The Commission held that a general ban on demonstrations can only be justified if there is a real danger of their resulting in disorder which cannot be prevented by other less stringent measures. The Commission decided that it was not disproportionate for the authorities to issue the ban. The association could have held its procession outside London or could have held a different type of protest, such as a meeting on private property.[16] Whether such

9.05

---

[15]   (1979) 17 D.R. 93.
[16]   *Christians Against Racism and Fascism* (1980) 21 D.R. 138.

restrictions are justified will depend on the availability and practicality of measures which fall short of a ban on assemblies. The interference with the freedom of assembly must be balanced against the scale of the disorder which is likely to ensue of the assembly takes place.

The Public Order Act gives power to a senior police officer who is present when a procession is taking place to impose conditions.[17] He or she may impose conditions before the procession has started once people are assembling with a view to taking part in the procession. The senior police officer may impose conditions if he or she reasonably believes that the procession may give rise to serious public disorder, serious damage to property or serious disruption to the life of the community, or that the purpose of the organisers is to intimidate others. Intimidation in this context means preventing people from doing what they have a right to do or compelling them to do something which they have no right to do. The senior police officer is the officer most senior in rank present at the scene. He need not be a high-ranking officer. Conditions may be imposed with regard to the time, place and manner of the procession. The conditions may be imposed only in so far as they are necessary to prevent serious disorder, disruption or intimidation. It is an offence to knowingly fail to comply with conditions imposed by the police on the day of a procession or to incite others to behave in a manner contrary to the conditions.[18] It is a defence for a person to prove that the failure to comply with the conditions arose from circumstances outwith his or her control.

Regulation Of Public Assemblies

9.06 Similar powers to those by which the police regulate processions are conferred on the police in relation to other public assemblies.[19] These would include political protests, picketing in the course of an industrial dispute, and social occasions. Conditions may be imposed if the senior police officer present reasonably believes that there is a probability of serious public disorder, serious damage to property or serious disruption to the life of the community, or intimidation. The police officer may make conditions regarding the location of the assembly, the duration and the maximum number of people who may attend. As with processions the conditions imposed must not be more stringent than is required to prevent serious disorder, damage to property or disruption. The powers apply to a public assembly. A public assembly is where 20 or more persons assemble in a public place which is wholly or partly open to

---

[17] Public Order Act 1984, s.12.
[18] *ibid.*, s.12(4) and (5)
[19] *ibid.*, s.14.

the air.[20] A public place means any road and any place to which at the material time the public or any section of the public has access, on payment or otherwise, as of right or by virtue of express or implied permission. A person who knowingly fails to comply with the directions of the police or who incites others to disregard the conditions is guilty of an offence.[21] Conditions may also be imposed in advance by the chief constable. Written notice of the conditions must be given to the organisers of the assembly.

Trespassory assemblies are prohibited.[22] A trespassory assembly is where 20 or more people assemble on land entirely in the open air, to which the public has no right or access or only limited right of access. If a chief constable reasonably believes that a trespassory assembly is about to take place and that it is likely to cause serious disruption to the life of the community or significant damage to the land or a building or a monument on it, he may apply to the local authority for an order prohibiting all trespassory assemblies for a period of up to four days in an area not exceeding a radius of five miles from the intended location of the assembly. This power applies where the land, building or monument is of historical, architectural, archaeological or scientific importance. Examples include Stonehenge at the time of the summer solstice and areas around Faslane naval base. Any person who organises or takes part in an assembly which trespasses onto land in the area for which a prohibition order is in effect commits a criminal offence. A uniformed police officer is entitled to stop a person who he reasonably believes to be on his way to an assembly which has been prohibited.[23] People can only be stopped in this way if they are within the area covered by the prohibition order. The police officer can direct him not to proceed in the direction of the assembly. Failure to comply with the instructions of the police officer is an offence.

The Criminal Justice and Public Order Act also confers powers in relating to specific types of assembly such as raves and music festivals.[24] It also confers powers to remove groups of trespassers from land which are aimed at controlling groups such as "new age travellers".[25] The offence of aggravated trespass is committed by a person who trespasses on land in the open air and does anything intended to obstruct or disrupt any lawful activity or to intimidate

---

[20] Public Order Act 1984, s.16.
[21] *ibid.*, s.14 (4) and (5).
[22] *ibid.*, s.14A and 14B. (These sections were inserted by the Criminal Justice and Public Order Act 1994, s.70.)
[23] Public Order Act 1984, s.14C, (inserted by Criminal Justice and Public Order Act 1994, s.71).
[24] Criminal Justice and Public Order Act 1994, ss.63–67.
[25] *ibid.*, ss.61, 62.

persons with a view to deterring them from engaging in lawful activity.[26] This offence is likely to be committed by hunt saboteurs or anti-road protesters.

9.07   It may be an offence to wear uniforms at a public meeting. The wearing of uniforms which signify association with a political organisation or for the promotion of any political purpose at a public meeting or in a public place may be an offence under the Public Order Act 1936.[27] This Act was passed to prevent uniformed fascists parading the streets in the 1930s. A uniform does not have to be a complete military outfit. The term uniform includes any article of clothing which is worn by each member of a group and which is intended to indicate his association with a political organisation or purpose. The article does not have to cover any major part of the body. The berets, dark glasses and dark pullovers worn by members of the IRA identify its members in the eyes of the public. Even members of a political organisation may wear uniforms in private and even in meetings at which the only people present are members of the organisation. The wearing of uniforms in public may be permitted by a chief constable if he is satisfied that there is unlikely to be any risk of public disorder. Uniforms such as badges or insignia may be worn by the stewards who are engaged to assist in the preservation of order at a public meeting, provided that the number of stewards is not excessive.

The Public Order Act and the Criminal Justice and Public Order Act have, like many statutes been drawn up to deal with a particular mischief which is perceived to be happening in society at the time. Sometimes, as in the case of the regulation of assemblies, the resulting statute has potential to be used in a wider range of circumstances. The powers which have been given to the police could be misused to prevent citizens gathering in groups to protest. Potentially the powers could be used against road protesters or anti-nuclear protesters. It is important that the powers to regulate public assemblies and processions are only used in order to achieve the legitimate purposes specified in Article 11(2). These are the protection of national security, or public safety, or for the prevention of disorder or crime, or for the protection of health or morals, or for the protection of the rights and freedoms of others. Article 11(2) now provides an additional ground for challenging decisions made by local authorities and the police if they prohibit assemblies or impose conditions which are disproportionate to the legitimate aims, or which are to achieve purposes which are not legitimate such as the suppression of political protest.

---

[26]   Criminal Justice and Public Order Act 1994, s.61.
[27]   Public Order Act 1936, s.1.

Indirect Restrictions on the Right of Assembly

Obstruction of the Highway

The Civic Government (Scotland) Act provides that any person 9.08
who, "in a public place—(a) obstructs, along with another or
others, the lawful passage of any other person and fails to desist on
being required to do so by a constable in uniform; or (b) wilfully
obstructs the lawful passage of any other person" is guilty of an
offence.[28]

It is not necessary for a street or footpath to be completely
blocked in order for the highway to be regarded as obstructed. It
may be classed as obstruction if there is still room for people to pass
by. People could, in theory be charged with the offence of
obstruction if they gathered in a road for a few minutes and
caused only a short delay to people wishing to use the road.

Obstruction of a Police Officer

It is an offence to obstruct a police officer in the execution of his 9.09
duty.[29] Prosecutions for the obstruction of a police officer are not
common. It is more usual for a person who has acted in a manner
which impedes the work of a police officer to be charged with
breach of the peace.

Breach of the Peace

The all-encompassing common law offence of breach of the peace 9.10
provides the grounds on which the police may prevent and control
any public disorder.[30] It is not necessary for a breach of the peace to
have occurred before a public assembly is dispersed or individual
participants are apprehended. It is sufficient for there to be, in the
opinion of the police, a reasonable probability that a breach of the
peace may occur. In Scotland breach of the peace is a criminal
offence in its own right. In *Alexander v. Smith*, a man was arrested
and convicted of breach of the peace for selling newspapers. He had
been selling National Front newspapers to football supporters. The
police, who were concerned for his safety, asked him to move on.
He refused to do so whereupon he was arrested.[31]

An arrest for breach of the peace may take place even though
there has been no rowdy conduct or loud noise. There have been
instances where simply standing still and not speaking has been held
justify a conviction for breach of the peace. In *Montgomery v.
McLeod*, a bystander was arrested in a hotel car park. There had

---

[28] Civic Government (Scotland) Act 1982, s.53.
[29] Police (Scotland) Act 1967, s.41.
[30] *ibid.*, s.17.
[31] *Alexander v. Smith*, 1984 S.L.T. 176.

been a disturbance in the car park earlier the same evening and the police returned to check that there had not been a reoccurrence. They found the accused standing in the car park waiting for a friend. The police asked him to move on. He refused and was then arrested. He was convicted of a breach of the peace and the conviction was upheld on appeal. It was said that an offence of breach of the peace could arise in two ways. First, any conduct which creates "disturbance and alarm to the lieges" constitutes breach of the peace. A second set of circumstances which could be classed as breach of the peace is where there has been conduct "such as to excite the reasonable apprehension" that mischief might ensue. Even where there had only been passive conduct a police officer could be deemed to be justified in believing that a breach of the peace might occur. It was held that "[t]here is no limit to the kind of conduct which may give rise to a charge of breach of the peace".[32] It is not necessary to prove that an individual accused person was acting in breach of the peace. A person may be convicted of breach of the peace if he was part of a crowd of people acting in a disorderly manner and he did not disassociate himself from the crowd. In the case of *Winnik v. Allan* the conviction was upheld of a man who had been part of a crowd of noisy and disorderly persons who shouted and swore and tore down a stone boundary wall and threw missiles at colliery buildings. His actions had not been singled out in the evidence at his trial but the evidence of the behaviour of the group was sufficient to give rise to the inference that he had supported, sympathised with and encouraged the actions of the crowd.[33]

This power to intervene is not restricted to assemblies held in public places. The police are also entitled to attend where a public meeting is being held on private premises. They can do so if they have reasonable grounds for believing that an offence such as a breach of the peace is imminent or even that there is a strong probability that there may be a breach of the peace.[34]

9.11   It is not necessary for there to be members of the public present for a breach of the peace to occur. So even if there are no "lieges" to be alarmed or disturbed the police may arrest a person on the grounds of a real or apprehended breach of the peace. So in *Wyness v. Lockhart*, the appellant was charged with breach of the peace after approaching two police officers in a street, patting them on the shoulders and asking for money. Neither the police officers nor any other bystanders were alarmed or upset. The High Court held that, nevertheless the conduct of the accused was such as might

[32] *Montgomery v. McLeod*, 1977 S.L.T. (Notes) 77.
[33] *Winnick v. Allan*, 1986 S.C.C.R. 35. See also *MacNeill v. Robertson*, 1982 S.C.C.R. 468; *Tudhope v. Morrison*, 1983 S.C.C.R. 262.
[34] *Thomas v. Sawkins* [1935] 2 K.B. 249.

reasonably be expected to cause alarm, upset or annoyance to members of the public.[35]

FREEDOM OF ASSOCIATION

The Convention right to freedom of association with others has 9.12 been held to be a right which the state must both permit and make possible.[36] The rights which Article 11 confers, to join or to refrain from joining an organisation, do not necessarily apply to every type of association. Public law organisations such as professional regulatory bodies may not fall within the scope of Article 11. In *Le Compte, Van Leuwen and DeMeyere v. Belgium*, members of a professional association for doctors claimed that the obligation to join the association was an infringement of their right to freedom of association. The association, the *Ordre des Medecins*, had been established by an Act of the Belgian Parliament and its disciplinary role was defined by a Royal Decree. All doctors practising in Belgium had to be registered with the *Ordre*. Doctors could also join other private organisations. The Court held that the *Order des Medecins* was not as association within the meaning of Article 11. Article 11 does not apply to organisations founded by legislation, which are integrated within the structures of the state, with the purpose of regulating a profession by rule-making and enforcement. Such organisations are public authorities. The state is under an obligation, however, to ensure that such regulatory organisations are not monopolistic and that practitioners can create and join their own supplementary professional associations if they desire.[37] Trade associations such as federations of taxi drivers do fall within the remit of Article 11.[38] In *Chassagnou v. France*,[39] the Court stated that the term "association" has an autonomous meaning in the context of the Convention. Whether an association falls within the ambit of Article 11 does not depend upon they way in which it has been classified under national law.[40]

Trade unions are without doubt organisations to which Article 11 applies. The right to form and join trade unions includes the right to choose not to join a trade union. In *Young, James and Webster v. United Kingdom*, the applicants complained that their rights had been infringed when they were dismissed from their jobs for refusing to join a trade union. Their employer had agreed only to employ union members. This was known as a "closed shop". Under employment law at that time their dismissals were deemed to be fair

---

[35] *Wyness v. Lockhart*, 1992 S.C.C.R. 808.
[36] *National Union of Belgian Police v. Belgium* (1979–80) 1 E.H.R.R. 578.
[37] *Le Compte, Van Leuwen and DeMeyere v. Belgium* (1982) 4 E.H.R.R 1.
[38] *Sigurdur A Sigurjonsson v. Iceland* (1993) 16 E.H.R.R. 462.
[39] (1999) 29 E.H.R.R. 615.
[40] *Chassagnou v. France* (1999) 29 E.H.R.R. 615.

and so they had no right to compensation. The Court held that the notion of freedom implies some measure of freedom of choice as to its exercise. An individual does not enjoy the right to freedom of association if, in reality, the freedom of action or choice which remains to him is either non-existent or so reduced as to be of no practical value. The interference with their rights under Article 11 was in accordance with the law and had the legitimate purpose of being for the protection of the rights and freedoms of others. It was not, however, necessary in a democratic society as the detriment to the individuals was not justified by the overall benefits to society.[41]

Deprivation of the right to join a trade union was considered in the case of *Council of Civil Service Unions v. United Kingdom.*[42] It was held that a ban on union membership at Government Communications Headquarters (GCHQ) was justified in the interests of national security. Staff at GCHQ had been allowed to belong to trade unions until 1984. Union members had occasionally taken part in industrial action such as one-day strikes and overtime bans. Under Article 4 of the Civil Service Order 1982, the Minister for the Civil Service had the power to make regulations for the controlling the conduct of the service and providing for the conditions of service for civil servants. In December 1983, the Prime Minister, Mrs Thatcher, (who was also Civil Service Minister), gave a direction that the conditions of service of all personnel employed at GCHQ should be revised to include a prohibition on membership of any trade union other than a staff association approved by the director of GCHQ. The Employment Protection Act 1975 and the Employment Protection (Consolidation) Act 1978 were then amended to exempt employees at GCHQ from the right to belong to a trade union for the purpose of safeguarding national security. Staff were offered the option of transferring to work in another civil service post, being made redundant, or remaining at GCHQ and receiving a payment of £1,000 in recognition of the loss of trade union membership rights. The applicants had unsuccessfully challenged the ban in the House of Lords.[43] The Commission found that there had been interference with the rights under Article 11(1). In terms of Article 11(2), the applicants fell into the category of members of the administration of the state and therefore the imposition of lawful restrictions on the exercise of these rights is specifically allowed. The term lawful in this context means that the measure must have been in accordance with national law. Staff at GCHQ were aware of the possibility that they may be subject to restrictions on trade union membership. The rules

---

[41]   *Young, James and Webster v. U.K.* (1982) 4 E.H.R.R. 38.
[42]   *Council of Civil Service Unions v. U.K.* (1988) 10 E.H.R.R. 269.
[43]   *Council of Civil Service Unions v. Minister for the Civil Service* [1984] 3 All E.R. 935.

restricting trade union membership were subject to judicial control by the domestic courts. The measures were, therefore, taken in accordance with national law. The Commission decided that the second sentence in Article 11(2) did not require that the interference should be necessary in a democratic society and the application was, therefore, declared inadmissible.

In *Gustafsson v. Sweden*, an employer complained that the state   9.13 had not protected him from actions taken by a union when he refused to be bound by a union collective agreement. Gustafsson ran a restaurant and youth hostel. He employed less than 10 employees and was not bound by any collective agreement with the relevant trade union. In 1987 the union asked Gustafsson to agree to be bound by a collective agreement, either by joining an employers' association or by signing a substitute agreement. Gustafsson refused. The union then declared a boycott against Gustafsson's premises and two other unions took sympathy action in support. Gustafson took proceedings against the Swedish Government, demanding that they intervene to prohibit the unions from boycotting his business. His claim was unsuccessful in the Swedish courts, and Gustafsson commenced proceedings under the Convention, claiming that the lack of state protection against the industrial action taken by the unions was a violation of his right to freedom of association under Article 11. It was held that Article 11 was applicable because the industrial action undertaken by the union affected his freedom of association. A compulsion to join a trade union was not always contrary to the Convention, but a form of such compulsion which strikes at the very substance of freedom of association would constitute an interference with that freedom. National authorities may in certain circumstances be obliged to intervene in relationships between private individuals by taking reasonable and appropriate measures to secure the effective enjoyment of the right to freedom of association. However, in assessing the appropriateness of state intervention to restrict union action aimed at extending a system of collective bargaining, the contracting states should enjoy a wide measure of appreciation in their choice of the means to be employed. Article 11 did not guarantee a right not to enter into a collective agreement. Since Gustafsson had not proved that that he provided conditions of employment more favourable than those required under a collective agreement, there was no reason to doubt that the union pursued legitimate interests consistent with Article 11 of the Convention, and having regard to the special nature of industrial relations in Sweden, there was accordingly no violation of Article 11.[44]

---

[44] *Gustafsson v. Sweden* (1996) 22 E.H.R.R. 409. See also *Sibson v. U.K.* (1994) 17 E.H.R.R. 193.

Although Article 11 mentions trade unions specifically and refers to the right to join trade unions as being "for the protection of interests", this does not mean that Article 11 gives a right to trade unions to be accorded any particular treatment or status. In *National Union of Belgian Police v. Belgium*, the National Union of Belgian Police complained that, because its membership had fallen below a certain number, the Government would no longer include the union in consultation processes. It was held that Article 11 does not secure any particular treatment to trade unions by the state. There is no right under Article 11 to guarantees that a trade union will be included in the process of collective bargaining. The state, like any other employer, can choose with which unions it will negotiate.[45]

Article 11 does not mean that private clubs are prevented from operating a membership policy provided that the purposes of the policy are legitimate. As a group of individuals the members of an association also have a right to freedom of association. In the English case of *Royal Society for the Prevention of Cruelty to Animals v. Attorney General*, the RSPCA sought a declaration that its rules permitted it to adopt and administer a selective membership policy. The Society wanted to exclude or remove from membership individuals who it suspected would not promote its aims and objectives. It was held that a society was justified by virtue of Article 11 in excluding from association those whose membership it believed would be damaging to its interests. It was not, however in the best interests of a large charitable organisation for there to be an arbitrary policy of exclusion which gave the excluded individual no opportunity to make representations in his defence. If such a membership policy was to be exercised, applicants had to be made aware of it upon receipt of the application form. Furthermore, a rejected applicant had to be invited to make representations as to why his admission to the society was appropriate. A potential member could not, however, maintain an entitlement to join the organisation in reliance upon a right to freedom of expression. The application was refused.[46]

9.14   The principle that a law which compels a person to join an association which is fundamentally contrary to his own opinions and beliefs may constitute an infringement of Article 11 was considered in the case of *Chassagnou v. France*, Chassagnou was owner of a small plot of land. He was opposed to hunting on ethical grounds but he was required under French national law to join an approved hunters' association and to allow its members to hunt on his land. Chassagnou complained that the law violated his rights to

---

[45] *National Union of Belgian Police v. Belgium* (1975) 1 E.H.R.R. 578.
[46] *Royal Society for the Prevention of Cruelty to Animals v. Attorney General* (2001) 98(11) L.S.G. 43.

and association under Article 11. It was held, that there was a breach of Article 11, since to force a person to join an association contrary to his own beliefs and to surrender his land to a use of which he disapproved went beyond what was necessary to protect the democratic participation in hunting. The right to hunt, in any event, was not a Convention right.[47]

The protection of the right to form and join political parties is also and important element of Article 11. In *Rekvenyi v. Hungary*, a police officer brought a complaint that the Constitution of Hungary which prohibited the police and army from joining a political party or carrying out any political activity, violated the rights of freedom of association in Article 11. It was held, although there had been interference with the right to freedom of association there had been no violation of the Convention. In the context of Hungary's recent history as a one party state in which the army and police force were closely linked, it was important for the state now to ensure that the police were seen to be politically separate from the governing party. The restriction was not an unreasonable or sweeping provision, and therefore justifiably outweighed the rights of the individual in the instant case.[48] Unjustified restrictions were held to have occurred in the case of *Socialist Party v. Turkey*. The Principal State Counsel in Turkey obtained an order from the Constitutional Court dissolving the Socialist Party on the basis that its political activities encouraged separatism which was incompatible with the Constitution and principles underpinning the Republic of Turkey and its founders and managers were banned from holding similar office in any other party. The Socialist Party maintained the dissolution was in breach their Convention rights including rights under Article 11. It was held that there had been a violation of Article 11 and Turkey was ordered to pay compensation for non-pecuniary damage. The dissolution of the political party pursued the legitimate aim of the protection of national security but the Court found that no evidence that the Socialist Party was engaging in violence or insurrection. Given the importance of political parties to democracy it was necessary to construe exceptions under Article 11 strictly. Even if there were problems associated with terrorism the Court concluded that the dissolution of the Socialist Party was disproportionate to the aim pursued.[49]

In relation to the United Kingdom the restrictions on the political activities of local government officers came under scrutiny in the case of *Ahmed v. United Kingdom*. The Local Government Officers (Political Restrictions) Regulations 1990 limited the right of local government officers holding "politically restricted posts" to

---

[47] *Chassagnou v. France* (1999) 29 E.H.R.R. 615.
[48] *Rekvenyi v. Hungary* (2000) 30 E.H.R.R. 519; 6 B.H.R.C. 554.
[49] *Socialist Party v. Turkey* (1999) 27 E.H.R.R. 51; [1998] H.R.C.D. 583.

participate in political activities. This meant that Ahmed, a local authority solicitor and holder of a politically restricted post, was unable to stand as a Labour candidate in local elections. He and a number of other people similarly affected applied unsuccessfully for judicial review of the Regulations. When their appeal was dismissed, Ahmed applied to the European Court of Human Rights, on the ground that the Regulations constituted an unjustified interference with his right to freedom of association, in breach of Article 11. It was held that the Regulations pursued the legitimate aim of protecting the rights of both council members and the electorate to effective local political democracy, which required political neutrality on the part of officers. Furthermore, the Regulations were "necessary in a democratic society", since they had been introduced as a result of a pressing social need to reduce the risk of abuse of power by local government officers. The Regulations did not represent a disproportionate interference with Ahmed's rights, given the margin of appreciation enjoyed by the state. It was held by a majority that there had been no violation of Article 11.[50]

9.15   The European Court of Human Rights has consistently held that only convincing and compelling reasons can justify restrictions on freedom of association. In determining whether a restriction is necessary within the meaning of Article 11(2), the states have only a limited margin of appreciation. This approach is shown in the case of *Sidiropoulos v. Greece*. Sidiropoulos and others, who lived on the border of the former Yugoslav Republic of Macedonia, decided to form a non-profit making association called "Home of Macedonian Civilisation". The objectives of the association included the cultural, intellectual and artistic development of its members and the protection of the region's natural and cultural environment. In June 1990 the applicants lodged an application under the civil code Article 79 with the local Court of First Instance for registration of their association. An application for registration of an association with the same name had been submitted to the same Court in January 1990, and the application had been refused in March 1990 on the ground that the objects included the words "the defence of national (*i.e.* Macedonian) independence". These words were held to indicate that the purpose of the association was contrary to the Greek national interest. The Court refused the second application on substantially the same ground, ruling that although the words "the defence of national independence" had been removed, the true object of the association was the promotion of the idea that there was a Macedonian minority in Greece, and that was contrary to the

---

[50]   *Ahmed v. U.K.* [1999] I.R.L.R. 188; (2000) 29 E.H.R.R. 1; 5 B.H.R.C. 111; (1999) 1 L.G.L.R. 94; [1998] H.R.C.D. 823.

Greek national interest and contrary to law. The applicants had appealed unsuccessfully in the national courts. The applicants contended that their right to freedom of association as guaranteed by Article 11 had been infringed. The Government argued that the restrictions on the applicants' right to freedom of association were in accordance with law and were "necessary in a democratic society in the interests of national security", as provided in Article 11(2). The Court held the Greek courts' refusal to register the applicants' association amounted to an interference with the applicants' exercise of their right to freedom of association. The main issue was whether that interference was prescribed by law, pursued one or more of the legitimate aims under Article 11(2) and was "necessary in a democratic society. The interference was "pre-scribed by law" under the civil code which allowed the courts to refuse an application to register an association where they found that the validity of its memorandum of association was open to question. Protection of national security and prevention of disorder was a legitimate aim in the light of the political unrest in the region. The aims of the association, being to preserve and develop the traditions and folk culture of the region, were perfectly clear and legitimate. In rejecting the application for registration the Greek courts had based their decisions on mere suspicions as to the true intentions of the applicants. If the possibility had become a reality the authorities could have acted to dissolve the association. Accordingly, the refusal to register the association was dispropor-tionate to the objectives pursued and there had been a violation of Article 11.[51]

PROTOCOL 4—PROTECTING CERTAIN ADDITIONAL RIGHTS

"Article 2
(1) Everyone lawfully within the territory of a State shall, within that territory, have the right to liberty of move-ment and freedom to choose his residence.
(2) Everyone shall be free to leave any country, including his own.
(3) No restrictions shall be placed on the exercise of these rights other than such as are in accordance with law and are necessary in a democratic society in the interests of national security or public safety, for the maintenance of the 'ordre public,' for the prevention of crime or for the protection of the rights and freedoms of others.

---

[51] *Sidiropoulos v. Greece* (1999) 27 E.H.R.R. 633; 4 B.H.R.C. 500; [1998] H.R.C.D. 707.

(4) The rights set forth in paragraph 1 may also be subject, in particular areas, to restrictions imposed in accordance with law and justified by the public interest in a democratic society."

9.16 This Protocol has not been ratified by the United Kingdom Government and thus the protections regarding the liberty of movement are not incorporated into the Human Rights Act 1998. However, freedom of movement is an important right and encompasses more than just the right to leave one country and enter another. It is recognised by the Treaties establishing the European Communities and, for the sake of completeness, there will be some discussion of this later in this section. The real impact of the right is often found to be in conjunction with other Articles and it is in these decisions of the European Court of Human Rights that the jurisprudence affecting the United Kingdom is to be found. Indeed there are comparatively few cases citing Article 2 of Protocol 4 as the foundation of the complaint.

Article 2 of Protocol 4 is concerned with restrictions on the freedom of movement, not the right to liberty which is dealt with by Article 5 of the Convention. It recognises that it is the right of an individual lawfully within a state to move freely within the state and to leave that state if he so wishes. The right is, however, heavily qualified by paragraphs 3 and 4. The qualifications in paragraph 3 are twofold: the restrictions must be "in accordance with law" and they must be "necessary in a democratic society" for four specific purposes. Paragraph 4 further qualifies the right under paragraph 1 to subject "particular areas" of a state to restrictions "in accordance with law and justified by the public interest in a democratic society".

The individual must be lawfully within the state for the article to apply. In *Piermont v. France*[52] a German Member of the European Parliament visited French Polynesia at the invitation of a local politician. When she arrived, government officials asked her to refrain from making political statements during her stay because elections were being held. Nonetheless she participated in demonstrations and made speeches criticising the government. As she was seated on the plane, about to leave, she was served with an order for expulsion and exclusion. She then flew to New Caledonia where she was allowed to pass through immigration but was then served with an exclusion order. She complained to the European Court on the basis of violations of Article 2 of Protocol 4 and Article 10. The Court held that although she had been served with the order in Polynesia when she was on the plane, she had had free movement until then. Once the exclusion order was served she was no longer

---

[52] (1995) 20 E.H.R.R. 301.

lawfully in the country and did not suffer any interference with the right to liberty of movement. The exclusion order for New Caledonia was served before she left the airport, so she had never lawfully entered the country and there was no breach of Article 2. There was however a breach of Article 10, freedom of expression.

The restriction on liberty of movement within one's own state 9.17 was examined in *Raimondo v. Italy*.[53] The applicant was suspected of being a member of a Mafia-type organisation but was acquitted of all charges. Preventative measures had been taken which involved confiscation of property and placing him under police supervision. He appealed against these measures and the decision allowing his appeal was filed on December 2, 1986 and made final on December 31, 1986. The European Court held that there had been a violation of Article 2 because his liberty of movement throughout Italy had been infringed as the police supervision had continued after December 2, 1986.

In the United Kingdom, the right of individuals to freedom of movement depends on the citizenship of the person and whether any restriction is required as a result of extradition or deportation proceedings. International law (including the Convention) accepts that a person should have freedom of movement within his own state. In Britain, a British citizen may freely move about the United Kingdom unless there are compelling legal reasons for preventing this. In *R v. Secretary of State for Home Department, ex parte McQuillan*[54] the applicant had been a member of a terrorist organisation but resigned in 1992. Exclusion orders preventing him from entering Great Britain were imposed on him under the Prevention of Terrorism (Temporary Provisions) Act 1989, section 5. He sought a review of the order and was interviewed by the Home Office. He claimed that his life was under threat while he was compelled to live in Northern Ireland. The Home Secretary refused to revoke the order and he then sought judicial review. The Court was asked to decide whether the decision contravened the applicant's rights under the Convention, Articles 2 and 3 and whether his right of freedom of movement was wrongly precluded by the 1989 Act contrary to EC Council Directive 64/221, Article 9. The Court referred the issue to the European Court of Justice but reasoned that the rights to life, freedom of movement and not to be subjected to torture or inhuman or degrading treatment were fundamental values of the common law. The Court would therefore scrutinise executive action that infringed such rights. However, the Court also noted that the interests of national security raised special questions. There was binding authority that the courts could not

---

[53] (1994) 18 E.H.R.R. 237.
[54] [1995] 4 All E.R. 400.

look into the rationality of a decision where it was made in the interests of national security.[55]

The European Convention does not give a person the right to enter, reside or remain in a particular country.[56] The European Court has recognised that states have the right to control who may enter or leave their jurisdiction[57] but this control must not violate any of the rights under the Convention, such as the right not to be tortured or suffer inhuman or degrading treatment (Article 3). Article 5(1)(f) allows the state to lawfully detain a person to prevent illegal entry to the country or to ensure that a person can be deported or extradited.

9.18   The admission of people into a state may be covered by Articles 3 or 8. Although there is no right given to enter a contracting state, once a person has entered a country, whether by lawful or unlawful means, then the protection of the Convention rights is engaged.

Article 3 may apply if the immigration policy of a state is found to be so discriminatory that the treatment of the applicant is degrading. In *East African Asians v. United Kingdom*[58] the Commission commented that discrimination based on race may be capable of reaching the threshold of degrading treatment.

> "Publicly to single out a group of persons for differential treatment on the basis of race might, in certain circumstances, constitute a special form of affront to human dignity; and the differential treatment of a group of persons on the basis of race might therefore be capable of constituting degrading treatment when differential treatment on some other ground would raise no such question."[59]

The exclusion of family members is not necessarily a breach of Article 8[60] and there is a presumption that the state is not obliged to admit family members. However, this presumption may be rebutted if it can be shown that it would be most difficult for the family to establish themselves elsewhere or there are special reasons why they should not be required to do so. Examples of such difficulties would be language difficulties, cultural religious and social practices, compelling health, employment or family issues. The European Court held in *Gul v. Switzerland*[61] that the extent of the state's

---

[55]   *R v. Secretary of State for Home Department, ex p. Adams* (No. 1) [1995] All E.R. (EC) 177.
[56]   *Soering v. U.K.* (1989) 11 E.H.R.R. 439.
[57]   *Chahal v. U.K.* (1996) 23 E.H.R.R. 413.
[58]   (1973) 3 E.H.R.R. 76 (EComHR).
[59]   *ibid.*, para. 207.
[60]   See *Abdulaziz, Cabales and Balkandali v. U.K.* (1985) 7 E.H.R.R. 471.
[61]   (1996) 22 E.H.R.R. 93.

obligation to admit relatives of settled immigrants will vary according to the particular circumstances and the general interest. Thus the refusal of leave to enter leading to the separation of an existing family, including an engaged couple, may amount to a violation of Article 8.[62] However, there is no right under the Convention to enter a country to found a new family.

Deportation

In the United Kingdom, the right to enter the country is governed 9.19
by the Immigration Act 1971 as amended by the British Nationality Act 1981. The 1971 Act introduced the idea of the "right of abode" which is the test for deciding whether a person has the right to settle and work within the United Kingdom without being the subject of immigration controls. A person will have the right of abode if he is a British citizen or a Commonwealth citizen who had right of abode as a Commonwealth citizen immediately before the 1981 Act came into effect.[63] The 1981 Act defines a British citizen as anyone who had the right of abode before the 1981 Act was enacted, or a person who is able to claim British citizenship after 1981 by virtue of birth, adoption by a British citizen, descent, registration or naturalisation. According to section 3(5) of the 1971 Act "a person who is not a British citizen shall be liable to deportation" in certain circumstances. A British citizen may not in any circumstances be deported.

The deportation rules are different for people who are citizens of the European Economic Area (EEA) and those who are not. The EEA includes all the European Union member states and Norway and Liechtenstein. EEA citizens are not British citizens and thus can be deported. However under European Community law, they have rights of free movement between member states for economic purposes. The power to deport under E.C. law is governed by Article 39 TEU and the Council Directive 64/221. These limit the power to grounds of public policy, public security and public health.

If an EEA citizen enters a country or wishes to enter they must have a reason for which free movement is guaranteed. The reasons include work, establishment of or joining a business, or to provide or receive services.

In *Van Duyn v. Home Office*[64] a member of the Church of 9.20
Scientology was excluded from the United Kingdom. The European Court of Justice upheld the exclusion by recognising that national authorities had "an area of discretion within the limits imposed by the Treaty". The whole point of Article 48 (now Article

---

[62] *Abdulaziz, Cabales and Balkandali v. U.K.* (1985) 7 E.H.R.R. 471.
[63] 1971 Act, s.2(1).
[64] [1974] 1 W.L.R. 1107.

39 TEU) was that freedom of movement was granted to nationals
of other member states but that freedom was subject to certain
restrictions. The Court emphasised in a later case that member
states could only rely on the "public policy" restriction where there
was "a genuine and sufficiently serious threat to the requirements of
public policy affecting one of the fundamental interests of
society".[65]

The decision in the *Van Duyn v. Home Office* case was narrowed
in *Adoui and Cournaille v. Belgian State*[66] where the European
Court of Justice decided that it would be difficult to regard conduct
as being sufficiently serious to justify deportation or exclusion on
public policy grounds unless some action had been taken by the
state against its own nationals who engaged in similar conduct. In
this case, the Belgian Government had tried to refuse residence
permits to two prostitutes. Prostitution was not illegal in Belgium
and so the government could not refuse residence for conduct which
was not illegal or controlled in its own citizens.

People who are not EEA nationals may be deported on three
grounds, these being set out in the Immigration Act 1971, section
3(5) and (6) as amended by the Immigration and Asylum Act 1999.
These are where deportation is deemed to be "conducive to the
public good", where someone in the person's family is to be
deported, or where a court has recommended deportation of a
person over the age of 17 years who has been convicted of an
imprisonable offence. In *P.P. v. United Kingdom*[67] the applicant and
her three children were deported from the United Kingdom in 1994,
leaving behind the children's father in prison. The mother had been
recommended for deportation after a drugs conviction. The
children complained that they had been constructively deported
as a result of their mother's deportation and that they would not be
able to see their father. In addition they maintained that, because of
his serious criminal record, he would not be able to join them in
Jamaica when he was released. The government asserted that there
were no obstacles to the father joining his family and the children
were all of an "adaptable age". All of the complaints were held to
be inadmissible. There were no elements concerning Article 8 which
outweighed the valid considerations for proper enforcement of
immigration controls. However, the Commission did leave open the
possibility that the children could make a fresh application if their
father was unable to join the family in Jamaica.

9.21   Where a person has breached the conditions of their entry to the
United Kingdom or has overstayed their permission to remain, they
will not now be "deported" but will be subject to removal by

---

[65]   *R v. Bouchereau* [1978] E.C.R. 1999.
[66]   [1982] E.C.R. 1665.
[67]   Appl. 25297/94, 16 January 1996, EComHR, unreported.

"directions" given by an immigration officer.[68] The main effect of this change was to reduce the scope for appeal.

Deportation on the ground of it being "conducive to the public good" allows the Secretary of State very wide discretion. Before making the deportation order, however, the Secretary of State must have regard to relevant matters such as the deportee's age, length of residence in the United Kingdom and the strength of connection with the United Kingdom, the character and conduct of the deportee, their employment record and any domestic or compassionate grounds. The phrase "conducive to the public good" is not defined but is used in four circumstances. First, it may be used where a person has been convicted of an offence but the court has not made an order for deportation.[69] Secondly, the deportation may be ordered where the deportee practiced deception to obtain settlement. An example of this would be "a marriage of convenience".[70] In a case before the Scottish courts, the person had been given entry clearance to participate in an arranged marriage.[71] However, the marriage lasted only a short time before divorce. A notice of intention to deport was served on him but he then hastily entered another marriage with an United Kingdom national. The man's arguments based on Article 8 were dismissed as a "side issue". The Secretary of State was obliged to give serious consideration to the effect of deportation on the deportee's family life but this did not necessarily mean that the marital home had to be in the United Kingdom.

The third example is where the deportee is practising or promoting political views which are regarded as dangerous or unduly offensive to certain members of the community. Fourthly, the presence of the deportee may be detrimental to national security. In *R v. Secretary of State for Home Department, ex parte Hosenball*[72] a United States journalist had lived in the United Kingdom for seven years but was served with a notice that he was to be deported. The grounds were that he had been trying to obtain information harmful to the security of the United Kingdom. The deportation was upheld on the grounds of national security. In *R v. Secretary of State for Home Department, ex parte Cheblak*[73] an Iraqi national was deported during the Gulf War because he was linked to an organisation which had indicated its intention to take terrorist action in support of the Iraqi regime. In *Secretary of State*

[68] Immigration and Asylum Act 1999, s.10.
[69] *R v. Nagari* [1980] 3 All E.R. 880.
[70] *R v. Immigration Appeal Tribunal, ex p. Khan* [1983] Q.B. 790.
[71] *Irfan Ahmed,* unreported, October 26, 1994, Outer House.
[72] [1977] 3 All E.R. 452.
[73] [1991] 2 All E.R. 319.

for Home Department v. Rehman[74] the court held that deportation on the grounds of national security could apply to someone who was likely to engage in international terrorism which would have no direct effect on the United Kingdom.

9.22   The deportations of non-EEA nationals must not breach any of the European Convention on Human Rights principles and it is not possible to deport someone, whatever the grounds, if the person will be subjected to treatment which is contrary to the Convention. Thus in *Chahal v. United Kingdom*[75] the applicant was able to show that deportation to India, his home country, would make him liable to suffer torture, inhuman or degrading treatment or punishment, contrary to Article 3. This was even where the applicant's political activities within the United Kingdom were held by the United Kingdom Government to be prejudicial to national security. Removal to a third country may be possible but only if there is no chance that the deportee would be removed to another country where there would be a real risk of ill-treatment. The European Court maintains that the country seeking to deport the applicant must undertake a thorough investigation of the implications of deportation.[76]

In Scotland, the courts have considered deportation cases in a more open and less harsh way. For instance, a deportation decision must take into account the impact on the deportee's spouse and children.[77] Thus a decision which will result in the permanent separation of a family will be so disproportionate as to be unreasonable.[78] However, Article 8 is not likely to be engaged where the deportee entered the country illegally and the family life started after that illegal entry and after enforcement action was commenced.[79]

Asylum Seekers

9.23   Many immigrants to the United Kingdom seek asylum when they arrive and special procedures will apply to them as a result of the Immigration and Asylum Act 1999. There is no right to asylum under United Kingdom law[80] and it is described as an "executive discretion restricted by statutory provision in relation to the destination to which the person refused entry asylum may be sent".[81]

---

[74] *The Times*, May 31, 2000.
[75] (1997) 23 E.H.R.R. 413.
[76] *Vilvarajah v. U.K.* (1991) 14 E.H.R.R. 248.
[77] *Malkiat Singh,* unreported, March 24, 1999, High Court of Justiciary.
[78] *Kulwinder Singh Saini,* unreported, March 12, 1999, High Court of Justiciary.
[79] *Saleem Ahmed,* unreported, March 28, 2000, Court of Session.
[80] *T v. Secretary of State for Home Department* [1996] 2 All E.R. 865.
[81] R. Stone, *Textbook on Civil Liberties and Human Rights* (3rd ed., 2000).

A person claiming asylum must be a refugee within the meaning of Article 1(A) of the Geneva Convention on the Status of Refugees 1951. The person must have a well-founded fear of persecution, which is more than discrimination or harassment. The reasons for the persecution must be based on race, religion, nationality, membership of a particular social group or political opinion. In *Islam v. Secretary of State for Home Department*[82] a Pakistani woman claimed asylum saying that if she returned to Pakistan she would be accused of adultery and punished according to Sharia law by stoning or flogging. The Court held that Pakistani women were capable of being a "social group" within the meaning of the Geneva Convention because of the existence of state-sanctioned discrimination against them.

Where asylum is claimed, the person will not be removed until the claim has been determined. The 1999 Act which governs this area has however a number of exceptions. An asylum seeker may be removed under section 11 to an European Union country which is party to the Dublin Convention of 1990. This states that such member states are to be regarded as "safe". The removal can only be made where the Secretary of State certifies that the member state has accepted responsibility under the Dublin Convention.

Asylum seekers may be removed to other countries under section 12 of the 1999 Act. There are two categories of states under this section. The first category includes those European Union countries which are not party to the Dublin Convention and other countries designated as "safe" such as Canada, the United Statses of America, Norway and Switzerland. An asylum seeker may be sent to one of these countries if the Secretary of State is satisfied that the applicant is not a national of that country, will not be threatened there and will not be sent on to another state except in accordance with the Geneva Convention. The second category includes all other states but the asylum seeker may appeal against the certificate of the Secretary of State and no deportation will take place until the appeal is heard.

Removal of an asylum seeker takes place in the many cases before the claim is decided. If, however, the person is to be removed under sections 11 or 12 and he has appealed against removal on the grounds that the removal is unlawful under section 6(1) of the Human Rights Act 1998, then he may not be removed until the issue is resolved. The Secretary of State may certify that the appeal is "manifestly unfounded" and this can then only be challenged by way of judicial review. The claimant is not, however, entitled to remain in the United Kingdom while the judicial review is proceeding.

9.24

---

[82] [1999] 2 All E.R. 545.

If a person has been served with a notice to remove he must give any additional ground for wishing to remain in the United Kingdom, including a claim to asylum or breach of human rights.[83] If, thereafter, he attempts to raise a claim of breach of human rights, the Secretary of State may certify under section 73 that the claim should have been made in the section 74 statement and there is no legitimate purpose in making the claim now. Once a certificate has been issued, the appeal is treated as having been finally determined. It is possible that section 73 (and section 72 which prevents the pursuit of an appeal from within the United Kingdom) may violate Article 6(1) of the Convention. It could be argued that having to leave the United Kingdom before pursuing an appeal is detrimental to the applicant's ability under Article 6 to pursue the action.

Extradition

9.25　Extradition is quite different from expulsion or deportation. It is a process whereby a person living in one country may be removed to another because that person is either accused of having committed a crime in the second country or has been convicted of a crime and escaped. The process of extradition is dependent on mutual arrangements between states either by a bilateral treaty or through the multi-lateral European Convention on Extradition. A British citizen may be extradited from the United Kingdom and this is the only way in which a British citizen can be forcibly removed from the country.

　　The main statute governing extradition is the Extradition Act 1989 but there are a number of other individual Extradition Acts from 1870 to 1932 which apply to countries with whom the United Kingdom has negotiated Treaties. These Treaties will eventually be superseded by ones concluded under the 1989 Act. Extradition arrangements with the Republic of Ireland are governed by the Backing of Warrants (Republic of Ireland) Act 1965.

　　Grounds for extradition depend on the state requesting the extradition and the alleged offence. The requesting state must have an extradition agreement with the United Kingdom or be a Commonwealth state. In addition, there must be an Order in Council in place under section 4 of the 1989 Act for a "foreign state" or under section 5 for a Commonwealth state. Where a country is a party to certain international treaties it may be viewed as having general extradition arrangements with the United Kingdom. Extradition for offences under these specific Conventions will be covered by specific Orders in Council. Examples of these Conventions include the 1963 Tokyo Convention on Offences and

---

[83]　1999 Act, s.74.

other Acts Committed On-board Aircraft, the 1979 International Convention Against the Taking of Hostages and the 1994 UN Personnel Convention on the safety of UN and Associated Personnel.

The alleged offence must be one as defined by section 2 of the 1989 Act, that is an offence punishable in the United Kingdom by 12 months' imprisonment and it must be punishable under the law of the state requesting extradition. It must also be an offence under English law at the time it was committed. In *R v. Bow Street Metropolitan Stipendiary Magistrate, ex parte Pinochet Ugarte (No.3)*[84] the former Chilean Head of State raised the definition of state immunity after the Government of Spain sought his extradition for conspiracy to murder, torture and hostage taking. The House of Lords confirmed the general principle that a Head of State had complete immunity while in office but after leaving office this immunity would be lost for private actions. It would be retained for official actions including "ordinary" criminal offences such as murder or conspiracy to murder. Crimes against humanity however were recognised by international law and it made no sense if such crimes were covered by the state immunity, since the main targets were state officials acting in their official capacity. Torture was an international crime against humanity under the 1984 Torture Convention and the United Kingdom had ratified this on December 8, 1988. Such actions were made criminal in England on September 29, 1988 by the Criminal Justice Act 1998, section 134. Any actions by Senator Pinochet before that date would not have been criminal in England. Actions before the ratification of the Convention were therefore immune and Senator Pinochet was protected for offences carried out before December 8, 1988.

There are restrictions on extradition. The target of the order must be a genuine criminal not a political offender. Section 6(1) refers to "offences of a political character" but section 6(8) excludes offences against the Head of the Commonwealth, that is the Queen. Genocide can never be categorised as a political offence.[85] The English Court of Appeal put forward a definition of political offence as being one which was incidental to and formed part of a political disturbance. There had to be a dispute about which side would govern.[86]

People who have committed acts of terrorism may claim their acts are political offences and thus they should not be extradited. The Suppression of Terrorism Act 1978 was passed to prevent international terrorists using this argument. The Act is based on the European Convention on the Suppression of Terrorism 1977 which

9.26

---

[84] [1999] 2 All E.R. 97.
[85] 1989 Act, s.23.
[86] *Re Castrioni* [1890] 1 Q.B. 149.

states that some offences may never be regarded as political. These include murder, manslaughter, rape, abduction, hostage taking and explosives and firearms offences. If a signatory state seeks extradition of a person the request cannot be refused on the basis that the offence was of a political character. If extradition is refused on another basis of the 1989 Act the person can be tried in the United Kingdom courts as if the offence had been committed here.[87]

9.27   In addition to these restrictions, an extradition will not be allowed if it appears to be a pretext to punish a person on grounds of race, religion, nationality or his political opinions, or it seems likely that a trial will be unfair because of one of these grounds. Section 12 of the 1989 Act gives other reasons to refuse the extradition request, such as triviality of the offence, lapse of time or bad faith on the part of the state making the request.

The European Convention on Human Rights does not give a person protection from extradition and many of the arguments noted above in deportation are relevant here. The Articles most likely to be used by an applicant are Articles 3 and 6. The European Court has stated that extradition powers have to be used within the limits of the Convention.

> "The decision by a Contracting State to extradite a fugitive may give rise to an issue under Article 3, and hence engage the responsibility of that State under the Convention, where substantial grounds have to be shown for believing the person concerned. . . faces a real risk of being subjected to torture or to inhuman or degrading treatment or punishment in the requesting country."[88]

The mere possibility of ill-treatment will not be enough to engage the Convention; there must be a real risk. In *Soering v. United Kingdom* the applicant was accused of murder and was to be extradited to the United States where, if convicted, he could be sentenced to death. The European Court held that if he were extradited and convicted, the prolonged appeal process would mean that there was a real risk that he would be subjected to inhuman or degrading treatment while incarcerated on "death row". In the event, Soering was extradited but only after the charge was reduced so that it was no longer a capital offence.

---

[87]   1978 Act, s.4.
[88]   *Soering v. U.K.* (1989) 11 E.H.R.R. 439 at para. 91

CHAPTER 10

FREEDOM FROM DISCRIMINATION

ARTICLE 14—PROHIBITION OF DISCRIMINATION

"The enjoyment of rights and freedoms set forth in this convention shall be secured without discrimination on any ground such as sex, race, colour, language, religion, political or other opinion, national or social origin, association with a national minority, property, birth or status."

There is a qualification to Article 14, (and Articles 10 and 11) which 10.01 follows.

ARTICLE 16—RESTRICTIONS ON POLITICAL ACTIVITIES OF ALIENS

"Nothing in Articles 10,11 and 14 shall be regarded as preventing the High Contracting Parties from imposing restrictions on the political activities of aliens."

Article 14 does not give protection against discrimination *per se*. It 10.02 gives protection against discrimination only in connection with other Convention rights. Article 14 therefore has no independent existence. A measure which is otherwise in conformity with the Convention may amount to a violation of Article 14 if it is of a discriminatory nature. The principle of equality of treatment is violated if any distinction on grounds of sex, race, colour, language, religion, political or other opinion, national or social origin, association with a national minority, property, birth or status has no objective and reasonable justification. In the case of *Abdulaziz, Cabales and Balkandali v. United Kingdom*, it was held that the immigration rules for entry into the United Kingdom were in violation of Article 14. Under the regulations it was easier for the wives of men residing in the United Kingdom to enter than it was for the husbands of wives residing in the United Kingdom. The applicants were women residing in the United Kingdom whose husbands were unable to join them. They claimed that this amounted to a breach of Article 8, the right to family life and to a breach of Article 14. The Government had argued that the difference in treatment between men and women was justified on the basis that immigration of men needed to be more tightly controlled in order to protect the domestic labour market. The Court was not convinced that the difference that may exist between the respective impact of men and women on the domestic labour market is sufficiently important to justify the difference of treatment complained of by the applicants. The court held that Article 8 had not been violated as it does not confer an unqualified right for married couples from different countries to reside in the same country but Article 14 had been violated by the difference in treatment accorded to men and women. The rules were amended as a result of the case.[1]

Article 14 does no more than provide a guarantee that people will not receive different treatment because of their sex, race colour, language, religion, political or other opinion, national or social origin, association with a national minority, property, birth or status. It does not create a positive obligation on a state to preserve the culture and language of minority groups. In the *Belgian Linguistic case (No. 2)*, the Court held that Article 14 does not guarantee to a parent or to a child the right to receive instruction in the language of his choice. The obligation under Article 14 is to ensure that the right to education shall be secured to everyone within its jurisdiction, without discrimination on the ground, for instance, of language.[2]

Often when claims are made to the European Court of Human Rights which include a contention that there has been a breach of Article 14 the issue of discrimination under Article 14 is not considered. This is because it is not deemed to be necessary to deliberate on the issue of differential treatment if the court finds that there has been a breach of another substantive right. This approach was explained in the case of *Dudgeon v. United Kingdom*, wherein it was stated that:

> "Where a substantive Article of the Convention has been invoked both on its own and together with Article 14 and a separate breach has been found of the substantive Article, it is not generally necessary for the Court also to examine the case under Article 14, though the position is otherwise if a clear inequality of treatment in the enjoyment of the right in question is a fundamental aspect of the case."

---

[1] *Abdulaziz, Cabales and Balkandali* (1985) 7 E.H.R.R. 471.
[2] *Belgian Linguistic case (No. 2)* (1968) 1 E.H.R.R. 252.

DEVELOPMENT OF DISCRIMINATION LAW IN THE UNITED KINGDOM

There are two ways in which freedom from discrimination can be   10.03
achieved. First, by regulation which makes discrimination unlawful
and which imposes penalties when discrimination has taken place.
The second approach is to protect individuals by providing them
with a remedy when they can prove that they have suffered
discrimination. Discrimination laws in the United Kingdom involve
both approaches. Remedies are provided for individuals who have
been discriminated against on grounds of race, sex or disability.
Regulations to prevent discrimination in general have been
developed in relation to disability and race but to a lesser degree
in relation to sex. In relation to race and disability a duty to prevent
discrimination has been imposed in certain circumstances.

The United Kingdom laws which protect citizens from discrimination are much narrower in scope than Article 14, being limited to
discrimination on grounds of sex, race, marital status or disability.
There is no protection against discrimination on grounds of
religion, political or other opinion, social origin, association with
a national minority, property, birth or status.

Influence of European Law

The laws which protect the citizen in the United Kingdom from   10.04
discrimination on grounds of sex, marital status, race, colour,
ethnic origin or disability all owe their existence to European
directives which required member states to establish protective
regimes. The development of protection against discrimination has
been an important aspect of European Law but it was not until
1997, when the Treaty of Amsterdam amended the Treaty of Rome,
that anti-discrimination was included as a basic founding principle
of the Union. Discrimination in relation to sex, racial or ethnic
origin, religion or belief, disability, age or sexual orientation is
contrary to Article 13 of the E.C. Treaty. The Treaty states:

> "Without prejudice to the other provisions of this Treaty, and
> within the limits of the powers conferred by it upon the
> Community, the Council, acting unanimously on a proposal
> from the Commission, and after consulting the European
> Parliament, may take appropriate action to combat discrimi-
> nation based on sex, racial or ethnic origin, religion or belief,
> disability, age or sexual orientation."

DISCRIMINATION ON GROUNDS OF SEX OR MARITAL STATUS

The laws to protect individuals in the United Kingdom from   10.05
discrimination on grounds of sex have been passed in order to

secure conformity with European Community law. Directive 76/
207/EEC, for example, provides for equal treatment as regards
access to employment and promotion, training, and working.
Article 2(1) of the Equal Treatment Directive[3] states that there be
"no discrimination on the grounds of sex either directly or
indirectly by reference in particular to marital or family status".
European Union directives are enforceable in the national courts
where the action is against an organisation under control of the
state.[4] They are not enforceable in the courts against private bodies
but an individual who suffers a loss caused by a private body due to
a failure by the state to implement a directive may have a claim
against the state.[5]

There is no general prohibition of discrimination on grounds of
sex in all circumstances under United Kingdom law. The two major
statutory provisions, the Equal Pay Act 1970 and the Sex
Discrimination Act 1975 (as amended by the Sex Discrimination
Act 1986) are limited in their application to specific spheres of
activity. The Equal Pay Act 1970 only applies to the contractual
aspects of employment. It makes it unlawful to discriminate
between men and women in respect of pay and other contractual
terms and conditions of employment. The Sex Discrimination Act
1975 ordains that it is unlawful to discriminate on grounds of sex or
marital status in respect of employment, training, education,
provision of goods and services, disposal and the management of
premises. The effects of the Sex Discrimination Act therefore relate
to many aspects of everyday life so, for example, it is unlawful for a
bank or building society to discriminate in the terms on which a
loan is offered. A public house cannot insist on women sitting at a
table if it allows men to stand at the bar. Although the spheres of
activity specified in the Act are fairly broad, questions do still arise
from time to time as to whether or not the Act applies to a
discriminatory act. In the case of *Graham v. Hawick Common
Riding Committee*, for example, the decision hinged upon whether
or not the common riding events could be categorised as "the
provision of services". Graham and other women had been
excluded from participation in certain events of the Hawick
Common Riding. They raised an action for declarator that their
exclusion was contrary to the Sex Discrimination Act 1975 section 1
and section 29. Hawick Common Riding argued that they did not
provide facilities or services in terms of section 29(1). They were a
voluntary organisation whose purpose was to organise the annual
common riding events. It was held that the provisions of the
constitution of the Common Riding organisation demonstrated

---

[3] 76/207/EEC.
[4] *Foster v. British Gas plc* [1990] 3 All. E.R. 897.
[5] *Francovich v. Italy* [1992] 21 I.R.L.R.84, [1991] ECR I-5357.

that they were concerned with the provision of "facilities" within the meaning of section 29(2)(e). It was also held that discrimination on grounds of sex was not justified by the fact that exclusive male participation in the events was a long established tradition.[6]

Definition of Discrimination

Section 5 of the Act defines "discrimination". Discrimination occurs where a person has been treated less favourably than a comparable person of the other sex has been or would be treated. The comparison of the cases of persons of different sex must be such that "the relevant circumstances in the one case are the same, or not materially different in the other".[7] It is not necessary to prove that a person of the other sex has received more favourable treatment, only that the person would have been better treated had they been of the other sex. First, it must be proved that there has been differentiation in treatment. Secondly, he or she must show that their treatment was less favourable, and thirdly, that the different treatment was on grounds of sex. Motive and intention are not relevant to determining whether or not an act amounted to discrimination. The test for discrimination is objective. Regard must be had to the actions which were taken and the consequences of those actions.[8] Discrimination exists if a person would not have received the same treatment from the defender but for his or her sex.[9] This "but for" test was applied by the House of Lords in *James v. Eastleigh Borough Council*. Mr James and his wife, both aged 61, used a local authority swimming pool. Pensioners were allowed to use the swimming pool without charge. As Mrs James was over the pensionable age for women she was admitted free, but Mr James being under 65 years old had to pay. It was held that the court had to apply an objective test and the appropriate question was whether Mr James would receive the same treatment as his wife of the same age but for his sex. The response to that question was "yes" and therefore Eastleigh Borough Council were in breach of the Sex Discrimination Act 1975.[10]

The "but for" test was also used in *Home Office v. Coyne*. Ms

10.06

---

[6]   *Graham v. Hawick Common Riding Committee,*1998 S.L.T. (Sh.Ct) 42; 1997 S.C.L.R. 917.

[7]   Sex Discrimination Act 1975, s.5(3).

[8]   *Birmingham C.C., ex p. Equal Opportunities Commission (No. 1)* [1989] A.C.1155, [1989] 1 All E.R. 769.

[9]   *Ibid.*

[10] James v. Eastleigh B.C., [1990] 2 A.C. 751; [1990] 3 W.L.R. 55; [1990] 2 All E.R. 607; [1990] I.C.R. 554; [1990] I.R.L.R. 288; (1990) 140 N.L.J. Rep. 926; (1990) 87(27) L.S.G. 41; (1991) 155 L.G. Rev. 205. See also, *Birmingham C.C. v. Equal Opportunities Commission (No.1)* [1989] A.C. 1155; [1989] 2 W.L.R. 520; [1989] 1 All E.R. 769; [1989] I.R.L.R. 173; 87 L.G.R. 557; (1989) 86(15) L.S.G. 36; (1989) 139 N.L.J. 292; (1989) 133 S.J. 322.

Coyne, a prison instructional officer, successfully brought a claim for unfair dismissal and sexual discrimination against the Home Office. She had claimed that a male member of staff had made indecent gestures toward her. She had made a formal complaint but the complaint was not dealt with for over two years. Coyne contended that she had been the victim of sexual harassment and that the failure to conduct a proper investigation into the situation constituted sexual discrimination. The Home Office appealed, contending that the failure to investigate the complaint was not related to Coyne's gender. It was held that the tribunal had erred in failing to adopt the "but for" test and had misdirected itself when concluding that the failure to investigate the complaint properly had constituted sexual discrimination by reason only of the complaint relating to sexual harassment. It had not been proved that a person of different sex would have been treated differently.[11]

The case of *Fire Brigades Union v. Fraser* concerned a male fire fighter who had been accused of sexual harassment. He was suspended from duty pending investigation of the allegations by the employer. The Fire Brigades Union decided not to give any support or legal assistance to Fraser as they were supporting the women who made the allegations against him. The union's equal opportunities policy stated that if a complainant was represented they would not represent a member accused of harassment. Fraser complained to an employment tribunal alleging that he had been discriminated against contrary to section 12(3) of the Sex Discrimination Act 1975 as the union had refused to provide him with legal services on the grounds of his sex.[12] The tribunal upheld his complaint, finding that a woman accused of harassment would have received the usual support from the union. The Inner House allowed an appeal. It was held that it was true that those complaining of harassment were treated more favourably than those who had been accused of harassment, but there was no evidence to support a finding that a woman accused of harassment would have been treated differently than a man.[13]

On Grounds of Sex

10.07   Discrimination is unlawful if the reason for the discrimination is the sex of the person who is the victim of the discrimination. Although the Act is generally regarded as being for the purpose of protecting women from discrimination, the Act makes it equally unlawful to discriminate against a man because of his masculine gender as

---

[11]   *Home Office v. Coyne* [2000] I.C.R. 1443; [2000] I.R.L.R. 838. See also *Chief Constable of Greater Manchester v. Hope* [1999] I.C.R. 338.

[12]   Sex Discrimination Act 1975, s.12(3).

[13]   *Fire Brigades Union v. Fraser* [1997] I.R.L.R. 671.

against a woman because of her female gender. Section 1(1) provides, *inter alia*, that "[a] person discriminates against a woman in any circumstances relevant for the purposes of any provision of this Act if ... on the ground of her sex he treats her less favourably than he treats or would treat a man". Section 2(1) provides that "section 1, and the provisions of Parts II and III relating to sex discrimination against women, are to be read as applying equally to the treatment of men, and for that purpose shall have effect with such modifications as are requisite." Section 5(2) provides that "woman" includes a female of any age, and that "man" includes a male of any age.

The word "sex" is not defined in the Act, but there are indications that the meaning of the word is intended to be the same as "gender". The word "gender" is used in section 2(A), which was inserted in 1999, in the context of gender reassignment. The expressions "either sex" and "the same sex" are also used in section 3, dealing with discrimination against married persons. Other phrases which are used include, "being a man",[14] "limited to one sex",[15] "single-sex establishment", "one sex only", "the opposite sex",[16] "one sex only",[17] "persons of one sex".[18]

DISCRIMINATION ON GROUNDS OF SEXUAL ORIENTATION

Discrimination on grounds of sexual orientation is not deemed to 10.08 be discrimination on grounds of sex in the United Kingdom. Discrimination on grounds of sexual orientation has been regarded as discrimination against homosexuals rather than discrimination against the members of one sex. In a case where a lesbian woman employed as a science teacher had been abused by pupils the employment tribunal held that the school which employed her would have been liable if sex discrimination had taken place. The employer had taken no steps to reduce the abuse. However, it was held that her subjection by pupils to abuse relating to her sexual orientation did not constitute sexual discrimination under the Sex Discrimination Act 1975. The teacher appealed, contending that the nature of the abuse had been gender specific and accordingly was discrimination on the ground of sex. The employment appeal tribunal held, however, that the teacher had been subjected to homosexual discrimination, not sexual discrimination, and as such there had been no breach of the 1975 Act which provided

---

[14] Sex Discrimination Act 1975, s.7.
[15] *ibid.*, s.19.
[16] *ibid.*, s.26.
[17] *ibid.*, s.33.
[18] *ibid.*, s.34.

protection from discrimination on the grounds of sex not sexual orientation. Abuse, albeit gender specific, directed at a person's sexual orientation did not amount to discrimination under the 1975 Act.[19]

The Ministry of Defence policy of excluding homosexuals from service in the armed forces came under scrutiny when several service men and women sought compensation after they had been dismissed from the armed forces on the grounds of their sexual orientation. The policy of excluding homosexuals from the armed forces was justified by the Ministry of Defence on the basis of national interest. The Ministry considered that operational difficulties could arise if homosexuals were admitted into the armed forces. Tribunals in the United Kingdom consistently held that discrimination on the grounds of sexual orientation was not sex discrimination. Sex discrimination was defined, in effect, as discrimination on the basis of gender. Eventually, after applications for judicial review of the Ministry of Defence policy were unsuccessful, as was a subsequent appeal to the House of Lords, a group of people who had been discharged from the armed forces brought a case to the European Court of Human Rights. All four applicants contended that the investigations into their private lives undertaken by the Ministry of Defence constituted an infringement of their right to respect for their private lives under the European Convention on Human Rights 1950, Article 8. They also claimed that the investigation and their subsequent discharge amounted to discrimination and was an infringement of Article 14. The applicants further contended that an application for judicial review in the United Kingdom did not afford them an effective domestic remedy as required under Article 13. The European Court of Human Rights held that the investigations, interviews and discharges amounted to an "exceptional intrusion" into the applicants' private lives, constituting a violation of Article 8. The Court accepted that some operational difficulties might arise where there were homosexual military personnel but that these could be countered by means of a code of conduct enforced by adequate disciplinary rules. Furthermore, opinion was expressed that the heterosexual armed forces personnel demonstrated apparent prejudice towards homosexuals. An adverse attitude to homosexuals could not of itself justify intrusions into the private lives of personnel any more than it could justify discrimination on the grounds of race or sex. The Court also found that the applicants did not have access to an effective domestic remedy as required by Article 13. So far as Article 14 was concerned, the Court considered

---

[19] *Pearce v. Governing Body of Mayfield Secondary School* [2000] I.C.R. 920; [2000] I.R.L.R. 548.

that the applicants' complaint under that Article, in conjunction
with Article 8, did not give rise to any separate issue. The issue of
whether the word "sex" in Article 14 included sexual orientation
was not addressed.

The Employment Appeal Tribunal subsequently held that it is
unlawful to discriminate on grounds of sexual orientation and that
the word "sex" in the Sex Discrimination Act 1975 should be
interpreted to include "on the grounds of sexual orientation" and
therefore applies to persons discriminated against on the grounds of
their homosexuality. An RAF officer whose employment had been
terminated by reason of his homosexuality, appealed against the
dismissal of his claim for sex discrimination and sexual harassment.
He submitted that "sex" within the meaning of the statutory
provisions had been wrongly construed so as to concern only
gender and to exclude sexual orientation. He contended that
interpretation of the legislation should have favoured a construction compatible with the European Convention on Human Rights
1950, Article 14. The Ministry of Defence appealed to the Inner
House wherein it was held that the Ministry of Defence had not
treated the respondent less favourably, on the ground of his gender,
than they would treat a woman. Although the Human Rights Act,
section 3(1) states that "[s]o far as it is possible to do so, primary
legislation and subordinate legislation must be read and given effect
in a way which is compatible with Convention rights", the Sex
Discrimination Act is not incompatible with the Convention.
Article 14 does not mention sexual orientation. It simply refers to
"grounds such as sex". Lord Kirkwood stated:

> "In my opinion, having regard to the context in which the
> word "sex" is used in sections 1 and 2 of, and elsewhere in, the
> 1975 Act it clearly and unambiguously relates only to gender
> discrimination and is not capable of being interpreted as
> including discrimination on the ground of sexual orientation."

He also pointed out that

> "if the word 'sex' in section 1(1) of the 1975 Act is read as
> meaning only gender, and does not include sexual orientation,
> such an interpretation is not incompatible with any Conven-
> tion right. The Convention does not contain any free-standing
> right not to be discriminated against. While Article 14 has
> been held by the European Court of Human Rights to
> prohibit discrimination on the ground of sexual orientation, it
> does so only when taken along with one of the substantive
> rights and freedoms which are guaranteed under the Conven-
> tion, and there is no Convention right or freedom which

relates specifically to employment."[20]

10.09　Whether the European Court of Human Rights is moving towards the inclusion of discrimination on grounds of sexual orientation in Article 14 is not entirely clear. With regard to discrimination on grounds of sexual orientation, the jurisprudence of the European Court of Human Rights includes the case of *Salguerio da Silva Mouta v. Portugal*. The Portuguese Court of Appeal had granted the applicant's ex-wife, rather than the applicant, parental authority over their daughter, and the applicant alleged that the decision had been taken purely on the ground of his sexual orientation as he was a homosexual and lived with another man. The applicant regarded this as a violation of Article 8 of the Convention, taken in isolation and in conjunction with Article 14. The Court concluded that the applicant and his ex-wife had been treated differently on the basis of the applicant's sexual orientation, and observed that that was a "concept which is undoubtedly covered by Article 14 of the Convention". Article 14 refers to "sex" and "other status". It was not made clear whether sexual orientation was included in the word "sex" or was included in the grounds of discrimination in a more general way, perhaps under the heading of "other status".[21]

DISCRIMINATION ON GROUNDS OF MARITAL STATUS

10.10　The Act outlaws discrimination on grounds of marriage in the context of employment.[22] It is permissible, however, to discriminate against a single person of either sex. The Sex Discrimination (Gender Reassignment) Regulations 1999 also make it contrary to the Sex Discrimination Act to treat a transsexual man or woman less favourably in recruitment, employment, pay, working terms and conditions, and dismissal, either before, during or after treatment.[23] The Regulations work not by comparing a man with a woman but by comparing the treatment of a transsexual person with that of a non-transsexual person, so they do not define any moment when a person changes sex. The Regulations allow for differential treatment in some circumstances, for example, where employees share living accommodation, or where a worker is providing personal welfare services to someone who is vulnerable (such as a mentally ill person). The Regulations make it lawful, for example, to require a man undergoing gender reassignment to leave

---

[20]　*Ministry of Defence v. MacDonald*, unreported, June 1, 2001.
[21]　*Salguerio da Silva Mouta v. Portugal* (2001) Fam. L.R. 2.
[22]　Sex Discrimination Act 1975, s.3.
[23]　See also *P v. S & Cornwall C.C.*, Case C-13/94 [1996] ECR 1-2143, [1996] IRLR 347.

a male-only post, if the employer can show that there is a single-sex genuine occupational qualification and that it is not possible to move the man to another post within the organisation. The Regulations also contain exceptions for work in a private home and for the purposes of an organised religion.

Under the European Convention single persons may be protected against discrimination on grounds of marital status, although only in connection with a contravention of another Convention right. This issue was considered in *B v. United Kingdom*. An unmarried father had applied for parental responsibility. The mother, took the child, B, to Italy. The father unsuccessfully sought B's return under the Hague Convention[24] with the court concluding that the father had no formal rights of custody. The father complained to the European Court of Human Rights that his rights as an unmarried father were not protected in the same way as those of a married father. The application was held to be inadmissible, there was an objective and reasonable justification why the father, who merely had contact with the child, should not be treated as being on an equal footing with someone who had the child in his care. There had been no discrimination as between married and unmarried fathers and that the United Kingdom courts had not in fact made any reference to F's marital status. Accordingly, the different treatment of the applicant was not in breach of the European Convention on Human Rights.[25]

Unlawful discrimination may take one of three forms: direct discrimination; indirect discrimination or victimisation.

(1) Direct Discrimination

There is direct discrimination if a person is treated less favourably   10.11
than a person of the opposite sex is or would be treated.[26]
Therefore, if a woman applied for a job selling cars and was told that it was not a woman's job that would amount to direct discrimination. However, if a feeble woman was rejected because the job needed a strong person to do it there would be no unlawful discrimination. She would have been rejected because she cannot do the job. However, if all women are rejected because an employer considers that all women are weak it would amount to unlawful discrimination.[27] A balance has to be achieved between the rights of employers to hire employees who are suitably equipped to do the job required and the right of each individual not to suffer discrimination.

---

[24] Hague Convention on the Civil Aspects of International Child Abduction 1980.
[25] *B v. U.K.* [2000] 1 F.L.R. 1; [2000] 1 F.C.R. 289; [2000] Fam. Law 88.
[26] Sex Discrimination Act 1975, s.1(1)(a).
[27] *Batisha v. Say* (1976) 19 Man. Law 23.

The purpose of the Sex Discrimination Act is to protect individuals from discriminatory acts. The motive of the person who discriminates against them is irrelevant. Whether or not he intended to discriminate is also irrelevant. Therefore it was held that, even where an employer acted on grounds which he thought were chivalrous, discrimination on grounds of sex would be unlawful. An employer who had refused to allow women to earn extra payments by working in an area that was very dirty was held to have discriminated against women. His policy preventing them from earning additional payments and also discriminated against his male employers by requiring them to work in different conditions from female employees.[28] Another successful claim was brought by a woman who had been prevented from starting her new job as a painter. The employer had withdrawn an offer of employment when another female applicant declined the job as Ms Greig would have had to work with a team comprised entirely of men. The employer genuinely thought it would not be in her best interests to work with an all-male team. Nevertheless the tribunal held that she had been the victim of unlawful direct discrimination.[29] In the case of *Schmidt v. Germany*, a man complained to the European Court of Human Rights because he was under a legal duty to either serve in the local fire brigade or to pay a levy in lieu of service. Women were not under the same duty. He argued successfully that service in the fire brigade was comparable for men and women and that account could be taken of the biological differences between the two sexes by sensible division of the various tasks. The concern to protect women did not justify a difference of treatment in this context. Women were also just as capable as men of paying the levy. It was held that there was a violation of Article 14.[30]

Different treatment may not always amount to discrimination. Whether a person has been treated "less favourably" is an objective matter, for the tribunal to determine. Dress codes which require men and women to dress differently are not always regarded as discrimination. In *Schmidt v. Austicks Books*, a female employee claimed that she had been discriminated against because she had been dismissed for wearing trousers. The employer had a rule prohibiting the wearing of trousers by women. However, there was also a rule forbidding the wearing of T-shirts by men. It was held that the applicant had not been discriminated against unlawfully as both male and female employees were restricted as to clothing.[31] In *Smith v. Safeway Plc*, the employer of Smith, a male delicatessen

---

[28] *Ministry of Defence v. Jeremiah* [1979] 3 All E.R. 833.
[29] *Grieg v. Community Industry* [1979] I.R.L.R. 158.
[30] *Schmidt v. Germany* (1994) 18 E.H.R.R. 513.
[31] *Schmidt v. Austicks Books* [1978] I.C.R. 85; [1977] I.R.L.R. 360.

Freedom From Discrimination

assistant dismissed for having long hair tied in a ponytail, appealed against an EAT ruling that a dress code requirement as to length of hair was unlawful as it discriminated against male employees. The employer argued that the rules on appearance were not discriminatory under the Sex Discrimination Act 1975 as they enforced a common standard of presentation for men and women and that, although individual items were different, including length of hair, neither gender was treated less favourably than the other. It was held, allowing the appeal, that to establish discrimination one had to show that one sex had been treated less favourably, not merely that they had been treated differently. The dress code was not of identical application to men and women and could legitimately take account of facial appearance or hair, to the effect that different appearances were acceptable for men and women. Taken as a whole, the employer's approach was even handed and the code did not treat either sex less favourably.[32] There is a distinction between discrimination between the sexes, which may be lawful, and discrimination against one sex which is a contravention of the Act.

A long-established tradition will not justify discrimination. When **10.12** women brought an action for a declarator that they had been unlawfully discriminated against by being denied an opportunity to participate in the Hawick common riding, it was held that the discrimination was unlawful. The fact that all of the roles had been traditionally taken by men did not justify the discrimination.[33] It is also direct discrimination where assumptions are made on the basis of gender, for example to refuse to let a flat to men because they are untidy or to operate a policy of never employing young mothers because they are unreliable. In the case of *Hurley v. Mustoe*[34] it was held that there had been unlawful discrimination when the manager of a bistro refused to employ a mother who had young children. Ms Hurley had applied for a job as a waitress. She was given a one-night trial to see if she was satisfactory. The manager was happy with her work but the owner instructed him not to give her a job because she had four children and he thought women with children were unreliable. She had previously worked for ten years as waitress and had a good work record. The bistro owner made no attempt to check this. He based his decision on his assumptions about working mothers in general.[35]

---

[32] *Smith v. Safeway Plc* [1996] I.C.R. 868; [1996] I.R.L.R. 456.
[33] *Graham v. Hawick Common Riding Committee*, 1998 S.L.T. (Sh.Ct) 42; 1997 S.C.L.R. 917.
[34] *Hurley v. Mustoe (No. 1)* [1981] IRLR 208.
[35] See also *Coleman v. Skyrail Oceanic Ltd* [1981] I.R.L.R. 398.

Sexual Harassment

10.13 Sexual harassment constitutes direct discrimination. Sexual harassment is defined as; "unwanted conduct of a sexual nature, or other conduct based on sex affecting the dignity of men and women at work. This can include unwelcome physical, verbal or non-verbal conduct."[36] Article 1 of the European Commission Recommendation on the Protection of the Dignity of Women and Men at Work recommended that member states take action to promote awareness that conduct of a sexual nature, including conduct of superiors and colleagues, is unacceptable if:

> (a) such conduct is unwanted, unreasonable and offensive to the recipient;
> (b) a person's rejection of, or submission to, such conduct on the part of employers of workers (including superiors or colleagues) is used explicitly as a basis for a decision which affects that person's access to vocational training, access to employment, continued employment, promotion, salary or any other employment decisions; and/or;
> (c) such conduct creates an intimidating, hostile or humiliating work environment for the recipient;

and that such conduct may, in certain circumstances, be contrary to the principle of equal treatment within the meaning of Articles 3, 4 and 5 of Directive 76/207/EEC. The Recommendation asked member states to implement a Code of Practice for employment within the public sector and to encourage its use in private sector. In the United Kingdom it appears that the Recommendation has been taken into account by tribunals in sexual harassment cases.[37]

Harassment may include bullying or unwanted sexual advances. This can amount to treating a person less favourably on grounds of sex contrary to the Sex Discrimination Act.[38] The most notable Scottish case involving sexual harassment is *Strathclyde Regional Council v. Porcelli*.[39] Mrs Porcelli was a laboratory technician in a school. She asked for a transfer to another school because of the behaviour of two male lab technicians. They sabotaged her work, let doors slam in her face as she was carrying equipment, and threw her personal possessions in the bin. They used obscene language, compared her body with nude pictures and one of them made suggestive remarks and brushed himself up against her. The

---

[36] European Commission Recommendation 92/131/EEC on the Protection of the Dignity of Women and Men at Work.
[37] See *Insitu Cleaning v. Heads* [1995] I.R.L.R. 4.
[38] Sex Discrimination Act s.1(1)(a).
[39] *Strathclyde R.C. v. Porcelli* [1986] I.R.L.R. 134.

employment tribunal held that if the two men had disliked a male colleague they would have treated him equally badly and dismissed her case. However, the Employment Appeal Tribunal and the Court of Session both found in Mrs Porcelli's favour. A man might have been treated badly, but the nature of the unpleasantness would have been different. The sexual element would not have been present. The Council who employed her was held liable because no action had been taken by management when she had complained.

Actual physical contact is not necessary to establish that there has been sexual harassment. Nor is it necessary to prove that there has been a prolonged series of acts of harassment. A single serious incident will be sufficient.[40] In *Wileman v. Minilec Engineering Ltd*,[41] Justice Popplewell stated at page 149 "'[s]exual harassment' is legal shorthand for activity which is easily recognisable as 'subjecting her to any other detriment'." Compensation for harassment relates to the degree of detriment and the courts have stated that evidence of the complainant's attitude to sexual matters is admissible in assessing injury to feelings. In *Wileman* a paltry sum of damages was awarded on the grounds that since the complainant had been scantily clad in posing for photographs, she had suffered little injury to her feelings.

It may be possible for a woman (or man) to claim a delictual remedy in the civil courts for sexual or racial harassment.[42] In such actions it would not be necessary for the pursuer to base their action on the inequality of treatment on the basis of gender, as would be required under the Sex Discrimination Act 1975. Harassment was recognised as a civil wrong in the case of *Khorasandjian v. Bush*.[43] 10.14

Unlawful discrimination may also occur where a woman is treated less favourably because she is pregnant. In the case of *Jennings v. Burton Group*[44] it was held that there had been unlawful discrimination by an employer against a pregnant employee. Mrs Jennings worked in store in Edinburgh and was dismissed when she was absent for five weeks because of a threatened miscarriage. She had less than two years' service and so could not (at that time) bring an unfair dismissal claim. The tribunal compared the treatment of the pregnant employee with the treatment which the employer

---

[40] *Bracebridge Engineering v. Darby* [1990] I.R.L.R. 3.

[41] *Wileman v. Minilec Engineering Ltd* [1988] I.R.L.R. 144.

[42] See, S. Middlemiss "Civil remedies for Victims of Sexual Harassment: Delictual Actions" Juridical Review 1997(4) 241.

[43] *Khorasandjian v. Bush* [1993] Q.B. 727. See also J. Dine and B. Watt "Sexual Harassment: Moving Away from Discrimination" (1995) M.L.R. 58(3) 362.

[44] *Jennings v. Burton Group* [1988] Edinburgh I.T.

would have afforded to a male employee who was sick and had to go into hospital.[45]

(2) Indirect Discrimination

10.15   Indirect discrimination occurs when a condition or requirement is applied equally to both sexes but the application has a disproportionate adverse impact on the members of one sex.[46] The Act provides that indirect discrimination arises:

(a) when a person applies a condition or requirement to another,

(b) but which is such that the proportion or persons from one sex who can comply with that condition or requirement is considerably smaller than the other sex,

(c) it cannot be shown that the condition or requirement is justified irrespective of the sex of the person to whom it is applied, and

(d) which is to that person's detriment because he/she cannot comply.

If, for example, an employer hiring labourers for a building site stated that applicants must be over six feet tall the condition would be applied to both sexes and so would not amount to direct discrimination. However, since the vast majority of women are less than six feet tall, it excludes a significantly larger proportion of women than men. It will therefore be classed as indirect discrimination and will be unlawful unless the employer can justify it. Indirect discrimination against a person on the ground of marital status is also covered.[47]

A woman must show that it was to her detriment that she could not comply with the requirement. The condition or requirement must amount to an absolute bar to employment or promotion, etc. There is no indirect discrimination if the employer has produced a list of characteristics he would prefer applicants to have. The case of *Price v. Civil Service Commission (No. 1)*[48] was a challenge to a requirement by the Civil Service that applicants for the job as executive officer had to be no older than 28 years. Mrs Price was 35 years old and was therefore barred from joining the Civil Service as an executive officer. The age requirement applied equally to men

---

[45] See also *Dekker v. Stichting Vormingscentrum voor Jonge Volwassen Plus* [1991] I.R.L.R. 27; *Webb v. EMO Air Cargo (U.K.) Ltd (No.2)* [1995] I.R.L.R. 645; *Gillespie v. Northern Health and Social Services Board* [1996] I.R.L.R. 214; *Ward v. Scotrail Railways Ltd*, 1999 S.C. 255.

[46] Sex Discrimination Act 1975, s.1(1)(b).

[47] *ibid.*, s.3(1)(b).

[48] *Price v. Civil Service Commission* [1977] I.R.L.R. 291.

and women, but Mrs Price argued that proportion of women who could comply with age requirement was considerably smaller than the proportion of men who could comply with it. Many women were out of the job market at that age because of childcare commitments. The employment tribunal dismissed her claim because they found that the numbers of men and women under 28 in the population were roughly the same. Therefore, the same proportion of women as men could comply with the age requirement. The employment appeal tribunal disagreed with this reasoning. The proper test was to look at proportions of men and women who could comply in practice with the requirement. Fewer women could comply than men and Mrs Price's claim was upheld.[49] In the case of *R v. Secretary of State for Employment, ex parte Equal Opportunities Commission*[50] the House of Lords held that statutory provisions requiring part-time workers to complete five years continuous service before they could claim unfair dismissal rights was unlawful on the grounds of indirect discrimination. The great majority of part-time workers were women while great majority of full-time workers were men. Service thresholds had a disproportionate adverse effect on women. This case led to the Employment Protection (Part-time Employees) Regulations 1995 which came into force on February 6, 1995 and removed all hours of work thresholds and granted part-time workers the same statutory employment protection rights as full-time workers.[51]

(3) Victimisation

It is important to provide protection from victimisation for individuals who bring complaints on grounds of discrimination. Victimisation occurs where a person is treated less favourably because: 10.16

(a) he or she brought proceedings under 1975 Act or Equal Pay Act 1970, or
(b) he or she gave evidence or information in connection with such proceedings, or
(c) he or she has done anything in relation to either Act to the discriminator or any other person, or
(d) he or she has alleged that a discriminator or other person has acted to contravene the 1975 Act or 1970 Act.[52]

---

[49] See also *Clarke & Powell v. Eley (IMI) Kynoch Ltd* [1982] I.R.L.R. 131; *The Home Office v. Holmes* [1984] I.R.L.R. 299; *Greater Glasgow Health Board v. Carey* [1987] I.R.L.R 484.

[50] *R v. Secretary of State for Employment, ex p. Equal Opportunities Commission* [1994] I.R.L.R. 176.

[51] These regulations were revoked and re-enacted in the Employment Rights Act 1996.

This protection only applies where the allegations of discrimination are made in good faith. An example of a successful claim on grounds of victimisation was *Chadwick v. Lancashire County Council*.[53] Ms Chadwick was a deputy headteacher who alleged that appointing committees in Lancashire discriminated against women candidates when appointing headteachers. After making these allegations she applied for two headteacher posts but despite having suitable qualifications and experience, she was not short-listed. She alleged she had been discriminated against by way of victimisation. The tribunal held that she had been excluded from the short-list because of her allegations and so she had been victimised under section 4.

DISCRIMINATION AGAINST MARRIED PERSONS

10.17 It is unlawful to discriminate against a person because he or she is married. Direct discrimination occurs where a married person is treated less favourably than an unmarried person of the same sex.[54] Indirect discrimination is also possible where a requirement or condition is such that a smaller proportion of married persons could comply compared with unmarried persons. In order to secure a remedy the married person must also show detriment. The discrimination may not be unlawful if it can be justified.

PROTECTION AGAINST SEX DISCRIMINATION IN RELATION TO EMPLOYMENT

10.18 In addition to the general protection against discrimination on grounds of sex, there are specific provisions which apply in relation to employment. It is unlawful for an employer to discriminate:

(1) in arrangements for seeking employees. This includes advertising, job descriptions, qualifications required and interviews;
(2) in terms of employment offered;
(3) by refusing or deliberately omitting to offer employment because of a person's sex or marital status;
(4) in respect of access to promotion, training, transfer or other benefits;
(5) by dismissing person because of their sex or marital status or subjecting them to detriment.[55]

---

[52] Sex Discrimination Act 1975, s.4(1).
[53] *Chadwick v. Lancashire C.C.* [1984] Liverpool I.T.
[54] Sex Discrimination Act 1975, s.3. See for example, *Hurley v. Mustoe* [1981] I.R.L.R. 208.

Originally the 1975 Act did not apply to provisions regarding death benefits or pensions. The Sex Discrimination Act 1986 was passed as a result of the milestone case of *Marshall v. South West Hampshire Area Health Authority.*[56] Ms Marshall had been forced to retire at the age of 62, although male colleagues could continue to work until they were 65 years old. Ms Marshall argued that her treatment was in breach of the Equal Treatment Directive.[57] The European Court of Justice held that different compulsory retiral ages for men and women were discriminatory. The Directive, having only vertical direct affect only applied to public sector employees. The government therefore passed the 1986 Act to extend the same provisions to private sector workers.

PERMISSIBLE DISCRIMINATION

Not all acts of discrimination are unlawful. Discrimination is 10.19 allowed in certain circumstances, for example, where it is necessary that a person of one sex undertake the duties of a job.

Genuine Occupational Qualification

When sex is a genuine occupational qualification, it is possible to 10.20 discriminate lawfully.[58] A genuine occupational qualification may exist where:

(a) A man or woman is required for reasons of physiology or authenticity. An example would be a requirement for a female model for advertisement.

(b) The job needs to be held by one sex for reasons of decency or privacy. Examples include lavatory attendants and changing-room attendants.

(c) Where the job is residential, there is only single sex sleeping and toilet accommodation and it would be unreasonable to expect the employer to provide additional facilities.

(d) The job is in a single-sex hospital, prison, or facility for persons requiring special care, attention and supervision, and it is reasonable for that job to be held by a person of that sex.

(e) The job involves provision of personal services for welfare

---

[55] Sex Discrimination Act 1975, s.6.
[56] *Marshall v. South West Hampshire Area Health Authority (No. 1)* [1986] I.R.L.R. 140.
[57] Equal Treatment Directive 76/207/EEC.
[58] Sex Discrimination Act 1975, s.7.

or education.

(f) The vacancy is for post overseas and the laws or customs of that country are such that the duties could not be performed by a person of a particular sex.

(g) The job is one of two to be held by a married couple.

An employer cannot plead that there is a genuine occupational qualification if he already has sufficient employees of that sex to perform the duties above.[59]

Positive Action

10.21 The Act does not permit positive or affirmative action in order to redress the effects of past discrimination. Positive action has been held to be contrary to the Equal Treatment Directive.[60] In *Kalanke v. Freie Hansestandt Bremen*, a man claimed that he had been discriminated against unlawfully when he was passed over for promotion. The job was given to a woman with the same qualifications as him.[61] This case was distinguished in *Marschall v. Land Nordheim-Westfalen*[62] where it was held that, for posts in the public service, where there are fewer women than men in a particular type of job, legislation may provide for preferential treatment for women. There must be a condition, however, that a woman is not to be given automatic priority if there is a factor in relation to an equally qualified male candidate which tips the balance in his favour. Therefore a rule will be within the scope of the directive provided that it does not guarantee absolute and unconditional priority to women.

Health Grounds

10.22 None of the provisions of the Act which deal with discrimination in employment shall make it unlawful for a person to treat a person of one sex differently where the different treatment is necessary in order to comply with a statutory provision concerning health and safety.[63] Therefore it is permissible to discriminate against women in order to protect them against specific health risks associated with pregnancy and childbirth. For example, airlines may prohibit pregnant cabin staff from working on flights. (It has recently been held, however, that their entitlement to additional payments for

---

[59] See *Wylie v. Dee & Co. (Menswear) Ltd* [1978] I.R.L.R. 103 and *Etam plc v. Rowan* [1989] I.R.L.R. 150.

[60] Equal Treatment Directive 76/207/EEC.

[61] *Kalanke v. Freie Hansestandt Bremen* [1995] I.R.L.R. 660.

[62] *Marschall v. Land Nordheim-Westfalen*, C-409/95 [1997] All E.R. (EC) 865, [1998] 1 C.M.L.R. 547, ECJ.

[63] Sex Discrimination Act 1975, s.51(1).

flying duties continues during the period of suspension from flying duties.)

Exceptions to the 1975 Act

The protection of the Sex Discrimination Act does not extend to 10.23 employment overseas.[64] Employment on ships registered in Great Britain is covered by the Act unless the work is done wholly outside Britain. Offshore oil and gas rigs in the United Kingdom sectors are within the scope of the Act. There are also exceptions in relation to certain types of employment including: police, prison officers, and ministers of religion.[65]

Remedies for sex discrimination

Actions under the Sex Discrimination Act are heard before an 10.24 industrial tribunal. There is no qualifying period or minimum number of hours. The claim must be made within three months of the prohibited act or omission unless the tribunal feels it is just and equitable to extend the limit.[66] If an applicant loses their case under United Kingdom law but then discovers that European Community law is wider, they can bring their claim in the tribunal relying on E.C. law. Such a claim must be brought within a reasonable time of the clarification.[67] The remedies which may be granted include: an order declaring rights of parties, compensation and a recommendation that remedial action is taken within a certain period.[68]

REGULATION OF SEX DISCRIMINATION

Certain discriminatory activities are rendered unlawful by the Act. 10.25 It is unlawful for a person who has authority over another to instruct that person to do an unlawful act.[69] It is also unlawful to induce another to do an unlawful act by offering a benefit or threatening a detriment or to aid a person to do an unlawful act.[70] Discriminatory advertisements are also unlawful.[71] The use of job descriptions which might be taken to indicate an intention to discriminate and the use of job descriptions with a sexual connotation contravenes the Act. The placing of a discriminatory

---

[64] *Haughton v. Olau Lines (UK) Ltd* [1986] 1 W.L.R. 504, [1986] 2 All E.R. 47.
[65] Sex Discrimination Act 1975, s.48. See *Kalanke v. Freie Hansestandt Bremen* [1995] I.R.L.R. 660.
[66] Sex Discrimination Act 1975, s.76.
[67] *Methilhill Bowling Club v. Hunter* [1995] I.R.L.R. 232.
[68] Sex Discrimination Act 1975, s.65.
[69] *ibid.*, s.39.
[70] *ibid.*, ss.40 and 42.
[71] *ibid.*, s.38.

advert does not, on its own, give rise to an individual right to a remedy.[72]

Equal Opportunities Commission

10.26 The Equal Opportunities Commission plays an important role in preventing discrimination as well as assisting persons who have suffered discriminatory treatment. The Equal Opportunities Commission may bring proceedings against the publisher of discriminatory advertisements within six months of publication. A non-discrimination notice may be issued. The Commission must inform the person of their intention, specifying the grounds, and give the alleged discriminator an opportunity to make oral or written representations. These must be taken into account. A register of non-discrimination notices is kept. Where discriminatory acts are repeated, an interdict may be sought from the sheriff court to restrain a person from repeating the unlawful act at any time within five years of a non-discrimination notice. The Commission provides advice and assistance to persons bringing complaints to tribunals. The Commission can assist a person in obtaining the necessary information. Questionnaires have been developed which can be sent to an alleged discriminator. The Commission may act as a mediator and may arrange and pay for legal representation. Its wider role includes the provision of assistance for research and other educational activities. It may carry out formal investigations at the request of the Secretary of State or on its own initiative. A person may be required to provide information or to attend a hearing. If a person refuses to comply with such request, the commission may apply to the sheriff court for an order requiring him to comply. It is a criminal offence to wilfully alter, suppress, conceal, or destroy a document or knowingly or recklessly to make a false statement.[73]

EQUAL PAY

Right to Equal Pay

10.27 The Equal Pay Act 1970 was passed to prevent discrimination between men and women as regards the terms and conditions in their employment. The Equal Pay Act 1970 did not come into effect until 1975, at the same time as the Sex Discrimination Act 1975. The delay in implementation provided a period of five years for employers to remove discrimination from their pay structures. A

---

[72] *Cardiff Women's Aid v. Hartup* [1994] I.R.L.R. 390.
[73] Sex Discrimination Act 1975, ss. 57–61.

claim for equal rights may fall under one or other of the two acts, but the claim will *not* fall under both.

The 1970 Act, as amended by Equal Pay (Amendment) Regulations 1983, seeks to ensure that terms in a woman's contract are no less favourable than the equivalent terms of a man's contract. Where a beneficial term is found in a man's contract and is not found in a woman's contract, it is treated as being included in the woman's contract, *e.g.* a man may be able to get an interest-free loan to buy a travel season ticket whereas there is no such term in the woman's contract.

Influence of European Law

The European Court has been very active in this area of employment law. The 1970 Act was amended by the Equal Pay (Amendment) Regulations 1983 to take account of Article 119 of the E.C. Treaty (now Article 141 E.C.) and the Equal Pay Directive.[74] Article 141 requires member states to ensure the application of the principle that men and women should receive equal pay for equal work. "Pay" in this context means ordinary, basic or minimum wage or salary and any other consideration whether in cash or kind which the worker receives directly or indirectly in respect of his employment. Article 119 is directly applicable in member states and its provisions are enforceable in domestic courts against employers, *i.e.* it has direct effect.[75] The case of *McCarthys Ltd v. Smith* illustrates how the principle of direct effect has extended the scope of the United Kingdom law. Ms Smith was being paid less as a manager than the man who had held the post prior to her appointment. [76] The Court of Appeal said that the 1970 Act allowed comparisons of contractual terms to be made only with men who were working at the same time as her. The European Court of Justice held that the comparisons under Article 119 were not restricted to comparisons with those working at the same time as her. The female applicant was entitled to compare herself with her male predecessor. In the case of *Garland v. British Rail Engineering,* the European Court of Justice held that benefits, such as the provision of concessionary travel for the dependants of retired rail employees, would fall within the definition of "pay" for the purposes of Article 119.[77] Similarly, the case of *Barber v. Guardian Royal Exchange* hinged upon the issue of whether benefits could be regarded as "pay" for the purposes of Article 119 and the Equal Pay Directive. In this case the benefits concerned were

10.28

---

[74] Equal Pay Directive 75/117/EEC.
[75] *Defrenne v. Sabena (No.2)* [1976] E.C.R. 445.
[76] *McCarthys Ltd v. Smith* [1980] 2 C.M.L.R. 205.
[77] *Garland v. British Rail Engineering* [1982] 2 E.C.R. 359.

connected with redundancy. The European Court of Justice decided that redundancy payments came within these provisions. The Court then went on to decide whether Article 119 was infringed if a man and woman of the same age were made compulsorily redundant but the woman then received an immediate private pension while the man's pension rights were deferred for another 10 years. In addition it appeared that the total value of the benefits received by the woman was greater than that received by the man. The Court decided that payments made by an employer in connection with redundancy must not discriminate on grounds of sex.[78]

The Equal Pay Directive[79] declared that the principle of equal pay for men and women outlined in Article 119 was to be taken as including the right to equal pay for work of equal value. This means that a woman who is doing a different job from a man may seek equal pay if her work is of equal value to his. The *Barber* case declared that pensions paid out under a contracted-out occupational pension scheme fell within the terms of Article 141. Such schemes must not be discriminatory. The Court declared in the *Ten Oever* case[80] that *Barber* was not retrospective and there could be enforcement of equalisation of pension benefits only in respect of service from May 17, 1990, the date of the *Barber* judgment. In the *Ten Oever* case a widower's claim for a pension on his wife's pension rights failed because his wife died before the *Barber* decision. In 1994, the European Court of Justice issued decisions on a number of cases concerned with pension rights. Part-time workers should have access to occupational pension schemes under Article 141. They can also make a retrospective claim back to 1976. This is particularly important where the pension scheme is non-contributory. If the scheme is voluntary the claimants have to finance their own backdated contributions.[81]

Following these decisions, the United Kingdom Government introduced the Occupational Pension Schemes (Equal Access to Membership) Amendment Regulations 1995,[82] which came into force on May 31, 1995. These Regulations outlaw both direct and indirect discrimination in relation to pension schemes. The Pensions Act 1995[83] implies into occupational pension schemes an equality clause in relation to pensions. The Act provides that, where a woman is employed in like work, work rated as equivalent or work

---

[78] *Barber v. Guardian Royal Exchange Group* [1990] I.R.L.R. 240.
[79] Equal Pay Directive 75/117/EEC.
[80] *Ten Oever* [1993] I.R.L.R. 601.
[81] *Vroege v. NCIV, Institut voor Volkhuisvesting BV* [1994] I.R.L.R. 651. *Fisscher v. Voorhuis Hengelo BV* [1994] I.R.L.R. 662.
[82] Occupational Pension Schemes (Equal Access to Membership) Amendment Regulations 1995 (S.I. 1995 No.1215).
[83] Pensions Act 1995, s.62.

of equal value, any terms which are less favourable than that of a man are to be treated as modified so that they are no less favourable. The *Barber* case did not apply to state pensions but the Pensions Act 1995 sets a common state pension age of 65 to be phased in between 2010 and 2020.

Provisions of the Equal Pay Act 1970 as Amended by Equal Pay (Amendment) Regulations 1983

An equality clause is implied into every contract of employment. 10.29
The effect of this is that, if a woman enjoys less favourable terms than a man does, her contract will be modified to equalise the terms. Similarly, if a beneficial term in a woman's contract is missing from a man's contract, it is deemed to be included in his contract.

Before these take effect the woman must show that one of the following three conditions is fulfilled:

(1) she is engaged in like work to that done by the man; or
(2) she is doing work rated as equivalent to that done by the man; or
(3) her work is of equal value to that done by the man.

Claims are brought to an employment tribunal at any time whilst in the relevant employment or within six months after leaving. The tribunal may declare the rights of the parties and award arrears of pay for up to two years. The woman must compare herself with a man who works for the same employer or an associated employer. The comparator must be a person of the opposite sex employed in the same employment as the applicant. In the case of *Leverton v. Clwyd County Council*, a nursery nurse claimed equal pay on the ground that her work was of equal value to that of a male comparator. She chose as comparators several male employees who worked in clerical posts at various locations. Ms Leverton and her comparators were under the same collective agreement. The men paid on a higher scale. Ms Leverton worked fewer hours and had longer holidays. The Council argued that the different workplaces did not share common terms and conditions. The House of Lords said that the fact there was a common collective agreement was sufficient to meet the test of being in the same employment. However, Ms Leverton's claim failed because there were genuine material factors which justified the difference in pay.[84]

In the case of *British Coal Corporation v. Smith*, 1,286 female canteen workers and cleaners employed by British Coal claimed that their work was of equal value to that done by 150 male clerical workers and surface mineworkers. The women were employed in 47

[84] *Leverton v. Clywd C.C.* [1989] I.R.L.R. 28.

establishments, and the men in 17. The issue in question was whether the women and their comparator were employed in different establishments and whether "common terms and conditions of employment" were observed at each. It was argued that the male surface mineworkers did not share common terms and conditions because of different local agreements on concessionary coal and incentive bonuses. The House of Lords held that there were common terms and conditions at the different establishments. Comparators did not need to share identical terms and conditions, provided that they were "sufficiently similar for a fair comparison to be made".[85]

In the case of *South Ayrshire Council v. Morton*[86] the Council appealed to the Employment Appeal Tribunal against a decision allowing Morton to use a teacher under the control of a different education authority as a comparator in her equal pay claim. Morton was a primary teacher claiming equal pay with secondary teachers. It was submitted that the comparator was not valid for the purposes of the Equal Pay Act 1970, section 1(6)(c) as the employers were not associated, and that as South Ayrshire Council had no control over the terms and conditions of the chosen comparator, he was not a relevant comparator. It was held, dismissing the appeal, that the tribunal's decision had been correct as there was, in Scotland, an education service giving rise to a sufficient connection in a loose and non-technical sense between the two teachers to justify use as a comparator.[87]

Like Work

10.30 The term "like work" means work which is the same or broadly similar to work done by the comparator. Any differences should not be of practical importance. In the case of *Capper Pass Ltd v. Lawton*, a female cook in the director's dining room sought equal pay with two male assistant chefs in the main canteen. She prepared up to 20 lunches per day whereas the men prepared around 350 over six sittings. Lawton was held to be doing like work to the men. Her work was broadly similar, similar skills were employed and, although they prepared more meals, she prepared more complex menus.[88] It has been held that a woman is not engaged on like work if the male comparator has more responsibility. In a case where a man and woman were employed as production schedulers, the woman dealt with less valuable items than the man. A mistake on

---

[85] *British Coal Corporation v. Smith* [1996] I.R.L.R. 399.
[86] *South Ayrshire Council v. Morton* [2001] I.R.L.R. 28.
[87] See also *Lawrence v. Regent Office Care Ltd* [2000] I.R.L.R. 608.
[88] *Capper Pass Ltd v. Lawton* [1976] I.R.L.R. 366.

her part would therefore have less serious consequences than a mistake by the man. His higher pay was justifiable.[89]

Where the contract of a man states that he may be required to perform additional duties this will not prevent a claim for like work if the man never has to perform those duties. Therefore, in a case where female assistants in a betting shop were paid 62 pence per hour and their male counterparts received £1.06 per hour because the men were contractually required to deal with violent or difficult customers it was held that the male and female employees were still engaged in like work. The men had never been called on to do deal with difficult customers and were not qualified to do so.[90] In the case of *Dugdale v. Kraft Foods*, it was held that differences in time at which work was done did not justify difference in basic rates of pay. Where workers work unsocial hours, the shifts should have a premium rate rather than a difference in basic rate of pay.[91]

Work Rated as Equivalent

Work may be rated as equivalent where a proper job evaluation 10.31 study has compared the work done by the claimant to that of a member of the opposite sex. The jobs are broken down into component parts and given a mark. Marks are awarded for qualifications and the amount of supervision required. Added together these give the work a total rating. The applicant has to establish that the rate for her job is the same as that of the comparator. The evaluation study must not be discriminatory.

Work of Equal Value

The right to equal pay on the ground that the work is of equal value 10.32 to that done by a member of the opposite sex was recognised by the 1983 Equal Pay Regulations. The work must be of equal value to that of members of the opposite sex in terms of effort, skill, decision making and other demands. However, the comparator may be in an entirely different job. The employment tribunal may determine the question of equal value immediately or appoint an independent expert to assess the value of the jobs. Both the employer and applicant may comment on any report and produce their own expert evidence. If the tribunal then decides that the jobs are of equal value, the employer has an opportunity to say that there is a genuine material factor which justifies the difference in pay.

In the early days of equal pay protection there was a concern that employers would avoid giving women equal pay by employing a token man on the same rate of pay as the women but in the case of

[89] *Eaton v. Nuttall* [1977] I.R.L.R. 71.
[90] *Shields v. E Coomes (Holdings) Ltd* [1978] I.R.L.R. 263.
[91] *Dugdale v. Kraft Foods* [1977] 1 W.L.R. 1288.

Pickstone v. Freemans plc, this tactic was discounted. In that case
five female packers in a warehouse claimed that their work was of
equal value to that of a male checker who was paid £4.22 per week
more than the women. There was a male packer who was paid at
the same rate as women. It was held that this did not prevent
women bringing a claim.[92]

In the milestone case of *Hayward v. Cammell Laird Shipbuilders
Ltd*, a canteen cook brought an equal pay claim on ground that her
work was of equal value to comparators who included a painter,
joiner and insulation engineer. The House of Lords held that an
applicant whose work is found to be of equal value to that of her
comparators is entitled to have each distinct contractual term in its
own right. Ms Hayward was entitled therefore to an increase in her
basic pay and overtime rates. Her comparators would then be
entitled to bring a claim to have their contractual terms regarding
holiday and sick pay improved to match those of Ms Hayward.[93]

Defences to an Equal Pay Claim

10.33 A claim for equal pay will not succeed if the employer can show
that there is a genuine material factor which justifies any difference
in contractual terms. In an early equal pay case where a female clerk
was engaged in like work but was paid less than a male clerk, the
employer argued that difference in pay was because the male clerk
had refused to do a job for less than when he was hired. It was held
that this was not a defence genuine material difference. In order to
justify a difference in pay there should be a personal difference such
as a difference in qualifications or experience.[94] However in 1987
the House of Lords held that genuine material factors may go
beyond the personal equation where the difference in pay can be
shown to be necessary to achieve a legitimate economic objective or
for sound administrative reasons. A health board had employed
outside contractors to fit artificial limbs. It was decided to set up a
prosthetic service within the National Health Service. There was no
established pay scale for prosthetists and so it was decided to pay
them the same as medical physics technicians. In order to encourage
qualified workers from the private sector, prosthetists transferring
would have the pay scale from their private sector employment
matched and maintained. The offer of transfer was made to 20
private sector workers who were all men. Rainey was a newly
qualified prosthetist who had not worked in the private sector and
so she was paid on the scale for medical physics technicians. She
sought equality of pay with her male colleagues but the need to

[92] *Pickstone v. Freemans plc* [1988] I.R.L.R. 357.
[93] *Hayward v. Cammell Laird Shipbuilders Ltd* [1988] 2 All E.R. 257.
[94] *Clay Cross (Quarry Services) Ltd v. Fletcher* [1979] 1 All E.R. 474.

establish the new service was held to be a valid objective justifying the difference in pay. Rainey did not succeed.[95]

In the case of *Ratcliffe v. North Yorkshire County Council*, the House of Lords looked again at what is necessary to constitute a genuine material factor where the defence is based on market forces. The work of three dinner ladies had been rated as equivalent to male road sweepers and refuse collectors. Their wages were cut when council set up a direct service organisation to compete with private firms bidding for school dinner contracts. The direct service organisation made the women redundant and re-employed them on lower wages. They brought a claim for equal pay. The House of Lords decided that this was female-dominated workforce which was paid less simply because it was female-dominated. Although the need to reduce the pay of the women so as to compete in the open market was a material factor, the factor was due to the difference of sex and so it amounted to a breach of the Act to reduce the pay of the women.[96]

Any differences in pay which are justified by a genuine material factor should be removed once the material factor has changed. In the case of *Beneveniste v. University of Southampton*, a female maths lecturer had been appointed at a salary lower than persons of her age and qualifications might expect. She was paid less than four male colleagues already in the post because the university was subject to severe financial restrictions at the time of her appointment. A year after her appointment, the financial situation improved but her pay did not. It was held that the fact that there was once a material difference did not justify a difference in pay forever.[97]

DISCRIMINATION ON GROUNDS OF RACE, COLOUR OR ETHNIC ORIGINS

The Race Relations Act 1976 provides that it is unlawful to discriminate on grounds of race in employment, training, education, union membership, provision of goods and services and in disposal and management of housing and other premises. This Act is modelled closely on the Sex Discrimination Act 1975 and the concepts of direct and indirect discrimination, victimisation and genuine occupational qualifications are all included in the 1976 Act. There are, however, some important differences. The Act applies to private clubs with more than 25 members and applies to segregation and transferred discrimination. These provisions have no counterparts under the Sex Discrimination Act. The influence of the E.U. is

10.34

---

[95] *Rainey v. Greater Glasgow Health Board Eastern District* [1987] I.R.L.R. 26.
[96] *Ratcliffe v. North Yorkshire C.C.* [1995] I.R.L.R. 439.
[97] *Beneveniste v. University of Southampton* [1989] I.R.L.R. 122.

less important. The Act outlaws discrimination on the ground of colour, race, nationality or ethnic or national origins.[98] None of these are defined.

Direct Discrimination

10.35   Direct discrimination occurs where persons are given less favourable treatment, or equal but segregated treatment, such as the provision of separate washing facilities. It will not amount to unlawful discrimination by an employer if workers segregate themselves and segregation is their choice, and has not been forced on them by their employer. An example of direct racial discrimination is the case of *King v. The Great Britain-China Centre*.[99] Ms King applied for job as deputy director at the china centre but she was not interviewed. She had been born in China but brought up in the United Kingdom. She spoke Chinese and had spent three months travelling in China in the year prior to her application. There was no satisfactory explanation as to why she did not receive an interview, but evidence was shown which proved that no ethnic Chinese were interviewed although five had applied, Ms King's qualifications met the job requirements, and the centre had never employed an ethnic Chinese person. It was held there was direct discrimination.[1]

Indirect Discrimination

10.36   Indirect discrimination on grounds of race, nationality or ethnic origin has four aspects:

> (1) There is a condition or requirement which is applied to all;
> (2) The condition or requirement has a disproportionate effect on a racial group;
> (3) The condition or requirement is not justifiable irrespective of race;
> (4) A member of the adversely affected racial group is unable to comply with the condition or requirement and this is to his detriment.

An example is the case of *J.H. Walker Ltd v. Hussain*.[2] Asian employees were disciplined for taking a day off work to mark the Muslim festival at the end of Ramadan. Muslim employees had previously been allowed to take time off for this festival but the

---

[98]   Race Relations act 1976, s.3(1).
[99]   *King v. The Great Britain-China Centre* [1991] I.R.L.R. 513.
[1]   See also *Wilson v. TB Steelworks*, IDS Brief 150; *Showboat Entertainment Centre Ltd v. Owens* [1984] I.R.L.R. 7; *Burton v. De Vere Hotels* [1996] I.R.L.R. 596.
[2]   *J.H. Walker Ltd v. Hussain* [1996] I.R.L.R. 11.

employers had introduced rule a that no employees could have time off during the firm's busiest time, which fell around this festival. The employees asked the employers to reconsider but they refused even although the employees agreed to make up the lost working time. A large number of Asian workers took time off and all were issued with final written warnings. The court held that there was no direct discrimination against the workers as Muslims because Muslims do not constitute a racial group, but there was indirect discrimination against the Asian workers since they had suffered a detriment.

If the employer can prove justification then there will be no discrimination. Therefore in the case of *Panesar v. Nestle Co Ltd*,[3] where a claim of indirect discrimination was brought against a rule prohibiting long hair, it was held that the rule was not unlawful because it was a condition justifiable in the interests of hygiene and safety. It had been argued that the rule against long hair indirectly discriminated against Sikhs in that a smaller proportion of Sikhs could comply with it compared to members of other racial groups.

Victimisation

It is unlawful to treat a person less favourably because he has: 10.37

(1) brought proceedings under the Act;
(2) given evidence or information connected with proceedings brought by another person;
(3) done anything under the Act in relation to the discriminator; or
(4) made allegations that a person has committed an unlawful act of racial discrimination.[4]

There is no need to prove that the victimisation is motivated by malice. This is shown in the case of *Chief Constable of West Yorkshire v. Khan*. Khan, a sergeant in the West Yorkshire Police force, had made a complaint of racial discrimination to an employment tribunal in relation to procedures for promotion to inspector. He then applied for an inspector's position in Norfolk. The Chief Constable declined to provide the reference, on the ground that to do so could prejudice his case in the pending employment tribunal hearing. Khan then amended his application to include a complaint of victimisation. The employment tribunal dismissed Khan's direct discrimination claim, but the victimisation complaint succeeded. On appeal, it was held the purpose of the victimisation provisions in the 1976 Act, was to safeguard those

---

[3] *Panesar v. Nestle Co Ltd* [1980] I.R.L.R. 64.
[4] Race Relations Act 1976, s.2.

who had brought proceedings alleging racial discrimination under section 2(1) from being victimised for having done the protected act. The "but for" test from the comparable provisions of the Sex Discrimination Act 1975 was equally applicable to the 1976 Act. If it had not been for the proceedings brought under the 1976 Act a reference would have been provided. Khan therefore had been victimised.[5]

It has now been held by the House of Lords, in the case of *Nagarajan v. London Regional Transport,* that it may not be necessary to prove that the action which lead to the claim of victimisation was motivated by an intention to discriminate. Nagarajan, of Indian origin, applied for a position as a travel information assistant with LRT, a position he had previously occupied for four months, during which time he had pursued various complaints of racial discrimination. Nagarajan was not appointed to the post and alleged that LRT treated him less favourably than the other applicants and they were therefore guilty of victimisation. The Court of Appeal dismissed Nagarajan's claim and he appealed. It was held by a majority, that it was sufficient to establish that employer had acted on a subconscious intention to treat an interviewee less favourably on the grounds of his race. Discrimination on the grounds of race was a form of direct discrimination and did not require a conscious motivation on behalf of the perpetrator. If an applicant received less favourable treatment than others in his position did, the tribunal had to examine the reasons why. Considerations of the mental state of the employer were crucial to the determination of those reasons. The tribunal was obliged to make certain deductions and inferences to establish the motivation behind any alleged discrimination because direct evidence was likely to be lacking, The motivation did not have to be conscious or possess any malice, as long as it represented a significant factor in the employer's decision.[6]

Racial Grounds

10.38 The Act defines racial grounds as: colour, race, nationality, ethnic or national origins.[7] National origin includes race and citizenship. Uncertainty has arisen from time to time with regard to the distinction between an ethnic group, who are protected from discrimination and a religious group who are afforded no

---

[5] *Chief Constable of West Yorkshire v. Khan* [2000] I.C.R. 1169; [2000] I.R.L.R. 324; (2000) 150 N.L.J. 308.

[6] *Nagarajan v. London Regional Transport* [2000] 1 A.C. 501; [1999] 3 W.L.R. 425; [1999] 4 All E.R. 65; [1999] I.C.R. 877; [1999] I.R.L.R. 572; (1999) 96(31) L.S.G. 36; (1999) 149 N.L.J. 1109(1999) 143 S.J.L.B. 21.

[7] Race Relations Act 1976, s.3.

protection under United Kingdom law. The case of *Mandla v. Dowell Lee*[8] hinged upon whether Sikhs were an ethnic or a religious group. It was held that an ethnic can be wider than a single race. Sikhs did constitute an ethnic group and were therefore a racial group for the purposes of 1976 Act. This means that some, but not all religious groups will come within the protection of the Act. For a group to be protected it should have shared characteristics such as:

(a) common geographical origin,
(b) descent from common ancestors,
(c) common culture and social customs,
(d) long shared history distinguishable from other groups,
(e) common language, literature and religion,
(f) be a minority group within larger community.

A common religion on its own is not enough to qualify as an ethnic group, the other factors must be present. So Sikhs and Jews may be protected, but Catholics and Muslims probably are not.

Although protection against discrimination on religious grounds is not yet provided for in domestic law the Scottish courts will now have to consider discrimination on religious grounds where the matter under consideration is one of other substantive rights under the European Convention on Human Rights. In *Hoffmann v. Austria*, the European Court of Human Rights held that a difference in treatment on grounds of religion was a breach of Article 14. The applicant was the mother of children who had been born when she was a practising catholic and was married to another catholic. When the marriage broke down she left her husband, taking the children and became a Jehovah's Witness. Custody of the children was granted to her husband as it was considered in their best interests not to be brought up as Jehovah's Witnesses. The Court found by a narrow majority that her rights under Article 14 had been infringed.[9] The minority of the judges found that she had not been discriminated against on grounds of religion but that the courts had attached significance to the effects of her beliefs on the welfare of her children. This would not have amounted to a contravention of Article 14. Even under the law of the European Convention there is a fine line between unlawful discrimination and lawful differential treatment which is justified in the circumstances.

In the case of *BBC Scotland v. Souster*, the Inner House considered whether discrimination against an English person in Scotland contravened the Act. Between 1995 and 1997, the BBC

---

[8] *Mandla v. Dowell Lee* [1983] I.R.L.R. 209.
[9] *Hoffmann v. Austria* (1993) 17 E.H.R.R. 293.

employed an English journalist, Souster to present "Rugby Special". Souster's employment took the form of successive contracts, but was not renewed in 1997. The BBC employed a Scottish woman to take his place and Souster complained of racial discrimination, maintaining that the major factor in his contract not being renewed was his "national origins". The BBC argued that "English" and "Scottish" were not distinct racial groups for the purpose of the Act. The BBC also argued that the phrase "national origins" meant no more than the nationality acquired by Souster upon his birth. It was held that Souster could claim racial discrimination on the grounds that he was English under the phrase "national origins", it being much more than "nationality" in the legal sense. There could be racial discrimination within Great Britain on the basis of a person being of Scottish or English national origin. Souster could not bring his claim on the basis of his ethnic origins as neither the English nor the Scottish are an ethnic group in the terms of the Act.[10]

Racial Discrimination in Employment

10.39   The Race Relations Act makes it unlawful to discriminate against a person before he is in employment as regards matters such as the arrangements for interview.[11] It is also unlawful to offer less favourable terms to a person on the grounds of his race. A person must not be refused employment because of his race. Once a person is in employment discrimination on racial grounds is unlawful as regards opportunities for promotion, training and transfer. It is unlawful to dismiss someone on the grounds of his race or subject him to detriment. An employer may insist on employing a person of a particular race where there is a genuine occupational qualification such as authenticity in an ethnic restaurant or where the holder of the job provides personal services to promote welfare of persons of the same racial group, such as a community relations officer.[12] The remedies are similar to those for sex discrimination.

Race Relations (Amendment) Act 2000

10.40   The Act fulfils the recommendation of the Stephen Lawrence inquiry report that the "full force" of race relations legislation should apply to the police. From now on members of the public will be able to take cases to court when they consider they have been racially discriminated against by the police.

In addition, the Act lays a duty on public bodies to work for

---

[10]   *BBC Scotland v. Souster* [2001] I.R.L.R. 150. See also *Northern Joint Police Board v. Power* [1997] I.R.L.R. 610.

[11]   Race Relations Act 1976, s.4.

[12]   Race Relations Act 1976, s.5.

racial equality in their employment practices and the services they provide. The Commission for Racial Equality will have the power to enforce this duty if public bodies do not fulfil this responsibility. The Race Relations (Amendment) Act 2000 strengthens and extends the scope of the 1976 Race Relations Act; it does not replace it. The new Act strengthens the 1976 Act in two major ways:

(1) it extends protection against racial discrimination by public authorities
(2) it places a new, enforceable positive duty on public authorities.

The Act also introduces other important changes:

(1) it makes Chief Officers of Police liable for acts of discrimination by officers under their direction or control
(2) it allows complaints of racial discrimination in certain immigration decisions to be heard as part of "one-stop" immigration appeals
(3) it prohibits discrimination by ministers or government departments in recommending or approving public appointments, and in the terms and conditions, or termination, of such appointments, or in conferring honours, including peerages; the Act will apply to any new arrangements for appointing members of the House of Lords
(4) it allows complaints of racial discrimination in education to be brought directly before county or sheriff courts without, as now, having to be referred first to the Secretary of State for Education
(5) it limits the circumstances in "safeguarding national security" can be used to justify discrimination.

The Commission for Racial Equality

The Commission for Racial Equality was established by the Race Relations Act 1976. It replaced the Race Relations Board, which was a statutory body which had no powers to investigate allegations of discrimination on racial grounds. The Commission for Racial Equality can assist claimants in the preparation of cases. It also has the power to initiate investigations, provided that it has a reasonable suspicion that acts of discrimination have taken place.[13] There must be a strong reason to suspect that discrimination is occurring.[14] The Home Secretary may direct the Commission to

10.41

---

[13] *R v. Commission for Racial Equality, ex p. Hillingdon Council* [1982] A.C. 779.
[14] *Commission for Racial Equality v. Prestige Group plc* [1984] 1 W.L.R. 335.

carry out an investigation. If the Commission finds that discrimination has occurred, it has powers to issue a non-discrimination notice. For a period of five years from the issue of such a notice the Commission may seek an interdict to prevent any recurrence of discrimination.

10.42 Disabled persons have not been protected against discrimination until relatively recently. The Disability Discrimination Act 1995 aims to end discrimination against disabled persons in employment, provision of goods, facilities and services, and in the disposal of premises. The Act requires schools, colleges and universities to provide information for disabled people. The Act also allows the Government to set minimum standards so that disabled people can use public transport more easily. The Act also allows individuals with a disability to seek unlimited compensation if they can establish unjustified discrimination on the part of the employer. The provisions relating to employment do not apply to employers with less than 20 employees.

Disability is defined as a physical or mental impairment which has substantial and long-term adverse effect on a person's ability to carry out normal day-to-day activities.[15] Physical impairment includes sensory impairment and severe disfigurement. Mental impairment is defined as mental illness which is "clinically well recognised". This includes mental disorders such as schizophrenia and manic depression. Protection against discrimination is not extended to people with anti-social disorders. Therefore it is not unlawful to discriminate against psychopaths, paedophiles and those addicted to tobacco, alcohol or drugs. Discrimination against a person whose disfigurement is self-inflicted by tattoos or body piercing is also not unlawful.

In order to qualify as a disability in terms of the Act an impairment must have long-term effects. It must be of a type which will last for 12 months or more. Persons with terminal illnesses who are expected to die within 12 months are, however, protected from discrimination. Conditions which recur, such as epilepsy or are progressive, such as cancer or multiple sclerosis are covered. The impairment must affect a person's normal daily activities. These include the ability to lift, mobility, manual dexterity, continence, speech, hearing, eyesight, memory or ability to concentrate, learn or understand. In the case of *Ashton v. Chief Constable of West Mercia* it was held that gender identity dysphoria did not constitute a

[15] Disability Discrimination Act 1995, s.1.

disability for the purposes of the Act. Ashton who had been born a male, had started gender reassignment. She had subsequently been moved to another department and had then been dismissed from her employment as a probationary police officer for poor work performance. It was held that, although Ashton's poor work performance was linked to the side effects of the medical treatment involved in gender reassignment, her condition did not fall within the definition of "disability" for the purpose of the Disability Discrimination Act 1995, section 1.[16]

It is unlawful to discriminate against a disabled person in relation to recruitment, training, terms and conditions of employment or promotion.[17] The Act does not apply to person working overseas, or to police, armed forces prison officers, fire-fighters. Employers are under a duty to take reasonable steps to make adjustments to any arrangements or physical features of premises which place disabled person at a substantial disadvantage. For instance, an employer could install ramps for wheelchairs, and obtain special equipment or allow the work to be carried out on the ground floor. The Act only requires that reasonable steps be taken. This means that the courts will take account of the cost involved, the financial resources of the employer and the amount of disruption in making the adjustment. The duty on employers is not a general one. It will apply only in individual cases when a person is affected by the lack of facilities. There is no express prohibition on indirect discrimination. The government argued that this was unnecessary because the terms of the prohibition on direct discrimination are so wide. Victimisation of a person who has made a complaint is unlawful. The remedies are similar to those available in cases of discrimination on grounds of race or sex. The tribunal can order a declaration of the parties' rights, compensation and a recommendation that the employer takes action. 10.43

Discrimination will occur if the person is treated less favourably than non-disabled persons are and such treatment is unjustified. So direct discrimination can be lawful if the employer can justify it. The Act is concerned with the consequences of the discriminatory acts rather than the motivation behind them. Discrimination can arise even where the discriminator has no knowledge of the actual disability suffered by the claimant. In the case of *Hammersmith and Fulham LBC v. Farnsworth*, Farnsworth had been offered a job by the council after an interview. The Council's occupational health physician discovered that Farnsworth had a history of mental illness and voiced concerns that a recurrence would affect her work attendance. The job offer was withdrawn on the grounds that

---

[16] *Ashton v. Chief Constable of West Mercia* [2001] I.C.R. 67.
[17] Disability Discrimination Act 1995, s.4.

satisfactory medical clearance had not been obtained and Farnsworth complained that she had been discriminated against under
the Disability Discrimination Act 1995, section 5. The employment
tribunal found that Farnsworth had been discriminated against
because of her disability. On appeal, the council argued that it had
no actual knowledge of the disability. It was held that knowledge
on the part of the council was not relevant for the purposes of
assessing whether there was, as a fact, discrimination under section
5(1)(a).[18]

Anyone who provides goods, facilities or services to members of
the public, whether paid for or free, must provide the same standard
of service to everyone. This could range from buying bread in a
supermarket, using the facilities in a launderette, or borrowing a
book from a public library. Private clubs are not included. It will
amount to unlawful discrimination to refuse to serve someone
because he or she is disabled, or because of a reason relating to his
or her disability. It is also unlawful to offer a disabled person a
service which is not as good as the service being offered to other
people or to provide a service to a disabled person on terms which
are different from the terms given to other people. It is also
discriminatory to run a service, or provide goods or facilities, in a
way which makes it impossible or unreasonably difficult for a
disabled person to use the service or goods. It is not against the law,
however, if the way the service is run is fundamental to the business.
For example, dim lighting could be considered essential to a
nightclub even though it causes difficulties for someone with poor
eyesight. People must provide equipment or other helpful items
which make it easier for disabled people to use their service, if it is
reasonable to do so. People must remove physical obstructions (for
example, widening entrance doors) or provide other ways of letting
disabled people use their services, if it is reasonable to do so. For
example, if a library's reference section is on the first floor and there
is no lift, library staff could offer to bring the reference books to the
disabled person. Service providers may not charge a disabled
person more to meet the cost of making it easier for them to use
their service. If the health and safety of the disabled person or other
people would be in danger, it would not be against the law to refuse
to provide the service to a disabled person or to provide it on
different terms. Other exceptions would arise if the customer was
not capable of understanding the terms of a contract or if providing
the service or the same standard of service would deny other
customers.

10.44   It is against the law for anyone who sells or lets land or property
(and their agents) to unreasonably discriminate against disabled

---

[18]   *Hammersmith and Fulham LBC v. Farnsworth* [2000] I.R.L.R. 691.

people. For example, a landlord could not charge a disabled person a higher rent than he would charge anyone else. A landlord who rents six or fewer rooms in his own home would not be affected. People selling or renting property do not have to make adjustments to make it accessible. If a disabled person feels they have been wrongly excluded from the provision of goods or services, or the selling or letting of land or property, they can go to court to seek damages for any financial loss they have suffered and for injury to their feelings.

The Government can set minimum standards for new public transport vehicles (taxis, buses, coaches, trains and trams) so that disabled people, including people who use a wheelchair, can use them. For example, disabled people who use wheelchairs will eventually be able to hire taxis in the street or at a taxi rank like everyone else. The Act ensures recognition of the needs of disabled people wishing to study and the provision of better information for parents, pupils and students. Schools must explain their arrangements for the admission of disabled pupils, how they will help these pupils gain access and what they will do to ensure they are treated fairly. Further and higher education institutions funded by the Further and Higher Education Funding Councils must publish disability statements containing information about facilities for disabled people. Local Education Authorities must provide information on their further education facilities for disabled people.

Discrimination will occur if the person is treated less favourably than a non-disabled person is and such treatment is unjustified. Consequently direct discrimination can be lawful if the person who acted in a discriminatory way can justify it. One example of this arose in the case of *Rose v. Bouchet*.[19] This case was an appeal against a sheriff court decision that there had been no unlawful discrimination. Rose contended that Bouchet had discriminated against him by refusing to let premises to him. Bouchet claimed that the refusal to let the premises was because the access was unsafe for a blind person. It was held that, although Bouchet had, *prima facie,* acted unlawfully by treating Rose less favourably on account of his disability, his treatment of Rose was justified if, in Bouchet's opinion, such treatment was necessary to avoid endangering Rose's safety. Evidence of the facts which gave rise to such an opinion could be considered in order to establish whether the belief that discriminatory treatment was justified was reasonable. This case is interesting because it does not set an objective standard for justifiable discrimination. Instead it establishes that discrimination will not be unlawful if the person who is discriminating believes, on reasonable grounds, that the discrimination is justified.

[19] *Rose v. Bouchet,* 1999 G.W.D. 20-958.

Discrimination on Grounds of Birth

10.45 A difference in treatment in relation to a Convention right may be a violation of Article 14 if a person is treated differently by reason of their birth. This usually means that discrimination against illegitimate children as opposed to those born to married parents will be seen by the Court as an infringement of Article 14. In *Marckx v. Belgium*, the Court observed that

> "at the time when the Convention was drafted, (1950), it was regarded as permissible and normal in many European Countries to draw a distinction between the illegitimate and the legitimate family ... The domestic law of the great majority of the member States of the Council of Europe has evolved and is continuing to evolve, in company with the relevant international instruments, towards full juridical recognition of the maxim *mater semper certa est.*"[20]

In *Inze v. Austria*, the applicant had been born to unmarried parents and the local laws of inheritance to farms provided that precedence should be given to legitimate children over illegitimate children. The Austrian courts refused to consider his claim to his dead mother's farm. He complained that this infringed Article 14, in conjunction with Article 1, Protocol 1 (right to property). The court held that very weighty reasons would have to be advanced before a difference of treatment on the ground of birth out of wedlock could be regarded as compatible with the Convention. There were no such justifications in this case and there was a violation of Article 14.[21] However, in judicial review proceedings in England it has been held that the Home Secretary is not in breach of Article 14 in exercising his discretion to refuse British nationality to an illegitimate child born abroad to a British father. British nationality is granted as a right to legitimate children born abroad to a British parent and to illegitimate children born to a British mother.[22] This is a case which was heard after the implementation of the Human Rights Act and therefore the decision has regard to the European Convention and to the jurisprudence of the European Court of Human Rights.

---

[20] *Marckx v. Belgium* (1979) 2 E.H.R.R. 330.
[21] *Inze v. Austria* (1987) 10 E.H.R.R. 394.
[22] *R v. Secretary of State for the Home Department, ex parte, Montana* [2001] 1 W.L.R. 552; [2001] 1 F.L.R. 449; [2001] 1 F.C.R. 358; [2001] H.R.L.R. 8; [2001] Fam. Law 94; (2001) 98(2) L.S.G. 41.

FUTURE DEVELOPMENTS

European Law

All of the uncertainty about discrimination on grounds of sexual 10.46
orientation will become merely academic in the near future, as will
the debate about the difference between religions and ethnic groups
because the United Kingdom will soon be obliged to introduce
legislation to prevent other types of discrimination, including
discrimination on grounds of sexual orientation. During 2000, three
important new measures to combat discrimination, based on Article
13 of the Treaty of Amsterdam, were adopted unanimously by the
Council of Ministers of the European Union. The measures are
intended to create a comprehensive set of anti-discrimination
measures and a minimum standard of legal protection against
discrimination that will apply across the European Union. The
general principles of Article 13 are not themselves legally binding.
To give effect to Article 13, the Council of Ministers have approved
two directives proposing minimum standards of legal protection
against discrimination throughout the European Union, and an
action programme to support practical efforts in the member states
to combat discrimination. The directives are,

(1) An Employment Directive, which requires member states to
make discrimination unlawful on grounds of religion or
belief, disability, age or sexual orientation in the areas of
employment and training and,
(2) A Race Directive, which requires member states to make
discrimination on grounds of racial or ethnic origin
unlawful in certain areas. The Race Directive applies to;
employment, training, education , access to social security
and health care, social advantages, and access to goods and
services, including housing.

Both directives set out clear definitions of direct and indirect
discrimination. The definition of direct discrimination is very
similar to that in United Kingdom legislation. The definition of
indirect discrimination however is broader than the one in current
United Kingdom law. The test for indirect discrimination is
whether "an apparently neutral provision, criterion or practice ...
would put persons of a racial or ethnic origin at a particular
disadvantage compared with other persons." The directives provide
that indirect discrimination will be unlawful unless the provision,
criterion or practice "is objectively justified by a legitimate aim and
the mains of achieving that aim are appropriate and necessary".
Harassment is to be regarded as a form of discrimination. It is
defined as unwanted conduct related to any of the grounds covered

by the directives, or conduct which is intended, or has the effect of, violating an individual's dignity and creating a humiliating, intimidating or hostile environment. Both directives recognise that equal treatment may not be sufficient to overcome the weight of accumulated disadvantage experienced by discriminated groups. They permit member states to take positive measures to "prevent or compensate for" situations of inequality.

The directives provide for exceptions where there is a genuine occupational qualification. Member states are permitted to allow difference in treatment on any of the grounds covered by the directives where the nature of a particular job, or the context in which it is carried out, justifies this. The Employment Directive also permits member states additional leeway to permit difference in treatment on grounds of religion or belief where the employment is in a church or other religious organisation. Both directives include protection against victimisation as a consequence of complaining of discrimination, or bringing or taking part in discrimination proceedings.

10.47   The aim of the directives is to ensure that anyone working, or simply travelling, within the European Union will be entitled to the same minimum level of protection from discrimination in all the member states. Both directives apply to any person who is within a member state when the act of discrimination occurs. Both directives, however, specifically exclude discrimination based on nationality and cannot be used to challenge conditions that a member state applies to the entry or residence of third-country nationals, and any treatment they receive as a result of their legal status. Discrimination on grounds of nationality is dealt with separately in the Treaty by Article 12, which provides that discrimination on grounds of nationality is prohibited. Article 12 has direct effect.

An action programme, which is to run from 2001-2006, will allocate 100 million euros over six years to fund practical action by member states to promote racial equality in all the areas covered by the two directives. The action programme aims to promote "transnational co-operation" between organisations in the 15 member states in tackling discrimination throughout the European Union, and to encourage the exchange of ideas and information. It will be administered by the European Commission, assisted by an advisory committee made up of representatives from all the member states.

One of the reasons for the proposals under Article 13 is that there has been no consistent level of protection in the European Union against discrimination on grounds of religion, disability, age or sexual orientation. In relation to the Employment Directive only, member states will be required to introduce protection against discrimination on the grounds of religion or belief, disability, age, sexual orientation, and racial or ethnic origin. In the United Kingdom, it is likely that new legislation will be required to provide protection against discrimination on grounds of sexual orientation and on grounds of religion or belief. Compliance with the Race Directive is required by July 19, 2003. Compliance with the Employment Directive in relation to religion and sexual orientation is required by December 2, 2003, and in relation to disability and age by December 2006. In the meantime, discrimination on grounds of religion or belief, age or social standing remains permissible under United Kingdom law. One exception to this is Northern Ireland where it is unlawful to discriminate on religious grounds. Article 12, which provides that discrimination on grounds of nationality is prohibited, has direct effect.

Protocol 12 to the European Convention on Human Rights

The Council of Europe has agreed a new Protocol 12 to the 10.48 European Convention on Human Rights which will replace Article 14 with a separate non-discrimination provision. This addresses the inherent weakness of Article 14 which is its failure to provide a separate right to be free from discriminatory treatment. This Protocol opened for signature in November 2000, but the United Kingdom Government has not yet ratified it. The Preamble to the protocol states that the principle of equality before the law and equal protection of the law is a fundamental and well-established general principle and an essential element of the protection of human rights. The principle of equality requires that equal situations are treated equally and unequal situations differently. Measures to promote full and effective equality are not prohibited by the principle of non-discrimination. States may be justified in treating different groups of people differently in order to redress past inequalities.
Article 1 states that:

"(1) The enjoyment of any right set forth by law shall be secured without discrimination on any ground such as sex, race, colour, language, religion, political or other opinion, national or social origin, association with a minority, property, birth or other status.

(2) No-one shall be discriminated against by any public authority on any ground such as those mentioned in paragraph 1."

This extends the scope of protection in Article 14, which only applies to the enjoyment of the rights and freedoms set forth in the Convention. It would apply to discrimination under national law and to acts or omissions by public authorities. The Article does not go so far as to impose an obligation on states to take measures to prevent or remedy all instances of discrimination in relations between private persons. States may be obliged to intervene in instances of grave forms of discrimination between private persons. This could be the case if a serious and widespread problem of religious discrimination in the workplace had arisen in a country where no protection was provided against religious discrimination. Protocol 12 will come into force once it has been ratified by 10 states. Until then Article 14 will continue to apply to all parties to the Convention and thereafter it will apply to those states which do not ratify Protocol 12.

CHAPTER 11

ARTICLE 1 OF PROTOCOL 1—RIGHT TO PROPERTY

"Every natural or legal person is entitled to the peaceful enjoyment of his possessions. No one shall be deprived of his possessions except in the public interest and subject to the conditions provided for by law and by the general principles of international law.

The preceeding provisions shall not, however, in any way impair the right of a State to enforce such laws as it deems necessary to control the use of property in accordance with the general interest or to secure the payment of taxes or other contributions or penalties"

Various writers have remarked that the right to property is a 11.01
strange right to include in a Treaty which is so overwhelmingly concerned with the rights and freedoms of people who are in difficulty. A number of the governments who set up the European Convention on Human Rights had similar thoughts. The protection of property rights was difficult for many of them to reconcile with their principles and proposals. Thus the British Labour Government opposed any inclusion of the right on the basis that they did not wish to be prevented from acquiring private property as and when they required it to fulfill their nationalisation proposals. There was a general fear that such a right might favour private interests at a time when a more "community" spirit was prevalent after the Second World War.

The European Convention signed in 1951 did not therefore include a right to property. However, it was obvious that such a right was required and the First Protocol was enacted in 1952 and came into force in 1954. Article 1 was a compromise and it is heavily qualified by a statement that the right may be restricted in the "public" or "general" interest. Its protection extends to both natural and legal persons. It is one of only two rights to invoke the public interest as a justification for state interference[1] and it is the

---

[1]   Fourth Protocol, Arts 2(1) and 2(4).

only clear economic guarantee found in the Convention.[2]

It has been stated that the protection in Article 1 of the First Protocol is so qualified that it might well be considered to be in a category of its own.[3] In cases involving property rights the question generally is whether there is a fair balance between the individual's right to property and the general public interest.

11.02   Any restriction on the peaceful enjoyment of property must be prescribed by law, legitimate, necessary and proportionate, and not discriminatory. Many cases involving the property related challenges also involve a violation of another Article, particularly the "due process" guarantee of Article 6(1) and the right to respect for private and family life found in Article 8.

A very wide margin of appreciation is left to the states and indeed, so far, no case has succeeded where an initiative was pursued by the state on the grounds of public interest. The actions of the state need to be so blatant that they cannot conform to the provisions of the Article. In *Stran Greek Refineries and Stratis Andreadis v. Greece*[4] the Greek Government passed retrospective legislation deliberately to deprive the company of an arbitration award made in its favour against a government body. This was found to be a blatant confiscation of property which could not be justified. In the United Kingdom, a similar occurrence took place in 1965 after *Burmah Oil Co. v. Lord Advocate*[5] where the House of Lords found in favour of the company that the government was liable to compensate them for the destruction of property during the Second World War. The government introduced the War Damages Act 1965 to retrospectively allow the destruction to have taken place without compensation. The government then delayed by six months a statement allowing the right of individual petition to the European Court at Strasbourg so that *Burmah Oil* would not have the right to challenge the government's actions.

WHAT IS A POSSESSION?

11.03 The first point to note about the word "possession" in the Protocol is that it has a wider meaning under Convention law than in either Scots or English law. The right to have and control property has been recognised in the United Kingdom jurisdictions for centuries and the United Kingdom courts have shown a willingness to overrule the decisions of central and local government where there

[2]   M. Smyth, *Business and the Human Rights Act 1998* (2000).
[3]   K. Starmer, *Human Rights Digest* (2001).
[4]   (1994) 19 E.H.R.R. 293.
[5]   [1965] A.C. 75.

is an interference with that right.[6] "Possessions" are not confined to land and buildings, furniture, jewellery, cash or stocks and shares. The term in the Convention has a wider definition and includes a variety of economic interests such as patents,[7] planning consents,[8] shares,[9] and money paid in tips.[10]

An interest is not a possession in United Kingdom law but it is capable of protection under Article 1 of the First Protocol and as a civil right under Article 6. The main principle is that there must be an interference with the right which then affects the financial value of the possession. In *Van Marle v. The Netherlands*[11] the applicants had carried on a business as accountants but when the government changed the law to regulate the accountancy profession they found that they could not be registered. The effect of the refusal to register them had a considerable impact on their business and the European Court held that they could invoke Article 1 of the First Protocol.

> "[T]he right relied on by the applicants might be likened to the right of property embodied in Article 1 (of Protocol 1); by dint of their own work the applicants had built up a clientele; this had in many respects the nature of a private right and constituted an asset."[12]

A licence is capable of being considered a possession within the Convention. Thus the revocation of a restaurant's liquor licence had an adverse effect on the value of the business and was contrary to Article 1 of the First Protocol.[13] If the licence creates a legitimate expectation that it will subsist for some time and the applicant will benefit from it, then it will be a possession.[14]

Article 1 of the First Protocol does not give a right to acquire property or possessions. However, there is a traditional and fundamental right to dispose of one's own property and this includes the right to bequeath property. In the leading case on this point, *Marckx v. Belgium*,[15] an unmarried mother complained that aspects of Belgian law limited her right to dispose of her property to her child. The European Court held that Article 1 of the First Protocol enshrined the right of everyone to peaceful enjoyment of

---

[6] *Att.-Gen. v. De Keyser's Royal Hotel* [1920] A.C. 508.
[7] *Smith Kline and French Laboratories v. The Netherlands* (1990) 66 D.R. 70.
[8] *Pine Valley Developments Ltd v. Ireland* (1991) 14 E.H.R.R. 319.
[9] *Bramelid and Malmstrom v. Sweden* (1982) 29 D.R. 64.
[10] although if these are included in a cheque or credit card payment, the tips belong to the employer – *Nerva v. U.K.* [2001] E.H.R.L.R. 98.
[11] (1986) 8 E.H.R.R. 483.
[12] *ibid.*, para. 41.
[13] *Tre Traktorer Aktiebolag v. Sweden* (1991) 13 E.H.R.R. 309.
[14] *Pudas v. Sweden* (1988) 10 E.H.R.R. 380.
[15] (1979) 2 E.H.R.R. 330.

their existing possessions but it did not guarantee the right to acquire possessions on intestacy or otherwise. However, the Belgian laws limiting the applicant's rights as a mother to make gifts or legacies in favour of her child were discriminatory and there was a breach of Article 14 in conjunction with Article 1 of the First Protocol.

11.04   Similarly the Convention does not protect the right to succeed while a testator is alive.[16] Recently the European Court ruled as inadmissible a claim by applicants that the transmission of titles of nobility through the male line was in breach of Articles 8, 14 and Article 1 of the First Protocol. It was claimed that the property rights included financial considerations inherent in a noble title and there were various items of property handed down to the holder of the title.[17]

Where there is a legitimate expectation of being able to carry out a proposed development of land, this may be construed as a component part of the property.[18]

A pending claim on civil proceedings will constitute a possession if it is sufficiently established. In *Pressos Compania Naviera SA v. Belgium*[19] the applicants claimed damages against the Belgian pilot service claiming that their ships had been damaged in collisions which were due to the negligence of the pilots. The government passed retrospective legislation to defeat the claims. The European Court held that there was a breach of Article 1 of the First Protocol because the claims for compensation had come into existence as soon as the damage occurred. The claims were assets amounting to possessions within the meaning of the Article and the retrospective legislation amounted to an interference with the peaceful enjoyment of possessions. The national authorities had a wide margin of appreciation in determining what was in the public interest but in this case the taking away of the property, *i.e.* the claims for damages, without payment of compensation was a disproportionate interference not justified by any exceptional circumstances.

11.05   The loss of value of a business or goodwill will not be a violation of Article 1 of the First Protocol. In *Ian Edgar (Liverpool) Ltd v. United Kingdom*[20] the company's business selling firearms suffered extensively after Parliament enacted stricter gun controls in 1996 and 1997. The company received substantial compensation for the stock they could not sell. However, they sought compensation for the diminution in the value of their business assessed by reference to their projected future income. The European Court held that the

---

[16]   *Inze v. Austria* (1987) 10 E.H.R.R. 394.
[17]   *De La Cierva Osorio de Moscoso and Others v. Spain*, Appl. 41127/98.
[18]   *supra*, no. 8.
[19]   (1995) 21 E.H.R.R. 301.
[20]   [2000] E.H.R.L.R. 322.

application was inadmissible and that the company had not suffered an excessive burden in relation to its possessions. The aim of the legislation was an important public interest and the company had no legitimate expectation of being able to trade.[21] The European Commission had previously found that future income only became a "possession" once it was earned or there was an enforceable right to it.[22]

The right to pursue a hobby is not a possession for the purposes of Article 1 of the First Protocol. In *RC, AW v. United Kingdom*[23] the Commission held that a complaint by 1,879 applicants was not admissible and they were not entitled to compensation in respect of loss of amenity because of the introduction of United Kingdom legislation to prohibit the ownership of handguns.

"Peaceful enjoyment" is another phrase often used and which requires some definition. It does not mean "enjoyment" in the aesthetic sense so as to give a right to enjoy possessions in a pleasant environment.[24] It is more a right which protects an owner or occupier from the exercise of adverse rights over the property.

INTERFERENCE WITH THE RIGHTS UNDER ARTICLE I OF THE FIRST PROTOCOL

It has been noted above that the right to peaceful enjoyment of possessions under Article 1 of the First Protocol is heavily qualified. The European Court has identified three distinct rules pertaining to the Article. These were derived from *Sporrong and Lonnroth v. Sweden*[25] and developed in *Allgemeine Gold-und Silberscheideanstalt v. United Kingdom (the AGOSI case)*.[26] The "*Sporrong* Rules" were described as follows: 11.06

> Rule 1—general nature of the principle of peaceful enjoyment of property—1st sentence of the 1st paragraph of Article 1 of the First Protocol;
> Rule 2—deprivation of possessions subject to certain conditions—2nd sentence of 1st paragraph;
> Rule 3—recognition of the right of Contracting States to control the use of property in accordance with the general interest—2nd paragraph of the Article.

---

[21] See also: *Pinnacle Meat Processors Co. v. U.K.* (1999) 27 E.H.R.R. C.D. 217.
[22] *Batelaan & Huiges v. The Netherlands* (1984) D.R. 41.
[23] (1998) 26 E.H.R.R. C.D. 210.
[24] *Powell v. U.K.* (1987) 9 E.H.R.R. 241.
[25] (1983) 5 E.H.R.R. 35.
[26] (1987) 9 E.H.R.R. 1.

The European Court further commented:

> "The three rules are not 'distinct' in the sense of being unconnected: the second and third rules are concerned with particular instances of interference with the right to peaceful enjoyment of property and should therefore be construed in the light of the general principle enunciated in the first rule."[27]

In *Sporrong and Lonnroth v. Sweden,* the applicants were owners of real property in Stockholm. Plans for redevelopment were proposed and expropriation permits were signed by the government. The local administration board then imposed prohibition notices on construction. The permits lasted 23 years and eight years respectively and the prohibition notices lapsed after 25 years and 12 years. The applicants were unable to seek compensation for the restrictions on their peaceful enjoyment of the property. The European Court held that there was a violation of Article 1 of the First Protocol because the expropriation permits affected the rights of the owners to use and dispose of their property. This interference was made more serious by the restriction on use imposed by the prohibition on construction. Although there was no deprivation of possessions or *de facto* expropriation, there was an excessive burden on the applicants which upset the balance between the owners' rights and the general interest. There were no remedies available under Swedish law for the applicants to seek a reduction of the time limits for expropriation or to claim compensation.

Rule 1—Principle of Peaceful Enjoyment of Property

11.07 The first sentence of the first paragraph of the Article sets out a general protection of the right to "peaceful enjoyment of property". The term "enjoyment" is wider than having and holding property. It will include rights to do anything lawful with one's possessions, such as disposal or destruction, sale or lease, lend or use the possession. The jurisprudence of the Convention suggests that "enjoyment" does not mean environmental amenity. The Convention does not guarantee a right of enjoyment "in a pleasant environment".[28] A complaint of damage to the environment such as aircraft noise is likely only to be considered under Article 1 of the First Protocol if there is an adverse effect on the value of the property.[29]

The principle implies that an interference with the peaceful enjoyment will engage the Convention right unless that interference

---

[27] *supra*, no. 25 at para. 48.
[28] *supra*, no. 24.
[29] *Rayner v. U.K.* (1986) 47 D.R. 5.

is identified as justifiable by the rest of the Article. Thus the Convention recognises that in certain circumstances it will be possible to deprive a person of his property (Rule 2) or to exert control over the property (Rule 3).

Unfortunately, the European Court does not always identify the rule that has been breached in making some of its decisions. There is a tendency to "assimilate all interferences with the peaceful enjoyment of property under the single principle of fair balance as set out in *Sporrong*".[30] However, the Court tends to apply the same benchmark in all three rules and thus it does not matter if none is identified. In *Papamichalopoulos v. Greece*[31] the Greek military junta passed a law which did not effect a legal transfer of the property concerned but did prevent the applicants from selling or making use of the land. This action was not a full legal expropriation but amounted to a *de facto* deprivation and thus breached Article 1 of the First Protocol. The European Commission were unable to decide whether the breach fell within the first rule or the second. The Court resolved the issue by making a general finding of a violation.[32]

Rule 2—Deprivation of Possession Subject to Conditions

The beginning of the second sentence of the first paragraph of the Article is written in positive terms, "[n]o-one shall be deprived of his possessions" but it is followed by three strong qualifications "except in the public interest and subject to the conditions provided for by law and by the general principles of international law". 11.08

The deprivation must be lawful and this term has the same meaning as elsewhere in the Convention.[33] This means that, to be lawful, the restriction must:

(1) Have an established legal basis in domestic law, such as legislation;
(2) Be accessible to those affected;
(3) Be foreseeable. The restriction must be sufficiently clear so that those affected can understand it and act accordingly.[34]

The degree of certainty of the restriction will depend on the circumstances of each case. Thus certainty must be absolute where the lawfulness of a deprivation of liberty is concerned.

The deprivation must be permanent, although there need not be a

---

[30] *supra*, no. 2 at 305.
[31] (1996) 21 E.H.R.R. 439.
[32] See also *Iatridis v. Greece* (2000) 30 E.H.R.R. 97.
[33] *James v. U.K.* (1986) 8 E.H.R.R. 123.
[34] *supra*, no. 3.

formal act of deprivation. The European Court will look at the whole situation to decide whether a *de facto* deprivation has occurred. "Since the Convention is intended to guarantee rights that are 'practical and effective' it has to be ascertained whether the situations amounted to a *de facto* expropriation."[35] In *Vasilescu v. Romania*[36] gold coins were seized from the applicant in 1966 after the local police searched her house without a warrant. The coins were deposited in the National Bank of Romania by the police. No charges were brought as a result of the search but the police kept the coins. After various attempts to retrieve the coins through the Romanian courts, the applicant complained to the European Court. A violation of Article 1 of the First Protocol was found. The applicant had been deprived of the use and enjoyment of her property since 1966 but remained the owner of it. She was the victim of a *de facto* confiscation of the property which was incompatible with her right to the peaceful enjoyment of property. In *Holy Monasteries v. Greece*[37] a statute was passed to modify the rules of administration of eight monasteries, transferring a large part of their estate to the Greek State. The European Court held that there had been an interference with their right to the peaceful enjoyment of property, creating a presumption of state ownership of the monasteries and making it difficult for them to prove title. The statute had failed to provide for compensation and thus there was no fair balance between the various interests.

11.09   In *Cyprus v. Turkey*[38] an action was brought under numerous articles against Turkey in respect of the Turkish military occupation of northern Cyprus since 1974. Among the claims were some relating to the interference without compensation with the property and homes of Greek Cypriots who had been displaced. The Commission found a violation of Article 1 of the First Protocol in that the Turkish authorities had failed to recognise southern Cypriots in inheritance law and to secure their property during their absence.[39]

Temporary interference will not be a deprivation. In *Air Canada v. United Kingdom*[40] the temporary seizure of an aircraft to enforce specific provisions in drugs legislation was held not to be a deprivation. The aircraft had arrived in the United Kingdom with drugs hidden on board. The aircraft was then seized under statutory powers of forfeiture. The European Court held that the seizure and subsequent release in return for payment was not a breach of

---

[35] *supra*, no. 25 at para. 63.
[36] (1999) 28 E.H.R.R. 241.
[37] (1994) 20 E.H.R.R. 1.
[38] [2000] E.H.R.L.R. 198.
[39] See also *Selcuk v. Turkey* (1998) 26 E.H.R.R. 477.
[40] (1995) 20 E.H.R.R. 150.

Article 1 of the First Protocol and was not disproportionate. The government's policy was to encourage Air Canada (which had a history of such events) to improve its security and it was acceptable to enforce that policy in the public interest.[41]

Where a deprivation of property has occurred, Rule 2 requires that compensation be paid. There is however no such presumption that compensation has to be paid with regard to a violation of Rules 1 or 3. The compensation paid will be part of the question of whether a fair balance has been struck between the rights of the individual and the public interest. It need not be the full market value of the possession; in this the states have a wide margin of appreciation. In *Lithgow v. United Kingdom*[42] the owners of aircraft and shipping companies nationalised in 1977 complained that they had not received proper compensation for their property. The relevant United Kingdom statute had a complex system for calculating the compensation payable. The government had admitted later that the terms of compensation had been grossly unfair to some companies. The European Court held that the policy goal of nationalisation had been debated extensively in Parliament and thus it could not be said to be in breach of the Convention. The Court considered whether the uniform basis for compensation was in principle acceptable and decided that the method of calculating the compensation was reasonable and within the margin of appreciation available to the government.

> "Compensation must normally be reasonably related to the value of the property taken but Article 1 of the First Protocol does not guarantee full compensation in all cases. The legitimate objectives of the public interest may justify reimbursement at less than the full market value; the nature of the property taken and the circumstances may be taken into account in holding the balance between public and private interests. The Court will respect the national legislature's judgment in this respect unless manifestly without reasonable foundation."

The Court reiterated the view that reasonable compensation for deprivation of property will be required in *Holy Monasteries v. Greece*.[43] "The taking of property without payment of an amount reasonably related to its value will normally constitute a disproportionate interference and total lack of compensation can be justifiable under article 1 only in exceptional circumstances."

---

[41] See also *Handyside v. U.K.* (1976) 1 E.H.R.R. 737; *Venditelli v. Italy* (1994) 19 E.H.R.R. 464.
[42] (1986) 8 E.H.R.R. 329.
[43] *supra*, no. 37.

11.10   The European Court has also found that the compensation
should be paid within a reasonable time and long delays in the
payment of compensation for expropriated land may be contrary to
the Convention. In *Sporrong* the Swedish Government was entitled
to designate private property for compulsory purchase but the
length of time taken (up to 23 years) was held to be an "individual
and excessive burden" on the landowners. In *Akkus v. Turkey*[44] the
applicant's land was expropriated as part of a dam building project.
She was given a compensation payment initially but a later study
commissioned by the water authority set a higher value on the land.
She applied for an order to increase the compensation plus interest
based on the rate of inflation. The water authority opposed this and
the matter went to appeal. However, before the appeal was heard,
she sought a remedy from the European Court complaining of the
delay in paying her compensation. The Court agreed that she was
entitled to be paid as quickly as possible once the initial award had
been made. The delay of 17 months coupled with the rate of interest
awarded meant that the value of the payment decreased when
compared with the annual rate of inflation. This amounted to a
breach of Article 1 of the First Protocol.[45]

Generally in the United Kingdom, property is not expropriated
without some form of compensation being available, but occasionally this does happen. In *Booker Aquaculture Ltd v. Secretary of
State for Scotland*[46] an order was made requiring the slaughter of
salmon on a fish farm to prevent the spread of disease. The
regulations under which the order was made, had been made to
implement an E.C. Council Directive.[47] There was no provision for
compensation. The pursuers claimed that the right to property
protected by Article 1 of the First Protocol of the European
Convention on Human Rights was recognised as a fundamental
right under Community law.[48] The Inner House of the Court of
Session decided to make a reference to the European Court of
Justice on whether the right to compensation should be determined
under Community law or national law.[49]

In *R v. Secretary of State for Health, ex parte Eastside Cheese
Co.*[50] an emergency control order was made under section 13 of the
Food Safety Act 1990 to prevent the use of certain cheese by a

---

[44] (2000) 30 E.H.R.R. 365.
[45] See also: *Almeida Garrett, Mascarenhas Falcao v. Portugal,* ECtHR, January 11,
    2000.
[46] 2000 S.C. 9.
[47] Diseases of Fish (Control) Regulations 1994.
[48] See *Hauer v. Land Rheinland Pfalz* [1980] 3 C.M.L.R. 42.
[49] See A. O'Neill "The Protection of Fundamental Rights in Scotland as a general
    principle of Community law—the case of *Booker Aquaculture*" [2000] E.H.R.L.R.
    18.
[50] [1999] 3 C.M.L.R. 123.

manufacturer. The cheese-maker was not entitled to compensation for cheese which was detained even if the cheese was not unfit for human consumption. The cheese-maker argued that the Secretary of State could not rely on Article 36 E.C. Treaty to justify his breach of Article 34 E.C. because making the order violated rights guaranteed by Article 1 of the First Protocol of the European Convention. The Court held that although the order interfered with the applicants' peaceful enjoyment of their property it did not deprive them of the property. Further, the rule that compensation was payable where there was a deprivation of property did not apply because the circumstances were sufficiently exceptional to displace the rule.[51]

In a recent case in Scotland, the livestock of a farm was due to be culled under the regulations made to curb the foot and mouth outbreak during the early part of 2001. In *Westerhall Farm v. The Scottish Ministers*[52] the animals were to be slaughtered because the farm was situated within a three kilometre radius of another on which the disease had been found. The petitioner argued, *inter alia,* that the slaughter policy was inflexible and disproportionate and it was a disproportionate invasion of property rights under Article 1 of the First Protocol. The petition was refused. Lord Carloway held that the Scottish Ministers had struck the right balance between the public interest and the petitioner's property rights. Thus the Convention was not engaged. He found there was nothing wrong with a rigid policy provided it did not fetter the Scottish Ministers' discretion in individual cases. The requirement for "swift and effective action" rendered the actions of the Scottish Ministers proportionate and the balance of convenience favoured the slaughter proceeding.

11.11

Under the Article 1 of the First Protocol, the state's interference with property rights must be proportionate and it is for the state to prove this. The policy adopted in the *Westerhall Farm* case was made in accordance with Council Directive 85/11/EEC, which recognised that natural boundaries might be sufficient to preclude slaughter within the three kilometre radius. In this case, the natural boundary between the two farms was an area of boggy ground unsuitable for the grazing of livestock. The Court however decided that the Directive set out minimum preventative measures which national authorities might extend, that is, there was a margin of appreciation in the implementation of the Directive.[53]

The second rule of the *Sporrong* case refers to deprivation being justified if it is in "the public interest". The European Court has generally been reluctant to interfere with the assessment of the

---

[51]   See also *Errington v. Wilson,* 1995 S.L.T. 1193 (The *Lanark Blue Cheese* case).
[52]   Outer House, April 25, 2001.
[53]   See also *Owen v. Ministry of Agriculture Fisheries and Food* [2001] E.H.R.L.R. 18.

public interest by the national authorities. However, there has to be a fair balance struck between the individual's property rights and the public or general interest. This issue of fair balance or proportionality is seen in other qualified rights under the Convention, such as Articles 8 to 11, but in this Article it is less exacting. The European Court looks to see whether the balance is excessively burdensome on the applicant. In *James v. United Kingdom*[54] the Court said "[t]here must be a reasonable relationship of proportionality between the means employed and the aim sought to be realised".[55] The case involved the Leasehold Reform Act 1967 which allowed tenants to purchase their homes in central London for amounts which were substantially below the market value. The landlord argued that the statute benefited individual tenants not the public at large and thus the public interest test could not be satisfied. The European Court held that "the notion of public interest is necessarily extensive" and this might involve considerations of political, economic and social issues. Remedying a perceived social injustice was a legitimate function of a democratic legislature and the absence of a direct benefit to the community at large did not mean that the judgment of the legislature was manifestly without reasonable foundation.

11.12   It follows from this that the community at large need not benefit if a legitimate social, economic or other policy is being pursued. Thus in *Spadea and Scalabrino v. Italy*[56] the state's legitimate aim was to prevent widespread homelessness and this was achieved by suspending eviction orders against the old and infirm and freezing rents. In *Mellacher v. Austria*[57] the state ordered significant rent reductions of up to 79 per cent to make accommodation available for the less affluent. The European Court held that the interference in the right to peaceful enjoyment of possessions was justified in the public interest of providing additional and affordable accommodation and it was not disproportionate in the circumstances.

The degree of risk taken on by the individual deprived of the possession will be relevant.[58] However, if the act of the national authority is truly arbitrary it is unlikely that a relationship of proportionality can be established. In *Papachelas v. Greece*[59] the applicants had their land taken compulsorily for a road improvement scheme. There was an irrefutable statutory presumption that landowners benefited from such road schemes and this influenced the amount of compensation payable. There was no right available

[54] *supra*, no. 33.
[55] *ibid.*, para. 51.
[56] (1995) 21 E.H.R.R. 482.
[57] (1989) 12 E.H.R.R. 391.
[58] *supra*, no. 8.
[59] March 25, 1999, ECtHR.

to an individual to plead that particular circumstances existed to vary the compensation.

There is a duty on the national authorities that their actions are provided for by law and by the general principles of international law. This will generally mean that the states must provide procedural safeguards for those affected and a compensation scheme. Where the property of non-nationals is subject to expropriation the deprivation must be in accordance with the general principles of international law. However, the European Court will also apply the principles of international law where national law does not allow reparation. In *Brumarescu v. Romania*[60] the Court found that it may "afford the party such satisfaction as appears to it to be appropriate". The applicant's parents' house had been nationalised in 1950 without compensation and there was no method whereby he could reclaim the property or receive compensation. The Court ordered the return of the property immediately or the payment of substantial damages by the state.

Rule 3—Recognition of the Right of Contracting State to Control the Use of Property in Accordance with the General Interest

This rule acknowledges that contracting states may require to control the use of property in the general interest to "secure payment of taxes or other contributions or penalties". The Article distinguishes between deprivation of property and control of the use of property. The former will usually be a violation of the Article particularly if no compensation is paid while violation of the latter is harder to prove. The measures taken by the state must be short of deprivation but must substantially interfere with the applicant's peaceful enjoyment of that property. For instance in *Scollo v. Italy*[61] a landlord applied in 1983 for an eviction order in respect of a flat he owned. Some years later, he required the flat for his own occupation because of ill-health and unemployment. The enforcement of the eviction order had been delayed because of government policy. Possession was eventually recovered in 1995 but the applicant had complained to the European Court in 1991. The Court held that the Convention reserved to the state the right to enact laws as they deemed necessary to control the use of property in accordance with the general interest. The Court would respect the state legislature's judgment unless it was manifestly without reasonable foundation[62] but any interference must strike a fair balance between the general interest of the community and the protection of the individual's fundamental rights. In this case, the

11.13

---

[60] [2001] E.H.R.L.R. 451.
[61] (1996) 22 E.H.R.R. 514.
[62] *supra*, no. 57.

Italian Government had failed to implement its emergency
legislative measures to give the applicant priority to enforce the
eviction. There had been inertia on the part of the administrative
authorities to ensure that the flat was re-possessed and therefore
there was a breach of Article 1 of the First Protocol and Article
6(1).

In a similar case, *Immobiliare Saffi v. Italy*[63] a statutory scheme to
alleviate a housing shortage allowed the use of the police to enforce
eviction orders. The applicants complained that since their case was
not deemed a priority, they were unable to obtain police assistance
to recover their property and thus were deprived of their right to
peaceful enjoyment of their property. The European Court held
that the practical effect of the state scheme was that non-urgent
evictions were never being enforced because of the number of
applications. There had to be safeguards against an arbitrary or
unforeseeable impact on the landlord's property rights. There was
an excessive burden on the applicants and this did not balance the
protection of the right of property with the requirements of the
general interest.

The state measures may require the applicant to use the property
in a particular way or may place restrictions on the use of the
property. Examples of these would include planning controls,[64] a
refusal to register the applicants as certified accountants[65] and
retrospective tax measures.[66] The Convention jurisprudence has
identified three aspects whereby the contracting state must justify
the control of use. First, the measure must be lawful. Secondly, it
must be in the public interest or aimed at securing the payment of
taxes, contributions or penalties. Thirdly, it must be deemed
necessary by the state. The term "lawful" has the same meaning as
discussed in Rule 2 above, that is, it must have an established legal
basis in the domestic laws, it must be accessible and it must be
foreseeable. An example of this aspect of the rule is found in
Hentrich v. France[67] where the applicant bought a large area of
land. The local Commissioner for Revenue considered that the price
was too low and invoked his powers under the French tax code to
pre-empt the sale by paying the purchase price plus a 10 per cent
premium. The power was used exceptionally to deter tax evasion
but there was no requirement on the French authorities to give
reasons for the intervention nor show fraudulent intent. There was
no way of challenging the order. The European Court found that
the basic procedural safeguards of Article 6(1) were missing and

---

[63]   (2000) 30 E.H.R.R. 756.
[64]   *supra*, no. 8.
[65]   *supra*, no. 11.
[66]   *National and Provincial Building Society v. U.K.* (1997) 25 E.H.R.R. 127.
[67]   (1994) 18 E.H.R.R. 440.

"the pre-emption was operated arbitrarily and selectively and was scarcely foreseeable".

In *Aston Cantlow and Wilmcote with Billesley Parochial Church* 11.14
Council v. Wallbank[68] landowners appealed against a finding that they had to contribute towards the cost of repairs to the parish church. The land had previously been part of the rectory. The church council was empowered to enforce the obligation to keep the church in good repair and sought to recover the costs. The Court of Appeal held that the liability of the owners to contribute to the repairs was a taxation that contravened Article 1 of the First Protocol since money constituted property. A tax which was arbitrary in nature and where an indeterminate liability could arise at any time was outside the limits of the state's power and breached the provisions of the Convention.

The meaning of "necessary" has, however, altered over the years. Originally the European Court gave the state authorities a wide discretion to assess necessity.[69] Now the test adopted is the "fair balance" test used in deprivation of property cases. This was acknowledged in *National and Provincial Building Society v. United Kingdom*.[70] Here a dispute involving another building society in respect of tax paid on interest was successfully settled in favour of the building society. Other societies tried to reclaim tax paid but the government passed legislation to close what they saw as a "tax loophole". The societies then claimed that there had been an interference with their rights to restitution. The European Court held that a successful claim to restitution would have amounted to a windfall for the building societies. It was noted that there was a clear intention by Parliament that this tax should be levied. The Court stated that

> "an interference, including one resulting from a measure to secure payment of taxes, must strike a 'fair balance' between the demands of the general interest of the community and the requirements of the protection of the individual's rights. The concern to achieve this balance is reflected in the structure of Article 1 as a whole, including the second paragraph: there must therefore be a reasonable relationship of property between the means employed and the aims pursued."[71]

In the *AGOSI* case[72] the applicants had sold Krugerrands to buyers

---

[68] [2001] 3 All E.R. 393.
[69] *Handyside v. U.K.* (1976) 1 E.H.R.R. 737; *Marckx v. Belgium* (1979) 2 E.H.R.R. 330.
[70] *supra,* no. 66.
[71] *ibid.* para. 80.
[72] *supra,* no. 26.

who defaulted on payment but attempted to smuggle the coins in the United Kingdom. They were seized and then declared forfeit by the Customs and Excise. Meanwhile, the applicants had obtained a declaration from a German court that the original transaction was void. The European Court found that the forfeiture was a legitimate exercise in control rather than deprivation. Its intention was to enforce an import prohibition and this was crucial for deciding whether it was deprivation or control.

11.15   Originally the phrase "secure payment of taxes or other contributions or penalties" was interpreted as distinguishing between the collection of taxes and the levying of tax. In *Gasus Dosier-und Fordertechnik GmbH v. The Netherlands*[73] the applicant company supplied goods against payment by instalments retaining title as security. When the purchaser became bankrupt, the Dutch revenue authorities seized the goods according to local law. The applicant challenged the seizure arguing that it neither knew about nor was responsible for the buyer's failure to pay taxes. The European Court gave a majority verdict in which it allowed the Dutch authorities power "to pass whatever fiscal laws they considered desirable, provided always that measures in this field did not amount to arbitrary confiscation". Three judges dissented from the judgment finding that the Dutch authority's actions were not proportionate.[74]

It is clear after *National and Provincial Building Society v. United Kingdom* that the provision applies to both the collection and levying of taxes. However, it is also clear that in the field of taxation, there is a wide discretion allowed to national authorities and only those tax measures which are wholly disproportionate or arbitrary or discriminatory will breach the Convention. Retrospective tax measures are not prohibited, although the national authorities may have to show they were introduced to counter a tax-avoidance scheme.[75] The measures should be proportionate and establish a fair balance between the individual and the general interest. In *Marks and Spencer v. Commissioners of Customs and Excise (No. 1)*[76] it was agreed that the company had overpaid VAT over a number of years. The Finance Act 1997 changed the length of period over which refunds of overpayment could be claimed, shortening the period from six to three years. It was held that this did not infringe Article 1 of the First Protocol "as it did not remove the possibility of a claim but merely imposed a limitation period".

If a penalty is imposed in taxation cases, there will be closer

---

[73] (1995) 20 E.H.R.R. 403.
[74] See also *Speyside Bonding Co. Ltd. v. Customs and Excise Commissioners*, 2001 W.L. 825611.
[75] See *A,B,C and D v. U.K.* (1981) 23 D.R. 203.
[76] [1999] 1 C.M.L.R. 1152.

scrutiny of the position. In *Smith v. United Kingdom*[77] the European Commission found that a 10 per cent surcharge was not a criminal sanction because failure to pay it would not convert it into a period of imprisonment. Generally, ordinary measures to enforce tax payment do not involve criminal charges or procedures within the meaning of Article 6 but a tax penalty which is punitively high may attract the Convention's safeguards. For instance, in *Perin v. France*[78] the tax penalties imposed were 30 to 50 per cent and in *Bendenoun v. France*[79] a surcharge of 500,000 francs was imposed.

Welfare Payments and Pensions as Possessions

There is no right created under the Convention to receive a welfare 11.16 benefit or pension but property rights may arise in certain circumstances. In *X v. Sweden*[80] it was found that the payment of contributions into a general pension fund might create a property right in a portion of a pension fund. A modification of the pension rights under the fund could therefore "in principle raise an issue under Article 1 of the First Protocol". This rule will apply to both compulsory schemes and those based on employment. The contributions made by an employer to a private pension plan may also amount to a possession.[81]

The right recognised by the Convention is to derive a benefit, not to receive a pension or welfare benefit of a particular amount. The European Commission in *X v. Sweden* acknowledged that the state social security system had to take account of public policy considerations especially financial policy, so that a reduction in the normal amount of pension would have nothing to do with a guarantee of ownership as a human right. As always the Convention requires a proportionate response by the national authority, so in this case, it was stated that a substantial reduction might destroy "the very essence" of the pension.

If contributions are paid by the applicant this may indicate the creation of property rights. In *Gaygusuz v. Austria*[82] a Turkish man had paid contributions to an Austrian state pension fund and then required emergency assistance. Any payments from the fund depended on contributions having been made. The applicant was excluded from the benefit because it was for Austrian nationals only. The European Court found this to be a violation of Article 1 of the First Protocol.

The non-payment of an elderly person's travel permit to a man 11.17

---

[77] (1996) 21 E.H.R.R. CD 74 (EComHR).
[78] Appl. 18565/91, December 1, 1992, EComHR.
[79] (1994) 18 E.H.R.R. 54.
[80] (1986) 8 E.H.R.R. 252 EComHR.
[81] *Stigson v. Sweden* (1988) D.R. 57/131.
[82] (1997) 23 E.H.R.R. 364.

aged 64 was scrutinised in *Matthews v. United Kingdom*.[83] The applicant argued that he should be entitled to the permit at age 64 since a woman aged 60 would be able to obtain one. Under the provisions of the London Regional Transport Act 1984 however a man had to be aged 65 to receive the permit. The applicant argued that Article 1 of the First Protocol applied because he would have an enforceable right to the travel permit were it not for his sex and therefore there had been discrimination in breach of Article 14 taken together with Article 1 of the First Protocol. The European Court admitted his claim. It is likely that there will be a "friendly settlement" in this case since the United Kingdom Government has recently recognised that there are discriminatory issues relating to the tax allowances and benefits payable to widows but not to widowers.[84] The United Kingdom Government has also lost a case before the European Court of Justice where winter fuel payments were paid to women at age 60 but men had to wait until they were 65.[85] This was contrary to the Equal Treatment Directive 76/707/EEC.

Planning Issues and Article 1 of the First Protocol

11.18 The rights of property include the right to dispose of and use that property as the owner wishes. However, rights in real property may be limited by planning and other development restrictions. The European Court has taken the view that contracting states are entitled to impose such planning restrictions as are required in the interests of the community as a whole. Thus the state may place restrictions on the use of property in order to preserve nature[86] or maintain the green belt[87] or protect the environment.[88]

There have been a number of cases involving the United Kingdom where planning matters have been at issue but these have mainly been complaints about the procedures used in the planning process. Thus the independence of the inspector employed by the Department of Environment was the issue in *Bryan v. United Kingdom*[89] where the applicant complained that the inspector was not an independent tribunal in terms of Article 6.[90] In *ISKON v. United Kingdom*[91] an enforcement notice had been served on a registered religious charity because there had allegedly been a

---

[83] Appl. 40302/98 [2001] E.H.R.L.R. 335.
[84] *Willis v. U.K.*, Appl. 36042/97, May 11, 1999.
[85] *Taylor v. U.K.*, Case C382/98, December 16, 1999.
[86] *Fredin v. Sweden* (1990) 13 E.H.R.R. 784.
[87] *supra*, no. 8.
[88] *Matos e Silva LDA v. Portugal* (1996) 24 E.H.R.R. 573.
[89] (1996) 21 E.H.R.R. 342.
[90] See also *County Properties Ltd v. The Scottish Ministers*, 2000 S.L.T. 965.
[91] Appl. 20490/92, 18 E.H.R.R. CD 133.

material change of use of the premises to a religious community. The applicants invoked Articles 9 (freedom of religion), 14 (freedom from discrimination) and Article 1 of the First Protocol. Although the European Commission noted that the enforcement notice interfered with their freedom of religion, the notice was held to be proportionate to the legitimate aims of the planning legislation and the decision had been based on proper planning considerations.

The use of green belt land for stationing a caravan was one of the issues in *Chapman v. United Kingdom*.[92] The applicant was a gypsy who wanted to live in a caravan on land she owned but the local planning authority refused to give her planning permission. She complained that the enforcement of planning restrictions to the land violated Article 8 and Article 1 of the First Protocol and additionally the decision constituted discrimination against gypsies as an ethnic group in breach of Article 14. The European Court held that although the planning decisions did hinder her enjoyment of the lifestyle which was common to her ethnic group, her individual desires had to be weighed against the environmental objections to the proposed use of the land. The interference with her enjoyment of the property was proportionate and fairly weighed against the requirements of Article 1 of the First Protocol.

One of the most drastic planning powers in terms of its impact on citizens is the ability of local authorities and certain other bodies to make a compulsory purchase order in respect of a citizen's property. The powers are statutory and strictly controlled as Lord Denning once remarked, "[i]t is a principle of our constitutional law that no citizen (is) to be deprived of his land by any public authority unless ... expressly authorised by Parliament and the public interest so demands."[93]   **11.19**

The two main Scottish planning statutes are the Town and Country Planning (Scotland) Act 1997 and the Local Government (Scotland) Act 1973. There is no doubt that by applying a compulsory purchase order to someone's property a public authority is interfering with that person's peaceful enjoyment of property in terms of Article 1 of the First Protocol and this has been acknowledged by the European Court in *Erkner and Hofauer v. Austria*,[94] although the United Kingdom legislation on compulsory purchase orders was successfully challenged in *Howard v. United Kingdom*.[95] Under the Convention such interference can be justified if there is a legitimate aim, the interference is in the public interest and it is proportionate. Springham suggests that public authorities

---

[92]   (2001) 10 B.H.R.C. 48.
[93]   *Prest v. Secretary of State for Wales* [983] 266 E.G. 527.
[94]   (1987) 9 E.H.R.R. 464.
[95]   (1987) 9 E.H.R.R. 117.

that intend to use compulsory purchase orders to acquire property should follow the rules of Article 1 of the First Protocol to ensure that their actions comply with the Convention. "Only when it is satisfied that the compulsory purchase order is the appropriate means to achieve the desired goal, and that the individuals whose property is to be acquired are not being unfairly burdened, would it be safe to proceed with the order."[96]

The owner of the property to be compulsorily acquired may object to the acquisition along with others with an interest.[97] If the owner, lessee or occupier (known as statutory objectors) object to the order, an inquiry must be held to investigate the matter. Other people may object to the purchase but an inquiry is not required to hear such "third party objectors" and they do not have an automatic right to be heard at any inquiry.

11.20   When an inquiry has been held, the reporter will make his recommendation to the minister and it will then be for the minister to exercise his discretion to confirm or reject the order. The minister need not follow the recommendation of the reporter but may take it into account in reaching his decision.[98] If the order is confirmed there remain two narrow statutory grounds of appeal. These are that there was no power to make the order or there were procedural defects that substantially prejudiced the application. The United Kingdom courts have interpreted these grounds as including others such as irrationality, illegality and breach of the principles of natural justice. It is therefore moot whether the Convention will add any protection to that already available in the United Kingdom courts.[99] The second aspect of a compulsory purchase order which may be the subject of challenge is the way in which compensation is calculated. There is no right at common law for someone to be compensated when they are deprived of their property but the courts will presume that the legislation intended to give compensation. The Convention does not require full compensation but there should be a fair balance of the individual's rights as against the public or general interest. In Scotland, if there is a dispute relating to the amount of compensation to be paid, the owner has the right to seek a determination by the Lands Tribunal for Scotland. There is little doubt that the Lands Tribunal will satisfy the requirements of Article 6 as regards a fair hearing.

Sometimes a development on neighbouring land will affect their peaceful enjoyment of the property. There is no right to

---

[96] K. Springham "Property Law" in *Practical Guide to Human Rights Law in Scotland* (Lord Reed, ed., 2001), p. 254.
[97] Acquisition of Land (Authorisation Procedure) (Scotland) Act 1947.
[98] *General Poster and Publicity Co. Ltd v. Secretary of State for Scotland*, 1960 S.C. 266.
[99] *supra*, no. 96 at 256.

compensation where planning permission is granted on a neighbouring property and this reduces the value of the complainant's property. The reduction in value of neighbouring land affected by a development is not a factor taken into consideration when a planning application is considered. The European Commission, however, has commented that such a detrimental effect on a complainant's property without compensation would breach the Convention.[1]

Current Issues involving Article 1 of the First Protocol

The Labour government elected in the United Kingdom in 1997   11.21
and the coalition Labour/Liberal Democrat government in Scotland have both embarked on various measures to change the way in which real property is held and controlled in their respective jurisdictions. There may be implications for Convention rights in each of these proposals.

(1) The "right to roam"—the Countryside and Rights of Way Act 2000

This Act was passed in the face of fierce opposition from the   11.22
Countryside Alliance and groups of landowners. It gives the public the right of access on foot "for open air recreation to open country". The landowners or occupiers will not be able to prevent such access. Arguably there is here a form of control of use of the land under the third *Sporrong* rule (discussed above) but it is likely that the government will be able to show that there is a legitimate aim in the legislation. The landowners may however argue that the measures are a disproportionate burden on them and that there is no compensation available for the infringement of their property rights. As discussed above, compensation is an important element in striking a fair balance and the lack of compensation would therefore be a reasonable argument to put forward. It is doubtful whether it would succeed because the government could argue, first, that the losses or costs are not material and so do not attract compensation. Secondly, the public interest requires that land is open to the enjoyment of the public at large.

(2) Hunting Rights

The issue of hunting as a sport is one of the most contentious issues   11.23
discussed by both the United Kingdom and the Scottish Parliaments. There has been little progress in the United Kingdom Parliament but the position is quite different in Scotland where a private member's bill is currently going through its stage two

---

[1] *S v. France* (1990) 65 D.R. 250.

scrutiny. The Protection of Wild Mammals (Scotland) Act 2002 prohibits the hunting of mammals such as foxes, hares and deer using dogs.

The European Court has had an opportunity to consider this issue in the context of property rights under Article 1 of the First Protocol. In *Chassagnou v. France*[2] a landowner objected on ethical grounds to be compelled to join an approved hunters' association, membership of which would transfer automatically the right to hunt over his land to the association. Only owners of land over a certain size had the right to object and this was held by the European Court to be a difference in treatment which was not justifiable in the public interest. The Court also found that compelling the applicant to transfer his hunting rights to others so that they could hunt over his land against his beliefs was a disproportionate burden and not justified under Article 1 of the First Protocol.

This case raises an interesting question: if hunting rights are rights of property protected by Article 1 of the First Protocol, what will happen when the 2002 Act comes into force? Will those who currently hunt over their own land, or allow their land to be so used, be able to argue that they have been deprived of these rights? A citizen exercising his hunting rights over his own land might find that his actions are criminalised by the Act. The issue of availability and adequacy of compensation was specifically excluded by Parliament from the Act. There remains the possibility therefore of challenges to the Act based on the issue of compensation.

(3) The Abolition of Feudal Tenure etc. (Scotland) Act 2000

11.24 This Act will abolish the current system of feudal tenure of land in Scotland on an "appointed day" which is expected to be at least two years after Royal Assent.

There will be no compensation available to the superior for the loss of the right to enforce feudal conditions or waive them in return for payment. The Act does allow the superior to invite the vassal to agree to retain the feuing conditions, although it is not clear why the vassal would want to do this. This invitation must be made before the appointed day[3] and if no agreement is reached the superior may apply to the Lands Tribunal for Scotland for a determination.[4]

The Act also acknowledges that the superior may have feued the land at either no or reduced consideration in the expectation that there will be a payment forthcoming if the land is able to be

---

[2]   (2000) 29 E.H.R.R. 615.
[3]   s.19.
[4]   s.20.

developed at a later date. Compensation may be paid to acknowledge the loss of the development value of the land. The superior must reserve the right to claim such compensation under section 35 by registering a claim before the appointed day. The compensation will be calculated according to section 37. If there is any dispute regarding the compensation amount, the European Court may very well take the view that the removal of the superior's rights was a legitimate aim of the government, in the public interest and thus the compensation regime is appropriate.

(4) Confiscation Orders

The Proceeds of Crime (Scotland) Act 1995 allows the Crown to 11.25
seek a confiscation order against a person who has been convicted of drug trafficking offences where the Crown believes that the person has property which was bought with the proceeds of that trafficking. A restraint order may be sought by the Crown to prevent the accused from dealing or disposing of his realisable property before the confiscation order is made. This would amount to a control of use of the property in Convention terms but such action has been recognised by the European Court as justified in the general interest and is not disproportionate.[5] However, if the criminal proceedings result in an acquittal, or no confiscation order is in fact made, the Convention will require the restraint order to be discharged quickly. In *Venditelli v. Italy*[6] an architect's flat was confiscated and action was taken against him for alleged infringement of planning regulations. On appeal, his conviction was quashed but the flat was not ordered to be returned to him by the court until 11 months later. This was held by the European Court to be a violation of Article 1 of the First Protocol.

In *H.M. Advocate v. McSalley*[7] an accused and his wife argued that a confiscation order deprived both of them of property and this was a violation of Article 1 because the family home would have to be sold to comply with the order. The High Court of Justiciary held that the order was not in excess of the value of their assets other than their home and thus they were not made homeless. The order did not infringe the principle of proportionality and the Court had in mind the underlying purposes of the statute in confirming the order.

The threat of a confiscation order being sought by the Crown will not interfere with an applicant's right to peaceful enjoyment of their property. In *H.M. Advocate v. Burns*[8] the Crown alleged that an

---

[5] *Raimondo v. Italy* (1994) 18 E.H.R.R. 237.
[6] (1995) 19 E.H.R.R. 464.
[7] 2000 S.L.T. 1235.
[8] 2000 S.L.T. 1242.

offender's former wife held property which fell to be treated as gifts from him. The woman sought a declaration that the confiscation of such property would create a real risk of interference with her right to peaceful enjoyment. The Court held that her application was premature because a confiscation order was a request to the Court to exercise its jurisdiction and until such jurisdiction had been exercised, no consequence of the order existed.

Conclusion

11.26 The right of property is one which affects virtually everyone within society and the European Convention recognises this partially by creating a right which is wider than most. However, the ability of the state to curtail the rights in property shows the difficulty encountered by the original contracting states. The scope of discretion given to states is so wide that it is only in the most extreme cases that a violation of the right will be upheld.[9] It also appears that so long as the compensation is forthcoming a state will escape sanction by the European Court.

---

[9] S. Greer, *The Margin of Appreciation: Interpretation and discretion under the European Convention on Human Rights* (2000).

CHAPTER 12

ARTICLE 2 OF PROTOCOL 1—RIGHT TO EDUCATION

"No one shall be denied the right to education. In the exercise of any functions which it assumes in relation to education and to teaching, the State shall respect the rights of parents to ensure such education and teaching is in conformity with their own religious and philosophical aims."

The Convention right to education given in Article 2 of Protocol 1   12.01
is not as strongly worded as other international treaties. For instance, the Universal Declaration of Human Rights 1948, Article 26 states "[e]veryone has the right to education". Such education "shall be directed to the full development of the human personality and to the strengthening of respect for human rights and fundamental freedoms". Parents "have a prior right to choose the kind of education that shall be given to their children". The International Covenant on Economic, Social and Cultural Rights, Article 3 states that the parties "recognise the right of everyone to education" and "education shall be directed to the full development of the human personality and the sense of its dignity". The United Kingdom is a signatory to these Treaties and the United Kingdom courts may use these as an aid to interpretation of any ambiguities in United Kingdom law.

The United Kingdom entered a reservation to the Protocol in March 1952, confining compliance to compatibility with "the provision of efficient instruction and training, and the avoidance of unreasonable public expenditure".[1] This means that the right to education must be balanced against the resources available. Unlike derogations, a designated reservation such as this one does not cease to have effect after five years.[2]

For the purposes of the Human Rights Act, public authorities in Scottish education will include schools, school boards and head-

---

[1]   Human Rights Act 1998, Sched. 3.
[2]   *ibid.*, s.16.

teachers. An independent school will likely be designated as a public authority when it is performing functions derived from the various Education Acts and when it is part of the state's system for providing education. Education is generally identified as a "public good" and a child must attend school, independent or otherwise, until the age of 16. Independent schools are registered and subject to inspection by Her Majesty's Inspectors of Schools and this state "interference" is legitimate to ensure a proper educational system is provided as a whole.[3] In *Costello-Roberts v. United Kingdom*[4] the European Court held that even if a state is not itself the education provider whose decision is being challenged, it is the state's responsibility under Article 1 of the Convention to secure the rights protected by the Convention to everyone within its jurisdiction. The right to education must be guaranteed equally to children in private and state schools.

12.02 A university will be regarded as a public authority in respect of most of its functions and will thus come within the ambit of the Human Rights Act and thus the Convention.

One area in which litigation might be expected is in the provision of denominational schools. The 1998 Act, section 13 requires a court or tribunal to "have particular regard to the importance of" the right to freedom of thought, conscience and religion. Any question which affects the exercise of a religious organisation of this right must be closely considered. It may be expected that a church school could still require that a head teacher is a practising member of that faith.

The right to education as a Convention right may not be used as a reason for the parents of a child to be granted exceptional leave to remain within the United Kingdom. In *R v. Secretary of State for Home Department, ex parte Holub,*[5] a Polish family were refused leave to remain in the United Kingdom, although they had pleaded that since their daughter had lived in the United Kingdom for five years, she would not be able to catch up in a Polish school and thus her hopes of attending university might be prejudiced. The Court of Appeal held that the right to education within the United Kingdom did not carry with it a right to remain in the United Kingdom.

12.03 The drafting of Article 2 of Protocol 1 caused problems because some states could envisage onerous positive and probably financial obligations on them. Originally the draft stated "[e]veryone has the right to education", as in the United Nations Declaration, but this was changed to the more negative "[n]o one shall be denied the right to education". A number of states were sensitive to the relationship that existed between the state sector and organised religion while

---

[3]	*Jordebo v. Sweden* (1987) 51 D.R. 125.
[4]	(1994) E.L.R. 1.
[5]	December 2000.

others wished to guard against state ideology in the schools. The right of parents to have their children educated as they wish is limited in the second sentence of the Article to those functions assumed by the state.

The right to education is not a traditional right in the same way as the right to freedom of expression or respect for private life. Rather, it is more of an economic or social right, and as such it is unusual in the Convention.

A number of states, including Germany, Ireland, Portugal and Sweden, attached reservations to the ratification of the First Protocol. The United Kingdom reservation states:

> "In view of certain provisions of the Education Acts in force in the UK, the principle affirmed in the second sentence of Article 2 is accepted by the UK only so far as it is compatible with the provision of effective instruction and training and the avoidance of unreasonable public expenditure."

The wording of the reservation reproduced the wording of the Education Act 1944 which was drafted to limit the obligation on education authorities to give effect to parental wishes.[6] However, a reservation such as that of the United Kingdom is not able to nullify the substance of the obligation imposed by the Article. The legal effect of a reservation upon a state's obligations is within the jurisdiction of the European Court of Human Rights and a reservation is only permitted to the extent that any specified national law at the time of ratification is not in conformity with a Convention provision.[7]

The meaning of the word "effective" within the reservation was considered in *M v. United Kingdom*[8] where a disabled child was held to be receiving an "adequate education" even though there was no lift within the school. The resource provisions of Article 2 gives a wide discretion to the relevant authorities on how to make the best use of their resources. The education provided must be "adequate and appropriate" and these will be assessed by the Convention authorities to ascertain whether they meet the meaning of those words. The Human Rights Act 1998, sections 1(2) and 15(1)(a) require national courts to interpret and apply the Convention rights to education subject to the United Kingdom reservation.

The validity of the reservation was questioned in *S.P. v. United Kingdom*[9] but on the facts of the case the Commission did not resolve the issue.

12.04

---

[6] Restated in the Education Act 1996, s.9.
[7] Art. 57; see *Belilos v. Switzerland* (1998) 10 E.H.R.R. 466.
[8] Appl. 29046/95, 27 E.H.R.R. CD 152.
[9] (1997) 23 E.H.R.R. CD 139.

There have been only four cases on Article 2 of Protocol 1 before the European Court but many more before the Commission.

First Sentence of the Article

12.05 The leading case for this Article is *Belgian Linguistics Case (No.2)*[10] where the European Court held that even though the sentence has a negative formulation it does enshrine a right, but this is narrow. The case involved consideration of whether children should be able to be taught in a language of their parents' choosing. The Court held that in every signatory state there was already a general educational system established so there was no question of a state being required to establish one. The right of every person was therefore "to avail themselves of the means of instruction existing at a given time".[11] The right would be meaningless if it did not imply the right to be educated in one of the national languages. However, it was not a requirement that states had to establish at their own expense, or subsidise, education of any particular type or at a particular level. In *R v. Secretary of State for Education and Employment, ex parte B (a Minor)*[12] the English courts referred to the *Belgian Linguistics* case. B applied for an extension of her assisted place to secondary school but this was rejected. She claimed statements made by Labour spokespersons before and after the 1997 General Election had given her a legitimate expectation that she would be able to continue on the scheme. Parliament had subsequently enacted legislation to abolish the assisted places scheme. The Court found that no legitimate expectation existed. The Secretary of State was obliged to implement statute and pre-election promises made by a party in opposition did not give rise to legitimate expectation because they were not a "public authority". There had been no violation of Article 2 of the First Protocol because the Article did not require states to establish at public expense education of any particular type or at any particular level.

The right must have a minimum content to have practical effect. Thus it implies the right to access to an educational institution existing at a given time, the right to an effective education, the right to be taught in a national language and the right to official recognition of qualifications obtained. It does not imply financial burdens such as the right to have children taught at state expense in a language of the parent's choice.

Thus there is no obligation to provide or subsidise a particular type of education.[13] The exception will arise where Article 14 is

[10] (1968) 1 E.H.R.R. 252.
[11] *ibid.* p.281.
[12] [1999] E.L.R. 471.
[13] *X. v. U.K.* (1978) 14 D.R. 179; *Simpson v. U.K.* (1989) 64 D.R. 188.

engaged. If the state funds some schools but not others, this may be discrimination if the schools are in a similar or same situation.

There is limited protection for further and higher education in the   12.06
Article. In *Campbell and Cosans v. United Kingdom*[14] the education
of a child was defined as:

> "the whole process whereby, in any society, adults endeavour
> to transmit their beliefs, culture and other values to the young,
> whereas teaching or instruction refer in particular to the
> transmission of knowledge and to intellectual development."

The Commission in the *Belgian Linguistics* case said that the right
to education includes entry to nursery, primary, secondary and
higher education. This was later distinguished by the Commission
in *X v. United Kingdom*.[15] There must be a universal right of access
to elementary education but in advanced studies individual rights
will be more limited. Later, in *X v. United Kingdom*[16] it was held
that it was not incompatible with the Convention to restrict access
to higher education to students who have attained a particular
academic level.

Second Sentence of the Article

This sentence was inserted because of fears that states would   12.07
attempt to indoctrinate children through the education system, a
not irrational fear given that the end of the Second World War had
only occurred seven years before and the Cold War was in its
infancy. The states are therefore required to take into account the
parent's religious and philosophical beliefs.

The sentence refers to the "functions" of the state in relation to
education and teaching. This has been interpreted as including all of
the state's involvement in education. In *Campbell and Cosans v.
United Kingdom*[17] the parents objected to the use of corporal
punishment and said that the exclusion of a pupil until he accepted
such punishment, was contrary to Article 2 of the First Protocol.
The government argued that the second sentence of the Article
applied to the curriculum content and functions such as discipline
were ancillary administrative matters. The European Court held
that the method of discipline used in a school could be an "integral
part" of the school's ethos and so the parents could object on
philosophical grounds.

More recently the European Court held that requiring the

---

[14] (1982) 4 E.H.R.R. 293, para. 33.
[15] (1975) 2 D.R. 50.
[16] (1980) 23 D.R. 228.
[17] (1982) 4 E.H.R.R. 293.

children of Jehovah's Witnesses to take part in a school parade to commemorate the outbreak of a war was within the scope of the Article. The Court, however, found that there had been no violation on the facts because there was nothing in the purpose of the parade that would offend the religious beliefs of the parents.[18]

12.08   The word "respect" in the sentence implies a positive obligation on the state to strike a balance between minority and majority views and to treat minorities fairly. There is, however, no absolute right for parents to have their child educated in accordance with their religious and philosophical beliefs, only to have these "respected". Thus in *W and K.L. v. Sweden*[19] the state was not required to provide financial assistance to alternative private schools such as Steiner schools. In *X v. United Kingdom*[20] the Commission held that there was no requirement on the state to fund a private non-denominational school in Northern Ireland if the parents' philosophical convictions could be respected within the existing education system.

The convictions of the parents have to be those "worthy of respect in a democratic society" and they must not be incompatible with other human rights. The parents' views have to be sufficiently serious, important and cogent to be referred to as "convictions".[21] The word "conviction" was held not to be synonymous with "opinion" or "idea" as in Article 10 but was closer in meaning to "beliefs" as in Article 9. Such convictions must not conflict "with the fundamental right of the child to education, the whole of Article 2 being dominated by its first sentence".[22] However, the Court ruled that "the applicants' views relate to a weighty and substantial aspect of human life and behaviour, namely the integrity of the person, the propriety or otherwise of the infliction of corporal punishment and the exclusion of the distress which the risk if such punishment entails."[23] The rights of the applicants in respect of the second sentence of Article 2 were violated; their views were weighty and substantive enough to satisfy the criterion of philosophical conviction and were not simply an opinion.

The parent's right is the right to protect the interests of the child with respect to education. Consequently the views of a parent who does not have custody of the child will not be given the same weight as the parent or guardian of the child. The parent's right will not overthrow the child's right to an education.

---

[18] *Valsamis and Efstration v. Greece* (1996) 24 E.H.R.R. 294.
[19] (1985) D.R. 143.
[20] (1978) 14 D.R. 179.
[21] *Campbell and Cosans v. U.K.* (1982) 4 E.H.R.R. 293.
[22] *ibid.*, p.305.
[23] *supra*, no.21.

In *Kjeldsen, Busk Madsen and Pedersen v. Denmark*[24] the parents 12.09
objected to their children receiving compulsory sex education at
state primary schools. They had attempted to have their children
exempted from these lessons but were refused. The European Court
decided that the sex education was not an attempt by the state to
indoctrinate the children and the education did not offend the
parents' religious and philosophical convictions. The lessons were
aimed at giving correct and precise knowledge and did not advocate
any specific kind of sexual behaviour. They did not prevent the
parents from providing their own guidance or educating their
children at home. However, the information or knowledge included
in the curriculum had to be presented in an "objective, critical and
pluralistic manner. The state is forbidden to pursue an aim of
indoctrination that might be considered as not respecting parents'
religious and philosophical convictions".[25] The setting of the
curriculum was for the state and parental rights did not extend to
demands on the school curriculum.

The right to education in Article 2 of the First Protocol overlaps
with a considerable number of other Articles such as Articles 3, 8, 9,
10 and 14. Article 10 (freedom of expression) is a qualified right
limited by various purposes including the protection of the rights of
others. The right of a teacher to freely express his views may be
legitimately restricted to protect the rights of pupils under Article 2
of the First Protocol. In *X v. United Kingdom*[26] a teacher was
forbidden to wear religious and anti-abortion stickers on his clothes
and he complained that this violated his right to freedom of
expression. The teacher worked in a non-denominational school
and the Commission found that he should therefore have regard to
the rights of parents to respect for their religious and philosophical
beliefs. The interference with his freedom of expression was
therefore justified.

Article 14 has implications for the right to education. It requires
that there is no discrimination between how Convention guarantees
are applied and in that sense, it broadens the protection of the other
Articles if they are applied in a discriminatory way. In the *Belgian
Linguistics (No. 2)*[27] the Court stated,

> "a measure which in itself is in conformity with the
> requirements of the Article enshrining the right or freedom
> in question may however infringe this Article when read in
> conjunction with Article 14 for the reason that it is of a
> discriminatory nature."

---

[24] (1976) 1 E.H.R.R. 711.
[25] *ibid.*, p.731.
[26] (1979) 16 D.R. 101.
[27] (1968) 1 E.H.R.R. 252 at para. 9.

Thus a state must ensure that any differences in treatment have a reasonable and objective justification and they pursue a legitimate aim. The differences must be proportionate as between the measures employed and the aim to be achieved.

12.10   In *Verein Gemeinsam Lernen v. Austria*[28] the applicant complained that higher state subsidies were allocated to private church schools than non-religious private schools such as his one. The non-religious schools had to satisfy a criterion of "need". The Commission found there was no discrimination because the church schools were so widespread that if the educational services they provided had to be provided by the state, there would be a substantial financial burden on the state.

Education and the Adult

12.11   It is clear from the wording of the first sentence that the Article does not apply only to children. The wording is "no-one" not "no child" and the implication must be that the education of adults is also covered by the Article. The main difference between the child's access to education and that by an adult to higher education is that the former is a universal right whereas access to higher education will be dependent on the aptitude of the person and the resources available. In *X v. United Kingdom*[29] a student who had failed his first year examinations and the resits complained that he had been excluded from the university. The state was able to show that the failures and the student's poor attendance were the reasons for the exclusion and the Commission accepted that there was no violation of the Article.

The second sentence of the Article refers to respect for religious and philosophical convictions of the parents. It is not clear whether such a right arises with regard to an adult student. Must the subject be taught so as not to offend the student's religious and philosophical convictions or would such a requirement violate the lecturer's freedom of expression under Article 10? There is no mention of academic freedom in the Convention but it is likely that the freedom of thought, conscience and religion promoted by Article 9 would apply here unless the teaching approach amounted to ideological indoctrination. In England, the articles of government of further education colleges requires the rules for academic staff to respect their academic freedom.

There have been a few cases before the Convention authorities regarding the education facilities provided for prisoners. In *Natoli v. Italy*[30] the Commission found that there was no obligation on states

---

[28]   (1995) 82 D.R. 41.
[29]   (1980) 23 D.R. 228.
[30]   Appl. 26161/95, May 18, 1998, EComHR.

to provide elementary education in prisons or to organise retraining programmes for prisoners.[31]

EDUCATION IN SCOTLAND

The right to education in Scotland is found in two main statutes, the Education (Scotland) Act 1980 as amended and the Standards in Scotland's Schools (Scotland) Act 2000.   12.12

The 1980 Act, section 1(1) provides that each education authority has a duty "to secure that there is made for their area adequate and efficient provision of school education". Thus the 1980 Act is not expressed as positive rights but has the more negative tone of the Convention. It simply places duties on the education authority and parents. However, the 2000 Act, section 1 states that "it shall be the right of every child of school age to be provided with school education by, or by virtue of arrangements made, or entered into, by an education authority". The right is conferred on children of school age only. Thus young people aged 16 to 18 years are excluded from the right to education although the education authority is required to secure their education in terms of section 2(1). Section 1 does not explicitly confer a right to mainstream education which campaigners for children with special needs found disappointing. However, section 15(1) requires that education should be provided in a mainstream school unless one of the circumstances in section 15(3) exists. The presumption is, however, that such circumstances will arise "only exceptionally". The three circumstances are that the education is not suited to the ability or aptitude of the child; or the education is incompatible with the provision of efficient education for children with whom the child would be educated; or the education would result in unreasonable public expenditure.

Section 2(1) of the 2000 Act goes on to place a duty on each education authority to secure education that is "directed to the development of the personality, talents and mental and physical abilities of the child or young person to their fullest potential". These words, taken from the United Nations Convention on the Rights of the Child, Article 29, require state education to be centred on the needs of the individual child. It is notable that there is no financial or policy qualification in section 2(1). Section 2(2) requires the education authority to consult with the child or young person regarding his or her education, although the form of consultation is very general. The education authority "shall have due regard, so far as is reasonably practicable, to the views of the child or young

---

[31] *Valasinas v. Lithuania,* Appl. 44558/98, March 14, 2000, EComHR.

person ... in decisions that significantly affect that child or young person, taking account of the child or young person's age and maturity". The duty only applies to education provided directly or indirectly by an education authority and does not therefore apply to independent schools.

12.13   There have been relatively few cases involving education issues before the Scottish courts and certainly the rise in education law cases seen in England has not been replicated here. In one case, the duty to provide "adequate and efficient" education was held to be a very "general" duty qualified by a number of factors such as resources, cost and practicability.[32]

"School education" in the 1980 Act is defined as "progressive education appropriate to the requirements of pupils in attendance at schools, regard being had to the age, aptitude and ability of such pupils".[33] No cases to date have centred on the education provided for children according to their "age, aptitude and ability".

A parent of a school age child is under a duty to provide efficient education suited to their child's age, aptitude and ability. The term "parent" is very wide and includes those who have parental responsibility and rights, has a duty to maintain and has care and control of the child.[34] Parents must fulfill their statutory duty to ensure their child receives appropriate education[35] or face criminal proceedings. The duty can be fulfilled by sending the child to a state school, another type of school or by any other competent means such as schooling at home. Where the child is sent to a state school, the education authority is under a duty to educate the child in accordance with the parent's wishes except where this is incompatible with the provision of suitable instruction and training and to avoid unreasonable public expenditure.[36] This wording echoes the Convention at Article 2 of the First Protocol and the United Kingdom's reservation to Article 2.

12.14   A recent case raised the issue of whether a parent should be prosecuted for the child's truancy where the parent could do nothing to prevent it. In *O'Hagan v. Rea*[37] a mother was charged under section 35 of the 1980 Act with failing to ensure her child attended school regularly. The sheriff found that section 35(1) was incompatible with the Convention because those liable to be found guilty would include those parents who could do nothing to prevent the actions. The court therefore reinterpreted section 42(1)(c) of the Act by including any reasonable excuse afforded by a parent, thus

---

[32]   *Walker v. Strathclyde R.C. (No. 1)*, 1986 S.L.T. 523.
[33]   1980 Act, s.5(1).
[34]   *ibid.*, s.135(1).
[35]   *ibid.*, s.35(1).
[36]   *ibid.*, s. 28(1).
[37]   2001 S.L.T. (Sh.Ct) 30.

allowing section 35(1) to be re-interpreted to let parents defend themselves against criminal liability.

An area of increasing concern among parents concerns a placing request for a child in a school which he or she would not normally attend because they do not live in that school's catchment area. If an education authority fails to educate the child in accordance with parental wishes, the decision may be challenged in court, either by way of statutory appeal, judicial review or now by mounting a Convention challenge. The 1980 Act, section 28A(1) provides for the "duty of the authority to place the child accordingly" unless one of 11 statutory grounds exist.[38] If the placing request fails an appeal is available to the sheriff court. The sheriff must consider all of the circumstances of the case and may not confirm the education authority's decision unless he finds the grounds stated for refusal exist and it is reasonable to confirm the decision.[39]

A parent may seek judicial review of a decision of the education authority in the pursuance of its statutory duties such as in proposed school closures. The Court of Session will not normally uphold such applications where the education authority is exercising its wide statutory discretion. In *Harvey v. Strathclyde Regional Council*[40] the Outer House judge considered the overwhelming parental opposition to a school's closure and held that the education authority had to show it had taken due regard of the wishes of the parents. On appeal, the Inner House considered the approach was wrong. "This Court may only interfere with the carrying out of the respondents' intention (to close the school) if it is satisfied that the decision to go ahead now is so obviously unreasonable that no reasonable education authority would have taken it."[41] Generally in cases of school closures parents have not been able to show that the decision was taken in breach of the authority's duty under section 28(1).[42]

In seeking judicial review of a decision or challenging a decision   12.15
using a statutory appeal procedure, the parents seek to challenge a specific decision made under statutory authority. If they attempted to mount a challenge under the Convention, this would involve showing that the education authority had not fulfilled its legal duties because of the operation of a state law, a difficult task.

Suspension and Expulsion from School

Suspending or expelling a child from school will not breach the   12.16

---

[38] s.28A(3).
[39] s. 28F.
[40] 1989 S.L.T. 25.
[41] Lord President, Lord Emslie at p.33.
[42] *King v. East Ayrshire Council*, 1998 S.L.T. 1287; *Regan v. City of Dundee Council*, 1997 S.L.T. 139.

Convention. However, there are two provisos: the expulsion must not prevent education being given elsewhere, and it must not breach another Convention right, such as Article 6. It may be possible to interpret education as a civil right thus bringing it within the ambit of Article 6. So procedures for suspending and expelling a child need to be within Article 6.[43] In England new guidance was given to schools on September 1, 2000. This was intended to strengthen the powers of headteachers in dealing with serious breaches of discipline and to prevent appeal panels from reinstating a pupil who has been permanently excluded for serious actual or threatened violence, sexual abuse, drug trafficking or persistent and malicious disruptive behaviour.[44]

In *P (by his mother and next friend) v. National Union of Schoolmasters/Union of Women Teachers*[45] a pupil with a very poor disciplinary record was permanently excluded from the school in June 2000 but was reinstated after an appeal to the school's governing body. In October 2000 he was again excluded for a fixed period of two days. The teaching staff at the school believed that the boy could not be taught in a standard classroom because of his disruptive behaviour. After the head teacher ordered that he be taught in a standard classroom, a teacher's union balloted its members in the school to take industrial action short of strike action and this was overwhelmingly agreed. The union members then refused to teach the boy and he was required to work on his own in a separate room with two supply teachers. He alleged that the industrial action had adversely affected his education and sued for damages. The Commercial Court confirmed that a school is entitled to put a disruptive pupil in a separate room so long as the action is taken for sound educational reasons. The segregation did not mean that there was any infringement of his right to education under Article 2 of the First Protocol.

In Scotland a child under 16 who is excluded from school has the right to appeal against the exclusion. The Standards in Scotland's Schools etc. (Scotland) Act 2000, section 41 states that if a child is 12 years or older[46] it is presumed that he "is of sufficient age and maturity to have understanding" sufficient to instruct a solicitor. Failing this the parent would appeal on the child's behalf.

The Rights and Duties of Children

12.17 Generally it is not possible for a child to pursue a violation of their

---

[43] *R v. Secretary of State for Education and Employment, ex p. B* [2001] EWHC Admin. 229.
[44] DfEE PN 357/00.
[45] 2001 *The Times*, May 3, 2001 (Comm. Court).
[46] Following the provisions of the Age of Legal Capacity (Scotland) Act 1991, s.2(4A) and (4B).

right to education independently; such action will be taken in the child's name by the parent or guardian. There are, however, anomalies here. For instance, a pupil raised an action for damages against the local authority after an accident at school.[47] This was possible because the child was competent to instruct a solicitor but under Scots law that same child could not seek a remedy if their right to education had been violated.

The Children (Scotland) Act 1995, section 6 requires parents to have regard to the views of their child when making major decisions about their education. The term "parent" is defined for the purposes of the 1995 Act in section 15 and it is a narrower definition than that in the education laws. The 2000 Act requires an educational authority to "have due regard, so far as is reasonably practicable, to the views (if there is a wish to express them) of the child or young person in decisions that significantly affect that child or young person, taking into account the child or young person's age and maturity".[48] The Act also gives a child the right to appeal against his or her exclusion where the child is competent to instruct a solicitor.[49]

The European Convention on Human Rights is not violated if a school implements a policy of compulsory school uniform.[50] However, there may be a violation where a school has a compulsory uniform which does not take into account the religious and cultural beliefs of its pupils to wear certain items of clothing, for instance, girls of the Muslim faith may wish to wear trousers and a headscarf. Issues of free speech arose in the United States where the courts have upheld the schools' policies which prohibit clothing which disrupts the academic environment of the school rather than trying to devise dress codes prohibiting all offensive messages and slogans.[51]

School Discipline

The European Court has held that school discipline is not a breach of the Convention in itself. In *Valsamis v. Greece*[52] the Court held that "the imposition of disciplinary penalties is an integral part of the process whereby a school seeks to achieve the object for which it was established, including the development and moulding of the character and mental powers of its pupils".

12.18

Disciplinary methods may not involve as a by-product a breach of another right such as searching a pupil's locker or school bag,

---

[47] *Taylor v. Fife R.C.*, 1991 S.L.T. 80.
[48] s.2(2).
[49] 2000 Act, s.40.
[50] *Stevens v. U.K.* (1986) 46 D.R. 245.
[51] M. Kuhn "Student Dress Codes in the public schools" (1996) J. of Law and Education, Vol. 25(1) 83.
[52] (1996) 24 E.H.R.R. 294.

which may breach Article 8. If it is justified and reasonable it will probably be accepted but the right of the child to dignity in disciplinary proceedings is important. This right was recognised by Article 28 of the United Nations Convention on the Rights of the Child 1989, to which the United Kingdom is a signatory and which was given effect by the Children Act 1989 in England and Wales and the Children (Scotland) Act 1995.

If a child is bullied at school, and the school authorities do not deal with it, this may violate the child's right under Article 3. It is possible that a refusal to exclude a bully from school or a direction by an appeals panel to reinstate a bully would breach the rights of the victim.

Special Educational Needs

12.19   Applicants have generally been unsuccessful in cases regarding special needs education before the European Court. The Commission has held that an education authority is entitled to withhold a place in a mainstream school where a placement would require costly special facilities for the child with special needs[53] and where the transport costs are too high.[54] The Commission has also held that parents may not insist on the child being placed in a special school where the education authority has decided that the child's special needs can be met within a mainstream school.[55] It is likely that Convention rights will not be violated where a local authority exercises its discretion in a proportionate way. However, it was held by the House of Lords in *R v. East Sussex County Council, ex parte Tandy*[56] that an education authority could not cut for financial reasons alone the educational provision for a long-term sick child who could not attend school. Complete withdrawal of the provision on financial grounds would probably have violated Article 2 of the First Protocol.[57]

In Scotland a child with special needs may have their education continued beyond the age of 16 and the duty to educate is owed until such education ceases.[58] The Disability Discrimination Act 1995, Part IV, Education, will start to come into operation in September 2002 for all education sectors. In addition, the Scottish Parliament is currently considering the Education (Disability Strategies and Pupils' Records) Bill which aims to improve access to education for children with disabilities.

---

[53]   *P.D. v. U.K.* (1989) 62 D.R. 292.
[54]   *Cohen v. U.K.* (1996) 21 E.H.R.R. CD 104.
[55]   *Simpson v. U.K.* (1989) 64 D.R. 188.
[56]   [1998] A.C. 714.
[57]   A. Bradley "Scope for Review: the Convention Right to Education and the Human Rights Act 1998" [1999] E.H.R.L.R. 395.
[58]   Education (Scotland) Act 1980, s.135 and ss.60–65.

CHAPTER 13

RIGHT TO AN EFFECTIVE REMEDY

ARTICLE 13—RIGHT TO AN EFFECTIVE REMEDY

"An effective remedy before a national authority must be secured to those whose rights and freedoms as set forth in the convention have been violated."

When the convention was incorporated into domestic law by the Human Rights Act there was one notable omission. Article 13 was not included.[1] The reason for the exclusion is that the Act lays down its own structure for remedies.[2] There was concern that the inclusion of Article 13 among Convention rights might undermine the interpretation of the Act itself. This could have lead to a period of uncertainty and confusion. Article 13 itself still provides a right which can be protected by a claim to the European Court of Human Rights where the remedies provided by domestic law are not effective. The action in such a case is against the state itself whereas the remedies provided under the Human Rights Act are against the individual public authority responsible for the infringement of a Convention right.

13.01

Article 13 is central to the co-operative relationship between the Convention and a national legal system. More comprehensive and effective national remedies mean that the number of applications to the European Court of Human Rights will decrease. The remedy need not be judicial. Remedies which consist of an appeal to a Minister will suffice provided that they are effective. The obligations of the state to provide an effective remedy will depend upon the particular Article which has been contravened. It was held in *Halford v. United Kingdom*,[3] that Article 13 had been violated in that the Interception of Communications Act 1985 did not apply to

---

[1]   Human Rights Act 1998, s.1(1)(a).
[2]   *ibid.*, ss.7–9.
[3]   *Halford v. United Kingdom* [1997] I.R.L.R. 471; (1997) 24 E.H.R.R. 253; 3 B.H.R.C. 31; [1998] Crim. L.R. 753; (1997) 94(27) L.S.G. 24.

calls made through Merseyside Police's internal telephone system and Halford had no other means of redress under United Kingdom law.

REMEDIES UNDER THE SCOTLAND ACT

13.02 The Scotland Act provides for challenges if the Scottish Parliament or the Scottish Executive acts outside its competence. An action taken under the Scotland Act raising an issue of the competence of the Parliament or the executive is referred to as a "devolution issue". Breach of obligations under the European Convention on Human Rights is one of the grounds for challenge. Devolution issues are defined as the following questions:

(1) Whether an Act of the Scottish Parliament, or a provision within it, is within the legislative competence of the Parliament.

(2) Whether a function is a function of a Scottish Minister or the First Minister or the Lord Advocate.

(3) Whether the exercise of a function by a member of the Scottish Executive would be within devolved competence.

(4) Whether the exercise of a function by a member of the Scottish Executive is or would be incompatible with E.C. law or Convention rights.

(5) Whether a failure to act by a member of the Scottish executive is incompatible with E.C. law or Convention rights.

(6) Any other question as to whether a function is within devolved competence and any other question arising by virtue of the Act about reserved matters.

A devolution issue may arise in any case, civil or criminal, anywhere in the United Kingdom. The issue may be raised by any party to the case but in criminal proceedings there are time limits for raising the issue. In cases on indictment the issue must be raised within seven days of the indictment being served and in summary cases the notice of devolution issue must be given before the accused is asked to plead.[4]

Schedule 6 sets out the rules as to which court or tribunal may hear the devolution issue and the appropriate rules of the courts in Scotland were amended accordingly.[5] Courts and tribunals else-

---

[4] Rules of Court 1999, Chap. 40.

[5] Act of Sederunt (Devolution Issue Rules) 1999 (S.I. 1999 No.1345) for civil proceedings and Act of Adjournal (Devolution Issue Rules) 1999 (S.I. 1999 No.1346) for criminal proceedings.

where in the United Kingdom are also detailed in the schedule.[6]

As the Lord Advocate and the Advocate General for Scotland 13.03 have a special interest in ensuring that devolution issues are resolved, the Scotland Act provides that either officer may institute proceedings to determine a devolution issue.[7] Devolution issues can also be raised by parties in any legal proceedings, whether they are proceedings instigated for the specific purpose of determining a devolution issue, or proceedings where the original purpose was the resolution of another matter but a devolution issue has arisen during the course of the proceedings. Devolution issues may be raised in both civil and criminal courts. They may be raised in courts at any level of the hierarchy. This means that in civil cases devolution issues may be raised in the sheriff court, the Court of Session and the House of Lords and in criminal cases devolution issues may be raised in the district court, sheriff court and High Court of Justiciary. If neither the Lord Advocate nor the Advocate General is a party to the legal proceedings, notice must be given to both the Lord Advocate and the Advocate General that a devolution issue is to be raised so that they may participate in the proceedings.

Under the Scotland Act 1998, where a declaration of incompatibility of an Act of the Scottish Parliament is made, the tribunal or court may make an order removing or limiting any retrospective effect of the decision, or suspending the decision for any period and on any conditions to allow the defect to be corrected.[8] Normally when a legal provision or action is found to be *ultra vires* the provision or action is treated as null and void. However, actions in court to challenge the validity of a provision or action made under the Scotland Act will take time to be heard and decided and before the case is raised the provision or action may have been acted upon. This would lead to uncertainty, as people could not rely on the provision in case a retrospective decision of invalidity was made. The Scotland Act therefore allows the court to remove or limit any retrospective effect of the decision. The court is also required to have regard to the effect of an order on persons who are not parties to the proceedings.

The Scotland Act 1998 gives powers to various bodies to correct defects in legislation, including defects which lead to Convention incompatibility. The powers are intended to allow amendment to be carried out as quickly as possible using a "fast track" procedure. Judicial review actions may be brought with regard to proposed legislation.[9] The Secretary of State may intervene to pass an order

---

[6] Scotland Act 1998, Sched. 6, para. 1.
[7] *ibid.*, Sched. 6, para. 4(1).
[8] *ibid.*, s.102.
[9] *ibid.*, s.33.

preventing the Presiding Officer of the Scottish Parliament from submitting a bill for Royal Assent where it is beyond the legislative competence.[10] The Act also provides that the Secretary of State may make an order to prevent an action of a member of the Scottish Executive which the Secretary of State believes is incompatible with an international obligation, other than the European Convention on Human Rights. A Secretary of State may also make an order requiring a member of the Scottish Executive to implement an international obligation. These measures should have the effect of preventing infringements of rights and reducing the number of challenges to Scottish legislation which may otherwise arise through the courts and tribunals

Definition of a Victim

13.04 Challenges on the basis of non-compliance with the Convention may only be raised by a person claiming to be a victim of a violation of their Convention rights.[11] This is a different standard from the normal standard of "title and interest" to sue. The concern that the incorporation of the European Convention on Human Rights could give rise to an unmanageable number of ill-founded actions is addressed in the Act. There is a provision that a devolution issue shall not be taken to arise in any proceedings merely because of any contention of a party to the proceedings, which appears to the court or tribunal before which the proceedings take place to be frivolous or vexatious.[12]

Title and Interest

13.05 The current test for standing to bring a case before the Scottish courts is that of title and interest to sue. This continues to be the appropriate test except when a devolution issue or a claim under the procedure under the Human Rights Act is brought. The general rule is that the Scottish courts can only exercise their jurisdiction when an action has been raised by an appropriate person. In order to qualify as an appropriate person to bring an action an individual or organisation must establish that he has *locus standi*, or standing.[13] Cases cannot be brought by persons whose rights and interests have not been affected by the decision which is being challenged.[14] An applicant who has interest but cannot establish that there is a relationship that gives him title has no standing to bring an action. In practice it is often difficult to separate title and

---

[10] Scotland Act 1998, s.35.
[11] *ibid.*, s.100, Human Rights Act 1998, s.7.
[12] *ibid.*, Sched. 6, para. 2.
[13] See Finch and Ashton, *Administrative Law in Scotland*, pp. 387–407.
[14] *D & J Nicol v. Dundee Harbour Trustees*, 1915 S.C. (HL) 7.

interest and in some circumstances judges may simply state that a person has or has not "title and interest" rather than deliberating separately on the qualifying title and interest.[15]

A definition of "title" was given in the judgement of Lord Dunedin in the case of *D and J Nicol v. Dundee Harbour Trustees.*[16] Lord Dunedin said that "[f]or a person to have title he must be a party (using the word in its widest sense) to some legal relation which gives him some right which the person against whom he raises the action either infringes or denies."

Even if a person qualifies as having title to raise an issue, the court must also be satisfied that he or she has an interest to do so. This requires that the particular issue is of real concern to the party and not an academic issue or merely something that is being raised as matter of general public-spirited concern.[17] The case which is regarded as the current leading authority in relation to title and interest is that of *Scottish Old People's Welfare Council Petitioners.*[18] The Scottish Old People's Welfare Council (commonly known as Age Concern Scotland) raised a petition for judicial review challenging the legality of a circular setting out the rules for extra social security payments in severe weather conditions. The chief adjudication officer argued that the petitioners had no title and interest. In relation to the issue of title it was held that any member of the public had a title to sue, and accordingly there was no reason in principle why members of the public should be deprived of that title simply because they combined together into an association. It was held, however, that the interest of the petitioners was too remote to give them a right to challenge the validity of the circular. An important factor was that Age Concern was an organisation whose purpose was to further the interests of elderly people. Its own membership did not necessarily include elderly people who would be in a position to benefit from a favourable decision. Age Concern Scotland was held, therefore, to have title but no interest to challenge the official guidance that limited the making of supplementary payment to old people during severe weather conditions

In the contrasting case of *Wilson v. Independent Broadcasting* 13.06 *Authority,*[19] a broader approach was taken to the issue of title and interest. Three members of a group campaigning in the period leading up to the referendum on devolution of political power to

[15] *Cockenzie and Port Seton Community Council v. East Lothian D.C.,* 1996 S.C.L.R. 209; *Lennox v. Scottish Branch of the British Show Jumping Association,* 1996 S.L.T. 353.
[16] 1915 S.C. (HL) 7.
[17] *Docherty v. Burgh of Monifieth,* 1971 S.L.T. 13.
[18] *Scottish Old People's Welfare Council Petitioners,* 1987 S.L.T. 179.
[19] *Wilson v. Independent Broadcasting Authority* (1979) S.C. 351.

Scotland were held to have title and interest to sue for an interdict to restrain the showing of certain political broadcasts by the Independent Broadcasting Authority. The broadcasts did not maintain a proper balance between opposing views. Lord Ross could see "no reason in principle why an individual should not sue in order to prevent a breach by a public body of a duty owed by that public body to the public".

Article 34 states that the European Court of Human rights may receive applications from any person, non-governmental organisation or group of individuals claiming to be a victim of a violation of the Convention.[20] This definition is not particularly helpful and decided cases have not shown a high degree of consistency in the approach which has been adopted to the issue of entitlement to sue. It is not always possible to separate consideration of standing from judgments on the merits of the particular case and the decisions have often depended on specific facts. Despite the wording of Article 34, an assertion that one's rights have been violated is not sufficient to qualify a person as a victim but there have been some decisions which seem to show that an actual infringement of rights of a specific individual may not always be required. In *Klass v. Germany* the Court accepted that a person may be a victim of a violation of a Convention right if a law exists which contravenes the Convention, even if it had not been proved that the law in question had ever been implemented to his detriment. The case was brought by five German lawyers who claimed that their rights under Articles 6, 8 and 13 had been infringed by a federal law which authorised the opening of letters and tapping of telephones. In that case it may have been difficult to identify victims as the law in question related to covert surveillance by the state. [21] Similarly in *Dudgeon v. United Kingdom*[22] the European Court of Human Rights held that the very existence of a law which made homosexual conduct a criminal offence, continuously and directly affects the private life of a homosexual man, even though he had not been prosecuted. The existence of the law meant that "either he respects the law and refrains from engaging ... in prohibited sexual acts, or he commits such acts and thereby becomes liable to prosecution". It appears therefore that a substantial risk that a person may be affected directly and personally may be sufficient.

---

[20] Art. 34 of the Convention, as modified by the 11th Protocol (formerly Art. 25).
[21] *Klass v. Germany* (1978) Ser. A, No.28, 2 E.H.R.R. 214, para. 34.
[22] *Dudgeon v. U.K.* (1981) Ser. A, No. 45, 4 E.H.R.R. 149, para. 41.

PROCEDURES FOR CHALLENGE UNDER THE SCOTLAND ACT

Civil Proceedings

Court of Session

Any devolution issue must be raised in the pleadings of the case. 13.07
The facts and points of law must be specified in sufficient detail to
allow the court to make an informed decision as to the existence of
a devolution issue.[23] This must be done before the proceedings
commence unless the court decides otherwise.[24] The Lord Advocate
and the Advocate General must then be given notice of the
devolution issue and they then have 14 days in which to decide
whether to take part in the proceedings. A further period of seven
days is allowed for them to make written submissions.[25]

Sheriff Court

The rules of procedure for the sheriff court are similar. A party 13.08
must raise a devolution issue before the formal hearing of evidence
before the sheriff commences, unless the sheriff determines
otherwise.[26] Notice must be given of the devolution issue to the
Lord Advocate and the Advocate General. The Lord Advocate and
Advocate General may be allowed 14 days, or such other period as
the sheriff may determine, to give notice if they wish to enter an
appearance as a party to the proceedings.

Criminal Proceedings

In the case of solemn proceedings, a party who intends to raise a 13.09
devolution issue must give written notice to the clerk of the court
within seven days of the indictment being served. This must be
copied to all of the parties and to the Lord Advocate and the
Advocate General for Scotland.[27] A party to summary proceedings
who wishes to raise a devolution issue must give written notice to
the clerk of the court before the accused is called on to plead. This
must be copied to all of the parties and to the Lord Advocate and
the Advocate General for Scotland.

---

[23] Act of Sederunt (Devolution Issue Rules) 1999 (S.I. 1999 No. 1345), r.25A.4(1) of
the Court of Session.
[24] r.25A.3(1) of the Court of Session.
[25] Act of Sederunt (Devolution Issue Rules) 1999 (S.I. 1999 No. 1345), rr. 25.A.5,
and 25.A.6.of the Court of Session.
[26] Act of Sederunt (Proceedings for the Determination of Devolution Issues Rules)
1999.
[27] Act of Adjournal)Criminal Procedure Rules) 1996, Chap. 40, added by Act of
Adjournal (Devolution Issue Rules) 1999 (S.I. 1999 No.1346).

Appeals

13.10 In order to avoid the possibility of inconsistency in judicial decisions the Judicial Committee of the Privy Council will act as a final court of appeal for all devolution issues. In criminal proceedings any court may refer any devolution issue which arises in the course of proceedings to the High Court of Justiciary for determination.[28] A criminal court comprising two or more Lords Commissioners of Justiciary may refer a devolution issue to the Judicial Committee of the Privy Council.[29] In civil proceedings in a court or tribunal a reference may be made to the Inner House of the Court of Session, even from a tribunal where there is usually no appeal to the Inner House. This may include a court or tribunal elsewhere in the United Kingdom.[30] Where a devolution issue arises in the House of Lords or a court of three of more Court of Session Judges, a reference may be made to the Judicial Committee of the Privy Council. This can be done either with the leave of the court concerned or with special leave from the Judicial Committee itself. This appellate role of the Judicial Committee in relation to Scottish cases is new. Previously, although it had an appellate function it was in relation only to appeals from certain Commonwealth countries, professional bodies and ecclesiastical courts.

Pre-enactment Scrutiny of Scottish Legislation

13.11 The Lord Advocate and the Advocate General for Scotland have the power to refer any bill which has been passed by the Scottish Parliament to the Judicial Committee of the Privy Council to determine whether the legislation is within the legislative competence of the Parliament. This must be done in the period before the Bill receives the Royal Assent and within four weeks of the passing of the Bill.[31]

Judicial Review of Scottish Legislation

13.12 Although the courts have no power to declare a provision in an Act of the Westminster Parliament invalid, the same principle does not apply to Acts of the Scottish Parliament. Acts of the Scottish Parliament are only valid if they are within the legislative competence, which has been devolved by the Scotland Act.[32] Acts of the Scottish Parliament and Scottish subordinate legislation are to be read as narrowly as is required for them to be within

---

[28] Scotland Act 1998, Sched. 6, para. 9.
[29] Criminal Procedure (Scotland) Act, s.124(2) as amended by Scotland Act 1998 (Consequential Modifications) (No.1) Order 1999 (S.I. 1999 No. 1042).
[30] Scotland Act 1998, Sched. 6.
[31] *ibid.*, s.33.
[32] *ibid.*, s.54.

competence. A court or tribunal may remove or limit any retrospective effect of the decision, or to suspend its effect for a period to allow correction of the defect if it decides that provisions are *ultra vires*.[33] This means than an individual may challenge the validity of an Act of the Scottish Parliament in any proceedings before a court or tribunal. This may only be done after a provision has received the Royal Assent and become an Act. The devolution issue procedures described above must be followed.

Judicial Review of Actions of the Scottish Executive

If a court or tribunal finds that an action of the Scottish Executive 13.13 infringes a Convention right or a principle of European Law the court or tribunal has power to strike down the offending action.

Remedies. The remedies which may be granted are the same as those 13.14 which may be awarded by the court in any other action. Therefore if the Court of Session finds in favour of the petitioner in relation to a devolution issue in judicial review proceedings the court may order, reduction, declarator, specific implement or damages. In the case of damages however, the Scotland Act restricts the remedy of damages to circumstances in which damages could have been awarded if section 8(3) and 8(4) of the Human Rights Act 1998 applied.[34] Section 8 is discussed below.

IMPACT OF THE HUMAN RIGHTS ACT

A failure by a public authority to act in a manner compatible with 13.15 Convention rights will render the act *ultra vires* on grounds of illegality. The Human Rights Act provides that a person who claims that a public authority has acted (or proposes to act) in a way which is unlawful may bring proceedings against the authority in the appropriate court or tribunal. Alternatively they may rely on the Convention right or rights concerned in any legal proceedings. An appropriate court or tribunal means such court or tribunal as may be determined in accordance with rules.[35] In making rules for proceedings regard must be had to section 9 which sets some limits on the avenues of recourse against courts and tribunals.[36] Proceedings against an authority include a counterclaim or similar proceedings as a contravention of a convention right may be used as a defence as well as grounds for an action. Legal proceedings

---

[33] Scotland Act 1998, s.102.
[34] *ibid.*, s.100(3).
[35] Human Rights Act 1998, s.7(9 (b). In this section in relation to proceedings before a court or tribunal in Scotland, rules mean rules made by the Secretary of State for those purposes.
[36] Human Rights Act 1998, s.7(10).

include proceedings brought by or at the instigation of a public authority and an appeal against the decision of a court or tribunal.[37] Proceedings brought by a public authority include for example proceedings for the prosecution of crimes and appeals. A private prosecution will also be included in the definition of proceedings.[38] Judicial review proceedings are also included in the category of legal proceedings. The intention behind this provision of the Act is that Convention rights may be relied on either offensively or defensively in any proceedings in which they are relevant. The Act does not make Convention rights directly enforceable against a private person or organisation.

Time Limits

13.16 The Act imposes a time limit. Section 7(5) provides that proceedings must be brought before the end of the period of one year beginning with the date on which the act complained of took place[39]; or such longer period as the court or tribunal considers equitable having regard to all the circumstances.[40] If there is a stricter time limit in relation to the procedure in question, that stricter time limit will apply. Some statutory appeal procedures have shorter time limits. There has up to now been no time limit for the instigation of judicial review proceedings in Scotland and so the Human Rights Act now creates an anomaly. Where judicial proceedings do not involve the infringement of a Convention right, there is no time limit but where the grounds of review include infringement of a Convention right there is a 12-month time limit. The time limit is not in any way entrenched and may be changed by rules and procedures such as Acts of Sederunt and Acts of Adjournal. The one-year time limit only applies to claims against public authorities for infringement of Convention rights.[41] It does not apply where a person relies on a Convention right or rights in any legal proceedings.[42]

Title and Interest to Sue

13.17 This right to bring proceedings under the Human Rights Act is only conferred on a victim of the unlawful act.[43] If therefore, the proceedings are made by way of a petition for judicial review in Scotland, the applicant shall be taken to have title and interest to

---

[37]   Human Rights Act 1998, s.7(6).
[38]   Hansard, H.C.Vol.314, col.1057.
[39]   Human Rights Act 1998, s.7(5)(a).
[40]   *ibid.*, s.7(5)(b).
[41]   *ibid.*, s.7(1)(a).
[42]   *ibid.*, s.7(1)(b).
[43]   *ibid.*, s.7(1). (The principle of unlawfulness in this context derives from s.6(1).)

sue in relation to the unlawful act only if he is, or would be, a victim of that act.[44] A person is only deemed to be a victim of an unlawful act if he would be a victim for the purposes of Article 34 of the Convention[45] if proceedings were brought in the European Court of Human Rights in respect of that act.[46] This creates the same practical problem as that which arises in relation to time limits. The effect of this provision is that a different test is to be used to establish whether a person is the appropriate person to bring an action where Convention rights are concerned than the usual standard of title and interest to sue which applies in judicial review proceedings. The "victim" test appears to rule out actions taken by pressure groups except in circumstances where the action, which is being challenged, has a direct impact on members of the organisations. This is consistent with decisions of the Scottish courts with regard to title and interest to sue but may be a less liberal test than that adopted by the English courts in recent years. The Lord Chancellor stated in the House of Lords debates that there was nothing in the act which would prevent pressure groups from assisting and providing representation for victims who wish to bring cases forward.[47] The European Court of Human Rights has, on occasion permitted third party interventions in cases in the form of written statements and even oral submissions.[48] The House of Lords and the Court of Appeal in England have been willing to accept third party interventions in recent years. Examples include *R v. Secretary of State for the Home Department, ex parte Thompson and Venables*,[49] in which Justice made submissions and *R v. Bow Street Stipendiary Magistrate, ex parte Pinochet Ungarte* (No. 3),[50] in which Amnesty International intervened. Written submissions have been accepted or very brief oral submissions.

Definition of a Public Authority

The Human Rights Act defines a public authority as 13.18

(a) a court or tribunal,
(b) any person certain of whose functions are functions of a public nature, but does not include either House of

---

[44] Human Rights Act 1998, s.7(4).
[45] Art. 34 of the Convention, as modified by the 11th Protocol (formerly Art. 25).
[46] Human Rights Act 1998, s.7(7).
[47] Hansard, HL Deb, 5 February 1998, col. 810.
[48] See *Young, James and Webster v. U.K.* (1981) 4 E.H.R.R. 38.
[49] *R v. Secretary of State for the Home Department, ex p. Thompson and Venables* [1998] A.C.407.
[50] *R v. Bow Street Stipendiary Magistrate, ex p. Pinochet Ungarte* [1999] 2 W.L.R. 827.

Parliament, or a person exercising functions in connection with proceedings in Parliament.[51]

This definition corresponds reasonably well with the tripartite relationship principle, which has been used to explain the nature of the supervisory jurisdiction of the Court of Session. The Human Rights Act will, however, add a new dimension to the debate and some of the actions against public authorities will fall outside the scope of the supervisory jurisdiction. Lord Hope in *West v. Secretary of State for Scotland*[52] stated that the Court of Session has power, in the exercise of its supervisory jurisdiction, to regulate the process by which decisions are taken by any person or body to whom a jurisdiction, power or authority has been delegated or entrusted by statute, agreement or any other instrument The sole purpose for which supervisory jurisdiction might be exercised is to ensure that the person or body does not exceed or abuse that jurisdiction, power or authority or fail to do what the jurisdiction, power or authority requires. The cases in which the exercise of the supervisory jurisdiction is appropriate involve a tripartite relationship constituted by the conferring, (whether by statute or private contract), of a decision-making power or duty on a third party to whom the taking of the decision is entrusted, but whose manner of decision-making might be controlled by the court.[53]

During Parliamentary debates in the course of enacting the Human Rights Act, Lord Irvine referred to Railtrack as an example of a private body exercising public functions. He said that it acts privately in its capacity as a property owner and developer but is a public authority when it exercises public functions in its role as safety regulator for the railways. This distinction is consistent with existing Scots Law as illustrated in the case of *Rooney v. Chief Constable of Strathclyde* which was a petition for judicial review raised by a former police constable who had submitted his resignation to his Chief Constable. He sought declarator that Chief Constable failed to follow proper procedures in accepting his resignation and refusing to accept his subsequent withdrawal of the resignation. Lady Cosgrove considered the issue of competency and found that the relationship between a police constable and a Chief constable was not simply a relationship of employer and employee. The functions of a police constable are conferred by section 17 of the Police (Scotland) Act 1967. The Chief Constable has statutory powers to direct constables and is also given disciplinary powers in terms of section 26 and there were also regulations and guidelines

[51] Human Rights Act 1988, s.6(3).
[52] 1992 S.L.T. 636, 1992 S.C.L.R. 385, *sub nom West v. Scottish Prison Service.*
[53] 1992 S.L.T. 636, 1992 S.C.L.R. 385, *sub nom West v. Scottish Prison Service,* at p. 643–651.

relating to matters such as procedures for resignation and dismissal. Judicial review was therefore held to be competent in that case.[54] It is likely that the criteria which the courts will take into account in deciding whether or not a body is a public authority will include whether, if the relevant body did not exist, the government itself would fulfil its function. It will also be relevant to consider whether any public funding is allocated to the organisation in question.

Courts with Jurisdiction

The Act is worded so as to allow all courts, at all levels to award the 13.19 remedies which would be awarded by the European Court of Human Rights. All courts and tribunals can consider arguments brought on the basis of infringement of Convention rights. Unlike the procedure for devolution issues under the Scotland Act there is no procedure for special notice to be given where an issue of Convention right infringement is going to be raised in a case. Legal proceedings are not defined in the Act and so there are some areas of uncertainty. One question is whether a complaint to an official appointed by statute, such as the Parliamentary Commissioner is classed as legal proceedings. Whether or not a referral to an ombudsman qualifies as legal proceedings, such officers are themselves public authorities and so must interpret the law, and act themselves in accordance with the Convention.

The majority of cases are likely to arise as judicial review proceedings and so will be dealt with by the Court of Session under judicial review procedure. Where the matter is one regulated by statute, for example, planning, or functions of local authorities under the Civic Government (Scotland) Act, the relevant statute will designate the court to which a statutory appeal should be made. This will usually be the sheriff court. The Court of Session has been designated, for the purposes of the Human Rights Act 1998, section 7(1)(a), as the forum in which proceedings may be brought that cannot be brought by exercising a right of appeal or raising a petition for judicial review.[55]

Remedies

Section 8 provides that, in relation to an act (or proposed act) of a 13.20 public authority which the court finds unlawful, it may grant such relief or remedy, or make such order, within its powers as it considers just and appropriate. These will be the same remedies as discussed in relation to the Scotland Act. In civil proceedings damages may be awarded. In respect of criminal proceedings,

---

[54] *Rooney v. Chief Constable of Strathclyde*, 1997 S.L.T. 1261; 1997 S.C.L.R. 367.
[55] Human Rights Act 1998 (Jurisdiction) (Scotland) Rules 2000 (S.S.I. 2000 No. 301).

indictments may be quashed, evidence may be excluded and proceedings may be stayed. The Act does not confer any additional power on a court or tribunal to award remedies except that the award of damages for infringement of a Convention right may be within the powers of tribunals such as employment tribunals.

Damages

13.21   Section 8(3) of the Human Rights Act 1998 provides:

> "No award of damages is to be made unless, taking account of all the circumstances of the case, including—
>
> (a) any other relief or remedy granted, or order made, in relation to the act in question (by that or any other court) and
> (b) the consequences of any decision (of that or any other court) in respect of that act, the court is satisfied that the award is necessary to afford just satisfaction to the person in whose favour it is made".

Section 8(4) then provides,
"in determining—

> (a) whether to award damages, or
> (b) the amount of the award,

The court must take into account the principles applied by the European Court of Human Rights in relation to the award of compensation under Article 41 of the Convention".

Article 41 of the Convention requires that, where the Human Rights Court has held that a violation of a Convention right has occurred and if the internal law of the state concerned allows only partial reparation to be made, the Court shall, if necessary, afford just satisfaction to the injured party.

In some cases the Court has judged that a finding that there has been a violation of human rights is a sufficient remedy in itself. In other cases damages have been awarded and they fall into three categories:

> (1) Pecuniary loss, where causation is shown between the pecuniary loss by the victim and the violation of rights;
> (2) Non-pecuniary loss, where it is proved that an infringement of rights has caused mental or physical harm resulting in pain and suffering experienced by the victim;

(3) Costs and expenses which have been incurred by the victim in bringing the case before the Court to enforce their Convention rights.

The European Court of Human Rights will only award damages where to do so is "just and appropriate". Damages are appropriate where, from the perspective of the person whose rights have been violated, financial compensation will effectively redress the harm done. In order for the court to consider that damages are a just award however, wider issues may be considered such as a balancing of the circumstances of the person whose rights have been infringed against the circumstances of the authority responsible for the infringement. This may also involve balancing the rights of the victim against wider issues such as the interests of society as a whole, or sections of society. This approach has already been adopted by the United Kingdom courts with regard to damage claims against public authority. In *X (Minors) v. Bedfordshire County Council*, it was held that the needs of the individual with regards to compensation had to be balanced against the interests of the local community. If damages were awarded it could cause local authorities to adopt a more cautious and defensive approach to their duties which would lead to poorer provision for the whole community.[56] This decision lead to a general reluctance on the part of the United Kingdom courts to award damages for breaches of statutory duty by local authorities to the extent that there was almost a blanket immunity from claims for damages. The Scottish courts however, have continued to be more willing to consider the individual circumstances in each case. In *Gibson v. Chief Constable of Strathclyde*, for example, the Outer House held that there was no immunity for a police force in performance of civil operational tasks concerned with human safety on the public roads and there was no overwhelming dictate of public policy to exclude the prosecution of such claims. It did not follow from the fact that civil and criminal police functions arose from the same statutory provision that the same considerations applied in respect of immunity from suit.[57]

The approach of the English courts has recently been to step back 13.22 from the concept of a blanket immunity from damages claims for breach of duty. The House of Lords considered the issue in *Phelps v. Hillingdon LBC*. Ms Phelps had claimed damages from the council on the grounds that the council's failure to provide adequate education for pupils with special educational needs had been a direct cause of her failure to find employment and the

---

[56] *X (Minors) v. Bedfordshire County Council* [1995] 2 A.C. 633.
[57] Gibson v. Chief Constable of Strathclyde, 1999 S.C. 420; 1999 S.C.L.R. 661; 1999 Rep. L.R. 78.

consequential loss of wages. It was held that a local education
authority could be vicariously liable for the acts of its employees
and there was no justification for a blanket immunity policy in
respect of education officers performing the authority's functions
with regard to children with special educational needs. Where a
duty of care existed, if that duty was breached by failing to diagnose
specific learning difficulties and failing to take steps to ameliorate
the condition, the local authority could be held vicariously liable for
the consequential loss suffered. However, the court also had to have
regard to any public policy reasons for not imposing such liability
and should be slow to find negligence since such a finding might
interfere with the performance of the authority's duties. A failure to
diagnose a congenital condition such as dyslexia and to take the
necessary action, resulting in a child's level of academic achievement being reduced and a consequential loss of wages, could
constitute damage for the purpose of a claim and could give rise to
a claim for personal injuries under the Supreme Court Act 1981,
section 33(2).[58] This case marks a reversal of the policy of general
immunity for local authorities in *X (Minors)* v. *Bedfordshire County
Council*. Instead, the courts should balance the interests of the
individual and the wider public interest in each case.

The European Court of Human Rights has recently held that the
blanket immunity which was previously afforded to local authorities social services departments constituted a breach of Article 13
as it deprived victims of Convention rights infringements of an
effective remedy. The European Court of Human Rights was ruling
in the case of four siblings who were subjected to "horrific" abuse at
the hands of their parents, despite reports of abuse to the local
authority. The court ruled they had been subjected to treatment
which violated the European Convention on Human Rights 1950,
and because they were unable to sue the local authority this
breached Article 13 of the Convention. The judges awarded
£350,000 to the four siblings and similar damages will now have
to be awarded in British Courts.[59]

Just Satisfaction

13.23   The Act states that no award of damages is to be made unless the
court is satisfied that the award is necessary to afford just
satisfaction to the person in whose favour it is made.[60] The term
just satisfaction is used in Article 41 (formerly Article 50) which

---

[58]   *Phelps v. Hillingdon LBC (sub nom Re G (A Child)* [2000] 3 W.L.R. 776; [2000] 4
      All E.R. 504; [2000] 3 F.C.R. 102; [2000] B.L.G.R. 651; [2000] Ed. C.R. 700;
      [2000] E.L.R. 499; (2000) 3 C.C.L. Rep. 156; (2000) 56 B.M.L.R. 1; (2000) 150
      N.L.J. 1198; (2000) 144 S.J.L.B. 241.
[59]   *Z and A v. U.K.*, May 11, 2001.
[60]   Human Rights Act 1998, s.8(3).

states that: if the court finds that there has been a violation of the Convention or the protocols thereto, and if the internal law of the High Contracting Party concerned allows only partial reparation to be made, the court shall, if necessary afford just satisfaction to the injured party. There are two aspects to this:

(1) A need to ensure that adequate reparation is made to he victim. This may involve the award of financial compensation in addition to remedies already awarded.
(2) A need to ensure that financial compensation is not awarded twice for the same loss.

The origins and intentions of Article 41 were explained in the case *De Wilde, Ooms and Versyp v. Belgium*. The Article is modelled on clauses found in a number of arbitration treaties, *e.g.* the German-Swiss Treaty on Arbitration and Conciliation 1921, Article 10, and the Geneva General Act for the Pacific Settlement of International Disputes 1928, Article 32. These clauses were inserted to deal with the situation that a state, although willing enough to fulfil its international obligations, for constitutional reasons is unable to do so without changing its constitution. Article 50 (now 41) should be interpreted as only allowing the Court to award damages when domestic law does not provide for financial compensation to be awarded.[61] In recent years the Court has moved away from this approach and takes a flexible approach to the award of damages.

Pecuniary Damage

The Court has awarded damages for pecuniary loss in a range of circumstances. In *Hentrich v. France*, damages were awarded for the wrongful seizure of property by the French tax authorities. The court held that, if the land was not returned, damages based on the current market value should be awarded. This was calculated as one million French francs, and 200,000 French francs that had already been paid to Mrs Hentrich was deducted.[62] In *Lopez Ostra v. Spain*, damages were awarded for the depreciation of value in a private home caused by industrial pollution. The applicant had claimed the value of a new home, moving expenses, and compensation for stress. The Court felt that the amounts claimed were excessive and balanced the amounts which she had claimed against assistance which she had already received and the fact that she still owned the original house. The Court said that the heads of damage did not lend themselves to precise quantification and awarded about 20 per cent of the original sum claimed.[63] In *Scollo v. Italy*, Scollo, who

13.24

[61] *De Wilde, Ooms and Versyp v. Belgium (No 2)* (1979–80) 1 E.H.R.R. 438.
[62] *Hentrich v. France* (1994) 18 E.H.R.R. 440.
[63] *Lopez Ostra v. Spain* (1994) 20 E.H.R.R. 277.

was disabled and unemployed, claimed compensation on the grounds of interference with his right to enjoy his property. He had been unable to enforce eviction of tenants from his flat so that he could occupy it himself. The Court held that he should be awarded the full amount of his claim for pecuniary and non-pecuniary damages and for costs and expenses.[64] On occasion the Court has even included the costs of fines paid as compensation where the conviction has been held to be a contravention of the convention. In *Jersild v. Denmark*, where a conviction for publishing racist material was held to be in breach of Article 10, the Court awarded reimbursement of the fine as compensation for pecuniary damage.[65]

In *Smith v. United Kingdom*, pecuniary damages were awarded to service personnel who had been dismissed from the armed services because of a policy of not employing homosexuals. The United Kingdom were held to be in breach of Article 8 because of the investigations which intruded into the private lives of the applicants. The applicants were awarded sums varying from £55,000 to £94,875 as pecuniary damages for losses, which included loss of earnings.[66]

Non-pecuniary Damage

13.25	There is no consistent approach towards the award of compensation for non-pecuniary damage. The declaration that rights have been infringed is often considered by the court to be adequate as "just satisfaction".[67] In *Nikolova v. Bulgaria*, an accountant in a state-owned enterprise had been arrested, detained and charged with misappropriation of funds. There was an infringement Article 5 as she had been detained on remand for three and a half months in circumstances which amounted to a violation of Article 5(4). The applicant's claim for loss of earnings suffered during her period of detention was dismissed. The only financial compensation awarded was part of her costs incurred with interest. The majority of judges rejected the request for non-pecuniary damages stating that, although in the past the Court has in certain cases granted relatively small amounts in respect of non-pecuniary damage for loss of liberty, in more recent cases the Court has declined to accept such claims. In some of the cases the Court noted that just satisfaction can be awarded only in respect of damage resulting from a deprivation of liberty that the applicant would have suffered

---

[64]	*Scollo v. Italy* (1996) 22 E.H.R.R. 514.
[65]	*Jersild v. Denmark* (1995) 19 E.H.R.R. 1.
[66]	*Smith v. U.K.* [1999] I.R.L.R. 734; (2000) 29 E.H.R.R. 493; (1999) 11 Admin. L.R. 879.
[67]	*Chahal v. U.K.* (1997) 23 E.H.R.R. 413.

if he or she had had the benefit of the guarantees of Article 5. In many cases the finding of the violation constituted sufficient just satisfaction in respect of any non-pecuniary loss suffered. A dissenting judge (Judge Bonello) stated:

> "I consider it wholly inadequate and unacceptable that a court of justice should 'satisfy' the victim of a breach of fundamental rights with a mere handout of legal idiom ... The Convention confers on the Court two separate functions: firstly to determine whether a violation of a fundamental right has taken place, and secondly to give 'just satisfaction' should the breach be ascertained. The Court has rolled these two distinct functions into one. Having addressed the first, it feels absolved from discharging the second. In doing so, the Court fails in both its judicial and its pedagogical functions, The State that has violated the Convention is let off virtually scot-free."

He then went on to say that the Court should carry out a careful balancing exercise when assessing the amount of compensation to be awarded. In certain cases it would be acceptable for the amount of damages to be modest.[68]

Non-pecuniary damage was awarded by a Grand Chamber of the Court in *Caballero v. United Kingdom*. Caballero, who was 70 years old, had been convicted of manslaughter and released in 1988. He was convicted of attempted rape and assault occasioning actual bodily harm in 1997, but no application for bail was made in view of the Criminal Justice and Public Order Act 1994, section 25 and in the light of his previous conviction. Caballero applied to the European Commission on Human Rights contending that the automatic refusal of bail violated the European Convention on Human Rights. He argued that but for section 25 he would have had a good chance of being released on bail prior to his trial. In the light of his age, ill-health and the length of his sentence, he may never have another chance to be at liberty. In accepting the United Kingdom Government's recognition of a violation, the Court granted compensation under Article 41 of £1,000 for non-pecuniary damage and £15,250 costs.[69] More substantial non-pecuniary damages have been awarded where claimants have suffered physical injuries.[70] Damages have also been awarded where applicants have not had an opportunity to represent their interests fully in the course of legal proceedings.

In *McMichael v. United Kingdom*, the applicants were awarded 13.26

---

[68] *Nikolova v. Bulgaria* (2001) 31 E.H.R.R. 3.
[69] *Caballero v. U.K.* (2000) 30 E.H.R.R. 643; [2000] Crim. L.R. 587.
[70] *Ribitsch v. Austria* (1996) 21 E.H.R.R. 573.

compensation for non-pecuniary loss because they had not been allowed to see official social welfare reports on their family in the course of a children's hearing. This was held to be violation of Article 8. The Court considered that, in addition to possibly losing a chance to make representations in reply to the social welfare reports, the applicants had suffered distress and anxiety and feelings of injustice. They were awarded £8,000.[71] In *Osman v. United Kingdom*, where an action for negligence against the police in respect of their conduct of the investigation of a crime was barred for reasons of public policy, contrary to Article 6(1). The Court awarded £10,000 to each applicant. The amount was decided on equitable grounds, the Court was not prepared to speculate on the remedy which might have been awarded by the domestic courts in an action for negligence.[72] In *Smith v. United Kingdom* non-pecuniary damages were awarded in addition to the damages for pecuniary loss because the investigations and dismissals were profoundly destabilising events in the applicants' lives. This had lead to long-term emotional and psychological effects. They were awarded £19,000 each.[73] The award of £350,000, in *Z and A v. United Kingdom*, contrasts strongly with the modest approach to financial compensation generally adopted by the Court, however, it must be noted that the compensation was for five applicants.[74]

The Law Commissions for England, Wales and Scotland have issued guidelines with the intention of ensuring that awards of compensation under the Human Rights Act 1998 will be higher than those awarded at the European Court of Human Rights in Strasbourg. The report stresses that the award should attempt to place that individual back in the same position they would have been in before their human rights were breached, but many cases heard at the European Court of Human Rights were only awarded with the costs of the proceedings. It is expected that the level of damages paid out under the Act will be similar to those already awarded by the British courts.[75]

According to section 8(2): "damages may be awarded only by a court which has power to award damages, or to order the payment of compensation, in civil proceedings". The general safety net of judicial review proceedings in the Court of Session provides a remedy where another court cannot award damages. The High

---

[71] *McMichael v. U.K.* (1995) 20 E.H.R.R. 205.
[72] *Osman v. U.K.* (2000) 29 E.H.R.R. 245; (1999) 1 L.G.L.R. 431; 5 B.H.R.C. 293; (1999) 11 Admin. L.R. 200; [1999] 1 F.L.R. 193; [1999] Crim. L.R. 82; [1998] H.R.C.D. 966; [1999] Fam. Law 86; (1999) 163 J.P.N. 297.
[73] *Smith v. U.K.* [1999] I.R.L.R. 734; (2000) 29 E.H.R.R. 493; (1999) 11 Admin. L.R. 879.
[74] *Z and A v. U.K.*, May 11, 2001.
[75] Damages under the Human Rights Act 1998, (Cm 4853).

Court of Justiciary, for example cannot award damages for a wrongful conviction but a victim of a rights infringement could petition for judicial review of the decisions which lead to his conviction. The Court of Session may award damages in combination with such other remedies as it considers appropriate. Where judicial review is not appropriate damages for delict may be sought through an ordinary action in the Court of Session or sheriff court. It is possible that in future, the rules of procedure for courts and tribunals which cannot award damages may be amended to include a procedure for a referral to the Court of Session for the issue of damages to be addressed. This would save the victim from the need to instigate another separate action for damages.

Exceptions

Section 9(3) provides that, in proceedings in respect of a judicial act 13.27 done in good faith, damages may not be awarded other than to compensate a person to the extent required by Article 5(5) of the Convention.[76] Article 5(5) guarantees a right to compensation if a person has been arrested or detained in violation of Article 5. An award of damages under this head is competent against the Crown but only if the appropriate person, if not a party to the proceedings, is joined. The appropriate person will be the Minister responsible for the court concerned or a person nominated to represent him. Such a claim for damages may be brought even where the judicial act was done in good faith. Where a judicial act is done in the absence of good faith, for example if the act was motivated by malice or undertaken without probable cause, then an action under section 8 may be brought.

RELATIONSHIP BETWEEN THE PROCEDURES UNDER THE SCOTLAND ACT AND PROCEDURES UNDER THE HUMAN RIGHTS ACT

Unlike the procedures under the Scotland Act where the approach 13.28 has been to develop special procedures for devolution issues, the intention of the Human Rights Act is to integrate the consideration of Convention rights into the existing procedures by which an individual obtains redress against a public authority.

There is an obvious overlap between the procedures under the Scotland Act and the procedures under the Human Rights Act. There are also some anomalies. The final court of appeal from the decisions of the Scottish courts in civil matters is the House of Lords. The House of Lords is the final court of appeal for matters relating to the Human Rights Act throughout the United Kingdom.

---

[76] Human Rights Act 1998, s.9(3).

However, in relation to devolution issues coming before the Scottish courts under the procedures laid down in the Scotland Act it is the Judicial Committee of the Privy Council which is the final court of appeal.[77] The same applies in respect of devolution issues from Northern Ireland and Wales. There is obvious potential for conflict between the two systems and for inconsistencies. The House of Lords is not bound by decision of the Judicial Committee of the Privy Council. The jurisdiction of the European Court of Human Rights cannot be regarded as a unifying influence on the two systems as, although the House of Lords is obliged by the Human Rights Act to have regard to decisions of the Court, it is not bound to follow them. Dissenting judgments are not even afforded a persuasive value. It is not clear at this stage whether the two separate frameworks for remedies are intended to continue indefinitely or whether they will eventually be merged into one framework.

Existing Remedies Under Scots Law

13.29   There are several routes for obtaining legal redress through judicial process. The appropriate action will depend on the source of the authority for the decision which is being challenged.

Acts Carried Out Under Authority of Statute

13.30   Where it is the exercise of a power derived from a statute which has caused an infringement of rights there may a specific right of recourse provided by the statute. For example Social Security Act 1980, section 14 gives a right of appeal on points of law from decisions of the Social Security Commissioners. The nature of a statutory right of appeal will depend on the provision in the relevant statute. It may allow a further inquiry into the factual basis of a decision, or it may be limited to reviewing the legality of the decision. The appeal may be to a court, (often the sheriff court) or there may be a right of appeal to a government minister or, occasionally, to a tribunal. As a general rule, where there is a statutory right of appeal a litigant must make use of that right rather than seeking judicial review at common law.

Where a right of statutory appeal is being exercised the right to challenge a decision is normally granted to a "person aggrieved" by the decision. The Town and Country Planning (Scotland) Act 1997, section 239(5) provides that where an authority has failed to follow the prescribed procedure in making a decision, the court should only intervene if the applicant has been "substantially prejudiced"

---

[77]   Scotland Act 1998, s.103(1).

by a failure to comply with any of the procedural requirements. In order to establish substantial prejudice it is not necessary to prove that the outcome would have been different if procedural requirements had been adhered to.

The fact that he has been deprived of the exercise of a right is sufficient alone to amount to substantial prejudice. In *Wordie Property Co. Ltd v. Secretary of State for Scotland*,[78] Lord Cameron said that "where an applicant has been deprived of the exercise of a right conferred on him by Parliament, that fact alone would appear ... to indicate that he has suffered substantial prejudice."

The grounds on which the courts can intervene through statutory 13.31 appeal procedures will depend on the wording of the statute. For example, the statutory right of appeal in relation to planning decisions allow appeal to be made on the grounds that the validity of a decision, notice or order can be questioned where;

(1) the decision in question is not within the powers of the relevant statute or statutes,
(2) there has been a failure to comply with a relevant statutory requirement.

Failure to Act to Prevent an Infringement of a Right

Where there is a statutory duty on an official or body, such as a 13.31 duty to provide a service, it may be possible for an individual to take action to enforce performance of that duty. A general power to enforce a statutory duty is provided by the Court of Session Act 1988,[79] which provides that the Court of Session may order the specific performance of any statutory duty. This section applies where a clear, definite duty is laid by statute upon some definite body or individual on whom the court can lay its hand and order the specific performance of the duty. It must be clear that the statute is imposing a duty, not merely conferring a power. In the case of *T. Docherty v. Burgh of Monifieth*,[80] the local authority was ordained to perform their statutory duty under the Burgh Police (Scotland) Act 1892 to construct sewers to the borders of land owned by Docherty.[81]

Acts Carried Out by Public Authorities and Certain Other Bodies where there is no Statutory Appeal

The Court of Session has a supervisory jurisdiction at common law 13.32

---

[78] *Wordie Property v. Secretary of State for Scotland*, 1984 S.L.T. 345.
[79] Court of Session Act 1988, s.45(b).
[80] *T. Docherty v. Burgh of Monifieth*, 1970 S.C. 200.
[81] See also *Strathclyde R.C. v. City of Glasgow D.C.*, 1988 S.L.T. 144.

to ensure that a decision-maker has acted within his powers. The procedure by which courts fulfil this function is known as judicial review. In Scotland the subject matter of the supervisory jurisdiction extends, not only to the actions of central government and of local authorities but also to some extent to voluntary associations and private bodies.[82] An application for judicial review is a remedy of last resort and, unless there are exceptional circumstances, judicial review is incompetent where there is an alternative remedy.[83]

Applications for judicial review are commenced by way of a petition to the Court of Session set out according to Form 58.6 of Rules of Court. The Court has a wide discretion as to the remedies which it can grant.

Petitions for judicial review may be sought of decisions made by a wide range of organisations including: inferior courts and tribunals, actions of the crown authorised by statute, public industries and services; nationalised industries and public boards, local authorities and certain decisions by the Parliamentary Commissioner for Administration.[84] The Court of Session may also review decisions made by various other statutory and non-statutory bodies such as:

(a) Disciplinary tribunals, *e.g.* Law Society of Scotland, Faculty of Advocates;
(b) Universities;
(c) Broadcasting Authorities such as the BBC and the IBA;
(d) Other bodies, *e.g.* Parole Board, Scottish Homes, Scottish Arts Council.

Conditions for Judicial Review

13.33 The following conditions must normally be fulfilled before judicial review procedure can be used to challenge an administrative decision;

(1) There are grounds for judicial review of acts complained of
(2) The person or body complained of is subject to judicial review
(3) The type of act complained of can be subject of judicial review
(4) The person bringing action has both title and interest to sue

---

[82] See Finch and Ashton, *Administrative Law in Scotland,* pp. 223–242.
[83] *Dante v. Assessor for Ayr,* 1922 S.C. 109; *Strathclyde Buses v. Strathclyde R.C.,* 1994 S.L.T. 724, *West v. Secretary of State for Scotland,* 1992 S.L.T. 636, 1992 S.C.L.R. 385.
[84] *R v. Parliamentary Commissioner for Administration, ex p. Dyer* [1994] 1 All E.R. 375; *R v. Parliamentary Commissioner for Administration, ex p. Balchin* [1996] E.G.C.S. 166; [1996] N.P.C. 147.

(5) The remedy sought is appropriate remedy and is available against the person complained of

(6) There is no appeal procedure still open to aggrieved person

Illegality as a Defence

In the course of defending a legal action, including a criminal 13.34 prosecution, the illegality of the action taken against the defender may be raised. The Human Rights Act makes it clear that Convention rights can be relied on defensively in this way. Indeed victims can rely on their Convention rights in proceedings brought against them by a public authority, even if the act in question took place before section 7 came into force.[85]

Where there has been an Infringement of Rights in Circumstances not Provided for by Other Remedies

An important "safety net" in Scots law is the extraordinary 13.35 jurisdiction of the Court of Session through the exercise of the *nobile officium*. The *nobile officium* provides a means to grant a remedy where justice requires it, but none is otherwise available. In the case of *Ferguson, Petitioners*,[86] an electoral registration officer wrongly removed the names of certain voters from the draft electoral register. There was no statutory procedure for revising the list of voters, however the court ordered the officer to reinstate the names on the register. The power is very useful as its existence means that the right to a remedy does not depend on the particular circumstances of a case having been foreseen and legislated for in advance.[87]

Grounds for Challenging Administrative Decisions

The fundamental ground on which a decision may be challenged by 13.36 judicial review proceedings is that there has been an excess of power on the part of the authority which made the decision. Every act or decision must be *intra vires*. The most widely recognised statement of the grounds for judicial review is that of Lord Diplock in the case of *Council for Civil Service Unions v. Minister for Civil Service*, Lord Diplock stated that the grounds are;

(1) illegality,
(2) irrationality,
(3) procedural impropriety.

---

[85] Human Rights Act 1998, s.22.
[86] *Ferguson, Petitioners*, 1965 S.C. 16.
[87] For further reading see Finch and Ashton, *Administrative law in Scotland*, pp. 218–223, pp. 425–426.

The unanswered question in relation to the incorporation of the European Convention into domestic law is whether or not it will create a new ground of challenge. It can be argued that an act which contravenes the Convention lacks lawful authority and is therefore *ultra vires* and illegal. If an action taken is disproportionate to the intended result then the decision may be challenged on the grounds of irrationality. Things are unlikely to be quite so straightforward however. The standard of *Wednesbury* unreasonableness, as discussed below, has already come under unfavourable scrutiny by the European Court. It is already apparent that compliance with Convention rights will lead to an increased level of accountability in the public sector.

Illegality

13.37 A decision may be quashed on grounds of illegality where a decision-maker has not understood correctly the law that regulates his decision-making power and has not given effect to that law.[88] Such a failure will render his decision unlawful. Illegality may arise where a public authority has:

    (a) Acted in excess of its statutory powers; or
    (b) Where a decision has been made by taking into account irrelevant considerations; or
    (c) Where a decision has been taken after failing to take relevant considerations into account; or
    (d) Where a statutory power has been used for an improper purpose or where a policy has been adopted which amounts to a fettering of a future discretion.

Irrationality

13.38 A decision may be quashed on the grounds of irrationality or unreasonableness. This applies to a decision which is so outrageous in its defiance of logic or of accepted moral standards that no sensible person who had applied his mind to the question to be decided could have arrived at it. In the case of *Associated Picture Houses v. Wednesbury Corporation*,[89] Associated Picture Houses challenged the validity of the decision by Wednesbury Corporation to grant permission for Sunday cinema performances only on condition that no children under 15 years of age should be admitted. The Sunday Entertainments Act 1932 gave a local authority power to permit cinemas to show films on Sundays "subject to such conditions as they see fit to impose". It was held

---

[88] *Malloch v. Aberdeen Corporation*, 1973 S.C. 227; *Adams v. Secretary of State for Scotland*, 1958 S.C. 279.
[89] *Associated Picture Houses v.Wednesbury Corporation* [1948] 1 K.B. 233.

that the local authority had not acted *ultra vires*, as the decision was not so unreasonable that no reasonable authority could ever have come to it. The term "Wednesbury unreasonableness" is often applied to a decision which is so unreasonable that no reasonable authority could have come to it.

Irrationality as a ground for challenging administrative decisions has been criticised by the European Court of Human Rights as providing too high a threshold of unreasonableness. The test of *Wednesbury* unreasonableness concentrates on the state of mind of the decision-maker. The test preferred by the European Court of Human Rights is a test of proportionality, which concentrates instead on the consequences of the decision. If the consequences of a decision are disproportionate to the purpose which was intended then the decision will be deemed to be unlawful. In the case of *Smith v. United Kingdom* several service men and women sought compensation after they had been dismissed from the armed forces on the grounds of their sexual orientation. Eventually, after applications for judicial review and an appeal to the House of Lords were unsuccessful, the case came before the European Court of Human Rights. The applicants contended that an application for judicial review in the United Kingdom did not afford them an effective domestic remedy as required under Article 13. The European Court of Human Rights held that the applicants did not have access to an effective domestic remedy as required by Article 13. Criticism was made of the standard of *Wednesbury* unreasonableness under which a decision will only be held to be *ultra vires* on the grounds of irrationality if it was so unreasonable that no reasonable authority could ever have come to it.[90] The Court held that this test of irrationality had been set at such a level that the United Kingdom courts were precluded from even considering whether the alleged interference with private lives could be justified on the basis of social need, national security or public order.[91]

In the case of *Ahmed, Petitioner*, Lord McEwen pointed out that the *Wednesbury* rules of unreasonableness and the Convention principles are seen to mix with each other and overlap. He said that this problem had been hinted at by Lord Ackner in *R v. Home Secretary, ex parte Brind*.[92] He said that it is a matter which requires rationalisation in the future.[93]

---

[90] *Associated Picture Houses v. Wednesbury Corp.* [1948] 1 K.B. 233.
[91] *Smith v. U.K.* [1999] I.R.L.R. 734; (2000) 29 E.H.R.R. 493; (1999) 11 Admin. L.R. 879.
[92] *R v. Home Secretary, ex p. Brind* [1991] 1 A.C. 696 at 762.
[93] *Ahmed (Nisar), Petitioner*, 2000 S.C.L.R. 761.

Procedural Impropriety

13.39   A decision may be quashed on grounds of procedural impropriety;

> (a) Where there has been a failure to observe the basic rules of natural justice; or,
> (b) Where there has been a failure to act with procedural fairness towards the person who will be affected by the decision; or,
> (c) Where there has been failure by an administrative tribunal to observe procedural rules.

Many of the challenges which are made on the grounds of procedural impropriety arise because a failure to follow procedures has caused a breach of the principles of natural justice. The two main principles of natural justice are *audi alteram partem*—both sides must be fairly heard—and *nemo judex in causa sua* (*potest*)—no one can be a judge in his own cause). The second of these is also known as the rule against bias.

Underlying these there is a third principle that justice must not only be done but must be seen to be done.

An example of a breach of the principle that both sides must be fairly heard arose in the case of *Barrs v. British Wool Marketing Board*,[94] a wool producer, Barrs, appealed to a tribunal against a valuation of his wool by the appraisers under a wool-marketing scheme. The tribunal examined the wool in the presence of a representative of the producer and the two appraisers who had originally valued it. The tribunal then retired for consideration. The representative of the producer was excluded at this stage but the two appraisers retired with the tribunal members although they took no part in the discussions. The tribunal dismissed the appeal and reduced the value of the wool by another penny per pound. Barrs successfully sought reduction of the tribunal's decision on the ground that it had reached its decision in circumstances which were contrary to natural justice.

13.40   This same principle applies where there has been a possibility that a person making a judicial decision has been biased. An example of possible judicial bias arose in the case of *Bradford v. McLeod*.[95] During a prolonged national strike by coal miners a conversation took place at a social function in Ayr in which the strike was discussed. A sheriff and a solicitor were both present. At one point the sheriff made remarks to the effect that he "would not grant legal aid to miners". Subsequently a miner represented by that solicitor appeared before that same sheriff accused of breach of the peace on

---

[94] *Barrs v. British Wool Marketing Board*, 1957 S.C. 72.
[95] *Bradford v. McLeod*, 1986 S.L.T. 244.

a picket line. The solicitor moved that the sheriff should declare himself disqualified from hearing the case because of the views which he had expressed. The sheriff declined to disqualify himself. The miner was convicted of the offence, as were 13 others in similar circumstances. They all sought to have their convictions and sentences suspended. It was held that there had been a miscarriage of justice. Although the sheriff himself might have been satisfied that he was not biased and would not act in a manner contrary to his judicial oath, circumstances existed which could create in the mind of a reasonable man a suspicion of the impartiality of the sheriff.[96]

Remedies

Where an appeal against a decision is being made under a statutory appeal procedure the remedies which may be granted will be laid down in the relevant statute. Where a decision is challenged by way of judicial review procedure in the Court of Session the Court has a wide discretion as to the remedies which it can grant. The remedies sought must be listed in the petition but the court is not limiting to awarding only the remedies which have been listed. It can even make an order for a remedy which has not been sought in the application, although Lord Clyde, in *Mecca Leisure Ltd v. City of Glasgow District Council*,[97] observed that "the court should not compel a petitioner to accept a remedy not sought and not desired by him or her". 13.41

The remedies which may be awarded include:

(1) declarator; a declaration as to the law;
(2) reduction; a decision that an act is invalid and is therefore reduced;
(3) damages;
(4) specific implement, requiring a person to perform an act;
(5) interdict, prohibiting an action.

A declarator is simply a declaration as to the law. The remedy of reduction is usually sought in conjunction with declarator. Reduction is a legal decision that a decision is invalid and is therefore reduced. Petitioners are sometimes disappointed with this remedy because it does not prevent a similar decision being made in the future. For example, if a decision to permit a quarry to open has been reduced because the proper procedures were not followed, the

---

[96] See also *Lockhart v. Irving*, 1936 S.L.T. 567; *London and Clydeside Estates v. Secretary of State for Scotland*, 1987 S.L.T. 459; *Wildridge v. Anderson* (1897) 25 R. (J) 27.

[97] *Mecca Leisure Ltd v. City of Glasgow D.C.*, 1987 S.L.T. 483 at p.486.

authority could then follow all of the procedures to the letter and then make the same decision. All that would have been gained by the petition for judicial review was a delay. The court may make an award of financial compensation where a person has suffered a financial loss because of an *ultra vires* decision. The Court may also make an order of specific implement. This requires a person to perform an act. For example, a local authority may be required to give a place in a school to a child. The remedy of interdict can be awarded as an interim order and as a remedy following the disposition of a case. Interdict is an order prohibiting an action or a series of actions. Interim interdict is especially useful as it can be used to maintain the status quo until a petition comes before the court for a hearing. This could be useful if, for example, a petition was sought to challenge a decision to allow a change of land use which could result in damage to the environment. An interim interdict could be sought to ensure that nothing was done before the case was heard. The Court of Session can therefore award any of the remedies which it has the power to award in ordinary actions between individuals when it is exercising its supervisory jurisdiction over public authorities under judicial review procedure. There are some exceptions. The remedies of interdict and specific implement are not available against the Crown. The remedies which can be granted against the Parliamentary corporation, the body set up to represent the Scottish Parliament in legal proceedings, are restricted. Orders for reduction, suspension, interdict, or specific performance including interim orders, may not be imposed against the Parliamentary corporation. The remedy of declarator is available. The Scottish Parliament will decide what action to take when an order of declarator has been made.

THE WAY FORWARD

13.42 An important principle of the Human Rights Act is that existing human rights are safeguarded. A person's reliance on a Convention Right does not restrict—

(a) any other right or freedom conferred on him by or under any law having effect in any part of the United Kingdom; or,

(b) his right to make any claim or bring any proceedings which he could make or bring apart from sections 7 to 9.[98]

The remedies are intended to be in addition to the existing

---

[98] Human Rights Act 1998, s.11.

common law and statutory remedies and not to restrict or limit them in any way. The 1997 Labour Party election manifesto stated that the incorporation of the Convention into domestic law "will establish a floor, nor a ceiling, for human rights".

The Scottish Executive has launched a consultation document on whether a Human Rights Commission should be established in Scotland. The Executive believes the creation of such a Commission could promote good practice among public bodies, provide advice to them and the general public on human rights and scrutinise draft legislation.[99]

A Human Rights Commission has already been established in Northern Ireland.[1] One of the functions of the Commission is to act as intervener in cases which raise issues about Convention rights.

---

[99] http://www.scotland.gov.uk/consultations/justice/porhr-00.asp.
[1] Northern Ireland Act 1998, s.68.

CHAPTER 14

DOMESTIC LAW AND THE CONVENTION

14.01 Throughout this book, we have made reference to the Human Rights Act 1998 and the Scotland Act 1998. In this chapter, we will explore how the Convention rights were "brought home" by the Human Rights Act and how devolution brought them home sooner to Scotland.[1] The Scotland Act placed obligations upon the Scottish Parliament and the Scottish Executive to comply with the terms of the Convention by virtue of sections 29 and 57 respectively. The Scottish Executive was first to become subject to the Convention, on May 6, 1999, followed by the Lord Advocate on May 20, 1999 and then the Scottish Parliament took up its powers and duties on July 1, 1999. Other public authorities in Scotland became liable to comply with the Convention along with the rest of the United Kingdom on October 2, 2000.

The Human Rights Act 1998

"Ordinary Britons will for the first time have a set of fundamental rights that can be enforced in the British courts".[2]

The idea of incorporating a form of Bill of Rights into United Kingdom law is not a new one. Various bills have been proposed by Members of Parliament and peers with no less than 25 bills being proposed in the years between 1970 and 1998. Many authors have commented on the need for a Bill of Rights but it was not until the Labour Government came to office in 1997 that government action was finally taken. The government announced its intention to incorporate the Convention into domestic law in the first Queen's Speech in May 1997 and shortly after a White Paper was published setting out the government's proposals. The White Paper was called "Rights brought Home: The Human Rights Bill"[3]and it gave the

---

[1] And Wales, although space precludes us from covering the effect of the Government of Wales Act 1998.
[2] From the *New York Times,* October 3, 1999, cited in F. Klug, *Values for a Godless Age: the Story of the United Kingdom's New Bill of Rights* (2000), p.25.
[3] 1997, Cm. 3782.

rationale for incorporation. One of the main reasons submitted by the government was a desire to put British people on the same footing as those in other European States where the Convention was part of the constitutional law. Seeking redress in the European Court of Human Rights was a difficult, time-consuming and expensive exercise for British applicants. The government recognised that some people would be deterred from pursuing a case to the European Court by these problems. The White Paper also observed:

> "Enabling courts in the U.K. to rule on the application of the Convention will also help to influence the development of case law on the Convention by the European Court of Human Rights ... enabling the Convention rights to be judged by British courts will also lead to closer scrutiny of the human rights implications of new legislation and new policies."[4]

The Human Rights Act requires that all public authorities in the United Kingdom must comply with the provisions of the Convention so far as these are incorporated into the Human Rights Act. Most of the substantive rights of the Convention are thus incorporated but there are some exceptions. The "Convention rights" are defined in section 1(1) of the Act and set out in Schedule 1. Section 1(4) gives power to the Secretary of State to make an order to amend the Act to take effect of the United Kingdom's ratification of any Protocol, although such an order will not come into effect until the Protocol in question is in force in the United Kingdom. Articles 1 and 13 of the Convention are not included, even though these were ratified by the United Kingdom many years ago. Only the First and Sixth Protocols[5] are included, thus excluding the Fourth and Seventh Protocols, neither of which have been ratified by the United Kingdom. During the Committee Stage in the House of Lords, the government indicated that both protocols had been reviewed to ascertain whether they could now be ratified. It was stated that Protocol 7 would be ratified as soon as a legislative opportunity arose "to remove some of the inconsistencies" between United Kingdom law and the Convention. Ratification of Protocol 4 would take longer because of the rights being enacted. Article 3 of the Protocol refers to the right of nationals not to be excluded from their home state. The government envisaged difficulties with this because of the variety of British nationals, some of whom do not have the right to settle in the United Kingdom.[6]

14.02

---

[4] *ibid.,* paras 1.14–1.17.
[5] Protocol 6 was originally excluded from the bill but was then added and the Protocol itself was ratified by the U.K. on January 1, 1999.
[6] Official Report, House of Lords, 18 November 1997, Vol. 583, col. 504.

It seems odd that the Human Rights Act does not include Article 1 which provides:

> "The High Contracting Parties shall secure to everyone within their jurisdiction the rights and freedoms defined in Section 1 of this Convention."

The government concluded that the implementation of the Act would in fact cover the provisions of Article 1 and therefore it was unnecessary to include it. A more controversial omission was Article 13:

> "Everyone whose rights and freedoms as set forth in this Convention are violated shall have an effective remedy before a national authority notwithstanding that the violation has been committed by persons acting in an official capacity."

The reason for the omission was that the Act sets out in some detail how proceedings may be brought (sections 7 to 9) and it was feared that there might be confusion between the Act and the Article.[7]

The main implications of the Act are:

(1) Interpretation of legislation where possible to give effect to Convention rights;
(2) Procedures to remedy any legislation not complying with the Convention;
(3) Requirement on public authorities to act in such a way so as to comply with the Convention.

14.03 In section 2(1), the Act enumerates the extent of the Convention jurisdiction to be taken into account. This extends to any:

(a) Judgment, decision, declaration or advisory opinion of the European Court;
(b) Opinion of the Commission given under a report adopted under Article 31 of the Convention;
(c) Any decision of the Commission in connection with Article 26 or 27(2) of the Convention; or,
(d) Any decision of the Committee of Ministers taken under Article 46 of the Convention.

It does not matter when these judgments, decisions, etc., were made or given, so long as the court or tribunal is of the opinion that

---

[7] Scottish Human Rights Service.

the judgment, decision, etc., is relevant to the current proceedings. It should be noted that paragraphs (b) and (c), referring to opinions and decisions of the Commission, are now largely historical because of the entry into force of Protocol 11 on November 1, 1998.

The expression used in the section is "must take into account". This is a mixture of the mandatory with the permissive or discretionary and thus indicates that the Convention jurisdiction will not be binding on the United Kingdom courts. This was deliberate. The government argued that the United Kingdom courts should not have to follow an opinion of the European Commission which was not consistent with subsequent European Court caselaw.[8] The European Court itself does not operate a rigid system of precedent, often referring to the Convention as "a living instrument" in its decisions.[9] It was felt also that the United Kingdom courts should be free to depart from decisions which were inappropriate in the circumstances of the case, such as decisions which did not involve the United Kingdom and involved the laws and practices of other states.

Normally reports of previous decisions are not treated as a matter of evidence; the court will "take judicial notice" of the decision. However section 2(2) requires that evidence of the judgments, decisions and so on stated in section 2(1) will have to be given in the United Kingdom courts using such rules of the court which may be made under section 2(3). The fact that the reports of previous decisions are "evidence" and have to be brought into the proceedings, reinforces the idea that the Convention is not made part of United Kingdom law by the Human Rights Act. Instead the Act gives effect to the Convention by using various devices of interpretation.

(1) Interpretation of Legislation

There are two main occasions when legislation may be found to be incompatible with the Convention: first, at the time of passage of new legislation and second, during court proceedings.   14.04

Before a United Kingdom government bill reaches its second reading, the sponsoring minister must provide a written statement under section 19 of the Human Rights Act that the legislation complies with Convention rights. This statement will either declare that, in the minister's view, the bill complies with the Convention or that he is unable to make a statement of compatibility but the government wishes the bill to proceed. It is likely that the courts, in interpreting the legislation later, will take notice of a statement of compatibility by the government. If the government states that it

[8] Official Report, House of Lords, Vol. 513, col. 514.
[9] *E.g. Soering v. U.K.* (1989) 11 E.H.R.R. 439.

cannot make a statement of compatibility, and Parliament proceeds to pass the legislation, it could be argued that Parliament was aware of the consequences and legislated specifically against the Convention. In this case, the courts might make a declaration of incompatibility but such a declaration might be ignored by Parliament. There could be no presumption that Parliament did not intend to legislate contrary to international law, because quite clearly and deliberately it had done so. The position with United Kingdom bills contrasts with those of the Scottish Parliament. Section 31 of the Scotland Act 1998 requires that both the Minister and the Presiding Officer must make a statements of compatibility, and there is no provision for a statement of incompatibility as in the Human Rights Act.

Existing (and future) legislation will be scrutinised by the courts and section 2 of the Act requires all United Kingdom courts and tribunals to take into account Convention law and Convention principles of interpretation when making a determination on a Convention rights issue. Section 3(1) requires: "[s]o far as it is possible to do so, primary legislation and subordinate legislation must be read and given effect in a way which is compatible with the Convention rights".

14.05   A definition of primary and subordinate legislation is given in section 21(1). Primary legislation is defined as:

- Public general Acts of the United Kingdom Parliament;
- Local and personal Acts of the United Kingdom Parliament;
- Private Acts of the United Kingdom Parliament;
- Measures of the Church Assembly and of the General Synod of the Church of England;
- Order in Council either made in exercise of the royal prerogative; or under section 38(1)(a) of the Northern Ireland Constitution Act 1973 or the corresponding provision of the Northern Ireland Act 1998; or amending an Act of United Kingdom Parliament.

It also includes other orders or instruments made under primary legislation by the United Kingdom Parliament where it operates to bring into force one of the provisions of primary legislation or amends another piece of primary legislation. The definition does not apply to orders or instruments made under primary legislation made by the National Assembly of Wales, a member of the Scottish Executive, a Northern Ireland Minister or a Northern Ireland government department.

Subordinate legislation is defined for the purposes of the Act as:

- Orders in Council, other than one included in the primary

legislation list above;
- Acts of the Scottish Parliament;
- Acts of the Parliament of Northern Ireland;
- Measures of the Assembly established under the Northern Ireland Assembly Act 1973;
- Acts of the Northern Ireland Assembly;
- Various other orders, rules, regulations, schemes, warrants, bylaws and instruments.

Section 3(1) applies to all primary and subordinate legislation regardless of whether it was enacted before or after the 1998 Act. This was made clear in *J.A. Pye (Oxford) Ltd. v. Graham*[10] where Lord Justice Mummery said, "[t]he principle of the interpretation of primary and secondary legislation contained in section 3 of the 1998 Act can be relied on in an appeal which is heard after that Act came into force, even though the appeal is against an order made by the court below before the Act came into force". This was confirmed by Lord Justice Keene in the same case, noting that section 3(1) applies to all cases before the courts on or after October 2, 2000 "irrespective of when the activities which form the subject-matter of those cases took place". It is also clear that the section will apply in previous cases where the Convention rights were not taken into account and thus the courts will not be bound by judicial interpretation of legislation in those cases.

The wording in section 3(1) is important to achieve the objective 14.06 of incorporating the Convention principles into the consideration of the courts. During the House of Lords debates, the Lord Chancellor said that

> "If it is possible to interpret a statute in two ways—one compatible with the Convention and one not—the courts will always choose the interpretation that is compatible. In practice this will prove a strong form of incorporation."[11]

Lord Steyn clarified the meaning of the words "so far as it is possible to do so".

> "Traditionally the search has been for the one true meaning of a statute. Now the search will be for a possible meaning that would prevent the need for a declaration of incompatibility. The questions will be (1) what meanings are the words capable of yielding? (2) And, critically, can the words be made to yield a sense consistent with Convention rights? In practical effect

---

[10] unreported, February 6, 2001.
[11] Official Report, House of Lords, Vol. 582, col. 1230.

there will be a rebuttable presumption in favour of an interpretation consistent with Convention rights." [12]

The section allows the court to choose between alternative possible meanings although obviously the court will not distort the meaning of a word or phrase where there is no alternative to it. In that circumstance, interpretation under section 3 will not be possible and the plain meaning of the words will be used.

The status of an Act of the Scottish Parliament is one of subordinate legislation under section 21(1) of this Act. Nonetheless, section 3(1) will apply to Acts of the Scottish Parliament and subordinate legislation made thereunder in the same way as any other subordinate legislation and the courts will have the duty of trying to read and give them effect in a way compatible with the Convention rights. If they are unable to do so, the provision may be quashed. The Scotland Act 1998, section 101(2) requires that any interpretation of an Act of the Scottish Parliament or subordinate legislation made by the Scottish Executive should be read "as narrowly as is required for it to be within competence, if such a reading is possible, and is to have effect accordingly". The intention of this section of the Scotland Act is therefore to give effect to legislation wherever possible, rather than declare it invalid.

14.07 Section 3(2)(a) clearly states that the Act is intended to apply to all legislation whenever it was enacted, and this will include future legislation as well as existing legislation. Section 3(2)(b), however, reasserts the doctrine of Parliamentary supremacy by declaring that the "validity, continuing operation or enforcement of any incompatible primary legislation" is not affected by section 3 and the need to interpret legislation to be compatible where it is possible to do so. Subsection (c) is a similar statement regarding incompatible subordinate legislation where the incompatibility cannot be removed because of the primary legislation under which it was made. It should be noted that section 3 does not affect the validity of any legislation; it operates only on the interpretation of the legislation. Nothing in the Human Rights Act affects the validity of primary legislation although section 6 affects the validity of subordinate legislation. Where the United Kingdom Parliament deliberately enacts a statute which is clearly contrary to the Convention, the validity of that statute will not be affected by the Human Rights Act and it will have full effect and will be fully enforceable.

---

[12] Lord Steyn "Current Topic: Incorporation and Devolution" [1998] E.H.R.L.R. 153 at 155.

(2) Incompatibility of Legislation

Section 4 of the Act deals with how legislation, which cannot be 14.08
given effect by section 3, is to be dealt with. Section 4(2) states that a
court may make a declaration of incompatibility where it is satisfied
that the provision of primary legislation is incompatible with a
Convention right. The term "court" is defined in subsection (5) as
the House of Lords; Judicial Committee of the Privy Council;
Courts-Martial Appeal Court; in Scotland, the High Court of
Justiciary sitting otherwise than as a trial court or the Court of
Session; in England, Wales and Northern Ireland, the High Court
or Court of Appeal. The section continues at subsection (6) to make
it clear that any declaration of incompatibility does not affect the
validity, continuing operation or enforcement of the statute in
question and is "not binding on the parties to the proceedings in
which it was made".

Section 4(3) and (4) deals with subordinate legislation where the
provision is incompatible but the primary legislation under which it
was made prevents removal of the incompatibility. The court in
these circumstances may make a declaration of incompatibility.

The power to make a declaration of incompatibility is permissive;
thus the power that the court "may make" a declaration is
discretionary, not mandatory. However, it is difficult to see any
circumstances, perhaps other than the public interest, under which a
court would refuse to make a declaration once it had come to the
conclusion that the statutory provision did not comply with the
Convention principles. The Act does not require the courts to make
the decision as to whether the provision should be repealed or
revised; that decision is left to Parliament and Parliament is not
obliged by the statute to act on the declaration.

Where the court finds that it will make a declaration of
incompatibility, it is required under section 5 to inform the Crown
of its intention. This enables the Crown to become a party to the
case in order to make submissions before any declaration is made.
Notice to the Crown can be given at any time. This section reflects
the political as well as legal impact any declaration of incompatibility may have and tries to ensure that the Convention issue is
brought out and not lost in the particular facts of the case before
the court.

Where a declaration of incompatibility regarding United King- 14.09
dom legislation is made, the relevant United Kingdom minister will
have power under section 10 to take remedial action. The power is
discretionary and will be used by the minister where he considers
"that there are compelling reasons for proceeding" to make an
order. The remedial order may amend or repeal the legislation and
the order requires the positive approval of both Houses of
Parliament. The power under section 10 may also be used where

the European Court of Human Rights has made a decision against the United Kingdom in a case decided after section 10 came into force. The ability to make a remedial order is a powerful tool and has been described as "an exceptionally drastic form of Henry VIII clause".[13] However, there are constitutional safeguards in place to ensure that the power is not abused. First, a declaration of incompatibility has to be made by a court. Section 10(1) requires that all appeals must have been given up by the parties, exhausted or time-barred. Alternatively the order may be made where a European Court of Human Rights decision has been made after October 2, 2000 that a legislative provision is in breach of the Convention. The judgment must be against the United Kingdom, otherwise it would not be binding on the United Kingdom. Secondly, a minister has to consider that "there are compelling reasons for" making such an order. The wording here implies that an order will be made only where the minister has considered the alternatives and found that this is the only practical way to give effect to the Convention rights. Thirdly, both Houses of Parliament must approve the order. The Parliamentary procedure for making the order is given in Schedule 2, paragraph 2. Both Houses have 60 days to consider the order and it must then be approved by a resolution of both Houses.

A remedial order can also be made to "correct" subordinate legislation which has been quashed or declared invalid as being incompatible with a Convention right.[14]

(3) Public Authorities

14.10 At section 6(1) it is declared that "it is unlawful for a public authority to act in a away which is incompatible with a Convention right". This will not apply if the provisions of the primary legislation mean that the authority could not have acted in any other way, or it was obliged to give effect to incompatible provisions made under primary legislation.[15] The latter application is meant to ensure that public authorities continue to apply and enforce the law even where it is known that the legal provision is incompatible with Convention rights. It is not for public authorities to decide whether to continue to implement legislation that is known to be incompatible; that is a matter first for the courts and then for Parliament to decide.

The term "act" in section 6(1) includes a failure to act[16] but not a

---

[13] W. Wade, "United Kingdom's Bill of Rights" in *Constitutional Reform in the United Kingdom* (1998, University of Cambridge Centre for Public Law), p.61 at p.66.

[14] s.10(4).

[15] s. 6(2).

[16] s.6(6).

failure to introduce legislation or make a remedial order. The effect of section 6(1) is described as making it unlawful for a public authority to make subordinate legislation that is incompatible, or commit an act (such as torture) which is incompatible, or for a court to give a judgment that is incompatible, or fail to provide relief where the Convention requires that it is given.[17]

There is no definition of the term "public authority" in the Act. This was deliberate and allows the courts to determine whether an organisation is acting in a public capacity or not. Section 6(3) states that the term includes any court or tribunal, or any person whose functions are wholly or partially of a public nature. It does not include either the House of Commons or the House of Lords or a person "exercising functions in connection with the proceedings in Parliament". The House of Lords acting in its judicial capacity is however a public authority.[18] A guidance note was issued by the Home Office Human Rights Unit to clarify the definition of a public authority. The guidance gave 3 broad categories. First, the term includes public authorities which are obvious, *e.g.* a minister, government department or agency, local authority, health body, the Armed Forces and the police. "Everything these bodies do is covered by the Act." Secondly, the courts and tribunals are always considered public authorities and thus must give decisions and act in a way compatible with the Convention. The third category concerns bodies which may on occasion be required to act as a public authority. For the purposes of the Human Rights Act, they will only be considered as a public authority when they are carrying out such public functions. An example given by the guidance note was Railtrack, which was required to act as a safety regulator for the railways and thus was a public authority for this function. It was not a public authority when acting as a commercial operator.[19]

The decision regarding the status of an organisation as a public authority will be made by the courts. However, there are characteristics which may suggest whether or not an authority is a public authority. These include: 14.11

- The body performs duties in the public domain as part of a statutory system performing public law duties;
- The duty is of public significance;
- Rights and obligations of individuals are affected by the performance.[20]

---

[17] Green's *Scottish Human Rights Service* (2000), p.B17.
[18] s.6(4).
[19] Human Rights Task Force "A New Era of Rights and Responsibilities: Core Guidance for Public Authorities" (1999) Human Rights Unit, Home Office, London.
[20] *ibid.*

If a person believes that a public authority has violated his Convention rights, he may bring an action directly in the United Kingdom courts. The person will still have the opportunity to seek redress in the Strasbourg court but only after he has exhausted all possible domestic remedies and he has leave to do so.

(4) Procedures

14.12 Section 7 of the Act sets out the procedure to be used in determining whether or not an infringement of the Convention rights has occurred. The person making the claim must comply with two conditions. First, the claim that the act was unlawful must either be brought in an action against the public authority or be raised as a Convention right during any other legal proceedings. Secondly, the person must be (or would be) a victim of the unlawful act.

As regards the first condition, it is important to note that "any legal proceedings" will include proceedings brought by a public authority, such as a prosecution, appeals and judicial review actions. During the Committee stage on the Bill in the House of Commons, the government minister reflected that

> "it is our expectation that the great majority of cases in which the Convention arguments are raised will fall within the scope of such proceedings. That is because, in most cases, it is likely that a victim of an act made unlawful by clause 6(1) will have available to him an existing course of action or other means of legal challenge, such as judicial review."[21]

It is therefore expected that direct proceedings against a public authority for breach of Convention rights will be less common than relying on Convention rights in an existing legal action.

The second condition of section 7(1) is that the person bringing the action must be a victim, or would be a victim, if the unlawful act is carried out by the public authority. The concept of "victim" comes from the European Convention on Human Rights where Article 34 allows applications to be received from "any person, non-governmental organisation or group of individuals claiming to be the victim of a violation of the Convention". According to section 7(7) the person claiming to be a victim under section 7(1) must fulfill the requirements to qualify as a victim under the terms of Article 34.

The jurisprudence of the European Court (and previously the European Commission) will be important for the United Kingdom courts in deciding whether a person will qualify as a victim. The person claiming to be a victim must be able to prove more than a simple allegation of a violation of their rights. A person will be a

---

[21] Official Report, House of Commons, 24 June 1998, vol. 314, col. 1056.

victim if a national law has been applied to their detriment and that law is incompatible with the Convention. In some circumstances the European Court has also considered that where there is a serious risk of a contravention of a Convention right, this may be sufficient to indicate that the person so affected is a victim. In *Open Door Counselling and Dublin Well Woman Centre Ltd v. Ireland*[22] women of child-bearing age were victims of an injunction to restrict abortion since they might "be adversely affected by the restrictions".[23]

Section 7(4) applies to judicial review proceedings in Scotland where a claim of breach of Convention rights is made. The applicant must "have title and interest to sue in relation to the unlawful act only if he is, or would be, a victim of that act". This is a different test of standing from that normally used in Scots law where the test is whether a person has title and interest to bring proceedings. The Lord Chancellor indicated during the Committee stage in the House of Lords that the bill was not intended to "alter the standing rules in relation to judicial review in either England or Scotland".[24] However, in the Third Reading debate, he acknowledged that "a narrower test will apply for bringing applications on Convention grounds than in applications for judicial review on other grounds".[25]

14.13

The European Court of Human Rights has maintained that there is no *actio popularis* available under the Convention.[26] Thus the developments in English law particularly where pressure groups or public interest groups are allowed to bring judicial review cases will not be possible under section 7(1) and (7). A public interest group will still be able to provide assistance to people who have been or may be affected by an unlawful act under section 6(1). It should be noted however that national and international non-governmental organisations are able to make written submissions to the European Court. This is already possible in the United Kingdom courts where non-governmental organisations have been able to intervene and file *amicus* briefs.[27] The Home Office minister indicated that the aim of the bill was to grant access to victims not to create opportunities for public interest groups to bring test cases which would "delay victims' access to the court".[28]

[22] (1992) 15 E.H.R.R. 244, para. 44.
[23] See also *Dudgeon v. U.K.* (1981) 4 E.H.R.R. 149.
[24] Official Report, House of Lords, 24 November 1997, vol. 583, col. 834.
[25] Official Report, House of Lords, 5 February 1998, vol. 585, col. 810.
[26] See *Norris v. Ireland* (1985) 44 D.R. 132 where an individual homosexual man had standing to challenge the Irish law criminalising homosexuality, but the National Gay Federation did not.
[27] *E.g.* Amnesty International in *R v. Bow Street Metropolitan Stipendiary Magistrate, ex p. Pinochet Ugarte (No. 3)* [1997] 3 All E.R. 97.
[28] Official Report, House of Commons Committee stage, 24 June 1998, vol. 314, col. 1086.

Section 7(5) requires that the proceedings must be brought within one year of the date on which the act occurred, unless there is a stricter time limit imposed by statute. There is discretion to the courts to allow proceedings to be brought after the one year has elapsed. However, in Scotland, this section will have the effect of placing a time limit on proceedings which are brought by way of judicial review. Currently there is no time limit for bringing such cases, although the Court of Session will not allow unreasonable delays. A petition may be barred by *mora,* taciturnity and acquiescence, that is, a period of delay followed by silence during which the person had full knowledge of the decision and did nothing to show he did not accept it.[29] Delay on its own is not necessarily a bar to an action, but "the absence of a strict time limit for bringing a petition does not mean that the decisions of public authorities will be open to challenge until the 20-year prescriptive period has expired".[30]

14.14   In section 9, the Act gives special provisions for the situation when a court or tribunal has acted unlawfully in respect of Convention rights. A court or tribunal is classified as a public authority under section 6. Section 9(1) declares that proceedings seeking remedy under section 7(1)(a) in respect of a judicial act may only be brought by exercising a right of appeal where such right exists, by petition for judicial review, or by any other route "as may be prescribed by rules". The scope of judicial review is not extended in any way[31] and no new route of appeal is offered, although there is the possibility of such route being created by rules made by the Scottish Ministers in Scotland or the Lord Chancellor in England and Wales. Where a claim of breach of Convention rights is successful against a judicial act done in good faith, damages are not payable except where the act was one of "arrest or detention in contravention of" Article 5(5) of the Convention. In these circumstances the award must be made against the Crown after joining the "appropriate person".[32] If the judicial act was not made in good faith, remedy under section 8 will apply, together with damages where appropriate.

(5) Remedies

14.15   Section 8 gives power to a court or tribunal to grant relief or remedy where a public authority has acted in a way which is

---

[29]   *Carlton v. Glasgow Caledonian University,* 1994 S.L.T. 549; *Perfect Swivel v. Dundee District Licensing Board (No. 2)* 1993 S.L.T. 112.
[30]   Finch and Ashton, *Administrative Law in Scotland* (1997), p.380.
[31]   s.9(2).
[32]   s.9(4).

incompatible with the Convention rights. The remedy granted must be one which the court is already able to make. The Act does not therefore create any new remedies or allow courts or tribunals to make any particular order, although it is possible under section 7(1) for a minister to add to the remedial jurisdiction of a court or tribunal so that it can provide an appropriate remedy. Damages can only be awarded by a court which has power to award such a remedy or order payment of compensation in civil proceedings. This ensures that damages cannot be awarded in criminal proceedings.

An award of damages can only be made if the court is satisfied that it is necessary "to afford just satisfaction to the person in whose favour it is made".[33] The wording mirrors Article 41 of the European Convention on Human Rights and indeed at section 8(4) the court is required to have regard to the case law of the European Court in awarding compensation under Article 41. The European Court's principles in awarding compensation are briefly as follows. The applicant should be put in the position he would have been if the Convention had not been breached.[34] Damages can be paid for pecuniary loss such as loss of business opportunities[35] or loss of income.[36] The European Court may also award damages for non-pecuniary loss such as frustration[37] or harassment, humiliation and stress.[38] Under the Human Rights Act, section 8(4) the amount of award must be at a level commensurate with those awards made by the European Court.

An award of compensation is not automatically made by the European Court where it has found in the applicant's favour. In many cases, the European Court has decided that the finding itself is a sufficient form of satisfaction. The European Court does not award punitive or exemplary damages, only amounts to bring the person to the place he would have been had the violation not occurred.

If, after exhausting all local remedies, a person is still dissatisfied with the action of a public authority and believes his Convention rights have been violated, he may still seek a remedy from the European Court of Human Rights. Section 11 clearly states that existing rights and freedoms are not restricted by the Human Rights Act and the right to bring an action in Strasbourg is untouched.

---

[33] s.8(3).
[34] *Piersack v. Belgium* (1984) 7 E.H.R.R. 251.
[35] *Allenet de Ribemont v. France* (1995) 20 E.H.R.R. 557.
[36] *Open Door Counselling and Dublin Well Woman Centre Ltd. v. Ireland* (1992) 15 E.H.R.R. 244.
[37] *Weeks v. U.K.* (1988)13 E.H.R.R. 435.
[38] *Young, James and Webster v. U.K.* (1982) 5 E.H.R.R. 201.

The section thus ensures that the rights granted by the Act are additional to the existing rights.

THE SCOTLAND ACT 1998

14.16 Prior to the passing of the Scotland Act 1998 and the Human Rights Act 1998, Scots law followed the principle that the European Convention on Human Rights was not part of the law of Scotland because it had not been incorporated into law by an Act of Parliament. This was strictly followed until the late 1990s, when the reasoning of the House of Lords in *R v. Secretary of State for Home Office, ex parte Brind*[39] was adopted by the Scottish courts. The House of Lords had considered that since there was a presumption that Parliament would not legislate to deny the United Kingdom's international obligations, such as the European Convention on Human Rights, then ambiguities in the legislation should be interpreted so as to conform with those Treaty obligations. The Inner House of the Court of Session accepted this reasoning in *T, Petitioner*[40] and a bench of five judges in the High Court of Justiciary agreed in *McLeod, Petitioner*.[41] These cases however involved the resolution of ambiguous legislative provisions. It was still the case that where legislation was clear and unambiguous, it had to be interpreted as such, even though the interpretation would lead to a violation of the Convention.[42]

The Scotland Act 1998 had the effect of importing Convention rights into Scots law at an earlier date than in England. The Human Rights Act came into force on October 2, 2000. In Scotland, the Scottish Executive took up most of its powers and obligations, including those to act compatibly with the Convention, on May 6, 1999, while the Lord Advocate's powers were brought into force on May 20, 1999. The obligations of the Scottish Parliament came into force on July 1, 1999. All other public authorities in Scotland became subject to the Human Rights Act on October 2, 2000.

(1) The Scottish Parliament

14.17 Sections 29 and 30 and Schedule 5 of the Scotland Act give the legislative competence of the Parliament. Subsection 1 of section 29 defines what the Parliament may not do, rather than taking a positive line on what it may do. All provisions of an Act of the Scottish Parliament must be within the legislative competence of the

---

[39] [1991] 1 A.C. 696.
[40] 1997 S.L.T. 724.
[41] 1998 S.L.T. 233.
[42] See White and Reid "The Legal Status of Human Rights in Scotland" *Scottish Law and Practice Quarterly*, 2000, Vol. 5(3) 289.

Parliament. Any provision which is "incompatible with any of the Convention rights or with Community law" is outside the legislative competence.[43] The term "Convention rights" has the same meaning as in the Human Rights Act 1998. Where an incompatible provision is enacted, it may be invalidated by the courts as being *ultra vires*. It must be remembered that Acts of the Scottish Parliament are considered to be subordinate legislation under section 21 of the Human Rights Act.

The section does not remove all powers on human rights legislation beyond the Scottish Parliament. The Parliament may legislate on human rights matters if the proposed legislation is not within one of the reserved matters of Schedules 4 or 5. In addition, if a declaration of incompatibility is made regarding a provision of a statute made by the United Kingdom Parliament and the subject matter is now one devolved to the Scottish Parliament, the issue of incompatibility may be resolved by one of the Scottish Ministers deciding whether or not to make a remedial order under section 10 of the Human Rights Act.

When a bill is to be presented to the Scottish Parliament, the member of the Scottish Executive in charge of the bill will make a statement that "in his view, the provision of the bill would be within the legislative competence of the Parliament".[44] The presiding officer must make a "decision" as to whether or not the bill is within the legislative competence and state his decision.[45] Both statements are published with the bill and explanatory and financial statements.[46] If the presiding officer decides that the bill is not within the legislative competence he must state this view but it will not prevent the Parliament from considering and passing the bill. These requirements create a pre-legislative scrutiny of a bill and are part of a series of checks to ensure that the competence of the Parliament is not breached.

After a bill has been passed by Parliament, it must be sent by the presiding officer to the Queen for Royal Assent. However, under section 32, he may not do so until additional hurdles relating to the competence of the Parliament are overcome. First, the Advocate General for Scotland, the Lord Advocate and the Attorney General may refer a question of competence of the bill to the Judicial Committee of the Privy Council[47] and these Law Officers have a period of four weeks to do so, counting from the passing of the bill in the Scottish Parliament. Secondly, the bill may not proceed to Royal Assent until such a reference under section 33(1) has been

14.18

---

[43] s.29(2)(d).
[44] s.31(1).
[45] s.31(2).
[46] r.9.3 of Standing Orders.
[47] s.33(1).

determined. Thirdly, any Secretary of State may intervene to prevent the bill receiving the Royal Assent if he has "reasonable grounds to believe (the bill) would be incompatible with any international obligations".[48] This controversial section gives power to the "Secretary of State" to make an order prohibiting the presiding officer from submitting the bill for Royal Assent. The Secretary of State referred to is not necessarily the Secretary of State for Scotland and it can be interpreted as referring to any Secretary of State of the United Kingdom Government. The Secretary of State must give reasons for his belief thus ensuring that his decision may be challenged by way of judicial review. Section 126(10) defines "international obligations" and specifically excludes the European Convention on Human Rights although other human rights treaties are included.

If a bill is deemed by the Judicial Committee of the Privy Council to be outwith the legislative competence of the Parliament, the presiding officer may not submit the bill unamended for Royal Assent. The bill must be returned to the Scottish Parliament for reconsideration.[49]

It should be noted that section 29(2)(c) prevents the Scottish Parliament from amending any of the provisions of the Human Rights Act 1998.

14.19   The final scrutiny of the legislation of the Scottish Parliament occurs after the legislation has been enacted. Section 100 allows the Lord Advocate, Advocate General, other Law Officers and any person who is a "victim" for the purposes of the European Convention on Human Rights Article 34, as defined by section 7 of the Human Rights Act, to seek judicial review of any legislation on the grounds that it is incompatible with Convention rights. An individual must be capable of being a "victim" but the Law Officers may act even if no victim is involved. The term "act" in this section applies to legislation and to the actions (or failure to act) of the Scottish Executive.[50] If the court finds that the legislation is incompatible, damages may only be awarded in accordance with the terms of section 8(3) and (4) of the Human Rights Act. Thus damages are limited to the sums which could be expected if the decision was made by the European Court of Human Rights.

(2) The Scottish Executive

14.20   Section 57(2) states:

"A member of the Scottish Executive has no power to make

---

[48] s.35(1)(a).
[49] s.36.
[50] s.100(4).

any subordinate legislation, or to do any other act, so far as the legislation or act is incompatible with any of the Convention rights or with Community law."

The section does not however apply to the Lord Advocate when his act is done to prosecute an offence or is done in his capacity as head of the systems of criminal prosecution and investigation of deaths in Scotland, where such an act would not be unlawful under section 6 of the Human Rights Act.[51] This section protects the prosecuting authorities when they are found to be prosecuting a violation of a statutory provision which is held to be incompatible with Convention rights. In addition, the section ensures that the Lord Advocate is able to bring a prosecution under United Kingdom legislation where the prosecuting authorities in England have been able to do so under the same legislation. This will ensure that United Kingdom legislation is applied in the same way across the United Kingdom.

Although the section does not specifically say so, the acts referred to will include those of the junior Scottish Ministers (now normally referred to as Deputy Ministers) and Scottish civil servants acting on behalf of Ministers. [52] This is based on the principle set out in *Carltona Ltd v. Commissioner for Works*[53] where it was recognised that Ministers cannot carry out all of their functions personally and must rely on civil servants to carry out some of them on their behalf.

Section 58 of the Scotland Act gives the equivalent power to the Secretary of State in respect of acts of the Scottish Executive as he has under section 35 in respect of the Scottish Parliament. The Secretary of State has power to make an order preventing a proposed action by a member of the Scottish Executive where the Secretary of State has "reasonable grounds to believe" that the action would be "incompatible with any international obligations".[54] The power is also given to revoke subordinate legislation which is either incompatible with international obligations or makes modifications to the law in matters which are reserved ones and the Secretary of State has reasonable grounds to believe will adversely affect the operation of that law.[55] In all cases where an order is made, the Secretary of State must state his reasons.

---

[51] s.57(3).
[52] White and Reid "The Legal Status of Human Rights in Scotland" *Scottish Law and Practice Quarterly*, 2000, Vol. 5(3) 289.
[53] [1943] 2 All E.R. 560.
[54] s.58(1).
[55] s.58(4).

(3) The "devolution issue"

14.21 A person seeking a remedy after being adversely affected by an act of the Scottish Executive or an Act of the Scottish Parliament will bring a "devolution issue" before the courts. The concept of the devolution issue is raised in section 98 which refers the reader to Schedule 6 where the devolution issue is defined. Basically, any alleged breach of the Convention under the Scotland Act will become a devolution issue for the purposes of Schedule 6. The validity of an Act of the Scottish Parliament cannot however be challenged on the grounds that the proceedings leading to its enactment were invalid.[56] In this respect, an Act of the Scottish Parliament in terms of its Parliamentary procedures is similar to an Act of the United Kingdom Parliament because neither may be challenged on these grounds.[57] During the passage of the Scotland Act through Parliament, the government indicated that there should be a distinction between an Act of the Scottish Parliament and subordinate legislation.

> "It is intended to make the position of an Act of the Scottish Parliament similar to that of an Act of the United Kingdom Parliament ... [and] in a different position from subordinate legislation which can be challenged on the basis that the procedure prescribed for making the subordinate legislation has not been complied with."[58]

In terms of human rights issues, Paragraph 1 of Schedule 6 defines a devolution issue as:

> "(a) a question whether an Act of the Scottish Parliament or any provision of an Act of the Scottish Parlament is within the legislative competence of the Parliament ...
> (d) a question whether a purported or proposed exercise of a function by a member of the Scottish Executive is, or would be, incompatible with any of the Convention rights or with Community law;
> (e) a question whether a failure to act by a member of the Scottish Executive is incompatible with any of the Convention rights or with Community law".

Proceedings for the determination of a devolution issue may be instituted by the Advocate General or the Lord Advocate[59] or by a

---

[56] s.28(5).
[57] *Picken v. British Railways Board* [1974] A.C. 765.
[58] Official Report, House of Lords, 28 October 1999, vol. 593, col. 1946.
[59] Sched. 6, para. 4.

person, who is a "victim" in terms of Article 34 European Convention on Human Rights, during the course of existing legal proceedings.[60] A devolution issue may therefore be raised in any court or tribunal proceedings but paragraph 5 of the Schedule requires that the Advocate General and the Lord Advocate are given intimation that a devolution issue has arisen. Either Law Officer may then become a party to the proceedings as far as it relates to the devolution issue. In criminal cases, it is possible to raise a devolution issue but this is subject to time limits. In cases brought on indictment the devolution issue must be raised within seven days of the indictment being served. In summary cases, the devolution issue must be stated before the accused has been asked to plead.

When a devolution issue is raised in a tribunal from which there 14.22 is no appeal, the tribunal must refer the devolution issue to the Inner House of the Court of Session; any other tribunal may choose to do so.[61] Any civil court (except the House of Lords or the Court of Session sitting with three or more judges) may refer the devolution issue to the Inner House.[62] Any criminal court (except the High Court of Justiciary sitting with two or more judges) may refer the devolution issue to the High Court of Justiciary.[63] These provisions are designed to ensure that where necessary a lower court may refer a devolution issue to a superior court and it will be dealt with by the superior court, not just passed upwards to another court. The superior courts may themselves refer a devolution issue to a higher court. This applies to the Court of Session convened as a court with at least three judges and the High Court of Justiciary convened with at least two judges. The court to which the reference will be made, in both civil and criminal cases, is the Judicial Committee of the Privy Council. This requirement creates for the first time an appeal route from the High Court of Justiciary acting in its appellate capacity.

Once a decision on a reference has been given, the right of appeal against that decision will come into operation. Where a reference has been made under paragraphs 7 or 8 to the Inner House of the Court of Session, appeal is to the Judicial Committee. Where the reference has arisen under paragraph 9 or the devolution issue has arisen in the ordinary course of proceedings before the High Court of Justiciary as an appeal court, then any appeal requires leave to appeal from the High Court or the Judicial Committee and is made to the Judicial Committee.[64] Where there is a reference to the Inner

---

[60] s.100(1).
[61] Sched. 6, para. 8.
[62] Sched. 6, para. 7.
[63] Sched. 6, para. 9.
[64] Sched. 6, para. 13(a).

House in a case from which there is no appeal to the House of Lords (*e.g.* the Lands Valuation Appeal Court) then appeal may be made to the Judicial Committee with leave of the Inner House or the Judicial Committee.[65] The routes for reference and appeal are set out in the table below.

Court in Which Devolution Issue is Raised	Court for Reference	Appeal
Any tribunal (except those where there is no appeal).	Inner House of Court of Session (para. 8).	Judicial Committee of Privy Council (para. 12).
Civil Court, *i.e.* sheriff court, Outer House of Court of Session.	Inner House of Court of Session (para. 7).	Judicial Committee of Privy Council (para. 12).
Criminal court, *i.e.* district court, sheriff court, High Court of Justiciary as trial court.	High Court of Justiciary as appeal court (para. 9).	Judicial Committee of Privy Council but only with leave to appeal (para. 13(a)).
Court of Session with at least three judges, but not if devolution issue was raised under paras 7 or 8.	Judicial Committee of Privy Council (para. 10).	Judicial Committee of Privy Council but only with leave to appeal and if no right of appeal to House of Lords (para. 13(b)).
High Court of Justiciary with at least two judges, but not if devolution issue was raised under para. 9.	Judicial Committee of Privy Council (para. 11).	Judicial Committee of Privy Council but only with leave to appeal (para. 13(a)).

Part III of Schedule 6 sets out the various routes for references from courts in England and Wales.[66]

14.23   On very rare occasions, the devolution issue may be first raised in proceedings before the House of Lords. In these circumstances the House may refer the issue to the Judicial Committee or deal with the matter itself.[67] The House of Lords therefore has no discretion

---

[65]   Sched. 6, para. 13(b).
[66]   See Ashton and Finch, *Constitutional Law in Scotland* (2000), p.221.
[67]   Sched. 6, para. 32.

in how to deal with the matter, but is bound to follow any previous decisions of the Judicial Committee since section 103 provides that any decision of the Judicial Committee is binding on all other courts. In any event, it is unlikely that the House of Lords would depart from the decisions of the Judicial Committee given that the two courts (for issues under the Scotland Act) have common members.

Where the devolution issue concerns the proposed exercise of a function by a member of the Scottish Executive, then the person making the reference must notify a member of the Scottish Executive that the issue has been raised.[68] The devolution issue may not have arisen in judicial proceedings but any of the Law Officers may refer the issue of the proposed exercise. Thereafter no member of the Executive may exercise the function until the matter is disposed of. If a member of the Scottish Executive does exercise the function, the Advocate General or any other person may bring proceedings against the Scottish Executive.

To all intents and purposes, the Judicial Committee is now the constitutional "court" for the United Kingdom with regard to matters involving devolution.[69] The Act does not require that the membership of the Judicial Committee when sitting to consider a devolution issue should include a judge from the country concerned. However, it is likely that a convention will develop whereby a Scottish judge will sit on cases involving the Scotland Act and this has been the case.

Normally when a legal provision or action is found to be *ultra* 14.24 *vires* the provision or action is treated as null and void. However, actions in court to challenge the validity of a provision or action made under the Scotland Act will take time to be heard and decided and before the case is raised, the provision may have been implemented or the action acted upon. This would mean that anyone who had relied on the provision or action would be in difficulty since any decision of invalidity will be retrospective. The Act accordingly allows the court to limit the effect of such a decision. Section 102(2) allows the court to remove or limit any retrospective effect of the decision or to suspend the effect of the decision pending its being corrected. The court is required to have regard to the effect the making of an order would have on persons who are not parties to the proceedings. Before an order is made the court must order intimation to the Lord Advocate, and, if the matter relates to a devolution issue, to the appropriate Law

---

[68] Sched. 6, para.35.
[69] The Judicial Committee of the Privy Council is technically not a court since it does not pass judgements; instead it offers advice to the sovereign which is then enacted by the government in an Order in Council.

Officer.[70] The Law Officer may then participate in the proceedings relating to the order.

Many of the devolution issues raised since May 1999 have been matters of criminal law and many of these, if not most, have been concerned with Article 6(1) of the Convention. We have discussed many of these cases elsewhere in this book but the most important decisions are worth recalling here.

The case of *Starrs v. Ruxton*[71] sent shockwaves through the Scottish legal establishment when it was held that temporary sheriffs appointed by the Lord Advocate could not be considered to be an impartial tribunal under Article 6(1). A similar contention that a lay justice appointed by the Scottish Ministers could not be an impartial tribunal was rejected.[72] In *Montgomery v. H.M. Advocate*[73] the Judicial Committee had to consider whether pre-trial publicity had made a fair trial impossible. In the event the judges decided that the trial had been fair given that proper directions had been made by the trial judge to the jury.

14.25 The question of self-incrimination was raised in *Brown v. Stott*[74] when a woman challenged the requirement under section 172(2)(a) of the Road Traffic Act 1988 that she state to the police who was the driver of a vehicle. There was no caution required or given and the woman made an incriminating statement and was subsequently found guilty of drink driving. The Judicial Committee interpreted the section 172 as being a requirement for the police to obtain the information requested but not a requirement for the Crown to use such evidence. Thus it did not infringe the accused's rights under the Convention.

---

[70] s.102(4): the appropriate Law Officers are the Advocate General for Scotland for cases in Scotland, the Attorney-General for cases in England and Wales and the Attorney-General for Northern Ireland for Northern Ireland cases.

[71] 1999 S.C.C.R. 1052.

[72] *Clark v. Kelly*, 2000 S.C.C.R. 821.

[73] 2000 S.C.C.R. 1044.

[74] 2000 S.C.C.R. 314.

CHAPTER 15

THE INTERNATIONAL CONTEXT

DEVELOPMENT OF THE EUROPEAN CONVENTION ON HUMAN RIGHTS
AND FUNDAMENTAL FREEDOMS

The European Convention on Human Rights and Fundamental 15.01
Freedoms was the first fully developed human rights treaty
although its development was partly a result of international
instruments of wider application. In 1945 the Charter of the United
Nations stated that the Peoples of the United Nations were
determined to, "reaffirm faith in fundamental human rights, in the
dignity and worth of the human person, in the equal rights of men
and women". The Council of Europe, which is an association which
has a wider membership than the European Community, was
established in May 1949. During the negotiations leading to the
establishment of the Council of Europe the need for some sort of
charter on human rights was considered. The aim was to ensure
that citizens would be protected against rights infringements such as
those which had taken place during the Second World War and the
period leading up to it. Article 3 of the Statute of the Council of
Europe stated that "[e]very Member of the Council of Europe must
accept the principles of the rule of law and of the enjoyment by all
persons within its jurisdiction of human rights and fundamental
freedoms". The Council set up a committee of experts to prepare
the European Convention which was signed in 1951. It entered into
force in 1953 after its ratification by eight countries: Denmark, the
Federal Republic of Germany, Iceland, Ireland, Luxembourg,
Norway, Sweden, and the United Kingdom. Over the years more
states have agreed to be bound by the terms of the Convention. The
following countries are now bound by the Convention: Albania,
Andorra, Austria, Belgium, Bulgaria, Croatia, Cyprus, the Czech
Republic, Denmark, Estonia, Finland, France, Georgia, Germany,
Greece, Hungary, Iceland, Ireland, Italy, Latvia, Liechtenstein,
Lithuania, Luxembourg, Malta, Moldova, the Netherlands, Nor-
way, Poland, Portugal, Romania, Russia, San Marino, the Slovak
Republic, Slovenia, Spain, Sweden, Switzerland, Macedonia,

Turkey, Ukraine and the United Kingdom.[1]

In order to provide a remedy for those whose rights were infringed or whose rights had not been adequately protected it was decided to set up a European Commission of Human Rights to which individuals could address petitions and a European Court of Human Rights to which the Commission could refer cases for judicial consideration. Several countries, which were willing to adopt the principles of the Convention, were not in favour of a European Court or Commission. The Committee of Ministers therefore decided to make both the jurisdiction of the Court and the right of individual petition optional. The United Kingdom was one of the states that was opposed to the idea of permitting legal actions to be taken against the state. It was not until 1966 that the United Kingdom recognised the right of individuals to take an action against the government to the European Court of Human Rights.

An action against the state can be brought where a public authority has interfered with the convention rights of an individual citizen. The infringement of rights could arise from either an act of the public authority or a failure to act. The Government's White Paper, "Bringing Rights Home", did not mention that the European Court of Human Rights in Strasbourg retains a residual jurisdiction for hearing cases where individuals believe that their Convention rights have been breached. However, notwithstanding the incorporation provisions in the Human Rights Act and the Scotland Act, individuals can still take a case to the Strasbourg Court where the incorporating legislation does not cover the alleged claim, or where the United Kingdom courts have decided a case but the claimant is not satisfied with the judgment.

PROCEDURE UNDER THE CONVENTION

15.02　After exhausting any effective and sufficient domestic remedies individuals may raise actions for compensation in the European Court of Human Rights in Strasbourg. The procedure until recently has been a two stage process with a filter stage to reduce the number of ill-founded petitions. Claims by both states and individuals went first to the European Commission on Human Rights, which was a body of independent experts. The Commission decided whether the application should be admitted for consideration on the merits. Only approximately 10 per cent of cases progressed beyond this filter stage. Petitions were rejected if they were out of time, or if the applicant had failed to exhaust all of the remedies available under

---

[1]　Council of Europe, Chart of Signatures and Ratifications of the Convention for the Protection of Human Rights and Fundamental Freedoms.

domestic law, or because for one reason or another they were "manifestly ill-founded".[2] If the Commission found an application admissible it proceeded to the Committee of Ministers who attempted to negotiate a friendly settlement. If this failed it proceeded to a hearing before the European Court of Human Rights.

Protocol 11 to the Convention, which entered into force on November 1, 1998, introduced a new procedure. The Commission and the European Court of Human Rights have been replaced with a single court. The conciliation stage carried out by the Committee of Ministers has been removed. There is now one single permanent court considering the interpretation of the Convention. As well as simplifying, and possibly speeding up procedures, this will increase the consistency of decision-making.

Although the new court is now in full operation it is still necessary to be aware of the role of the European Commission of Human Rights as the decisions made by the Commission with regard to admissibility of applications are an important part of the jurisprudence of the European Convention.

The European Commission of Human Rights

The Commission was originally established as a filter, which would 15.03 weed out frivolous or mischievous petitions in order to prevent a deluge of cases descending on the Court. Its stated purpose was to ensure the observance of the engagements undertaken by the High Contracting Parties. This involved three principal functions;

(1) Filtering complaints through admissibility proceedings.
(2) Mediating disputes through the process called friendly settlement.
(3) Fact-finding and reporting on admitted but unsettled disputes.

These functions have now been absorbed into the reformed European Court of Human Rights.

A member was elected from each of the states which were parties to the Convention. The Commission met in Strasbourg for periodic sessions lasting about two weeks. As the number of petitions increased the number of sessions increased. In 1992 it met for a total of 16 weeks. As the Commissioners were appointed on a part-time basis many of them had other employment commitments and the high workload was seen as a problem. They were assisted by a professional full-time secretariat of about 95 persons.

All complaints about violations of Convention rights were sent

---

[2] ECHR, Art. 27.

first to the Commission. Complaints could be from states complaining about the activities of other states. Where a state permitted such petitions, private individuals could also bring complaints.

Filtering Complaints

15.04 Having received an application, the first task of the Commission was to consider its admissibility. One member of the Commission was appointed as a Rapporteur for each petition. He or she considered the petition and then reported to the Commission as a whole. If he or she reported that the petition was inadmissible the Commission could:

(1) Accept the report and adopt a decision rejecting the petition.
(2) Call for written papers.
(3) Hold an oral hearing.

In the course of these procedures the Commission was entitled to enquire into the facts of the case. The Commission then adopted its decision on admissibility. It was obliged to give reasons for its decisions. These were published in the Council of Europe publication, "Decisions and Reports".

Friendly Settlements

15.05 Where it decided that a petition was admissible the Commission was obliged to attempt to mediate a friendly settlement. The Commission produced a report on the petition, which was sent to the State or States concerned and to the Committee of Ministers. The report was also published. If a friendly settlement was not achieved, the Commission gave an opinion on whether or not the facts disclosed a breach of the Convention. The report was not binding on any of the parties. Once the Commission had transmitted its report, it or one of the states concerned was entitled to refer the matter to the Court within three months. If no such reference was made, the Committee of Ministers decided whether there had been a breach of the Convention. The decision of the Committee of Ministers was expressed in the form of a resolution.

The Committee of Ministers

15.06 The Committee of Ministers is the executive body of the Council of Europe. It is formally composed of the Foreign Ministers of member states, but deputies undertake most of the work on their behalf. These are normally ambassadorial members of state's diplomatic services. The Committee fulfilled a quasi-judicial role when considering reports of the Commission to decide whether there had been a breach of the Convention. The political nature of the Committee of Ministers meant that it was not really suitable for this quasi-judicial role. This decision-making role in respect of applications has now been abolished.

The European Court of Human Rights

The original Court came into existence in 1959 and ceased to exist in 1998. The original court was a part-time court but the new European Court of Human Rights is full-time. Although the title of the original court has been retained the Court now has new functions, new powers and a new composition. There are as many judges as the number of states which are party to the Council of Europe. Each judge serves for a period of six years after which he or she can be re-elected.[3] Judges have to retire when they reach the age of 70.[4] The judges must be suitably qualified and must be independent from national states.[5]   15.07

Applications to the Court

Actions may still be brought by states against other states[6] or by individuals against states.[7] The admissibility criteria for applications have not been changed.[8] Very few inter-state actions have been made because of the detrimental effects on economic and political relations between states. The few that have arisen have tended to relate to severe and widespread abuses of rights.[9] The majority of applications are from individuals and the number of individual applications has increased year by year. Any person, non-governmental organisation or group of individuals claiming to be a victim of a violation by one of the High Contracting Parties (the member states) of the rights set forth in the Convention, may petition. The tem "any person" includes both natural persons and artificial legal persons and so applications may be made by bodies such as companies.[10] Non-governmental organisations are bodies who do not perform official duties assigned to them by Law. Governmental organisations may not petition as it is inappropriate   15.08

---

[3]   ECHR, Art. 22.
[4]   *ibid.*, Art. 23.
[5]   *ibid.*, Art. 21.
[6]   *ibid.*, Art. 33.
[7]   *ibid.*, Art. 34.
[8]   *ibid.*, Art. 35.
[9]   For example, *Ireland v. U.K.* (1978) 2 E.H.R.R. 25.
[10]   For example, *National & Provincial Building Society v. U.K.*, Joined Cases: *Leeds Permanent Building Society v. U.K.; Yorkshire Building Society v. U.K.* [1997] S.T.C. 1466; (1998) 25 E.H.R.R. 127; 69 T.C. 540; [1997] B.T.C. 624; [1998] H.R.C.D. 34.

to permit one level of government, such as a local authority, to make an application with regard to its treatment by another level of government. Political groups, trade unions and religious groups may make applications.[11] Groups whose only interest in common is the violation of a Convention right may also apply as a group.[12] In order to be classed as a victim a person, group, or organisation has to show that they are directly affected by some form of state action or failure to act. Applicants also have to exhaust all available remedies under domestic law before applying to the European Court. There are six additional criteria upon which the admissibility of an application depends:

(1) Applications may not be made anonymously but an applicant may request that the publications arising out of the action are in anonymous form.
(2) Applications may not relate to a matter already adjudicated upon by the Court. This means that a person may not bring a new application relating to the same circumstances on which he based a previous application.
(3) Applications may not be made to the European Court if the same matter is also being adjudicated by another procedure of international investigation or settlement. This criterion is of little practical significance as there are very few international adjudication procedures.
(4) The application must not be incompatible with the provisions of the Convention. This means that the rights, which have been infringed, must fit the categories of those described in the Convention.
(5) Applications which are "manifestly ill-founded" are not admissible. This means that there must be at least a *prima facie* case against the respondent state.
(6) Applications will not be accepted from a person who has abused the right of petition. The case of *M v. United Kingdom* was brought by a man who had made four previous applications and whose wife had made one application. The applications concerned a long-running dispute over the way in which they had been treated by the civil courts in England. The application was declared to be inadmissible as it was an abuse of the right of petition. [13]

Composition of the Court

15.09 The court has an elected President and Vice-Presidents. The plenary

[11] For example, *National Union of Belgian Police v. Belgium* (1975) 1 E.H.R.R. 578.
[12] For example, *Hatton v. U.K.,* October 2, 2001, unreported.
[13] *M v. United Kingdom,* 54 D.R. 214 (1987).

Court, *i.e.* all the judges sitting together, established four sections, which form the basic operating units of the Court. Each judge is a member of one section. The composition of each section is intended to be balanced in terms of gender and geography and is designed to reflect the variety of legal systems of the member states. The sections are appointed for three years. The presidents of the sections are the two vice-presidents of the Court and the two presidents of chambers. Chambers are groups of judges who determine the merits of the majority of cases. Each chamber consists of seven judges. The president of the section to which the particular case is allocated is a member of the chamber. The judges in the section who are not involved in determining the case may be brought in as substitute judges. Any judge who has a personal involvement with the case or who has previously participated in proceedings related to the case must not take any part in consideration of the case. A unanimous committee of three judges may declare an application inadmissible. The president of the Court, after consulting the presidents of the sections, decides how many committees should be established. Each committee lasts for 12 months.

The grand chamber[14] is responsible for dealing with cases relinquished to its jurisdiction by chambers or where it accepts a request for a referral (a re-hearing of a case) following a judgment by a chamber. The grand chamber is made up of 17 judges together with three substitute judges. It always includes the president of the court, the presidents of the chambers and the relevant national judges. The remaining members are appointed on rotation from one of two groups of other judges so as to reflect the geographical balance and range of legal systems. A screening panel, of five judges, controls access to the grand chamber under the referral procedure.[15] No national judges from the concerned state may sit on the screening panel.

The organisation of the Court is complex but the aim is to ensure that it is possible to achieve the diversity of judicial backgrounds necessary for proper consideration of the most complex cases while maintaining a core of experienced judges in the grand chamber.

Hearings

Hearings are normally held in public, but may be held in private 15.10 where the interest of morals, public order, national security, juveniles or the protection of the private lives of the parties so requires. Parties who request confidentiality must give reasons and must specify which hearings and which documents they wish to be confidential. Individuals may represent themselves or be repre-

---

[14] Created by ECHR, Art. 27(1).
[15] ECHR, Art. 43.

sented by a qualified legal representative. The president of the chamber may direct that a legal representative must represent the applicant. Legal aid may be granted to individual applicants if it is necessary for the proper conduct of the case and the applicant has insufficient means to meet all or part of the costs.

Individual applications must be made on an official application form issued by the registry. The form consists of factual information about the applicant, a brief statement of the facts and the alleged violation and any claims for just satisfaction. Applicants must also provide supporting documents to show that they meet the admissibility criteria. Inter-state applications need not be made on an application form but similar information must be provided.

One judge is appointed by the president as a rapporteur for each case. The rapporteur decides whether the application will be referred to a committee for a declaration that it is inadmissible or to a chamber for a declaration of its admissibility. If it is referred to a committee, the rapporteur must produce a report giving a brief statement of the facts and the reason why he or she considers it inadmissible. If the committee comes to a unanimous agreement that it is inadmissible, that decision is final. No detailed reasons for the decisions are required. If the committee cannot agree the application is forwarded to a chamber. When the application is sent directly to a chamber, the rapporteur may express a provisional opinion on the merits. The chamber may decide to hold a hearing before reaching a decision regarding admissibility, in which case the merits of the application may also be considered. The chambers must give reasoned decisions for their admissibility findings.

15.11   The chamber may indicate interim measures which it considers should be adopted in the interests of the parties or for the proper conduct of the proceedings before it. The Court Rules do not expressly state that interim measures are binding on the parties. When it is considering the merits of an admitted case, the chamber may invite further evidence and written observations from the parties. Members of the chamber may also conduct inquiries and investigations. If the Court decides to hold a hearing on the merits of the application, either party may request that the consideration of the merits at the admissibility stage should be ignored. Witnesses and experts may testify before the Court. Third party interventions may be permitted from organisations, such as pressure groups like Amnesty International or Greenpeace, at the discretion of the Court. The registrar takes a leading role in negotiating friendly settlements but the Court has the right to ensure that any friendly settlement will respect human rights.

Where a case raises a serious question of interpretation of the Convention or where the resolution of the case may lead to inconsistency with an earlier decision, the chamber may relinquish the case to the grand chamber. The parties are given one month to lodge any objection to relinquishment. Judgments contain the facts of the case, a summary of the submissions of the parties and the reasons for the decision in relation to points of law. Where the chamber has found a violation of the Convention it may give a ruling on any claim for just satisfaction or set a later date for such a ruling. Where a case has been decided by a chamber, either party, within three months of the decisions may submit a written request for the case to be referred to the grand chamber for a re-hearing. The request must show that there is a serious question affecting the application of the Convention or a serious issue of general importance, which warrants examination by the grand chamber. The screening panel examines the case on the basis of the existing case file. The panel need not provide reasons if it refuses a request for a re-hearing. If the request is accepted a full hearing takes place before the grand chamber.

Where an adverse judgment is given against it, the United Kingdom comes under an international legal obligation to change national law so as to comply with the Articles of the Convention. However, if the government does not wish to change the law it may enter a derogation from an aspect of the relevant Article.

Derogations

The United Kingdom entered a derogation from Article 5(3) of the Convention (which requires prompt judicial review following arrest) to legitimise the Prevention of Terrorism (Temporary Provisions) Act 1989. The European Court of Human Rights accepted that the derogation was justified in *Brannigan and McBride v. United Kingdom*.[16] The United Kingdom domestic legislation therefore governed the length of time terrorist suspects might be held without charge. However the peace settlement in Northern Ireland changed the emergency situation and therefore the grounds under which the derogation was made no longer existed. The Terrorism Act 2000 provided for judicial authorisation of detention of terrorist suspects and, as a result of the implementation of the Terrorism Act 2000, the government withdrew its derogation on February 19, 2001.

Article 15 of the Convention permits contracting parties to derogate from the Convention "in time of war or other public emergency threatening the life of the nation ... to the extent strictly required by the exigencies of the situation". It is not, however, possible to derogate from the following Articles:

(1) Article 2, (the right to life), except in respect of deaths

15.12

---

[16] *Brannigan and McBride v. U.K.* (1994) 17 E.H.R.R. 539.

resulting from lawful acts of war,
(2) Article 3 (prohibition of torture),
(3) Article 4(1), (prohibition of slavery and servitude),
(4) Article 7, (no punishment without law), or
(5) Protocol 6 (abolition of the death penalty) save as provided by Article 2 of the Protocol.

Section 14 of the Human Rights Act made the derogation from Article 5(3), which was in existence in the United Kingdom at the time when the Act was passed, a "designated derogation" so that the Convention rights could take effect in the United Kingdom subject to it.[17] The Human Rights Act enables subsequent derogations to be made and designated by the Secretary of State. Designation orders require parliamentary approval within 40 days and must be reconfirmed every five years.[18]

THE EUROPEAN UNION AND HUMAN RIGHTS

"It is well settled that fundamental rights form an integral part of the general principles of law whose observance the Court ensures. For that purpose, the Court draws inspiration from the constitutional traditions common to the Member States and from the guidelines supplied by international treaties for the protection of human rights on which the Member States have collaborated or of which they are signatories."[19]

15.13 The foundation Treaties of the European Communities did not include human or fundamental rights because they were created in 1951 and 1957 in the same time period as the Council of Europe was creating the European Convention of Human Rights. The issue was not however dismissed as irrelevant; rather it was thought the aim of the E.C. Treaties was to seek economic integration and this would not interfere with human rights. "Rights only warranted protection if they were necessary for the furtherance of this economic ideal".[20] European law was to be the instrument to bring about a change in the member states to bring them closer together, and human rights became limitations on the discretion of the Community institutions. The changes being effected in the E.C./E.U. now may change the emphasis of human rights from

---

[17] Human Rights Act 1998, s.14.
[18] Human Rights Act 1998, s.16.
[19] ECJ Opinion 2/94 [1996] E.C.R. I-1759, para. 33.
[20] Fredman, McCrudden, and Freedland "An EU Charter of Fundamental Rights" [2001] P.L. Summer 178.

limitation to determination, bringing the human rights principles to the centre of E.U. policies.[21]

Problems did arise in the early years when the European Court of Justice was developing the doctrine of supremacy of E.C. law. The doctrine raised the question that if E.C. law was supreme over national (constitutional) law and human rights were not protected by E.C. law, then how would those human rights protected by the individual constitutions of each member state be protected?[22] National courts could not override Community law and it was not possible for the ECJ to apply national law. If the application of Community law violated "the constitutionally guaranteed human rights" of the individual, there would be no redress available to him in either jurisdiction. The issue was addressed in *Stauder v. City of Ulm*[23] where a German national complained that he had been required to give his name contrary to the German constitution, in order to show his entitlement to buy discounted Community butter. The Community act setting out the scheme had been translated into different languages but the translations were different thus giving different eligibility requirements. The ECJ said that the most liberal translation of the Community act should prevail if it gave effect to the act's objectives. The ECJ further indicated that human rights principles were enshrined in the general principles of Community law and they are part of the law which Article 164 TEC requires to be observed "in the interpretation and application of the Treaty". The Court noted: "[i]nterpreted in this way, the provision at issue contains nothing capable of prejudicing the fundamental human rights enshrined in the general principles of Community law and protected by the Court".

The way in which the ECJ tackled the omission of human rights in the EEC Treaties is discussed by Betten and Grief.[24] The phrase "general principles of Community law" has been shortened to "general principles of law". However, this is not the same as human rights which normally are set out in some constitutional document or treaty and which create "an area of freedom to be respected by public authorities". A general principle of law on the other hand is not necessarily documented in the same way. They may be presumptions for instance that a public authority will act proportionately. The unwritten nature of the general principles were ideal for use by the ECJ to introduce the idea of human rights into Community law. Thus in *Internationale Handelsgesellschaft*[25]

---

[21] Von Bogdandy "The EU as a Human Rights Organization? Human Rights and the Core of the EU" [2000] C.M.L.Rev. 1307.
[22] Betten and Grief, *EU Law and Human Rights* (1998), p.56.
[23] Case 29/69 [1969] E.C.R. 419.
[24] Betten and Grief, *EU Law and Human Rights* (1998), p.57.
[25] Case 11/70 [1970] E.C.R. 125.

the ECJ stated "the protection of such (human) rights, whilst inspired by the constitutional traditions common to the Member states, must be ensured within the framework of the structure and objectives of the Community".

15.14   Some years later, the ECJ started to refer to specific Articles of the European Convention on Human Rights to provide guidelines for human rights protection in E.C. law. In *Rutili v. Minister for the Interior*[26] the ECJ used the provisos present in Articles 8 to 11 ECHR and Article 2 of Protocol 4 on freedom of movement to interpret the public policy limitations on freedom of movement set out in Article 48(3) EEC. However, citing an article of the ECHR as a justification is not always accepted by the ECJ. In *National Panasonic v. Commission*[27] the company alleged a breach of Article 8 European Convention on Human Rights, respect for private and family life, home and correspondence after an unannounced "raid" by Commission officials to scrutinise the company's books. The ECJ considered the whole Article and held that the action was justified by Article 8(2) which allows interference in certain circumstances. Examples include national security or public safety considerations or the economic well being of the country. The Commission could carry out investigations without prior notification to avoid distortion of competition.

In the *Wachauf case*[28] the proposition was made that member states must also observe fundamental rights when implementing Community law.

> "Since those requirements [of the protection of fundamental rights in the Community legal order] are also binding on the Member States when they implement Community rules, the Member States must ... apply these rules in accordance with those requirements."

In addition if a member state seeks to derogate from the Treaty, any measures enacted or taken by the member state must take into account the principle of fundamental rights.

It became obvious in the 1970s that the notion that progress on social rights would follow from economic progress was flawed. Thus the European Commission implemented measures to give the Community a more "social face".[29] The principle of equality of pay between men and women was boosted by the Equal Pay Directive 75/117 and then the Equal Treatment Directive 76/207.

15.15   The Single European Act 1986 states that member states are determined to "work together to promote democracy on the basis

---

[26] Case 36/75 [1975] E.C.R. 1219.
[27] Case 136/79 [1980] E.C.R. 2033.
[28] Case 5/88 [1989] E.C.R. 2609.

of the fundamental rights recognised in the Convention".[30] The ECJ has not, as yet, indicated that a particular article of the European Convention on Human Rights is part of Community law, rather it uses the Convention as an aid to interpretation of the general principles of law.

In 1976, the European Commission asked the European Parliament and the Council of Ministers whether the European Community should accede to the European Convention on Human Rights. The discussion concluded that since the principles of the Convention were already binding in E.C. law, accession was unnecessary. However, the Commission concluded that the position would be strengthened if the Community's political institutions declared their respect for human rights. The three institutions published a non-binding declaration in 1977.

By 1989 however the Commission had decided that legal certainty in human rights was lacking and accession would resolve this. The 1977 Resolution was expanded in 1989 to become the Declaration of Fundamental Rights and Freedoms.[31] This included a list of fundamental rights and called upon member states and institutional bodies to associate themselves with it. In 1994, the ECJ was asked for its opinion on the legal aspects of accession to the European Convention on Human Rights. The Commission asked: "Would the accession of the E.C. to the Convention on Human Rights and Fundamental Freedoms of 4 November 1950 be compatible with the Treaty establishing the European Community?"[32]

The question was asked pursuant to Article 228(6) TEC which aims 15.16 to prevent complications arising from legal disputes as to the compatibility with the Treaty of international agreements which are binding on the Community. The request for an opinion raised questions concerning the legal basis of accession to the Convention and whether accession was compatible with the E.C. Treaty. The second issue was particularly relevant to the position of the ECJ because Articles 164 and 219 TEC confer exclusive jurisdiction on the ECJ where there is an action between a member state and a Community institution.

The opinion was delivered on March 28, 1996. The ECJ concluded that it was not possible to rule on the issue of the accession of the Community to the Convention because various issues had not been resolved. The Court believed that such

[29] Fredman, McCrudden, and Freedland, "An EU Charter of Fundamental Rights" [2001] P.L. Summer 178.
[30] SEA Preamble, 3rd Recital.
[31] Resolution adopting the Declaration of Fundamental Rights and Freedoms (De Gucht Report) 12 April 1989, A2-3/89 OJ C-120.
[32] OJ 1994, No. C-174/8.

accession would require a substantial modification of the Community system on human rights and thus significant amendment of the Treaty.[33] The Court was particularly concerned with how its powers would be affected by the decision of the European Court of Human Rights. An accession to the European Convention on Human Rights would make the ECJ subordinate to the Strasbourg Court in human rights issues and there is little doubt that the European Court of Human Rights would find difficulty with the notion of the supremacy of the ECJ. Fredman *et al* suggested that this could be resolved by using a similar technique to the Human Rights Act 1998, where the decisions of the Strasbourg Court must be taken into account but they are not binding.[34]

The Court went on to declare that respect for human rights is a condition of lawfulness of Community acts and this was implicit from the Court's jurisprudence. "As Community law now stands, the Community has no competence to accede to the Convention". In addition, the Court stated that "no Treaty provisions confer on the Community institutions any general power to enact rules on human rights or to conclude international conventions in this field".[35]

15.17   The apparent inability of the E.U. to accede to the European Convention on Human Rights gave rise to an anomaly: although all member states have incorporated the European Convention on Human Rights into their national law the E.U. has no similar regime in force for E.U. institutions.

There is no doubt whatever that the Convention is part of the European Union's Constitutional order. This is seen in Article 6(2) TEU[36] and by the fact that the ECJ will follow the Strasbourg case law to interpret and apply the rights and freedoms in the Article. The new Article 6(2) TEU states:

> "The Union is founded on the principles of liberty, democracy, respect for human rights and fundamental freedoms, and the rule of law, principles which are common to the Member States. The Union shall respect fundamental rights, as guaranteed by the European Convention for the protection of Human Rights and Fundamental Freedoms ... and as they result from the constitutional traditions common to the Member States as general principles of Community law."

The Article is drafted more restrictively than the ECJ Opinion 2/94.

---

[33] Betten and Grief, *EU Law and Human Rights* (1998) p.113.
[34] Fredman, McCrudden, and Freedland, "An EU Charter of Fundamental Rights" [2001] P.L. Summer 178.
[35] ECJ Opinion 2/94 [1996] E.C.R. I-1759, para. 27.
[36] Formerly Art. F(2).

The ECJ referred to "international treaties for the protection of human rights on which the Member States have collaborated or of which they are signatories". These international documents such as the European Social Charter and the various Protocols of the European Convention on Human Rights, have been drawn on by the ECJ in its jurisprudence, even though not all of the member states had ratified them. Arguably this was an important factor for the ECJ's development of a human rights dimension in E.C. law.

The Maastricht Treaty on European Union 1992 confirms the commitment "to the principles of liberty, democracy and respect for human rights and fundamental freedoms and the rule of law". The Second Pillar on Common Foreign and Security Policy states that one of the policy's objectives shall be "to develop and consolidate democracy and the rule of law and respect for human rights and fundamental freedoms".[37] The Third Pillar on Co-operation in Justice and Home Affairs refers to matters of common interest in Article K1 and states that these will comply with the European Convention on Human Rights and the Convention relating to the Status of Refugees 1951 (the Geneva Convention) and will have regard to "the protection afforded by Member States to persons persecuted on political grounds". This Article also refers to freedom of movement of persons and deals with asylum, immigration policy and police co-operation to prevent international crime. These are areas of the most fundamental human rights.

In 1997, the Treaty of Amsterdam was negotiated and this added   15.18
a new Fourth Recital to the Preamble of the TEU.

> "Confirming their attachment to fundamental social rights as defined in the European Social Charter ... and the 1989 Community Charter of the Fundamental Social Rights of Workers."

A large part of the TEU's Third Pillar (the CJHA) is now within the E.C. Treaty and is subject to the interpretation of the ECJ.

The Amsterdam Treaty established various procedures to secure the protection of human rights. Article 6 TEU states the general principle of respect for human rights and fundamental freedoms while Article 7 TEU allows the European Union to suspend certain rights of a member state if that member state is in serious and persistent breach of the human rights principles. Any country wishing to join the E.U. must indicate its respect for human rights under Article 49 TEU and the ECJ has been given power to ensure respect for fundamental rights and freedoms by the European institutions.[38] In addition, equality is a stated aim of the Union and

---

[37] Art. J.1(2) CFSP.

Article 13 E.C. allows the Community to legislate against many forms of discrimination. It could be argued that these provisions taken with the E.U. Charter of Fundamental Rights (discussed below) will create a yardstick for determining whether a state is fulfilling its obligations. For instance, Article 49 TEU requires a state seeking membership to indicate its respect for human rights. It may not be able to do so if it still operates the death penalty, which would be a contravention of Article 2(2) of the Charter.[39] The requirements for suspending a member state's rights under Article 7 TEU are more stringent than those which challenge the "candidate" states. The Article is not however reviewable by the ECJ, indicating that the action of suspending a member state's rights is largely a political one, not a legal matter. It also allows other member states to choose whether or not to recognise that a breach of human rights has occurred; again a political decision. An indication of the difficulties which might be encountered by the member states is their reaction to the coalition government of the Austrian People's Party and the Austrian Freedom Party in late 1999. The Austrian Freedom Party was allegedly an extreme right wing group which espoused xenophobic and racist views. No legitimate action could be taken under Article 7 TEU because Austria had done nothing wrong and had not breached the Treaties. However in January 2000, the other 14 member states showed their concern by drafting a statement restricting bilateral relations with the Austrian government. This was not an act of the Council.

　　The ECJ does not have jurisdiction with respect to certain measures on international border controls where these relate to the maintenance of law and order or the safeguarding of internal security.[40] The abolition of border checks for those member states within the Schengen acquis is similarly outwith the jurisdiction of the ECJ although the Schengen agreement itself is incorporated into European law.

15.19　　The ECJ does have jurisdiction over Article 6(2) TEU after Article 46 TEU[41] was amended "with regard to an action of the institutions, insofar as (it) has jurisdiction under the Treaties establishing the E.C. and under this Treaty". This does not however mean that the basis of the ECJ's jurisdiction on human rights protection has been changed; human rights protection will still be founded on "general principles of law" rather than the European Convention on Human Rights.

---

[38]　Art. 46 TEU.
[39]　For discussion of the E.U.'s policy on "candidate" states for membership see A. Williams "Enlargement of the Union and Human Rights Conditionality: a policy of distinction?" (2000) 25 E.L.Rev. 601.
[40]　Art. 68(2) E.C.
[41]　Formerly Art. L.

There are a number of areas of European Community legislation which are exempted from human rights protection. For instance, Article 3(2) of Directive 95/46/E.C. "[o]n the protection of individuals with regard to the processing of personal data and on the free movement of such data" exempts certain processing operations relating to public security, defence, state security and activities of the state in areas of criminal law.

It is clear from the foregoing that fundamental rights are recognised within the jurisprudence of the ECJ and that the court will make decisions which recognise these rights. There is a difficulty between E.U. law and European Convention on Human Rights law and that which one will be the final arbiter of human rights law. It could easily happen that both courts give interpretations on human rights on the same topic, which are at odds with one another. Since the decisions of the ECJ are binding on member states, this could lead to them violating the Convention because they are obliged to follow the ruling and interpretation of the ECJ. The question is one of scope and jurisdiction. Decisions of the ECJ are applicable to those areas of activity which are within the ambit of the European Community Treaties. Thus if a member state decides to restrict religious broadcasting to achieve a balance of faiths the member state will be able to justify a derogation from the Treaty on public policy grounds. There is no discrimination against broadcasters from any other member state. The restriction might be challenged on the ground of fundamental rights of one particular faith but there is no challenge available under Community law. No breach of Community law is exposed by the restriction and a challenge would not be admissible. The issue is one for the national courts to determine with regard to any breach of fundamental rights.[42]

European Union Charter of Fundamental Rights

The Charter was finalised in October 2000 and adopted by proclamation of the Council, Commission and Parliament at the Nice European Council in December 2000.[43] In many ways the Charter is a compromise. Some of those who participated in its creation believe that it is merely a public relations exercise with no or few legal consequences and certainly none leading to a binding instrument. Others view it as a Bill of Rights for the European Union which will lead to the promise of a federal Europe. It is, however, difficult to know how it will be viewed by the ECJ and whether it will eventually become justiciable.

The origins of the charter appear to lie in the German Presidency

15.20

---

[42] F. Jacobs "Human rights in the EU: the role of the Court of Justice" E.L.Rev. 2001, Vol. 26(4) 331.
[43] [2000] OJ C-364/8.

of the Union in the early half of 1999. A report of an expert group on fundamental rights chaired by Professor Spiros Simitis[44] focused on the need for an E.U. Bill of Rights and the German Presidency decided to propose a European Charter in April 1999 at a conference called to consider it. There were many who opposed such a charter arguing that human rights are already incorporated into E.C. law through the jurisprudence of the ECJ. Another argument was that if the member states had wanted to ensure the binding nature of the human rights principles upon the institutions of the E.U., then it would have been possible to amend the Treaties to allow accession to the European Convention on Human Rights. The political will to do so had apparently been absent.

The aim of the charter however appeared to be an exercise to raise the awareness of the public so that the European Union could inform its citizens that there was a Community commitment to human rights. In April 1999, the conference in Germany noted in its conclusions, "[t]here appears to be a need, at the present stage of the Union's development, to establish a Charter of Fundamental Rights in order to make their overriding importance and relevance more visible to the Union's citizens". A large group of representatives was convened from the member state governments, the Commission, the European Parliament and national Parliaments. There were observers from the ECJ and the Council of Europe. All the hearings were held in public and other bodies and groups were invited to give their views to the group. The construction of the group was noticeably different from those which were usually set up to discuss and prepare documentation for the E.U. Its openness and transparency and the high-profile nature of its membership ensured that its conclusions and the charter itself would be taken seriously.

15.21   The charter has not been given legal force. In fact, it was drafted without its authors knowing whether it would be legally binding or not. The final decision on enforceability was not taken until the Nice summit itself. The majority of member states took the view that it should not have binding force but the question of the status of the charter will be discussed again at the next Inter-Governmental Conference in 2003/4. In the next few years however it is likely to be used as a source in cases before the ECJ.[45] It may in the event become the standard for interpreting the "general principles of law".

The idea was to consolidate all of the existing rights into a single comprehensive text and accordingly it includes a catalogue of traditional civil and political rights together with economic and social rights. Specific fundamental rights are granted by Commu-

---

[44] "Affirming Fundamental Rights in the EU: Time to Act" Report of the Expert Group on Fundamental Rights, February 1999.

[45] Lord Hope of Craighead, House of Lords Hansard, 16 June 2000, col. 1852.

nity law to citizens of the Union. Some members of the drafting group were adamant that the charter should only include existing rights and not create additional rights. "The Charter is not about creating new rights enforceable in the domestic area; it is not about giving Brussels new powers to control our lives. It is about restricting the powers of Brussels so that it respects the fundamental freedoms that we all have."[46]

Some of the rights have little to do with the stated functions of the E.U., *e.g.* there is a prohibition of the death penalty in Article 2, a laudable provision but one which has little to do with the economic well being of the European Union. The inclusion of both existing Community rights and some which have little to do with the Community could have created uncertainty but the position is clarified in Article 51(1) and Chapter VII "General Provisions". The Article states "[t]he provisions of this Charter are addressed to the institutions and bodies of the Union ... and to the Member States only when they are implementing Union law".

The protection of the fundamental rights in Article 6 TEU is   15.22
welcome but there are some problems associated with it. The wording lacks legal certainty and depends on the "constitutional traditions common to the Member States", phrasing which is not specific enough. The charter on the other hand is clear, succinct and up-to-date and identifies the fundamental rights and the limitations of those rights. In this respect, the charter is different from, and arguably better than, the Convention itself. Its stated principles are more relevant and cover a wider range of rights than the Convention. Another difficulty is that the Convention contains very few economic rights since it concentrates on civil and political rights. However some of the "rights" are more aspirations than definite agreed rights. The charter is not legally binding and thus its status is not the same as that of the Convention which also has wider application throughout Europe. The lack of legally enforceable provisions in the charter arguably is a retrograde step. The ECJ has after all built up an extensive jurisprudence on human rights within E.U. law and these cases are legally binding. However, the political difficulties of creating a legally enforceable charter resulted in the authors stating that enforceability was a future battle.

While most of the civil and political rights in the charter attracted little controversy the same cannot be said for the social and economic rights under the heading of "Solidarity". Members were unhappy that rights such as the right to collective bargaining and action, fair and just working conditions, social security and social assistance, were included, since these were traditionally within the

---

[46] *per* Lord Goldsmith, House of Lords Hansard, 16 June 2000, col. 1879.

exclusive jurisdiction of the member states. It was noted that the method of achievement of these rights was essentially a political issue and there were differences among the member states about such issues. Despite evidence from various groups and organisations that these social and economic rights were necessary, in the event the terms of the charter are more limited in scope and the "Solidarity" rights were not given the same importance as civil political and citizenship rights.

The charter draws on many sources for its validity. For instance, the sources of the rights in Chapter 1, "Dignity" come from the Preamble to the 1948 Universal Declaration of Human Rights, the European Convention on Human Rights, the Convention on Human Rights and Biomedicine of the Council of Europe, the Statute of the International Criminal Court and the Europol Convention. Other articles draw on the E.C. Treaties, Council Directives and ECJ caselaw. [47]

15.23   It was recognised that conflicting interpretations of rights could be given by the European Court of Human Rights and the ECJ. However the charter allows both courts to have regard to the jurisprudence of each other in reaching decisions and Article 52(3) provides that the meaning and scope of those rights which appear in the European Convention on Human Rights shall be given the same meaning and scope in the charter.

The charter has 54 Articles, divided into seven chapters whose titles express their broad content. The chapters are Dignity (Articles 1–5), Freedoms (Articles 6–19); Equality (Articles 20–26); Solidarity (Articles 27–38); Citizens' Rights (Articles 39–46); and Justice (Articles 47–50). The final chapter is a technical chapter of general provisions.

The rights in the charter fall into four broad categories. First, rights and freedoms and procedural guarantees. These come mainly from the European Convention on Human Rights and the constitutional traditions of the member states. They include procedural guarantees, the principle of equality, respect for private life and rights such as freedom of the press, freedom of conscience, freedom of assembly and freedom of association. They are part of Community law as general principles according to the caselaw of the ECJ and already apply in the member states and are applied to the Community institutions.

15.24   Secondly, there are rights which apply only to citizens of the European Union. These are taken from the Treaty establishing the European Community (TEC) Part Two "Citizenship of the Union". The provisions include the union's electoral laws, common

[47] See Europa website for list of sources. http://europa.int/comm/justice_home/unit/charte/en/charter02.html (07.05.01)

diplomatic protection and the right to petition the European Parliament and refer cases to the ombudsman. Thirdly, there are economic and social rights including provisions on labour law and social law. The former laws include the right to join a trade union and the right to strike, the right to minimum pay, the right to professional training and the right of the disabled to "occupational integration". Social laws include social protection and the right to health care.

The final group could be called "modern rights". They include the protection of personal data and the right of access to administrative documents of the Community institutions and the right to good administration. Rights connected with bioethics are included to meet the challenges of developments such as genetic engineering and information technology.

INDEX